Developmental Disabilities

DELIVERY OF MEDICAL CARE
FOR CHILDREN AND ADULTS

DEVELOPMENTAL DISABILITIES:

DELIVERY OF MEDICAL CARE
FOR CHILDREN AND ADULTS

I. LESLIE RUBIN, M.D.

Director of Pediatrics
Developmental Evaluation Clinic
The Children's Hospital

Assistant in Medicine
The Children's Hospital

Assistant Professor of Pediatrics
Harvard Medical School

and

ALLEN C. CROCKER, M.D.

Director, Developmental Evaluation Clinic
The Children's Hospital

Associate Professor of Pediatrics
Harvard Medical School

Lecturer in Maternal & Child Health
Harvard School of Public Health

BOSTON, MASSACHUSETTS

Lea & Febiger • 1989 • Philadelphia • London

Lea & Febiger
600 Washington Square
Philadelphia, PA 19106-4198
U.S.A.
(215) 922-1330

Library of Congress Cataloging-in-Publication Data

Rubin, I. Leslie
    Developmental disabilities.

    Includes bibliographies and index.
    1. Developmentally disabled children—
Medical care. 2. Developmentally disabled—
Institutional care. I. Crocker, Allen C.
[DNLM: 1. Child Development
Disorders. 2. Delivery of Health
Care. 3. Handicapped. 4. Mental
Retardation. W 84.1 R8955d]
RJ506.D47R83   1987   616.89   87-2840
ISBN 0-8121-1082-X

PRINTED IN THE UNITED STATES OF AMERICA

Print No. 3 2 1

PREFACE

This book brings together the observations made and conclusions drawn by various specialists who have had experience in providing medical care for children and adults with developmental disabilities. It fulfills a long awaited need by offering a broad and deep clinical perspective and the necessary insight for dealing with such children and adults.

Although pediatricians have treated this population for many years, the lack of formal training in this specialized area did not equip them to deal effectively and efficiently with the often complex medical problems or with the additional psychosocial, habilitative, and educational issues.

For internists the problem has been more confounding. Among the many reasons for this is their lack of exposure, since in the past, adults with developmental disabilities usually received services through the large state residential facilities in which they lived. Although not all adults with developmental disabilities lived in these situations, medical services for this population were, by and large, provided within this system. Because such services were provided outside the mainstream of academic and clinical practice, there is a noticeable lack of literature on medical management.

The social revolution of the last two decades, however, has brought about a major demographic shift in which children and adults with developmental disabilities have gone from institutions into the community and thus into the usual settings of medical practice. Our book reflects the culmination of two developments in this process of change.

First, major teaching hospitals have become involved in providing medical care to large state residential facilities. Thus, when the Children's Hospital of Boston and the Brigham and Women's Hospital (both affiliated with Harvard Medical School) established a contractual arrangement with the State of Massachusetts to provide "Health and Habilitative Services" to the Wrentham State School, this allowed for a fresh clinical approach to some of the challenges presented by developmentally disabled persons. Similar contractual arrangements have also been established elsewhere in Massachusetts as well as in other states. The second factor can be attributed to the simultaneous appearance of deinstitutionalization and a philosophy of normalization, with the result that community services could, increasingly, be drawn upon.

Although much clinical practice is readily applicable to this group of people, certain situations require special consideration and reflection. For example, physicians (except for pediatricians) obtaining a medical history may not be accustomed to getting information from a third party, and these informants may know very little about the patient's past medical problems. In addition, many children and adults with developmental disabilities often have a complex set of medical problems, as well as serious psychosocial and habilitative difficulties. Our text has been developed with these factors in mind.

It has been our intention to provide pediatricians and internists, generalists and specialists, nurses, nurse practitioners, and clinical therapists with guidelines on clinical management, and to bring into focus the diverse aspects involved. Another purpose in developing this text has been to bring insights to the medical and nursing professions about this specialized clinical field of practice and therapy, and to generate for it visibility and respectability. In addition, we hope the text will provide a base for the improvement of clinical practice and for the advancement of knowledge through study and research. As will also be apparent, we are concerned with the "right to treatment" in its full sense, including supports, so that individuals can reach their optimal personal outcome.

The book is divided into four sections: Part I defines the population and gives an overview of the clinical needs and the various settings in which these needs can be addressed. Part II presents the main body of clinically relevant material in a spectrum going from early infancy to the geriatric age group, and from a broad clinical perspective to specific and specialized concerns. Part III discusses services provided within large state residential facilities. Although this may be seen as an anachronism in an era when community services are being stressed, this section documents, first, the fact that we have learned much by becoming involved in these systems and, secondly, the fact that continuing requirements for care exist. Part IV looks at the broader issues of planning and policy.

In providing medical care for children and adults with developmental disabilities, there should be a coordinated resolve to ensure and improve the quality of life for these individuals and for their families.

Boston, Massachusetts   I. Leslie Rubin
                                           Allen C. Crocker

CONTRIBUTORS

Norberto Alvarez, M.D.
Director of Neurology
Seizure Control Program
The Children's Hospital Health and Habilitative
    Services Program
Wrentham State School
Wrentham, Massachusetts
Assistant in Neurology
The Children's Hospital
Assistant Professor in Neurology
Harvard Medical School
Boston, Massachusetts

Dale Antanitus, M.D.
Primary Care Physician
The Children's Hospital Health and Habilitative
    Services Program
Wrentham State School
Wrentham, Massachusetts
Instructor in Medicine
Harvard Medical School
Boston, Massachusetts

Stuart B. Bauer, M.D.
Associate in Urology
The Children's Hospital
Assistant Professor of Surgery and Urology
Harvard Medical School
Boston, Massachusetts

Barbara Begin, R.N.*
Formerly Assistant Director of Nursing for Clinical
    Services
Wrentham State School
Wrentham, Massachusetts

* Deceased.

Rita Benezra, M.D.
Developmental Pediatrician
Institute for Child Development
Hackensack Medical Center
Hackensack, New Jersey

Allen I. Berliner, M.D.
Chief, Dermatology Section
Norwood Hospital
Norwood, Massachusetts
Staff Dermatologist
University Hospital
New England Medical Center
Assistant Clinical Professor of Dermatology
Tufts University School of Medicine
Boston, Massachusetts

Kathleen A. Blaber, R.N.
Marketing Manager
General Rehabilitation Services
Teaneck, New Jersey

Paula L. Blinkhorn, R.N.
Nursing Coordinator
Developmental Services Department
Wrentham State School
Wrentham, Massachusetts

Elizabeth R. Brown, M.D.
Director of Neonatology
Boston City Hospital
Associate Professor of Pediatrics
Boston University Medical Center
Boston, Massachusetts

Christina M. Browne, R.N.-C., B.S.N., M.S., M.M.H.S.
Director of Nursing
Massachusetts Mental Health Center
Boston, Massachusetts

Edward A. Cavallari, M.S., R.Ph.
Director of Pharmacy Services
The Children's Hospital Health and Habilitative
   Services Program
Wrentham State School
Wrentham, Massachusetts

Frank Crantz, M.D.
Clinical Associate Professor of Medicine
Georgetown University School of Medicine
Washington, DC

Allen C. Crocker, M.D.
Director, Developmental Evaluation Clinic
The Children's Hospital
Associate Professor of Pediatrics
Lecturer in Maternal and Child Health
Harvard Medical School
Boston, Massachusetts

Marie Cullinane, R.N., M.S.
Director of Special Services and Nurse Specialist in
   Developmental Disabilities
Developmental Evaluation Clinic
The Children's Hospital
Adjunct Assistant Professor of Maternal-Child
   Nursing
Boston College
Boston, Massachusetts

Sandra J. Curtis, R.N.
Director of Nursing
Wrentham State School
Wrentham, Massachusetts

Ann T. Cutler, M.D.
Attending, Chronic Disease Division
La Rabida Children's Hospital and Research Center
Assistant Professor of Clinical Pediatrics
Developmental Institute
Michael Reese Hospital
University of Chicago
Chicago, Illinois

Philip W. Davidson, Ph.D.
Director, University Affiliated Program for
   Developmental Disabilities
Department of Pediatrics

University of Rochester Medical Center
Associate Professor of Pediatrics
University of Rochester School of Medicine and
   Dentistry
Rochester, New York

Jocelyn Douglass, R.N.-C., M.S.
Nurse Practitioner
The Children's Hospital Health and Habilitative
   Services Program
Wrentham State School
Wrentham, Massachusetts

Mairin B. Doherty, M.D.
Chief, Day Hospital Program
E.P. Bradley Hospital
East Providence, Rhode Island
Assistant Professor of Psychiatry and Human
   Behavior
Brown University Program in Medicine
Providence, Rhode Island

Frances Medaglia Dwyer, R.N.C.
Formerly Program Director
Senior Citizen's Health Center
Lawrence Memorial Hospital of Medford
Medford, Massachusetts

Ellen Roy Elias, M.D.
Assistant Pediatrician, Clinical Genetics
New England Medical Center Hospitals
Instructor in Pediatrics
Tufts University School of Medicine
Boston, Massachusetts

Theodor Feigelman, M.D.
Chief Hospital Physician
The Children's Hospital Health and Habilitative
   Services Program
Wrentham State School
Wrentham, Massachusetts
Assistant in Medicine
The Children's Hospital
Instructor in Pediatrics
Harvard Medical School
Boston, Massachusetts

Ellen M. Friedman, M.D., F.A.A.P., F.A.C.F.
Associate in Otolaryngology
The Children's Hospital
Assistant Professor of Otolaryngology
Harvard Medical School
Boston, Massachusetts

David R. Fulton, M.D.
Cardiologist
Floating Hospital for Infants and Children
New England Medical Center
Assistant Professor of Pediatrics
Tufts University School of Medicine
Boston, Massachusetts

Naom Gavriely, M.D., D.Sc.
Head, Respiratory Physiology Unit
Rappaport Family Institute for Research in the
    Medical Sciences
Senior Lecturer, Faculty of Medicine
Technion-Israel Institute of Technology
Haifa, Israel

Samuel Z. Goldhaber, M.D.
Associate Physician
Brigham and Women's Hospital
Assistant Professor of Medicine
Harvard Medical School
Boston, Massachusetts

Adria S. Hodas, R.N., F.N.P.
Health Care Coordinator
Toward Independent Living and Learning
Dedham, Massachusetts

Kristen L. Johnson, M.D.
Anesthesiologist
Children's Hospital Medical Center of Northern
    California
Oakland, California

Kirtly Parker Jones, M.D.
Assistant Professor of Obstetrics and Gynecology
University of Utah Health Sciences Center
Salt Lake City, Utah

Lawrence C. Kaplan, M.D., Sc.M., F.A.A.P.
Director, Birth Defects Service
The Children's Hospital
Instructor in Pediatrics
Harvard Medical School
Boston, Massachusetts

Jacqueline M. Keane, R.N.
Director of Health Services
The May Institute
Chatham, Massachusetts

Catherine McNiff, R.N.
Nurse Practitioner
The Children's Hospital Health and Habilitative
    Services Program
The Children's Hospital
Boston, Massachusetts

Marc Manigat, M.D., M.P.H.
Physician and Chairman, Infection Control
The Children's Hospital Health and Habilitative
    Services Program
Wrentham State School
Wrentham, Massachusetts
Clinical Instructor in Pediatrics
Harvard Medical School
Boston, Massachusetts

Harold L. May, M.D.
Director of Medical Services
The Children's Hospital Health and Habilitative
    Services Program
Wrentham State School
Wrentham, Massachusetts
Associate Surgeon
Brigham and Women's Hospital
Assistant Clinical Professor of Surgery
Harvard Medical School
Boston, Massachusetts

Sharon R. Menkveld, M.D.
Orthopedist
Milwaukee Medical Clinic
Consultant Orthopedist
Children's Hospital of Wisconsin and Columbia
    Hospital
Milwaukee, Wisconsin

David L. Meryash, M.D.
Associate Director, Child Development Center
Rhode Island Hospital
Assistant Professor of Pediatrics
Brown University Program in Medicine
Providence, Rhode Island

Joseph E. Murray, M.D.
Chief of Plastic Surgery Emeritus
The Children's Hospital
Professor of Surgery
Harvard Medical School
Boston, Massachusetts

Priscilla S. Osborne, M.S.
Clinical Director of Physical Therapy
Developmental Evaluation Clinic
The Children's Hospital
Adjunct Clinical Associate Professor
Sargent College of Allied Health Professions
Boston University
Boston, Massachusetts

Judith S. Palfrey, M.D.
Chief, Division of Ambulatory Services
The Children's Hospital
Associate Professor of Pediatrics
Harvard Medical School
Boston, Massachusetts

Frederick B. Palmer, M.D.
Director of Inpatient Services and Vice-President
  for Medical Affairs
Kennedy Institute for Handicapped Children
Associate Professor of Pediatrics
The Johns Hopkins University School of Medicine
Baltimore, Maryland

Joel Pearlman, D.M.D.
Director of Dentistry
Tufts Dental Facility for the Handicapped
Wrentham State School
Wrentham, Massachusetts
Associate Chief Dentist
Tufts Dental Facilities for the Handicapped
Preceptor and Clinical Instructor
Tufts University School of Dental Medicine
Boston, Massachusetts

Ingram M. Roberts, M.D.
Associate Professor of Medicine
Division of Gastroenterology
George Washington University Medical Center
Washington, DC

Mai-Lan Rogoff, M.D.
Assistant Professor of Psychiatry and Pediatrics
University of Massachusetts Medical Center
Worcester, Massachusetts

Shirley A. Roy, R.N.
Clinic Nurse
Department of Otolaryngology
The Children's Hospital
Boston, Massachusetts

I. Leslie Rubin, M.D.
Director of Pediatrics
Developmental Evaluation Clinic
The Children's Hospital
Assistant Professor of Pediatrics
Harvard Medical School
Boston, Massachusetts

Aruna Sachdev, M.D.
Clinical Associate, Children's Service
Massachusetts General Hospital

Pediatrician
Spaulding Rehabilitation Hospital
Boston, Massachusetts

Richard R. Schnell, Ph.D.
Director of Psychology and Senior Associate in
  Psychology
Developmental Evaluation Clinic
The Children's Hospital
Associate in Pediatrics (Psychology)
Harvard Medical School
Adjunct Associate Professor of Psychology
Boston College
Boston, Massachusetts

Bruce K. Shapiro, M.D.
Director of Outpatient Services and Director of
  Training
Kennedy Institute for Handicapped Children
Baltimore, Maryland
Associate Professor of Pediatrics
The Johns Hopkins University School of Medicine
Baltimore, Maryland

Eunice Shishmanian, R.N., M.S.
Director of Nursing
Developmental Evaluation Clinic
The Children's Hospital
Clinical Associate in Nursing
Boston College
Adjunct Assistant Clinical Professor of Nursing
Boston University
Boston, Massachusetts

Howard G. Smith, M.D.
General Director
Boston Children's Deafness Network
Senior Associate in Otolaryngology
Department of Otolaryngology
The Children's Hospital
Assistant Clinical Professor of Otolaryngology
Harvard Medical School
Boston, Massachusetts

Richard U. Staub, M.D.
Senior Pediatrician
The Children's Extended Care Center
Groton, Massachusetts
Clinical Instructor
Tufts New England Medical Center
Boston, Massachusetts

Stephen B. Sulkes, M.D.
Pediatric Discipline Coordinator, University
  Affiliated Program for Developmental Disabilities
Coordinator, New York State Developmental
  Disabilities Medical Fellows Program
Assistant Professor of Pediatrics
University of Rochester School of Medicine and
  Dentistry
Rochester, New York

Ludwik S. Szymanski, M.D.
Director of Psychiatry
  Developmental Evaluation Clinic
The Children's Hospital
Assistant Professor of Psychiatry
Harvard Medical School
Boston, Massachusetts

Holly Tomlinson, R.P.T.
Assistant Supervisor
Physical Therapy Department
The Children's Hospital
Boston, Massachusetts

Carol A. Walsh, R.N.-C., B.S.N., M.P.H.
Director, Nurse Practitioner/Physician Assistant
  Program
The Children's Hospital Health and Habilitative
  Services Program
Wrentham State School
Wrentham, Massachusetts

Robert Wharton, M.D.
Director of Pediatrics
Spaulding Rehabilitation Hospital
Director, Prader-Willi Clinic
The Children's Hospital
Instructor in Pediatrics
Harvard Medical School
Boston, Massachusetts

Philip R. Ziring, M.D.
Chairman
Department of Pediatrics
Pacific Presbyterian Medical Center
Associate Clinical Professor of Pediatrics
University of California San Francisco School of
  Medicine
San Francisco, California

Johan Zwaan, M.D.
Associate Surgeon and Director
Pediatric Eye Service
Massachusetts Eye and Ear Infirmary
Associate Professor of Ophthalmology
Harvard Medical School
Boston, Massachusetts

CONTENTS

Part I

OVERVIEW OF NEEDS AND SYSTEMS

1

PARTNERSHIPS IN THE DELIVERY
OF MEDICAL CARE

Allen C. Crocker, M.D.

There is an array of clinical challenges presented to the medical care team by persons with developmental disabilities. A consideration of relevant processes and systems most commonly utilized by workers in the pursuit of treatment goals is only part of the medical story. Of equal importance are a clarification of the purposes intended and opportunities offered in the provision of health care and an affirmation of the vitality of medical partnerships in the whole human service concept.

OPTIMAL MEDICAL CARE

Although in the United States appropriate health care is an expectation, it does not have the features of entitlement found in key civil rights issues and in free public education. General emergency care may be assured in most community systems; a compassionate design may exist for providing basic primary care, particularly for the economically needy; and some components of disease prevention may be secured within health departments of cities and states. The deficit occurs, however, in the more searching aspects of health maintenance, and in quality assurance for attention to chronic issues.

For persons with developmental disabilities, a "right to treatment" statement is found in every listing of acceptable provisions. For example, such a statement appears in Article II of the Declaration of General and Special Rights of the Mentally Retarded, promulgated on October 24, 1968, by the International League of Societies for the Mentally Handicapped:

The mentally retarded person has the right to proper medical care and physical restoration and to such education, training, habilitation, and guidance as will enable him to develop his ability and potential to the fullest possible extent, no matter how severe his degree of disability. No mentally handicapped person should be deprived of such services by reason of the costs involved.

Although treatment ordinarily implies the utilization of modern medical assistance and other allied services, it should be noted that this "right" is culturally determined and not legally based (except regarding bias in life-sustaining measures). The comprehensiveness of medical care is not standardized, and it relies in good part on the integrity of the prevailing societal forces and the energy of service providers. In university centers and other locales where patient advocacy is well developed, there are palpable pressures for accountable professional performance. Beyond this we ultimately depend on the gradual evolution of additional knowledge and a refined sense of mission.

Individuals with developmental disorders carry with them a variety of somatic disabilities, the origin of which is often related to whatever produced the developmental aberration. Obvious examples of the medical work that needs to be done to assure the best health and ability to function are effective management of seizure disorders, orthopedic intervention in the complications of cerebral palsy, and surgical treatment of congenital heart disease in Down syndrome. Much less obvious are effective psychiatric assistance for a troubled and severely retarded client, regular screening for hearing impairment in a child

3

with multiple anomalies, reconstructive surgery for facial anomalies, and consideration of the role of gastroesophageal reflux in chronic pulmonary disease in seriously handicapped persons.

Besides these rather discrete medical interventions are the many more inquiring and creative aspects of simple good health maintenance, including a continuing look at growth and weight gain, the best management of recurrent infection, the monitoring of vision, and a concern for how the person feels. All this is part of normal health care, perhaps more strategic than usual in a person with special limitations. The urgency of some first-order bodily problem may produce a flurry of diversion, with the result that less vigorous attention may be given to basic health needs than is appropriate. Behavioral atypicality in a client may confound the resolve of medical providers to go "the rest of the way" in meeting health responsibilities.

Two examples illustrate deficiencies in our planning and counseling. First, there is very limited information available about longevity for persons with Down syndrome, assuming that cardiac issues have been controlled. We really do not know what the outlook is for the person with this anomaly because all previous studies have been based on the unusual circumstances of institutional living. Second, the true long-term natural history of cerebral palsy is not documented, and it is not known whether moderate degrees of motor handicap in the setting of diffuse cortical disease inevitably show significant further functional loss as the decades proceed.

The search for optimal medical care must include a look at associated issues. Families tell us, when we stop to ask them, that medical services leave them with important continuing needs in the following areas:

Basic information on the patient's underlying condition
Difficulties with transportation and parking costs
Assistance in home health care personal services and respite for family caregivers
Adaptation of the home to special needs
Counseling, mental health care, and support groups
Obtaining various special therapies
Nonreimbursed financial obligations

The factors listed above are in a direct sequence in the follow-through of health care activities; a host of additional elements exists in other spheres.

In the care of individuals with bodily abnormalities, it is important to avoid placing undue emphasis on the concept of "illness" with its attendant psychological limitations. When the anomaly is as fully compensated as possible, the person should no longer be considered ill. Stressing wellness by acknowledging achievements in adaptation is a more positive approach. For example, children with spina bifida whose bladder functions are well managed by clean intermittent catheterization are not ill; nor are adults whose seizure disorders have responded adequately to anticonvulsant therapy. Because the idea of wellness depends in part on the person's ability to perform social and daily living tasks, the health care provider must be aware of factors related to age and gender, and of social and ethnic components.[12] Wellness is promoted by paying attention to good nutrition, proper sleep, adequate exercise and relaxation, and stress control. Ultimately, self-understanding and self-actualization form the bases for securing wellness; for individuals with developmental disorders, these precious accomplishments require substantial assistance. The clinical team can make valuable contributions not only in the abatement of illness, but also in the attainment of wellness.

Conceptual problems also arise when considering the terms "disability" and "handicap." In human service work, if not in the dictionary, it is now widely agreed that there is an appropriate distinction between these words. A disability is an established aberration or abnormality with potential functional significance. A handicap is the degree of limitation or hindrance the disability produces. A disability can be objectively defined; a handicap has subjective and relative elements. For example, an amputation or a serious hearing impairment represents unmistakable disabilities, but the degree of the handicap will depend on the success of the person's rehabilitation and accommodation. All disabilities are to some extent handicapping, but the more generic term is more applicable to most situations.

Nomenclature can become depersonalizing and also bewildering. For instance, when the media speak of handicap-free disabilities, attention is diverted from the barriers that persist for most disabled individuals.[1] Koop[8] has described well the quiet gains achieved by young people born with congenital difficulties:

The presence of a physical or mental disability should not suggest or presuppose that an emotional or spiritual disability is also present. If we cannot make these kinds of distinctions, then we are the ones with the more serious disabilities—the disability of imprecision, the disability of discrimination, and the disability of being a casual generalist.

PRINCIPLES IN THE PROVISION OF MEDICAL CARE

Currently, the public has become involved in ethical decisions about the quality and intensity of medical and nursing care for newborn infants with serious clinical problems. A relationship exists between the assurance of life-sustaining nourishment and intervention for these infants, without regard to the degree of disability, and whether or not medical facilities will receive federal reimbursement for services. The actions of the Justice Department in the "Baby Doe" tragedy of 1982 drew on the anti-bias provisions of the Section 504 amendment of the Vocational Rehabilitation Act (regulations in 1977), an unexpected extension of this basically nonmedical, adult-oriented legislation. Although some controversy remains about the operational elements of these regulations (and of later ones based on child abuse laws), an interesting effect has been the evocation of resolves on behalf of disabled newborn infants. Representatives of parent groups, the clinical professions, religious and legal interests, various administrators, and hospital-based infant committees have come together for discussion. A benchmark for these coalitions was the joint signing on November 29, 1983, of the "Principles of Treatment of Disabled Infants." (This statement has been subscribed to by the American Academy of Pediatrics, the American Association of University Affiliated Programs for Persons with Developmental Disabilities, the National Down Syndrome Congress, the Association for Retarded Citizens/ U.S., the Spina Bifida Association of America, The Association for Persons with Severe Handicaps, the American Association on Mental Deficiency, and the American Coalition of Citizens with Disabilities.) The statement says:

Discrimination of any type against any individual with a disability/disabilities, regardless of the nature or severity of the disability, is morally and legally indefensible.

Throughout their lives, all disabled individuals have the same rights as other citizens, including access to such major societal activities as health care, education, and employment.

These rights for all disabled persons must be recognized at birth.

NEED FOR INFORMATION

There is a need for professional education and dissemination of updated information which will improve decision-making about disabled individuals, especially newborns. To this end, it is imperative to educate all persons involved in the decision-making process. Parents should be given information on available resources to assist in the care of their disabled infant. Society should be informed about the value and worth of disabled persons. Professional organizations, advocacy groups, the government, and individual care givers should educate and inform the general public on the care, need, value, and worth of disabled infants.

MEDICAL CARE

When medical care is clearly beneficial, it should always be provided. When appropriate medical care is not available, arrangements should be made to transfer the infant to an appropriate medical facility. Consideration such as anticipated or actual limited potential of an individual and present or future lack of available community resources are irrelevant and must not determine the decisions concerning medical care. The individual's medical condition should be the sole focus of the decision. These are very strict standards.

It is ethically and legally justified to withhold medical or surgical procedures which are clearly futile and will only prolong the act of dying. However, supportive care should be provided, including sustenance as medically indicated and relief of pain and suffering. The needs of the dying person should be respected. The family also should be supported in its grieving.

In cases where it is uncertain whether medical treatment will be beneficial, a person's disability must not be the basis for a decision to withhold treatment. At all times during the process when decisions are being made about the benefit or futility of medical treatment, the person should be cared for in the medically most appropriate ways. When doubt exists at any time about whether to treat, a presumption always should be in favor of treatment.

GOVERNMENT AND COMMUNITY SUPPORT

Once a decision to treat an infant has been made, government and private agencies must be prepared to allocate adequate resources for appropriate services as needed to child and family for as long as needed. Services should be individualized, community-based, and coordinated.

The Federal Government has an historical and legitimate role in protecting the rights of its citizens. Among these rights is the enforcement of all applicable federal statutes established to prevent and remedy discrimination against individuals with disabilities, including those afforded by Section 504 of the Rehabilitation Act. States also have legitimate roles in protecting the rights of their citizens and an obligation to enforce all applicable state laws.

The components of this declaration would not seem in themselves to be controversial. The form of it and its message of broad commitment constitute a useful clarification for medical facilities. The affirmation of the need for allocation of "adequate resources for appropriate services as needed to child and family for as long as needed" may be ahead of reality.

In another effort to place on record key factors in modern care for disabled children, Project BRIDGE of the American Academy of Pediatrics has developed a statement of "Principles of Health Care for Children"[7] as follows:

Preface. As prologue to the health care guidelines, we present a set of general statements, or principles, written to express the underlying philosophy of our approach. These statements are broad in scope because they are intended for all professionals who provide health care services to children.

We wish to emphasize that these principles refer to optimal health care for *all* children and their families. Accordingly, the following statements have been designed to facilitate the delivery of health care services to both the able-bodied child and the child with chronic illness or disability.

In the principles listed below, there are frequent references to the family. The reader should note, however, that "or guardian" should be added wherever appropriate. We also wish to emphasize that the word "family" refers not only to parents, but also to siblings.

OPTIMAL HEALTH CARE FOR CHILDREN SHOULD:

1. consider the child and his or her family as the focus of health care services.
2. be based on child and family needs, determined by comprehensive and relevant evaluations.
3. encourage normal patterns of living within the home and community.
4. provide guidance in creating an environment which supports and nurtures developmental progress.
5. insure access to a comprehensive range of health, educational, and social services.
6. encourage the child and the family to become educated consumers by fostering their knowledge and understanding of the health care system.
7. reflect an efficient and effective allocation of resources.
8. contribute to an ongoing process of coordination and communication between the child and family, the school, and all other relevant agencies.
9. improve the functional independence of the child and his or her family.
10. protect the fiscal integrity of the family unit.

This valuable document broadens the scope of traditional medical support by indicating the importance of providing care that is child and family focused, developmentally oriented, coordinated with school and other services, accompanied by patient and parent education, attentive to environment, and thoughtful about resources. Regrettably, no group has brought out a comparable declaration for adults.

TEAMS AND NETWORKS

Because of the multifactorial nature of developmental disabilities and their consequences, medical activities are often appropriately carried out in the setting of teams.[4] These functions may occur at service facilities, such as early intervention programs and cerebral palsy treatment centers; at diagnostic units, such as child development clinics; and at school meetings for educational teams. For some physicians these encounters are stimulating and fulfilling; for others they may seem redundant or confounding. The two team models most commonly employed are the multidisciplinary and the interdisciplinary types (see Fig. 1-1).

A multidisciplinary team is a loose coalition of professionals, each of whom contributes pertinent material (assessment studies, etc.) to a coordinator who has the responsibility of tying it all together. The diverse reports may be presented only in writing or can involve personal discussion as well. An interdisciplinary team, in comparison, sees the patient at one facility and meets shortly thereafter. Members of this team have relatively equal professional stature and decide by a system such as rotation who will serve as coordinator. They remain accessible for follow-through activities. Interdisciplinary teams may require subsidization because of the difficulty of reimbursing expenses to the group. When these teams are small enough they can provide mobile services and visit areas where special needs exist.

Physicians may require some training before serving in an interdisciplinary team because its egalitarian structure is in contrast to usual medical problem-solving behavior. Doctors are seldom involved in transdisciplinary activities, in which the other disciplinary roles are subsumed for purposes of leadership and communication by a single managing professional. In collaborative practice the action is taken by a small team and is a true sharing between involved professionals, such as between physician and nurse or nurse practitioner.

Overall, the alliance of medical personnel with their clinical colleagues to plan programs for persons with developmental disabilities has been one of the most productive features of child study in the last two decades. This time period has seen the emergence of developmental pediatrics as a specialty and of developmental-behavioral pediatrics as a field. It has been natural for pediatricians, family practitioners, and internists to work with psychiatrists, physiatrists, and other medical specialists and with dentists, nurses, physical therapists, occupational therapists, speech and language pathologists, audiologists, clinical psychologists, and social workers. New ground has been carved out as they have learned to interact with special educators, vocational counselors, creative art therapists, environmental design experts, clergy, lawyers, and public planners. (For descriptions of other disciplinary roles, see the sections on nursing services in Chaps. 4 and 27; the sections on physical therapy and psychology in Chap. 5; the discussion of nutrition in Chap. 10; and the discussion of pharmacy services in Chap. 29.)

Forming a team in behalf of a client with developmental disabilities commonly requires reaching out to agencies and interest groups. As the diagram of Cullinane shows (Fig. 1-2), a pattern evolves of shared responsibility for the diverse services that are appropriate during various periods of life.[3] Medical contributions con-

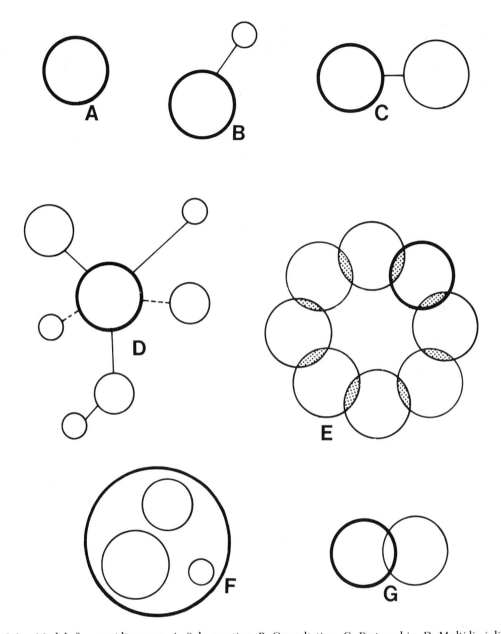

FIG. 1-1. Models for providing care: *A.* Solo practice. *B.* Consultation. *C.* Partnership. *D.* Multidisciplinary team. *E.* Interdisciplinary team. *F.* Transdisciplinary team. *G.* Collaborative practice. Size of circle is correlated with importance of contribution by that team member. Darker ring indicates person providing coordination and communication. (From Crocker, A.C., and Cullinane, M.M.: Coordination of services. *In* Developmental-Behavioral Pediatrics. Edited by M.D. Levine, W.B. Carey, A.C. Crocker, and R.T. Gross. Philadelphia, W.B. Saunders, 1983.)

tinue throughout, with varying intensity (black wedges in Fig. 1-2). A major challenge is the need to coordinate the components that are interacting with the child or adult and the family. In some states services are coordinated by the Department of Health for clients from birth to age 2 or 3; by the Department of Education during the school years; and by Vocational Reha-

bilitation and the Department of Mental Health (or Mental Retardation/Developmental Disabilities) in the adult years. Also involved are the Department of Social Services (or welfare); special agencies such as the Commissions for Blindness, Deafness, and Elderly Affairs; voluntary agencies, parent support groups, and advocacy organizations. Physicians need help in learning

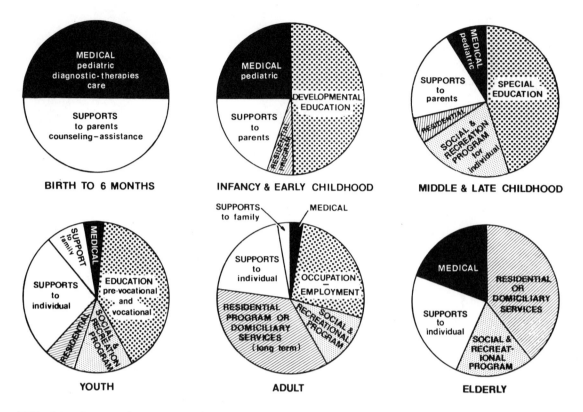

FIG. 1-2. Sequential program needs of individual with early onset of mental retardation and other developmental disabilities. (From Crocker, A.C., and Cullinane, M.M.: Coordination of services. *In* Developmental-Behavioral Pediatrics. Edited by M.D. Levine, W.B. Carey, A.C. Crocker, and R.T. Gross. Philadelphia, W.B. Saunders, 1983.)

about these resources (e.g., by contact with the Developmental Disabilities Planning Office).

In writing for the guidance of families who were caring for children with progressive central nervous system disorders, Cullinane suggested the term "the helping network" to describe the collection of community based supports that can be marshaled for assistance.[9] For direct medical care this assistance includes the community pediatrician, the local hospital, and the medical center. Nursing services may be available through community nursing, home nursing, and consultation from hospitals. Relief in the home is provided by home health aides and other respite arrangements and by hospice programs.

For family support there are parent groups sponsored by consumer organizations (including the National Tay-Sachs and Allied Diseases Association Parent Peer Group); resource parents; and social workers from various sources. Child development services, including home and center-based early intervention programs, can now also accommodate small children with serious disabilities. City or state agencies counsel on the availability of Supplemental Security Income

(SSI), Medicaid, and other benefits. In some states toll-free telephone numbers are maintained to assist parents in locating sources of assistance.[5] Parents can call the National Self-Help Clearinghouse (212-840-1258) for names of appropriate self-help groups in their state. Siblings can obtain a useful newsletter on supports for brothers and sisters published by the Sibling Information Network (Department of Educational Psychology, U-64, University of Connecticut, Storrs, CT 06268). The many helpful articles in a book edited by Mulick and Pueschel[10] are recommended for people interested in partnerships between parents and professionals.

THE MEDICAL MODEL— AND WHAT WENT WRONG

Historically the person with a developmental disorder was viewed as having a disease, particularly if there were also bodily elements in the situation (congenital anomalies, cerebral palsy, etc.). Medical judgments were given substantial credence, even if the knowledge base was limited. Other service professions in the late nineteenth and early twentieth centuries had only a minor commitment to the developmentally disabled population, and medical experts filled the void; this included their prognostication about developmental potential. It is embarrassing to note that medical involvement often resulted in nihilism, segregation, and banishment.

Nowhere was the medical model more indurated than in the large state residential facilities for mental retardation, the institutions. In both architecture and organization, institutions were patterned to resemble monolithic hospitals. Residents were called patients; they lived in wards and were cared for by nurses.[11] Wolfensberger[13] has pointed out that earlier in these settings the chief administrative officer (superintendent) was a physician and that physicians made a vast number of decisions about nonmedical care and regulations. Further, it was assured by law that the commissioners of mental health and/or mental retardation in the states were also physicians.

Medical dominance of the direction of long-term care has waned rapidly in the past two decades. Clinical and behavioral psychology, special education, and the various therapies have developed strong professional perceptions about the best course and guidance for persons with disability syndromes. Family advocacy and self-advocacy have enriched the scene. Team management is customary, with strong family and individual input. Physicians now only infrequently serve as institutional superintendents. Instead of being a "Medical Director," a physician is more often a "Director of Medical Services," with medicine joining as a partner in the program. It is of interest to learn how the administration of Boys Town in Nebraska came to deplore the medical model that had characterized their facility and changed over to a teaching-family model.[2] The medical model seems to have been equated with the entire institutional structure as compared with the smaller organizational unit associated with sensitivity to individual developmental needs.

Some residual fear regarding medical models still exists in community based services. There is a concern that medical pronouncements, with insinuations of illness, will subvert the thrust toward normalization in behavioral and educational programming. Better education in developmental matters for physicians and the presence of a more informed public would work against

such a possibility. It is also helpful for physicians to look thoughtfully at their own attitudes about disability.[6]

Optimal medical care is critical in realizing the greatest progress for children, adults, and their families in the presence of developmental disabilities. Medical contributions in the valued circumstances of direct doctor-patient relationships, in the joint planning of teams for individual persons, and in public planning make up the spirit and the activities of partnerships in the delivery of medical care.

REFERENCES

1. Cheever, R.: Too great a burden? UCPA News, Apr.-June, 1985.
2. Coughlin, D.D., et al.: Implementing the community-based teaching-family model at Boys Town. *In* Programming Effective Human Services. Edited by W.P. Christian, G.T. Hannah, and T.J. Glahn. New York, Plenum Press, 1984.
3. Crocker, A.C., and Cullinane, M.M.: Coordination of services. *In* Developmental-Behavioral Pediatrics. Edited by M.D. Levine, W.B. Carey, A.C. Crocker, and R.T. Gross. Philadelphia, W.B. Saunders, 1983.
4. Crocker, A.C., and Cullinane, M.M.: The function of teams. *In* Developmental-Behavioral Pediatrics. Edited by M.D. Levine, W.B. Carey, A.C. Crocker, and R.T. Gross. Philadelphia, W.B. Saunders, 1983.
5. Davidson, P.W., et al.: Direction services: a model facilitating secondary prevention of developmental handicapping conditions. Ment. Retard., 22:21, 1984.
6. Forman, M.A., and Hetznecker, W.: The physician and the handicapped child; dilemmas of care. J.A.M.A., 247:3325, 1982.
7. Healy, A. Personal communication, 1985.
8. Koop, C.E.: Who are the disabled among us? J. Adolesc. Health Care, 6:156, 1985.
9. Mackta, J. (ed.): One Day at a Time. Cedarhurst, N.Y., National Tay-Sachs and Allied Diseases Association, 1984.
10. Mulick, J.A., and Pueschel, S.M. (eds.): Parent-Professional Partnerships in Developmental Disability Services. Cambridge, MA, Ware Press, 1983.
11. Nelson, R.P., and Crocker, A.C.: The medical care of mentally retarded persons in public residential facilities. N. Engl. J. Med., 299:1039, 1978.
12. Steele, S.: Health Promotion of the Child with Long-term Illness. Norwalk, Conn., Appleton-Century-Crofts, 1983.
13. Wolfensberger, W.: The Origin and Nature of Our Institutional Models. Syracuse, N.Y., Human Policy Press, 1975.

2

THE SPECTRUM OF MEDICAL CARE FOR DEVELOPMENTAL DISABILITIES

Allen C. Crocker, M.D.

DEFINITION AND PREVALENCE OF DEVELOPMENTAL DISABILITIES

The term "developmental disabilities" embodies the very useful concept, first established by Elizabeth Boggs in the late 1960s, of clustering early-onset disorders of development according to their needs for supportive services. As a general term, in lowercase letters, its meaning extends beyond the study and planning regarding conditions that originate in childhood and are characterized by mental retardation, to include any circumstance that in its effects significantly impinges on development. Examples are neuromuscular disorders, such as cerebral palsy and muscular dystrophy; multiple congenital anomaly syndromes; sensory impairments, such as blindness and deafness; serious seizure disorders, such as epilepsy; autism; and certain physical disabilities and chronic illnesses. As will be discussed, these conditions can have similar etiologies and sometimes coexist, and they are of life-long duration.

When capitalized, the term "Developmental Disabilities" (DD) conveys these concerns as they are conceptualized in public planning and in legislative issues. This concept has now had 15 years of trial in federal, state, and community settings and has become a meaningful focus for the application of human service resources. It first appeared on the national scene with the passage in 1970 of the Developmental Disabilities Services and Facilities Construction Act Public Law (P.L.) 91-517. As with the other DD acts that followed, this legislation was largely concerned with policy and planning.

The population under consideration were individuals of all ages with mental retardation, cerebral palsy, epilepsy, and related neurological disorders.[4, 19] The Developmentally Disabled Assistance and Bill of Rights Act of 1975 (P.L. 94-103) added autism and severe dyslexia, and a study was begun to seek a functional rather than categorical definition. This was achieved in the Rehabilitation, Comprehensive Services, and Developmental Disabilities Amendments of 1978 (P.L. 95-602), which defined DD:

A severe, chronic disability of a person which (A) is attributable to a mental or physical impairment or combination of mental and physical impairments; (B) is manifested before the person attains the age twenty-two; (C) is likely to continue indefinitely; (D) results in substantial functional limitations in three or more of the following areas of major life activity: (i) self-care, (ii) receptive and expressive language, (iii) learning, (iv) mobility, (v) self-direction, (vi) capacity for independent living, and (vii) economic sufficiency; and (E) reflects the person's need for a combination and sequence of special interdisciplinary, or generic care, treatment, or other services which are of life-long or extended duration and are individually planned and coordinated.

The specifications in the Amendments of 1978 are a commendable listing of the true issues. Diagnostic and functional notations are usually blended as programs are developed. The subsequent Developmental Disabilities Act of 1984 (P.L. 98-527) retains the definition's elements. Included in the provisions of the various DD acts have been supports for state planning councils, protection and advocacy agencies, university affiliated facilities, and various special projects, as directed by the federal Administration on Developmental Disabilities.

Attempts to estimate the number of persons with various types of developmental disabilities are seriously hampered by intrinsic methodological variables. My comments here draw extensively on the excellent review by Kiernan and Bruininks,[18] who say that the five most common techniques for tallying this clientele use (1) key informants, (2) community forums, (3) rates under treatment, (4) social indicators, and (5) field surveys. Conclusions about prevalence for any given population will be influenced by the effects of such factors as age, culture, availability of service programs, and enrollment criteria.

Mental retardation, for example, receives its predominant identification during the school years, and the illusion is created that its incidence is reduced as adult life proceeds. Mild mental retardation (IQs in the range of 50 to 70) constitutes 85% of the total population with intellectual subnormality, and many do not have serious functional liabilities (see DD definition in P.L. 95-602). Likewise, persons with well-managed and/or mild epilepsy or cerebral palsy will not be counted in a census of true developmental disability. Significant mortality rates for such conditions as muscular dystrophy and certain other hereditary syndromes cause prevalence figures for these conditions to be higher in younger population groups. Diagnostic custom influences the apparent numbers of some rare conditions such as autism.

Kiernan and Bruininks[18] consider 1.0% the most reasonable prevalence figure for mental retardation for all ages in the general population, although they acknowledge that many other studies report up to $2\frac{1}{2}$–3%. They suggest overall prevalence figures of 0.75% (7.5/1000) for epilepsy, 0.35% for cerebral palsy, and 0.05% for autism. Gortmarker and Sappenfield[15] put the averages at 0.35%, 0.25%, and 0.04% for these three categories, with low rates for neural tube defects (0.04%) and for muscular dystrophy (0.006%). Tables 4-1 and 4-2 provide experiential reporting for these disorders in private pediatric practice.

Because of the prevalence of issues related to developmental problems, two other groupings should be kept in mind. First, 8 to 16% of the pupils in public schools have difficulties that currently justify individualized educational plans (IEPs), with special services provided, although these numbers are influenced by the practices and resources of the respective school districts. The majority of these young persons have learning or language disabilities (see Fig. 3-1), but some have other problems including mental retardation and sensory handicaps. Second, the Vanderbilt study concluded that 5 to 10% of the children in the United States have moderate or severe physical disability or chronic illness, often with developmental inhibition (though many of these are not provided with IEPs). Although the exact percentages are not available, it is certainly true that a considerable number of children, and probably a similar quantity of adults, have what can be considered significant developmental disabilities.

ORIGINS OF DEVELOPMENTAL DISABILITIES

In searching for the causes of disorders of development, one must give foremost consideration to supports for the growth and function of the brain—constitutional elements, nurturance during embryologic formation, insults in the birth period, later stresses, and interference with learning. Presented below is a scheme for thinking about possible mechanisms that may have been operative in any given situation. This guide has been found useful in the Developmental Evaluation Clinic of The Children's Hospital in Boston.

Heredity

Some potential disturbances are programmed by the genotype of the parents and can thus be said to have an origin prior to conception. These syndromes commonly have multiple somatic effects and may have a progressive course. Some degree of variation in expression can be anticipated, even in the same pedigree, as single-gene influences interact with other genic and environmental forces. A family history can provide clues, although in recessively transmitted disorders other involved relatives may not be apparent at the time when the first child is encountered.

Inborn Errors of Metabolism. The expressed biochemical aberrations include disturbances in amino acids (PKU), carbohydrates (galactosemia), lipids (Tay-Sachs disease), and mucopolysaccharides (Hurler syndrome).

Other Single-Gene Abnormalities. Included are many inherited conditions, some with X-linked transmission (Duchenne muscular dystrophy) and some with dominant transmission (neurofibromatosis, tuberous sclerosis).

Chromosomal Aberrations. The translocation syndromes and the fragile-X syndrome are examples.

Polygenic Familial Syndromes. Various combinations of altered genes are inherited, with a diversity of expression in the pedigree.

Early Alterations in Embryonic Development

Sporadic events may affect mitosis or embryogenesis, resulting in significant phenotypic alteration. The developmental implications will be determined by involvement of the central nervous system or other complications. The disability can be expected to be relatively stable after birth (if there are no further untoward happenings).

Chromosomal Aberrations. It is assumed that chromosomal aberrations such as nondisjunction, which produces a trisomic state as in Down syndrome, occur somewhat before, during, or very shortly after conception.

Prenatal Influence. The causes of so-called embryodysgenesis are usually of mysterious nature, although their origin must reflect some unfavorable element in organ differentiation in the first half of pregnancy. Occasionally, the force is known, as in congenital rubella and fetal alcohol syndrome; more often it is not. It is said that it requires 85 separate operations to make an Acushnet Titleist golf ball and about 26,000 to assemble a Chevrolet. To produce a human must involve uncountable small and large events. It is not surprising that there will be notable sensitivity to host and environmental influences (and their combinations). Included in this category are the many congenital anomaly syndromes (discussed in Chap. 6).

Other Pregnancy Problems and Perinatal Morbidity

Once morphogenesis is complete there remains in pregnancy a long period of growth and maturation. Premature termination of this support period results in the birth of a small, vulnerable baby. Compromise in the maintenance of central nervous system integrity due to immaturity or trauma at this time produces neurological lesions with many types of potential disabilities, basically stable in nature but with gradually increasing degrees of expression.

Placental Insufficiency. Infarction, infection, abnormal implantation, uterine tumor, toxemia, and multiple pregnancy can lead to fetal malnutrition, with altered growth and progress. The cause of intrauterine growth retardation can also be obscure, sometimes linked to the presence of fetal malformation.

Perinatal Difficulties. Now largely the dilemma of the premature infant, perinatal difficulties have elements of potential insult from asphyxia, acidosis, intraventricular hemorrhage, hypoglycemia, hyperbilirubinemia, and infection. (Care for these infants is discussed in Chap. 5.) Occasionally, full-term large and normal-sized babies are involved in obstetrical complications.

Acquired Childhood Diseases

Certain postnatal hazards can cause an acute modification of developmental status. These discrete events do damage from which varying degrees of recovery are possible.

Central Nervous System Infection. Types include the various viral encephalitis pictures, late-treated and complicated bacterial meningitis, and the vascular and metastatic effects of general sepsis.

Cranial Trauma. Commonly thought to result predominantly from vehicular accidents involving passengers and pedestrians, cranial traumas may be more frequently caused by accidents occurring in the household.

Other Mishaps. Cardiac arrest, near drowning, brain tumors, acquired hypothyroidism, and poisoning (including by lead) are childhood hazards.

Environmental and Behavioral Problems

A child's developmental progress is sensitive to limitations in nurturance and support and to the deviations inherent in constitutional disturbances in behavior. These more dynamic influences can sometimes be counterbalanced by appropriate intervention.

Deprivation. Decompensated parenting, child abuse and neglect, and particularly harsh and limited environmental elements are implied.

Parental Neurosis, Psychosis, and Character Disorder. A skewed setting can be produced for the child, particularly with maternal schizophrenia.

Emotional and Behavioral Disorders. Origins vary. Developmental progress, including learning, is deflected.

Childhood Psychosis and Autism. Some of the puzzling developmental effects may be intrinsic. Serious atypicality and pervasive developmental disorder require intense intervention if adequate personal gains are to be experienced.

Unknown Mechanisms

After all the usual special causes of developmental disability are considered, a substantial number of individuals remain for whom the operative influences are obscure. This testifies, in part, to our incomplete understanding of the many factors in developmental processes. When histories include a number of potentially deleterious elements with none of serious magnitude, the outcome may well be due to multifactorial effects. Sometimes no reasonable inferences can be drawn.

Our outline of origins of disorders can serve as a diagnostic checklist for single or multiple factors during investigations of causes. Distribution patterns for causative elements and settings vary with different disabilities and with the sources from which the individuals came. Various authors submit that there may be a subjective or interpretive component as well in judgments about probable causation.

In the Developmental Evaluation Clinic, a tertiary hospital referral clinic for the study of children with mental retardation, many years of experience have shown the percentages of causative factors to be 4 to 5% each for hereditary disorders and for acquired childhood diseases; 10 to 12% for perinatal difficulties; 17 to 20% for environmental and behavioral problems; and just over 30% each for early alterations of embryonic development and for "unknown" causes.[11] The children involved were referred for general evaluation and were not patients in special project areas. Among individuals found in pediatric nursing homes (see Chap. 4) and state residential facilities, there is usually a higher percentage of mental retardation due to trauma or infections.[22] On the other hand, the experience of the pupil–personnel services division of a busy public school district shows that the majority of children with retardation have a background of environmental and behavioral problems.

The matrix of causes for other developmental disabilities is similar to that for mental retardation. In cerebral palsy, perinatal factors and cerebral dysgenesis are thought to constitute the two largest causes of the disability, with the effects of infection, trauma, and progressive encephalopathies lesser causes.[2, 26] For the major seizure disorders, hypoxic ischemic insults, trauma, infection, malformations, and hereditary elements are all operative.[1, 6] Hearing impairment can be considered in two categories. For sensorineural loss, hereditary conditions are the most important causes, followed by prematurity and its sequences, congenital infections, and meningitis. For conductive hearing loss, middle ear effusions and eustachian tube dysfunctions are the principal issues.[31] For serious

FIG. 2-1. A 3-year-old boy with Hurler syndrome, enjoying a whale watch cruise with his father. He has had a ventriculoperitoneal shunt for hydrocephalus, repair of a large umbilical hernia, and two sets of P-E tubes to aid hearing impairment from serous otitis media.

visual impairment, congenital anomalies are critical, plus tumors, complications of prematurity, cortical disease, and hereditary syndromes.[13]

As could be anticipated, origins in common for central nervous system morbidity will often set the scene for clinical expression of multiple disabilities. In fact, either by shared causation or as a complication or sequential phenomenon, multiple elements can be considered usual. Accardo and Capute[3] have commented that "of all developmentally disabled children, approximately one-third have one handicap, another third have two handicaps, and the remaining third have three or more handicaps." Again, the numbers vary with author and population. Accardo and Capute report that among persons with mental retardation, about 4% will have epilepsy and 10% will show cerebral palsy. For the adult population with retardation at Wrentham State School, Nelson and Crocker[23] list about one third with a seizure disorder and one third with a cerebral palsy type of physical disability. For children with cerebral palsy, it is anticipated

Table 2-1. *HEALTHWATCH for the Child with Hurler Syndrome*

Concern	Clinical Expression	When Seen	Management
Phenotypic changes	Full forehead, flat nose joint restriction, synophrys, hirsutism	Gradually apparent in 1st yr	None necessary
Growth pattern	Accelerated at first, then stops (maximum 42 in.)	1st 1–2 yr; stops by 3 yr	None necessary
Hernias	Inguinal in most boys; umbilical in both sexes	Early months	Repair optional; will recur if not reinforced
Joint restriction	Flexion contracture of all joints; progressive for some yrs.	Elbows by few months; other joints gradually apparent	ROM exercises of limited use; encourage general activity
Kyphos	Beaking of L-1, with sharp angulation of spine	Early months; more when upright	None necessary (no spinal cord pressure)
Corneal clouding	Hazy appearance	1–2 months	None necessary
Hearing problems	Middle ear effusions, ankylosis of ossicles, hearing impairment	1–2 yr	Treatment of infection, ventilation tubes; possible amplification
Hepatosplenomegaly	Firm organomegaly; limited progression	During 1st yr	None necessary (no functional handicap)
Subarachnoid cysts	Increased intracranial pressure; hydrocephalus	Variable; 1–3 yr	Shunting may be advisable
Seizures	Primary generalized	2–4 yr	Usual anticonvulsants; will have time limitation
Cardiac problems	Thickened valves, coronary narrowing, cardiac myopathy	Murmur in 1st yr; other issues by 3+ yr	May require treatment for congestive failure
Airway problems	Large adenoids, tonsils; increased secretions; thickening, narrowing of larynx, trachea; obstructive sleep apnea	Slowly progressive	In later years may need oxygen therapy; rarely tracheostomy; great care in anesthesia

that 30 to 70% will have mental retardation ("generally, the more limbs involved, the more significant the retardation") and that 25 to 35% will have seizures.[27] Sensory problems are seen more frequently among individuals with retardation: in a typical series, 10 to 20% will have significant hearing impairment and about 5 to 10% will have serious visual impairment.[24] Behavioral and psychiatric disorders are also common (see Chap. 20).

SPECIAL MEDICAL CARE

While informed primary and specialty medical care is due for persons with developmental disabilities, a balance must be sought between the appropriateness of providing usual, "generic" care and being concerned with the special vulnerabilities of this population. This is the alike-unalike dilemma. Much of the health care is usual, but particular extra knowledge is needed. Topics of customary medical study,

such as cardiology, ophthalmology, etc., are discussed in the other chapters of this book, where basic principles can be emphasized along with their application for the large number of syndromes. For detailed consideration of specific disabilities, the reader is referred to the bibliography of textbooks at the end of this chapter.

The necessary considerations in providing medical care for developmental disabilities can be illustrated by examining four types of disorders: hereditary disease (Hurler syndrome), chromosomal aberration (Down syndrome), prenatal influence syndrome (myelodysplasia), and possible perinatal difficulties (cerebral palsy).

Hurler Syndrome

The inborn error of mucopolysaccharide (MPS) metabolism represents homozygous expression (autosomal recessive transmisson) of l-iduronidase deficiency, and the clinical difficulties center around altered MPS functions in key locations.

In the proband child, diagnosis is typically established during the second half of the first year of life and confirmed by enzyme assay on white blood cells. As is usual for large-molecule inborn errors, there is a period of reasonable personal progress (1 to 2 years) and a middle time of slowed development (2 to 4 years); then functional losses occur, with death in early middle childhood. Good resolve is required by family and community to acknowledge the involved limitations and embrace the special existence and charm embodied by these children (Fig. 2-1).[10]

A bill of rights was put together in the 1970s,[9] emphasizing the opportunities for positive support. Table 2-1 presents a HEALTHWATCH synopsis of special needs of children with Hurler syndrome. At the present time the possibility of useful enzyme replacement from bone marrow transplantation remains in the research realm. (See networks that can assist the family in Chap. 1.) Parental support, referrals, and information are available at the National MPS Society in Hicksville, NY (516-931-6338) and at the National Tay-Sachs and Allied Diseases Association in Newton, MA (617-964-5508).

Down Syndrome

Down syndrome is the clinical expression of a surfeit of material in chromosome 21 (trisomy, translocation); it is often referred to as the leading clinical cause of mental retardation. It occurs universally at an incidence of 1 per 1,000 births, is diagnosed at birth, has high public recognition, and has its own lore (some mythic). Individuals with Down syndrome have been traditional victims of stereotyping and segregation, but in the last decade and a half vastly improved opportunities have been secured in education, vocation, and independent living (Fig. 2-2).

Changes in outcome have been revolutionary. First, we are seeing the results of education and support; mental retardation is now more commonly mild in degree than moderate, as it was formerly. Second, we are seeing changes in such critical areas as mortality rates from repair of serious congenital cardiac anomalies. The adoption of young children with Down syndrome has become commonplace, with waiting lists in many metropolitan areas. Significant medical care issues exist, as summarized in Table 2-2. (See discussions in Chaps. 8, 12–15, 18, 20.) A particularly sensitive time for best contributions from the medical team is when information is supplied during the first diagnostic interview with parents.[25] A headquarters for information and advocacy is maintained by the parent-formed

National Down Syndrome Congress in Park Ridge, IL (1-800-232-NDSC outside of Illinois).

Children formerly had a high early mortality rate, but in current times prompt and continued intervention is managing many of the complications and producing good survival (Fig. 2-3). Extensive ethical discussions have affirmed the need for maximum assistance, early and ongoing. For example, an 8-year-old girl, Amber Tatro of Irving, Texas, was recently supported by the Supreme Court in claiming the right to have clean intermittent catheterization at school.[19] Because the natural history of clinical difficulties in myelodysplasia is variable, no time frame is given in the HEALTHWATCH chart in Table 2-3. Renal failure from the difficulties complicating a neurogenic bladder remains the most common cause of death. (Chap. 17 gives information on the best management of urologic problems.) It is clear that there will soon be a new cohort of young people reaching adult life with moderate to severe disability and adequate health. The Spina Bifida Association of America has headquarters in Chicago (312-663-1562).

Cerebral Palsy

The term cerebral palsy is applied to a disorder of movement and posture due to a nonprogressive lesion of the immature brain. The diagnosis is a matter of clinical judgment but is useful for the development of services. As in planning regarding myelodysplasia, significantly involved individuals will make optimum progress when they are provided with guidance from an interdisciplinary specialty team.[30] As Taft and Matthews have pointed out,[29] there is an evolution of motor problems and associated dysfunctions, with difficult times arriving in middle to late childhood. The story becomes more complex in the adult because it is often difficult to determine the basis for the diminishing function in mobility, language, and independence. Table 2-4 presents some of the major items in care. (See also Chaps. 9–11, 23, 26.) Information and resources are available from the United Cerebral Palsy Association in New York (212-481-6300).

Myelodysplasia

The cluster of congenital anomalies identified as neural tube defects (spina bifida, meningocele, myelomeningocele, and anencephaly) are prenatal influence syndromes, with apparent multifactorial elements. (Risk for repeat pregnancies ranges from 1 per 20 to 1 per 40.) The term myelodysplasia is used to describe spinal defects in which there is cord involvement and

FIG. 2-2. *A.* A young lady with Down syndrome, sharing her joy with a friend after winning third place in Special Olympics track events. *B.* The same girl (#1) with her tentmates at an integrated overnight camp.

loss of nerve function. Such a condition can be viewed as a prototypic developmental disability, with a varying degree of abnormality and a complex set of personal effects requiring a team of devoted professionals to accomplish optimal habilitation.

PASSAGES

Life-long planning is appropriate for developmental disabilities, which are defined in P.L. 95-602 as being "manifested before the person attains the age of twenty-two" and "likely to continue indefinitely." Nevertheless, human services tend

Table 2-2. *HEALTHWATCH for the Person with Down Syndrome*

Concern	Clinical Expression*	When Seen	Prevalence	Management
Congenital heart disease	Endocardial cushion defect, ventricular septal defect, tetralogy of Fallot	Newborn or first year	34%	ECG, chest X ray, cardiac consultation, surgical repair
Hypotonia	Reduced muscle tone, increased range of joints, motor function problems	Throughout; improvement with maturity	All	Guidance by physical therapy, early intervention
Delayed growth	Typically at or near third percentile	Throughout	All	Early nutritional support; check heart
Developmental delays	Some global delay, variable degrees; special language problems	1st yr; continues	All	Early intervention, special education language therapy
Hearing problems	Serous otitis media, small ear canals, conductive impairment	Check by 1 yr; review regularly	70%	Audiology, tympanometry, ENT consultation
Ocular problems	Refractive errors, strabismus, cataracts	Eye exam by 1 yr, then follow-ups	50% 35% 15%	Ophthalmologic consultation
Cervical spine abnormality	Atlantoaxial instability, potential long-track signs	X ray by 3 yr; occasional repeat	10% ± 1–2% +	Orthopedic neurologic help; possible restriction, fusion
Thyroid disease	Hypothyroidism (rare hyper-), decreased growth	Some congenital; most 2nd + decade; check 2 yr, repeat	15%	Replacement therapy as needed
Obesity	Excessive weight gain	2–3 yr, 12–13 yr, and in adult life	Common	Caloric restriction, activity
Seizure disorders	Primary generalized (also hypsarrhythmia)	Any time	5–10%	Usual management
Emotional problems	Inappropriate behavior, depression, other emotional disturbances	Mid to late childhood, adult life	Common	Mental health assistance, family guidance
Premature senescence	Behavioral changes, functional losses	4th, 5th decades	Unknown (increased rate)	Special support

* Additional variable occurrences include congenital gastrointestinal anomalies, constipation, Hirschsprung disease, leukemia, keratoconus, dry skin, hip dysplasia, diabetes, hepatitis B carrier state, and mitral valve prolapse.

to be designed to provide for separate periods in life with different groups of workers for each period—infancy, preschool, childhood, youth, adult, and elderly. These intervals and the preponderance of different agencies at different times, including coordinating services, cover only part of the life story of each individual and family, and the potential for discontinuity is troubling. Recently, more attention has been given by planners to transitions. Particular heed is being given, first, by health departments, private groups, and school departments to the transfer of 3-to-5-year-olds from early intervention programs to public schools; second, by various agencies to the transfer of people in their late teens and early twenties from special education programs to vocational programs or employment.

The design for medical care also risks discontinuity, especially during the major shift from pediatric attention to adult medical services. Understandably, pediatricians tend to con-

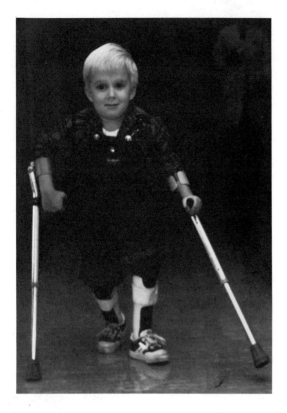

FIG. 2-3. A 6-year-old boy with a lumbar myelo-meningocele and shunted hydrocephalus. He requires intermittent urinary catheterization, is ambulatory with the aid of crutches, and attends regular classes in school.

tinue in the care of adults because of their personal knowledge of the problems of these patients, but this pattern of care must also be viewed as an abdication of internal medicine; the new group must take over.

Birth to Three Years Old

Infants thought to be at risk regarding developmental disabilities are commonly grouped as follows: "established risk" refers to those with medical syndromes known to have outcomes of concern, such as Down syndrome. "Biological risk" refers to those with histories of prenatal or perinatal events that can result in difficulties. "Environmental risk" refers to those whose life circumstances may interfere with their making the best progress. An effort is being made to identify such children and to provide special stimulation and training in early intervention programs. In Massachusetts in 1984, 2,500 children, or 1.1% of the population group from birth to 3 years old, attended such programs.[28] More than half had been referred by physicians or hos-

pitals, and the others came from family self-referrals, other agency programs, or Child Find outreach programs in the school district. Estimates vary of the total number of infants and toddlers for whom early intervention is appropriate; many estimates are from 5% to 10%. In the Massachusetts program, enrollment for children with cerebral palsy and Down syndrome (both frequently reported) was closer to the expected prevalence rates for these conditions than enrollment for less common ones: for cerebral palsy, enrollment was 46% of expected prevalence; for Down syndrome it was 72%.[28]

Early intervention programs have focused attention on the total needs of the birth-to-3-year-old group, with a resultant enhancement of medical study as well. For infants from newborn intensive care nurseries, some state health departments now have tracking systems that assure monitoring of progress and services. A recent study in New England[15] found that 35 to 50% of those from neonatal intensive care units went on to infant follow-up clinics in hospitals. Many also had home visiting at first by community nursing services; and most attended early intervention programs, where they constituted an average of 28% of the total enrollment. All infant follow-up programs and most early intervention programs maintain contact with the community pediatrician, who shares in the guidance of the families of these small children (see Chap. 5).

During the past decade, most noncategorical support programs for infants and young children have attempted to apply the risk categories described above in providing services and have tried to maintain an open-ended view of ultimate developmental outcomes. For many of those in the "established risk" classification, this approach gives added hope for improved learning and adaptation. These services add enormously to what the physician can say to families at the time of diagnosis regarding potential for activity and progress. When the moment comes for the transition to the programs of the school district, these young people are much better known and accommodated.

School Years

Medical care services during the school years involve the establishment of partnerships between community teams, schools, private physicians, hospitals, residential programs, and Crippled Children's Services clinics (see Chaps. 1, 3, and 4). It is often in this period that definitive diagnostic conclusions are formed and key patterns of intervention are established. Serv-

Table 2-3. *HEALTHWATCH for the Person with Myelodysplasia*

Concern	Clinical Expression*	Management
Myelomeningocele	Exposed meninges and spinal cord	Repair in 1st 24–48 hrs.
Hydrocephalus	Increased intracranial pressure; ventricular enlargement	Scans, ventriculoperitoneal shunting in early wks.
Shunt failure	Vomiting, irritability, headache, drowsiness, strabismus	Consultation; possible revision
Loss of muscle action	Flaccid paraplegia degree per motor level can cause some spasticity	Assisted ambulation (orthoses) or wheelchair
	Muscle imbalance potential for contractures, dislocations	Training, preventive physical therapy later, muscle lengthening and transfer, release of contractures
	Scoliosis, plus complications	Bracing, surgery
Loss of sensation	Potential for skin trauma; decubitus	Care, inspection, hygiene
Neurogenic bladder	Incontinence Poor emptying, reflux Pyelonephritis Renal failure	Intravenous pyelograms, urodynamic studies; clean intermittent catheterization; padding, collecting devices; anticholinergics, antibiotics; possible vesicostomy, artificial sphincter
Neurogenic bowel	Incontinence, constipation	Training, suppositories, mini-enemas
Cortical deficiencies	Mental retardation and/or perceptual disabilities; strabismus; seizures; other developmental problems	Assessment of function plus early intervention; special education programs, vocational education, counseling; anticonvulsants
Chronic deprivation, and interruptions of activities	Adjustment problems; obesity	Support by habilitation team; counseling, therapy, recreation

* Additional difficulties include sexual dysfunction and other congenital anomalies.

ices can also originate from the Early and Periodic Screening, Diagnosis, and Treatment (EPSDT) Program, provided for in an amendment to Title XIX (Medicaid) (P.L. 90-248):

... early and periodic screening and diagnosis of individuals who are eligible under the plan and are under the age of 21 to ascertain their physical or mental defects and such health care, treatment, and other measures to correct or ameliorate defects and chronic conditions discovered thereby, as may be provided in regulations of the Secretary.

This ambitious program may be the "largest public secret in the human services domain."[21]

Youth and Young Adult Years

The interest in support programs for youth and young adults has been heightened in recent times by the improved survival rates for many chronic illnesses and by the continuing presence in the community of young people who were formerly in residential programs. The special vulnerability and sensitivity of the teen years compound the adjustment process[22]:

Youths with chronic illness or disability confront a much more uncertain future. Their childhood has probably created an even greater dependence on parents and other adults than it has for other young people. The arduous adolescent process of exploring limits, reality testing, and self-image development may be severely delayed or compromised. Future options may be perceived as dependent, not on ability or motivation, but on the status of the health conditions.

In adolescence the process of self-discovery must also include learning positive perceptions about one's special problems, learning habits of good health maintenance, and learning about the local support systems with which one can interrelate.[7] The medical care team plays an important role in this educational process. The entire March 1985 issue of the *Journal of Adolescent Health Care*[5] reports on discussions at the Conference on Youth with Disability held in Minnesota in June 1984.

Adult Years

Medical care services for adults with serious developmental disabilities are irregularly organized. A recent review[8] documented "serious

Table 2-4. *HEALTHWATCH for the Person with Cerebral Palsy*

Concern	Clinical Expression	Prevalence	Management
Central nervous system abnormality	Infancy: variation in tone, delayed motor milestones, asymmetry, hyperreflexia, primitive reflexes	All	Early-intervention programs
	Preschool: development of motor, posture, and movement patterns		Orthopedics and physical therapy (see below)
	Childhood: motor tasks more difficult, deformities may occur		
	May present with spasticity, dyskinesia (athetosis, choreoathetosis, dystonia), ataxia, mixed syndromes		
Altered muscle function	Slow, weak movements	All	Physical therapy: muscle stretching, stimulation, positioning
	Combinations of extremity involvement: diplegia, hemiplegia, quadriplegia		
	Imbalance leading to contractures, dislocations, leg-length discrepancy, scoliosis		Orthopedics: bracing, corrective surgery, possibly Valium, dantrolene
Associated dysfunctions	Mental retardation	50%	Assessment, special education
	Visual problems: strabismus, visual field defects, amblyopia	>50% (common)	Ophthalmologic collaboration
	Hearing impairment (sensorineural)	5–15%	Audiologic collaboration
	Seizures—all forms	30%	Anticonvulsant treatment
	Communication disorders: speech (oromotor function), language (central processing, etc.)	Common	Speech therapy collaboration
	Urinary tract infections	Common	Medical surveillance
Emotional and coping issues	Adjustment problems, especially in adolescents, adults	Common	Psychosocial support in many areas
	Loss of function in adults		Rehabilitation, physiatry

gaps and omissions" in physician training in the areas of course work and clinical practice. A survey by the same authors suggested that the most common health problems were seizures, skin disease, behavioral disorders, and obesity.[8] Other studies have named orthopedic handicaps, hearing impairment, respiratory disease, ocular problems, and severe dental and periodontal disease.[12, 23] Discussions have often questioned whether the best setting for care of the adult with severe disabilities is a state residential facility with a stable and experienced medical staff or the open and less certain circumstances of community residences.[14]

Superintendents of institutions have been known to draw up lists of clients whose medical problems allegedly disqualify them from being discharged from the facility. This contention ignores the capacity of community health services to mobilize when needed. It also discounts the good progress of many multiply disabled adults who have always been based in the community. The best conclusion would appear to be that with good will and agency assistance effective medical care plans for all adults can indeed be implemented in the community, regardless of the complexity of the disabilities. Recently there has been increased interest in utilizing medical staffs from state residential facilities for the establishment of outpatient services for discharged adults. Such medical staff participation should also extend to providing functional assessments and evaluations of continuing health problems.

Later Years

The arrival of the senior years begins a period of less fluid intelligence, but with some continued plasticity. A dissolution of prior family supports may occur, and often important new concerns arise in health maintenance. The pressure for models of institutional residence or nursing homes must be modulated by coordinate consideration of the satisfaction from home-based services, including day habilitation programs, social and recreational options, meals at home, personal care attendants, and special agency supports. Human services should be a blend of the viewpoints expressed in programs for mental health, mental retardation, and developmental disabilities and the viewpoints of the Older Americans Act, councils on aging, offices of elderly affairs, etc.

To be old is not necessarily to be dependent, and stereotypes should be avoided. Insinuations about the special aging vulnerabilities of persons with developmental disabilities (e.g., Down syndrome, cerebral palsy) should be countered by accurate, individualized assessment and management. The Joseph P. Kennedy, Jr., Foundation is providing a fresh direction for thinking about creative programs for elderly persons with developmental disorders. As a culture we have been slow to perceive opportunities. Medical care teams can offer positive contributions in study, treatment, and advocacy. The thrust for wellness among the elderly is of especially critical value. (See the discussion of the geriatric population in Chap. 24.)

To be involved with a developmental disability is a life-long adventure. There are personal implications and service components in each of life's stages. We have not yet found the way to naturalize the process, but grace and redemption can be felt during many moments along the trip. It is particularly rewarding when this is achieved for the aging population by those who love them.

REFERENCES

1. Abroms, I.F.: The child with a seizure disorder. *In* The Practical Management of the Developmentally Disabled Child. Edited by A.P. Scheiner, and I.F. Abroms. St. Louis, C.V. Mosby, 1980.
2. Abroms, I.F., and Panagakos, P.G.: The child with significant developmental motor disability (cerebral palsy). *In* The Practical Management of the Developmentally Disabled Child. Edited by A.P. Scheiner, and I.F. Abroms. St. Louis, C.V. Mosby, 1980.
3. Accardo, P.J., and Capute, A.J.: The Pediatrician and the Developmentally Delayed Child. Baltimore, University Park Press, 1979.
4. Birenbaum, A., and Cohen, H.J.: Community Services for the Mentally Retarded. Totowa, N.J., Rowman & Allanheld, 1985.
5. Blum, R.W., and Leonard, B.: Conference on youth with disability: the transition years. J. Adolesc. Health Care, 6:77, 1985.
6. Bresnan, M.J., and Hicks, E.M.: Seizure disorders. *In* Developmental-Behavioral Pediatrics. Edited by M.D. Levine, W.B. Carey, A.C. Crocker, and R.T. Gross.

Philadelphia, W.B. Saunders, 1983.
7. Brunswick, A.F.: Health services for adolescents with impairment, disability, and/or handicap: an ecological paradigm. J. Adolesc. Health Care, 6:141, 1985.
8. Buehler, B.A., Smith, B.C., and Fifield, M.G.: Medical Issues in Serving Adults with Developmental Disabilities. Logan, Utah State University, 1985.
9. Crocker, A.C.: Present status of treatment of the mucopolysaccharidoses. Birth Defects, 10:113, 1974.
10. Crocker, A.C., and Cullinane, M.M.: Families under stress; the diagnosis of Hurler's syndrome. Postgrad. Med., 51:223, 1972.
11. Crocker, A.C., and Nelson, R.P.: Mental retardation. *In* Developmental-Behavioral Pediatrics. Edited by M.D. Levine, W.B. Carey, A.C. Crocker, and R.T. Gross. Philadelphia, W.B. Saunders, 1983.
12. Crocker, A.C., and Yankauer, A.: Community health care services for adults with mental retardation: The Sterling D. Garrard Memorial Symposium. Ment. Retard., 25:189, 1987.
13. Davidson, P.W.: Visual impairment and blindness. *In* Developmental-Behavioral Pediatrics. Edited by M.D. Levine, W.B. Carey, A.C. Crocker, and R.T. Gross. Philadelphia, W.B. Saunders, 1983.
14. Garrard, S.D.: Health services for mentally retarded people in community residences. Am. J. Public Health, 72:1226, 1982.
15. Gilkerson, L., Crocker, A.C., and Mayer, R.: Access to Developmental Services for NICU Graduates. Boston, Wheelock College, 1985.
16. Gortmarker, S.L., and Sappenfield, W.M.: Chronic childhood disorders: prevalence and impact. Pediatr. Clin. North Am., 31:3, 1984.
17. Hobbs, N., Perrin, J.M., and Ireys, H.T.: Chronically Ill Children and their Families. San Francisco, Jossey-Bass, 1985.
18. Kiernan, W.E., and Bruininks, R.H.: Demographic characteristics. *In* Pathways to Employment for Adults with Developmental Disabilities. Edited by W.E. Kiernan, and J.A. Stark. Baltimore, Paul H. Brookes Publishing Co., 1986.
19. Kiernan, W.E., Smith, B.C., and Ostrowski, M.B.: Developmental disabilities: definitional issues. *In* Pathways to Employment for Adults with Developmental Disabilities. Edited by W.E. Kiernan, and J.A. Stark. Baltimore, Paul H. Brookes Publishing Co., 1986.
20. Klein, S.D., and Schleifer, M.J.: Related school services—a legal right, an educational dilemma. Exceptional Parent, 14:10, 1984.
21. Meisels, S.J.: Prediction, prevention, and developmental screening in the EPSDT program. *In* Child Development Research and Social Policy. Edited by H.W. Stevenson, and A.E. Siegel. University of Chicago Press, 1984.
22. Nelson, R.P.: Political and financial issues that affect the chronically ill adolescent. *In* Chronic Illness and Disabilities in Childhood and Adolescence. Edited by R.W. Blum. New York, Grune & Stratton, 1984.
23. Nelson, R.P., and Crocker, A.C.: The medical care of mentally retarded persons in public residential facilities. New Engl. J. Med., 299:1039, 1978.
24. Nelson, R.P., and Crocker, A.C.: The child with multiple handicaps. *In* Developmental-Behavioral Pediatrics. Edited by M.D. Levine, W.B. Carey, A.C. Crocker, and R.T. Gross. Philadelphia, W.B. Saunders, 1983.
25. Pueschel, S., and Murphy, A.: Counseling parents of infants with Down's syndrome. Postgrad. Med., 58:90, 1975.

26. Rubin, I.L.: Perinatal factors. *In* Comprehensive Management of Cerebral Palsy. Edited by G.H. Thompson, I.L. Rubin, and R.M. Bilenker. New York, Grune & Stratton, 1983.
27. Shapiro, B.K., Palmer, F.B., Wachtel, R.C., and Capute, A.J. Associated dysfunctions. *In* Comprehensive Management of Cerebral Palsy. Edited by G.H. Thompson, I.L. Rubin, and R.M. Bilenker. New York, Grune & Stratton, 1983.
28. Shonkoff, J.P.: Early intervention collaborative study. Personal communication, 1985.
29. Taft, L.T., and Matthews, W.S.: Cerebral palsy. *In* Developmental-Behavioral Pediatrics. Edited by M.D. Levine, W.B. Carey, A.C. Crocker, and R.T. Gross. Philadelphia, W.B. Saunders, 1983.
30. Thompson, G.H., Rubin, I.L., and Bilenker, R.M. (eds.): Comprehensive Management of Cerebral Palsy. New York, Grune & Stratton, 1983.
31. Ziring, P.R.: The child with hearing impairment. *In* Developmental-Behavioral Pediatrics. Edited by M.D. Levine, W.B. Carey, A.C. Crocker, and R.T. Gross. Philadelphia, W.B. Saunders, 1983.

BIBLIOGRAPHY

Anderson, E.M., and Spain, B.: The Child with Spina Bifida. London, Methuen, 1977.
    Good account of life guidance for the young person with myelodysplasia.
Batshaw, M.L., and Perret, Y.M.: Children with Handicaps: A Medical Primer. Baltimore, Paul H. Brookes, 1986.
    A sound review of pathogenesis and clinical concerns.
Bergsma, D. (ed.): Birth Defects Compendium, 2nd Ed. New York, Alan R. Liss, 1979.
    The ultimate reference for definition of genetic diseases and birth defects.
Blackman, J.A. (ed.): Medical Aspects of Developmental Disabilities in Children Birth to Three. University of Iowa, Iowa City, 1983.
    Brief, thoughtful reviews, with excellent diagrams.
Crocker, A.C., and Yankauer, A.: Sterling D. Garrard Memorial Symposium: Community health care services for adults with mental retardation. Ment. Retard., 25:189, 1987.
    The entire issues of the journal surveys special care needs in adults, plus planning for services.
Levine, M.D., Carey, W.B., Crocker, A.C., and Gross, R.T. (eds.): Developmental-Behavioral Pediatrics. Philadelphia, W.B. Saunders, 1983.
    An extensive review of all aspects of normal and altered development in children.
Pueschel, S.M., Tingey, C., Rynders, J.E., Crocker, A.C., and Crutcher, D.M.: New Perspectives on Down Syndrome. Baltimore, Paul H. Brookes Publishing Co., 1987.
    Modern presentation of all aspects of Down syndrome.
Scheiner, A.P., and Abroms, I.F. (eds.): The Practical Management of the Developmentally Disabled Child. St. Louis, C.V. Mosby, 1980.
    The finest book of its kind, strongly recommended.
Smith, D.W.: Recognizable Patterns of Human Malformation, 3rd Ed. Philadelphia, W.B. Saunders, 1982.
    A classic text, valuable guide to congenital anomaly syndromes.
Thompson, G. H., Rubin, I.L., and Bilenker, R.M. (eds.): Comprehensive Management of Cerebral Palsy. New York, Grune & Stratton, 1983.
    Modern commentary on scientific and clinical aspects.
Umbriet, J. (ed.): Physical Disabilities and Health Impairments: An Introduction. Columbus, OH, Charles E. Merrill, 1983.
    Written for educators, also good for parents.

3

HEALTH CARE NEEDS OF CHILDREN IN SPECIAL EDUCATION PROGRAMS

Judith S. Palfrey, M.D.

Since the passage in 1975 of the Education for All Handicapped Children Act, Public Law (P.L.) 94-142, increased emphasis has been placed on the provision of appropriate health and health related services to children in special education programs in public schools. It is important to look at the provisions of this act, the population of children covered, and the implications for health practice.

PROVISIONS OF P.L. 94-142

The major provision of P.L. 94-142 is a free appropriate public education for all children regardless of the presence or severity of handicap. When the law was passed, the most severely disabled children were emphasized first because they had least access to educational services. The philosophy of the act includes two important goals: (1) the removal of all barriers to education (including medical barriers) in order to allow children access to normal academic experiences; (2) the provision of services within the "least restrictive environment" to afford children with disabilities as normal a social experience as possible. To accomplish these goals, the law has four major components: identification, evaluation, health related services, and parent advocacy.

Identification. It is the responsibility of school systems to identify all children with educationally handicapping conditions at the earliest possible time. Because the regulations of the act are not specific, the states have undertaken various methods of identification. Some states have nothing more than a toll-free phone number to call. In others a formal screening procedure has been set up for the 3- to 5-year age range. In still

others collaborative arrangements have been made between the education and health sectors to ensure the earliest possible identification of physical and developmental disabilities.

Evaluation. The federal statute defines evaluation in great detail. Children with developmental disabilities are to have triennial reviews with annual reviews as necessary. The evaluation of the Individualized Educational Plan (IEP) must consist of at least two standardized tests performed in the child's own language. In addition, consultations may be requested with professionals who know the child well. Considerable variation exists among states in the consultative role designated for physicians.[7] Table 3-1 details the state regulations regarding the involvement of physicians. Three major patterns are evident: (1) the requirement that a physician evaluate *all* children referred for special education; (2) the requirement that a physician evaluate children with certain specific categories of handicaps; and (3) the recommendation that all or certain specified children have an evaluation.

The content of the evaluation also varies. Some states require a form that can be filled out using information from the child's previous visits to a physician. Others require a current physical examination. Still others request that the physician address specific questions about the child's functioning in the school environment. After the evaluations have been made, a formal meeting is called. The child's parents and teachers, a representative of the special education division, and appropriate consultants attend this meeting to write a plan for the child's curriculum and for any "related services" the child may need in order to

Table 3-1. *Physician Participation in Evaluation of Children for Special Education*

Disability Group	States Requiring					States Recommending				
All disabilities	CT	MA	MI	NJ		AR	CA	DE	LA	ME
	NY	RI	TX	VA		MD	NH	SD		
Hearing	AL	AR	DC	HI		AK	ID	LA	MI	MO
	IL	IN	MI	MO		NV	NH	OR	PA	SC
	NM	NB	NC	ND		TX	VT			
	NY	OH	OK	RI						
	TX	VA	WV	WI						
Vision	AK	AR	IL	MI		AL	DE	FL	GA	ID
	NB	NH	ND	RI	UT	IN	LA	MO	MT	NV
	VA	WV				NC	OK	OR	SC	TN
						VT	WA	WI		
Physical and health	AL	AK	AR	DC		NH	NJ	NM	NC	ND
	FL	GA	HI	ID	IL	OH	OK	OR	PA	SC
	IN	KS	KY	LA		TN	VT	WA	WI	WV
	MI	MS	MT	NB	NV					
Emotional and social	AL	FL	OH	OR	VA	AL[1]	AR[1]	CA	DC[1]	
	NJ	PA				FL[1]	HI	IN[1]	IA[1]	
						KY[1]	LA	MI[1]	MN	
						MO[1]	MS[1]	MT[1]	NM[1]	
						NC	NY[1]	ND[1]	RI[1]	
						TN[1]	TX[1]	UT[1]	WA[1]	
						WV[1]				
Speech and voice disorder	AK	GA	IN	LA	MI	AZ	FL	ID	NY	OH
	NM		WA			OR	PA			
Mental retardation	NM[2]	OR[2]	VA[2]	DC[2]		CA[2]	HI[2]	NC[2]	WV[3,4]	
	GA[4,5]	NC[4,5]	PA[5,6]	VT[6]						
Learning disabilities	AL[7]	DC[7]	NJ[7]	OH[7]		AR[7]	CA	ID	KS	
	PA[7]	TX	VA	WA		KY	LA	MI[7]	MT	
						NC	OR	RI[7]	WV	
						MI				

Data from Twarog, W.T., Levine, M.D., and Berkeley, T.R.: Patterns of physician participation in the evaluation of handicapped children for special education programs: a report on state regulations. BEH PR# 45113H70139, 1979. Used with permission.

[1] Physician should be a psychiatrist.

[2] For all degrees of retardation.

[3] For mild or educable retardation.

[4] For moderate or trainable retardation.

[5] For severe retardation.

[6] For profound retardation.

[7] Includes a neurological exam.

benefit from the school's program.

Health Related Services. In order to make access to educational programming available to children, schools can provide services that include special transportation, special nursing, health evaluations, counseling, audiology, occupational therapy, and physical therapy.[1] These services are generally decided upon when the IEP is set up and are provided through funding of the school system or through funding of other state agencies that is funneled through the schools.

Because the provision of related services is a nontraditional role for the education sector, considerable debate has taken place about financing, licensing requirements, and supervision. This debate may well increase over the coming years as more and more children who depend on medical technology enter the community through the school systems. In addition to needs for intermittent clean urinary catheterization, provisions may have to be made for children with gastrostomies, hyperalimentation, tracheostomies, and other respiratory problems.[9]

Parent Advocacy. The Education for All Handicapped Children Act was passed in large measure because of parents' concerns about the education of their disabled children.[4] As a result, it is heralded by many as a consumer's law. Its emphasis is on the due process rights of parents and children. Parental signature is required on the individualized educational plan, and if parents are unhappy with their child's program, they may request reevaluation or a hearing in front of an impartial observer to decide whether the school system should provide services other than those recommended by the IEP team.

THE POPULATION OF HANDICAPPED CHILDREN

According to the Education for All Handicapped Children Act, the children eligible for special education and related services include "mentally retarded, hard of hearing, deaf, speech impaired, visually handicapped, seriously emotionally disturbed, orthopedically impaired or other health impaired who by reason thereof require special education and related services or who have specific learning disabilities." Aside from the services provided to children in these categories, the reporting requirements of the law have in themselves produced a major benefit: the provision of services has generated useful data on the population of handicapped children. The knowledge base for planning and research is much better now than it was in 1975.

The yearly reports resulting from implementation of P.L. 94-142 have established that approximately 10% of the nation's children fit the "special needs" criteria of the public schools. Figure 3-1 shows the breakdown into federally established criteria. As apparent from the figure, the largest categories of disability are speech and learning disabilities. Mental retardation and emotional disturbance each account for 10 to 15% of the population. The residual categories of the physical and orthopedic and the sensory handicaps are constituted by only 7% of the children, less than 1% of the total school population.

Clearly, the population of children now in special education is heterogeneous. At one extreme, children with very serious disabling conditions are considered eligible for educational services, with education broadly construed to include services previously considered rehabilatative (such as training in ambulation, feeding, toileting, and dressing). At the other extreme, children with mild to moderate speech and learning problems are also considered handicapped.

The inclusion of children with learning disabilities and speech impairments (disorders known for their high prevalence and low severity) has subtle but definite ramifications. On the positive side, public acknowledgment that learning problems are developmental deviations underscores the need for innovative approaches, including the assessment of neurodevelopmental status, attentional ability, memory, sequencing, language processing, and perceptual understanding. In addition, the recognition that such problems are beyond the control of these children protects them and their families from a variety of moral condemnations.[3] On the negative side, the "handicapped" designation can stigmatize children with low severity disorders in the eyes of their parents, teachers, and peers, which can lead to a spiral of self-doubt and even poorer performance.[2] Physicians need to join with other professionals in making the positives outweigh the negatives.

Two groups of disabled children continue outside the program. One is made up of the most profoundly involved, multiply handicapped children. These youngsters remain in pediatric nursing homes and state institutions. Primarily they receive custodial care. The second group is disabled but does not fit the provisions of the Education for All Handicapped Children Act. These youngsters have chronic illnesses but unimpaired learning potential.[9] Some states have attempted to cut programs for physically disabled children who are not intellectually impaired.

A Collaborative Study of Children with Special Needs

In 1983 and 1984, a study was made of the health care provisions for children in the special education programs of five large urban school districts. The study looked at health profiles, functional status, and academic performance of children in the programs of the Education for All Handicapped Children Act. In particular, the study examined arrangements for health care and for augmenting functional status and ability to attend school with other children.

The study consisted of a parent interview, a teacher interview, a physician interview, and a record review for a representatative sample of children from each of the five nationally dispersed sites, which had a total enrollment of 20,000 students. The sample was generated in such a way that stable estimates could be made for each of the handicapping conditions included within the population of disabled children.

The study helps us understand health care relationships for children in large cities, but the findings cannot be generalized to all situations since the experiences of some suburban and rural communities may be quite different.

Sources of Health Services

Table 3-2 shows the regular source of health care for children in the five sites studied.[6] It is evident that most of the children had a regular source of care; but the type of care received varied considerably with geographic locality, and the source of medical care depended on economic and social factors. Each area in the study had different eligibility criteria for welfare assistance and Aid to Families with Dependent Children. The relationship between welfare and Medicaid eligibility and regular source of care was striking. From the analysis of the collaborative study, it is clear that participation in the special education program affords little or no protection against social and economic compromise of health care accessibility. The study also showed that although children with more serious disabilities have better access to care than those with less severe problems, socioeconomic and ethnic inequities are still apparent within disability categories.

Table 3-3 depicts the type of physician providing care by parent classification of handicap. The vast majority of children are being followed by pediatricians or pediatric specialists. This finding contrasts dramatically with the national fig-

Table 3-2. *Percentage of Children in Special Education Programs Regularly Served by Various Sources of Health Care, by Site**

Source of Care	Site				
	I	II	III	IV	V
No regular source of care	12	15	5	2	2
Doctor's office	63	58	59	48	85
Hospital outpatient	16	17	29	25	9
Emergency room	4	3	3	2	0
Other (including company, government, school and unspecified clinics)	6	6	3	22	5

Data from Singer, J.D., Butler, J.A., and Palfrey, J.S.: Health care access and utilization among children with disabilities. Med. Care, 24:1, 1986.

* Percentages do not add to 100 because of rounding.

ure of over 50% of children seeing general practitioners,[5] suggesting that this group of children has moved into pediatric care. The study indicated that 21% of the children had changed medical care providers because of dissatisfaction. It is important to consider what it is that parents are seeking by these changes.

IMPLICATIONS FOR PHYSICIANS

The philosophy behind the special education program has been an increase in access to education for children with disabilities. In fact, P.L. 92-142 was very much a civil rights law for children with handicapping conditions. The onus has been placed on professionals to find appropriate services for enhancing the functional capabilities of children. What does all this mean for the practicing pediatrician and pediatric specialists? There are a number of obvious implications.

First, it is incumbent upon physicians dealing with the disabled population to ask themselves, each time they see a child, whether they have done everything they can to make it possible for the child to take part in society. Five areas need to be considered: mobility, activities of daily living (including feeding, dressing, and toileting), communication, academic performance, and social and emotional interactions.

Mobility

It is important that physicians join with other professionals and charitable organizations in assuring adequate facilities and equipment for youngsters whose mobility is impaired. In addition, because of the availability of the Special Olympics and other sports programs, physicians have to understand how to write prescriptions for athletic competitions for children with disabilities. Since youngsters can participate in many different activities, the physician must be aware of the consequences of sports medicine for children with a variety of handicapping conditions.

Activities of Daily Living

How the activities of daily living are handled will often determine whether a child can attend a regular or a special school. Toileting is an important consideration when decisions are being made about school placement for youngsters. To the extent possible, physicians need to be aware of the various options available, including clean intermittent catheterization, the use of constipating medications, and even colonic diversion. In writing letters to schools, it is extremely helpful to give as much detail as possible on the as-

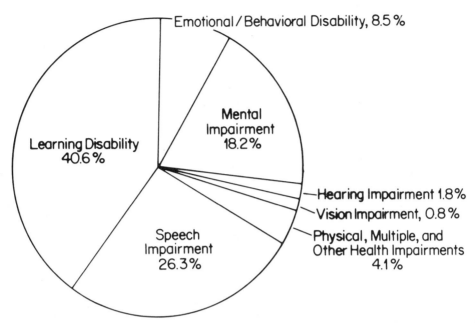

FIG. 3-1. Distribution of primary handicapping conditions as defined by the schools. From U.S. Office of Special Education and Rehabilitation Services: Fifth Annual Report to Congress on the Implementation of P.L. 94-142. Washington, DC, Government Printing Office, 1983.

pects of daily living, especially for children with very complicated medical problems.

Communication

Computer technology has made new communication devices available to children, and physicians can consult specialists in this area to determine what is appropriate for their patients. In addition, typewriters and tape recorders can make communication possible for learning-disabled children who have difficulty in formulating their thoughts using pencil and paper. The use of sign language also opens up the area of communication for children with mental retardation because it enables them to use cognitive processes that are more representational and less abstract. Physicians can refer young retarded patients for speech and language evaluations with a specific query about the appropriateness of sign language. In some disabled children (particularly those with Down syndrome), meticulous attention to associated middle ear problems has resulted in better language function. Pediatricians should follow this aspect of their patients' care carefully and ask schools to be alert to fluctuations in hearing levels.

Academic Performance

Sophistication in the areas of child development, education, and pediatrics is increasing with regard to the understanding of academic performance among children, particularly among children with perceptual and cognitive handicaps. It is becoming increasingly clear that these children do not see the world the way the majority of individuals do. The extent to which learning disabilities can be identified and intervention undertaken depends on this increased sophistication.

As in all diagnostic areas, a differential pediatric approach is needed. Is the child failing in school because of a serious medical problem, an iron deficiency, a mild to moderate hearing loss, or a previous neurologic insult? Is the basic problem one of attentional weakness? How does the child process information? Does he understand language concepts? How does he use active memory; does he have proper storage and recall mechanisms? Does sequential information give him more trouble than nonsequential?

For physicians, a major decision is how extensive a diagnostic workup is needed to unravel these questions. At a minimum, a thorough history and physical are warranted, not only to look for specific medical etiology, but also to ascertain parents' explanations of what is going on. Many parents live with hidden guilt about some event or health habit they feel has contributed to the child's disability. Often, airing that worry can go a long way to help parents confront present problems.

Beyond the traditional medical evaluation,

Table 3-3. *Percentage of Children in Special Education Programs Regularly Served by Various Types of Physicians, by Parent Classification of Handicap*

Handicap	Type of Physician			
	No Regular Physician	General Practitioner	Pediatrician	Pediatric Specialist
Speech	25.2	17.0	56.6	2.7
Learning	32.2	20.0	46.1	2.9
Other dev	24.7	25.0	50.4	4.4
Hyperactivity	26.0	19.2	47.7	7.9
Emotional	29.7	14.3	55.6	1.0
Mental retardation	18.1	22.4	57.8	7.8
Down syndrome	7.4	23.6	69.0	4.8
Hearing	8.8	15.3	62.2	16.5
Vision	33.8	32.5	41.6	20.2
Cerebral palsy	12.3	8.0	66.2	23.9
Other neurologic	12.5	11.8	49.2	37.3
General medical	14.2	4.1	70.8	19.1

Data from Singer, J.D., Butler, J.A., and Palfrey, J.S.: Health care access and utilization among children with disabilities. Med. Care, *24*:1, 1986.

developmental observation can be very helpful. A variety of models now exist for obtaining such information, including developmental disability clinics, school team evaluations, and partnerships between pediatric and educational specialists. Physicians can contribute special perspectives to any one of these settings because of their longitudinal relationship with the child, their understanding of both the parents and the youngster, and an awareness of the potential contribution of a variety of influences to the child's ultimate performance. Physicians need to resist the temptation of having the last word in these cases, but they should not hesitate to make contributions as team members because their observations may be unique and critically important.

Social and Emotional Factors

We are only beginning to understand the major impact of social and emotional factors on children with disabilities. Physicians can play a major role in helping schools, parents, and children understand the nature of the disability and in dispelling notions that the child is failing in order to "get back" at the parents or the school. Counseling directed at specific aspects of the child's day-to-day needs can be extremely reassuring and helpful to the family. The more specific the suggestions, the more useful. In situations in which emotional distress is great, referral to a child psychologist or psychiatrist can be of major benefit. Often this cannot be accomplished without a series of prior meetings.

For children, school represents the major area of functional performance. Because of the current emphasis on careful evaluation and planning for children with disabilities, physicians and other professionals have new opportunities to become active and creative in devising interventions that build on children's strengths and minimize their weaknesses. Physicians are in a unique position. Their voices can be heard in the community as advocates for individual children and for groups of children. With an awareness of the progress being made in schools throughout the country, physicians can make sure their local education and health agencies are coordinating activities to ensure the full range of services to every child with developmental handicaps.

REFERENCES

1. Greene, D.: Local Implementation of P.L. 94-142: Education Agency Responsibility for "Related Services." Menlo Park, CA, SRI International, 1980.
2. Hobbs, N., Egarton, J., Matheny, M.H.: Classifying children. Child. Today, Jul-Aug.:21, 1975.
3. Levine, M.D., Brookes, R., and Shonkoff, J.: A Pediatric Approach to Learning Disorders. New York, John Wiley & Sons, 1980.
4. Pennsylvania Association for Retarded Citizens v. Commonwealth of Pennsylvania, Vol. 343F, Suppl., p. 279, 1972.
5. Select Panel for the Promotion of Child Health. Better Health for Our Children. Vol. III. DHHS (PHS) Pub. No. 79.55071. Washington, DC, U.S. Dept. of Health and Human Services, 1981.
6. Singer, J.D., Butler, J.A., and Palfrey, J.S.: Health care access and utilization among children with disabilities.

Medical Care, *24*:1, 1986.

7. Twarog, W.T., Levine, M.D., and Berkeley, T.R.: Patterns of physician participation in the evaluation of handicapped children for special education programs: a report on state regulations. BEH PR# 45113H70139. Washington, DC, U.S. Government Printing Office, 1979.

8. U.S. Office of Special Education and Rehabilitation Services: Fifth Annual Report to Congress on the Implementation of P.L. 94-142. Washington, DC, Government Printing Office, 1983.

9. Walker, D.K.: Care of chronically ill children in schools. Pediatr. Clin. North Am., *31*:221, 1984.

4

SYSTEMS OF HEALTH CARE DELIVERY

PRIVATE PRACTICE

Allen C. Crocker, M.D.

A significant prototype for the provision of medical care is the direct relation between the physician and the patient (and often the family) in a private office. In the area of developmental disabilities, the activities of pediatricians in private practice are known and documented. Many of these activities are appropriate not only for other physicians who deal with children such as family practitioners, but also for physicians who see only adults, e.g., internists, and other types of adult physicians.

The range of activities in the pediatric care of persons with developmental disabilities is broad. It includes steps for prevention, anticipatory guidance, management of specific symptoms, evaluation as part of team studies, referral for other assistance, counseling, education, and advocacy. In some of the developmental disorders, medical care activities are ascendant; in others, the doctor's role is less central. Hardly ever can the doctor be the sole determinant of the "service package," and determining the most fruitful contribution is a large part of skillful coordination.

DEVELOPMENTAL DISABILITIES IN PRACTICE

Simply on the basis of usual prevalence, it is to be expected that physicians who care for children will find a significant number of young people with developmental disabilities in their practice. A most useful documentation of this frequency was a survey in five New England states of 97 pediatricians involved in solo and group practices of various sizes in rural and urban settings.[9] Usually 100 to 200 children were seen per week, and Table 4-1 presents the pediatricians' perceptions of the number with handicapping conditions. The total patient panel for these offices is not known, but it probably included 1,000 to 2,000 children. Hence, it would appear that the prevalence of children with mental retardation was similar to the usual figure of 2 to 3% of the child population. Cerebral palsy appeared about half as often, hearing impairment still less commonly, and blindness much less often.

A more recent survey was conducted through mailed questionnaires by Project SERVE. Sponsored by the Division of Maternal and Child Health, it was a review of resources in Massachusetts for the care of children with developmental handicaps and/or chronic illness. Eighty-four replies from members of the Massachusetts chapter of the American Academy of Pediatrics contained sufficient detail for analysis. The responses in this study are summarized in Table 4-2.[3] The smaller practices accounted for 40% of the sample. Some of the prevalence figures are lower than those in the earlier study. One wonders whether the true levels are higher than those perceived by the respondents. For comparison, the average figures for the index condition of asthma were 20 and 64 for the smaller and larger practices.

It is apparent that for the average practitioner it is difficult to sustain familiarity with the health and general service needs of children with certain serious developmental disorders when only one to three of the total patients have such conditions. Seizures, mental retardation, and cerebral palsy are seen often; neural tube defects, autism, muscular dystrophy, and sensory handicaps are rare. Of these Massachusetts practitioners, 59% felt that the medical care needs of handicapped and/or chronically ill children were being met adequately; 74% thought that important nonmedical needs were unfulfilled.

Table 4-1. *Pediatricians' Estimates of the Number of Children in Their Practices with Handicapping Conditions*

Condition	Mean	Range
Language and/or speech impairment	29	0–100
Mental retardation	27	0–250
Cerebral palsy	14	0–150
Hearing impairment	11	0–250
Legally blind	2	0–50

From Shonkoff, J.P., et al.: Primary care approaches to developmental diseases. Reproduced by permission of Pediatrics. *64*:506, 1979.

Table 4-2. *Pediatricians' Views of Prevalence of Developmental Disorders in Their Practices*

Disorder	Smaller Practices (<100/week)	Larger Practices (>100/week)
Seizure disorders	11	24
Mental retardation	14	14
Down syndrome	3	6
Cerebral palsy	6	14
Autism	2	2
Spina bifida	1	2
Muscular dystrophy	1	1
Severe hearing impairment	3	4
Severe visual impairment	2	3

From Crocker, A.C., et al.: Report of Project SERVE. Unpublished report, 1985.

CONFIGURATIONS OF PRACTICE

Physicians interact in different ways with patients who have developmental disabilities. Using the activities of pediatricians as a basis, one can describe various types of physician involvement with such patients. Three conceptual levels of involvement are present here, ranging from minimal specific involvement ("Physician A") to total concentration on developmental disabilities ("Physician C"). *Physician A* is a usual community based primary care pediatrician such as most of the doctors polled in the studies mentioned above, with no special training in developmental pediatrics or in care for handicapped children. Physician A has had a long career of handling all manner of children, and has attained notable wisdom about human variation and a good sense of special family dynamics. Most significantly, he is trusted by the families of his patients and has come to know them and the child well, and he has a fine sense of setting and values. Most of the acute care for children with disabilities in this country is provided by this type of doctor, a person prepared to respond to the family's most significant concerns. The challenge of long-term health care guidance and special problem solving may be more difficult, and here Physician A commonly uses consultants and referral assistance. A distinct opportunity exists for advocacy in behalf of the child and family, and the primary care pediatrician can be an important ally in the community and school.

Physician B is more common in recent years. He also runs a primary pediatric care office, but for a variety of possible reasons he has a special empathy for children with developmental disabilities. He has had conventional pediatric training, but he regularly attends continuing education courses on handicapping conditions, commonly buys and reads new textbooks in the

field, and tends to have a closer relationship with pediatric consultants. Without specifically intending to do so, he has developed a subtle concentration on children with special needs: he may find that he is caring for six of the seven young people with Down syndrome who live in his town. Further, he has come to serve as pediatrician for the local Easter Seal program or pediatric nursing home, and he is invited to talk at the P.T.A. meeting on learning problems.

Physician B is palpably frustrated because of his involvement in sustained health care and the time demands placed by such children and their families. He characteristically finds himself required to set aside some special time in the week (1 half-day, 2 half-days, or 1 day) when appointments as long as 1 or 1½ hours can be booked—so that he can truly turn to the family and ask "How are things going?" and deal with the replies. He participates in discussions with the school district or local day programs even though such activities are time-consuming and tend not to be reimbursible.

Physician B could solve some of his reimbursement problems by holding conferences in his office instead of at the school, or at times and in places where overhead costs are less. Physician B needs to learn to adapt to the special mind-set of developmental discussions, which are more collaborative and less directive than in the acute care world. Life is not easy for Physician B, but his contributions are substantial.

Physician C is a full-time specialist in developmental disabilities. He works for a salary, in a secondary or tertiary facility such as a child study center, a child development clinic, or a

University Affiliated Facility for Developmental Disabilities (UAF). He has had specialized post-residency training and has a career commitment to handicapped individuals and their families. Because of his optimal circumstances he is expected to provide state-of-the-art diagnostic studies (chromosomal, metabolic, radiologic, electroencephalographic, etc.), arrangements for therapeutic interventions (orthopedic, ENT, reconstructive surgery, cardiologic, ophthalmologic), and family counseling. He is part of a team operation, probably interdisciplinary, which can look at diverse special needs and assist in program design. It is expected that he will undertake investigative studies that contribute new knowledge in the field, and he is involved in teaching. Physician C has little time to devote to primary care, but he can be valuable in managing hospital admissions when he is needed, and he serves as a consultant for Physicians A and B.

This classification of medical activities is similar to that described by Dworkin[4] as "primary care physician without special interest," "primary care physician with special interest and expertise," and "full-time specialist in developmental-behavioral pediatrics." He further speaks of the complications in pediatric role definition, including issues of diagnostic and prognostic uncertainty, the multiplicity of problems of a given child, the involvement of multiple professions, and the complex effects on families.

Scheiner[7] provides useful reflections on the dynamics of the consultative process for children with developmental disabilities, pointing out that deterrents exist for the most effective functioning of this process, deriving from both the primary care physician and the consultant:

Deterrents presented by the primary care provider

1. Lack of recognition of significant problems
2. Misdiagnosis and improper referral
3. Objectives of consultation not clear to family or consultant
4. Inadequate support and coordination of the consultative process
   a. Poor communication with consultant
   b. Lines of responsibility not clear
5. Inadequate discussion with the family of the results of the consultation

Deterrents presented by the consultative or referral source

1. Referral process too cumbersome
   a. Application too complex, unclear, and lengthy
   b. Appointment times inconvenient
2. Poor "fit" between consultant and family
3. Misdiagnosis
4. Treatment plan inappropriate
   a. Poor communiction with primary care physician
   b. Plan impractical and too complex
   c. Not well explained to family
   d. Lines of responsibility not clear
5. Excessive use of jargon with the family and primary care provider

Green[5] describes the shifts occurring in pediatrics: children are healthier now, infectious and nutritional problems are less demanding, and children with long-term disorders survive longer. He too suggests a three-tiered scheme for developmental and behavioral pediatrics. Level I is ambulatory office care by the general pediatric physician and pediatric nurse, encompassing health supervision and management of acute illness episodes. There is some developmental assessment, parent education and support, and promotion of positive parent-child interactions. Early intervention is sought for identified problems, and consultation and referral are used as needed.

Level II in Green's scheme is represented by pediatricians with special interests such as developmental disabilities or adolescent health. These pediatricians collaborate readily with other team members, on site or elsewhere, to allow better description of the child's needs and the planning of programs. Pediatricians in groups are well suited to practice at this level.

Level III care is provided by specialists, particularly in academic settings. Included here are full-time teachers and researchers, and the unique "master general pediatric clinician." Nonpediatric scientists often play an important role, and Level III pediatricians may work full- or part-time in community or regional diagnostic and treatment centers.

In southeastern Massachusetts, Minihan and Dean[6] assessed the potential community physician resources available for the care of adults with serious developmental handicaps who were being discharged from a state residential facility. They concluded that there were sufficient primary care physicians for that region and that the number of wheelchair-accessible physician offices was also adequate. They thought that some key specialty services were well covered, such as dermatology, gastroenterology, pulmonary disease, cardiology, urology, and ophthalmology, but they found inadequate resources in neurology, behavioral neurology and psychiatry, and orthopedic services for multiply-handicapped persons.

ACTIVITIES IN PRIVATE PRACTICE

In a busy primary care medical office, some adaptations are required to accommodate patients with developmental disabilities. These clients tend to have multi-system abnormalities, with long problem lists. They are usually receiving concurrent services from many other facilities, some of which can be perceived as anti-physician in attitude. It is necessary to establish a good interim rapport with family members (many nonpressured visits), so that when a crisis arises there is a base of trust and understanding. Families can be taught to differentiate between the need for a brief office appointment to deal with a discrete acute problem and the need for a more extensive review of issues. Having to complete a large number of reports and forms is a burden. Attendance at team meetings (including educational and rehabilitation conferences) is occasionally required but can be replaced by telephone discussions with key persons in schools and agencies.

Private physicians vary greatly in the way they inform families about congenital anomaly syndromes in newborns, in the vigor with which they refer for early intervention services, and in their use of consultants for diagnostic assistance. Their customs are no doubt influenced by their personal training, experiences, and convictions. In the report of Shonkoff et al.,[9] virtually all pediatricians felt that early identification of hearing and visual impairments was of value, but there was less agreement regarding mental retardation and cerebral palsy. Pediatricians in groups were more likely (53%) than those in solo practice (31%) to favor the delegation of responsibility for developmental assessments to a nurse practitioner. Referrals to pediatric neurologists for consultation has long been traditional for children with significant developmental delay, but this pattern is shifting as larger numbers of child development centers become available. Pediatricians eventually communicate with a child study team when they or the family have important concerns.[10]

In Palfrey's report of the usual source of primary health care for children with special needs (see Chap. 3), general practitioners provided 15 to 25% of pediatric care and pediatricians contributed 45 to 70%. Specialists were more likely to be active in primary care for those with cerebral palsy and other neurologic disorders.

TRAINING AND PHILOSOPHY

More persons with developmental disabilities are now being seen in the offices of private physicians. This trend can be attributed to their presence in usual community settings, their improved survival capability, and the commitment to more active treatment and service plans.[8] The avoidance of institutional care has added over 100,000 such persons of all ages to the cities and towns, but probably an even greater factor is the attitudinal change in families and in the clinical professions. It is gratifying to note that mentally retarded and other handicapped persons have obtained certain rights of citizenship in the medical office.

Physicians' residency training programs do not provide adequate preparation, accurate knowledge, or sufficient familiarization regarding persons with developmental disabilities. In the teaching of internal medicine and family practice, experience with retarded and multiply handicapped patients is sparse and nonsystematic. When 7,000 recent graduates responded to the American Academy of Pediatrics Task Force on Pediatric Education in 1978, insufficient training was indicated by 40% in the area of chronic cerebral dysfunction, by 51% in the area of child advocacy, and by 54% in the care of patients with psychosocial and/or behavioral problems.[1] More extensive developmental education in pediatric residencies is currently being stressed, particularly in centers where there is a UAF.

Continuing education courses after graduation are also an important source of information. The American Academy of Pediatrics course "New Directions in Care for the Handicapped Child" has been broadly offered. The majority of practicing pediatricians in the Project SERVE study indicated a desire for courses about newer therapies, work with families, psychosocial issues, and nutrition. One-third of the respondents asked for instruction regarding community resources for handicapped or chronically ill children.

The practicing physician has a unique opportunity to contribute to optimal personal progress through health maintenance, family support, and appropriate referrals. For disabled persons the respected milieu of the medical office can offer education, enhancement of belief in self, and a platform for advocacy.

REFERENCES

1. Battle, C.U.: The role of the primary care physician. *In* The Practical Management of the Developmentally Dis-

abled Child. Edited by A.P. Scheiner, and I.F. Abroms. St. Louis, C.V. Mosby, 1980.

2. Browder, J.A.: Pediatric diagnosis and management of children with developmental disabilities. J.D.B.P., 4:92, 1983.

3. Crocker, A.C., et al.: Report of Project SERVE. Unpublished report, 1985.

4. Dworkin, P.H.: Pediatric role definition. *In* Developmental-Behavioral Pediatrics. Edited by M.D. Levine, W.B. Carey, A.C. Crocker, and R.T. Gross. Philadelphia, W.B. Saunders, 1983.

5. Green, M.: The Role of the Pediatrician in the Delivery of Behavioral Services. Address at National Conference on Behavioral Pediatrics, Easton, MD, March 4, 1985.

6. Minihan, P.M.: Planning for community services prior to deinstitutionalization of mentally retarded persons. Am. J. Public Health, 76:1202, 1986.

7. Scheiner, A.P.: Referral processes. *In* Developmental-Behavioral Pediatrics. Edited by M.D. Levine, W.B. Carey, A.C. Crocker, and R.T. Gross. Philadelphia, W.B. Saunders, 1983.

8. Schor, E.L., Smalky, K.A., and Neff, J.M.: Primary care of previously institutionalized retarded children. Pediatrics, 67:536, 1981.

9. Shonkoff, J.P., Dworkin, P.H., Leviton, A., and Levine, M.D.: Primary care approaches to developmental disabilities. Pediatrics, 64:506, 1979.

10. Szymanski, L.S., and Crocker, A.C.: Mental retardation. *In* Comprehensive Textbook of Psychiatry/IV. Edited by H.I. Kaplan, and B.J. Sadock. Baltimore, Williams & Wilkins, 1985.

My appreciation is extended to G.L. Fuld, M.A. Gilchrist, and G. Storm for personal communications on pediatric practice.

CONSULTATION SERVICES TO SCHOOLS AND RESIDENCES

Stephen B. Sulkes, M.D.

In recent years much of the care for developmentally disabled persons has been shifted from large residential facilities to smaller family-like settings in the community. Professionals and government agencies have responded to this trend toward deinstitutionalization with decreased admissions to large facilities. This has been necessarily and appropriately combined with improved support for family care, supervised group homes, and community-based intermediate care facilities (see Fig. 4-1).[3] In conjunction with this trend, the role of physicians based in institutions has decreased as the role of community based primary care physicians has blossomed. Primary care physicians in private practice are frequently called on to provide consultative services to schools and small residential facilities.[2]

Consultative roles take several forms, depending on the nature of the facility and its community resources. At one end of the spectrum, physicians serve on agency boards; at the other end, they serve as primary medical caretakers and key members of interdisciplinary ha-

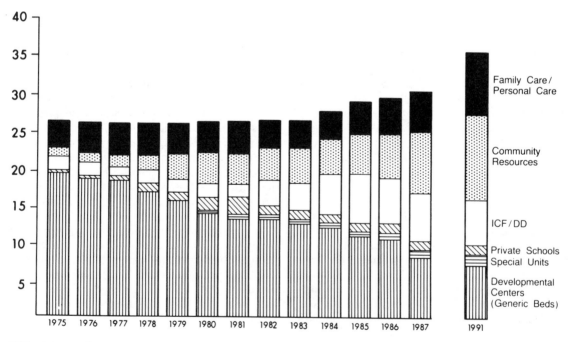

FIG. 4-1. Utilization of residential program beds, in thousands, 1975 to 1991, in New York State. (Courtesy of John Jacobson, Bureau of Program Research and Planning, New York. State Office of Mental Retardation and Developmental Disabilities, 1984.)

bilitative teams. Between these extremes is a range of roles, including intake screening, evaluation, coordination of other medical professionals, staff education, community outreach, and follow-up.

DAY SCHOOL PROGRAMS

Health Screening

In many ways, the physician working with a day program is a classic school physician with an expanded job and a necessarily expanded time commitment. Such a "school doctor" is involved primarily with public health issues such as immunization, sensory screening, preathletic evaluation and treatment, and infection control. In educational programs for children with developmental disabilities, health screening remains a major issue. As in programs for typical children, basic preliminary health screening must conform with state and federal law. This includes confirmation of adequate immunization for diphtheria, pertussis, tetanus, polio, measles, mumps, and rubella and of skin testing for tuberculosis exposure.[8]

Additional screening to prevent introduction of other infectious diseases into the school population is sometimes warranted. For example, a school in which many children have associated chronic medical conditions may recommend or provide annual influenza immunization. Similarly, if students previously lived or are currently living in large residential facilities, screening for hepatitis B immunity and carrier status may lead to appropriate precautionary measures and active immunization programs with hepatitis B vaccine. Precautions include postexposure prophylaxis with hepatitis B immune globulin and hepatitis B vaccine (Heptavax—Merck Sharpe & Dohme) for students or staff members who have sustained injuries involving blood or secretions of identified carriers. The decision to provide preexposure prophylaxis to susceptible individuals, either with or without antibody status screening, depends on an analysis of cost effectiveness for the individual facility (see Chaps. 30 and 31).[4, 5, 9]

Some schools screen for the chronic carrier status of certain viruses, such as the cytomegalic inclusion disease virus, that leads to developmental disability when prenatally acquired. The evidence that such screening will be effective is limited. First, restricting the activity of carriers has little significant impact on prevention of congenital infection in others because the organisms are ubiquitous in the community. Secondly, ef-

fective treatment for such congenital infection and vaccines for immunization of susceptible adults are currently not available; therefore, specific therapeutic responses when a carrier is identified are impossible. With improved technologies for immunization of susceptible individuals, it is hoped that screening for these carriers will become reasonable in the near future. Meanwhile, if liability toward staff remains the concern, screening for staff susceptibility seems more appropriate than barring services to a needy individual because of viral carrier status.[8]

Screening for Athletics

Screening for sports becomes an expanded job for the physician providing care for persons with chronic disability. Instead of acting as a barrier to sports participation, the physician, working with physical, occupational, and recreational therapists, can play an important role in facilitating this area of growth. The medical consultant should be ready to provide suggestions for physical, educational, and team sports activities that are geared to foster the strength, skills, and developmental abilities of each student. For example, the child who has problems with fine motor planning and attention deficits may do better in swimming or bowling than in competitive sports using a small ball. Accentuating areas of strength enhances the student's self-image, improves social skills, and reinforces acceptance by peers.[14]

Neuromuscular and orthopedic problems are of concern in the planning of sports programs, and adapting activities that can circumvent such impairments can result in uniquely rewarding outcomes. For example, the Special Olympics program for the involvement and training of handicapped persons 8 years old and older in sports activities and guided competition has been enormously successful.

Safety must also be considered. The seizure-prone student requires close monitoring during water sports with as high as a one-to-one ratio of staff to students. Other chronic illnesses, such as congenital heart disease, asthma, and diabetes mellitus, may impose limitations and special preparations for athletic activity. The growth of the Special Olympics and other organized competitions necessitates an expansion of preparticipation sports assessment.[13] Recent recognition of atlantoaxial instability as a problem in as many as 10% of the individuals with Down syndrome has made cervical spine roentgenograms a requirement prior to participation in competitions involving abrupt flexion and extension of the neck.[11] Medications taken for a variety of legitimate medical problems can affect athletic performance and lead to accusations of inappropriate drug use. It is the role of the involved physician to be an advocate for the athlete, and to provide counseling about safety and the appropriate participation in athletics. As in all other areas of special educational programming, physical education must be individualized.

Admissions

Physicians are often involved in the school admissions process, the entry point of the educational system. They must consider, with other interdisciplinary team members, the goals of a school's programs and the anticipated characteristics of the students. Although a heterogeneous mixture of disability types can be served in a relatively small setting, staffing issues often demand some similarity of students within a single classroom. In many states the educational labeling system (mentally retarded, physically impaired, and multiply handicapped) provides some distinctions in classroom types. Wide variability exists in the types of disabilities that lead to these educational placements, however, particularly when movement to less restrictive settings is attempted. Thus, a typical moderately mentally retarded class may be a mix of physically unimpaired children and children with Down syndrome, cerebral palsy, myelodysplasia, and sensory impairment—all of whom happen to function in a similar range of mental retardation.

The medical consultant must monitor the safety of individual students in such a mix. For example, if children are working on ambulation skills, the presence of children whose behavior is hyperactive or aggressive may be hazardous. On the other hand, by reassuring the education staff about other combinations that are relatively safe, the physician can foster student growth through mainstreaming. Reducing anxiety about the physical frailness of developmentally disabled students can also foster greater social acceptance. In one situation, a young woman had recently gotten a seizure disorder under improved control and was happy when the school was reassured that she wouldn't fall and injure herself; she could stop wearing her helmet on the school playground, where her classmates had found the helmet an irresistible target for stone throwing.

Physical Plant Evaluation

Strict codes exist for the design and construction of school buildings, residential facilities, and other public buildings. In most cases public health and safety agencies provide initial and ongoing evaluations of a building's conformity with such regulations. When buildings are being chosen for programs for disabled persons, however, additional factors must be considered.

Two extremes are to be avoided in this regard. The first is ignoring basic accessibility requirements. All too frequently, buildings serving children (or staff) who have decreased ambulation skills are multilevel structures without wheelchair accessibility. Even worse are buildings with ramps at out-of-the-way doors, subtly implying second-class status for those regularly using them in addition to limiting egress in emergency situations. Hallways and doors should provide adequate clearance for wheelchair users, and bathrooms and dining areas should have appropriate fittings. At the opposite extreme is the totally functional, utilitarian, and institutional building designed for optimal safety and ease of maintenance. Not only do such buildings lack human warmth, but removing all conceivable environmental challenges also removes a potential area of mastery for the student. There is no reason for not incorporating bright colors and stimulating designs and textures into decorating plans.

Committees on the Handicapped

Whether physicians are included on a school system's committee on the handicapped depends on the community and the state. The role of physicians on such committees was suggested by the Education for All Handicapped Children Act of 1975 (P.L. 94–142) and has received extensive comment (Chapter 3).[6, 10] From such an advisory position, the physician can interpret medical data to educators and influence recommendations for education programs. In many cases, physicians are the only professional committee members not employed by the school system, and they are therefore able to plead the cause of the child without being subject to conflicts of interest. The physician's involvement allows for a flow of information about the school's educational workings and classroom groupings and about the attitudes and styles of school personnel. The physician also acts as a liaison between the medical and educational establishments, interpreting jargon and facilitating a school's communication with other physicians. Finally, the physician committee member can bring the concerns of the school to the attention of other medical specialists.

Staff Education

Staff education and in-service programs are other areas in which physicians can apply their knowledge. A school staff may have limited understanding about specific medical conditions and limited access to current references. Arrangements can be made with other physicians who have special interests. Providing regular medical in-service programs increases staff knowledge of medical topics and also helps dispel misconceptions and inappropriate folklore. Having educated staff members as allies in monitoring and providing health care multiplies the number of observant eyes focused on the patient. Communication between medical and education systems can be fostered—for example, a physician will be more receptive to hearing concerns about seizure activities from a teacher who has heard him lecture on the subject. Similarly, including parents in the audience broadens the network of informed observers and health care consumers. Lists of helpful readings for staff and families are available, and material can be assembled through the school, the public library, or a medical facility.

Liaison

The school medical consultant acts as liaison between the educational establishment and other health care providers. Gathering and interpreting medical information for the education staff can occur during the intake, evaluation, or program-planning phase of the child's experience at the school. Interpreting the morass of jargon and illegible handwriting related to medical communications can be of enormous help to school personnel. Transmitting information back to other physicians is another important role. All too often, physicians are inaccessible when members of the educational community attempt to share data. The school doctor can also bring the results of screenings performed at school to the attention of the primary physician. Medical consultants will necessarily develop some expertise in areas of medicine closely related to learning, behavior, and development, and they can provide valuable "over the shoulder" consultation to the primary practitioner in areas related to education.

COMMUNITY RESIDENCES

In working with residential schools and group homes, the medical specialist has the opportunity of expanding on the roles mentioned with regard to day programs.[4,5,8] Small residences provide the physician (and also the medical group, as is becoming increasingly common) with the chance to function more actively as a member of the habilitative team. All roles that are applicable to day programs still exist for admission screening, physical plant evaluation, staff education, etc. Often, however, physicians become more deeply involved when their role is primary medical care provider for the entire population of a community residence. A new set of responsibilities arises when a substantial adult population of residents is involved.

Barriers to Providing Care

Primary care as usually practiced in the typical office setting is not immediately transferable to the community residence setting. Despite moves to improve the relationship between medical consultant and residence staff, numerous barriers to the provision of optimal care exist.[7]

Time Barriers. Perhaps the most imposing barrier to care provision is the factor of time. Because of the frequent multiplicity of chronic problems presented by each individual, a single brief visit to the residence is often insufficient if the physician is to be brought up to date on the status of each resident in the facility. Similarly, a visit to the physician's office for routine care that addresses each chronic problem often takes extra time.

Communication Barriers. Difficulty in communication is an even greater obstruction in residential life than it is in other settings when caring for developmentally disabled persons. In addition to the communication problems inherent in many types of disabilities (e.g., mental retardation, autism, severe spasticity), multiple caretakers are usually providing the information about clinical problems. Compounding the difficulty are shift-to-shift differences in staffing ratios, leading to variability in closeness of observation, and differences in recordkeeping by staff members with unequal knowledge and experience. Such a situation can make history-taking a frustrating task.

Administrative Barriers. With close governmental supervision of residential care, an increased paperwork load is often presented to the health care provider. One particularly onerous administrative burden is the requirement of a physician's signature on myriads of papers, from monthly renewals of orders to extensive physical examination forms. This requirement, which may have no relevance to the process involved, is in many cases a remnant of the classic "medical model" of service provision, in which the physician was also the administrative head of the residence. Such paperwork can be lessened through the assistance of the on-site medical coordinator discussed in a later section. In the final analysis, however, it should be remembered that each bit of paperwork represents someone's good intention toward the patient and that the person providing the signature is ultimately responsible for the statement signed.

Diagnostic Barriers. Diagnostic dilemmas can further complicate the communication process. It is not uncommon for the physician to be faced with a complex behavior problem that requires elaboration about whether it represents seizure activity, pharmacologically treatable psychiatric disease, environmentally related reaction formation, or some combination thereof. Hidden agendas can arise on the part of patients, families, and residence staff members. Extended history-taking sessions can be helpful, as can the use of an interdisciplinary evaluation team.

Financial Barriers. Remuneration remains a significant barrier to quality medical care that is community-based. The American Academy of Pediatrics[1] has called for appropriate compensation for the extra time and effort required by physicians in diagnosing and caring for developmentally disabled persons. Ongoing work with third-party payers is focusing on the decreased expense involved when developmentally disabled persons are medically evaluated and managed as outpatients. Frequently, a contractual relationship can be developed between a residence and a medical care provider whereby predetermined services are provided according to a model similar to that for a health maintenance organization. This relationship allows a freer flow of information between physician and residence because time is "purchased" in advance and billing for individual services is decreased. It may also facilitate on-site visits by the medical consultant.

Organizing Residential Care

Although persons living in community-based residential facilities may enjoy a degree of general health greater than that of their institutionalized peers, the chronic medical problems common to populations with developmental disabilities are still manifest. Whether annual physical examinations and periodic chart reviews are mandated by governmental regulations or not, they are useful in keeping abreast of complex chronic problems. Several studies have shown

that by concerted effort and close management, polypharmacy can be reduced (Chapter 8). It has also been observed[14] that when chronic problems are closely monitored, they do not erupt in acute decompensations. Acute interventions can then be of the same type (and nearly the same frequency) as those for age-related nondisabled peers. Utilizing an approach that is problem oriented and based on what is known of the etiology of disability, the functional capabilities leading to residential groupings, and the chronic concerns common to a developmentally disabled population, the primary physician can streamline and organize interactions between physicians and patients and simultaneously improve care.

Screening

Screening has an expanded role as care becomes broader. The screens and preventive methods used in day programs are applicable, but in residential programs the screening must be for all chronic conditions affecting persons with developmental disabilities. Screening should be used not only to monitor appropriateness and therapeutic efficacy of medications being used (e.g., anticonvulsant drug levels), but also to detect hearing and vision problems; scoliosis; occult gastrointestinal bleeding due to unrecognized gastritis, esophagitis, or constipation; and lead poisoning in populations with a high prevalence of pica behavior. Etiology-directed ongoing screening would include monitors for hypothyroidism with Down syndrome, for urinary tract infection in patients with neural tube defects, and for contractures in individuals with spasticity. Establishing regular schedules and routines for such screenings can be extremely beneficial in minimizing oversights and preventing significant secondary disability.

Etiologic Workups

Usually, people move to community residences either from home, due to problems with behavior management, unacceptable family stresses, or simply maturation, or from larger institutions in which sufficient skills to "make it" in the community have been demonstrated. In either instance, there are often gaps in the patients' etiologic or functional workup. A goal the consultant can help address is the pursuit of an etiologic diagnosis. This can be intellectually stimulating for the practitioner in addition to providing an important service to the person and family regarding, for example, genetic counseling, education about the underlying cause of the disability (with attendant alleviation of long-term guilt feelings), and greater availability of services to the resident.

The occasion of a shift in residence and primary care physician provides a rare opportunity to have all previously obtained data at hand and a fresh team of professionals to provide important evaluative services. It is all too often the case that this valuable opportunity is missed during the admission and adaptation of a client to a facility, when old records are relegated to a storeroom and the team's focus turns to treatment and ignores important past history. The consultant can help other staff members focus their evaluative capacities and make the most of these infrequent turning points.

Subspecialty Coordination

Perhaps the most critical role of the medical caretaker's interaction is in the area of coordinating referrals to other specialists. Athough acute care needs can be minimized with a well organized program of preventive measures, the variety of complex chronic needs in this population requires input from a coterie of consultants. One study reported an almost fifteen-fold greater frequency of chronic problems in this population as compared with nonretarded age-matched peers (also Chapter 23).[12] The average small residential facility designed as an intermediate care facility for mental retardation (ICF/MR) will send each resident to off-site consultations eight times a year (S.B. Sulkes, I.L. Rubin, and E.P. McDonald. Personal communication, 1987). This requires an extensive time commitment and a closely knit group of consultants who communicate readily and well with the primary physician. The physician's input is essential in making these primary linkages. An on-site medical coordinator can be an enormous asset in organizing and arranging the flow of appointments (see discussion below).

When a physician consultant to a residential program becomes an integral member of an interdisciplinary habilitative team, he is not only an evaluator but also a provider of service. This increases the intimacy of the medical caretakers' understanding and interaction with residents and families, which in turn increases his opportunity for advocacy. The seemingly simple task of maintaining a developmentally disabled individual in the community can be a life-long battle that can be waged more effectively if the physician is a deeply involved ally. Staff education and staff health maintenance can become additional components of the primary physician's interaction with the small residence, usually as an outgrowth of screening procedures and public health monitoring. Acting as a communication liaison with the medical community, the physician can also be an ambassador to the community at large, broadening the interaction between residents of the community facility and their neighbors and expanding on educational experiences in community life.

Acute Care Arrangements

Despite the best efforts of the primary care physician to forestall the occurrence of acute medical problems, patients occasionally require emergency room care and hospitalization. To hospital personnel unfamiliar with developmentally disabled patients, much less with the problems of a given individual patient, performing the usual emergency procedures can be difficult. Communication barriers are compounded by anxieties of patient, residence staff, and family members in the situation of an acute illness. How to approach a developmentally disabled patient may not be the first thought in the minds of emergency personnel, and this can lead to resistance to treatment and the development of reciprocal resentments and control issues.

If inpatient treatment is needed, unfamiliarity can also breed contempt. The disabled adolescent or adult is sometimes rejected by pediatric services because of age, and by adult medical services because of associated behavior problems. Unnecessary physical or pharmacological restraints are sometimes utilized when the presence of a familiar staff or family member would suffice. The needs of the patient for basic comforts may be ignored because of the patient's inability to communicate effectively.

The primary care physician can smooth the process of acute care management to a large degree simply by being present. In too many cases, physicians abdicate care to hospital personnel, missing the chance to influence both patient care and medical education. By making an appearance and demonstrating a calm and reassuring manner to hospital staff, the physician can affect not only the care of the particular patient being seen, but also the manner in which subsequent patients with disabilities are treated.

Another method for ensuring quality treatment and maintaining good communications between acute care and residential facilities is the development of a transfer agreement. With this method, each facility is clear on the capabilities and responsibilities of the other in acute care situations, and administrative barriers to care delivery are minimized. The medical consultant to the residence presumably has admitting privileges at the hospital of choice and can bring together the individuals needed in making such an arrangement. In the long term, a transfer agreement with a single hospital can aid in the development of a close working relationship between the two facilities.

On-Site Health Care Coordinator

Because of the limited client base inherent in the community-residence model, it is unlikely that a physician will be present at the residence on anything approaching a full-time basis. Depending on the number and frequency of medical problems in a given residential group, it may be prudent to have an on-site health care coordinator present on a daily basis if not on a 24-hour schedule. In fact, certification of a facility often depends on the presence of a qualified professional to organize the administration and storage of medications. This person (usually a nurse) can expand the role of coordinator dramatically and greatly enhance the primary physician's ability to provide care. (See section on "Nurses in Community-Based Residential School Programs" in this chapter.)

Triage for Acute Problems. An initial and obvious role for the on-site health care coordinator is triage of the occasional medical problem. Extensive institutional nursing protocols are frequently developed for the handling of acute problems by nurses and by medically untrained aides. When nurses are not available around the clock, aides must be aware of basic emergency responses in order to avoid complications while exercising some degree of discretion. The physician and nurse together can draft guidelines uniquely suited to the requirements of the staff, clients, geography, physical plant, and style of physician practice. The residential base can approximate an extension of the physician's office, handling acute problems as well as routine illnesses. When present, the on-site health coordinator can evaluate, monitor, and determine the urgency of a particular acute problem, deciding whether it can wait hours or days for a physician's attention or needs immediate medical input.

Monitoring of Chronic Problems. In the area of chronic problems, the on-site coordinator can make a major contribution. The coordinator has a trained eye, is on the scene most often, and can observe patterns as chronic problems develop and are manifested. For example, the association between behavioral outbursts and

menstrual cycles may only become apparent when data are charted and monitored by this member of the team. Seizure charting, essential to optimal anticonvulsant management, must be the responsibility of this coordinator, even if other staff members are collecting data as well. Similarly, regular monitoring of weight, skin care, and nutrition is a classic role assigned to the coordinator. In some cases, the charting of stool patterns to aid in managing constipation is organized by the coordinator.

Organizing Appointments with Specialists. Although the development of linkages to other professionals and specialty services is the job of the medical overseer, scheduling, preliminary data collection, and coordination of appointments falls to the on-site coordinator. As a representative of the primary physician and as surrogate family member, the coordinator can eliminate many confused and unproductive interactions. For example, an aide might bring a child with multiple contractures to the orthopedist without any knowledge of why the appointment has been scheduled. Although consultant requests from the physician can clarify issues and the primary physician is helpful in greasing entry wheels to the medical system, at the moment when consultant sees patient a medically knowledgeable representative of the resident is a great asset.

Liaison between Physician and Treatment Team. As the member of the habilitative team who is the primary communicator with the physician, the on-site health coordinator plays a key liaison role. Even when physicians are actively and energetically involved in team activities and decisions, they are not available constantly, and they therefore suffer decreased influence in team decision making. The health coordinator can transmit the physician's input to the team, and the team's to the physician, allowing for a closer working relationship. On-site coordinator is an ideal role for a person with training as a nurse practitioner. Such a person can expand the job from one of basic nursing to one of more active decision making and take on many tasks previously ascribed to the physician, who can then play a role more supervisory than directive.

Site Choices for Primary Health Care

A well-established model for on-site provision of primary medical care is the one in large institutions. In the community, however, practitioners have traditionally cared for patients in private offices or clinics. Which of the models should be adopted for individuals who are both community-based and residential? For this group each model has advantages and disadvantages.

On-site health care offers several attractive features. First, it is a familiar environment for the individuals being treated. They can be examined in their own beds or in the room just down the hall where they receive medication daily. Behavior problems arising from strange environments should be considered, and if assistance is needed in gaining patient cooperation, the on-site staff will be familiar to the resident, will know the resident intimately, and will be able to lend reassurance. This staff will also be available to aid in information gathering. As with house calls, the physician will have the opportunity to observe problems related to the residence. For example, safety hazards, staff-resident and resident-resident interactions, and treatment methods sometimes require adjustments. Compliance with medical suggestions will improve as a result of better communication with the staff, and the staff will more readily accept the physician as a habilitative team member.

The disadvantages of the on-site visit, as with any home visit, relate to the extent of immediately available technical assistance. No residential health station is as well equipped as a physician's office (e.g., there may be no table on which to perform a pelvic exam). Few medications will be immediately at hand, and instruments for minor surgical repairs may not be available. The physician may be unfamiliar with the facilities, and improvisation may be necessary—using a spoon in place of an unfound tongue depressor, for example. Finally, and perhaps most significantly, it is time-consuming for a busy physician to leave a finely tuned office setting to venture forth into territory not as well known or well organized.

It follows from the foregoing that there may be advantages in providing care in an off-site location, such as the physician's office. The office is a familiar, comfortable, and efficient environment for the physician. Diagnostic and treatment facilities are present and in good condition. Time management is streamlined. When the physician is reimbursed on a fee-for-service basis, provision of care in the physician's office establishes a clearer basis for third-party billing. From the point of view of the developmentally disabled patient, it is a "normalizing" experience to go to the doctor's office the way one's nondisabled peers do, and the sense of responsibility required for a community outing can turn the medical visit into a learning experience.

In certain respects, however, the disadvan-

tages can be greater than the benefits. The unfamiliar and potentially threatening office environment may make the individual less comfortable and result in undesirable behavior. Fewer staff people are available to provide history and background information. Office flow may necessitate waiting and shortened interactions with the physician. The physician may not develop as close a relationship with the resident staff and may therefore be a less involved member of the treatment team. Certain records may not be available. Without appropriate preparations, nondisabled patients may be put off by disruptive residential patients who appear to get more attention from the doctor.

How is this dilemma to be resolved? Optimal medical care should be provided while the person's comfort is preserved. Yet in order to engage the best physicians to provide care, some bending to physicians' needs is appropriate. Which is more important, medical mainstreaming for the benefit of the patient and society, or maximizing information transfer and the physician's team involvement? Clearly, both are important.

One resolution may involve a mix of on-site and off-site visits for routine care, with the physician making weekly or biweekly visits to the residence for review of orders, team discussions, and general patient reviews. Behavior problems can be addressed on the site, where observations can be made in the individual's usual context. The medical needs of residents might then be evaluated in the physician's office, with extra time allotted for history-taking and explanations. Depending on the size of the residence and the medical needs of the patient, a regular block of office time can be set aside for addressing issues related to health maintenance and to chronic problems, with acute situations being scheduled into the regular office flow as needed. Naturally, this scheme would have to be manipulated to suit the nature of the residential facility, the specific medical needs of the people living there, and the physician's practice style. This solution would combine the maximum number of advantages in each method and, over time, minimize the disadvantages.

As physicians become increasingly involved in consultation to schools and residences, they can begin to develop close and rewarding relationships with other caretakers and with community-based children who have developmental disabilities. In the short term, physicians can learn an enormous amount about the variation among individuals with disabilities and about methods for providing services. At the same time, they can become involved with the interdisciplinary habilitative team, forming a unique liaison not usually possible elsewhere in the practice of primary medicine. By this means, a medically challenging population can receive increasingly intimate and enlightened health care. In the long term, these relationships will flourish and ultimately benefit not only those directly involved but also the entire community.

REFERENCES

1. American Academy of Pediatrics Committee on Children with Handicaps: Financial compensation for evaluation and therapy of children with developmental disabilities. Pediatrics, 62:602, 1978.
2. Browder, J.A.: Pediatric diagnosis and management of children with developmental disabilities. J.D.B.P., 4:99, 1983.
3. Byrne, R.: A decade of triumph! Journal for the Office of Mental Retardation and Developmental Disabilities, 1:6, 1984.
4. Center for Disease Control (Recommendation of Immunization Practices Advisory Committee): Postexposure prophylaxis of Hepatitis B. M.M.W.R., 33:285, 1984.
5. Center for Disease Control (Recommendation of Immunization Practices Advisory Committee): Preexposure prophylaxis of Hepatitis B. M.M.W.R., 30:423, 1981.
6. Fitzgibbons, P.M., and Ferry, P.C.: It's the law: mandatory public education for handicapped children. Am. J. Dis. Child., 113:476, 1979.
7. Gillick, M.R.: Is the care of the chronically ill a medical prerogative? N. Engl. J. Med., 310:190, 1984.
8. Klein, J.R. (ed.): Report of the Committee on Infectious Diseases. 19th Ed. Elk Grove Village, IL, American Academy of Pediatrics, 1982.
9. McPhillips, J.C., Collins, J.C., and Spigland, I.: Hepatitis B virus infections transmitted from retarded children to their families during brief home exposure. J. Pediatr. Gastroenterol. Nutr., 3:69, 1984.
10. Palfrey, J.: Commentary: P.L. 94-142: the Education for All Handicapped Children Act. J. Pediatr., 97:417, 1980.
11. Pueschel, S.M., Scola, F.H., Perry, C.P., and Pezzullo, J.C.: Atlanto-axial instability in children with Down syndrome. Pediatr. Radiol., 10:129, 1981.
12. Schor, E.L., Smalky, K.A., and Neff, J.M.: Primary care of previously institutionalized retarded children. Pediatrics, 67:536, 1984.
13. Smith, N.J.: Sports participation for children and adolescents with chronic health problems. In Sports Medicine: Health Care for the Young Athlete. Elk Grove Village, IL, Academy of Pediatrics, 1983, pp. 104-119.
14. Weitzman, M.: Schools and peer relations. Pediatr. Clin. North Am., 31:59, 1984.

PEDIATRIC NURSING HOMES
Richard U. Staub, M.D.

One of the options available for sustained residential care of seriously handicapped and chron-

ically ill children is the pediatric nursing home. Small units of such skilled pediatric nursing facilities have existed for many years, often founded and managed by a devoted nurse with a personal mission to contribute to the support of very troubled children. Such nurses were commonly in alliance with a community physician who shared their commitment. These enterprises were affected by agency pressures as resolves for broader habilitative programs challenged the use of simplistic nursing and medical models.

The movement in the 1960s and early 1970s toward rejection of large state residential facilities as suitable environments for children with mental retardation resulted in the deinstitutionalization of many young people and a resistance to further admissions to institutions. Consequently, a sizable new population developed, consisting of seriously retarded and multihandicapped children who had no out-of-home living arrangements. Specialized foster care was a possibility, but usually difficult to secure. Most of the need for care was filled by the establishment of pediatric nursing homes, but some of these children were moved into existing adult nursing homes.

POPULATION AND ADMISSION

In Massachusetts four privately owned pediatric homes were opened between 1972 and 1975. These homes, which offered skilled care (level II) and intermediate care (level III), admitted a total of 256 children during the first three years.[1] Applications for admission came from families, from acute care hospitals, and from state residential facilities. All children became publicly supported, primarily through Medicaid for primary services and through assistance from school districts for day programs. Occasionally, the motivations for application are the need for respite because of a disordered situation in the home and the need for transitional care, including convalescence after debilitating illness and complex surgical interventions. More commonly, however, extended admission (not time-limited) is sought, after families have reached a state of exhaustion or desperation. Although developmental issues are invariably intense, strong medical concerns are the central theme, and experienced nursing care is required. Some children are admitted late in the course of a terminal illness. A classification of children admitted to these four Massachusetts pediatric nursing homes between 1972 and 1980 is presented in Table 4-3.

Table 4-3. *Classification of Handicapping Conditions by Etiologic Mechanism in 421 Children Admitted to Pediatric Nursing Homes between 1972 and 1980*

Classification		Number of Children
Hereditary disorders		
Inborn error of metabolism		10
Other single-gene abnormalities		19
Polygenic familial syndrome		11
	Subtotal	40 (9.5%)
Early alterations of embryonic development		
Chromosomal changes		21
Prenatal influence syndromes		124
	Subtotal	145 (34.4%)
Other pregnancy problems and perinatal morbidity		
Fetal malnutrition		34
Perinatal difficulties		96
	Subtotal	130 (30.9%)
Acquired childhood diseases		
Infection and postinfectious encephalopathy		25
Cranial trauma		24
Neoplasm		3
Other trauma, cardiac arrest, intoxication, asphyxia		25
	Subtotal	77 (18.3%)
Unknown causes		29 (6.9%)
	Total	421

From Glick, P.S., Guyer, B., Burr, B.H., and Gorbach, I.E.: Pediatric nursing homes; implications of the Massachusetts experience for residential care of multiply handicapped children. Reprinted by permission of the New England Journal of Medicine. *309*:640, 1983.

The Montrath Pediatric Nursing Center

The challenges and opportunities inherent in pediatric nursing-home settings are exemplified by the Montrath Pediatric Nursing Center in Groton, Massachusetts, where this author has been medical director. The facility has 76 beds and is consistently fully occupied. All patients are afflicted with serious central nervous system dysfunction and consequent mental retardation. Most have cerebral palsy and epilepsy. The orthopedic complications of cerebral palsy include contractures, scoliosis, and hip subluxation and dislocation. Other common problems include severe behavioral disturbances, gastroesophageal reflux, malnutrition secondary to the latter and to pharyngeal incoordination, and recurrent pneumonia. In addition there is a high incidence of congenital anomalies that affect numerous or-

gan systems (Chapter 23). The mean age on admission has been 5 years.

The director of nursing and the social worker serve as admitting officers and are responsible for the dissemination of information to the various services of the nursing home. An initial examination is made by the physician and the team, with reassessment in about 2 weeks, after the results of early studies are available. A special meeting between physician and family allows for questions, suggestions, and a critique of care. Agreements about philosophy and communications are established.

MEDICAL CARE PROCEDURES

Standing Orders

At Montrath, routine standing orders include plans for a number of problems:

Constipation. A high-fiber diet is emphasized, with an attempt to minimize suppositories, enemas, and disimpaction. When necessary, pediatric Fleet enema is used for patients over 40 pounds, soapsuds enema for smaller children.

Fever. Acetaminophen is given according to weight.

Nasal Congestion.

Diarrhea. For infants, electrolyte solution is graduated to half-strength and then full-strength lactose-free formula; for older children, a restricted diet is given at first and then a full diet.

Vomiting. A period of nothing by mouth is followed by electrolyte solution by mouth or per gavage.

Dehydration. Observation protocol.

The Medical Record

A problem list is maintained in the medical record. Diagnoses are listed at each reevaluation and coded according to the International Classification of Diseases (ICD) for computer storage and retrieval. The medical record is problem-oriented. The format is: Subjective-Objective-Assessment-Plans (S-O-A-P). Flow sheets are used for the following:

Seizure monitoring (type of movement, body part involved, duration, state of consciousness)
Seizure frequency
Anticonvulsant dosage and blood level
Growth: weight monitored monthly, weekly for special problems; length every 3 to 6 months; head circumference when pertinent (e.g., with hydrocephalus or shunt)

Immunizations (including influenza, pneumococcal vaccine, hepatitis vaccine, and PPD)
Range of motion (updated every 3 months)
Troubleshooting for other chronic problems such
as wheezing and vomiting
Rehabilitation services (occupational and physical therapy; problem-oriented and updated
every 3 months)

Order Sheet and Daily Rounds

The physician's order sheet is organized as a
standard sequence of categories. It is reproduced monthly on a word processor to include
changes, and new orders are handwritten in the
interval. Daily rounds are conducted to deal
with problems brought to the attention of the
care team by the charge nurse. The care team
consists of physician, charge nurse, nursing supervisor, director of nursing, and social worker.
An aide or therapist may be asked to participate.
The patient is examined, the problem discussed,
the diagnosis and treatment plan formulated,
and a note dictated. The social worker serves as
the first liaison with the patient's family and
reminds the team of the particular needs and
preferences of the family.

Reassessment

Each child's problems receive a comprehensive reassessment every 3 to 6 months, depending on the severity of the child's condition. This
is done at the bedside by an enlarged care team
(physician, charge nurse, nursing supervisor, director of nursing, social worker, occupational
therapist, physical therapist, and special education persons). The problem-oriented approach is
used. The status of each problem is reviewed,
studies are ordered, the care plan is revised if
necessary, and disposition is established.

Routinely discussed topics include nutrition,
growth, development, immunizations, and physical and occupational therapy. Vision and hearing are assessed annually. The nurse supervisor
is responsible for seeing that all shifts are informed about changes in the care plan and for
bringing the results of diagnostic studies to
the attention of the physician. The social worker
apprises the family regarding the findings of reassessment and changes in the care plan. In addition, the social worker makes appointments for
consultations, admissions, and laboratory and
X-ray studies and maintains a tickler file for follow-up appointments.

Consultations

On site consultations are both cost-effective
and less traumatic for patient and family. The
cost of a round trip for an ambulance or chair
car is avoided. Orthopedic and pediatric neurology rounds are made at the nursing home at
least monthly. Orthopedic and orthotic rounds
are the most frequent of the specialty consultations, and are attended by medical director,
nurse, occupational and physical therapists, social worker, and family. The presence of the
family and the care team at the orthopedic consultation provides the surgeon with data that
tend to modify surgical recommendations so that
they more appropriately meet the needs of the
child. Electroencephalograms done at a fixed
site are preferable to those done by a portable
unit. Occasionally, pediatric developmental and
psychological consultations are obtained on site.
The latter are useful when treatment of severe
behavior disorders utilizes behavior modification techniques because these techniques necessitate educating all shifts and careful follow-up.

Conferences with Parents

When a major decision has to be made, the in-
house comprehensive reassessment done by the
care team is followed by a team conference with
the parents. Such a conference would take place,
for example, if a recommendation has been
made for spinal fusion in a child with scoliosis
who also has severe recurrent pneumonia. These
sessions are informative for parents. Pros and
cons are frankly discussed, and often more information or a consultation or second opinion is
requested. Decisions may be delayed. Parents
are asked not to attempt to reach a decision at
the meeting. They are advised to take time for
consideration at home and communicate the decision within a few weeks.

ETHICAL DILEMMAS IN
DECISION MAKING

Decisions about Institutionalization
and Care

Multihandicapped children whose medical conditions clearly require care in a skilled pediatric
nursing facility are usually admitted from acute
care facilities or rehabilitation institutes. Some
multihandicapped children, however, have been
cared for at home for years. Long-term care for
such children can eventually overwhelm family
resources. The responsible factors may be medical, social, emotional, or a combination. The decision to relinquish care for a child is a wrenching
experience for the family, and parents tend to
feel guilty for "abandoning" their child. Close

and continuing support by the social worker, relatives, and the child's physician is critical if the family is to make a healthy adaptation to the move.

Parents can and should have a say about the intensity of medical care their child will receive. Comfort and function must always be preserved, and the physician should give the parents the opportunity to express preferences. For example, should a child who has pneumonia with mild distress be treated with antibiotics at the nursing home or be admitted to a hospital? A handicapped child may be more comfortable in the familiar surroundings of the nursing home, where he is cared for by people with familiar faces and voices. Despite the higher level of technical care at a hospital, nurses and aides at a nursing facility are more adept at delivering hands-on care. Because of their familiarity with the individual, they can observe the child more accurately.

Decisions about Major Surgery

The most common major surgical procedures performed on handicapped children are orthopedic and gastrointestinal. Orthopedic surgery is used to correct complications of cerebral palsy; gastrointestinal surgery includes gastrostomy to facilitate feeding and Nissen fundoplication to correct gastroesophageal reflux. The progression of contractures, dislocations (e.g., hip), and worsening scoliosis become indications for surgical intervention when they are not controlled by physical therapy, medications, splinting, and casting.

Many seriously multihandicapped children are not nourished adequately by oral feeding, even when high-calorie thickened formulas, blended foods, and special feeding techniques are used. Gastrostomy must then be considered. Recurrent vomiting, malnutrition, recurrent pneumonia, and "asthmatic bronchitis," raise the possibility of gastroesophageal reflux. Should studies confirm the presence of reflux, Nissen fundoplication (Chapter 10) should be considered. The decision is not simply a medical one, a case of find it and fix it. Occasionally, the best interest of the child may be served by concluding not to operate.

The care team and surgeon attempt to reach consensus in the recommendation for or against surgery. Alternatively, they simply define the pros and cons and discuss them at a meeting that includes parents, physicians, social worker, and perhaps a nurse who is close to the family and patient. Such a meeting includes answers to when and why to do surgery and should also address risk assessment. The decision on when surgery must be performed takes into account the present degree of deformity (severity of disease), the anticipated rate of progression, how much time is left before problems are no longer correctable or preventable (e.g., in scoliosis), and whether the risk of surgery will increase if surgery is delayed. There are three general indications for performing surgery:

Prevention of Pain. The presence of pain for persons in this population can be difficult to assess. They can't tell us, and we can't measure it. One of the objectives of release procedures is to prevent "painful contractures," such as may occur around the hip. Although contractures may indeed happen, they are by no means an invariable complication. Some patients do not survive long enough to experience the complication, whereas others do not give evidence of pain despite the presence of severe contractures or dislocations.

Enhancement of Quality of Life. Treatment of contractures "to facilitate care" is frequently cited as an indication for surgery, but the presence of contractures may not interfere significantly with the care of these children in the setting of a skilled nursing facility. Preserving function, however, is a strong argument for surgery. For example, it is important to preserve the ability to maintain a vertical position. To be able to sit upright is critical for effective interaction with the environment and for having eye contact. Safe and pleasurable eating requires an upright position. Pulmonary complications supervene when such positioning is no longer possible.

Prolongation of Life. Prolonging life with certain surgical procedures can be an immediate or a long-term objective. Gastrostomy might be required to prevent progressive malnutrition when special feeding techniques and high-calorie supplements become inadequate. Spinal fusion might prolong life by preventing pulmonary compression secondary to severe scoliosis. In these situations complex questions exist regarding survival goals and potential.

Clearly, the operative mortality and morbidity of multiply disabled children in this population are increased due to compromised pulmonary function; poor gag, swallow, and cough reflexes; undernutrition; obtunded state of consciousness; and seizures. The degree of these dysfunctions must be assessed prior to surgery. It is possible that this population experiences complications of major surgery and anesthesia that are not recognized, such as developmental regression, less social awareness, more seizures, and weight loss. These factors are thoughtfully considered by the care team and the consultants and then presented clearly and openly to the family in a deliberate and supportive manner. In this way the family can make an informed decision that is consistent with the best interests of the child and with their own convictions.

MEDICAL ADMINISTRATION

A medical director's responsibilities and authority are documented in contractual form. The many responsibilities of medical administration include establishing policies for the medical staff and for patient care; coordinating services; and interfacing with agencies, facilities, community, and parents.

Staff and Patient Policies

The medical director develops and assures adherence to medical staff bylaws, rules, and regulations. Attending physicians at a pediatric nursing facility should be pediatricians, and the medical director reviews their qualifications and approves their credentials. The medical staff meets monthly to review and analyze clinical management and medical records and to review utilization of the facility. Rules and regulations include standing orders, admission orders, and admission protocol. The medical director is responsible for maintaining the schedule for 24-hour medical coverage and for adherence to the facility's standards for keeping medical records.

The medical director also develops and implements policies for patient care. Admission procedures have been discussed earlier in this chapter. Discharge planning actually begins early in the child's stay and is coordinated by the social worker and continually updated. This involves a careful monitoring of the circumstances of care needed by the client and an analysis of where care can be best provided.

Coordinating Medical Services with Nursing and Administration

A weekly administrative meeting is a useful device to ensure coordination between the three departments and to provide a forum for discussing and resolving problems. Representatives from other services are invited on an informal basis. Weekly meetings often avert crises and facilitate the management of crises that do occur. For example, in response to the need to establish a protocol to prevent hepatitis B, the medical director might recommend testing and a protocol for vaccination; the administrator might

point out state recommendations, rules, and regulations for nursing homes, and give cost considerations; the director of nurses might reflect nurses' concerns regarding the risk to themselves, to their families, and to newborns as well as to patients. Weekly administrative meetings can prevent the occurrence of interservice conflicts and misunderstandings by serving as a vehicle to air problems and to coordinate problem-solving efforts.

Coordinating Delivery of Diagnostic Services

The most convenient and inexpensive source of laboratory diagnostic services is a commercial laboratory, state approved, with an established reputation for prompt sampling and reporting as well as for effective quality control. Samples are collected daily on a routine basis. Pediatric normal values for hematologic studies and chemistries appear on the report. Some labs are providing terminals for nursing homes, by means of which reports are promptly delivered. Radiologic services are usually provided by the local hospital. Results of diagnostic studies are reviewed and acted upon promptly by the attending physician. A routine established by the medical director and director of nurses ensures that attending physicians are made aware of the results of diagnostic studies.

Coordinating Delivery of Consultative Services

The medical director and administrator make arrangements for the provision of medical consultations and dental services. Some medical consultations are required frequently and are provided on the site, for example, orthopedic, orthotic, neurological, and developmental pediatric consultations. Dental services should also be made available on site, and the dentist should be experienced in dealing with multiply handicapped children.

For medical specialty consultations provided outside the facility, a communication routine is required to assure the accurate transmission of clinical information in each direction. The record sent to the consultant includes a tabbed indexed copy of physical examination, progress notes, lab and X-ray reports, the notes of other consultants, and flow sheets. Consultants are encouraged to refer to this record rather than to depend on an aide to answer their questions. The reasons for the referral are briefly stated on the consultation form attached to the record. The consultant is requested to use the S-O-A-P format. The consultant's notes are reviewed by the attending physician on rounds and in the presence of the care team so that appropriate action can be taken. For consultations outside the facility, the social worker makes the appointment, arranges for the transportation, and informs parents.

Interfacing

State and Federal Agencies. The medical director and administrator respond to periodic requests from state and federal agencies for monitoring the quality of care.

University Hospitals. Ideally a pediatric nursing facility should have a relationship with a university hospital. The child population is best served by a system that delivers a continuum of care provided by a university hospital, a rehabilitation hospital, a pediatric nursing home, and a local hospital. A contact person at the university hospital (nurse or physician) serves as coordinator for arranging multiple consultations on the same day, team evaluations at the hospital, and admission if needed. The coordinator should be well informed about the needs of the child and should be familiar with the circumstances of the nursing home. A university hospital also serves as a resource for other diagnostic and therapeutic modalities, for example, for electroencephalography, audiology, brain stem evoked potentials, pharmacology, and nutrition.

Local Acute-Care Facilities. Patients with acute medical problems requiring more intensive care than can be provided at the nursing home are transferred to a local hospital. The pediatric unit of that hospital develops expertise in caring for the multihandicapped child. Emotional and professional support of pediatric nurses at the acute care facility is provided through visits by care-team members and aides from the nursing home.

In-service Education Programs. The medical director assists the director of nursing in arranging for or providing in-service education programs. The university hospital, the local hospital, pharmaceutical firms, and commercial laboratories serve as resources for the programs.

Parents. Meetings with parents are arranged and managed by social service persons. The meetings serve as a support group for parents. Periodic attendance by the medical director supplements individual conferences with parents.

REFERENCE

1. Glick, P.S., Guyer, B., Burr, B.H., and Gorbach, I.E.: Pediatric nursing homes; implications of the Massachusetts experience for residential care of multiply handicapped children. N. Engl. J. Med., 309:640, 1983.

COMMUNITY NURSING SERVICES

Marie Cullinane, R.N., M.S.
Eunice Shishmanian, R.N., M.S.

Community nursing, or public health nursing, is the specialty concerned with providing health care to people in their homes and in other local community settings. Community nursing services incorporate many roles and usually involve interdisciplinary collaboration. Community nurses seek to provide humanistic, accessible, and comprehensive care, and they function in many roles that extend broadly into areas of prevention, health education, planning and coordination, individual and public education, and consumer advocacy. The approach used by health care systems in the prevention of developmental disabilities includes a spectrum of programs in which nurses make contributions. They are particularly significant in programs for adolescent health, prenatal care, nutrition, immunization, screening and monitoring, and intervention projects.

Community nurses are avid health educators with a strong commitment to teaching a wide range of subjects, including individual self-care, the promotion of health, and the prevention of illness. Traditionally, nurses have also been strong and energetic advocates for their patients' right and needs. They are in a particularly strategic position to inform families and individuals of available services and to assist them in obtaining access to services. At the local, state, and federal levels public health nurses represent the health needs of the community. They frequently serve on advisory boards and planning committees. Nursing groups advocate for the right of patients to receive quality services. By calling attention to inadequate or unjust treatment, these nurses help make the human service systems more aware of, and responsive to, human needs.

AGENCIES, ACCREDITATION, AND FINANCING

Of the providers presently administering community nursing services there are several major types: public agencies operated by state or local units, such as municipal or county health departments; voluntary agencies such as the Visiting Nurse Associations (VNAs); proprietary agencies, which are privately owned for-profit agencies; and combined agencies, which are operated under the dual sponsorship of a governmental unit and a voluntary agency. In recent years some voluntary agencies, including VNAs, have come into affiliation with hospitals and now operate under the hospitals' corporate umbrellas. Another newly evolving model is the community service agency that is certified as a home health agency as well. Examples of this are certain Easter Seal and Catholic Charities programs.

Accreditation of home health programs is provided chiefly by the Joint Commission for Accreditation of Hospitals (JCAH) and most crucially by Medicare. More than 5,000 certified Home Health Agencies exist in the United States, according to 1984 statistics (see Table 4-4). The quality and appropriateness of individual programs for particular patients is best assessed through acquaintance with the local agency and its reputation for consumer satisfaction as expressed by those who have used the services.

Financing of services comes from diverse sources. The major portion of government funding comes from the federal programs of Medicare (Title XX) and Medicaid (Title XIX). The Medicare program is not set up for chronic care and is therefore restricted in its ability to support longer term needs for home care. Guidelines are stringent. Medicaid coverage is more broad in scope, but its reimbursement rate is less. Medicaid policies are fluid and subject to frequent changes. Some authorities in home health care anticipate a prospective prepayment plan for such services in the near future.

SETTINGS

For purposes of discussion, the numerous and varied settings of community nursing services can be grouped into several major categories: homes, ambulatory services, independent nursing practices, schools, and occupational health settings.

Homes

The home is one of the most frequently used sites. Persons discharged from hospitals, rehabilitation facilities, and other inpatient settings are regularly referred to community health agencies for continued care and follow-up. At home the service can be individualized and adapted to the context of family and household circumstances. With the assistance of local nursing services, it is possible for individuals who might otherwise require admission to a nursing care facility to remain at home. People with disabil-

ities in various areas of social, physical, and occupational functioning who live in community group residences and supervised apartment settings rightfully come under the purview of home-based nursing care.

Ambulatory Care Settings

The variety of places to which clients go for day service or ambulatory care include community health centers; hospital outpatient departments and continuing care programs; local health departments; neighborhood multiservice centers; and other highly accessible locations such as store fronts, shopping malls and public buildings. In remote rural and island areas, traveling health teams hold clinics in mobile vans or using helicopters or planes to provide specific programs or regular health care. Programs that offer services to migrant worker camps, Native American reservations, and remote mountain communities also utilize community nursing.

Independent Nursing Practices

In many communities services are being offered through the independent private practices of professional nurses who are trained in family health care and numerous subspecialties such as pediatrics, maternity, psychiatry, gynecology, and geriatrics. These nurses see patients in their offices or in home visits. They work in cooperation with physicians, therapists, and other professionals who are part of the network of community care and service.

Schools

The school, on all levels, is a major setting in which community nurses practice. Public schools are served by local nursing agencies or departments of public health, and may hire nursing services directly by individual contract. Private schools also receive nursing services through agencies or by individual contract.

School health services across the nation vary greatly, as do the specific functions that school nurses are authorized to perform. Some schools are used as primary care provider, some deliver a limited number of services, and some act solely as intermediary between the child's daily environment and the health care system.

The services provided depend largely on the specific community, the needs of the population, and the general availability of health care for school age children. The major areas of responsibility in which school nurses function are screening programs, preventive care, control of communicable diseases, response to ill or in-

Table 4-4. *Medicare/Medicaid-Certified Home Health Agencies as of December, 1984*

Region		No. of Agencies	Region		No. of Agencies
I. Connecticut		115	VI. Arkansas		163
Maine		16	Louisiana		136
Massachusetts		147	New Mexico		38
New Hampshire		38	Oklahoma		127
Rhode Island		13	Texas		447
Vermont		20		Total	911
	Total	349			
			VII. Iowa		134
II. New Jersey		55	Kansas		126
New York		139	Missouri		189
Puerto Rico		41	Nebraska		31
Virgin Islands		1		Total	480
	Total	236			
			VIII. Colorado		114
III. Delaware		22	Montana		20
District of Columbia		10	North Dakota		26
Maryland		103	South Dakota		17
Pennsylvania		231	Utah		23
Virginia		100	Wyoming		29
West Virginia		34		Total	229
	Total	500			
IV. Alabama		112	IX. Arizona		52
Florida		150	California		333
Georgia		73	Guam		1
Kentucky		64	Hawaii		10
Mississippi		135	Nevada		13
North Carolina		103		Total	409
South Carolina		37			
Tennessee		336	X. Alaska		4
	Total	1,010	Idaho		25
			Oregon		65
V. Illinois		222	Washington		43
Indiana		105		Total	137
Michigan		174			
Minnesota		154			
Ohio		218			
Wisconsin		113	Total for all Regions		5,247
	Total	986			

From Health Care Financing Administration: Health Services and Quality Bulletin, January 1985, p. 45.

jured children, team core evaluation for pupils with special needs, evaluation of health for placement in classrooms and planning activities, liaison between school and families, health education programs, and sexuality education and counseling.

In special education programs for children with disabilities or major chronic health impairment, school nurse services are particularly important. As members of the Core Evaluation Team, which plans and implements individualized educational programs and therapies, nurses participate in conferences and identify health needs and their effects on the child's ability to use the educational environment and curriculum. Nurse personnel are most knowledgeable about health services and community resources, and they can provide invaluable assistance in determining how the student's needs can best be met. Through interaction with families, often in home visits regarding health, nurses often bridge the two major environments of a child and thereby facilitate the communication and coordination that is necessary in providing a unified home-school experience.

Children with special health care requirements are included under the Education for All Handicapped Children Act (P.L. 94-142) (Chapter 3). Those who were formerly excluded from public school classrooms because of their need for special health care procedures are increasingly being accommodated by school personnel, thus permitting participation with classmates in the normal environment of neighborhood schools.

By ruling of the Supreme Court in July 1984, obligation was placed upon public schools to administer health care procedures that nurses have competence to perform. The landmark case brought by school officials in Irving, Texas, involved the need for intermittent urinary catheterization at 3-hour intervals by Amber Tatro, an 8-year-old girl with spina bifida. Groups representing public school administrators nationwide expressed interest in the case and were concerned that a ruling in favor of the child would broadly expand their obligations under the Education for All Handicapped Children Act.

In his decision, Justice Berger relied heavily on the fact that the catheterization procedure can be carried out easily, either by nurses or by other persons with a reasonable amount of training. He ruled, therefore, that the procedure cannot be classified as a special medical service that would burden the school board. The court unanimously ruled that the obligation of public schools to provide a normal education for handicapped children includes the responsibility to administer procedures that school nurses can perform.

Occupational Health Settings

Business and industry have long recognized that employee health services make a vital contribution to individual workers as well as to productivity. Nurses in such settings are particularly significant to employees with disabilities and health problems. In addition to teaching sound health practices and providing care for ill or injured employees, nurses also function as advocates, ensuring appropriate job placements for workers and adequate treatment for work-related illness or injury.

HOME HEALTH PROGRAMS

Home health care has been defined as any arrangement for providing, under medical supervision, needed health care and supportive services to sick or disabled persons in their homes. An array of services can be brought into the home for individuals of all ages who require such services because of acute illness, chronic illness, or disability. Home care services required by individuals range from specialized medical therapies to help with activities of daily living and household management. Some in-home programs are directed toward concentrated medical care activities; some emphasize social and supportive assistance.

Respite care for families of developmentally disabled children and adults who are living at home is a service commonly provided under public auspices through contract with home health agencies. By definition, respite care programs are designed to provide for the brief or periodic relief of care responsibilities for the family, thus alleviating stress and promoting family well-being. These programs are state funded and are usually administered by the state's Department of Social Services, Department of Mental Health, or Department of Mental Retardation, as determined by the human services structure of the particular state. Sometimes the service is provided in the family's home setting; sometimes the individual is cared for in an alternative family home or respite center.

Home health care is provided at an intensive (concentrated) level, an intermediate level, or a maintenance (basic) level. The central administration and coordination for the network of home care workers, equipment, and schedules is based in a hospital department or, more commonly, in a community nursing agency. As with other programs offered by a variety of providers and direct service workers, it is advisable to ascertain the quality of services by inquiring into local consumer satisfaction as well as into the provider agency's credentials for staff certification.

HOSPICE PROGRAMS

A hospice program provides family-centered care for persons near death. This approach is significant when a family member is affected by a progressive metabolic or neurological disorder and is experiencing terminal phases of the illness. The emphasis is on relief of symptoms and psychological and spiritual support to patient and family. Some hospice programs can provide direct nursing care when necessary. The spectrum of hospice services is comprehensive and holistic in design, and each program determines which services will be offered to individual families. Possible hospice services include skilled nursing care; personal care services; physical, speech, and occupational therapies; medical supervision and care; and psychological or spiritual support. Although a hospice may not provide all of these services, a referral system is usually developed with other agencies so that a comprehensive spectrum of services can be delivered. In the United States hospices have taken various forms. The most common are home health care organizations, free-standing facilities, volunteer organizations with no facilities, hospital-based units, and units of skilled nursing services.

Paying for Hospice Care. The five major

sources of funding are private donations, membership fees, hospital revenues, private and governmental project grants, and federal, state, and local contracts. Medicare, Medicaid, Title XX, and the Older Americans Act pay for various specific services when eligibility criteria are met. In most states, Blue Cross/Blue Shield plans provide coverage with selected health care providers, and in some states, such as Ohio and Colorado, they are mandated to do so under state law. The quality of care provided by hospice programs is monitored by the Joint Commission for Accreditation of Hospitals.

PERSONNEL

The popularly held, traditional concept of nursing encompasses innumerable kinds of responsibilities, caring activities, and levels of professional and vocational preparation. Most broadly based community nursing programs and agencies rely on combinations of professional and vocational personnel for the varying degrees and types of assistance needed by their patients. It is probably safe to presume that every community nursing program has at least one registered nurse in a position of supervisory responsibility on its staff. Additional registered nurses may also be involved, both in professional nursing care and in supervision (see Table 4-5).

Registered Nurses and Nurse Practitioners

Registered nurses (RNs) are graduates of approved schools of professional nursing who are licensed by the states in which they practice. Beyond this basic RN preparation is the master's degree level for nurses who are specialists in particular clinical areas, such as public health, pediatrics, geriatrics, and developmental disabilities. Nurse practitioners attend a specialized program within a continuing-education program or a baccalaureate or master's degree curriculum. The nurse practitioner has advanced skills in physical assessment and measures of primary health care (Chapters 4 and 27). Certification is required to practice in this role.

Practical (Vocational) Nurses

Practical (vocational) nurses are licensed by the state in which they practice. To be a licensed practical nurse (LPN) or a licensed vocational nurse (LVN) in California or Texas, an applicant must be a graduate from a state-approved school of practical nursing and must pass a state board examination. These practitioners provide nursing care under the supervision of an RN or a licensed physician. They administer appropriate treatments and basic nursing care and sometimes assist in supervising nursing aides and assistants.

Nursing Assistants and Nursing Aides

Nursing assistants, nursing aides, and home health aides are usually provided with training in a nursing agency or through a community college program and are granted certification by the training facility. They offer appropriate measures of assistance, receiving instruction and supervision from an RN.

Table 4-5. *Personnel Categories*

Title	Licensure	Education	Usual Length of Training
Registered Nurse	RN by state board exam or interstate reciprocity	Diploma	2–3 yr
		Associate degree	2 yr
		Baccalaureate degree	4 yr
Nurse Practitioner	RN plus practitioner certification	RN plus nurse practitioner program	RN plus 1–2 yr practitioner program
Clinical Nurse Specialist	RN	RN with master's degree in clinical specialty	5–6 yr
Licensed Practical (Vocational) Nurse	LPN LVN	Vocational training	1 yr
Nursing Assistant Nursing Aide Home Health Aide	Certification	Agency in-service training	1–3 mo

SPECIFIC POPULATIONS SERVED BY COMMUNITY NURSING SERVICES

High-Risk Infants

Infants with low birth weights who are discharged from neonatal intensive care units (NICUs) and need the services of community health nursing are a relatively new population (see also Chapter 5). Referrals to community nursing agencies are appropriate for certain infants discharged from NICUs: those who go home with medical conditions warranting further follow-up; those who are at biological risk for future developmental problems; and those for whom concerns are raised regarding the psychosocial circumstances of their parents. Examples of the latter group include adolescent mothers, parents involved in substance abuse, and parents with psychiatric disorders. When there is a need for additional support in the home, various services are provided by community health nurses: assistance with home medical management and health care monitoring for infant and mother in cooperation with the primary physician; family assessment and support specific to the needs of the infant; parent education and assistance in obtaining access to services of other agencies and programs that may be needed; and ongoing periodic developmental screening of the infant.

Project ACCESS, a joint project of Wheelock College and the Children's Hospital in Boston, examined access to services for infants at risk after discharge from NICUs in New England. They reported a great variation in the ability of community nursing programs to provide such follow-up. Identified as major determinants of an agency's capabilities in providing this kind of service were the agency's eligibility criteria, financial and geographic factors, and the availability of nursing expertise in infant follow-up (see Chapter 2).

Eligibility Criteria

In some states all newborn infants are referred to community nursing; in others only first births and premature infants are referred. Criteria vary among states and regions, but risk factors for child and family, financial qualifications, and geographic area are considerations. Usually eligibility criteria are mandated by state departments of health or special project funding, or they are developed by advisory and directorial committees. Most community nursing programs are able to accept referrals for any infants diagnosed at risk for established, biological, or environmental factors.

Financial and Geographic Issues

Some programs must adhere to financial criteria or mandates to accept families who are economically disadvantaged. Payment for the care of high-risk infants is a problem for many agencies. Third-party reimbursement is a significant factor. Medicaid and other third-party payers strongly influence the kinds of medical problems agencies can follow. Most community agencies only provide services within specific areas.

Availability of Nursing Expertise

The quality of services delivered depends largely on the availability and employment of nurses with professional preparation in maternal and child health, particularly in relation to the special needs of high-risk infants and their families. A widespread need exists for more community nurses with updated training in the screening and appraisal of early childhood developmental problems, in the special health care requirements and techniques used for post-NICU infants, and in the psychosocial implications for the whole family. Parents report that visiting nurse services are invaluable when individual nurses are expert in comprehensive basic home care for infants and are able to correlate well with other support services, developmental intervention programs, the primary care physician, and the tertiary center.

Children with Major Health Impairment

Many children with major body system anomalies and with progressive central nervous system disorders require special measures in their daily care at home (Chapter 2). Parents can learn to perform procedures such as gastrostomy or nasogastric tube feeding, tracheostomy care and suctioning, postural drainage, chest percussion, oxygen and inhalation therapy, and urinary catheterization. With assistance from community nurses and backup by the primary care physician, they can provide such care without neglecting the needs of other children or jeopardizing parental equilibrium. Visiting nurses can offer the instruction and moral support that helps parents become competent and confident in caring for the involved child. In some respite situations, nurses assume direct care responsibilities on a regularly scheduled basis.

Molly

Molly is a 3-year-old girl with multiple major anomalies that include atonic bladder, gastrointestinal dysfunction with nutritional failure, and spastic quadriparesis. Her parents perform nasogastric tube feedings and urinary bladder catheterization at 3-hour intervals during the day and evening. The local community nursing agency provided direct care in the home during her mother's surgical and obstetrical hospitalizations, and it continues with respite care on a regular basis. This plan has allowed the child to remain at home with her father during her mother's absence and has permitted the parents to devote time and energy to their second daughter.

Carlos

Carlos, a 7-month-old boy whose difficulties include phocomelia, cleft palate, choanal atresia, and diaphragmatic hernia, was discharged from the hospital after complications of upper airway obstruction, congestive heart failure, and severe nutritional difficulties necessitated placement of a gastrostomy tube (see Chapter 6). His home care provides tracheostomy care, gastrostomy feedings, and physical therapy. The community nursing service provides a period of daily direct care that is paid for by private health insurance, supplemental respite care that is funded through the state program, and physical therapy funded through an early intervention program sponsored by the state department of public health. Such services are critical to the parents' ability to cope with the long-term stresses of providing for such a special child.

The outlook for these and other children with long-term serious health impairments and with probable episodic childhood illnesses made more acute by medical vulnerability calls for a number of elective hospital admissions throughout childhood and for elective habilitative procedures.

Children with Progressive Disorders

With progressive disorders the needs of children and families are similar in some ways to needs in other types of chronic illness. They are different in that the course of the disorder is expected to be one of gradual loss of function and eventual demise. Parents usually develop special care skills and adapt the design of home life gradually, which allows them to master one phase before coping with the next. During the earlier stages, care promotes and maintains functional capabilities. The philosophy for care in later times, however, calls for acceptance of the realities of declining function, with emphasis on pleasurable experiences, prevention of discomfort, and gentle support to waning life systems. As with aggressive habilitative programs, community nurses are called on to provide relief of parental stress through direct care and through emotional support that helps parents maintain their commitment to home care until the eventual death of their child.

Robbie

Four-year-old Robbie is a boy with an inborn metabolic disorder (I-cell disease) involving severe skeletal dysplasia, respiratory tract difficulties, and psychomotor retardation. In the advanced stages of illness his complex needs have required a highly demanding regimen of home care involving supporting nursing measures, inhalation therapy, oxygen administration, special diet and feeding techniques, and numerous medications. His parents are devoted to home management and are in difficult financial straits. Both are employed out of the home in order to provide for their household and 2 other children. They find it necessary at this time for Robbie to have a knowledgeable, trained, competent person available to him in their absence. Through a combination of public and private funding sources, they are able to have a nurse with him 6 hours a day, 5 days a week. Difficulties in insurance coverage have arisen because of the long duration of his illness. In the situation of this child and others like it, the strong advocacy of physicians is a major factor in obtaining the continued coverage needed for long-term community nursing services. Robbie's parents say, "Knowing that our nurse is there gives us the strength and peace of mind to continue on."

Technologically Assisted Children

The small but growing number of children being discharged from hospitals with continuing long-term requirements for highly technological ("high-tech") assistance constitutes a significant new population to be served by local community health programs. Among this group are children with respiratory disorders who are dependent on ventilators (Chapter 11), children with chronic renal disease that is managed by dialysis, and children with severe nutritional disorders who are maintained by parenteral nutrition. All require sophisticated equipment and ongoing medical and nursing management in order to survive. The needs of such children and their families present a major challenge to health care planners, funding sources, medical equipment suppliers, community nursing programs, and other human service groups involved in the delivery of health, educational, and social services.

Both historically and in current times, programs and services for children with special needs have been developed as a result of the pressure and leadership of parents working with professionals and other involved individuals to generate strong and effective consumer advocacy movements. The national volunteer organization known as Sick Kids need Involved People (SKIP) is a group of parents, professionals, providers of medical equipment and services, and other involved individuals who are committed to assisting families in preparing and maintaining a network of safe, coordinated home care. In many states the local chapters or affiliates of this organization are actively involved in the development of state plans for such home health care programs.

As children receiving technological assistance reach school age, school systems are called on to adjust to their requirements. The ability of school systems to accommodate these children is influenced by decisions in federal policy regarding whose needs will be determined to be within the province of school services and whose will be excluded. Nursing services to and within school systems are heavily implicated, and they vary widely depending on the availability and funding of specialized nursing expertise.

BIBLIOGRAPHY

Blackwell, M.: Care of the Mentally Retarded. Boston, Little, Brown, 1982.

Levine, M., Carey, W., Crocker, A., and Gross, R.: Developmental Behavioral Pediatrics. Philadelphia, W.B. Saunders, 1983.

Spradley, B.: Community Health Nursing—Concepts and Practices, Boston, Little, Brown, 1981.

Symposium on Community Nursing. Nurs. Clin. North Am., *15*:321, 1980.

NURSES IN COMMUNITY-BASED RESIDENTIAL SCHOOL PROGRAMS

Adria S. Hodas, R.N., F.N.P.
Kathleen A. Blaber, R.N.
Jacqueline M. Keane, R.N.

Illness and disability can be mysterious, especially to people associated with individuals who have developmental disabilities. Misconceptions and confusion often exist. As health care providers, nurses help unravel the mystery and clarify the problems. This is done by recognizing the unique needs of ill and disabled individuals and by striving to help them achieve their highest level of functioning. The nurse's role in a community-based residential school program is multifocused and complex. It encompasses a variety of clinical nursing functions as well as teaching, administrative, and child-centered functions. The nurse is in a leadership position and therefore acts as a resource person for staff, students, and families. The nurse is also the primary spokesperson in the facility for health care issues.

PROGRAMS, PERSONNEL, AND FUNDING

With the current trend toward community-based care for individuals with serious developmental disabilities, many children who formerly would have been in state institutions are now residing in various types of residential facilities within the community. The degree of structure and supervision in these facilities depends on the functional level of the students. A residential school provides a type of program that has evolved to serve the growing needs of these individuals. Its goals are to promote normalization and assist children in reaching their highest potential for self-sufficiency in major life activities. A structured environment is provided in which the student can work on the development of skills related to self-care, communication and language, cognition, mobility, independent living, and economic self-sufficiency.

Services are provided for individuals with developmental disabilities who cannot be served in the home or in local school programs or who are making a transition from a long-term care facility to more independent living. The setting promotes skills in independent living and active participation in the community. Each student's program is individualized to meet the needs of cognitive, functional, developmental, and physical status. Families are encouraged to remain actively interested and involved with the student. Although the program is usually separated into a residential and a day school component, each with a specific focus, many of the goals intertwine. The residential goals focus more on self-help and skills related to the activities of daily living; the day component emphasizes academics, cognitive development, and prevocational and vocational training. Sometimes both programs concentrate on communication, mobility, and socialization. In some cases the programs share the same building; in others they are separated into group homes and the school. Some residential schools also have provisions for serving day students who live at home.

The personnel in these special programs come from varying disciplines and backgrounds. The direct care providers are special education teachers, child care workers, and case managers. Usually, additional personnel provide counseling, health care, physical therapy, occupational therapy, recreation, transportation, music therapy, speech therapy, social services, and protective and legal services.

Funding comes from various local and state agencies. Since the passage of Public Law 94-142, which requires that local school systems provide individualized special education services to all handicapped individuals between the ages of 5 and 21, a majority of pediatric and adolescent developmentally disabled students placed in residential schools receive funding from local school systems. Some cost-sharing arrangements are made between appropriate state agencies and the school systems. In order to augment tuition funds, many programs seek grants and contributions from government and private sources.

COMMON HEALTH CONCERNS

The health care needs of individuals with serious developmental disabilities are much more intricate than those of the normal individual, and many of them persist into adulthood. Of the long list of problems that can be identified, some are more common and outstanding. Management of these problems usually includes more than just nursing interventions and often requires medical intervention and the assistance of a wide range of disciplines.

Infection

For the developmentally disabled child an important health care concern is the prevention and treatment of infection. In a residential setting, infections are easily transmitted by close contact, drooling, and mouthing of objects. Prevention includes teaching good personal hygiene to staff and students and establishing rational infection-control procedures. An ongoing part of the health care program should consist of educating staff and families about common infectious diseases and control procedures. Prevention should also include maintaining complete immunizations, annual tuberculosis testing, and hepatitis B screening.

Trauma and Accidents

Trauma and accidents are common when individuals have physical and developmental disabilities. They often have problems of spasticity, abnormal gait patterns, and poorly developed protective reflexes, all of which can contribute to falls and accidents. Some have sensory impairments, such as hearing or visual deficits, which can reduce safe mobility and prevent the recognition of dangers in the environment. Many do not have the cognitive ability to comprehend and avoid danger. Their lack of self-preservation skills necessitates constant supervision and a secure environment. Seizures, which are a common occurrence, are an additional source of accidents, and some students require helmets to prevent head injury. Self-injurious and assaultive behavior can result in trauma that ranges from minor to life-threatening (see Chapter 2).

The nurse working with the interdisciplinary team needs to identify children at risk and plan interventions that reduce the frequency and severity of accidents. Such diverse approaches can be used as physical therapy for gait training and protective reflex conditioning. Visually impaired individuals can receive training in mobility and orientation. Others need self-preservation skills, particularly fire-drill techniques. Accident prevention may also mean working with a neurologist on seizure control and a psychologist on programs for behavior management regarding behavior disorders. Incident reports can be a useful source of information for identifying the nature, frequency, and features of accidents and trauma.

Nutrition

Nurses in residential settings are sometimes responsible for monitoring nutritional status. Regularly recording heights and weights on established growth curves helps in observing growth spurts, growth delays, and excessive weight loss or gain. Growth spurts may require an increase of foods rich in calcium and additional calorie intake. Growth delays, which are not unusual in this population, sometimes require endocrine evaluation. Obesity can be associated with Down, Laurence-Moon-Biedl, and Prader-Willi syndromes, and these may require weight monitoring and control programs (Chapter 10).

Sometimes when students refuse meals the reason is not apparent. They may have food preferences or dislikes that they cannot express; they may be showing the first sign of illness or dental problems; or they may be responding to stress or problems in the dining room environment. All these possibilities need to be considered when mealtime or appetite problems arise. An evaluation of eating skills will indicate whether there is a need for special techniques, modified food textures, or adaptive equipment. Unusual weight loss can be caused by physical or emotional disorders, but before an emotional or behavioral cause can be implicated, medical causes should be ruled out. Food intake records and documentation of mealtime behavior can be useful in the assessment of weight and eating disorders. Clinical nutritionists can be extremely helpful in assessing normal as well as problem situations and can offer guidelines and nutritional plans for individual nutritional needs. It is also useful to consult with a feeding specialist, such as an occupational therapist, about clients with mouth closure and swallowing difficulties.

Pica

Ingestion of nonfood substances is frequently

seen, and if this compulsive behavior is not controlled, it can result in serious consequences. Ingestion of toxic substances and materials that cause bowel obstructions can lead to emergency situations. Pica can cause elevated lead levels, which require monitoring, treatment, examination of the environment, and elimination of the source of lead. Lead screenings are indicated for new admissions to a school program and periodically, for students at risk. The nurse should work with the clinical team to develop behavioral interventions to control pica behavior. Pica may need to be considered in the differential diagnosis of unexplained illnesses, particularly in children with gastrointestinal symptomatology (Chapter 20).

Constipation

Another common disorder in this population is constipation, which can result in development of bowel obstructions and distension if not well managed. The initial approach should be a dietary program of high-fiber food, sufficient fluids, an exercise program, and daily monitoring of bowel movements. If this is not effective, mild stool softeners or bulk laxatives may be necessary, although long-term use of laxatives and cathartics should be avoided if possible. In order to develop good bowel patterns, the individual should be allowed adequate quiet toileting periods (Chapter 10).

Seizures

Management of seizure disorders may take up a large portion of the nurse's time. It is necessary to become familiar with the current accepted terminology, the international seizure classifications, commonly used anticonvulsant medications, and seizure first aid. The nurse should work closely with the neurologist, following each student in order to facilitate optimal seizure management. Seizures can be frightening to staff members and to families who are unprepared. The nurse needs to teach seizure first aid, which means how and when to intervene and proper safety procedures. A seizure profile on each child can be used for staff training and parent education and can accompany students whenever they leave school to be seen by a neurologist, to be admitted to a hospital, to attend camp, or to be discharged to another program (Chapter 8).

Sexual Development

Once the child reaches puberty, his sexuality needs emerge and must be recognized. Girls need to be taught about menstruation and appropriate personal hygiene habits during menses. When possible, this teaching should be initiated prior to the onset of menstruation. Irrespective of cognitive levels, an individual needs to learn appropriate social conduct and sexual expression. This includes the need for privacy from others and for others. Staff members need to respect this privacy and to remember that they act as role models for students. Many developmentally delayed individuals need to be taught how to recognize and relate to strangers and how to reject inappropriate and undesired attention from others. Sexuality training based on the person's cognitive and functional level needs to be included in the individualized service plan. The sexual education curriculum can include such topics as anatomy, menstruation, relationships, masturbation, intercourse, contraception, sexually transmitted diseases, and sexual abuse (Chapter 16).

Menstruation, masturbation, and sexual excitement are indications to parents that their child is reaching physical maturity. For parents this knowledge can accentuate the developmental delay that is present and make them more aware of their child's changing needs. This can be an emotionally difficult time for parents who are trying to understand and cope with the knowledge that their developmentally disabled child is reaching adulthood and with the issues of their child's sexuality. Counseling and teaching for the parents is just as important as sexuality training for the child, and it should not be left until a crisis has developed.

Health Needs Assessment

Meeting the health care needs of individuals with developmental disabilities is not always an easy task. Often they are not able to express their needs and discomforts adequately. They may be unable to understand explanations or instructions. Their frustrations and discomforts may be expressed through such inappropriate behaviors as self-injury and aggression. The first step in meeting their needs is to obtain a thorough history from as many sources as possible. From the history, the nurse can develop a problem list and identify areas that warrant monitoring. This will provide a basis for assessment when illness is suspected or apparent. It can also be used to develop a health care maintenance plan.

In residential settings nurses have the advantage of seeing a student often, perhaps daily. This gives them the opportunity to learn about a student's habits, mannerisms, and communication methods and to develop a good relationship with each student. The most valuable information about a child sometimes comes from the direct care staff or family members, who may be the first to notice the subtle indications that a problem is developing. The first signs of illness are often minor changes in routines and habits. If a student displays alterations in mood, activity level, appetite, sleep, or urinary or bowel patterns, or indicates pain by touching a part of the body, the nurse should be alerted to the presence of a problem and the possible need for an evaluation.

Examinations

Examinations and diagnostic tests can produce anxiety in normal individuals. They produce even more anxiety in these young people, who may not be able to understand what is occurring and may be frightened by an unfamiliar environment with unfamiliar people. Previous troubling experiences can compound the problem and make individuals tactilely defensive. If they become anxious and resistive and restraints are used, it is likely to establish a pattern that is difficult to break. Eliciting compliance by reducing anxiety is a better approach, even if it takes more time and effort. When a child lacks or has limited expressive language skills, this does not necessarily mean that receptive language skills are equally impaired. It is important, therefore, to communicate to children during exams and to be conscious of the content of anything that is said about them in their presence. Students' anxiety can be reduced by having a familiar person present, by giving continual reassurance and explanations at their level of comprehension, by using a gentle voice and touch, and by avoiding false promises. Trust may need to be built slowly, and it may develop more easily if exams take place when children do not have an illness so that the significance of the exam and the anxiety are not so great. If anxiety becomes too great, more than one session may be needed. Exams should begin with the least-threatening components and advance through the more anxiety-provoking procedures, even if this alters the usual order of the examination. Since an entire exam may not be possible, the clinician needs to set such priorities before starting. Once the anxiety threshold is reached, it may be impossible to accomplish anything further at that time.

Health Education

Many students have good communication skills and are able to learn basic health care concepts. This provides the nurse with an opportunity to teach concepts such as wellness and health care maintenance. By gearing the teaching to the cognitive and functional level of young people, the nurse can teach them to manage and monitor some of their own health care needs and self-medication procedures and to understand when and how to seek assistance. Not all students are candidates for this type of teaching. For students with serious cognitive and physical impairments, the nurse aims more at teaching them how to take medications without resisting and with the least amount of difficulty.

CHILD-CENTERED NURSING ROLES

Coordination of Health Care

The nurse coordinates the health care of students according to their individual needs and in compliance with state regulations pertaining to mandated levels of care and screening. Since individuals with developmental disabilities have multiple medical and mental health needs, many residential facilities have contractual arrangements with a hospital or a physician for the provision of medical services. These services are given in the school itself, in the physician's office, or at a hospital-based clinic (see section on consultation services in this chapter). The role and degree of involvement of the physician depend on whether he or she is acting as physician to individual students or as consultant to the school. Most children are eligible for third-party funding and make use of services that are paid through this funding mechanism.

Young people with complex medical problems requiring special attention are usually referred to medical and allied health specialists. More than one specialist may be involved in the management of a particular problem or a particular child. The nurse must make sure that appointments are coordinated, that each clinician receives the necessary information, and that the program receives all reports and test results. Recommendations from specialists are integrated into health care plans and individual service plans. The direct care staff may be responsible for carrying out recommendations, for example, for a regimen of physical therapy exercise. In some cases the nurse may have to see that the staff receives necessary training. The nurse can either do the training or bring in a consultant. It is sometimes advantageous to use specialists for training of staff and parents.

Liaison

Nurses act as liaisons between teachers, child

care workers, parents, and health care providers. They have flexibility in moving between school, home, and medical settings, and they facilitate communication by interpreting health care information and issues and by providing education for parents and school staff.[1] Nurses also function as liaisons between the program, the health care providers, and the funding agencies, which require accurate information on health care status and its implication for patients. The nurse relies heavily on direct care providers for information related to changes in health care status. An effective communication system enables the student to receive immediate medical attention. Certain procedures in combination have been successful in keeping both nurse and staff abreast of current health care concerns: regular contact with day and residential supervisors; communication log describing daily behaviors and health concerns; daily nursing rounds for general physical assessment of each child and communication with direct care staff; and weekly memos or newsletters for staff with updates on treatments, medication changes, and general health care issues.

Community Resource Expert

The nurse takes an active role identifying and utilizing community resources. These resources might include local hospitals and clinics, mental health facilities, specialty clinics provided by state health departments, visiting nursing agencies, social service agencies, respite care services, and legal services.[3] Some associations for various disabilities and syndromes provide in-service programs, literature, funding for special equipment, and support services for families. Most children qualify for third-party payment, such as Medicaid, and it is essential to learn about the public welfare system and to know the details of the special programs available through state agencies so that each student can receive necessary health care funding.

Interdisciplinary Team Member

The interdisciplinary team model has been successful in the management of complex problems (see Chapter 1). Nurses are active members of interdisciplinary teams and can be considered "generalists" among specialists because their knowledge incorporates anatomy, physiology, psychology, sociology, and development.[1] The exact make up of a team varies depending upon the nature and scope of the child's problems and the resources of the program. In many cases nurses identify a problem and initiate some in-terventions, but because problems are often multifaceted, a nurse may need to rely on other members of the team to develop a comprehensive plan of care. The plan provides all team members with a complete assessment and explanation of the needs of the individual. Members of individual disciplines have an opportunity to share ideas and plans and learn more about how other disciplines carry out their roles. For children the final service plan is created in coordination with the special education administration of the involved school district.

Child Advocate

"At all levels of our judicial system, litigation on behalf of patients and clients is increasing. At issue are the rights of these citizens to adequate care, privacy and confidentiality, informed consent, due process, and protection from all practice and procedures that threatens their dignity as human beings."[2] Advocating a child's rights and the ability to provide optimal health care without violation of these rights are crucial components of the health care system. The advocacy role is well served by nurses and health care professionals who are familiar with the problems of a developmentally disabled person and can readily anticipate and assess his needs.

It is appropriate that nurses develop strategies and advocacy plans for health care. In doing so, they must (1) take the initiative for preparing the child, family, and staff regarding interventions related to the individual's problems; (2) increase utilization and development of community resources when necessary, for example, assist the family with financial concerns by providing for specialty services; (3) intervene when there is an unmet need for a second medical opinion, necessary evaluation, follow-up, medication, or treatment; (4) become involved as nonlegal advocates by testifying or acting as witnesses in legal issues; (5) promote the provision of services at the student's highest level of independence and in the most appropriate and least restrictive setting; (6) assure the child's rights of confidentiality; and (7) understand and comply with the principles of human rights and provide an environment that respects and fosters human dignity.

The Nurse Practitioner

The expanded role of the nurse practitioner is well suited to assuming primary care responsibilities in a residential setting. The nurse practitioner uses clinical assessment and medical management skills to promote health care based on wellness and other principles of health care maintenance. These skills are used in developing a comprehensive plan that addresses the medical, nursing, psychosocial, and developmental needs of the student. Nurse practitioners can provide education and counseling. They are valuable as resource persons for staff, other nurses, families, and children. A nurse practitioner on the staff lessens the need to refer students to clinics and emergency rooms for medical evaluation of episodic illness. Instead, children can receive prompt treatment from a familiar person in a familiar environment. Chronic problems can be managed and medications adjusted by the nurse practitioner within her scope of practice and in coordination with specialty clinics. Medical management of episodic and chronic problems is based upon protocols established by the nurse practitioner and the primary care physician (see also Chapter 27).

ADMINISTRATION

Supervision of Staff

The delivery of health care services includes the utilization of professional and other personnel according to the organizational structure of the program. Because the nurse is responsible for all health care activities within the program, she must develop methods for orienting, training, and supervising to ensure competence and safety. To facilitate these administrative and supervisory tasks it is necessary to develop written guidelines, work performance standards, and evaluation procedures for personnel whose duties are related to health care.

The delegation of responsibilities is based on the structure and personnel in the program. Responsibilities might be interchangeable or might overlap. For example, a health care assistant might help in scheduling and transporting students to medical evaluations, in maintaining medical records, in ordering supplies, or in the initial triaging of health care problems. The staff nurse would be responsible for direct care and direct and indirect administration of medications through supervision of staff. Other nursing responsibilities include documentation in clinical progress notes, provision of necessary immunizations, and administration of first aid and emergency care when necessary.

Policies and Procedures

Health Care Manual

In order to develop and implement a health care system that meets the needs of the student and the individual program, it is essential to establish policies and procedures and to compile them in a manual. The purpose of the manual is twofold: to provide a written statement of the health care policies and procedures of the individual program, which may be required by state licensing agencies, and to serve as a basic source of information regarding medical, nursing, first aid, and general issues for administrators, health care providers, and the entire staff. The first step in the development of policies and procedures is to review the sources that effect the program, such as local, state, and federal laws; agencies that regulate and license the program; standards that are imposed by third-party funding sources; professional codes of ethics; accepted standards of practice; and goals and objectives of the program. The information reviewed should address all areas of the health care program and should be clearly written so that it is easily understood by each member of the staff. Just as health programs change from time to time, so do laws and guidelines. Therefore, revisions and/or updating should be done annually and according to need. The manual should be reviewed with staff, especially when changes are made, and should be available to all staff members at all times.

Programs

The role of the nurse in a residential program often extends beyond the provision of direct care and teaching into administration. As a member of the clinical administrative team, the nurse must demonstrate to the team the health care needs of the program and identify the policies and procedures that are necessary in order to meet these needs. This may encompass policies that affect the utilization of direct care staff for health care purposes, the utilization of a primary care physician and consultants, the prioritization of funds used in meeting health care needs, and the development of staff orientation and in-service training programs. In addition, the nurse integrates individual and programmatic health care needs with the goals of education and support services for the individual and the program. This takes place during the intake and discharge processes, and is also part of the annual development of individual service plans. As the program grows and changes in response to the needs of the community, the nurse brings the health care perspective to the changing philosophy, goals, and methodologies of the program. As nurses participate in these processes, they are able to contribute a holistic point of view.

Coordination of Health Care Records

A permanent record commonly referred to as the medical record or chart should be maintained for each student in accordance with accepted professional standards. These records may have to be separate from the child's central record in order to promote better access to health care information. Comprehensive health care requires complete and ongoing collection of data regarding the child. All health status data should be readily available and easily understood. Problem-oriented record keeping is very useful in the residential schools. This system provides organized health data and information concerning active and inactive problems. The format can be adapted easily to include nursing diagnoses, thereby facilitating the planning of nursing care and contributing to the clarity of communication within the nursing profession. Each program should have a policy that regulates the use and flow of records. Things to consider are record retention period, forwarding copy of record or abstract for students transfer to other facilities, protection of clinical record information against loss or unauthorized use, consent for release of information, and secure storage. The health care record should provide the following information:

1. Identifying information
   Student's name, permanent address, date of birth, sex, admission date, allergies, hospital numbers
   Parent and/or legal guardian, with address and home and work telephone numbers
   Alternative emergency contacts, with addresses and telephone numbers
   Primary and specialty care physicians, with addresses and telephone numbers
   Pharmacy address and telephone number
   Insurance information
   Consent forms
2. Immunization information
3. Health care information
   Past medical history, including birth and development, hospitalizations, illnesses, surgery, injuries
   Diagnoses, including medical, etiologic, psychological, functional
   Problem list, including active and inactive problems
   Initial and annual assessments, including physical examination, laboratory data, behavior, and functional status
   Health care treatment plan
   Clinical evaluations, including medical, den-

tal, vision, hearing, other specialty areas
   Diagnostic evaluations and laboratory data
   Medication history
   Physician's orders
   Clinical progress notes
   Growth charts, seizure charts, menstrual records
   Discharge summary

EDUCATION AND RESOURCES

In-Service Training and Staff Orientation

All staff members, whether directly involved in health care or not, need to understand the nature of children's disabilities and health problems. Many people in direct care come to the program with little knowledge of health care and may have misconceptions or be unprepared to incorporate the student's needs into the daily program of care. An orientation program introduces staff members to the program's health care policies and procedures and provides basic information on health care issues. Some useful items in an orientation program are an information packet, discussions, lectures, and a demonstration of applicable procedures. For staff members who will be directly involved with health care, a more involved orientation can include a walk-through of the routines for as many days as deemed necessary. The orientation is particularly essential to nonprofessional staff members who will be assigned the responsibility of performing health care tasks.

On-the-job training is an extension of the orientation process. For health care this might include the procedures for checking vital signs, minor treatments, first aid, and administration of oral medications. This training method has the advantage of providing the new employee with a role model, and it gears the orientation to the special needs of individual children and employees. After the initial orientation, a written test can be administered, emphasizing the program's key features and issues. A follow-up meeting can be scheduled so the nurse can observe the new employee's competence. Only after adequate training, proper supervision, and evaluation is the staff member assigned to health care responsibilities. In some facilities experienced staff members are appointed on a continuous basis. In others, all staff members are prepared to take on health care tasks, and a senior staff member delegates the responsibilities according to staff availability and children's needs.

In-service training is provided on a continuous basis to introduce new procedures, discuss child health care needs, and present educational programs on subjects such as dental hygiene, seizure management, nutrition, and emergency procedures. Because staff turnover is common in residential programs, the need to orient and educate new staff members is continuous. As new admissions come in or new problems arise, education is needed about the health care problems that confront the staff. It is not always possible to present an in-service program around one specific student's needs. It is important, however, to meet with the direct care staff either in small groups or individually to provide them with the knowledge they need and often seek. Such education takes place almost continually because of the intricacies of the problems. In many ways this is one of the nurse's most important roles. The nurse can help the direct care staff to understand the children, and this understanding has a direct impact on the quality of care that the children receive.

Resources for Families

Residential programs that meet a child's needs effectively do not eliminate the involvement of the family. Communication with families is an area in which the nurse can work closely with the social worker. The nurse is often the bearer of troubled tidings, calling when a problem has arisen. It is important to establish a good rapport with the family and to maintain regular contact. A problem will produce less anxiety if the family has been kept regularly informed of child's health care status. Such contact provides the opportunity for teaching and including the family in routine health care planning. Together with the other clinical staff, particularly with the social worker, the nurse needs to assess the family system and determine where interventions from a health care provider are necessary. The family may require teaching or counseling in order to meet the needs of their child more effectively.

The family may also need assistance with finances or in managing medical appointments. The ultimate aim is to keep the parents optimally involved by teaching them how to advocate effectively for their child and maneuver in the health care system. In some situations families are unable to maintain full involvement, and school or state agencies must take on some of the responsibilities. In these cases nurses may find themselves working with court-appointed guardians, case workers, or foster families. The nurse must keep the appropriate person well informed about the health care issues so that proper decisions will be made.

Along with the movement for normalization and deinstitutionalization, we have seen wide changes in the scope of care to developmentally disabled persons, which present a unique challenge to the nurse working in a community-based residential school. The needs of individuals can be varied and complicated, but meeting them means contributing to their quality of life. Meeting such needs requires a wide knowledge base, many different resources, and the ability to integrate multiple therapeutic modalities and disciplines. Nurses will find themselves performing nontraditional roles as they use their knowledge, theories, and skills to provide optimal health care to an individual. Within the educational structure of the community-based residential school program, the holistic approach of a nurse helps the children attain maximal health and self-sufficiency.

REFERENCES

1. Bumbalo, J.A.: The clinical nurse specialist. *In* Early Intervention—a Team Approach. Edited by K.E. Allen, V.A. Holm, and R. Schiefelbusch. Baltimore, University Park Press, 1978.
2. Christian, W.P.: Legal issues relevant to child development and behavior. *In* Developmental-Behavioral Pediatrics. Edited by M.D. Levine, W.B. Carey, A.C. Crocker, and R.T. Gross. Philadelphia, W.B. Saunders, 1983.
3. Kenny, T.J., and Clemmens, R.L.: Behavioral Pediatrics and Child Development. Baltimore, Williams & Wilkins, 1975.

BIBLIOGRAPHY

Blackwell, M.W.: Care of the Mentally Retarded. Boston, Little, Brown, 1979.
Hannah, G.T., Christian, W.P., and Clark, H.B.: Preservation of Client Rights, a Handbook for Practitioners Providing Therapeutic, Educational and Rehabilitative Services. New York, The Free Press, 1981.
Massachusetts Department of Public Health, Division of Family Health Services. The Administrators Guide for the School Health Program, 1979.
Robinson, N.M., and Robinson, H.B.: The Mentally Retarded Child. New York, McGraw-Hill, 1976.
Siantz, M.L.: The Nurse and the Developmentally Disabled Adolescent. Baltimore, University Park Press, 1977.
White, S.L.: Managing Health and Human Services Programs, a Guide for Managers. New York, The Free Press, 1981.

SERVICES FOR CHILDREN WITH SPECIAL HEALTH CARE NEEDS (Formerly Called Crippled Children's Services)

Allen C. Crocker, M.D.

Fifty years ago Title V of the Social Security act was passed, and Crippled Children's Service

(CCS) programs were thus established in the states. This legislation, conceived by Dr. Martha Eliot and the Children's Bureau, reflected concern regarding the adequacy of services then available for children who had disabling conditions such as poliomyelitis, cerebral palsy, tuberculosis of bone, and congenital skeletal anomalies. The programs were designed

For the purpose of enabling each state to extend and improve (especially in rural areas and in areas suffering from severe economic distress), as far as practicable under the conditions in such states, services for locating crippled children, and for providing medical, surgical, corrective, and other services and care, and facilities for diagnosis, hospitalization, and aftercare, for children who are crippled or who are suffering from conditions which lead to crippling (Title V, Section 501).

Each state was given supporting federal funds, partially as a basic grant and partially in a formula based on child population and identified need. State matching funds were required in order to obtain the money. Although total appropriations through the years have been modest, the CCS programs have been a stable and important component in the health care system for children with disabilities.

In the early times of the CCS clinics the particular concern with orthopedic care implicit in the legislation (and in the program name) was apparent. Individual orthopedic surgeons often contributed special leadership in the formation of a state network of clinics, with a sustaining relation to tertiary care centers. As the years went on, the sponsoring agencies (almost always the state Departments of Health) assumed a broader definition of functional handicap, and other chronic and recurring medical problems came to be included.[2] In the 1950s the American Academy of Pediatrics petitioned for the addition of rheumatic and congenital heart disease,[3] and later cystic fibrosis became an important inclusion. The distribution of clinics in Massachusetts in 1983, shown in Table 4-6, can be considered representative. It will be noted that a large number of the clinics are within the general categories of developmental disabilities. The word *crippled* in the original CCS title has become increasingly inappropriate and disfavored. Alternate terminologies were gradually established in many of the state programs. Finally, responding to this general dissatisfaction, the 99th Congress in 1987 officially changed the designation from "Crippled Children" to "Children with Special Health Care Needs," and this will now become the standard usage. Either "programs for . . . " or "services for . . . " can be

Table 4-6. *Distribution of Crippled Children's Service Clinics in Massachusetts in 1983, by Specialty*

Regional Clinics	Number	Hospital Clinics	Number
Orthopedic	17	Cystic fibrosis	4
Neurology	10	Hemophilia	4
Cardiac	7	Inborn errors of metabolism	3
Genetics	6		
Developmental	4	Seizure	3
Myelodysplasia	3	Orofacial	1
Orofacial	3	Total	15
Cerebral Palsy	2		
Scoliosis	1		
Brace	1		
Total	54		

added to describe the organizational structure of these Title V activities. The CCS terminology, however, has obvious historic relevance.

In the traditional formula for running CCS state clinics, the families served were not charged directly. Coverage for service included clinic visits, medications, and appliances and also extended to inpatient costs for related reparative surgery. In recent years, especially in the CCS specialty clinics based in teachings hospitals, the trend has been to utilize available family insurance, including Medicaid, using Title V funds only when no other support can be found. Different state legislatures have shown varying willingness to invest in these public clinics beyond the contributions received from federal Title V funds, but in 1981 the average ratio was 2.2 state dollars per federal dollar.[4]

The size of the enrollment is also quite variable. As shown in Table 4-7, some states serve less than $\frac{1}{2}$% of their child population, while others serve 1 to $1\frac{1}{2}$%. These percentages often represent a significant proportion of the total number for children with certain diagnoses (e.g., hemophilia, phenylketonuria (PKU), muscular dystrophy, cleft palate, cystic fibrosis). For many others, even among those with usual CCS categorical diagnoses, it is a small fraction of the actual prevalence. The total number of children enrolled in the United States was 650,000 in 1979, a year in which the combined state and

Table 4-7. *Children Served in State Crippled Children's Service Programs in 1979 as Percentage of State's Childhood Population*

State	%	State	%
Midwest		**Northeast**	
Illinois	0.43	Connecticut	0.46
Indiana	0.27	Delaware	2.66
Kansas	0.42	Maine	0.31
Iowa	1.18	Massachusetts	0.46
Michigan	0.37	New Hampshire	0.96
Minnesota	0.89	New Jersey	0.80
Missouri	0.76	New York	0.46
Ohio	0.66	Pennsylvania	0.98
Wisconsin	0.48	Rhode Island	0.65
Upper Northwest		Vermont	1.84
Idaho	0.71	**South**	
Nebraska	0.75	Alabama	1.15
North Dakota	1.01	Arkansas	1.04
Oregon	1.04	Florida	1.46
South Dakota	0.55	Georgia	1.06
Washington	0.38	Kentucky	1.06
Wyoming	1.36	Louisiana	0.83
West and Southwest		Maryland	1.05
Arizona	1.50	Mississippi	0.76
California	0.80	North Carolina	1.24
Colorado	0.58	South Carolina	0.58
Hawaii	0.82	Tennessee	0.58
Nevada	1.48	Virginia	1.21
New Mexico	1.06	West Virginia	1.76
Oklahoma	0.52		
Texas	0.30		
Utah	0.88		

From Ireys, H.T., Hauck, R.J., and Perrin, J.M.: Variability among state Crippled Children's Service. Programs: pluralism thrives. Am. J. Public Health, 75:375, 1985.

federal expenditure for CCS was estimated at $275 million.[1]

Patterns in the maintenance of clinic services also vary substantially. Included are operations run by professionals directly employed by states, clinics conducted under contract from the health department, and fee-for-service activities for children seen in private offices and hospitals. Clinic teams commonly include, beyond the medical consultants, nurses, physical and occupational therapists, social workers, speech pathologists, and nutritionists, all utilized when appropriate. The general federal guidelines that have existed through the years regarding CCS design have been largely abandoned since the conversion of Title V funds to a Maternal and Child Health Block Grant.

After the Supplemental Security Income/Disabled Children's Program (SSI/DCP) was estab-

lished in 1976, there was a slow increase in funding for coordinated care planning and more extensive case management for children in CCS facilities. SSI/DCP activities have not been limited to CCS clients, however.

The existence of the Services for Children with Special Health Care Needs has a greater importance than the size of the system would indicate. Starting as a pioneering service mode for a needy group of children, the CCS operation provided a dependable source of specialty care in many environments for children with disabilities or chronic illness. It offered team attention to complex problems, brought clinical workers of high quality into the communities, focused on family problems, gave good follow-up care, and was available to those with special economic limitations. In our society the CCS system has been the principal base for steadfast public provision of long-term care.

As many commentators have observed, however, the time is appropriate for a fresh consideration of the mandate in the light of accumulated experience.[2] It has been pointed out that the CCS program has been generally very well accepted by private physicians, who tend to view its secondary care as helpful.[1] On the other hand, many pediatricians have been unfamiliar with CCS, and this explains some of the underuse of the services. The private sector, including teaching hospitals, now reaches out more broadly into child populations with disability or chronic illness and is capable of sustained assistance. The system of categorical diagnoses employed by CCS clinics has allowed some useful concentration on demanding problems, but there is an element of arbitrariness (including among states) regarding coverage of the larger field of disability that is frustrating and often difficult to defend. CCS programs have begun to include child development clinics in some states, but the general utilization of the medical model has limited their practicality. In fact, CCS facilities, in spite of good intentions, suffer from constraints in the area of true interagency collaboration. Many new kinds of disabled children, including those with so-called high-technology needs, are not part of the usual CCS plan.

Hence it is likely that the freedom now available for public health planning under the open design of the Maternal and Child Health Block Grant will lead to revisions in the public care system (see Chapter 32). The accomplishments of the Services for Children with Special Health Care Needs will be an important guide in this evolution.

REFERENCES

1. Ireys, H.T., Hauck, R.J., and Perrin, J.M.: Variability among state Crippled Children's Service programs: pluralism thrives. Am. J. Public Health, 75:375, 1985.
2. MacQueen, J.C.: The integration of public services for handicapped children: myth or reality. In Developmental Handicaps: Prevention and Treatment II. Edited by E.M. Eklund. Silver Spring, Md., American Association of University Affiliated Programs for Persons with Developmental Disabilities, 1984.
3. McPherson, M.G.: Community based services for disabled/chronically ill children and their families. In Developmental Handicaps: Prevention and Treatment III. Edited by E.M. Eklund. Silver Spring, Md., American Association of University Affiliated Programs for Persons with Developmental Disabilities, 1985.
4. Nelson, R.P.: Rationale for a Statewide Program. Address given at the Second Crippled Children's Services Institute, Columbus, Ohio, July 22, 1985.

OUTREACH PROGRAMS FROM TERTIARY HOSPITALS

Philip R. Ziring, M.D.

HEALTH CARE FOR PERSONS LIVING IN THE COMMUNITY

It is now clearer than ever that the forces of deinstitutionalization, increasingly supported by parent groups, court-ordered reform, and news media exposés during the past decade, have reshaped the system of services for children and adults with developmental disabilities and have engendered a change in public attitudes about such individuals. Persons with mental retardation are now admitted to residential facilities only under exceptional circumstances, and community-based residential and vocational services continue to undergo expansion to accommodate people who are either being discharged from these facilities or who have been living at home.

As this trend continues, it is also becoming increasingly evident that the provision of community-based health services for this population has not kept pace with progress in other areas of human services. It was expected that private physicians in local communities would be able to provide all necessary services to these often medically complex individuals, especially adults, in a manner that would satisfy responsible government and private agencies. In this expectation, policymakers and case managers have often been disappointed. For example, primary care physicians have too frequently been unfamiliar with the special needs of persons with mental retardation who are Hepatitis B carriers. In addition, physicians have often been unable to give proper guidance to staff caring for clients who are being given psychotropic drugs for problematic behavior.

The need to participate in an interdisciplinary process, to fill out seemingly endless forms for state agencies, and to be reimbursed at a level of financial compensation often lower than they receive to care for patients with less-complex needs have proven to be major disincentives for the average private practitioner. This situation has unfortunately led to the reinstitutionalization of a number of individuals who could not be accommodated in the community because their medical or behavioral needs could not be met, and this, in turn, has resulted in calls for new models of health care delivery to supplement the existing generic system of health services. One such model has been in operation in Morristown, New Jersey, since 1982.

THE MORRISTOWN MODEL

Morristown Memorial Hospital is located in Morristown, New Jersey. It is a modern 621-bed community hospital and a major teaching affiliate of the College of Physicians and Surgeons of Columbia University. Its fully accredited residency programs in pediatrics, internal medicine, surgery, dentistry, and other specialties have the support of the medical staff, hospital administration, and board of trustees. Most state-of-the-art radiologic services can be provided, and a full range of clinical laboratory services is maintained, including cytogenetics. The hospital is conveniently located along major interstate highways, is a 45-minute drive from New York City, and is 30 minutes away from two large state residential facilities for developmentally disabled persons.

The department of pediatrics provides medical supervision for all patients in the hospital nurseries (including the intensive care nursery) and in the pediatric inpatient service and has pediatric subspecialists in endocrinology, cardiology, adolescent medicine, genetics, and other areas. The department includes a child development center to provide evaluation and referral of children with developmental delay and to coordinate the high-risk newborn follow-up program. A case management unit is responsible for registering all handicapped children in Morris County with the state health department.

The Developmental Disabilities Center was established in the department of pediatrics in October 1982 through a contract with the State Department of Human Services, Division of Mental Retardation (recently redesignated Division of Developmental Disabilities). As originally conceived, the center was to provide the following:

1. Comprehensive medical and dental evaluation for any clients registered with the Division of Mental Retardation living in communities in northern New Jersey, including adults as well as children
2. Primary health care services for persons who had no private physician or dentist
3. Subspecialist services for individuals and special medical consultation services to staff of the Division of Mental Retardation
4. In-service education for case managers, group-home staff, and others regarding the special health needs of their clients
5. In-patient medical care as needed for clients of the Division of Mental Retardation
6. Linkages with state developmental centers and assistance in coordinating health service planning for persons being transferred to community living arrangements
7. Identification on an ongoing basis of gaps in the health care delivery system for developmentally disabled persons, which includes bringing these deficiencies to the attention of the Division of Mental Retardation and presenting proposals to remedy them.

To carry out these responsibilities, the Developmental Disabilities Center was staffed with three nurse practitioners, a consultant in internal medicine, a genetic counselor, a pedodontist with a background in the care of developmentally disabled patients, and a secretary. The program has been under the clinical and administrative supervision of the chairman of the department of pediatrics since its inception. Patients are seen in the outpatient department of the hospital every day of the week, both by appointment and on an emergency basis. The staff is on call on a rotating basis for patients in urgent need on nights and weekends.

Prior to their employment in the Developmental Disabilities Center, many members of the staff had no special experience or training in developmental disabilities. Furthermore, residents in pediatrics and internal medicine at Morristown Memorial Hospital had received no specific training or experience in the care of such patients.

Program Outcome

By the conclusion in September 1985 of its third year of operation, the Developmental Disabilities Center had registered 546 patients for ongoing health services. Persons from 15 New Jersey counties had come to Morristown for care, the majority coming from the northern tier of the state (Fig. 4-2). The 297 males and 249 females ranged in age from children under 10 years of age to elderly individuals in their seventh decade of life (Table 4-8). Approximately two-thirds were living in group homes or sponsored apartments, and the remainder were still living at home with their families. Thirty-eight group homes were being served, nearly half of the individuals having had a history of living in a state residential facility (Table 4-9).

Many patients had a number of handicapping conditions in addition to mental retardation, in-

Table 4-8. *Number of Patients Registered at Morristown Memorial Hospital Developmental Disabilities Center between October 1982 and September 1985, by Sex and Age*

Age	Male	Female
0–10	25	25
11–20	66	38
21–30	96	73
31–40	54	40
41–50	29	34
51–60	16	30
61–70	8	9
71–80	3	0
All ages	297	249

Table 4-9. *Community Living Arrangements of Patients Registered at Morristown Memorial Hospital Developmental Disabilities Center from 1982 to 1985*

Living Arrangement	No. of Patients
Current	
Living with family	209
Living in group home*	131
Living in supervised apartment or with "sponsor"	188
Living in public residential facility	18
	Total 546
Previous	
Lived in public residential facility	249
Never lived in public residential facility	244
Previous institutional status unknown	53
	Total 546

* Patients came from 38 group homes.

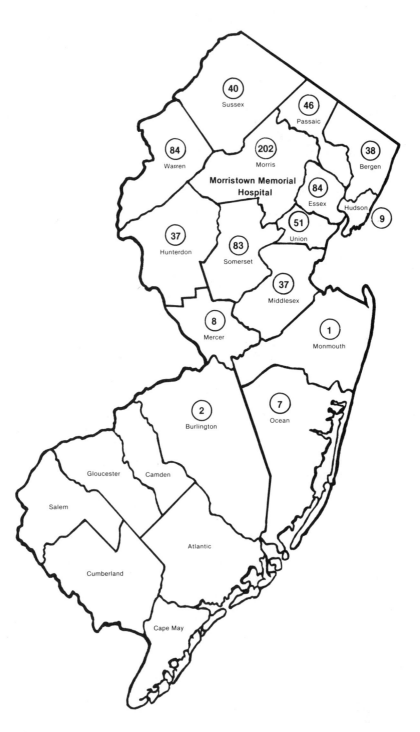

FIG. 4-2. Distribution of patient population at the Developmental Disabilities Center, Morristown Memorial Hospital, by New Jersey county of origin, as of November 1986.

Table 4-10. *Associated Handicapping Conditions in 546 Patients at Morristown Developmental Disabilities Center*

Hearing loss	43
Severely profound hearing loss	13
Hearing loss not previously diagnosed	14
Legally blind	23
Nonambulatory	17
Evidence of spasticity on neurological exam	63
Seizure disorder (by history)	112
Under active follow-up by center	27

cluding epilepsy and significant disorders of hearing and vision. Of the 43 with significant hearing loss, 14 had not been diagnosed prior to their evaluation at the Center (Table 4-10). Seventeen were nonambulatory.

INPATIENT SERVICES AT MORRISTOWN

Admission to the hospital is coordinated by nurse practitioners, whose liaison function between hospital staff and agency and group home staff is critical to the relatively smooth manner in

Table 4-11. *Patients Admitted to Morristown Memorial Hospital*

Reason for Hospitalization	Number
Dental procedure under general anesthetic	15
Pulmonary disorder	7
Cardiac disorder	4
Seizure disorder	3
Endocrine disorder	5
Surgery	11
Sickle cell crisis	1
Psychiatric disorder	2
Comprehensive developmental disability evaluation	4
Dilantin toxicity	1
Malnutrition/sepsis	1
Down syndrome with unexplained weight loss	2
Renal disease	2
Second-degree burns	1
Vascular disorder	1
Gynecological procedure	1
Total	61

which inpatient care and discharge planning are carried out. Caring for potentially disruptive patients with significant mental retardation on a general medical or surgical inpatient service was not welcomed by the hospital staff at first. In a relatively short period of time, however, the efforts of the Center staff overcame considerable bias through provision of in-service training for staff nurses and arrangement for supervision of difficult patients. This assured the hospital that their nursing staff was relieved of much of the administrative burden associated with caring for these patients, while experienced staff remained available to intervene if urgent problems arose. A listing of the reasons for hospitalization of 61 patients is provided in Table 4-11.

The Diagnostic Related Groups (DRG) system for reimbursing hospitals for all inpatient care is worthy of special consideration because the average length of stay for developmentally disabled individuals is generally longer than for persons without such coexisting conditions. Since reimbursement to the hospital is based on the diagnosis for which the patient is admitted and not on a per diem basis, it is in the hospital's best interest to keep the patient in the hospital for the fewest possible number of days and to keep inpatient utilization of the laboratory and X-ray departments at a minimum. This means that caring for significant numbers of patients with mental retardation on an inpatient basis without sufficient attention to the details of efficient inpatient management and early discharge planning could result in financial loss for the hospital. This factor is another reason the nurse practitioners' coordinative efforts are especially helpful. The DRG system, now spreading nationwide, needs to be explained carefully to all members of the state human service agency staff so that they do not refer patients for inpatient care if the same service can be provided on an outpatient basis and if admission cannot be medically justified.

ADMINISTRATION OF THE CENTER

The clinical responsibilities of service for patients under 21 years of age are supervised by the chairman of the department of pediatrics. For adults they are supervised by a board-certified internist. Initial intake, including medical and behavioral screening, is carried out either by pediatric or adult nurse practitioners in accordance with the age of the patient. Nurse practitioners arrange for assembling all available past medical records, order initial laboratory work, and coordinate referral to subspecialists. Coordi-

Table 4-12. *Endocrine Disorders at Morristown Developmental Disabilities Center*

Hypothyroidism	19
Down syndrome	14
Turner syndrome	1
Etiology unknown	4
Not previously diagnosed	8
Diagnosed but requiring medication adjustment	4
Hyperthyroidism	3
Down syndrome	1
Etiology of mental retardation unknown	2
Not previously diagnosed	2

nating the services for all patients at the Center, regardless of age or hospital department, is of major importance in providing continuity of care. This is also a useful training perspective for students and house staff. The ready availability of thorough screening, evaluation, and subspecialist consultation has led to some important new diagnoses being made in many patients. For example, eight patients with hypothyroidism not previously diagnosed have been identified (Table 4-12). In addition, a new appreciation has been possible regarding the higher than expected prevalence of mitral valve prolapse in patients with Down syndrome (Table 4-13).

BEHAVIOR DISORDERS

The ability to manage individuals with serious behavioral impairment in a community setting remains a major problem. It is an issue that in-

creasingly affects the rate of transfer from public residential facilities because many residential patients have a long history of severe problematic behavior. The mental health system seems ill-equipped to deal with this issue, and persons with a "dual diagnosis" of both mental retardation and mental illness are referred to the local mental retardation professional for service. Community-based psychiatrists have generally been turned to by case managers when patients demonstrate "acting out" behavior to gain attention. These physicians are usually unprepared by training or experience to counsel patients or staff, and they rely instead on established psychotropic medication. The result is that many of these patients have been taking high doses of these medications, or more than one psychotropic drug (polypharmacy), in the absence of a clear-cut psychiatric indication. It is one of the ironies of deinstitutionalization that psychotropic drug use has declined in public residential settings while inappropriate psychotropic drug use in the community has been increasing. At the Center, requests for management of problematic behavior is a daily occurrence. The list below shows the most common serious behavior disorders encountered; similar behavior is seen at inpatient residential facilities.

Aggressive, assaultive (spontaneous)
Stubborn, uncooperative, leading to assaultive verbal or physical behavior
Self-injurious
Severe hyperactivity
Depression

Table 4-13. *Cardiac Status in 546 Patients at Morristown Developmental Disabilities Center*

Status	Number
Congenital heart disease	69 (12.6% of total)
No previous cardiac diagnosis	43 (7.9% of total; 62.3% of those with heart disease)
Previously diagnosed but requiring treatment or follow-up	20 (3.7% of total; 28.9% of those with heart disease)
Down syndrome	48 (69.6% of those with heart disease)
Referred for cardiac evaluation and echocardiography	60
Referred for cardiac catheterization and/or surgical treatment	4
Not surgical candidate because of advanced heart disease (prophylaxis for subacute bacterial endocarditis recommended)	3
Surgery not indicated (SBE prophylaxis recommended)	36
Cardiac medication prescribed	2
No treatment indicated	12
Treatment recommendation pending	4

Anxiety
Rage attacks
Autistic

As might be expected, more males than females are under our care for such disorders. With the cooperation of staff, we reduced the overall rate of psychotropic drug use to 21% (Table 4-14). The management of persons with significant behavioral impairment is a subject of ongoing in-service education, and the use of psychotropic medication is seen as only one possible part of the management plan. At this time, 82 patients are taking a single psychotropic medication and 22 are being given propranolol hydrochloride (Inderal) in addition to a major tranquilizer (Table 4-15). Propranolol hydrochloride, a beta blocker used for many years in the management of patients with hypertension and other disorders, appears to be of exceptional value in selected patients whose behavior is severely aggressive. Use of this drug has enabled us to reduce dependency on major tranquilizers considerably and thereby lower the risk of patients' acquiring symptoms of tardive dyskinesia and other complications associated with these drugs.

OTHER SERVICES

Hepatitis B.   Despite the availability of a vaccine to prevent hepatitis B and other well-established control measures, the management of mentally retarded carriers of hepatitis B continues to be a source of much concern in the community. The staff of the Center has been active in providing in-service education at group homes and workshops, in providing consultation to local physicians and administrative staff of the state agency, and in providing hepatitis screening and vaccination of clients and staff. Education regarding the natural history of hepatitis and how to prevent it remains ongoing for all staff working with developmentally disabled persons living in the community. Such education has been one of the principal missions of the staff of the Center. Our experience in serologic screening of 265 of our first 546 patients for evidence of past infection by hepatitis B is summarized in Table 4-16. Of the 82 persons who had antibody to hepatitis B, 25 had never lived in a public residential facility and 6 of 35 individuals identified as carriers acquired their infections in the community. As has been shown in other studies, persons with Down syndrome are at especially high risk of becoming carriers of hepatitis B. Of the 79 patients with Down syndrome tested, only 23 are still susceptible to hepatitis B;

Table 4-14.   *Patients with Behavior Disorders at Morristown Developmental Disabilities Center*

Patient Class	Number
Patients with behavior disorders	166 (30% of all patients)
Female	68 (41% of all females)
Male	98 (59% of all males)
Patients receiving psychotropic medication	115 (21% of all patients)

20 have antibodies, and 29 are carriers (Table 4-17).

Genetics.   One of the special features of the Center is the screening of patients by a genetic counselor. As part of the regular intake evaluation, 230 patients have undergone such screening, and 208 of these have had a karyotype constructed (Table 4-18). The results of these evaluations are summarized in Table 4-19. It is of interest to note the new diagnoses made in this process and to consider the impact on prevention of mental retardation through subsequent family counseling. It is a tribute to the administration of the state Division of Mental Retardation that it has recognized the need to incorporate genetic counseling as part of the overall health care program for their clients.

Dental Care.   One of the most popular services offered at the Center is comprehensive dental care. It is not surprising that dental care is one of the greatest unmet health needs among developmentally disabled persons. Many suffer from infected, decaying teeth or long-standing gum disease. The availability of a pedodontist

Table 4-15.   *Psychotropic Medication Review at Morristown Developmental Disabilities Center (320 Patients)*

Patient Class	Number
Receiving single psychotropic drug	82
Receiving two psychotropic drugs	33
Major tranquilizer plus propranolol hydrochloride	22
Major tranquilizer plus lithium carbonate	4
Two major tranquilizers	2
Other combinations	5
Receiving new psychotropic drug or higher dose	28
Receiving lower dose, or medication discontinued	39

Table 4-16. *Hepatitis Immune Status of 265 Patients at Morristown Developmental Disabilities Center*

Status	Number
Immune (HB$_S$Ag−, Ab+)	82 (31% of total)
History of institutionalization	57 (22% of total)
Susceptible (HB$_S$Ag−, Ab−)	117 (44% of total)
History of institutionalization	47 (18% of total)
Carriers	35 (13% of total)
HB$_S$ Ag+, eAg+	7 (6 with Down syndrome)
HB$_S$ Ag+, eAg−	10 (5 with Down syndrome)
HB$_S$ Ag+, eAg unknown	18 (14 with Down syndrome)
History of institutionalization	29 (82.9% of carriers)
Indeterminate	
HB$_S$ Ag−, antibody unknown	31 (12% of total)
Given hepatitis B vaccine (Heptavax)	31
Known susceptible	15
Hepatitis status untested	16

with special training in developmental disabilities, together with an approved general practice dental residency, has added an important dimension to the comprehensiveness of services. One important side benefit of this program is research by the program's periodontist on new approaches to preventing premature loss of teeth from diseases of the gingiva in patients with Down syndrome, who seem to be predisposed to this problem.

Table 4-17. *Patients with Down Syndrome and Hepatitis at Morristown Developmental Disabilities Center*

Immune Status	Number
Patients with Down syndrome registered at center	115
Tested for hepatitis B	79
Immune	20
History of institutionalization	19
Susceptible	23
History of institutionalization	14
Carriers	29
eAg+	6
eAg−	5
eAg unknown	18
History of institutionalization	24
Indeterminate: Ag−, antibody unknown	7

Table 4-18. *Genetic Evaluations at Morristown Developmental Disabilities Center*

Complete genetic evaluation	230
Including chromosome analysis	208
No chromosome analysis (etiology of mental retardation clearly nonchromosomal)	22
Chromosome analysis (some repeated)	259
Fragile X analysis	26

The program at the community teaching hospital in Morristown has demonstrated that medically and behaviorally complex persons with developmental disabilities can be maintained successfully in community living arrangements while at the same time a setting is provided for the training of physicians, dentists, and other health professionals. It has also demonstrated that programs based at hospitals in the community can make an important contribution to research in mental retardation and to efforts in primary, secondary, and tertiary prevention.

Other models for delivering community health care to developmentally disabled persons may

Table 4-19. *Results of Genetic Evaluations*

Normal karyotype	125
Pending analysis	28
Fragile X	9
New diagnoses (chromosomal)	
Down syndrome	
Trisomy 21	64
Translocation Down syndrome	3
Mosaic Down syndrome	3
Other chromosome abnormalities	
Translocation (familial)	1
Deletion #13	2
Turner syndrome	1
Ring chromosome (mosaic)	1
Sex chromosome (mosaic)	4
Down syndrome and rearrangements	1
Fragile X positive	1
Derivative #10	1
Derivative #8	1
Derivative #7	1
Duplication #13	1
New diagnoses (nonchromosomal)	
Noonan syndrome	2
Saethre-Chotzen craniosynostosis	1
Pendred syndrome	1
Rett syndrome	1
Oculo-dental-digital syndrome	1
Changed diagnoses	
Not Down syndrome	3
Not tuberous sclerosis	1
Not fetal alcohol syndrome	1

be in the offing. Programs sponsored by proprietary health care corporations may soon be developed as counterparts to the institutional health services they provide. The rapidly growing health maintenance organizations could also incorporate services especially designed for persons with developmental disabilities. The number of individuals in need of service now and in the future is very large, and the existing services are fragmented and lacking in overall comprehensiveness. Room exists, therefore, for the testing and evaluation of several models of care. The Morristown model represents one type of approach. The record is open to scrutiny and should be given careful consideration by health and human service planners who wish to expand services for persons with developmental disabilities.

Part II

CLINICAL PROBLEMS

5

OUTCOMES FOR INFANTS AT RISK

INFANT FOLLOW-UP, TRACKING, AND SCREENING
I. Leslie Rubin, M.D.

The etiology for developmental disabilities encompasses a wide spectrum, most of which are either prenatal or perinatal (see Chaps. 2 and 6). In a review of more than 2,200 children with mental retardation seen in the Developmental Evaluation Clinic at The Children's Hospital in Boston, Crocker (see Table 7-4) documented that one-third had diagnosable prenatal influences, approximately 10% had perinatal factors contributing to their disabilities, and one-third had unknown causes for their disabilities.[7] This leaves only 21% who had postnatal causes. Of the postnatal causes, the most striking involved socioeconomic factors (17%) and medical conditions that affected the central nervous system (4%), for example, meningitis and head injury. Therefore, for almost 80% of the infants, children, and adults with developmental disabilities, prenatal or perinatal causes are likely, whether clearly identified or not.

To the pediatrician this means that disturbances in central nervous system function will be manifested at an early age. Indeed, in their review of the age at which disorders of development present, the child development group at the John F. Kennedy Institute in Baltimore[29] reported that motor problems tend to become manifest toward the end of the first year and early in the second year of life; speech delays, late in the second year and in the third year of life; and behavioral disturbances, from the third year of life upward. Obviously, learning disabilities will present in the school-age years. This implies that the pathologic disturbances underlying most developmental disabilities are present from early infancy, and it is important to identify the problem as early as possible to assure an optimal outcome.

IDENTIFICATION

In the area of child development, the mission becomes one of early identification of handicaps, with attention to parent-child relationships, to cognitive, motor, and social development, and to encouragement of achievement of full developmental potential.[10,12] If one considers, in addition, that developmental disabilities might possibly occur in up to 10% of children, identification becomes a relatively common pediatric challenge. Because pediatricians are likely to monitor infants in the first years of life, it devolves upon them to be aware of normal development, deviations in development, and identification of these disorders. In order to do this, it is important to develop an approach to the screening of children for possible developmental deviance. Three groups of infants require screening: infants at established risk, biologic risk, and environmental risk (Fig. 5-1). (See Chapter 2.)

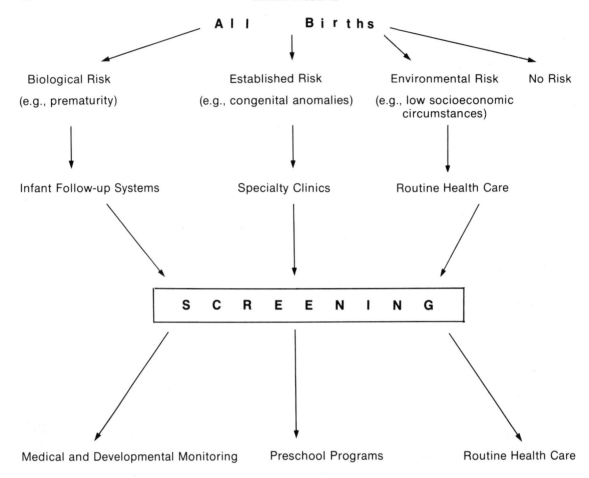

FIG. 5-1.   Screening of infants at risk for developmental disabilities.

Established Risk. The group with established risk have obvious and readily identifiable conditions associated with developmental deviance. Included are chromosomal disorders, most notably Down syndrome, syndromes with multiple congenital anomalies, and congenital infections (see Chap. 6). Although not all infants with congenital anomalies have developmental disorders, they are more likely to occur within this group, and the management of the child in the family presents an additional set of medical and psychosocial concerns.

Biologic Risk. Close surveillance is also required for infants who have had adverse perinatal experiences generally associated with high risk, e.g., asphyxia, extreme prematurity, and trauma and those for whom related factors have played a part, such as small for gestational age and high-risk pregnancy (e.g., maternal diabetes).

Environmental Risk. Infants at environmental risk[31] are those born to young mothers (sometimes unwed)[48] and to those with limited

education and, more broadly, low socioeconomic circumstances.[25] With or without established or biologic risk, this group of infants clearly has a higher morbidity and mortality rate. This is seen most dramatically in underdeveloped countries,[37] but similar factors operate even in the most sophisticated cities.[46,47] Unfortunately the distribution of health care and educational resources is not equitable, and this factor contributes to the adverse outcome. If anything, it is this group of infants who should receive the closest attention vis-à-vis health and developmental monitoring.

No Risk. The vast majority of infants have no identifiable physical features, no perinatal factors, and no environmental risk factors associated with developmental deviance. Yet, given the data presented above, a number of infants in this group will manifest developmental disorders. The pediatrician may find the greatest difficulty in identifying developmental concerns or sharing these concerns with the family when handling this group of infants.

SCREENING

The concept of screening has taken a prominent place in medical practice. It suggests that the early identification of a clinical condition, before it exerts its pathologic effects, will result in prompt attention and hence improved outcome.[10] Examples of mass screening programs include those for tuberculosis, streptococcal throat infections, children's growth rates, lead toxicity, and other conditions. Screening does not necessarily involve large populations, although neonatal mass screening for phenylketonuria (PKU) and hypothyroidism has proven efficacious when centralized and well controlled.

Screening operations often take place in the pediatric or health care office. Whereas screening in the traditional medical realm involves biochemical tests (e.g., PKU and hypothyroidism) or technologic methods (e.g., roentgenography or ultrasonography), screening to identify developmental problems involves a different set of factors that rely on the clinical skills of the examiner.

Many aspects of a physical examination can be considered elements of screening. In the routine examination of a newborn infant, for example, feeling for femoral pulses is a "screening" for coarctation of the aorta, and measurement of the head circumference and examination of "primitive reflexes" (grasp, the Moro, suck, root) can lead to identification in the neonatal period of neurologic problems with developmental implications. Extending the neurologic examination of the newborn infant into a formal screening process requires a much more thorough and time-consuming approach, but with a higher degree of sensitivity and specificity this might identify potential developmental problems in the newborn period. Prechtl[36] has devised such a newborn neurologic screening approach, and when the model was tested, it was found to have good predictive value.[42] It is when screening techniques of this nature are extended into general use that the experience and skill of the examiner will be important.

The Brazelton Neonatal Behavioral Assessment Scale[5] uses the neurologic integrity of the infant but extends this into behavioral and interactional areas. This adds another dimension of screening to the identification of problems that will have developmental consequences. This particular assessment scale, however, requires specific training on the part of the examiner and is more lengthy, and for practical purposes it may not be much better than the neurologic examination alone. What remains important, therefore, in screening newborn infants for developmental concerns is a thorough physical examination with attention paid to physical features, alertness, responsiveness, muscle tone, and reflex activity. Although this does not differ much from traditional practices in the examination of the newborn, it should be stressed that any deviation should be thoughtfully noted and followed through with close monitoring.[11]

In the early stages of infancy, indications of potential developmental deviance include irritability, hypotonia, lethargy, difficulty in feeding, and unusual sleep patterns. These should alert the pediatrician to the possibility that something is amiss, and again close monitoring and follow-up are crucial. As the infant grows and develops, the pediatrician's attention to the routine issues of appropriate physical growth, feeding, sleeping, and social behavior becomes part of the screening process. Within the first year of life, the identification of "milestones" that represent major developmental achievements, such as rolling over, sitting, transferring objects, crawling, walking, and talking, is important.

The timing of developmental milestones within the first year of life is not difficult to remember, but as the infant gets older and developmental achievements become more complex, it may be helpful to refer to standardized developmental screening tests. The one most widely used by pediatricians is the Denver Developmental Screening Test (DDST),[13] which offers the opportunity for the pediatrician to check the development of the infant against norms for a specific age. If there is any difference, an index of suspicion is raised, and the problem can either be followed through immediately or kept under close surveillance.

Another screening protocol, developed by Amiel-Tison,[1] involves screening for neurologic maturation in the first year of life. This is more sensitive for neurologic development than the DDST; however, it requires a degree of discipline and attention to detail that may not be possible in standard clinical practice. Other screening tests for development are available. Of primary importance, however, is awareness of the patterns of development and the implications of developmental problems.

The most sensitive albeit nonspecific clue to any developmental problem will most likely come from an expressed concern on the part of the parents. This cannot be stressed strongly enough because most parents are sensitive to their child's developmental progress. They may compare the development of their child to the development of other children, e.g., older siblings or children of relatives and neighbors, and they like clarification about whether or not their concerns are appropriate. This issue becomes somewhat difficult to address because parents who raise concerns want to be reassured that nothing is wrong and may not be fully satisfied unless this is the case.

If the developmental assessment by the pediatrician shows that the delay or deviation is not of major significance, then reassurance and reassessment at a follow-up visit are appropriate. If the pediatrician suspects that the developmental concern has some realistic basis, however, it is appropriate to refer the child for further assessment to a developmental pediatrician, neurologist, psychologist, or developmental center. If the decision is to wait and see, a time limit should be set for the follow-up visit, and if the developmental concern is still present, a referral for assessment should then be made. This assessment may or may not confirm the developmental problem, but at least the responsibility of the pediatrician has been met, the parents have been satisfied, and the relationship between parents and pediatrician can be maintained with mutual trust and respect.

After the presence of a developmental problem has been identified, the next step is involvement in a therapeutic or educational program with a developmental focus.[9] What may emerge, in addition, is the need for coordination of other medically oriented consultations, for example, neurologic, orthopedic, and ophthalmologic. The pediatrician fulfills the role of coordinator by helping the family to cope with the impact of the diagnosis and with the multiple services often necessary in the long-term management of children with multiple problems.

When perinatal problems have been present, the pattern of screening, follow-up, and surveillance is quite different. This group of infants is at biologic risk. For purposes of discussion we can examine the perinatal features and long-term sequelae of the very low birth weight infant and of the term infant who has experienced perinatal asphyxia.

PROBLEMS OF PREMATURITY

The improvement in the survival of very low birth weight infants as a result of advances in obstetric and neonatal management has contributed significantly to the evolution of systems designed to monitor growth and development in these infants. Infant follow-up systems were initially designed to evaluate and modify neonatal practices, but as time went on it became appreciated that the quality of survival was significantly impaired by adverse neonatal experiences. Indeed, the lower the birth weight of these infants, the higher the incidence of handicap, to the point that as many as 50% with a birth weight less than 1,000 g have significant handicaps[38] (Fig. 5-2). This does not include function in the school situation, in which more sophisticated demands result in identification of more subtle consequences.[39]

Not only birth weight but also gestational age and the relationship between birth weight and gestational age are factors in eventual outcome. Follow-up studies of very low birth weight infants have consistently shown that those who are small for their gestational age (SGA) do less well than those who are appropriate for gestational age (AGA).[6,44] In fact, correlations between intrauterine head growth and later developmental outcome suggest that for infants whose head growth slowed before 26 weeks (postconceptual age), the outcome was more of a problem than for those whose head growth slowed after 26 weeks.[21] These findings support the notion that adverse outcome may be more strongly correlated with intrauterine than with extrauterine factors. Each of these factors, as well as those that resulted in the premature delivery, creates a series of hazards in the neonatal period and, in effect, a cascade of clinical problems.

The vulnerability of premature infants is largely a factor of physiologic immaturity, which contributes to their inability to survive the extrauterine environment. Technologic advances in neonatal and perinatal care that have been developed to support life functions have contributed to the survival of these infants beyond the neonatal period. Although much of the work done in the systematic follow-up of these infants has concentrated on their neurodevelopmental status, they are susceptible in the newborn period to multiple organ system involvement, and involvement of any organ system can result in significant chronic disability. It is important to be aware of the complications and chronic problems that can result from prematurity and to address these issues in monitoring health, growth, and development.

Respiratory System

The incidence of hyaline membrane disease (HMD), or respiratory distress syndrome (RDS), increases with the degree of prematurity. Apart from the biochemical and metabolic stresses of

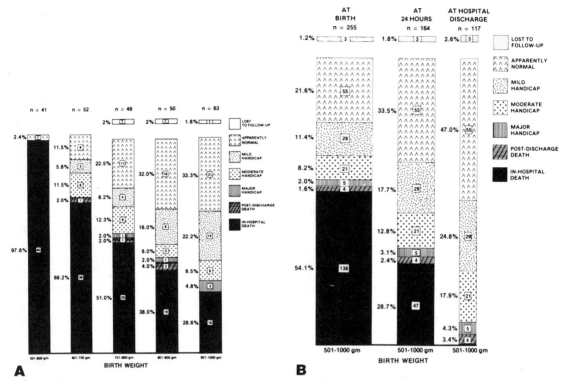

FIG. 5-2. Outcomes for infants weighing 1,000 grams or less. *A.* Correlation between birth weight and outcome. *B.* Correlation between postnatal age and outcome (to age 3). As infant passes critical life-threatening phases, likelihood of survival is greater and proportional rate of disability becomes higher. (From Saigal, S., Rosenbaum, P., Stoskopf, B., and Sinclair, J.C. Outcome in infants 501 to 1000 gm. birth weight delivered to residents of the McMaster Health Region. J. Pediatr., *105:*969, 1984.)

hypoxia and acid-base disturbances associated with RDS there are the complications of therapy with oxygen and assisted ventilation. These two factors correlate significantly with the consequent persistence of pulmonary pathology (bronchopulmonary dysplasia), in which prolonged ventilator therapy and prolonged requirement for oxygen are part of the clinical picture. In addition, such infants appear to have an increased susceptibility to chest infections and reactive airway disease, particularly in the first year of life (see Chap. 11).

Other complications of therapy include the development of pneumothorax, pneumomediastinum, and hemothorax. These disorders do not carry with them significant local morbidity but can affect outcome by dramatically altering cerebral blood flow. Indeed, it may well be that the effects of RDS on developmental outcome are a consequence of the metabolic and mechanical alterations in cerebral blood flow, thus predisposing to hypoxic-ischemic insults or precipitating periventricular and intraventricular hemorrhage.[34]

Infants who require recurrent intubation are susceptible to developing local trauma to the vocal cords, which may result in airway narrowing and susceptibility to stridor and croup. In addition, the recurrent laryngeal nerve may be interrupted during surgery on patent ductus arteriosus (PDA), which causes unilateral vocal cord paralysis.

Heart

The major cardiac complication of prematurity and RDS is the persistence of PDA. In the neonatal period, this may result in cardiac failure and refractoriness to attempts at weaning from assisted ventilation. In an attempt to close the ductus, surgical ligation may be necessary or, as in recent practice, the use of prostaglandin inhibitors, such as indomethacin. The other major cardiac complication is cor pulmonale, usually in association with severe chronic lung disease.

Gastrointestinal System and Nutritional Problems

The major gastrointestinal complication is necrotizing enterocolitis (NEC). The consequences of this condition exist along a spectrum. The mildest cases usually have no complications or sequelae. Damage to the gastrointestinal tract, however, can cause strictures that may manifest in intermittent obstruction. In severe conditions, perforation can result, which necessitates resection of the affected portion of the bowel. If this portion is small and an end-to-end anastomosis can be performed, the sequelae will be limited to the anastomosis site, which could also develop into a stricture. If the resected portion of bowel is large, a colostomy or ileostomy may be necessary as a temporary measure. The risks of short bowel syndrome with resultant malabsorption and failure to thrive may pose a major clinical problem in providing adequate nutrition, even though later reanastamosis can improve the situation.

The nutritional challenge in the neonatal period is that of providing adequate calories and protein to encourage growth. For this, prolonged intravenous feeding may be necessary, and complications can be infectious or hematologic or involve impairment of liver function.

In the later growth phase, the infant may fail to thrive, in which case, two causes should be considered—a feeding disorder and organic disease (see Chap. 10).

The feeding disorder is either an inability to take in adequate fluids due to immaturity or neuropathology with lethargy, hypotonia, or inadequacy of oral musculature and disorders of swallowing.

Failure to thrive in the presence of prematurity and organic disease (other than central nervous system) is related primarily to chronic lung disease but also to renal and gastrointestinal problems, or to gastroesophageal reflux accompanied by excessive vomiting and, possibly, aspiration syndrome.

Renal Problems

If asphyxia was present, acute tubular necrosis can result in temporary or permanent renal impairment. Renal impairment can also be a cause of failure to thrive, and should be looked for in any event because congenital anomalies of the urinary tract are not uncommon (Chap. 17).

Vision and Hearing Problems

One of the first complications of prematurity to be identified was retrolental fibroplasia (RLF), which causes blindness. The administration of high concentrations of oxygen was identified as the major causative factor, but the pathogenesis may be more complex.[40] If mild, the retinopathy of prematurity can resolve completely or result in refractory errors, but with more severe pathologic conditions, retinal detachment can occur with complete loss of vision. Therefore, regular ophthalmological examinations are mandatory (Chap. 13). Infants with grades III and IV RLF are also at higher risk for neurodevelopmental problems.[43]

Complications of prematurity can also result in hearing loss.[4] Screening for this is important, either with standard hearing tests or, if there is any doubt, with brain stem auditory evoked potentials (Chap. 8).

Central Nervous System

The major consequences of prematurity are found in the central nervous system. The susceptibility of premature infants to periventricular and intraventricular hemorrhage (PVH/IVH) is well known.[34] Although the exact association between PVH/IVH and outcome has not been clear, it is becoming clarified.[35] Prior to the advent of computerized tomography it was thought that the consequences of intraventricular hemorrhage were uniformly fatal because of the dramatic clinical presentation: a bulging fontanelle, shock, and poor response to resuscitation. However, since then the manifestations and degrees of PVH/IVH have been elucidated.[26]

If the hemorrhage is small and localized, the outcome can be satisfactory. If the hemorrhage is severe, and particularly if it involves the perenchyma, the outcome is almost invariably the clinical picture of cerebral palsy. Attempts to clarify the significance of radiologic PVH/IVH have resulted in a preliminary report suggesting that precise definition of extent, location, and pathologic condition may be preferable to grading the hemorrhage.[27] The grading system continues to be used, however, and it does have some practical significance in its relative simplicity. In the final analysis, it is the continued follow-up of infants that reveals the extent of the problem.

In the early grading of intraventricular hemorrhage, special mention is made of ventricular dilation and hydrocephalus for grades III and IV. It has become clear, however, that ventricular dilation does not always represent hydrocephalus. In fact, it appears that ventricular dilation is frequently the result of cerebral atrophy,[18] with prognostic implications different from those for hydrocephalus.

In many situations, the monitoring of head circumference demonstrates catch-up growth.[19] In the early stages, such growth can be dramatic and can cross percentile lines, which may raise the concern about hydrocephalus. In this situation a dilated ventricular system can be demonstrated by careful interpretation of CT scan or ultrasound, but it does not necessarily mean hydrocephalus. The careful monitoring of head size, of CT scan findings, and of the clinical picture is, therefore, vital. Hydrocephalus does remain a significant complication of prematurity, particularly if there has been PVH/IVH. Early identification and prompt management are important. Sometimes a response to repeated spinal or ventricular taps occurs, but the placement of a shunt might be necessary. Because the presence of a ventricular shunt (usually ventriculo-peritoneal) raises further concerns about the risks of malfunction or infection, vigilance is advised.

The presence of white matter lesions, or periventricular leukomalacia, in association with prematurity has been correlated with the clinical picture of spastic diplegic cerebral palsy.[8] Atkinson and Stanley, however, have accumulated data suggesting that intrauterine factors are more strongly associated with spastic diplegia.[2]

PROBLEMS OF FULL-TERM INFANTS WITH ASPHYXIA

Neonatal hypoxic-ischemic insults caused by intrauterine or intrapartum asphyxia present clinically at birth and reflect significant central nervous system injury.[22] Fetal monitoring techniques and other advances in obstetric management have reduced the incidence of this condition, but it still occurs with disturbing frequency. Apgar scores are invaluable in documenting the status of infants at birth. The scores are recorded at 1 and 5 minutes. If the results are satisfactory at 5 minutes, scoring is discontinued; if not, scores can be recorded again at 10, 15, and 20 minutes. In general, low Apgar scores indicate severe physiologic stress, as in compromised respiratory, cardiac, and neuromuscular function.

The recording of Apgar scores can provide a helpful indicator of significant perinatal stress. In addition to stresses in the immediate perinatal period, low Apgar scores also imply the risk of permanent organ damage and permanent disability. Long-term follow-up of infants with low Apgar scores indicates that a significant proportion of these infants have central nervous system damage. If Apgar scores are still low at 10 and 20 minutes, the likelihood of central nervous system damage is far greater.[32]

Infants who are asphyxiated at birth and suffer immediate intrapartum hypoxic stress might be susceptible to this stress as a result of intrauterine factors. Possible causes are insults that disturb central nervous system development in the first trimester during embryogenesis and stresses of placental insufficiency during the second and third trimesters. This point deserves emphasis because sometimes neither the Apgar scores nor the clinical diagnosis of hypoxic-ischemic injury fully explains the later neuropathological manifestations.[32] The distinction in causation is important and may have implications for future pregnancies, and it warrants thoughtful consideration. Making the distinction clinically is often difficult, but evaluation of the degree of perinatal stress and the pattern of recovery from this stress needs to be closely examined.

Volpe stresses the importance of the immediate postnatal course of the infant with asphyxia in relation to the risk of central nervous system damage and the risk of later handicap.[45] The correlation of degree of hypoxic-ischemic stress, and rate of recovery, with later developmental handicap is strong. Risks for later handicaps are small when infants recover completely during the first week of life. Risks are greatly increased, however, when symptoms of central nervous system depression and/or irritation (for example, severe hypotonia, unresponsiveness, and particularly seizure disorders) persist beyond the first week of life.[30]

The relationship between perinatal stress and the long-term sequelae of central nervous system damage manifested in disorders of movement, posture, cognition, and socialization was first described by Little in 1862.[28] This condition is now known as cerebral palsy. Many other secondary and tertiary effects can arise, however, and they need to be closely monitored. The clinical effects of hypoxic-ischemic stress are not limited to the central nervous system; nearly all organ systems are affected.

Cardiovascular System

Hypoxic-ischemic stress can cause myocardial injury, presumably through severe acidosis, and this will be manifested in the neonatal period with physiologic instability and electrocardiographic changes. There is no evidence, however, of long-term sequelae.

Gastrointestinal Tract

Ischemia related to the gastrointestinal tract can result in susceptibility to necrotizing enterocolitis (see section on prematurity).

Respiratory System

The metabolic stress of hypoxia can result in the passage of meconium in utero, and severe hypoxic stress can result also in gasping. The presence of meconium and the act of gasping can result in meconium aspiration, and severe meconium aspiration can result in chronic lung disease. The risks of meconium aspiration have been significantly reduced through the clinical practice of examining for and clearing meconium from the airways prior to initiating assisted ventilation.

The clinical syndrome of persistent fetal circulation (PFC) is strongly associated with asphyxia in the newborn period. Presumably, extrapulmonary arteriovenous shunting occurs, and blood flow to the lungs is severely decreased. This results in poor arterial oxygenation, and assisted ventilation with a high percentage of oxygen is often required for prolonged periods. The high pulmonary vascular resistance associated with PFC may have its origins in the prenatal period,[14]—further evidence that prenatal stress can be a major determinant in adaptation to extrauterine life.

Kidneys

Awareness that hypoxia can cause acute tubular necrosis and acute renal failure has led to the restriction of fluids for newborns with asphyxia, and this practice has reduced the severity of complications. Severe renal impairment can result, however, and renal function has to be closely monitored.

Vision and Hearing Problems

Although retrolental fibroplasia is extremely rare in full-term infants, it remains a possibility when extremely high doses of oxygen are required for extended periods. More commonly, ocular manifestations of hypoxic-ischemic insult occur through central nervous system damage, and the result can be a spectrum of disabilities from minor refractory errors to ocular motor disturbances and blindness caused by interruptions of the neural pathways of vision. For this reason, it is mandatory to monitor visual function with regular ophthalmologic examinations and to use visually evoked brain stem responses when necessary (Chaps. 8 and 13).

As with visual disturbances, neural pathways of hearing can also be interrupted. Auditory evoked brain stem responses are helpful in identifying this problem. In any event, it is important to monitor hearing status.

Central Nervous System

The major manifestations of pathologic conditions become evident in the central nervous system, and they occur across a wide spectrum of clinical involvement (see Fig. 5-3).

Seizure Disorders. Seizure disorders are extremely common and can occur in the immediate neonatal period in association with the acute clinical picture. If these seizures disappear, weaning from anticonvulsants is possible. Seizures can reappear, however, at almost any age.[16]

Motor Problems. Motor problems caused by central nervous system dysfunction are manifestations of cerebral palsy and can present as hypotonia, spasticity, or movement disorders, involving limbs and trunk control.

Feeding Problems. Feeding disorders occur frequently in the child who has had central nervous system insults. Problems can involve sucking and swallowing, and at later stages, the chewing and handling foods with texture. Unless these problems are identified early, disorders of nutrition will result in failure to thrive. If parents attribute this to their lack of competence, the relationship between parents and infant can be adversely affected (Chap. 10).

Sensory Modalities. Vision and hearing are discussed above, but it should be appreciated that touch and proprioception can be affected.

Cognitive Effects. Mental retardation is the term used to describe a central nervous system insult that is manifested in significant cognitive effects. In early infancy, however, the discrepancy between developmental age and chronological age is usually described as developmental delay. One should be cautioned about using absolute and permanant labels; terminology should be accompanied by explanations to parents (see section on psychological assessment in this chapter). Cognitive limitations that result from central nervous system insult are of major concern, and they occur across a wide spectrum of severity. In general, the more severe the insult and consequent central nervous system damage, the

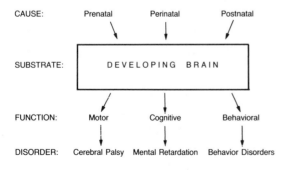

FIG. 5-3.   Patterns of injury and potential disorders.

more significant the developmental discrepancy and risk of mental retardation. Also, as a general rule, the more significant the developmental delay, the earlier it will be identified[29] (Table 5-1). Therefore, with early evidence of a delay in development other than of motor features, the likelihood is greater that there will be significant permanent cognitive deficit.

Learning and Perceptual Problems. Merely defining the sequelae of central nervous system insult in terms of motor and mental deficits is not sufficient if the spectrum of possible consequences is to be appreciated. More subtle manifestations make their presence felt in more sophisticated settings, such as the school.[41] It is in school that many children manifest difficulties in various aspects of learning, for example, in auditory and visual processing and in visual-motor integration.

Behavior Problems. Central nervous system damage can result in disturbances in behavior, either alone or in combination with manifestations such as mental retardation and cerebral palsy. The most common of these disorders is hyperactivity with attention deficit. Other problems involve loss of impulse control, aggression, and self-injurious behavior. At the severe end of the spectrum are disorders of communication and socialization with behavior problems similar to those of children with autism (Chap. 23).

Speech Problems. Disorders of speech and communication are extremely common. Indeed, speech therapy is the most common service required by children in special education (Chap. 3). Speech is vital not only for communication, but for socialization and development. Disorders of speech in children who have central nervous system damage can occur as a primary involvement of the speech center and as an involvement of overall cognition. These disorders can also arise secondarily in the clinical picture of cerebral palsy as a result of poor motor control of oral musculature.[3]

Although any of the sequelae of asphyxia discussed above can exist independently, they are more often found in combination. The presence of one clinical feature would, therefore, strongly suggest an exploration of other elements (see Fig. 5-4).

INFANT FOLLOW-UP PROGRAMS

Advanced technology in the management of pregnancy and labor and in the care of the fragile newborn infant has resulted in increased survival rates for infants and in lower rates of infant mortality and perinatal mortality. Developed and industrialized countries have experienced an unprecedented phenomenon—the gratifying likelihood that a pregnancy will result in a live born infant who will reach adulthood. For professionals, this has created a concern about the developmental outcome for such infants, and the hope that the beneficial effects technology has had on pregnancy, labor, and the care of sick newborn infants will also be translated into a lower incidence of developmental disabilities.[23]

Table 5-1. *Developmental Characteristics*

Degree of Retardation	Preschool (0–5 yrs)	School Age (6–20 yrs)	Adult (21 and Over)
Mild: IQ 53–67; 89% of all retarded persons	Often not diagnosed until later age	Learns academic and prevocational skills with some special training	Lives and works in the community; may not be easily identified as retarded
Moderate: IQ 36–52; 6% of all retarded persons	Fair motor development; can learn to talk and care for basic needs	Learns functional academic skills and can be independent in familiar surroundings	Performs semiskilled work under sheltered conditions; may achieve competitive employment
Severe: IQ 21–35; 3½% of all retarded persons	Slow motor development and some communication skills; may have physical handicaps	Can talk or learn to communicate; cares for personal needs	Can contribute to self-maintenance with supervision in work and living situations
Profound: IQ 20 or less; 1½% of all retarded persons	Overall responsiveness is minimal; often has secondary physical handicaps	Motor development is slow; can be taught basic self-care skills	Some communication skills; cares for basic needs and performs highly structured work activities

Reproduced from "About Mental Retardation" with permission, © 1978, Channing L. Bete Co., Inc., South Deerfield, Massachusetts, 01373.

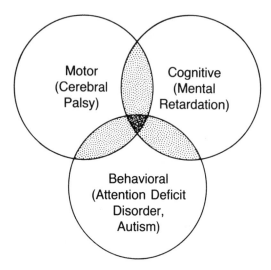

FIG. 5-4. Any insult to the developing brain can result in dysfunction in more than one area, as overlap demonstrates.

The establishment of neonatal intensive care units (NICUs) in tertiary care hospitals has led to the question of how to manage the infants so as to minimize risk of adverse developmental outcome. Prospective and retrospective studies have looked at specific NICU practices and at how these practices have affected the survival rates and quality of life of infants. The most dramatic example was the identification of oxygen therapy for premature infants as a factor in the pathogenesis of retrolental fibroplasia. Also identified were factors such as high concentrations of oxygen and high pressures on ventilators in the pathogenesis of bronchopulmonary dysplasia (Chap. 11). Other findings were related to preventing cardiovascular instability and maintaining adequate arterial oxygenation in the prevention of hypoxic-ischemic brain damage and intraventricular hemorrhage in premature infants.

Unfortunately, the establishment of systematic follow-up for all survivors of neonatal intensive care units (NICUs) has been slow. Follow-up is important for all institutions that have such nurseries, for the infants and their families, for neonatologists caring for the infants, and for health and educational professionals whose care of infants involves developmental problems that can be directly attributed to perinatal experiences.

The difficulties in establishing follow-up programs are manifold, and discussion around them can only take place by examining each factor and analyzing the possible reasons. In its study of the interrelationships between NICUs and early in-

tervention programs in the six New England states, Project ACCESS was able to identify some of the complex issues affecting health and developmental services for this population. It was evident that follow-up services depended strongly on the type of population and geographic location, on whether the infant follow-up programs focused on research, screening, or service, and on what resources were available in the community.[15] A mission for the future is to develop guidelines for the appropriate organization of various components of systems providing services to infants whose adverse perinatal circumstances necessitate admission to NICUs and affected developmental outcome by causing some degree of central nervous system dysfunction.

Neonatal Intensive Care Units

Neonatal intensive care units focus on survival. Dramatic life-and-death issues make it necessary for the NICU staff to respond immediately to changes in the clinical picture, and they must be sensitive to and aware of what these changes mean so that homeostasis can be reestablished. The philosophy underlying this work is far different from the analytical approach required for the systematic follow-up of infants at high risk for developmental concerns. A strong desire and need exist, however, to correlate NICU practices with developmental outcome, and a strong emphasis is being placed on discharge planning.

Pediatricians

More often than not, discharge from a neonatal intensive care unit means that the health and development of the infant will be entrusted to a private pediatrician chosen by the parents. Fortunately, more and more graduate pediatricians are gaining experience in NICUs. Some are also getting experience in formal infant follow-up programs, and they will be familiar with medical, developmental, social, and emotional issues related to the high-risk infant. Concern remains on the part of pediatricians and families that hospital services in infant follow-up systems are duplicating pediatric services in the community.

Visiting Nurse Agencies (VNAs)

More VNAs are playing a role in the support systems that encourage services to infants at risk. This continues the tradition of providing a link between family and health care system. Whether support for VNAs is private or public, the public services are increasingly taking on the burden of monitoring the well-being of infants at risk. The retraining of nurses for this population may not be wholly adequate in these systems, and this needs to be pursued.

Systems for Infant Follow-up

Infant follow-up systems are by no means uniform. Some have risen out of NICUs, and they examine specific clinical questions on the basis of certain protocols. Others have grown up because developmental pediatricians were concerned that infants graduating from NICUs would require closer surveillance due to the increased likelihood that problems would develop. The last 10 years has seen the growth of infant follow-up systems and a marriage between NICU services and developmental programs, with a view toward optimum follow-up for all infants at risk for developmental disabilities. Although these systems are not uniform in philosophy or practice, the common thread is repeated follow-up that includes developmental assessment with identification of deviance or confirmation of normality. The developmental assessment is usually made by a team of two or more developmental professionals and may involve a pediatrician, neurologist, psychologist, physical therapist, speech pathologist, and social worker, although not all are available in all clinics and programs.

Funding

In the evolution of funding for infant follow-up programs, support initially came from research funds that were generated to look at specific issues. When these funds ran out, developmental programs and, notably, university affiliated facilities helped support these follow-up programs. The hiatus in support for these vital components in the practice and services of NICUs is receiving increasing attention.

Although the time and personnel involved in infant follow-up programs can be expensive, billing must be reasonable and within the framework of procedures for outpatient visits. Because the programs are not cost-effective, much funding comes from federal, state, and even city grants. A more cost-effective system involving rapid turnover of patients would not be appropriate in this setting. Developmental assessment is a time-consuming process if it is done correctly.

The Family

Ever since Klaus and Kennell[24] emphasized the need to establish a relationship between parents and premature infants, an appreciation of this bond has become part of accepted, standard NICU practice. Parents are encouraged to visit daily, to stay over in some situations, to telephone at any time; and they are kept informed of every change in the infant's clinical picture. The revolutionary idea introduced by Klaus and Kennell in the mid-seventies that parents should be encouraged to touch and hold even the sickest of premature infants has had beneficial effects on the outcome of these infants. The emotional toll that affects parents, however, cannot be fully assessed or appreciated, given the daily concerns about life and death crises and contact with a busy NICU.

As the infant passes the critical phase, the expectation of feeding competence and nutritional support is focused on growth and eventual discharge. Once parents leave this dramatic environment, memories, fears, and emotional stresses are preferably swept aside and forgotten as the focus turns to a hoped-for normal development for the child. These parents would like nothing better than an opportunity to get on with the process of parenthood, and to appreciate the infant who has come home and is apparently doing well. Consciously or unconsciously they and the staff of the NICU may avoid thinking about their fears of possible bad news concerning central nervous system damage during this neonatal period.

Such a possibility represents painful questions and further torment for parents and to some degree a sense of failure for staff, even though they appreciate the need to address such problems scientifically and examine them critically. For infants of very low birth weight and short gestational age the average length of stay in NICUs is 2 months; complications of feeding, nutrition, and medical illness, such as the development of bronchopulmonary dysplasia, often require a stay of a year or more. These situations pose a different set of conditions and problems for infant and family.

Infants are cared for optimally in the perinatal period, with prompt attention to health and survival and with much investment of money, time, staff, and technology. Unfortunately, the consequences of perinatal experiences are not fully appreciated, and staffing and support for infant follow-up programs are not receiving the same amount of attention. The responsibility of a hospital that supports a neonatal intensive care unit should include ensuring care for these infants through the developmental years and even until their entrance into the educational system as mandated by Public Law 94-142.

What remains for the future is the development of guidelines for the appropriate organization of the various components of systems providing services to these infants. All things considered, it should be remembered that obvious and dramatic perinatal factors contribute to only 50% of children with cerebral palsy and 15% of children with mental retardation.[7,20,32,33] Although many children with developmental disabilities have identifiable prenatal influences (Chaps. 2, 6) a large group remains (30%) in whom no identifiable causes can be found (this figure may be somewhat lower for cerebral palsy).[7] These statistics have three major implications:

1. Because many factors operating in utero influence central nervous system development,[17] it is important to continue to strive to identify these influences with a view toward prevention (Chap. 31) and genetic counseling (Chap. 7).
2. The influence of socioeconomic circumstances on development cannot be underestimated.[25,31] Environmental factors may be the most significant potentially preventable cause when the term "psychosocial mental retardation" is invoked[31] (see also Chap. 31). Because of such factors and the higher mortality rates this population[47] should receive greater attention regarding health and development.
3. Systematic and conscientious screening should include all infants—not just those who are statistically at higher risk for developmental disabilities because of identifiable factors at birth.

REFERENCES

1. Amiel-Tison, C., and Grewier, A.: Neurologic Evaluation of the Newborn and the Infant. New York, Masson, 1983.
2. Atkinson, S., and Stanley, F.J.: Spastic diplegia among children of low and normal birth weight. Dev. Med. Child Neurol., 25:693, 1983.
3. Bashir, A., and Shane, H.C.: The child with speech and language deficits. In The Practical Management of the Developmentally Disabled Child. Edited by A.P. Scheiner and I.F. Abroms. St. Louis, C.V. Mosby, 1980.
4. Bergman, I., et al.: Cause of hearing loss in the high-risk premature infant. J. Pediatr., 106:95, 1985.
5. Brazelton, T.B.: Neonatal behavioral assessment scale. Clinics in Developmental Medicine. No. 50. London, William Heinemann, 1973.
6. Commey, J.O.O., and Fitzhardinge, P.M.: Handicap in the preterm small-for-gestational-age infant. J. Pediatr., 94:779, 1979.
7. Crocker, A.L., and Nelson, R.P.: Major handicapping conditions. In Developmental Behavior Pediatrics. Edited by M.D. Levine, W.B. Carey, A.L. Crocker, and R.T. Gross. Philadelphia, W.B. Saunders, 1983.
8. Davies, P.A., and Tizard, J.P.M.: Very low birth weight and subsequent neurological deficit. Dev. Med. Child Neurol., 17:3, 1975.
9. Donovan, C.M., and Scheiner, A.P.: Early intervention. In The Practical Management of the Developmentally Disabled. Edited by A.P. Scheiner and I.F. Abroms. St. Louis, C.V. Mosby, 1980.
10. Drillien, C., and Drummond, M.: Development, screening and the child with special needs. Clinics in Developmental Medicine. No. 86. London, William Heinemann, 1983.
11. Dubovitz, L., and Dubovitz, V.: The neurological assessment of the preterm and full term infant. In Clinics in Developmental Medicine. No. 79. Philadelphia, J.B. Lippincott, 1981.
12. Frankenburg, W.K.: Developmental assessment. In Developmental-Behavioral Pediatrics. Edited by M.D. Levine, W.B. Carey, A.C. Crocker, and R.T. Gross. Philadelphia, W.B. Saunders, 1983.
13. Frankenberg, W.K., Goldstein, A.D., and Camp, B.W.: The revised Denver developmental screening test: its accuracy as a screening instrument. J. Pediatr., 49:988, 1971.
14. Geggel, R., and Reid, L.: Structural basis of T.P.H.N. Clin. Perinatol., 11:525, 1984.
15. Gilkerson, L., and Crocker, A.C.: Access to Developmental Services for NICU Graduates. Wheelock College, Boston, 1985.
16. Gillam, G.L.: Convulsions following birth asphyxia/birth trauma—are long-term anticonvulsants necessary? Aust. Pediatr. J. 18:90, 1982.
17. Golden, H.L., and Rubin, I.L.: Intrauterine factors and the risk for the development of cerebral palsy. In Comprehensive Management of Cerebral Palsy. Edited by G.H. Thompson, I.L. Rubin, and R.M. Bilenker. New York, Grune & Stratton, 1983.
18. Graziani, L.J., et al.: Clinical ultrasound and clinical studies in preterm infants. J. Pediatr. 106:269, 1985.
19. Gross, S.J., Oehler, J.M., and Eckerman, C.O.: Head growth and developmental outcome in very low-birth-weight infants. Pediatrics, 71:70, 1983.
20. Hagberg, B., Hagberg, G., and Olow, I.: Gains and hazards of intensive neonatal care: an analysis from Swedist cerebral palsy epidemiology. Dev. Med. Child Neurol., 24:13, 1982.
21. Harvey, D., et al.: Abilities of children who were small-for-gestational-age babies. Pediatrics, 69:296, 1982.
22. Holden, K.R., Mellits, E.D., and Freeman, J.M.: Neonatal seizures. I. Correlations of prenatal and perinatal events with outcomes. Pediatrics, 70:165, 1982.
23. Kiely, J.L., et al.: Cerebral palsy and newborn care. II. Mortality and neurological impairment in low birth weight infants. Dev. Med. Child Neurol., 23:533, 1981.
24. Klaus, M.H., and Kennell, J.H.: Maternal-Infant Bonding. St. Louis, C.V. Mosby, 1976.
25. Knobloch H., et al.: Considerations in evaluating changes in outcome for infants weighing less than 1,501 grams. Pediatrics, 69:285, 1982.
26. Krishnamoorthy, K.S., et al.: Evaluation of neonatal intracranial hemorrhage by computerized tomography. Pediatrics, 59:165, 1977.
27. Kuban, K., and Teele, R.L.: Rationale for grading intraventricular hemorrhage in premature infants. Pediatrics, 74:358, 1984.
28. Little, W.J.: On the influence of abnormal parturition, difficult labours, premature birth and asphyxia neonatorum, on the mental and physical condition of the child especially in relation to deformities. Trans. Obstet. Soc. Lond., 2:293, 1862.
29. Lock, T.M., Shapiro, B.K., and Capute, A.J.: Factors affecting referral of the developmentally disabled. Presented at the meeting of the American Academy of Cerebral Palsy and Developmental Medicine, Washington, D.C., 1984.

30. Mellits, E.D., Holden, K.R., and Freeman, J.M.: Neonatal seizures. II. A multivariable analysis of factors associated with outcome. Pediatrics, 70:177, 1982.

31. Moser, H.W.: Prevention of psychosocial mental retardation. *In* Comprehensive Management of Cerebral Palsy. Edited by G.H. Thompson, I.L. Rubin, and R.M. Bilenker. New York, Grune & Stratton, 1983.

32. Nelson, K.B., and Ellenberg, J.H.: Apgar scores as predictors of chronic neurologic disability. Pediatrics, 68: 36, 1981.

33. Paneth, N., and Stark, R.I.: Cerebral palsy and mental retardation in relation to indicators of perinatal asphyxia. Am. J. Obstet. Gynecol., 147:960, 1983.

34. Pape, K.E., and Wigglesworth, J.S.: Hemorrhage, ischemia, and the perinatal brain. *In* Clinics in Developmental Medicine. No. 6970. Philadelphia, J.B. Lippincott, 1979.

35. Papile, L-A., Musick-Bruno, G., and Schaefer, A.: Relationship of cerebral intraventricular hemorrhage in early childhood neurological handicaps. J. Pediatr., 103:273, 1983.

36. Prechtl, H.F.E.: The neurological examination of the full term newborn infant. *In* Clinics in Developmental Medicine. No. 63. Edited by R.L. Samilson. London, William Heinemann, 1977.

37. Rubin, I.L.: Perinatal factors. *In* Comprehensive Management of Cerebral Palsy. Edited by G.H. Thompson, I.L. Rubin, and R.M. Bilenker. New York, Grune & Stratton, 1983.

38. Saigal, S., Rosenbaum, P., Stoskopf, B., and Sinclair, J.C.: Outcome in infants 501 to 1000 gm. birth weight delivered to residents of the McMaster Health Region. J. Pediatr., 105:969, 1984.

39. Sell, E.J., Gaines, J.A., Gluckman, C., and Williams, E.: Early identification of learning problems in neonatal intensive care graduates. Am. J. Dis. Child., 139:460, 1985.

40. Shohat, M., et al.: Retinopathy of prematurity: incidence and risk factors. Pediatrics, 72:159, 1983.

41. Siegel, L.S.: The prediction of possible learning disabilities in preterm and full-term children. *In* Infants Born At Risk. Edited by T. Field, and A. Sostek. New York, Grune & Stratton, 1983.

42. Touwen, B.C.L., Van Eedenberg, M.D., and Van Der Zee, A.J.: Neurological screening of full term newborn infants. Dev. Med. Child Neurol., 19:739, 1977.

43. Vohr, B.R., and Garcia Coll, C.T.: Increased morbidity in low birth-weight survivors with severe retrolental fibroplasia. J. Pediatr., 106:287, 1985.

44. Vohr, B.R., and Oh, W.: Growth and development in preterm infants small for gestational age. J. Pediatr., 103:941, 1983.

45. Volpe, J.J.: Observing the infant in the early hours after asphyxia. *In* Intrauterine Asphyxia and the Developing Fetal Brain. Edited by L. Gluck. Chicago, Year Book Medical Publishers, 1977.

46. Wegman, M.E.: Annual summary of vital statistics. Pediatrics, 74:981, 1984.

47. Wise, P.H., Kotelchuck, M., Wilson, M.L., and Mills, M.: Racial and socioeconomic disparities in childhood mortality in Boston. N. Engl. J. Med., 313:360, 1985.

48. Zuckerman, B.S., et al.: Adolescent pregnancy: biobehavioral determinants of outcome. J. Pediatr., 105:857, 1984.

REFERRALS FOR PHYSICAL THERAPY EVALUATION

Priscilla Osborne, M.S.

Infants are referred for physical therapy evaluation so that motor behavior can be assessed and, if necessary, recommendations for therapy can be developed. The primary reasons for referral are the presence of abnormal movement patterns and/or postures and delayed acquisition of the motor skills that represent milestones in development. Various underlying reasons for the development of motor problems include neurological abnormalities and musculoskeletal anomalies. A physical therapist sometimes screens infants for motor deficits or delays as part of an interdisciplinary team in the context of a follow-up clinic for high-risk infants. The infants most commonly seen in this manner include those whose birth weights were very low, those with intraventricular hemorrhage,[11,14] and those who suffered perinatal asphyxia. Other infants frequently seen in a team approach are those born with congenital anomalies or disabilities associated with deficits in motor development or motor control, such as infants with Down syndrome.

ASSESSMENT OF MOTOR FUNCTION

Motor function is assessed for patterns of movement and for developmental aspects, or appropriateness of motor behavior for the age of the infant. Observational data related to speed and timing and to ease and variability of movement are also noted and described. The combined findings reflect the level and quality of motor function.

Factors that Influence Motor Testing

The motor, physical, cognitive, communicative, and emotional aspects of development are interdependent, and evaluation in one area should take into consideration any difficulties in other areas. Strengths and weaknesses of the infant's overall development should be defined, and the motor dysfunction should be regarded within the infant's overall developmental achievement.

Accurate assessment of motor function is possible only if the infant is physically well and the setting is comfortable. Any assessment done while the infant is physically ill, anxious, irritable, or uncooperative will not adequately reflect the developmental status and quality of motor function. Motor function is significantly influenced when premature infants have suffered from bronchopulmonary dysplasia and when infants with congenital anomalies have significant cardiac disease, and these health-related factors should be taken into consideration when interpreting findings. Acute illnesses, such as viral and ear infections, can compromise cooperation as well as function, and in such cases it is preferable to defer assessment.

During the assessment both spontaneous movement and elicited movement should be observed because they show different facets of movement. Such observation allows the examiner to determine the variability and adaptability of the infant's movements and the specific responses to stimuli. Serial assessments are helpful in determining the direction and rate of motor development, particularly in the infant who has experienced major health problems.

Movement Patterns

The physical components underlying the development of normal movement patterns include tone, muscle strength, joint range of motion, and sensory perception. Primitive reflexes and postural reactions reflect the more automatic combinations of muscle action, which are essential in the development of motor function. Each component is initially assessed independently, with particular attention to its influence on function.

Tone is evaluated by assessing the passive resistance to movement and by observing active movement patterns and posture.[1] Muscle strength is assessed through an adaptation of the principles defined by Daniels and Worthingham,[6] an evaluation based on the ability of muscles to take weight against gravity. Assessment of strength in infants and children is most often based on observations made during functional activities. Joint range of motion is assessed through passive flexion, extension, and rotation of the limbs through the available arc of movement for a particular joint.

Sensory perception is vital for the learning and modification of movement. It is assessed by observing responses to touch and auditory and visual stimuli and responses to movement in space. Unfortunately, age-related norms for these physical components have not been fully defined, although research is ongoing and some guidelines are available.

When present normally, primitive reflex patterns are thought to provide a basis for volitional movement; however, if they persist or are abnormally strong or weak in their presentation, they may interfere with the development of functional movement patterns.[4] Righting reactions, elicited by tactile and proprioceptive stimuli, allow the infant to maintain body alignment and adapt to upright positioning. Equilibrium reactions are necessary for maintaining a center of gravity by use of postural adjustments, thus allowing the infant to maintain a posture in space and to move without losing balance.[2]

Integration and maturation of these reflexes and responses influence the infant's ability to perform volitional movement.[12] Available norms for such integration and maturation are only approximations, but they can be useful as guidelines for normal development.[2] Muscle tone, muscle strength, and joint range of motion may influence the infant's ability to express these reactions; therefore, as with the other physical components, they cannot be assessed in isolation.

To understand the significance of an abnormality in any one area, it is necessary to look at the interaction of the various components and to observe the impact on motor development. The significance of a positive finding varies with the degree of abnormality and with the integrity of the other components that influence movement. Because of the multiplicity of factors involved, the motor outcome cannot be predicted by any one factor alone, for example, by abnormal muscle tone or muscle weakness. The significance of subtle abnormal findings is variable. The influence of subtle abnormalities in tone may not be manifested until the emergence of more highly coordinated and integrated movements. Subtle abnormalities of tone may also be transient, but such transient abnormalities have been associated with later nonmotor learning problems.[13]

Developmental Aspects

Motor development is assessed through the use of standardized tests that correlate motor achievements with developmental age. The results are then expressed as an age level or developmental quotient, which compares the age level achieved on the test to the child's chronological age. The most commonly used standardized tests for measuring motor development in infants are the Revised Gesell Developmental Schedules,[10] the Bayley Scales of Infant Development,[3] and the Peabody Developmental Motor Scales.[9] Each scale has its strengths and weaknesses, and these must be considered in determining the scale's appropriateness. The Peabody Developmental Motor Scales are unique in their attempt to provide a method of scoring that allows for partial completion of an item, thus noting the emergence of a skill.

All of these tests measure motor function in relation to a cross-section of infants of the same age. A wide variation from normal in the absence of abnormal movement patterns indicates that the child is delayed in motor development. The significance of lesser variations needs more consideration because the normal ranges in which an infant accomplishes a specific motor task vary and are not well defined. The significance of lesser variations from the norm is unclear, particularly when only one test result is considered. In order to evaluate developmental progress, more than one point in time should be considered. With testing at two separate points in time, the rate of development and direction of development can be better assessed. Considering the results of motor testing within the context of the infant's functional development provides more information as to the meaning of a noted delay.

In general, the quality of movement patterns is not addressed in standardized testing. Therefore, a complete motor assessment should include developmental testing and assessment of movement and posture. For example, an infant who has abnormal movement patterns will show a scatter of skills that can only be expressed as a delay, thus misrepresenting the infant's motor function as delayed rather than abnormal. There has been an attempt to combine the assessment of tone, primitive reflexes, automatic reactions, and volitional movement in infants less than 1 year of age in the nonstandardized Movement Assessment in Infants.[5] This test can be used to assist the examiner in assessing movement patterns and development of volitional movement.

A score expressed as a developmental quotient or age level will be an overview of the child's motor performance. Further examination and description of motor performance are necessary in order to delineate specific strengths and weaknesses. Observational information concerning speed, variability, and ease of movement should be obtained during the motor testing and added to the description of the infant's movement abilities.

The results of motor development testing must be considered in conjunction with assessment of the various components underlying the development of normal movement patterns, the results of other developmental testing, and information about the health of the infant.

TREATMENT

In general, the goal of physical therapy intervention is the development of optimal motor function. Types of intervention range from anticipatory guidance for parents to direct therapy for an infant. Sometimes an infant who has been hospitalized for a prolonged illness shows a delay in motor development but no movement disorder. Such an infant benefits when the physical therapist provides the parents with anticipatory guidance to further their understanding of motor development and of how to encourage their child's motor function. Infants who demonstrate abnormal movement patterns, however, require direct treatment from the therapist in order that the abnormal pattern of movement can be modified and more effective patterns established. The type of treatment and frequency should be considered in light of other therapeutic, emotional, and social demands being made on the infant and family.

Approaches

Many approaches to physical therapy can be used for infants with motor impairment. The most effective approach is an integrated model that draws on the components of various methods in order to obtain the best response from the infant.[8] The two primary principles common to most approaches relate to (1) the view that motor function has a developmental basis and (2) the use of techniques based on neurophysiologic theory. Developmental factors include cephalocaudal progression, the establishment of stability, and mass movement preceding fine movement.

In all approaches, sensory modalities are used to influence movement. An essential part of treatment is consideration of tactile, kinesthetic, proprioceptive, vestibular, auditory, and visual sensory modalities when positioning, handling, or encouraging movement of the infant throughout the day. Developmentally appropriate play activities can incorporate the use of sensory modalities to alter inappropriate movement patterns. This method elicits the active participation of the infant in establishing new movement patterns.

It is important that the family understand and become involved in the treatment of the infant so there is consistency and carry-over of treatment goals throughout the day. Instruction to the family about the proper positioning and handling of the infant should be given frequently, and the family's help should be enlisted in developing new activities. The frequency of treatment varies with the developing and changing needs of the infant.[15] When a skill is emerging, frequent guidance or treatment may be indicated; once a skill has emerged and is being established, less frequent involvement is required. Therefore, flexibility is needed regarding frequency, duration, and type of treatment (direct versus consultation). Periodic reassessment of the effectiveness and appropriateness of a treatment mode is also essential.

Settings

When referring an infant for physical therapy, certain factors should be considered in choosing the setting. Because of the interrelationship of the various aspects of development in infancy, an interdisciplinary approach is preferred. The potential for treatment in the home and the availability of consultation to the parents are important. Treatment at home may be chosen because of health reasons or because of the possibility of adapting instructions to the home setting. The physical therapist providing the service should have experience with normal movement in infancy and with infants who have movement dysfunction.

Early intervention programs provide multidisciplinary treatment services for infants and children from birth to age 3 years, and they sometimes provide services in the home. Other settings are public health and private agencies that specialize in the treatment of infants. A physical therapy department in a pediatric hospital can provide outpatient treatment for an infant and can also coordinate efforts with a multidisciplinary approach and provide home visits. The setting should meet the needs of the specific infant and family.

REFERENCES

1. Amiel-Tison, C.: A method for neurological evaluation within the first year of life. Curr. Probl. Pediatr., 7:1, 1976.
2. Barnes, M., Crutchfield, C., and Heriza, C.B.: The Neurophysiological Basis of Patient Treatment. Vol. 2: Reflexes in Motor Development. Morgantown, W. Va., Stokesville Publishing, 1978.
3. Bayley, N.: Manual for Bayley Scales of Infant Development. Berkeley, Calif., The Psychological Corporation, 1969.
4. Bobath, B.: Abnormal Postural Reflex Activity Caused by Brain Lesions. London, William Heinemann, 1965.
5. Chandler, L.S., Andrews, M.S., and Swanson, M.W.: Movement Assessment of Infants: A Manual. Rolling Bay, Wash., 1980.
6. Daniels, L., and Worthingham, C.: Muscle Testing, Techniques of Manual Examination. 3rd Ed. Philadelphia, W.B. Saunders, 1972.
7. Easton, T.: On the normal use of reflexes. Am. Scientist, 60:591, 1972.
8. Farber, S.D. (ed.): Neurorehabilitation: A Multisensory Approach. Philadelphia, W.B. Saunders, 1982.
9. Folio, R.M., and Fewell, R.R.: Peabody Developmental Motor Scales and Activity Cards: A Manual. Allen, Tex., D.L.M. Teaching Resources, 1983.
10. Knobloch, H., and Pasamanick, B.: Gesell and Amatruda's Developmental Diagnosis. 3rd Ed. Hagerstown, Md., Harper & Row, 1974.
11. Ment, L., et al.: Neonates of less than 1,250 grams birth weight: prospective neurodevelopmental evaluation during the first year post-term. Pediatrics, 98:292, 1982.
12. Milani-Comparetti, A., and Giodoni, E.A.: Pattern analysis of motor development and its disorders. Dev. Med. Child Neurol., 9:625, 1967.
13. Nelson, K., and Ellenberg, J.H.: Children who "outgrew" cerebral palsy. Pediatrics, 69:529, 1982.
14. Pape, K.E., Buncic, R.J., Ashby, S., and Fitzharding, P.M.: The status at two years of low birth weight infants born in 1974 with birth weights of less than 1,001 gm. J. Pediatr., 92:253, 1978.
15. Shea, A.: Physical therapy. In Developmental-Behavioral Pediatrics. Edited by R. Gross, M. Levine, W. Carey, and A. Crocker. Philadelphia, W.B. Saunders, 1983.

PSYCHOLOGICAL ASSESSMENT
Richard R. Schnell, Ph.D.

REFERRAL

Regardless of age, a child should be referred for psychological assessment when there is any question about learning ability or developmental progress. Frequently, children are not referred until everyone is convinced that a major problem exists. This often delays effective intervention and puts parents through an agonizing period of uncertainty. Pediatricians are in a position to refer a child, particularly an infant, for further assessment because of their frequent contact with children and their families. Questions have arisen, however, about the predictive utility of infant tests and the detrimental effects of labels. Reluctance to refer is sometimes based on pessimism about the effects of early intervention. A growing body of research now demonstrates the effectiveness of intervention. Intervention may not mean problems are removed, but it lessens their impact by helping a child become more competitive with both handicapped and normal children. With early identification of problems, family expectations may be more appropriate. The family may, therefore, have a better understanding of the child and relate to the child better.

Pediatricians often rely on the infant's history of milestones in achievement and on clinical judgment when deciding whether an infant needs to be referred. The elasticity of the time at which infants acquire skills makes milestone delay a less than dependable indicator of developmental difficulty. Milestones such as sitting, standing, and walking are within normal limits for one-half of all mentally retarded children. The best practice is to do routine screening of the development of infants using instruments such as the Denver Developmental Screening Test[7] and the Gesell scales.[10] The administration and interpretation of screening techniques require significant training and sufficient time. The apparent simplicity of the screening scales often leads professionals to the erroneous conclusion that they need no training to use them appropriately. A rule of thumb is to refer a child for psychological assessment when cognitive development appears to be 25% or more below chronological age and when this delay is not due to prematurity or specific motor and sensory deficits.

Frequently, busy physicians do not have time to engage in developmental screening. If the physician or parent has a cause for concern, referral to ascertain whether a developmental problem exists is better than waiting, even though many potential problems seem to disappear with time. Referral is especially important if the child also has a history of "at risk" factors, such as low birth weight or significant prematurity. A number of child psychologists in most areas of the country have had significant experience and training in assessing infants. Appropriate psychologists are often associated with infant follow-up programs.

ASSESSMENT

Psychological procedures assess behavior as a means of ascertaining the functioning maturity of the central nervous system as well as the impact of environmental experiences. In measuring the development of children, the assumption is made that behavior develops in regular patterns and is therefore predictable. Children do not develop at the same rate, however, and normal differences in learning rates and styles have caused confusion because developmental age is not necessarily a direct measure of intellectual potential or disability. Children greatly delayed in developmental age usually have significantly lower scores on later tests of intelligence and achievement, whereas children advanced in development may not eventually prove to have above-average intellectual skills. Results from longitudinal follow-up studies with impaired children show that infant scales are effective predictors of continued patterns of disability but are less reliable at characterizing normality. By the age of 1 year, moderate or greater mental retardation can be detected, and confirmation can be made by 18 to 24 months of age. Mild retardation is frequently suspected by 2 years of age and confirmed by

3 years of age. Table 5-1 describes the developmental characteristics for each degree of retardation.

The younger the child, however, the less predictive the scores on tests of cognitive development will be regarding later school-age test scores and academic performance. Many indicators of later specific learning difficulties and behavior problems are not easily measurable with current techniques before the age of 6 years. With normal children, scores on infant tests do not correlate with later measures before 18 to 24 months of age. To further complicate the issue, major changes in psychological development occur around certain chronological age levels, changes that involve the disappearance of old cognitive structures and the emergence of new structures. Factor analytic studies[14] of the Bayley Mental Scale of Development have found major shifts at 3, 8, 13, and 20 months. Correlations of scores were higher within a developmental stage (e.g., 3 and 7 months) than between stages (e.g., 3 and 8 months). Measures of early sensorimotor development did not predict later scores on language scales. As a child's age increases, the correlation of scores with later scores increases, so that by 4 years of age there begins to be a solid relationship. The older the child and the less time between tests, the higher the correlation between test scores. Intelligence at age 17 can be accounted for by the following developmental pattern: 20% developed by 1 year of age, 50% by 4 years of age, 80% by 8 years of age, and 92% by 13 years of age.[2]

Although correlation coefficients increase with children's ages, the scores of an individual can fluctuate a great deal. Extreme changes in environment can significantly change a developmental quotient or IQ. As much as 30 points can separate the intellectual performance of advantaged versus disadvantaged children.[11] The availability of information about the child's environment can improve developmental prediction. The research literature is replete with data demonstrating that the socioeconomic status of the family is a strong predictor of intellectual skills.

Impairments in motor and/or sensory development also directly affect test performance, but standardized infant assessment techniques do not provide guidelines for adapting test materials. Current practice is to adapt the test material to the child and describe the child's performance qualitatively. The great number of items requiring good perceptual motor skills within the first year is an obstacle to a child with motor and/or sensory problems. Lower scores will be the result. The kind and degree of the motor and/or sensory problem and its influence on performance should always be described in presenting assessment results.

For a more extensive treatment of standardized psychological testing, the chapter by Schnell in Developmental Behavioral Pediatrics is suggested[17]; for more detail, the text by Sattler,[16] which provides a thorough review of the assessment of children's intelligence. The text edited by Lewis[12] presents a comprehensive discussion of cognitive functioning in the first years of life, and Kopp's chapter in the *Handbook of Child Psychology*[11] reviews risk factors in early development.

Assessment Techniques

Descriptions of tests frequently used for assessing infant development are presented in Table 5-2. These tests are not downward extensions of the tests used for assessing older children because this procedure has in general not worked well. The skills measured in infants often relate to less differentiated and changing competencies, such as sensorimotor adaptations and conceptual skills that are qualitatively different from those required for later performance. Meier[15] has developed a three-stage model for the assessment of children that covers primary screening through intervention. At stage I, brief tests and interviews by paraprofessionals provide a rough sorting of children who may have or may acquire developmental problems. Group measures are often used at this level. At stage II, one professional or each individual on a team of professionals makes an assessment of the child in order to determine whether the child has significant problems. Individually administered standardized tests provide much of the data. In stage III, children who have been found to have significant problems are referred for appropriate programs and follow-up procedures.

The two most widely used screening techniques are the Denver Developmental Screening Test[7] and the Gesell Developmental Schedules. Both require that a series of developmental observations be made and that test items similar to those routinely used by a pediatrician be presented. Items from the Gesell test have been widely used in other tests. The four scales used on the Denver test are similar to the four used on the Gesell. The scales are not scored but interpreted impressionistically. Age approximations can be obtained from the Gesell test, whereas the Denver test results are judged as to normal-

ity. Little data exist regarding the reliability and validity of the Gesell test. The reliability of the Denver test can be good if the examiners are well trained. Recent studies, however, question the usefulness of the Denver test.[24] Neither test is based on adequately defined norms.

A test with more adequate norms that can be used for screening is the Vineland Adaptive Behavior Scale.[21] This test measures the adaptive behavior of children—behavior that is effective in meeting the natural and social demands of the environment.[8] It has four scales similar to those in the Gesell test, but instead of observing the child directly they rely on parental report. Standardized scores and age equivalents are available for the total instrument as well as for each scale. The Vineland test is often used with children who are thought to be developmentally delayed, and data in this area can be compared to data for the same children from measures of cognitive development. Other scales for adaptive behavior are available, some for special groups of children. The Maxfield-Bucholz[13] adaptation of the old Vineland Social Maturity Scale is used with blind children, and the Callier-Azusa Scale[22] is used with deaf and blind children.

The Bayley Scales of Infant Development[1] are the most frequently used individual developmental assessment techniques in the clinical assessment of infants. Of its three scales, the mental scale is most often employed because it produces an estimate of cognitive development. The items for this scale were empirically derived, not based on developmental theory, and they make a determination of the infant's abilities based on the number of developmental milestones achieved. The norms for the mental and motor scales are adequate. The scores generated allow the examiner to compare the child's rate of sensorimotor development with a normative sample consisting of other children of similar chronological age. Only a single developmental index score is derived for each scale, although an age equivalent can also be estimated.

Tests like the Bayley Scales do not provide direct information about sequential patterns of development because of their empirical base. Data on the infants' stage or stages of development must be gathered incidentally or by means of another test, such as the Infant Psychological Development Scale developed by Uzgiris and Hunt.[23] This test, based on Piagetian tasks, provides ordinal scales of development. The scales assessing object permanence and the development of means and ends relationships are the best developed and most frequently used of the

Table 5-2. *Examples of Tests Frequently Used for Assessing Infant Development*

Test	Age Range	Description	Scores
Denver Developmental Screening Test[7]	Birth to 6 years	Developmental screening procedure consisting of 4 scales: personal-social, fine motor, gross motor, and language. It involves minimum equipment and is administered in approximately 20 minutes	Results are judged abnormal, questionable, or normal depending on the number and distribution of items among the scales on which the child was found to be delayed (items which 90% of children normally pass at a younger age)
Vineland Adaptive Behavior Scale[21]	Birth to 19 years	A general assessment of adaptive behavior in 4 major domains: communication, daily living skills, socialization, and motor skills. Each domain is divided into 2 or 3 subdomains. A parent is given a semistructured interview about the child to obtain the test data. The interview requires 20 to 60 minutes. A scale of maladaptive behavior is optional.	For each domain and the total score (adaptive behavior composit) the following scores may be obtained: standard scores (mean = 100, standard deviation = 15, national percentile ranks, adaptive levels, and age equivalents. For each sub-domain the following scores are obtained: adaptive level, supplementary norm, group adaptive levels, and age equivalents
Bayley Scales of Infant Development[1]	Birth to 2½ years	An empirically derived test of developmental status made up of 2 tests and a rating scale. The Mental Scale assesses early perceptual motor skills, memory, learning, problem-solving ability, and the beginning of language development and abstract thinking. The Motor Scale assesses gross motor and a few fine motor skills. The Infant Behavior Record rates the nature of the infant's social and objective orientation toward the environment. The Mental Scale requires 20–30 minutes for administration, the Motor Scale 15–20 minutes, and the Infant Behavior Record, scored after the infant has left, requires 15–20 minutes	For the Mental and Motor Scales standard scores can be obtained (mean = 100, standard deviation = 16) and age equivalents estimated. For the Infant Behavior Record percentile ranks are available for each of the 24 ratings
Infant Psychological Development Scale[23]	Birth to 2 years	A test of developmental status based on Piagetian theory, it is composed of 6 subscales: the development of visual pursuit and the performance of objects, the development of means for obtaining desired environmental events, the development of vocal imitation and gestural imitation, the development of operational causality, the construction of object relations in space, and the development of schemes for relating to objects. It takes 40 to 60 minutes	No formal scores are computed; the score is the highest number reached on each scale. From these data the sensorimotor stage or stages the child is performing in can be estimated

Table 5-2. *Continued.*

Test	Age Range	Description	Scores
Home Observation for Measurement of the Environment[3]	Birth to 3 years	The Home Environment scale assesses some of the intangible qualities of animate and inanimate stimulation available to the young child through the use of 6 factorially derived subscales: emotional and verbal responsiveness of mother, avoidance of restriction and punishment, organization of environment, provision of appropriate play material, maternal involvement with the child, and opportunities for variety in daily stimulation. The observation and interview procedure requires approximately 60 minutes.	Raw scores are computed for each of the 6 subscales and the total score, and they may be contrasted with the raw score means and standard deviations of various groups using such variables as the mother's marital status, race and level of education, and the child's age.

six scales. No commercial test kit is available, but Uzgiris and Hunt describe the standard materials and test procedures in their book.[23] Other sensorimotor scales based on Piagetian theory are also broadly used, such as the Casati-Lezine[5] and the DeCarie.[6] These descriptive Piagetian scales are not good predictors of future development, but they give a picture of the sequential pattern of development and can be used to help parents understand their infant's behavior. Parents can modify their behavior when they have a better understanding of the meaning of their infant's behavior.

Another instrument that can lead to direct parental intervention is the Home Observation for Measurement of the Environment (HOME),[3] which is intended to measure the quality and quantity of social, emotional, and cognitive support available in the child's home. Data are gathered from interviews with parents and observations in the home. Observing how parents behave with their child can lead to direct suggestions for modifying their behavior to make it more effective. Scores on the HOME during the first 2 years of a child's life were found to relate to later mental development.[4] A limitation of this scale is the requirement for a home visit; several researchers have developed versions adapted for clinic use.

The Vineland Adaptive Behavior Scale, the Bayley Scales, the Infant Psychological Development Scales, and the HOME Inventory might all be profitably used to evaluate the same child.

The Vineland test can provide information about the child's development from the parents' perspective. This information can be compared to the child's performance on an objective test of development, such as the Bayley Scales, and contrasted to the parents' actual behavior, as measured by the HOME. The Uzgiris-Hunt scale can supplement the milestone approach of the Bayley Scales by providing data on the child's developmental sequences.

Interpretation of Assessment Results

Although questions remain about the long-term prediction of development, infant scales do provide a measure of the infant's present level of development. Despite their limitations, current infant assessment techniques are effective in identifying infants at risk for developmental disabilities. Identification of risk status makes it possible to provide early intervention services aimed at prevention and/or amelioration of potential problems. Assessors of infants must be well trained professionals who have not only a sound background in child development but also training in the use of the measures and an understanding of their strengths and limitations.

When interpreting infant assessments, the context in which the child exists must always be taken into account. Environmental and personal factors include the socioeconomic status of the parents, family stability and characteristics, and the child's health history. Past events, such as prematurity, may have led to medical issues, such as intraventricular hemorrhage or broncho-pulmonary dysplasia, and these issues need to be taken into consideration because they influence risk. We know little, however, about how the interaction of risk factors affects risk. Many significant perinatal problems and medical concerns have not been associated with problematic developmental outcomes,[20] and these must be sorted out from the real contributors to risk.

Parents' expectations and characteristics must be taken into account if assessment results are to be effectively communicated to them.[18] Explanations of results through the use of labels must be handled carefully. Only labels that really fit and can be satisfactorily explained should be used. Labels present hazards for both parent and child, as Hobbs indicates in his excellent book[9]:

> Classification can profoundly affect what happens to a child. It can open doors to service and experiences the child needs in order to grow in competence, to become a person sure of his worth and appreciative of the worth of others, to live with zest and to know joy. On the other hand, classification, and the consequences that ensue, can blight the life of a child, reducing opportunity, diminishing his competence and self-esteem, alienating him from others, nurturing a meanness of spirit, and making him less a person than he would become.

Although labeling can often lead to negative consequences, it is essential in a number of situations. Labeling may make it possible for services to be obtained for children, for children's programs to be planned and organized, and assist in describing the outcomes of intervention efforts. A good approach is to avoid labels when possible, and instead describe the child's behavior and particularly the child's needs. This approach leads to a focus on meeting the needs of the child rather than coding deficits. Second, a combination of techniques should be used in evaluation. Taking a single score from a measure like the Bayley Scales and using it alone to represent the child is not appropriate. Developmental levels in different areas such as adaptive skills, gross and fine motor skills, language, and cognition give a more rounded picture of the child and might improve prediction. Scores on infant scales greater than one standard deviation below the mean are indicators of developmental risk. The use of developmental age scores with the parents, rather than standard scores (which often seem to parents like IQ scores) should be encouraged. Reporting performance as falling within a range rather than at a specific age level also will give a more realistic picture of the infant. Normative measures such as the Bayley yield developmental levels and scores, but they

may not lead parents to any better comprehension of their child's behavior. Piagetian measures such as the Uzgiris-Hunt scales are not good predictors of future development, but may be employed to help parents understand how their children comprehend the world and respond to it. Adding information about the qualitative nature of the child's performance can also aid parents in understanding their child. Parental insight can often lead to better parent-child interactions.

Third, prediction about an infant's development made to parents and others should initially be tentative and short-term. As an infant progresses in developing various skills, over specific periods of time and under known conditions, better developmental predictions can be made. The developmental assessment results of premature infants raise special problems because the scores on infant scales are frequently contrasted to the infant's chronological age. Most assessors make a correction for the length of the prematurity. If an infant is two months premature his performance is compared to his chronological age minus the 2 months of prematurity. Correction has often continued until 2 years of age, and some assessors have continued correcting beyond 2 years. Siegel's longitudinal study of the results of correcting developmental test scores for prematurity suggests that correction stop at 1 year of age. She found that corrected scores during the first year of life were more highly correlated with scores in later tests, but after 12 months of age uncorrected scores were more highly correlated.[19]

Infants at significant risk for developmental handicaps should be assessed at regular intervals. These assessments should be primarily for the parents to ask questions about the infant and to get to know their infant better. Only secondarily should the assessments be an exercise in discovering disability. With such an emphasis, assessment would be less anxiety-provoking and a regular contribution to parenting.

REFERENCES

1. Bayley, N.: Manual for the Bayley Scales of Infant Development. New York, Psychological Corporation, 1969.
2. Bloom, B.S.: Stability and Change in Human Characteristics. New York, John Wiley & Sons, 1964.
3. Bradley, R.B., and Caldwell, B.M.: Early home environment and changes in mental test performance in children from six to 36 months. Dev. Psychol., *12*:93, 1976.
4. Bradley, R.B., and Caldwell, B.M.: The relation of infants' home environments to mental test performance at 54 months. A follow-up study. Child Dev., *47*:1172, 1976.

5. Casati, I., and Lezine, I.: Les Etapes de l'Intelligence sensorimotrice. Paris, Les Editions du Centre de Psychogie Appliquee, 1968.

6. Decarie, T.G.: Intelligence and Affectivity in Early Childhood. New York, International Universities Press, 1965.

7. Frankenburg, W., et al.: Denver Developmental Screening Test, Reference Manual. Rev. Ed. Denver, Ladoca Project and Publishing Foundation, 1975.

8. Grossman, H.J. (ed.): Manual on Terminology and Classification in Mental Retardation. Ref. Ed. Washington, DC, American Association on Mental Deficiency, 1977.

9. Hobbs, N.: The Futures of Children. San Francisco, Jossey Bass, 1975.

10. Knoblock, H., and Pasamanick, B. (eds.): Gesell and Amatrudas Developmental Diagnosis. 3rd Ed. New York, Harper & Row, 1974.

11. Kopp, C.B.: Risk factors in development. *In* Handbook of Child Psychology. 4th Ed. Vol. II. Edited by Paul H. Mussen. New York, John Wiley & Sons, 1983.

12. Lewis, M. (ed.): Origins of Intelligence. 2nd Ed. New York, Plenum Press, 1983.

13. Maxfield, K.E., and Bucholz, S.: A Social Maturity Scale for Blind Preschool Children: A Guide to its Use. New York, American Foundation for the Blind, 1957.

14. McCall, R.B., Eichorn, D.H., and Hogarty, P.S.: Transitions in Early Mental Development. Monogr. Soc. Res. Child Dev., 42:171, 1977.

15. Meier, J.H.: Developmental and Learning Disabilities. Baltimore, University Park Press, 1976.

16. Sattler, J.M.: Assessment of Children's Intelligence and Special Abilities. 2nd Ed. Boston, Allyn & Bacon, 1982.

17. Schnell, R.R.: Standardized psychological testing. *In* Developmental Behavioral Pediatrics. Edited by M.D. Levine, W.B. Carey, A.C. Crocker, and R.T. Gross. Philadelphia, W.B. Saunders, 1983.

18. Schnell, R.R.: The psychologist's role in the parent conference. *In* Psychological Assessment of Handicapped Infants and Young Children. Edited by G. Ulrey, and S.J. Rogers. New York: Thieme-Stratton, 1982.

19. Siegel, L.S.: Correction for prematurity and its consequences for the assessment of the very low birth weight infant. Child Dev., 54:1176, 1983.

20. Sigman, M., and Parmelee, A.H.: Longitudinal evaluation of the preterm infant. *In* Infants Born at Risk: Behavior and Development. Edited by T.M. Field, A.M. Sostek, S. Goldberg, and H.H. Shuman. Jamaica, NY, Spectrum, 1979.

21. Sparrow, S.S., Balla, D.A., and Cicchetti, D.V.: Vineland Adaptive Behavior Scale: Interview Edition, Survey Form Manual. Circle Pines, MN, American Guidance Services, 1984.

22. Stillman, R.D.: Assessment of Deaf-Blind Children: The Callier-Azusa Scale. Dallas, Callier Hearing and Speech Center, 1975.

23. Uzgiris, I.C., and Hunt, J.M.: Assessment in Infancy: Ordinal Scales of Psychological Development. Urbana, University of Illinois Press, 1975.

24. Wacker, D.: Diagnostic Efficiency of the Denver Developmental Screening Test. Paper presented at annual meeting of the American Psychological Association, Montreal, September 1980.

6

ASSESSMENT AND MANAGEMENT OF INFANTS AND CHILDREN WITH MULTIPLE CONGENITAL ANOMALIES

Lawrence C. Kaplan, M.D.

Perhaps no other clinical pediatric situation is as challenging as the process of diagnosis and planning for the care of the child with multiple congenital anomalies. In accepting the responsibility to care for these patients, the pediatrician must be able not only to draw upon general medical knowledge but also to recognize the complex problems unique to disorders of morphogenesis. This chapter will present an approach to the diagnostic evaluation and treatment of the infant and child with multiple congenital anomalies.

THE EXTENT OF THE PROBLEM

Major Anomalies

Major anomalies represent errors in morphogenesis that have serious medical and surgical implications. They are estimated to be present in approximately 2% of all newborn infants of at least 20 weeks gestation. This number increases to approximately 4% when one considers those major anomalies which present by the end of the first year of life such as disorders of the central nervous system, cardiovascular system, spine, and kidneys (Table 6-1). This group of anomalies carries with it significant mortality and morbidity. For example, approximately 9% of deaths in the perinatal period and 18% of deaths by the end of the first year of life are attributable to complications related to major anomalies, thus making major congenital anomalies the second most common cause of neonatal death after extreme prematurity. Nearly one-fifth of deaths directly related to major anomalies occur in the first day of life, half by the end of the first month, and nearly three-quarters by the end of the first year.

The etiology of major anomalies was analyzed by Holmes in a 3-year study of 18,155 newborns of at least 20 weeks gestation. Of these infants, 2.4% had major anomalies, nearly 60% of which could be explained on the basis of genetic, uterine, and maternal causes.[21,22] These data are summarized in Table 6-2.

Minor Anomalies

Minor anomalies represent unusual features detectable by physical examination that have no medical consequences to the patient (Table 6-3). When considered in the context of major anomalies, however, some important relationships emerge. As illustrated in Figure 6-1, most infants (85%) in the study by Marden, Smith, and McDonald[34] had no minor anomalies, and very few of these patients had major anomalies. Ap-

Table 6-1.   *Examples of Major Congenital Anomalies and Their Significance*

Physical Feature	Origin and Significance	Clinical Clues to Diagnosis
Central nervous system		
Anencephaly	Defective closure of neural tube	Elevated 2nd trimester amniotic fluid alpha-fetoprotein level
Myelomeningocele		Abnormal fetal ultrasound
		Decreased fetal movement
Spina bifida occulta	Defective closure of neural tube	Decreased fetal movement
		Sacral dimple
		Sacral hair tuft
		Diminished anal wink
Holoprosencephaly	Defect in development of prechordal mesoderm	Small midface
		Microphthalmia
		Neurologically abnormal
Craniofacial/orofacial		
Cleft lip	Abnormal fusion of lat. nasal, maxillary, and med. nasal swellings	Physical examination
Cleft palate	Failure of closure of maxillary palatine shelves	Physical examination
		Feeding difficulties
		Speech problems
Cardiac		
Ventriculoseptal defect	Abnormal closure of ventricular septum	Cardiac murmur
		Congestive heart failure
Transposition of the great vessels	Defective development in bulbus cordis septum	Cyanosis
		Respiratory distress
Gastrointestinal tract		
Intestinal malrotation	Abnormal intestinal loop rotation	Failure to gain weight
		Gastrointestinal obstruction
Duodenal atresia	Duodenal recanalization	Vomiting
		Absent lower intestinal bowel gas pattern
Diaphragmatic hernia	Pleuroperitoneal canal closure defect	Scaphoid abdomen
		Respiratory distress

Adapted from Smith, D.W.: Recognizable Patterns of Human Malformation. Philadelphia, W.B. Saunders, 1982.

proximately 13% of infants had a single minor anomaly, and the relative frequency of major anomalies in this group remained low. As the number of minor anomalies increased, the likelihood of major defects increased dramatically, and in those 0.5% of babies with 3 or more minor anomalies, 90% were shown to have 1 or more major anomalies.

These observations all underscore the importance of recognizing the potential for life-threatening disease among patients whose visible anomalies may not appear serious. This concept can apply to both the neonate undergoing initial evaluation and the child experiencing significant chronic disease.

Who Provides Care?

The responsibility for the outpatient care of children handicapped by congenital anomalies varies with the problems of each patient, but some general patterns are known. In one study, it was noted that specialists or specialty clinics provided 63% of the coordinated care of patients with myelodysplasia, other sources provided 25%, and primary care physicians alone provided 10%. Well-child care, specifically the responsibility for immunizations, growth and developmental assessment, and dietary evaluation, was provided by primary care physicians in 73% of cases, and by specialists in 23%. No one was identified as a primary care provider in 14% of the cases, and 30% of parents questioned felt that they received no support (listening and showing concern) from any source.[27]

Data from the National Ambulatory Medical Care Survey done in 1980 suggest an increase in the contribution of chronic conditions to practices in the primary care setting.[14] Chronic care problems account for 10% of office visits to primary care providers and for one-third of the pediatric visits to medical or surgical subspecialists.[14]

The Cost of Care

The cost of treating individual birth defects continues to be tremendous. Myelodysplasia, for example, with a prevalence in the United States in 1975 of 58,000, resulted in estimated annual expenditures by the Crippled Childrens' Services of $11,458,000.[31] The significance of this is appreciated when one considers that patients with myelodysplasia comprised only 4.6% of the total number of patients with birth defects treated in 1975.

A cost study done in a representative tertiary-care hospital for the 3-year period between 1981 and 1983 indicated a mean cost of hospitalization of $37,327 in constant 1984 dollars for patients with myelodysplasia. The first year of care represented 89% of all costs. Costs during the first year of life rose significantly when back closure was delayed rather than immediate. In addition, costs increased as a function of the level of the

Table 6-2. *Etiology of Major Anomalies (Malformations) among 18,155 Newborns at Boston Hospital for Women, 1972–1975*

Cause	Incidence (%)
Genetic abnormalities	
Multifactorial inheritance	0.6
Single mutant genes	0.1
Chromosomal abnormalities*	0.1
Uncertain inheritance	0.3
Uterine factors	0.1
Drugs taken by mother	0.01
Maternal conditions	0.1
Unknown etiology	1.1
Total	2.4

From Holmes, L.B.: The Malformed Newborn: Practical Perspectives. Boston, Massachusetts Developmental Disabilities Council, 1976.

* 0.14% had a clinically recognizable chromosomal abnormality. Most chromosome abnormalities such as 47,XXX, 47,XXX, and 47,XXX cause no physical abnormalities that are apparent in newborn infants.

spinal lesion, higher lesions resulting in higher costs in all 3 years.[18] These data imply that not only is the type of lesion related to hospital cost, but that decisions concerning various treatment options can have far-reaching financial as well as emotional consequences.

Table 6-3. *Examples of Minor Anomalies and Their Significance*

Physical Feature	Origin and Significance	Clinical Example
Calvarium		
Large fontanel	Delayed ossification	Congenital hypothyroidism
Small fontanel	Insufficient brain growth	Cerebral dysgenesis
Upper 3rd of face		
Epicanthal fold	Redundant skin folds secondary to low nasal bridge or excess skin	Down syndrome (trisomy 21)
Ocular hypertelorism	Widely spaced eyes and orbits	Frontonasal dysplasia
Brushfield spots	Abnormal iris pigment pattern	Down syndrome
Oral region		
Prominent lateral palatine ridges	Defective tongue thrust against hard palate	Neurologic disease
Auricular region		
Preauricular tags	Accessory Hillocks of Hiss	Hemifacial microsomia
Limb		
Single palmar crease	Planes of folding of hands prior to 11 weeks	Trisomy 18 Down syndrome (trisomy 21)

Adapted from Smith, D.W.: Recognizable Patterns of Human Malformation. Philadelphia, W.B. Saunders, 1982.

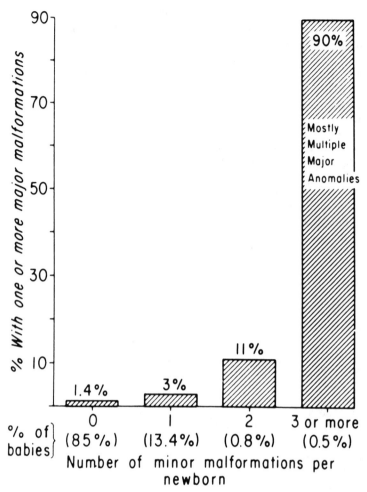

FIG. 6-1. Frequency of occurrence of major malformations in relation to number of minor anomalies detected in a given newborn baby. (From Marden, P.M., Smith, D.W., and McDonald, M.J.: Congenital anomalies in the newborn infant, including minor variations. J. Pediatr., *64*:358, 1964.)

PATTERNS AND MECHANISMS OF ABNORMAL MORPHOGENESIS

It is often easier to offer prognoses for developmental and functional outcomes when abnormal physical or laboratory findings comprise well-understood syndromes such as Down syndrome, Brachman-de Lange syndrome, or Beckwith-Wiedemann syndrome. Much can be predicted on the basis of the known features of each of these entities.[2,4,43,51] For the patient with multiple anomalies who may not fit into a readily recognized group, some general principles of dysmorphology can serve as a guide in evaluation and should enable the physician to generate some predictions concerning growth and development.

Specific anomalies can be classified depending on their presumed pathogenesis, as being either malformations, deformations, or disruptions. De-

tailed descriptions of these concepts, introduced and refined by D.W. Smith,[43] are summarized with reference to how form can influence function in Table 6-4. Regardless of the types of specific anomalies identified, one's approach should be guided by attempts to explain multiple anomalies on the basis of a single cause or a single abnormal mechanism influencing morphogenesis.

Malformation

Malformation implies abnormal formation of tissue or abnormal tissue interaction. A single initiating malformation may give rise to a cascade of other structural defects comprising a malformation sequence, e.g., hydrocephalus and myelomeningocele secondary to abnormal neural tube closure. The primary malformation here is the neural tube defect. Consideration of a genetic cause for such defects is important since

Table 6-4. *Overview of Congenital Anomalies of Prenatal Onset*

Problem in Morphogenesis			
Malformation of Tissue due to Single Cause—Genetic, Chromosomal, Teratogenic, Unknown		**Disruption of Normally Formed Tissue by Mechanical or Infectious Destruction of Tissue**	**Deformation of Normally Formed Tissue by Abnormal Mechanical Force Exerted Against Tissue**
Multiple Localized Defects	**Single Localized Defect**		
SYNDROME			
Multiple malformation	Malformation	Deformation	Disruption
	Malformation sequence	Deformation sequence	Disruption sequence
EXAMPLES			
Trisomy 21	Agenesis of corpus callosum	Hip dislocation	Rubella syndrome
Trisomy 18	Microcephaly	Breech head	Digital amputation secondary to amniotic bands
Cornelia de Lange syndrome	Close-set eyes	Torticollis	Hemifacial microsomia secondary to vascular disruption
	Neurological impairment	Scoliosis	
	Equinovarus deformity	Genu recurvatum	
		Equinovarus deformity	
TREATMENT			
Underlying cause not correctable; individual defects treatable depending on type and on available therapy	Underlying cause usually not correctable; defects treatable depending on type and on available therapy	Surgery Physical therapy	Underlying cause usually not correctable; defects treatable depending on type and on available therapy
PROGNOSIS			
Frequently poor, especially when central nervous system is involved	Depends on structures involved	Generally improves with removal of abnormal forces and/or surgery or physical therapy	Depends on extent, nature, and timing of disruption; CNS disruptions can be severe

Adapted from Smith, D.W.: Recognizable Patterns of Human Malformation. Philadelphia, W.B. Saunders, 1982, p. 1.

abnormally formed tissues are commonly associated with monogenic or chromosomal syndromes. Malformations generally do not improve or resolve in the extrauterine environment. Specific correction of a malformed structure is usually a function of the extent and severity of the defect and the interventions available.

Because malformations occur early in embryogenesis (i.e., by completion of organogenesis at approximately 9 weeks), one must also anticipate the likelihood of poorly *functioning* tissue and organs. Central nervous system dysgenesis (as in trisomy 18 syndrome, for example) is usually severe, contributing to demise of 90% of these patients by the end of the first year of life.[49] When localized malformation involves only one of a pair of structures (as in unilateral renal agenesis), prognosis may be good because of the compensatory ability of the remaining organ.

Deformation

Deformation or deformation sequence generally implies no intrinsic abnormalities in tissue but rather abnormal mechanical forces on an otherwise normally developing embryo or fetus. Examples of such deformations include plagiocephaly or talipes equinovarus deformity secondary to fetal compression from an abnormally shaped or crowded uterus.[6,10,11,42] Deformation may also occur if normal tissue overlying or opposing intrinsically *abnormal* tissue is affected by that tissue. Examples include separation of the nasal bones by a frontal encephalocele, or joint contractures due to a congenital myopathy causing poor movement in utero.

As a group, deformations caused by abnormal extrinsic forces frequently improve in response to removal of the abnormal mechanical forces.

This is usually accomplished by extrauterine growth. The child with plagiocephaly and normal sutures is likely to achieve normal head shape once the head is allowed to grow unconstrained, because normal brain growth helps in this process.[6] Physical therapy can benefit the child with joint contractures (arthrogryposis) caused only by fetal compression since intact neurologic function helps insure success of therapy. This situation should be differentiated clinically from the infant with joint contractures secondary to neuromuscular disease in which abnormal mechanical forces persist.[16]

Another example of deformations caused by extrinsic forces is micrognathia due to face presentation: once outside the uterus, the normal mandible is permitted to grow unimpeded.[42] This type of deformation should be differentiated from micrognathia secondary to probable abnormal migration of the neural crest as seen in Treacher Collins syndrome (mandibulofacial dysostosis), where postnatal mandibular growth is limited and the micrognathia represents a malformation.[39,46] The therapeutic implications of this observation are important, since mandibular catch-up growth of the infant with Treacher Collins syndrome will be minimal and tracheostomy may be a protracted necessity. The child with a deformed mandible may not require such drastic airway support.

Finally, severe deformation may be secondary to early compression, as, for example, in limb reduction and body wall defects secondary to early rupture of amnion, chorion, or yolk sac.[28,36]

Disruption

Disruptions or disruption sequences can occur when an otherwise normal embryo or fetus is exposed to an event that results in destruction of normal tissue. This may be mechanical, as, for example, when parts of a normal fetus become tethered or amputated by fibrous amniotic bands.[25] In such a case, surgical correction may be possible, and if the central nervous system is spared, developmental potential may not be altered. On the other hand, if the disruption occurs as a result of an infection (e.g., rubella or toxoplasmosis) the consequences may be manifold).[8] As a rule, the degree of injury to the fetus by disruption depends on the timing of the disruptive event as well as the nature of the process.

Although minor and major anomalies provide clues to associated anomalies that may not be so obvious, the constellation of findings can offer clues as to how growth and development might proceed. Cohen[5] and Jones and Robinson[24] provide excellent discussions of these concepts.[5,24]

CLINICAL EVALUATION OF THE INFANT AND CHILD WITH MULTIPLE CONGENITAL ANOMALIES

A systematic evaluation of obvious multiple congenital anomalies should be undertaken without undue pressure over as much time as needed to define the extent of involvement. An exception to this is, of course, the medically unstable newborn, for whom emergency care is required in the delivery room. Once stabilized, however, an extensive evaluation including family and gestational histories and physical examination should be completed. Frequently, a genetic diagnosis can be strongly suspected in the neonatal period, but such suspicion should not cause one to defer confirmatory workup and laboratory testing. By the same token, the older infant or child who carries a previously made diagnosis should be approached objectively. This child's medical course and development will provide additional data that might disprove the original diagnosis.

History

In addition to a detailed family history including information about cousins, parents, and grandparents, some additional key information should be obtained (Table 6-5). The mother's past obstetric history should focus on possible miscarriages or infertility, since an association exists between chromosome abnormalities and first-

Table 6-5. *Selected Elements of History and Physical Examination*

Family history	Umbilical cord
	Length of cord
Gestational history	Number of vessels
Size-date discrepancy	Thrombosed vessels
Oligohydramnios/	
polyhydramnios	Physical examination
Drug or toxin exposure	Height, weight, and
Maternal fever, infection	head circumference
Maternal uterine	Extrauterine position of
malformation	comfort
Predominant fetal	Symmetry
position	Head shape and suture
Unusual back pain	patterns
	Scalp-hair pattern
Placenta	Midface anthropometrics
Evidence of deceased	Palate
co-twin	Ear shape and size
Vascular anastamoses	Back and anus
Thrombosed vessels	Neurologic reflexes and
Inflammation	symmetry

trimester miscarriage. When possible, information from fetal pathology reports should be sought. Attention should be given to any discrepancy between fetal size and estimated date of delivery, to the presence of oligohydramnios or polyhydramnios, and to the onset, duration, and vigor of fetal movements, and this information should be correlated with data obtained from fetal ultrasonograms if available. In addition, a history of maternal fever and drug or toxin exposure should be obtained, with particular attention to known exposure to teratogens and infectious agents. The parents and obstetrician should be asked if any known abnormalities exist in the mother's reproductive tract, noting in particular the existence of a bicornuate or septate uterus or uterine fibroids, which may cause fetal deformation.[35] Obtaining the history of the predominant fetal lie can be helpful when correlating this information with the newborn's and infant's position of comfort in the extrauterine environment.

Placenta and Umbilical Cord

Information about the placenta and umbilical cord should be reviewed and any pathologic findings documented. In the newborn setting, direct examination of these structures is very helpful. One should note the number of blood vessels in the cord, the length of the cord, the presence of placental vessel thrombosis or anastomosis, the presence of a nonsurviving co-twin, or evidence of placental inflammation. These data can all be useful in determining the mechanisms of abnormal morphogenesis and are valuable regardless of the patient's age (Table 6-6).[3]

The General Physical Examination

The details of a complete dysmorphology examination are beyond the scope of this chapter; however, certain key elements are presented that are critical to the evaluation of the patient with multiple congenital anomalies (Table 6-5). The size and relative proportions of the infant

Table 6-6. *Examples of Congenital Anomalies with Reference to Gestational History*

Gestational History	Significance	Clinical Examples
Oligohydramnios	Insufficient amniotic fluid Production of circulation	Renal agenesis, pulmonary hypoplasia, ureteral valves, atresia, amnion nodosum
Polyhydramnios	CNS disease, poor swallowing, fetal gastrointestinal obstruction	Hydrocephalus, anencephaly, esophageal atresia, duodenal atresia, trisomy 18, trisomy 21
Maternal hyperthermia	Maternal fever more than 38.9°C Variety of congenital anomalies reported with hyperthermia 4–14 weeks after conception	Microphthalmia, microcephaly, cleft lip, cleft palate, neurogenic contractures, micrognathia
Size/date discrepancy	Prenatal growth retardation	"Multiple malformation syndromes," chromosome anomalies
Diminished fetal movement	Abnormal central nervous system Uterine constraint, e.g., bicornuate uterus	Holoprosencephaly, anencephaly, anterior horn cell disease, plagiocephaly
Abnormal fetal position	Neurologic disease Uterine malformation Twin pregnancy	Anterior horn cell disease, unilateral craniosynostosis, twins
Uterine malformation	Maternal origin	Plagiocephaly, redundant skin
Abnormal umbilical cord	Short cord Single umbilical artery	Amniotic bands, "multiple malformation syndrome"
Deceased co-twin noted in placenta	Potential for thrombogenic material released into circulation of surviving twin	CNS anomalies, thrombosed renal artery
Chorioamnionitis of placenta	Gestational infection	Cytomegalic inclusion disease, rubella, toxoplasmosis, syphilis

should be noted, with particular reference to whether the child's height, weight, and head circumference are small, large, or appropriate for gestational age, and if any of these measurements is discordant with the others. This check can be helfpul in identifying prenatal growth problems as well as problems in head growth frequently signifying defects in brain. Standard reference charts are available for this purpose.[12] The examiner should carefully observe for evidence of asymmetric size or movement of the extremities, the number of digits, and any evidence of cutaneous lesions.

Abnormalities of situs (laterality) usually reflect abnormal symmetry in morphogenesis and suggest that such errors have occurred within 30 days of gestation. Their significance depends on whether defects in laterality are "bilaterally left- or right-sided." Both situations are associated with other major anomalies, the most extreme example being serious cardiac anomalies when situs inversus and levocardia occur together (bilateral right-sidedness sequence).[48] Palpation of the liver and auscultation of the heart to note the point of maximal impulse are important steps in assessing errors in laterality.

Finally, a careful lung examination is critical, especially for infants with congenital diaphragmatic hernia, in which abdominal contents may occupy the thorax, or for infants with Potter's malformation sequence, in which pulmonary agenesis occurs.

Examination of the Head

Measurement of head circumference remains the single most useful screening technique for assessing the degree of pre- and postnatal brain growth, and is useful even in the presence of newborn moulding of the calvaria. Note the position and integrity of the cranial sutures, searching for evidence of craniosynostosis, size and position of the anterior and posterior fontanels, and the presence of overlapping or widely split sutures. These all provide clues not only to brain shape and growth, but also to any abnormalities in the reflections of the dura and the size of the base of the skull. The child with an abnormally large anterior fontanel may have congenital hypothyroidism, for example, and the bilateral coronal craniosynostosis seen in Apert's syndrome represents a very different pathogenesis from the unilateral coronal craniosynotosis seen in plagiocephaly caused by uterine constraint.[15]

Note the scalp hair pattern. This is established by the 18th week of gestation and reflects underlying brain growth and stretching of the scalp. Aberrant scalp hair patterns thus provide the examiner with clues of an abnormal brain. Most important, abnormal hair patterns time such central nervous system defects, helping one to determine whether they are pre- or postnatal.[44]

Note ear shape, size, and rotation. Pits and tags can be important clues to other anomalies, especially those involving the branchial arch and its derivatives, and to sensorineural and conduction deafness.[13,23]

Examination of the Face

Midface

Evaluate the midface, looking primarily for evidence of poor frontal brain growth, or asymmetry. The impression of an abnormal-appearing face can usually be substantiated and quantitated by describing the shape of the palpebral fissures, the pattern of skin around the palpebral fissures, by measurement of the inner and outer canthal and interpupillary distances, and by noting the size of the eyes. This information is useful because it pertains to the presence of central nervous system malformation.

Mouth and Palate

Examine the palate, noting the shape of the arch and the presence of clefts. In general, a V-shaped cleft palate suggests malformation and warrants a search for other anomalies because it originates from an arrest of fusion of the palatal shelves rather than from interference with closure by the tongue. Examples of this latter situation include congenital myopathy: poor tongue thrusts lead to a tendency of the tongue to press against the palate, impeding closure.[17]

Examination of the Limbs and Back

Carefully examine the back. Neural tube defects may present at any age, as sacral dimples, hair tufts, or lipomatous lesions.

Examination of the Perineum

Anus

It is important to determine the patency and position of the anus because anal abnormalities are seen in a number of recognized associations and syndromes. Anterior displacement of the anus is frequently associated with constipation and encopresis, which can be problematic in later childhood.[19]

Genitalia

Ambiguous genitalia should always alert the examiner to the possibility of adrenogenital syndrome and to the possibility of urinary tract abnormalities. If one is unsure of the presence of kidneys upon routine abdominal examination, genital anomalies should certainly prompt a re-examination. Simple documentation of first voiding and passage of meconium in the newborn period can help determine gastrointestinal and genitourinary tract integrity. Urine analysis should be a part of the evaluation of all infants and children with multiple congenital anomalies because it can be useful in evaluating renal function in patients with congenital obstructive uropathy. Hypospadius, particularly third-degree hypospadius with extension to the scrotum, should also alert one to the possibility of structural genitourinary defects.[32] In the neonatal period, buccal smear analysis of X-chromatin (Barr bodies) or Y-fluorescence to identify the presence of a Y-chromosome are not as reliable as full chromosome analysis to evaluate ambiguous genitalia; a full karyotype should be available in the final discussions concerning sex assignment. Furthermore, absence of the Barr body may indicate an XO situation as well as XY.[33]

The Neurologic Examination

This part of the evaluation should emphasize the degree of symmetry and whether neurologic impairment represents central or peripheral pathology. Furthermore, with the help of a detailed reflex examination, one should attempt to differentiate between lesions at the level of the upper motor neuron and lesions at the level of the lower motor neuron. The volume and pitch of the newborn cry and the integrity of newborn reflexes may be the most objective physical information obtainable in the neonatal period and should be documented in order to be able to determine whether results of later examinations represent deterioration or improvement.

A bell or loud noise, as well as information by parents, can provide useful hearing screening at most ages, and shining the light of an otoscope into the eyes can establish reflex to light. It must be emphasized that these screening maneuvers do not quantitate visual or auditory acuity.

IMMEDIATE INTERVENTIONS IN THE NEWBORN PERIOD

A number of interventions may play a crucial role in minimizing the risk of postnatally acquired encephalopathy and subsequent developmental handicaps. The following issues should be considered in the immediate newborn period.

Airway Patency

Airway patency should be established in an infant with significant respiratory distress. This can be done simply, e.g., by passing a #5 French nasogastric tube through each nostril. This maneuver will establish patency of the nares and choanae but does not quantitate choanal diameter. The diagnosis of choanal atresia can also be made by direct visualization of the choanae with otoscope and speculum, and, when there is doubt, by computerized tomography. The passage of a tube per nares into the stomach while defining nasopharyngeal patency does not rule out lower respiratory tract obstruction as in the case of laryngeal webs, vascular rings, hemangioma, or atresia of the larynx.[41] Persistent stridor or difficulty ventilating the infant following endotracheal intubation in the presence of patent nares and choanae should alert the examiner to one of these conditions.

Ventilation

Bag and mask ventilation with oxygen is usually adequate to ventilate the infant with a patent airway in respiratory distress. Exceptions to this include infants with congenital diaphragmatic hernia or pulmonary atresia. With this in mind, nasotracheal or orotracheal intubation can be considered an "elective" maneuver when mechanical ventilation is indicated or when transport of the infant is required. Once the tube is in the trachea, difficulty ventilating the patient implies significant anatomic defects, and adequate ventilation with poor oxygenation suggests right to left shunting of blood at either the cardiac or pulmonary level. Attention to these basic principles will help to decrease the risk of hypoxic ischemic injury to the infant.

Metabolic Status

The infant under stress in the newborn period, regardless of the reason, is prone to hypoglycemia. Determination of serum glucose levels by heel stick will guide the decision to administer intravenous glucose, which can prevent hypoglycemic seizures. Persistent hypoglycemia is often seen in infants of diabetic mothers and in infants with Beckwith-Wiedemann syndrome and nissidioblastosis and should prompt one to consider other congenital anomalies.

After approximately 12 hours of life, serum calcium should be checked in an unstable infant or an infant who may have a defect involving derivatives of the fourth branchial arch and the third and fourth pharyngeal pouches, such as in the DiGeorge syndrome (sequence) where levels may be low.[7] High serum calcium levels are seen in Williams syndrome and should call attention to the possibility of congenital heart disease in such a patient.[26] Other serum electrolytes should be evaluated, especially if there are adrenal or renal anomalies or alterations, any of which could lead to seizure or cardiac arrhythmias.

Cardiac Status

Cardiovascular disease can rarely be diagnosed with accuracy in the delivery room but is suggested by the presence of persistent cyanosis, especially with oxygen administration, a loud murmur, or absent or diminished pulses, particularly in the femoral arteries. Tachypnea with no radiologic evidence of lung disease may also suggest cyanotic heart disease. A right radial arterial PO_2 determination with the infant in 100% oxygen, roentgenography of the chest, and electrocardiography aid in the diagnosis of congenital heart disease.

Congenital heart lesions that can be life-threatening in the first hours of life include transposition of the great vessels with intact ventricular septum, critical pulmonary stenosis or atresia, and totally anomalous pulmonary return. Lesions that depend on the patency of the ductus arteriosus, such as transposition of the great vessels with ventricular septal defect, tetralogy of Fallot, and hypoplastic left heart, frequently present clinically as the ductus closes.[37] These lesions, and other lesions involving the conotruncus, should alert the examiner to other midline defects and to consideration of anomalies of the central nervous system and gastrointestinal tract.

FURTHER ASSESSMENT AND INVESTIGATION

A significant amount of information can be derived from relatively noninvasive diagnostic tests and key diagnostic questions. These are presented to increase the accuracy of evaluating the child with multiple congenital anomalies.

Radiology

An anteroposterior roentgenogram of the chest and a flat plate film of the abdomen provide use-

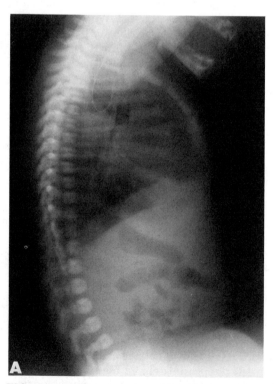 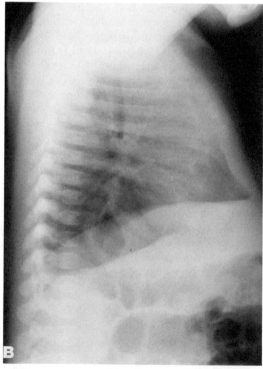

FIG. 6-2. *A.* Roentgenogram showing nasogastric tube coiled in upper thoracic esophagus of patient who had respiratory distress at 1 day of age. *B.* Dilated proximal esophageal pouch after tube was partially withdrawn and air was injected into it. Patient underwent successful surgical correction for esophageal atresia. (Courtesy of Dr. S. Borden.)

ful information concerning heart size, lung volume, pulmonary blood flow, the skeleton, and bowel gas patterns. The absence of thymus tissue would suggest the diagnosis of branchial arch defects or of long-standing in utero stress (e.g., infection). Defects in rib shape and density are often seen in myopathies and neuropathies at any age; vertebral anomalies are associated often with other defects including defects of the anus, tracheoesophageal fistula, ear anomalies, renal anomalies, limb defects, and congenital heart disease.[20]

Abnormal bowel gas patterns often suggest such entities as duodenal atresia, pyloric stenosis, Hirschsprung's disease, and tracheoesophageal fistula with or without esophageal atresia. One helpful aid in diagnosis is to obtain the chest roentgenogram with a nasogastric tube in place, which can help define gastrointestinal tract anatomy (Figs. 6-2, 6-3, and 6-4).

Cranial Transillumination, Ultrasound, and Computerized Tomography

A simple bedside transillumination of the skull can help support the suspicion of hydrocephalus, or subdural fluid collection. Cranial ultrasound in conjunction with the physical examination can delineate structural central nervous system lesions in adequate detail for syndrome identification (Fig. 6-5). Cranial CT scanning can provide detailed information concerning choanal patency, posterior fossa anatomy, and details of the ventricular-aquaductal systems. CT scanning is particularly useful if detailed craniofacial and intracranial information is needed simultaneously.

Electrocardiography

A 12-lead electrocardiogram provides the examiner with information on cardiac axis and ventricular forces—two elements that can help in diagnosing congenital heart disease.

Abdominal Ultrasonography

Abdominal ultrasonography has its greatest utility in assessment of genitourinary tract anomalies, particularly obstructive uropathy, and polycystic kidney disease. In expert hands, it may also be helpful in diagnosing defects in pelvic anatomy, in the gastrointestinal tract, and intra-abdominal masses.[47]

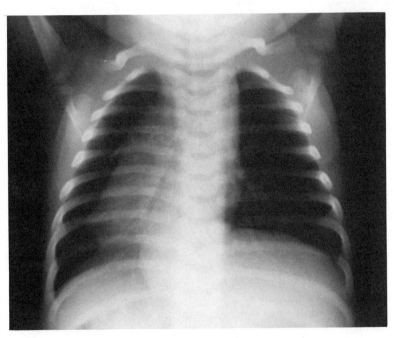

FIG. 6-3. Roentgenogram of newborn male, cyanotic without respiratory distress, who fed poorly and had nonbilious, nonprojectile vomiting, a right-sided cardiac impulse, and a murmur. Roentgenogram shows dextrocardia, a left aortic arch, symmetrical bronchial branching, liver shadow, and an air-containing retrocardiac structure. Patient had asplenia (bilateral right-sidedness) with double-outlet right ventricle, common atrioventricular valve, common atrium, midline liver and absent spleen, hiatal hernia, and intestinal malrotation. (Courtesy of Dr. T. Ben-Ami.)

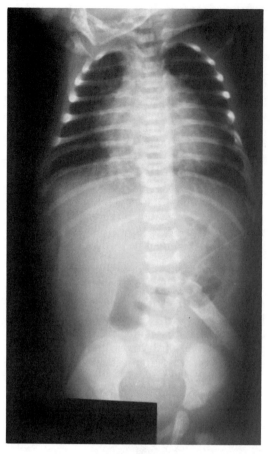

FIG. 6-4. Anteroposterior roentgenogram of chest and abdomen of dysmorphic child who had vomiting at 1 day of age reveals "double bubble" configuration of duodenal obstruction and an enlarged heart. Iliac wings are flared, and acetabular angles are shallow. Physical examination was consistent with Down syndrome, in which duodenal atresia, endocardial cushion defect, and these bony abnormalities are frequently seen. (Courtesy of Dr. C. D'Orsi.)

Eye/Vision

All newborns and children with multiple congenital anomalies should have a thorough ophthalmologic examination. Abnormalities of particular relevance include retinal and iridial colobomata, aniridia, cataracts, optic nerve atrophy or hypoplasia, chorioretinitis, vascular malformations, epibulbar dermoids, and weakness of the extraocular muscles. The suspicion of central nervous system anomalies or injury warrants a formal ophthalmology examination because defects of the brain are often reflected in specific eye findings, and this evaluation should be performed by an ophthalmologist. The importance

of knowing the visual status of the patient cannot be overemphasized because this will have a bearing on developmental interventions.[40]

Hearing

The most effective means of assessing hearing in the newborn and infants with multiple congenital anomalies as well as in the child with mental retardation in whom audiometry may be difficult to interpret is with auditory evoked brain stem potentials. In the absence of visible congenital anomalies this test should be considered when there is a suspicion of hearing loss. The child with isolated microtia or other auricular deformities may have an intact cochlea and eighth cranial nerve to that ear and may exhibit conductive hearing deficits only. The infant with holoprosencephaly or other central nervous system malformations may have normal-appearing external ears and yet have sensorineural deafness. Audiometry has utility for the older child, who is able to demonstrate acknowledgment of pure tones through his behavior.

Chromosome Analysis and Other Investigations

Specific indications for chromosome analysis are discussed in Chapter 7. In general, chromosome analysis with banding on peripheral lymphocytes is indicated in patients for whom a particular recognized chromosomal disorder is suspected or who exhibit multiple major and minor anomalies that do not fit a particular diagnosis. Chromosome analysis should always be done for the child with ambiguous genitalia. In addition, for future genetic counseling of parents, the child with congenital anomalies who dies or is stillborn should be photographed, and skin and/or lung tissue should be obtained for karyotype analysis (lymphocytes from such infants may not grow well in tissue culture). Extended-prophase chromosome analysis can uncover interstitial chromosome breaks, deletions, or rearrangements.[52]

Screening tests for newborn infants with inborn errors in metabolism vary from state to state, but most centers screen for phenylketonuria and thyroid disease. Assays for galactosemia, maple syrup urine disease, homocystinuria, and tyrosinemia are less consistently offered. Although children with these disorders do not constitute a large group among children with multiple anomalies, review of their test results and/or repeat urine screening in infancy and childhood should be considered if metabolic derangement is considered.[30]

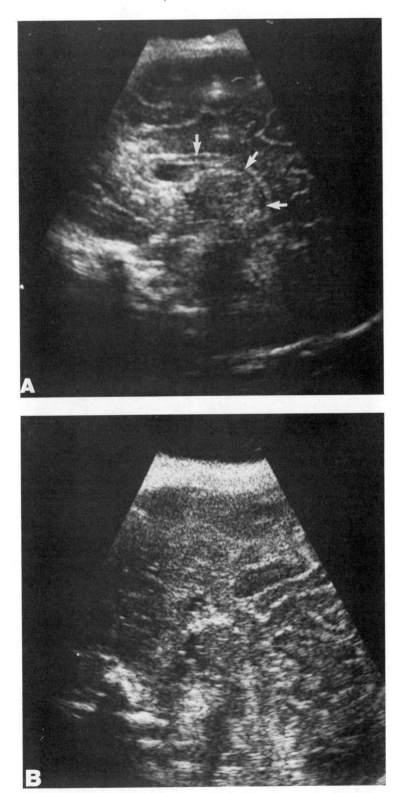

FIG. 6-5. *A.* Center sagittal head ultrasonogram of normal infant showing normal appearance of the corpus callosum (arrows). *B.* Absence of corpus callosum in infant whose neurologic examination disclosed abnormality and microcephaly. (Courtesy of Dr. R. Teele.)

If mucopolysaccharidoses are included in the differential diagnosis, particularly in later infancy or childhood, mucopolysaccharides are detectable by urine screening.[9] Specific diagnosis will require assay of enzyme activity in leukocytes or fibroblasts.

The serologic measurement of antibodies to known congenital infections such as toxoplasmosis, rubella, cytomegalic inclusion disease, and herpes (TORCH) should be considered when an infant's features dictate this.[38] TORCH titers cannot be used to confirm the diagnosis of congenital TORCH infections in the child or teenager, given the potential for acquiring antibodies following postnatal infection.

DIAGNOSIS

Synthesizing the Diagnosis

Many congenital multiple-anomaly syndromes can be diagnosed on the basis of one's familiarity with them, and the diagnosis can be confirmed by specific tests; diagnosis of less-familiar syndromes, however, requires systematic use of the approaches detailed earlier in this chapter:

1. Attempt to classify the child's anomalies as either minor or major and predict from this classification the likelihood of finding multiple major anomalies that may be serious.

2. Evaluate each anomaly in terms of the likelihood of its being a malformation, deformation, or disruption, with a special attempt to identify a *single cause* for multiple problems, be it monogenic, chromosomal, teratogenic, maternal, or interuterine/mechanical. Abnormal development of the earliest prenatal onset should prompt the greatest attention to find other major anomalies.

3. If a diagnosis cannot be confirmed by definitive test (e.g., chromosome analysis, biochemical assay) and the diagnosis remains questionable, proceed with the appropriate general evaluation and follow the child over time. Phenotype changes with age and may be more evident at a later age.

4. If a cogent diagnosis cannot be offered, individual defects should be explained in terms of the possible mechanism of their pathogenesis. This can allay parental guilt and helps parents recollect relevant obstetric or perinatal history.

5. In the older child, in particular, review the past history by looking at actual test reports and roentgenograms, because interpretations may vary and better quality studies may be needed.

The Role of the Geneticist/ Dysmorphologist

Recent advances in genetics and dysmorphology plus technical advances in cytogenetics and molecular genetics have helped refine diagnostic accuracy for a number of syndromes. Examples include special techniques for identifying chromosomal heteromorphisms, DNA probes for individual chromosomes, chromosome break stress-testing (in the diagnosis of Fanconi anemia) and high-resolution banding. Also, new clinical entities and anomaly associations have been recognized.[1,29] Consultation with specialists in genetics and dysmorphology can provide both clinical evaluation and education concerning these advances. Even when minor anomalies are detected, the geneticist or dysmorphologist can provide valuable insights into their significance and understands the natural history of certain disorders important in evaluation of the older patient or for follow-up of newborns.

Informing the Parents

Telling parents about significant errors in morphogenesis needs to be done in a gentle but forthright and confident manner. The information should not be incomplete or hastily put together. It can be particularly stressful for parents to hear of drastic changes in prognosis based on a new finding made in the course of the workup. When the diagnosis is evident by physical examination alone (e.g., in Down syndrome), informing parents of the need to do confirmatory tests is justified. A tentative diagnosis should be explained as a diagnosis based on one's current understanding of a child's physical features, the history, and the child's clinical course thus far. Final diagnosis should reflect a reasonable synthesis of these elements plus the best available diagnostic and laboratory tests. Thus, it is appropriate to tell the parents of a child with Down syndrome, for example, that you believe their baby has Down syndrome, that this diagnosis is based on your experience seeing other children with this condition, but in order to confirm this and to tell them more about recurrence risks, the baby's chromosomes need to be tested. While this may take some time, at present your best judgment is that the child has Down syndrome.

If the child presents with severe major anomalies, it is best to inform the parents early in that you are worried about serious complications; reticence tends to make parents feel abandoned. Always tell parents about those aspects that appear to be normal, since this helps them understand and accept less-encouraging information.

A frequent mistake made by physicians during the first discussions about an affected child is to assume parents cannot express their feelings and desires for management under the emotion-charged circumstances. Their words may, in fact, be quite representative of their current understanding and wishes about their child. It is vitally important, therefore, that parents be given plenty of opportunity to speak with the physician assessing their child and to ask questions.

Parents usually invest tremendous emotional energy to assure that the pregnancy is healthy. If one can confidently reassure parents that their child's problems are not related to problems with egg or sperm, with their own states of health, or with events or exposures during the pregnancy, then one should do so. Shock over the birth of a child with multiple congenital anomalies quickly mixes with and gives way to feelings of guilt because most parents worry about but never expect to have a child with such disorders. It can be reassuring to the parents of a child with congenital anomalies to learn that the intrauterine environment supporting the pregnancy was a healthy one and that such an ill baby could have been lost were it not for the mother's ability to carry even the sickest child.

LONG-TERM MANAGEMENT

Areas of Concern

Four important concepts are presented for the developmental follow-up of children with multiple congenital anomalies.

1. Optimizing the receptive skills of hearing and vision. These are extremely important for developmental performance and for learning, especially in children with major malformations of the central nervous system. A prescribed plan of vision and hearing testing is indicated, and where necessary, speech and hearing therapy should be included in the early-intervention plans.

2. Minimizing hospitalizations. Whenever possible, early intervention or formal schooling should continue during hospitalizations, especially prolonged ones. One outgrowth of effective communication between medical providers is the coordination of invasive tests and surgeries so that they can be done during the same hospital visit. This helps prevent missed school days.

3. Parental participation. If supports for parents are in place and effective, parent participation in home developmental therapies can facilitate education of the child.

4. Early-intervention programs. Referral to an early-intervention program is likely to be more beneficial than waiting for resolution of problems related to the child's physical handicaps. This also serves to extend the number of individuals who may be in a position to recognize new problems.

5. Family support. Parent support groups provide needed contacts for parents. Respite care can further provide parents with professional help in the day-to-day care of the child. Parents may not ask for referral to this resource and need to have it suggested in a supportive way, stressing the notion that choosing temporary respite care is an extension of a parent's concern for the child and does not represent failure to care for him. This is especially important since parents of multiply handicapped children frequently have difficulty finding baby-sitters who can provide the complex care needed.

The Primary Care Provider

Three major themes dominate the role of the primary care provider in caring for children with multiple handicaps: the monitoring of growth and nutrition, well-child care, and record-keeping.

Monitoring Growth and Nutrition. Monitoring of growth and nutrition is important for a number of reasons. Patients who undergo the physical stresses of major surgery and whose postoperative courses are difficult, those who have long unstable periods between staged surgical procedures, and those who experience debilitating medical complications may not achieve their full growth potential. These children require careful nutritional care because their caloric requirements can greatly exceed those of normal children. Second, additional nutrition may be required in children whose anomalies may demonstrate some somatic catch-up growth, as for example, in the extrinsically deformed mandible with the Robin sequence. Third, there remains a significant risk to children whose normal development is interrupted by frequent medical and surgical intervention. They can either fall behind in the acquisition of normal feeding skills or not develop them at all. Some children with poor feeding skills will not be able to obtain the necessary calories and nutrients even though their metabolism is normal. At times, it may be necessary to use alternative feeding practices, e.g., nasogastric or gastrostomy feeding tubes. Table 6-7 illustrates some general guidelines for meeting the nutritional needs of children with various congenital anomalies. It should be stressed that if a child is able, attempts at introducing solids and encouraging self-feeding in as normal a manner as possible should be a goal. The primary care provider

Table 6-7. *Nutritional Concerns for Representative Congenital Problems*

Clinical Entity	Significant Nutritional Issues	Suggestions
Congenital heart disease	Increased oxygen consumption Decreased body fat Risk of congestive heart failure with too much volume 21% of patients below 5th percentile for weight by 5 years	Usual caloric need: 150–180 kcal/kg/day Range of formula caloric density: 20–30 cal/oz.
Cleft lip	Infant usually learns to feed despite defect Certain feeding devices can interfere with surgical correction	Breck or Mead Johnson feeder Hold head above chest level, minimizing regurgitation
Cleft palate	Child usually adapts to soft-palate cleft. In hard-palate clefts the child may develop no suction	
Robin sequence	Retrognathic jaw with U-shaped cleft palate places child at risk for tongue obstructing airway; nasogastric or gastrostomy tube until jaw grows	Introduce Breck or Mead Johnson feeder once breathing or swallowing becomes coordinated
Hemifacial microsomia	Cleft of corner of mouth, abnormal occlusal plane, and neurologic dysfunction of palate produce poor seal and coordination until repair	Hold cheek of affected side upward Face forward Lamb's nipple preferable
Choanal atresia	Frequent use of stents makes feeding difficult Obligate nose-breathing may make feeding difficult	Clear nasal airway of mucus Plastic airway through nipple useful to develop suck
Macroglossia	Attempt feeding if sucking and swallowing can coordinate without aspiration	Use long lamb's nipple Water after feedings Oral hygiene important
Tracheoesophageal fistula with esophageal atresia	Most patients need gastrostomy tube High association with gastroesophageal reflux Esophageal dysmotility problems Stress with oral feeding	Attempt to wean G-tube Small feedings Encourage pacifier and oral feeding
Myelodysplasia	Any new feeding problem may indicate shunt malfunction Poor sucking may indicate brain stem or spinal cord pathology; symptomatic Arnold-Chiari Type II malformation	Monitor for reflux and aspiration Feeding difficulties can be symptom of shunt malfunction; further neurologic evaluation required

Adapted from McDonald, D.M.: *In* Nutrition and Feeding of Infants and Toddlers. Edited by R.B. Howard, and H.S. Winter. Boston, Little, Brown, 1983.

should work with nutritionists and parents to this end. Feeding can often be an enormous job, and many referral centers have feeding teams composed of individuals who specialize in feeding problems to help parents and physicians.

Well-Child Care. Despite the complexity of a child's multiple problems, or the number of consulting specialists contributing to the child's care, it is important to devise a plan for health care. A health care plan affords parents the opportunity to express their feelings and to ask questions on a regular basis. It can shorten visits by allowing more problems to be addressed individually over time rather than in clusters. Finally, it strengthens the role of the primary care physician as first contact for the patient's problems. A well established relationship in the well-child care format, even if the child is ill, permits attention to immunizations, drug allergies, follow-up vision and hearing screening, and to communicable infectious diseases representative of the community in which the child lives.

Record-Keeping. Because the child with multiple congenital anomalies has complex problems, the office medical record should follow a Problem-Oriented Medical Record (POMR) format, presumably to parallel the problem list used in the patient's hospital care.[50] Disorganized office notes result in neglect of active or unresolved problems when addressing new problems. Because of the premium on time in a busy office practice, searching through notes to determine the status of a particular problem is inefficient. Three approaches to using the Problem-Oriented Medical Record are suggested:

1. Use of a problem list relevant to the child with multiple congenital anomalies. Tables 6-8 and 6-9 offer examples of categories important in this patient population.

2. Use of interim summary worksheets to update a patient's progress at regular intervals. The worksheets are designed to be distributed to any persons involved in the patient's care including physicians, nurses, physical therapists, and social service personnel (Table 6-10). Done properly, these summaries communicate current information on medications and provide documentation for insurance companies, schools, social welfare agencies, hospital admitting offices, house-officers, and legal offices. Furthermore, they can accompany the patient and family to other locations and are helpful if the patient requires care in another office or hospital.

3. Use of standardized forms for correspondence. Formal letters of referral and authorization for specific therapies can be standardized to cut down on the redrafting of such correspondence. Use of a microcomputer and word-processing system can speed up correspondence and generation of interim summaries.

The Multidisciplinary Clinic

Multidisciplinary clinical programs for the comprehensive care of handicapped children permit efficient coordinated provision of care. They allow specialists and paramedical support staff to work together to address each of the patients' problems in detail. Typical programs in the hospital and community include those for myelodysplasia, cerebral palsy, craniofacial anoma-

Table 6-8. *Example of Typical Problem-List Categories for Children with Multiple Congenital Anomalies*

Problem List
1. Health care maintenance
2. Description of the syndrome or diagnosed entity

   a. Central nervous system
   b. Vision
   c. Hearing
   d. Cardiovascular
   e. Respiratory
   f. Otorhinolaryngological
   g. Gastrointestinal
   h. Orthopedic
   i. Genitourinary
   j. Nutrition and feeding
   k. Metabolic/endocrine

3. Social and family
4. Immunization status
5. Educational/development

lies, cleft lip and palate, limb anomalies, scoliosis, and Down syndrome. These clinics represent a prototype for similar multidisciplinary groups in a variety of medical and surgical clinics.

Usually, the pediatric nurse clinician serves as the first contact for the patient, triaging individual problems. An administrative coordinator arranges for clinic appointments, test requisitions, and billing matters. The patients may have individualized schedules for each clinic meeting, and they are provided with these when arriving at the clinic. These programs work best when all members meet to review and update each patient's total plan of care. Record-keeping is most efficient when the Problem-Oriented Medical Record format is followed.

These programs should not be confused with the provision of primary care. Indeed, success of the multidisciplinary program depends on reciprocal communication with primary care providers, since each can mistakenly assume that the other is attending to details important for the patient.

The multidisciplinary clinic also affords parents the opportunity to meet with one another, to have formal and informal discussion groups, and to maintain liaison with local, state, and national family-support groups. Attended often by the social service member of the team, these sessions with parents and support groups often facilitate identification of deficient services in the hospital, clinic, and community.

Table 6-9. *A Problem List Generated for a 3-Year-Old Child with the CHARGE Association (Colobomata, Heart Disease, Choanal Atresia, Retarded Growth and Development, Genital/Renal Anomalies, External Ear and Hearing Anomalies)*

1. Health care maintenance: Dr. _____ The Children's Hospital

2. Diagnosis:
     CHARGE association
     S/P neonatal respiratory arrest in the delivery room

    a. CNS:
     S/P hypoxic encephalopathy
     Mild residual hemiparesis
     Cognitive functioning age appropriate
     Right seventh nerve palsy
     Gross motor delay
     Fine motor delay

    b. Vision:
     Bilateral retinal colobomata
     Requires corrective lenses
     Legally blind
     Refuses to wear glasses

    c. Hearing:
     70 db bilateral sensorineural hearing loss
     Hearing aids
     American sign language

    d. Cardiovascular:
     Tetralogy of Fallot
     S/P repair on June 1, 1982—inactive

    e. Respiratory:
     Reactive airway disease, bronchodilator treatment
     Recurrent pneumonia February 1981, May 1981,
     June 1981, January 1982—inactive

    f. ENT:
     Bilateral bony choanal atresia
     Recurrent restenosis S/P laser X2
                      S/P transpalatal X3—resolved
     Chronic sinusitis, on trimethoprim/sulfa
     Velopharyngeal discoordination

    g. GI:
     S/P gastroesophageal reflux—resolved
     S/P gastrostomy tube—resolved

    h. Orthopedic:
     Bilateral metatarsus adductus—resolved
     Scoliosis watch—inactive

    i. Genitourinary:
     No problems

    j. Nutrition and feeding:
     S/P postnatal growth retardation—resolved.

    k. Metabolic/endocrine:
     No problems

3. Social, family:
     Intact family
     5-year-old male sibling doing well

4. Immunizations:
     UTD

5. Educational/development:
     _____ School
     Home tutor
     Developmental evaluation pending

Table 6-10. *Interim Summary Worksheet*

This will summarize the past medical history and present clinical status of _____, as of

_____. The following individuals are involved in _____'s care and

should be contacted if you need further information:

1. Pediatrician (address)
2. Neurologist
3. Orthopedic surgeon
4. Neurosurgeon

5. Primary nurse
6. Social worker
7. Physical therapist
8. Other

I. Problem List

   A. Health care maintenance (active, inactive, resolved, unresolved)

   B. _____

   C. _____

II. Medications

MEDICINE	DOSE	SCHEDULE	WHEN STARTED

III. Gestational/neonatal history

IV. Past medical history (by problem)

   A. Health care maintenance

   B. _____

   C. _____

V. Summary of hospitalizations

PROBLEM	TREATMENT	DISCHARGE DIAGNOSIS

VI. Allergies

VII. Immunization status

VIII. Transfusions

IX. Trauma

X. Relevant childhood illnesses

XI. Relevant family history

XII. Social history

XIII. Development/current developmental status

XIV. Current treatment plans

   A. _____

   B. _____

   C. _____

XV. Legal status and guardianship

XVI. All copies of treatment records, agency reports, and correspondence should be sent to: _____

_____
Signature and title

REFERENCES

1. Averbach, A.D., Adler, B., and Chaganti, R.S.K.: Prenatal and postnatal diagnosis and carrier detection of Fanconi Anemia by a cytogenetic method. Pediatrics, 67:128, 1981.
2. Beckwith, J.B.: Macroglossia, omphalocele, adrenal cytomegaly, gigantism, and hyperplastic visceromegaly. Birth Defects, 5:188, 1969.
3. Benirschke, K.: Placental pathology. *In* Neonatal-Perinatal Medicine. Edited by R.E. Behrman. St. Louis, C.V. Mosby, 1977, p. 1.
4. Berg, J.M., McCleary, B.C., Ridler, M.A.C., and Smith, G.F.: The DeLange Syndrome. Oxford, Pergamon Press, 1970.
5. Cohen, M.M., Jr. The Child with Multiple Birth Defects. New York, Raven Press, 1982.
6. Clarren, S.K., Smith, D.W., and Hanson, J.W.: Helmet treatment for plagiocephaly and congenital muscular torticollis. J. Pediatr., 94:43, 1979.
7. Conley, M.E., et al.: The spectrum of DiGeorge Syndrome. J. Pediatr., 94:883, 1979.
8. Cooper, L.Z.: Congenital rubella in the United States. *In* Infections of the Fetus and Newborn Infant. Edited by S. Krugman, and A.A. Gershon. New York, A.R. Liss, Inc., 1975, pp. 1-22.
9. Crocker, A.C.: Inborn errors of lipid metabolism: early identification. Clin. Perinatol., 3:99, 1976.
10. Dunn, P.M.: Congenital sternocleidomastoid torticollis: an intrauterine postural deformity. Arch. Dis. Child. 49:824, 1974.
11. Dunn, P.M.: Congenital postural deformities. Br. Med. Bull., 94:43, 1976.
12. Feingold, M., and Bossert, W.H.: Normal values. Birth Defects, 10:1, 1974.
13. Gorlin, R.J., Pindborg, J.J., and Cohen, M.M., Jr.: Syndromes of the Head and Neck. 2nd Ed. New York, McGraw-Hill, 1976.
14. Gortmaker, S., and Sappenfield, W.: Chronic childhood disorders: Prevalence and impact. Pediatr. Clin. North Am., 31:3, 1984.
15. Graham, J.H.: Craniostenosis: A new approach to management. Pediatr. Ann., 10:27, 1981.
16. Hall, J.G.: An approach to congenital contractures (arthrogryposis). Pediatr. Ann., 10:15, 1981.
17. Hanson, J.W., and Smith, D.W.: Prominent lateral palatine ridges: Developmental and clinical relevance. J. Pediatr., 89:54, 1976.
18. Henderson, K.: Hospital costs of spina bifida children in the first three years of life. Second Symposium on Spina Bifida, A multidisciplinary approach, 1984 (in press).
19. Hendren, W.H.: Constipation caused by anterior location of anus and surgical correction. J. Pediatr. Surg., 13:505, 1978.
20. Heyman, M.B., et al.: Esophageal muscular ring and the VACTERL Association: A case report. Pediatrics, 67:683, 1981.
21. Holmes, L.B.: The Malformed Newborn. Practical Perspectives. Boston, Massachusetts Developmental Disabilities Council, 1976.
22. Holmes, L.B.: Congenital malformation. *In* Manual of Neonatal Care. Edited by J.P. Cloherty, and A.R. Stark. Boston, Little, Brown, 1980, pp. 91-96.
23. Jaffe, B.F.: Pinnea anomalies associated with congenital conductive hearing loss. Pediatrics, 57:332, 1976.
24. Jones, K.L., and Robinson, L.K.: An approach to the child with structural defects. J. Pediatr. Orthop., 4:238, 1983.
25. Jones, K.L., et al.: A pattern of craniofacial and limb defects secondary to aberrant tissue bands. J. Pediatr., 84:90, 1974.
26. Joseph, M.C., and Parrott, D.: Severe infantile hypercalcemia with special reference to the facies. Arch. Dis. Child., 33:385, 1958.
27. Kanthor, H., et al.: Areas of responsibility in the health care of multiply handicapped children. Pediatrics, 56:779, 1974.
28. Kaplan, L.C., et al.: Ectopia cordis and cleft sternum: Evidence for mechanical teratogenesis following rupture of the chorion or yolk sac. Am. J. Med. Genet., 21:187, 1985.
29. Latt, S.A., et al.: Molecular genetic approaches to human diseases involving mental retardation. Am. J. Ment. Defic., 89:420, 1985.
30. Ledley, F.D.: Metabolic diseases. *In* Manual of Pediatric Therapeutics. Edited by J.W. Graef, and T.E. Cone. Boston, Little, Brown, 1985, pp. 341-350.
31. Ma, P., and Piazza, F.: Cost of treating birth defects in State crippled children's services, 1975. Public Health Rep., 94:420, 1979.
32. McArdle, R., and Lebowitz, R.: Uncomplicated hypospadius and anomalies of the upper urinary tract: Need for screening? Urology, 5:712, 1975.
33. McLean, N.: Sex chromatin surveys of newborn babies. *In* The Sex Chromatin. Edited by K. Moore. Philadelphia, W.B. Saunders, 1966, pp. 202-209.
34. Marden, P.M., Smith, D.W., and McDonald, M.J.: Congenital anomalies in the newborn infant, including minor variations. J. Pediatr., 64:358, 1964.
35. Miller, M.E., Dunn, P.M., and Smith, D.W.: Uterine malformation and fetal deformation. J. Pediatr., 94:387, 1979.
36. Miller, M.E., et al.: Compression-related defects from early rupture: Evidence for mechanical teratogenesis. J. Pediatr., 98:292, 1981.
37. Nadas, A.S.: Heart disease in children. Hosp. Pract., 12:103, 1977.
38. Nahmias, A.J.: The TORCH complex. Hosp. Pract., 9:65, 1974.
39. Poswillo, D.: Mechanisms and pathogenesis of malformation. Br. Med. Bull., 32:59, 1976.
40. Reinecke, R.D.: Ophthalmic examination by the pediatrician of infants and children. Pediatr. Clin. North Am., 30:995, 1983.
41. Richardson, M.A., and Cotton, R.T.: Anatomic abnormalities of the pediatric airway. Pediatr. Clin. North Am., 31:821, 1984.
42. Smith, D.W.: Recognizable Patterns of Human Deformation. Philadelphia, W.B. Saunders, 1981.
43. Smith, D.W.: Recognizable Patterns of Human Malformation. Philadelphia, W.B. Saunders, 1982.
44. Smith, D.W., and Gong, B.T.: Scalp hair patterning as a clue to early fetal brain development. J. Pediatr., 83:374, 1973.
45. Smith, G.F., and Berg, J.M.: Down's Anomaly. 2nd Ed. Edinburgh, 1976.
46. Sprintzen, R.J., and Berkman, M.D.: Pharyngeal hypoplasia in Treacher Collins Syndrome. Arch. Otolaryngol., 105:127, 1979.
47. Teele, R.L.: Ultrasonography of the genitourinary tract in childhood. Radiol. Clin. North Am., 15:109, 1976.
48. Van Mierop, L.H.S., Genner, I.H., and Schiebler, G.L.: Asplenia and polysplenia syndrome. Birth Defects, 8:74, 1972.
49. Weber, W.W.: Survival and the sex ratio in Trisomy 17-18. Am. J. Hum. Genet., 19:369, 1967.
50. Weed, L.L.: Medical Records, Medical Education, and Patient Care. Cleveland, Case Western Reserve University Press, 1969.
51. Wiedemann, H.R.: Complexe malformatif familial avec hernie ombilicale et makroglossie—un "Syndrome nouveau"? J. Hum. Genet., 13:223, 1964.
52. Yunis, G., and Chandler, M.E.: High resolution chromosome analysis in clinical medicine. Prog. Clin. Pathol., 7:267, 1977.

7

THE GENETIC APPROACH

David L. Meryash, M.D.

Genetic disorders can affect any organ system. The treatment of these disorders depends not so much on the etiology, but on the organs involved and their accompanying physiologic aberrations. The responsibilities of the physician or medical team caring for the individual with developmental disabilities fall into five areas: (1) medical treatment and follow-up, (2) coordination of educational and related therapies (occupational, physical, and speech), (3) diagnosis, (4) family support and counseling, and (5) prevention.

Individuals whose disabilities are the result of a genetic disorder must receive attention in all five of the areas listed above. But, if a disorder is genetic, and especially if it is hereditary, the last three require particular emphasis. This chapter addresses the special issues involved when the etiology of developmental disabilities might have a genetic basis. Although the primary care physician may find it necessary to obtain the assistance of a clinical geneticist in establishing a diagnosis, in counseling a family, or in prevention-oriented activities, he can largely incorporate these issues into management of his patient.

When parents are first faced with the knowledge that their infant or young child has a handicapping condition, their reactions are usually shock and disbelief. They might wonder what they did wrong to deserve such an occurrence. Once they have grieved the loss of the normal child they had expected, and they begin to accept their situation, their attention turns to how to help their child. They want to know what

medical complications to expect, and how these can be treated. They are concerned about the child's developmental potential, whether milestones will be delayed, whether he can be expected to walk or talk. They seek information regarding the child's educational potential and, looking to the future, his prospects for employment.

Eventually the parents' attention to the child's needs broadens into concern for the family. For example, the parents of a young child with mental retardation may ask about the risk of having another affected infant. A couple who have completed their family may not raise this question until their unaffected children have reached an age when they themselves might become parents. If parents or other relatives do not ask about recurrence risk, a primary care physician has the responsibility of offering some insight and suggesting carrier testing and prenatal diagnostic procedures where indicated.

The process involved in addressing the question "Can this happen again?" constitutes the genetic approach to developmental disabilities. The process has two phases. The first is evaluation and falls within the physician's role as a diagnostician. The second phase, genetic counseling, is an important responsibility of the physician as an advocate for the health of the family.

Before a description of the two components of the genetic approach is presented, a brief discussion of the classification of genetic disorders is in order.

CLASSIFICATION OF GENETIC DISORDERS

A condition or disorder is genetic if it is a direct result of the presence of abnormal genetic material in an individual. Genetic disorders can either be inherited or arise de novo. A condition is inherited if one or both parents contributed to their affected child the genetic material resulting in the disorder in question. If both parents are genetically normal with respect to the condition, it is a de novo occurrence in their child.

Genetic disorders are divided into single-gene disorders, chromosome abnormalities, and multifactorial conditions.

Single-Gene Disorders

In single-gene (mendelian) disorders, there is an abnormal sequence of DNA bases at a discrete location within the genome. Because it is thought that a single gene codes for one protein, it is presumed that single-gene disorders affect the normal production of only a single enzyme. The single-gene disorders include those inborn errors of metabolism (phenylketonuria or galactosemia, for example) for which the affected enzyme has been identified. For the majority of known single-gene disorders, however, the gene product normally produced has not been identified. Single-gene disorders are heritable, that is, capable of genetic transmission from one generation to the next. They exhibit one of four basic modes of transmission: autosomal dominant, autosomal recessive, X-linked recessive, and X-linked dominant. Of these, the first three are the most important to the area of developmental disabilities.

Chromosome Disorders

Chromosome disorders are of two types: those in which there is extra chromosomal material, and those in which a portion of chromosomal material is missing from an individual's genome. In order to be detected microscopically, chromosomal abnormalities must involve large amounts of genetic material. They can involve entire chromosomes as in trisomy 21 (Down syndrome), or portions of chromosomes as in 5p- (cri-du-chat syndrome). Modern cytogenetic techniques have enabled the observation of fairly small deletions of chromosome material in some conditions, for example: the Prader-Willi syndrome (chromosome 15), bilateral retinoblastoma (chromosome 13), and the aniridia–Wilms tumor association (chromosome 11). However, even in each of these instances, at least several genes are probably involved.

Trisomy 21 (Down syndrome) is an example of a chromosome disorder that can either be sporadic or inherited. In either case the affected person has three copies of chromosome 21 instead of two. In the more common situation (95% of cases), the affected individual has 47 chromosomes with 3 separate copies of chromosome 21. The extra copy arises from nondisjunction of the pair of 21s during either the first or second meiotic division in the production of either the mother's ovum or the father's sperm. Each parent, however, has 46 chromosomes and only 2 number 21 chromosomes. Since they are genotypically normal, the condition was not inherited. Nondisjunction can also occur during mitosis once the sperm and egg have united and at least 1 cell division has occurred. This will lead to a mixture of 2 populations of cells, 1 with 47 chromosomes and an extra 21 and 1 with 46 chromosomes and 2 number 21s. The result is a mosaic pattern, which is not inherited.

In 3 to 5 percent of the instances of Down syndrome, the extra chromosome 21 is attached to ("translocated" onto) one of the other acrocentric chromosomes—either 1 from the D group (13, 14, or 15) or 1 from the G group (21 or 22). This is a de novo occurrence about half of the time, but in the remaining instances the translocation chromosome came from 1 or the other parent. The parent who has the translocation chromosome has a total of 45 chromosomes with 2 copies of number 21, 1 copy being involved in the translocation. Since the parent has a normal amount of chromosome material, he or she is phenotypically normal and is said to have a balanced translocation. If such an individual transmits the translocation chromosome along with the other 21 to his or her child, this will result in trisomy 21 in the offspring (Fig. 7-1).

Virtually any of the 46 chromosomes can be involved in translocations, though some are more frequently involved. The translocation associated with Down syndrome is called a Robertsonian translocation. In a Robertsonian translocation the long arms of 2 acrocentric chromosomes combine at their centromeres. The short arms are lost, but in acrocentric chromosomes these are thought not to contain significant genetic material.

Translocations involving nonacrocentric chromosomes are the result of breaks occurring in important portions of 2 different chromosomes

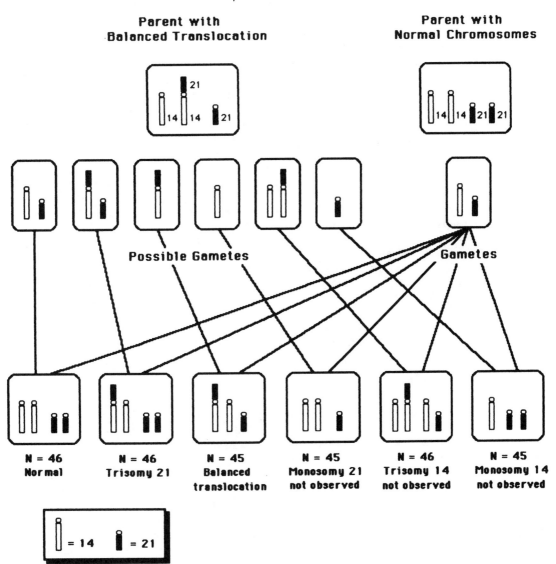

FIG. 7-1. Chromosome complements of possible offspring of individual with balanced 14/21 transloca-tion. Three combinations are nonviable and lead to early spontaneous abortion. Live-born offspring have either normal chromosomes, unbalanced translocation with Down syndrome, or balanced translocation with normal phenotype.

with either a mutual exchange of material or loss of some of the material. The cri-du-chat syn-drome is associated with a loss of the distal por-tion of the short arm of chromosome 5. In a few instances of cri-du-chat, one parent has the same deficient chromosome as the child; however, the portion of the number 5 that is missing in the child is attached to another chromosome in the phenotypically normal parent. This is another example of a phenotypically normal parent with a balanced translocation having an offspring who is chromosomally unbalanced and phenotypically abnormal.

Multifactorial Conditions

There are some conditions for which there is a familial predilection but which cannot be ex-plained on the basis of mendelian (single-gene) inheritance or a chromosome abnormality. They appear to occur as the result of the combined effect of several genes contributed by both par-ents. In addition, it appears that these genes are expressed only in the presence of an unknown environmental trigger. An example of a condi-tion causing developmental disabilities that fits this pattern of inheritance is meningomyelocele.

EVALUATION

History and Physical Assessment

One aim of the evaluation of the child with developmental disabilities is to arrive at an etiologic diagnosis. If there has been no clearly documented adverse external influence during the prenatal, perinatal, or newborn periods, the possibility of a genetic etiology should always be entertained until proven otherwise. Although the causes of developmental disability are traditionally divided into those that are genetic and those that are environmental, it is not always easy to make a distinction in individual cases. A child's ultimate growth and development depend on both genetic and environmental influences.

If the etiology of a particular child's developmental disabilities is proven or assumed to be primarily genetic, the fundamental goals are to determine whether the condition is hereditary and to establish the mode of transmission.

In a genetic evaluation, the identified patient is known as the proband. The evaluation of the proband starts with a complete history and physical examination. Details regarding the pregnancy (e.g., health of the mother, drugs ingested, febrile illnesses, environmental exposures, length of gestation) should be obtained first. Then, it is important to examine carefully the perinatal history, including the details of labor and delivery, abnormalities noted at birth, and the health of the newborn infant. If possible, actual birth records should be obtained so that no items suggesting a perinatal insult are overlooked. When the health history is complete a developmental history is important to determine the extent of the child's disabilities.

The family history is the single most important component of a genetic evaluation. Starting with the proband's parents, one should "walk the pedigree," identifying each relative by name and obtaining information on as many individuals as possible. Details about the health and development of each individual should be obtained, using a set of standard questions. The questions should elicit information in the following areas of concern (list modified from Riccardi[4]):

1. Family members other than proband who were mentally retarded, had learning disabilities, speech problems, or did not achieve as much as their siblings
2. Family members other than proband who had "nerve" or "muscle" disorders
3. Presence of other heritable or congenital disorders in family members other than proband
4. Presence of birth defects in family members other than proband
5. Age of parents at conception of first affected individual
6. Ethnic backgrounds of family members
7. Consanguinity
8. Incest
9. Nonpaternity
10. Frequent miscarriages or stillbirths
11. Occupations of family members

Highest grade attained in school, enrollment in special education classes, a history of speech problems, adult occupation, and the presence of birth defects or "mental" or "nervous" conditions all provide useful information about a person's development. Simply asking the informant whether his relatives were mentally retarded often yields responses that are clouded by his own cognitive abilities and subjective perceptions. If abnormal development is present in other family members, it is important to determine to what extent their features match those of the proband. Members of the family who have had repeated miscarriages should also be identified because this pattern may indicate a chromosome abnormality. It may often be necessary to obtain medical records from hospitals and institutions or to question additional relatives in order to fill in gaps in the family history initially provided.

A positive family history is highly indicative of a heritable disorder, but the absence of a positive family history does not rule out the possibility that the condition is hereditary. The family history can be negative even when the condition is hereditary because of any of the following reasons: (1) inadequate history, (2) nonpaternity, (3) new mutation, (4) variable expression or penetrance, (5) initial occurrence in a family of autosomal recessive or multifactorial disorder, or (6) X-linked condition with relatively small sibships.

In the physical examination one should look for congenital anomalies or subtle dysmorphic features that in combination may suggest a particular syndrome, and for features suggestive of specific inborn errors of metabolism or progressive neurologic disorders suggested by the medical and developmental history.

It is often helpful to examine other affected members of the family. If a particular condition is being seriously considered, the characteristic features might be more recognizable in some family members than in others.

Once all possible sources about family history have been exhausted and all available affected individuals have been examined, enough infor-

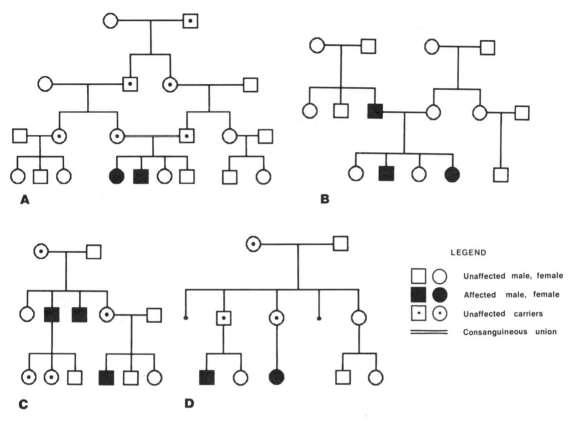

FIG. 7-2. Pedigrees demonstrating the most common modes of transmission of hereditary conditions that can cause developmental disabilities. *A.* Autosomal recessive. *B.* Autosomal dominant. *C.* X-linked recessive. *D.* Chromosome abnormality (translocation).

mation may have been obtained to suggest strongly a specific mode of inheritance. Figure 7-2 shows pedigrees typical of autosomal dominant, autosomal recessive, and X-linked recessive inheritance, and of a family in which there is an inherited translocation (such as one involving chromosomes 14 and 21 leading to Down syndrome).

Although there is personal satisfaction to be gained by making a syndromic diagnosis, there is little practical advantage in doing so unless as a result important information can be provided to the family such as recurrence risk or further insight regarding causality. If after a careful evaluation the physician cannot provide a specific diagnosis, but has established that a condition is hereditary and has determined the mode of transmission, he has provided an important service to the family.

Hundreds of syndromes of multiple congenital anomalies have been described. For many the cause has been determined to be either a single gene abnormality or a chromosome abnormality. For others environmental insults have been clearly implicated (e.g., fetal alcohol syndrome, rubella syndrome). For the majority, the occurrence is sporadic and the etiology is unknown.

Unless a syndrome has a constellation of pathognomonic features, or a chromosomal analysis can demonstrate a specific defect, a perfect fit of a particular patient to the description of a syndrome is not achievable. One can only talk about possible diagnoses or the most likely diagnosis. Further difficulties arise from a great deal of overlap of features among syndromes which themselves are very rare. There are several excellent texts that catalogue dysmorphic syndromes. One of the most valuable is David Smith's *Recognizable Patterns of Human Malformation* (see list of additional readings at the end of this chapter).

A clinical geneticist may sometimes be able to establish that a child has a certain rare syndrome if he has seen several cases himself. The genetic consultant, however, is too often regarded by the referring physician simply as a "syndromologist." The physician who refers a diagnostic dilemma with the expectation of an answer to the question "What syndrome is this?" or "Is this syndrome Z?" will more often than not be disappointed by the outcome. One way in which the geneticist may be able to assist is by suggesting appropriate further diagnostic testing.

Further Investigation

At one time, a chromosomal analysis was recommended if a child had three or more congenital anomalies. Chromosome abnormalities involving every chromosome have now been demonstrated. With newer technologies more subtle abnormalities can be observed. At the same time it has been shown that some children with developmental disabilities who have nearly normal physical appearances can demonstrate either chromosome abnormalities (the young child with XXY karyotype who has speech problems) or a cytogenetic marker indicative of a single-gene disorder that causes mental retardation (fragile-X syndrome). Any individual who has mental retardation without a specific etiologic diagnosis should have a chromosome analysis.

The inborn errors of metabolism and the degenerative neurologic disorders are virtually all single-gene disorders. If such a disorder is suspected, consultation from a neurologist, nerve conduction studies and/or muscle biopsy, or metabolic testing of blood and urine are usually required to establish the specific diagnosis.

GENETIC COUNSELING

When the medical history and physical examination of the proband and other affected family members have been completed and all resources regarding family history have been exhausted, the evaluation phase has reached a critical juncture. One of several outcomes will have been achieved:

1. The cause of the disabilities was determined with reasonable certainty to be environmental, a major genetic cause being effectively ruled out.

2. A recognizable condition with a known mode of genetic transmission was diagnosed.

3. Although a specific diagnosis was not made, the family history is strongly suggestive of a genetic disorder and the mode of transmission is apparent.

4. The etiology remains unknown and the family history can neither implicate nor rule out hereditary factors. Examination of the patient may not suggest a named syndrome.

Genetic counseling is an information-sharing process. It is often regarded as mysterious or threatening, but it should be neither. The American Society of Human Genetics provides an apt description:[1]

Genetic counseling is a communication process which deals with the human problems associated with the occurrence, or the risk of occurrence, of a genetic disorder in a family. This process involves an attempt by one or more appropriately trained persons to help the individual or family (1) to comprehend the medical facts, including the diagnosis, the probable course of the disorder, and the available management; (2) to appreciate the way heredity contributes to the disorder, and the risk of recurrence in specified relatives; (3) to understand the options for dealing with the risk of recurrence; (4) to choose the course of action which seems appropriate to them in view of their risk, their family goals, and their ethical and religious standards, and to act in accordance with that decision; and (5) to make the best possible adjustment to the disorder in an affected family member and/or to the risk of recurrence of that disorder.

Thus genetic counseling covers a good deal of territory. Depending on the outcome of the evaluation and the expertise of the professionals involved, some of it may appropriately be covered by the primary medical team, but other aspects may require consultation with someone more knowledgeable in genetic principles and available procedures.

Cause Determined to be Environmental

If an intrauterine infection (e.g., congenital rubella) or drug effect (e.g., fetal alcohol syndrome) is clearly apparent from the medical history and physical examination, the determinants of recurrence in the family are clear. The mother who had rubella is now immune and cannot infect future children; the mother who drank heavily during one pregnancy may or may not do so during future ones. The object of counseling in these situations is to present the facts about the relationship of the particular environmental influence on fetal development. The idea that mothering (and fathering) of a child should begin prior to conception should be discussed with the parents of an already affected individual.

If it is probable from the history that the cause of a child's disabilities was birth asphyxia, the risk for recurrence should not be increased above that for the general population. One point of caution, however, is that perinatal difficulties tend to occur more frequently among infants who have genetic disorders; therefore clearly documented problems at birth do not necessarily exclude genetic determinants.

Recognizable Condition with a Known Mode of Inheritance

Examples of conditions that cause developmental disabilities are shown in Table 7-1. When

Table 7-1.   *Etiology of Some Conditions Associated with Developmental Disability*

Autosomal Dominant
  Apert syndrome
  Neurofibromatosis
  Tuberous sclerosis
 	
Autosomal Recessive
  Galactosemia
  Homocystinuria
  Hurler syndrome
    (mucopolysaccharidosis I)
  Phenylketonuria
  Seckel syndrome
  Smith-Lemli-Opitz syndrome
  Wilson disease
 	
X-linked Recessive
  Fragile-X syndrome
  Hunter syndrome
    (mucopolysaccharidosis II)
  Lesch-Nyhan syndrome
  Menkes syndrome
  Oculocerebrorenal (Lowe) syndrome
  Renpenning syndrome
	Multifactorial
	  Meningomyelocele
	
	Chromosome Disorders
	  Aniridia-Wilms tumor (11p−)
	  Cri-du-chat syndrome (5p−)
	  Down syndrome (+21)
	  Prader-Willi syndrome (15q−)
	  Retinoblastoma (13q−)
	  XXY (Klinefelter syndrome)
	  XYY syndrome
	
	Sporadic Syndrome—
	Etiology Unknown
	  Cerebral gigantism (Sotos syndrome)
	  Noonan syndrome
	  Rubinstein-Taybi syndrome
	  Williams syndrome
	
	Environmental
	  Fetal alcohol effects
	  Fetal hydantoin effects
	  Fetal rubella effects
	  Maternal PKU fetal effects

the cause of disabilities is a single-gene disorder, determination of the risk of recurrence and identification of relatives at risk for having affected children are fairly straightforward.

Autosomal Recessive Disorders

In autosomal recessive disorders two copies of the abnormal gene must be present for the condition to be expressed. The affected individual inherited one copy of this gene from each parent. Both parents are phenotypically normal, although specific biochemical testing or, occasionally, specialized examination techniques might disclose minor manifestations of the condition. For each subsequent pregnancy that same couple has a 1-out-of-4 chance of having a child with the same disorder. The situation in which the single offspring of 2 persons heterozygous for a particular condition is affected is an important example of the occurrence of a hereditary disorder when the family history is otherwise negative. Each subsequent child has a 50-percent chance of being an unaffected carrier of the abnormal gene. Unless such an individual marries another carrier, his risk for having an affected child is zero. The chance of marrying another carrier depends on the frequency of the gene in the general population. The likelihood of a mate also being a carrier increases dramatically if the mate is a relative. For example, if a person who is heterozygous marries a first cousin, the likelihood of that first cousin also carrying the gene is 1 out of 16.

Autosomal Dominant Disorders

In autosomal dominant conditions, only one copy of the abnormal gene need be present for the condition to be expressed. A person who has the gene for an autosomal dominant disorder usually has features of that disorder. It usually can be assumed that this dominant gene was inherited from one or the other parent. There are, however, additional characteristics of autosomal dominant conditions which must be considered. First, many autosomal dominant conditions have variable penetrance. This means that some individuals with a gene for a particular disorder can be affected while some of their relatives with the same gene might be unaffected. Detection of the manifestations of a condition often depends on the technology available and the degree of sophistication in examination. Second, dominant conditions may vary considerably in the degree to which individuals who have the condition are affected; that is, autosomal dominant conditions have variable expression. Third, autosomal dominant conditions frequently occur as a result of a new mutation. For example, in 90% of the cases of Apert syndrome neither parent carries the gene; consequently one would not expect the proband's siblings to be affected. Because of these considerations, the possibility that anyone with developmental disabilities has an autosomal dominant condition should not be eliminated if the family history is negative.

Table 7-2. *Risk of Meningomyelocele for Relatives of Affected Individuals Based on Experience in the United States*

Relationship to Affected Individual(s)	Risk (%)
Unrelated person (general population)	0.05
Sibling	2–4
Sibling of 2 affected individuals	6–8
Son or daughter	2
Niece or nephew	0.5–1.0

Data from Leonard, C.O.: Counseling of parents of a child with meningomyelocele. Pediatr. Rev., 4:317, 1983.

X-Linked Recessive Disorders

In X-linked disorders, the deleterious gene is located on the X chromosome. Males who have such a gene will usually have manifestations of the corresponding disorder. A female who has a deleterious recessive gene on one of her two X chromosomes will usually not be affected because the normal corresponding gene on her other X chromosome will compensate. If a woman who is a carrier for an X-linked disorder is affected, it is usually to a milder degree than an affected male.

X-linked disorders can be transmitted by either sex. Affected males who are capable of reproducing will transmit the gene for the disorder to each of his daughters but to none of his sons. The daughter of a female carrier has a 50% chance of being a carrier. The son of a female carrier has a 50% chance of being affected by the disorder. Since X-linked disorders are usually transmitted

Table 7-3. *Risk of Recurrence of Down Syndrome*

Category	Risk (%)
Any couple in general population	0.1
Couple with 1 child with	
Trisomy 21	1
D/G translocation, mother is carrier	10–15
D/G translocation, father is carrier	5
21/22 translocation, mother is carrier	10–15
21/22 translocation, father is carrier	5
21/21 translocation, either parent is carrier	100
Translocation, both parents normal	<1
Mosaicism	<1

Modified from Skinner, R.: Genetic counseling. *In* Principles and Practice of Medical Genetics. Edited by A.E.H. Emery, and D.L. Rimoin. New York, Churchill Livingstone, 1983.

by normal women, many women in a family may unknowingly be at risk for having affected children. One must be concerned not only for the mother of the identified patient, but also for her sisters, her mother or father's sisters, their daughters, and their daughters' children. The presence of small sibships with few or no males will have a tendency to mask the presence of an adverse X-linked gene in some branches of the family.

X-linked disorders that diminish the reproductive capacity of affected males, like autosomal dominant conditions, also have a fairly high rate of new mutation. For example, one-third of the males with Duchenne muscular dystrophy and one-half of the carriers for this disorder have a new mutation.

Thus in X-linked disorders the family history is often negative. Since there is subtlety in identifying such a pattern, a careful and extensive family history is important if an X-linked recessive disorder is suspected.

Multifactorial Conditions

When a couple has had a child with a multifactorial condition, the risk to any subsequent child is about 3 to 5%. The risk of meningomyelocele for various relatives of the proband is shown in Table 7-2.[2]

Chromosome Disorders

If a chromosome disorder is sporadic, the recurrence risk is relatively small. The recurrence risk for a couple with one child with trisomy 21 unassociated with a translocation is empirically about 1%. This is somewhat greater than the risk for the general population (about 0.1%), and the reason is unknown. The risk is of different magnitude if one or the other parent has a balanced translocation. The recurrence risks for the different possible cytogenetic findings associated with Down syndrome are given in Table 7-3.[5]

The recurrence risk for other less common translocations is based on pooled data, since each possible translocation alone is too rare to provide meaningful data. The general risk of a live-born child with an unbalanced translocation is estimated to be 10% to 20% if the mother is a balanced carrier and 5% to 10% if the father has a balanced translocation.[3]

Carrier Detection and Prenatal Diagnosis

For many of the inborn errors of metabolism, there are biochemical assays that reveal reduced levels of specific enzymes or abnormal products in the blood or other tissues of carriers. Similar assays can be performed on amniotic fluid or cells obtained from the fluid for prenatal diagnosis. If a diagnosis is made prenatally, options can be discussed through genetic counseling. For most single-gene disorders, however, biochemical identification of carriers is not possible and prenatal diagnosis unavailable.

Virtually any chromosome disorder can be detected by amniocentesis. Any couple who has had one child with a chromosome disorder should be offered amniocentesis for subsequent pregnancies.

Elevated alpha fetoprotein (AFP) in the serum of a pregnant woman can be indicative of an open neural tube in the fetus; this can be confirmed by elevated AFP in the amniotic fluid and by ultrasonography, through which the anatomic defect can be visualized. Measurement of maternal serum alphafetoprotein (MSAFP) is simple and inexpensive and is increasingly being offered to women as a screening procedure even when they are not at risk by history.

In certain X-linked disorders, even in the absence of definitive carrier testing, a genetic counselor can calculate the probability that any woman in the family is a carrier. Several factors can be considered in such an analysis. For example, in Duchenne muscular dystrophy, 80% of carriers have moderately increased levels of creatine phosphokinase (CPK). A woman with a normal CPK level whose mother is a carrier for muscular dystrophy is herself less likely a carrier than her sister who has an elevated CPK level. Prior to testing, she could be given a 50% risk of being a carrier. Once her CPK level is known to be normal her probability of being a carrier is reduced to about 17%. The presence of unaffected males in the family can also be figured into the risk calculation. For example, a woman who has a brother with muscular dystrophy is much less likely to be a carrier if she has had 5 normal sons. This method of calculating the probability of being a carrier is known as Bayesian analysis and is part of the repertoire of trained genetic counselors.

Diagnosis Unknown with Mode of Inheritance Apparent

The most appropriate genetic counseling is provided when an accurate specific diagnosis is made, but even if a specific diagnosis is not possible, recurrence risks can often be given to concerned relatives if the mode of inheritance is apparent. The principles described above apply. In the absence of a specific diagnosis, of course,

carrier testing is impossible. When a major structural abnormality is a feature of the underlying disorder, however, prenatal diagnosis by ultrasonography may be possible, in which case it should be offered.

Etiology Unknown

When the etiology remains unknown and the family history is not conclusive for any of the mendelian modes of inheritance, little information can be provided regarding recurrence risk. Sporadic occurrences of such conditions may be the result of primarily environmental factors (recurrence risk as low as 0), a rare autosomal recessive disease (recurrence risk 25%), or multifactorial inheritance (recurrence risk about 5%). Many genetic counselors present an overall recurrence risk of about 5% but caution that it may be close to 0 or as high as 25%. In any case a couple should not be left with the impression either that there cannot be a recurrence or that recurrence is certain, neither of which is ever true.

If a child has multiple congenital anomalies, the parents can be told with certainty that whatever the adverse influence, it was present prior to the tenth week of gestation. This is because all of the fetus' organs are fully formed by that point. This information regarding the timing of the insult may be important to the family if they are concerned that the cause is something they did (or did not do) during the second or third trimester.

NEW DEVELOPMENTS

Technological Advances

In recent years there have been many new technological developments which will aid in the diagnosis of genetic disease. The techniques involve recombinant-DNA technology. Carriers for some diseases can now be detected by determining, on a molecular level, the presence of the gene itself in the DNA of individuals at risk. In other diseases carriers can be detected by knowledge of linkage of the abnormal genes to areas of normal variation within the genome, called "restriction fragment length polymorphisms." These methods, which are rapidly being developed, are also potentially useful for prenatal diagnosis.

Meanwhile cytogeneticists have expanded their ability to band chromosomes in different ways and have identified additional chromosomal abnormalities. Many laboratories are able to prepare longer chromosomes for analysis, enabling identification of smaller and smaller deletions.

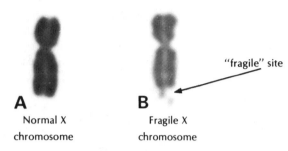

A
Normal X
chromosome

B
Fragile X
chromosome

"fragile" site

FIG. 7-3. *A.* Normal X chromosome. *B.* X chromosome with fragile site at distal tip of the long arm. Arrow indicates fragile site.

The Fragile-X Syndrome

The fragile-X syndrome is a newly recognized X-linked condition which, after Down syndrome, is the second most common genetic cause of mental retardation. It has been estimated to affect 1 out of every 2,000 males. The cognitive level of affected males ranges from borderline intelligence (I.Q. 70 to 84) to severe mental retardation (I.Q. 20 to 40). One out of 3 female carriers also has some form of developmental disability.

Males with the fragile-X syndrome can be recognized by certain characteristic physical features that include macrocephaly relative to height, dolichocephaly, a long, narrow face, prominent ears, and a prominent mandible. Macroorchidism (large testes) is also a frequent finding, particularly in the postpubertal individual.

Diagnosis of the fragile-X syndrome is confirmed by chromosome analysis. Affected males as well as one-third of carrier females demonstrate a characteristic finding on the X chromosome. The distal end of the long arm of the chromosome is pinched off and in many cases has actually broken off. This "fragile" appearance of the X chromosome gives the syndrome its name (Fig. 7-3). The laboratory performing the study must be notified that the individual is being examined specifically for the fragile-X syndrome in order that they employ special procedures required to demonstrate the abnormality.

The fragile-X syndrome can be transmitted by either a male or female who carries on an X chromosome the gene responsible for the syndrome. A male with the fragile-X gene will pass it on to each of his daughters, but to none of his sons. A daughter of a woman with the fragile-X gene has a 50% chance of carrying the fragile X gene. Most males who have the gene have the condition described above, but some have functioned adequately enough in their lifestyles and occupations not to have been recognized by their families as having any disorder. Moreover, these individuals have had families, thus passing on the gene to their descendants.

A large number of the relatives of a person with this anomaly will be at risk for transmitting the gene and having offspring who are mentally retarded. Thus it is the responsibility of the physician who made the diagnosis to disseminate this information to members of the patient's family and to offer them genetic counseling.

The pedigree in Figure 7-4 shows how a large number of individuals in one family may be affected by the fragile-X syndrome. Any two members of the family who are at risk for having affected children, or who already have had affected children, may be so distantly related that they do not know each other. It is up to the physician, together with the family, to explore the genealogy and attempt to contact the various branches of the extended family.

Optimal methods for prenatal diagnosis, carrier detection, and treatment of this condition are all subjects of ongoing research.

THE ROLE OF THE GENETICIST

The Geneticist as Consultant

It should be apparent from the above discussion that much of the activity that constitutes the genetic approach is an integral part of the routine evaluation and management of a patient with developmental disabilities. The primary care physician should be capable of performing a physical examination and recognizing phenotypic abnormality as well as obtaining a thorough family history. Once the diagnosis is made, it is important that accurate genetic information and estimates of risk are provided. This often requires the expertise of someone who has specialized training in genetic principles and in genetic counseling.

Most clinical geneticists are physicians who received their initial training in pediatrics (less commonly in internal medicine or obstetrics) and who have special interest in genetic disease. Others, with Ph.D.s in genetics, also provide genetic services. Medical genetics is one of the newest medical subspecialties, and there are relatively few formal training programs. The establishment of the American Board of Medical Genetics in 1981 formalized the specialty by requiring certification for training programs in clinical genetics, cytogenetics, and genetic counseling, and for certifying practitioners on the basis of training, experience, and examination.

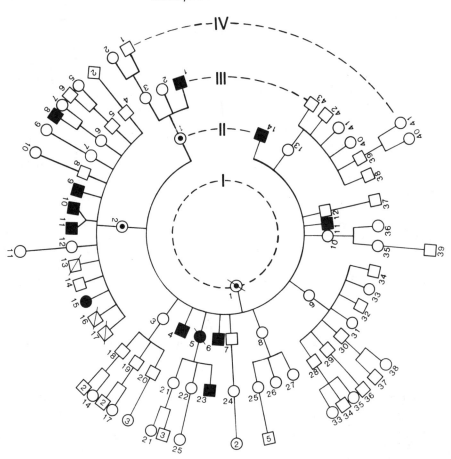

FIG. 7-4. Pedigree of family with fragile-X syndrome demonstrates how distantly related individuals might be affected by an X-linked condition. Ten males (black squares) and two females (black circles) are mentally retarded. In addition, four women with normal intelligence (circles with black dot) are obligate carriers.

Genetic counselors or genetic associates work closely with clinical geneticists. These individuals usually have masters degrees in genetic counseling. They are trained in genetic principles and techniques of interviewing and counseling.

Most clinical geneticists are allied with laboratories capable of modern chromosome analysis. The personnel in these laboratories should be trained in the various methods of chromosome preparation and banding and should know the most appropriate tests for demonstrating a suspected diagnosis. The most helpful chromosome laboratory is one from which the personnel will not merely turn out a laboratory result, but also be capable of providing suggestions for appropriate tests and further workup. As genetic laboratories mature in their capabilities and move to molecular diagnostic techniques, more selective requisitions will have to be made for each patient. A clinical description and family history should accompany every blood sample sent to a laboratory for chromosome analysis. If a specific diagnosis is suspected, this should be noted so that the laboratory will use the appropriate techniques for demonstrating the associated abnormality.

The decision to refer a patient and family to a genetic consultant will depend on the knowledge and expertise of the referring physician. As a general guide, referral to a clinical geneticist is indicated by a need for (1) confirmation or assistance in establishing an etiologic diagnosis; (2) assurance of a comprehensive and adequate family history; (3) assistance in interpretation of a family tree; (4) determination of the persons at risk for having affected children and the magnitude of risk; (5) discussion with the family concerning the mode of transmission of a disorder and other genetic factors; (6) assistance in setting up carrier testing and prenatal diagnosis procedures; and (7) discussion of reproductive options for couples determined to be at risk.

The Genetic Approach in an Institutional Setting

A large percentage of individuals living in institutions for mentally retarded persons do not have an etiologic diagnosis. During the process of admission most had an evaluation of some sort; this probably included all the appropriate screening tests for mental retardation available at the time. The majority of individuals in most institutions were born or admitted prior to 1960. Since that year, we have witnessed the initiation of newborn screening for PKU and other metabolic defects, a maturation of cytogenetic techniques with the introduction of chromosome banding, and the recognition of the fragile-X syndrome. With these advances more individuals can be diagnosed as having genetic conditions. There should be a continued concern for the patient and his relatives in this regard. Although specific treatment for genetic diseases is not available, the mentally retarded adult can benefit if the attendant staff has a better understanding of the diagnosis or behavioral features. In addition, relatives who may be planning families must be informed if they are at risk for having children with conditions that cause mental retardation, especially if the option for prenatal diagnosis is available.

Attending to genetic concerns within an institution must take into consideration circumstances not encountered in the community-based practice of medicine. First, information gathering is more difficult. The parents of many residents are deceased or unavailable. The family histories documented in admission records are often sketchy and have not been updated. Second, although establishing a genetic diagnosis may not greatly benefit the individual in the institution, one must seriously consider that there may be relatives somewhere who might benefit from learning a genetic diagnosis. Because contact between family members and the individual who is institutionalized is often minimal, a special effort must be made to locate people who may be at risk.

Within institutions today there is an honest and appropriate concern for the privacy of residents. The rights of the mentally retarded adult must be respected. However, although the mentally retarded individual might not always benefit directly from a genetic evaluation, the rights of other family members must also be taken into consideration. The benefits of genetic evaluation outweigh any potential risks so long as any diagnostic procedures employed meet the standards of quality and appropriate medical care.

The physician who cares for mentally retarded persons in an institution should seek an etiologic diagnosis for each of his patients. He should keep abreast of new developments in the field of genetics that may provide new diagnoses, and he should continue to update family information, which can assist in making a diagnosis. The birth of another affected individual, for example, might reveal the mode of inheritance.

GENETICS AND COMPREHENSIVE HEALTH CARE

As advances continue to be made in genetics, the physician caring for individuals with developmental disabilities will have to become more knowledgeable in this area. As mentioned already, there is not always a clear distinction between environmental and genetic factors in the etiology of developmental disability. Table 7-4 shows the etiologic classification used in the Developmental Evaluation Clinic at the Children's Hospital in Boston and the experience with over 2,000 children over a 16-year period. Although those listed as "Hereditary issues" are clearly such, those children presenting with "early influences on embryonic development" almost certainly include many in which there were predominant hereditary factors as well as those in which an environmental insult predominated. At present it is not always possible to separate these. More telling is the high percentage of children for whom it is not possible to determine a cause or even to suspect a likely cause on the basis of history and examination. It is hoped that, in the future, capabilities will improve for diagnosing as well as preventing developmental disabilities. In the meantime one should never

Table 7-4. *Diagnostic Classification of Developmental Disabilities (2,536 Children with Mental Retardation Examined in the Developmental Evaluation Clinic at the Children's Hospital, Boston, 1967 to 1983)*

Classification	Number (%)
Hereditary issues	121 (5)
Early influences on embryonic development	812 (32)
Other pregnancy problems and perinatal morbidity	276 (11)
Acquired childhood disease	112 (4)
Environmental and behavioral problems	442 (17)
Unknown causes	773 (31)

close the book on children or adults whose diagnoses are undetermined. The search for a diagnosis should be an ongoing quest; it should be the first listing on the individual's problem or needs list and should be addressed at least annually. Meaningless diagnoses such as "congenital encephalopathy" or "familial retardation" should not be used. If the diagnosis is unknown, it should be clearly listed as such.

The two processes that comprise the genetic approach, evaluation and genetic counseling, relate closely to the responsibilities of the primary care physician. In performing these functions, however, the physician must broaden his scope to recognize the entire family as his patient, and consider prevention rather than treatment as the primary concern. Although the mechanism of how genes cause disease is poorly understood, and ways of correcting genetic processes even more elusive, our knowledge regarding identifying and ameliorating certain genetic disorders is expanding at a rapid pace. The knowledge that is currently available can be invaluable to the families of developmentally disabled individuals. Thus, consideration of the genetic aspects of an individual's developmental disabilities should be an integral part of his or her comprehensive health care.

The author wishes to thank Dr. Ricardo Barrera and his Macintosh for assistance with the illustrations and Dr. Dianne Abuelo for reviewing the manuscript.

REFERENCES

1. American Society of Human Genetics Ad Hoc Committee on Genetic Counseling: Genetic counseling. Am. J. Hum. Genet., 27:240, 1975.
2. Leonard, C.O.: Counseling of parents of a child with meningocele. Pediatr. Rev., 4:317, 1983.
3. Ludman, M.D., Gilbert, F., and Hirschhorn, K.: Risk of recurrence of chromosomal abnormalities. Pediatr. Rev., 6:141, 1984.
4. Riccardi, V.M.: The Genetic Approach to Human Disease. New York, Oxford University Press, 1977.
5. Skinner, R.: Genetic counseling. *In* Principles and Practice of Medical Genetics. Edited by A.E.H. Emery, and D.L. Rimoin. New York, Churchill Livingstone, 1983, p. 1430.

ADDITIONAL READING

Emery, A.E.H., and Rimoin, D.L. (eds.): Principles and Practice of Medical Genetics (two volumes). New York, Churchill Livingstone, 1983.

> An extensive compendium of genetic aspects of various disorders arranged by organ systems; also contains several chapters on basic areas such as genetic counseling, prenatal diagnosis, treatment of genetic diseases, and parentage testing.

Levine, M.D., Carey, W.B., Crocker, A.C., and Gross, R.T. (eds.): Developmental-Behavioral Pediatrics (Chapter 18, Heredity, development, and behavior, by J.G. Leroy, and Chapter 19, Chromosomal determinants, by P.S. Gerald, and D. Meryash. Philadelphia, W.B. Saunders, 1975.

> The first major textbook in developmental and behavioral pediatrics; covers all aspects of the field and includes practical guides to consideration of genetic aspects of developmental disability and workup of the dysmorphic child.

McKusick, V.A.: Mendelian Inheritance in Man. 6th Ed. Baltimore, Johns Hopkins University Press, 1983.

> The widely accepted definitive catalogue of all single-gene disorders that have been described, including those occurring frequently as well as those for which only several cases have been described; conditions are arranged by mode of inheritance and include abstracts from journal articles in which they were first reported.

Milunsky, A.: The Prevention of Genetic Disease and Mental Retardation. Philadelphia, W.B. Saunders, 1975.

> A good basic text of genetic principles as they apply to the individual with mental retardation.

Riccardi, V.M.: The Genetic Approach to Human Disease. New York, Oxford University Press, 1977.

> A good basic overview of genetic principles. Clearly written and directed to the clinician.

Smith, D.W.: Recognizable Patterns of Human Malformation. Philadelphia, W.B. Saunders, 1982.

> An encyclopedia of dysmorphology syndromes with good pictures and short reference lists for each condition.

8

NEUROLOGY

Norberto Alvarez, M.D.

EPILEPSY

Most children and adults with epilepsy have normal psychomotor development. A number of recent books include material on diagnosis and management of epilepsy (e.g., refs. 8, 19). This chapter will focus on epileptic disorders in persons with developmental disabilities. It is not within the scope of this chapter to discuss the intellectual or behavioral deterioration that may be seen in children or adults with normal intelligence after they have developed epilepsy.

BASIC PRINCIPLES AND CLASSIFICATION OF SEIZURES

Epilepsy is a symptom-complex that results from an "occasional excessive and disorderly discharge of nerve tissue."[39] The intensity and the extent of the neuronal discharge determine whether the epileptic event is limited to electroencephalographic changes alone or produces a clinical event (epileptic seizure). These seizures can have different topographies as presented in Table 8-1.[11]

Epileptic seizures are divided into two basic groups: partial and generalized. A third category, "unclassified," is reserved for cases in which data are incomplete or the seizures cannot be classified.

Partial Seizures

In partial seizures the neuronal discharges are limited to part of one cerebral hemisphere. When consciousness is not impaired the seizure is partial simple. When consciousness is impaired the seizure is partial complex. The complex partial forms are more likely to have bilateral brain involvement. A simple seizure may evolve into a complex seizure, and any seizure may become generalized.

Many of the clinical features of partial seizures are subjective; it is therefore difficult to diagnose them in an individual who is mentally retarded. Similar problems in diagnosis apply for complex partial seizures. It is not unusual for persons with mental retardation to exhibit periods of "loss of consciousness" or "detachment" with or without stereotyped behaviors that may simulate "psychomotor seizures." This makes the differential diagnosis with real epileptic seizures very difficult in some cases.

Generalized Seizures

Generalized seizures with predominantly motor manifestations are the most common in mentally retarded persons. It is probable that most are of the focal type with secondary generalization, but that the early focal component, the "aura," which is subjective, cannot be elicited. This is important because auras are said to occur in approximately 50% of patients with complex partial seizures[16] and in 15% of patients with generalized tonic-clonic seizures.[29] As Ajmone-Marsan and Gumnit[1] found in persons with normal IQs, the aura can be the only manifestation of an epileptic event. In some patients in their study the auras were followed by loss of consciousness with or without motor components. There was also a high incidence of visceral symptoms and disturbances of taste and/or smell. Auras may also take the form of fears, abdominal sensations, numbness, or visual disturbances.[16]

The problem of identifying the auras has not been systematically addressed in children or in adults with mental retardation. It is not known how often persons with mental retardation, who exhibit sudden, abrupt changes in behavior, not followed by any other recognizable clinical manifestation of epilepsy, have focal epileptiform changes in brain wave activity at the time of this event. In these circumstances the simultaneous recording of the questionable behavior and the electroencephalogram (EEG) is the best way to answer the question, but this is difficult to achieve.

Petit Mal Seizures

In its true sense the term petit mal should be restricted to the typical absence seizures, lasting 5 to 10 seconds at the most, with abrupt loss of consciousness followed by a rapid complete recovery with no postictal behavior. During the crisis the patient will usually present some associated signs, most commonly eyes blinking or arms jerking, and occasionally rigidity or loss of muscle tone. The other distinctive feature is the presence through the ictal event of generalized 3 cycles per second spike and wave discharges on the EEG. Often, however, the term petit mal is misused to refer to brief seizures of any kind. This usage is misleading because the typical absence seizures have a specific treatment and different prognosis. This type of seizure should, theoretically, occur as frequently in children with mental retardation as it does in the general population.

In the "atypical absence" the alteration of consciousness is less complete, onset is gradual, the seizure lasts longer, cessation is also gradual, and some confusion may follow. The EEG pattern is also different, characterized by a slow (2 to 2½ cps) spike and wave pattern during the ictal event and the presence of abnormalities between seizures. This type of seizure is more frequent in children with mental retardation.

Table 8-1. *International Classification of Epileptic Seizures*

I. Partial (focal, local) seizures

    A. Simple motor seizures (consciousness not impaired)
- 1. With motor signs: focal with or without march, versive postural, phonatory
- 2. With sensory symptoms: somatosensory, visual, auditory, olfactory, gustatory, vertiginous
- 3. With automatic symptoms or signs: epigastric sensations, pallor, sweating, flushing, piloerection, pupillary dilatation
- 4. With psychic symptoms (rarely occur without impairment of consciousness): dysphasic, dysmnesic (deja vu), cognitive (e.g., dreamy states), distortions of time sense, affective (e.g., fear, anger), illusions (e.g., macropsia, micropsia), structure hallucinations (e.g., music, scenes)

    B. Complex partial seizures (so-called "temporal lobe or psychomotor seizures," consciousness impaired)
- 1. Simple partial onset, followed by impairment of consciousness
  - a. With simple partial features (described in A1–A4) followed by impairment of consciousness
  - b. With automatisms
- 2. With impairment of consciousness at onset
  - a. With impairment of consciousness only
  - b. With automatisms

    C. Partial seizures evolving to secondarily generalized seizures (tonic-clonic, tonic, or clonic)
- 1. Simple partial seizures (as described in A) evolving to generalized seizures
- 2. Complex partial seizures (as described in B) evolving to generalized seizures
- 3. Simple partial seizures evolving to complex partial seizures, evolving to generalized seizures

II. Generalized seizures (convulsive or nonconvulsive)

    A. 1. Absence (petit mal) seizures: impairment of consciousness only, or with clonic, atonic, or tonic component, or with automatisms or automatic component (more than one component may be observed)
- 2. Atypical absence: may have changes in tone that are more pronounced than in A1 and onset and/or cessation that is not abrupt

    B. Myoclonic seizures

    C. Clonic seizures

    D. Tonic seizures

    E. Tonic-clonic seizures

    F. Atonic seizures (astatic seizures) (Combination of the above may occur, e.g., B and F; B and E)

III. Unclassified epileptic seizures

From International League Against Epilepsy. Commission on Classification and Terminology: Proposal for revised clinical and electroencephalographic classification of epileptic seizures. Epilepsy, 22:489, 1981.

Myoclonic Seizures

Myoclonic seizures are characterized by brief involuntary muscle contractions, involving one or several muscles, that may or may not produce body movements. Myoclonus may or may not be epileptic in origin. Myoclonus can be one of the most frequent causes of pseudoseizures.[52]

Tonic Seizures

Tonic seizures consist of a stiffening of muscle groups, usually of brief duration (10 or 15 seconds to a minute), with changes in level of consciousness if the patient is awake. They frequently occur during sleep, more often in non-REM periods, and can disrupt the sleep cycle. Usually the whole body is involved, and the patient will raise his arms and flex his legs. Some clonic twitching can be seen at the end of the seizure. This is a frequent seizure type in children with brain damage.

Atonic Seizures

Atonic seizure refers to a sudden loss of muscle tone, followed by a fall. A person undergoing an atonic seizure collapses like a marionette when all its strings are cut at once. This is an-

Table 8-2. *Types of Seizures Found at Wrentham State School*

Type		Number
Generalized		
Tonic-clonic		74
Tonic		30
Myoclonic, akinetic, atypical absence		25
Myoclonic, typical absence		2
Focal		
With generalization		56
Without generalization		30
Unclassified		30
	Total	247

From Alvarez, N., and Hazlett, J.: Seizure management with minimal medications in institutionalized mentally retarded epileptics. A prospective study: First report after 4½ years of follow-up. Clin. Electroencephalogr., *14*:164, 1983.

The seizures were classified following the international classification of epileptic seizures. Most of the clinical information was obtained from descriptions by staff. In several cases the epileptic seizures were observed by medical staff or at time of EEG recording. Videotape recording and radiotelemetry were used in a few patients. Direct information from patients was almost nil due to the degree of mental retardation. It is possible that some patients classified as having generalized tonic-clonic or generalized tonic seizures in fact had focal seizures with secondary generalization. The unclassified group consisted mostly of patients with infrequent seizures.

other type of seizure frequently seen in children with brain damage.

"Minor Motor Seizures"

In the past this term was used in reference to myoclonic, atonic, short-lasting tonic seizures with or without "atypical absence," and it can still be found in some textbooks and in old medical records. The term has been abandoned by epileptologists. It should no longer be used, because it describes the epileptic event very poorly. The word "minor" is misleading, suggesting a benign course, which is usually not the case with these seizures.

Mixed Seizures

So far I have described seizures as isolated events, but in practice more than one type of seizure may coexist in the same patient.

A paradigm of epileptic disorders, as they present in children with brain damage, is the Lennox-Gastaut syndrome.[28] This consists of a combination of atypical absence, myoclonic seizures, atonic seizures, tonic seizures, and episodes of generalized tonic-clonic seizures. This clinical picture starts at an early age, is strongly associated with brain damage, and usually responds poorly to antiepileptic treatment. Even though this syndrome is seen in only 10% of epileptic children, it is frequently observed in children with brain damage. It can also extend into adulthood.

Table 8-2 shows the types of epileptic seizures Hazlett and I found in a survey of an institutionalized population of individuals with mental retardation.[3]

EPIDEMIOLOGY

Methodological Problems in Evaluating Surveys

Even though it is generally appreciated that there is a close relationship between brain damage, mental retardation, and epileptic disorders, it has been difficult to determine the prevalence and incidence of epileptic disorders in persons with mental retardation.

Epidemiologic studies have run into serious methodological difficulties. One of the main problems has been to define mental retardation and epilepsy. For epidemiologic purposes, mental retardation can be defined either on the basis of IQ (psychometric criterion) or on the basis of criteria established for admission to institutions or programs for the mentally retarded (administrative criteria). Both approaches have limitations. For example, if performed in a large population, a study in which the psychometric criterion is used requires intense use of manpower. It is also probable that some children with sociocultural disadvantage will be classified as mentally retarded. Use of administrative criteria facilitates epidemiologic studies because the study population is defined, but children with mental retardation and epilepsy who are not of school age will be excluded. Studies using administrative criteria will also be influenced by the admission criteria used in each situation: systems with more resources are likely to admit more children with mental retardation and epilepsy.

It can also be difficult to define epilepsy in specific population groups, especially when the group is large. Much of the information in such a survey would need to be obtained on a retrospective basis or from clinicians who may have different diagnostic criteria—for example, some authors will include children with febrile seizures. In some epidemiologic studies it is not specified how the diagnosis of epilepsy was made or what clinical forms of epilepsy were included. It is also probable that the nonconvulsive forms of epilepsy are underrepresented in some studies.

The populations in which studies are done also affect the results. Studies done in community settings give different results compared to those done in institutions, and among the latter the results vary according to whether the institution includes epilepsy as a criterion for admission or exclusion. Studies done in institutions may also reveal a predominance of the more severe forms of epilepsy, because the most profoundly handicapped, who usually have the most severe forms of epilepsy, tend to predominate in institutions.

The age of the patient at the time of the survey should also be considered. Some forms of epilepsy associated with severe brain damage manifest frequently, and sometimes only, at an early age (e.g., infantile spasms), or are associated with serious congenital malformations that result in early death. These children are not represented in epidemiological studies of school-age children. Adults with later-onset epilepsy are also excluded.

Some of these problems can be avoided with prospective studies, but these are difficult to organize, require intensive use of resources, and a considerable number of patients, usually with the more severe forms of epilepsy, are lost to follow-up.

Down syndrome is a good example of the methodological difficulties encountered in the evaluation of epileptic disorders in persons with mental retardation. In general the prevalence of epilepsy in persons with Down syndrome is higher than in the general population.[55] There are two peaks of incidence of epilepsy, the first in early infancy and the second in the fourth or fifth decade of life. The first peak, with a predominance of infantile spasms and/or myoclonic seizures, is probably the consequence of superimposed brain damage or cerebral dysgenesis. During school age, adolescence, and early adulthood, and excluding convulsive disorders related to cerebrovascular accidents, usually associated with cyanotic heart disease, the prevalence decreases because the infantile spasms resolve and children with severe congenital malformations die. In the fourth and fifth decades, generalized tonic-clonic seizures are an early sign of the Alzheimer's degeneration that affects a number of patients with Down syndrome.[50] In later stages tonic-clonic seizures are replaced by myoclonic seizures.

Table 8-3[12,22,25,35,38,42,53,59,61,67] summarizes a number of epidemiologic studies of the prevalence of epilepsy in persons with mental retardation. In spite of the limitations already mentioned, some generalizations are possible.

Epilepsy and the Etiology of Mental Retardation

Patients with mental retardation are not a homogeneous group, and different etiologies of mental retardation have different epileptogenic potentials. Table 8-4[12] illustrates the differences. For example, epileptic attacks are more frequent when there is damage to the cerebral cortex than when the mental retardation is the result of chromosomal aberrations. The prevalence of epilepsy in children with cerebral palsy may vary from as low as 22%[64] to as high as 58%.[70] The spastic forms have a much higher prevalence than the dystonic choreoathetotic forms (Table 8-5).[13,35,38,65] In addition, the epileptic crises of the extrapyramidal forms have a better prognosis with more spontaneous resolutions (Table 8-6).[12] In some forms of epilepsy, the underlying etiology and age are interrelated (Table 8-7).[37]

Age at Time of First Seizure

There is a higher prevalence of brain damage and mental retardation in newborns who undergo their first seizure in the first 3 days of life than in those who experience them in the second half of the first week, probably because of the higher incidence of metabolic disorders in the latter.[47] Also, children with mental retardation present with seizures early in life. Richardson et al.[59] found that 68% of children with IQs lower than 50 and only 5% with IQs higher than 60 had their first seizures in the first year of life. In an adult population with mental retardation and epilepsy, the seizures began in the first year of life in 46% and before the fifth year in 74%.

In an institutionalized population of around 1,200 people (mean age 38), only 31 new cases of seizures were observed in a 4-year period. In several, acute pathology was found to be responsible. It is unusual for a person with mental retardation to present with a first epileptic seizure after adolescence, and if that happens, other causes should be explored.

Age and Prevalence of Epilepsy

The prevalence of epilepsy is higher in early infancy and declines in adolescence. This can, in part, be explained by the mortality in the early ages, loss of cases to follow-up, and some spontaneous remissions.[13,31] Prevalence again increases in early adulthood.

In the Camberwell study[12] it was found that children with IQs lower than 50 and under 5 years of age had an incidence of seizures of 25% in the year preceding the study. Seizure incidence was 18% in those between 5 and 10 years, and 5% in those between 10 and 15 years. In an institutionalized population, Richardson et al.[59] found a prevalence of 24% in those younger than 16 years and 37% in those older than 16 years.

Table 8-3. *Epidemiologic Studies on Prevalence of Epilepsy in Mentally Retarded Persons*

Author(s)	Percent Epileptic	Study Population
Ingram et al.[38]	32 (Edinburgh) 38 (Dundee)	Edinburgh: 125 persons 8–22 years of age with cerebral palsy, identified by 2 previous studies. Reevaluation by interview and IQ test. Dundee: 75 persons, same criteria
Eyman et al.[22]	35 (Institution A) 34 (Institution B) 21 (Institution C)	6,029 persons: total populations of 3 institutions for the mentally retarded in the U.S. excluding nonambulatory, deaf, blind
Corbett et al.[12]	23 (IQ 50–70) 23 (IQ 35–49) 28 (IQ 20–34) 50 (IQ <20)	155 persons 0–15 years of age in Camberwell, England, included in study on basis of IQ tests
Richardson et al.[59]	27	192 persons transferred from regular schools to school for retarded before age 16. Diagnosis of epilepsy on basis of 1 or more convulsions
	20 (IQ 60–75) 39 (IQ 50–59) 47 (IQ <50)	49 persons with IQ <75 in 2 evaluations at 7 and 9 years of age
	12	Prospective study: patients 0–22 years of age were included on basis of IQ test. Clinical data obtained from parents and examination of patients
Alvarez and Hazlett[3]	28	860 persons transferred from regular schools to school for retarded in Wrentham, MA before age 16
Floyer[25]	29	Children with cerebral palsy
Kirman[42]	45	Children with cerebral palsy
Hilliard and Kirman[35]	45	Children with cerebral palsy
Tizard and Grad[67]	20 14	Institutionalized mentally retarded persons Mentally retarded, not institutionalized
Payne, Johnson, and Abelson[53]	31	Institutionalized mentally retarded persons
Rutter, Tizard, and Whitmore[61]	16	Children with cerebral palsy
Skatvedt[64]	22	Children with cerebral palsy
Woods[70]	58	Children with cerebral palsy

Gender and Prevalence of Epilepsy

Epilepsy and mental retardation are both found more often in males than in females. There is also a higher prevalence of epilepsy in males with mental retardation,[12,33,60] but it is not clear whether this pattern reflects the trend in the general population or is the result of the causes that produced the mental retardation.

Emotional and Psychiatric Problems

Even though the idea of the epileptic personality is no longer accepted, recent studies suggest that certain factors may predispose both children and adults to emotional and psychiatric disorders. One identifiable factor is brain damage. The risk is even higher in children with epileptic crises.[30] Studies done in patients with normal IQ suggest that some personality traits are more frequently observed in epileptic individuals than in nonepileptics, and, among the epileptic group, more often in those with focal epilepsy in the limbico-temporal area.[69] If these findings hold true, common traits should be found in persons with mental retardation and epilepsy.

Analysis of this problem is complex. Extensive brain lesions are more frequently associated with lower IQs, severe epileptic disorders, usually more' than one type of seizure, and polypharmacy. These factors alone could increase the risk of psychopathology in the patients.[17,34] Eyman et al.,[22] in a study done in three institutions for the mentally retarded, found that aggression and hyperactivity were more common in persons with epilepsy. In the same group there was a high incidence of language disorders and motor

Table 8-4. *Percentage of Children with Seizures for Different Diagnoses in Children with IQ Less Than 50*

Diagnosis	Number	Seizures (%)
Infections and intoxications	23	34
Trauma and other physical agents	9	33
Metabolic	6	51
Gross brain disease	8	100
Other prenatal causes	16	41
Chromosomal	35	16
Others with family history	13	23
Others with no family history	30	30

From Corbett, J.A., Harris, R., and Robinson, R.G.: Epilepsy. *In* Mental Retardation and Developmental Disabilities, Vol. VIII. Edited by J. Wortis. New York, Brumer Mazel, 1975, pp. 79-111.

coordination problems in the upper limbs, suggesting that the epileptic group had a higher incidence of brain damage. In the Camberwell study[12] there was no significant difference in prevalence of emotional or behavioral problems in their mentally retarded population with or without epilepsy. In that sample, only 25% of the subjects were living in institutions, most of them had their seizures during childhood, and the seizures were more severe in the children with the most serious forms of cerebral palsy, the very group in whom the manifestations of emotional and behavior problems are most difficult to diagnose.

In summary, and in spite of the methodological limitations already mentioned, it is obvious

Table 8-5. *Percentage of Mentally Retarded Patients with Brain Damage and Epilepsy in Several Studies*

Type of Cerebral Palsy	Authors			
	Crowthers and Paine[13]	Hilliard and Kirman[35]	Ingram et al.[38]	Stephen and Hawks[65]
Hemiplegic				
Congenital	55	17	51	17
Acquired	72	—	—	—
Quadriplegic, diplegic	33	50	31	50
Extrapyramidal	23	4	25	4
Other	—	29	15	29

Dashes in table indicate no information available.

Table 8-6. *Spontaneous Resolution of Epileptic Seizures*

Type of Cerebral Palsy	Spontaneous Resolution (%)
Hemiplegic	
Congenital	47
Acquired	24
Quadriplegic, diplegic	61
Extrapyramidal	91

From Corbett, J.A., Harris, R., and Robinson, R.G.: Epilepsy. *In* Mental Retardation and Developmental Disabilities, Vol. VIII. Edited by J. Wortis. New York, Brumer Mazel, 1975, pp. 79-111.

that there is a higher incidence of epilepsy in individuals with mental retardation. These epileptic disorders are more predominant and severe in individuals with more severe intellectual and motor deficits. Most of the epileptic disorders in the mentally retarded start in childhood, before adolescence. Epileptic disorders that start after adolescence may be due to other causes not related to the primary etiology responsible for the retardation. The different causes that produce mental retardation have different epileptogenic potentials, and even in patients of the same etiologic category, e.g., cerebral palsy, there are subgroups with different prevalences and prognoses. It is also probable that there is a higher prevalence of emotional and psychiatric problems in persons with brain damage, mental retardation, and epilepsy.

Table 8-7. *Age and Frequency of Seizures in Patients with Tuberous Sclerosis*

	Number of Patients	
Age in Years	With Seizures	Without Seizures
0–2	7	
3–5	21	
6–10	29	2
11–15	14	
16–20	9	
21–30	2	5
31–40		6
41–51		2
All ages	82	15

From Hunt, A.: Tuberous sclerosis: A survey of 97 cases. I. Seizures, pertussis immunization, and handicap. Dev. Med. Child. Neurol., 25:346, 1983.

CLINICAL AND THERAPEUTIC ASPECTS OF EPILEPSY IN THE MENTALLY RETARDED

Clinical Aspects

Problems in Diagnosis

With the possible exception of children and adults with mild mental retardation, it is almost impossible to obtain valid information about seizures from the patients. On some occasions the physician might have the chance to observe an epileptic attack, but an attack hardly ever occurs at the time of an EEG recording. In practice the diagnosis is made on the basis of information obtained from third parties, e.g., parents, teachers, or friends, so maximal effort should be made to educate these persons about the patient. Failure to do so would lead to inadequate descriptions such as "petit mal seizure" for what in reality is a short tonic seizure. It is more important that observers describe the event and the circumstances that preceded and followed it; diagnostic terms can be applied by the physician.

In some circumstances the diagnosis of epilepsy should be made cautiously. The presence of "generalized tonic convulsions" or "focal tonic convulsions," at times associated with "clonic components," when reported in persons with marked spasticity, is one such situation. These patients often present tonic crisis as a consequence of pain, skin lesion, abdominal distention, urinary tract infections (which are frequent in children and adults with neurogenic bladder and spasticity), chronic constipation, and other situations that produce massive spinal cord stimulation with consequent massive reflex response. Environmental factors should be closely monitored: for example, the comment of the mother or nurse that the "tonic seizures" subsided with an enema should not be regarded lightly. This situation should be suspected in cases resistant to antiepileptic medications, when the crisis often occurs under similar conditions, when the interictal EEG is consistently normal or with isolated epileptiform activities, and always if the "ictal" EEG is normal. Other precipitating factors have to be excluded before committing the patient to long-term treatment with antiepileptic medication, which would probably fail anyway.

The use of psychotropic medications presents an additional problem. These medications are said to decrease the threshold for seizures,[15] although this has not been an important problem in my experience. More commonly the presence of abnormal movements (dystonic posturing, oculogyric crises) can be mistaken for convulsive epileptic crises. Extrapyramidal motor involvement that produces slowness in motor responses with periods of "lack of response" or "absent look" might mimic "petit mal seizures" or "psychomotor crisis." In my experience most of the episodes of "absence" or "staring spells" reported in mentally retarded persons have not been necessarily epileptic.

Pseudoseizures (sometimes referred as hysterical seizures or hysteroepilepsy) are behaviors that resemble epileptic seizures and are frequently observed in mentally retarded persons. Pseudoseizures have been studied extensively in persons with normal intelligence,[23] but little has been done in the mentally retarded.[36] In our experience 25 to 30% of the patients referred for evaluation of epileptic disorders were cases of pseudoseizures.[52]

The diagnosis of epilepsy is even more complex in patients who present with sudden, unexpected, and unexplained changes in behavior. Some of them also have abnormal EEGs. In these circumstances the diagnosis of epilepsy can be very difficult because the behaviors can be a manifestation of the underlying seizure disorder. I have already commented on how frequently subjective symptoms are reported in nonretarded people with epilepsy in association with simple and partial complex seizures, and on the difficulties in diagnosing "auras" in retarded individuals. One wonders therefore what the reaction would be of a mentally retarded person who has "auras" of visual or auditory origin or who experiences déjà vu phenomena.

Electroencephalography and Other Diagnostic Procedures

Even experienced clinicians have problems in differentiating epileptic from nonepileptic behaviors in mentally retarded individuals. In these circumstances electroencephalography can be of great help; presently it is the most useful diagnostic procedure for the diagnosis of epilepsy. Even though several EEG patterns have been identified that are frequently associated with epileptic disorders (epileptiform patterns),[51] the EEG tracing alone is not enough; in some situations it can even be misleading. Electroencephalography reaches its maximum diagnostic potential when a supposedly epileptic behavior is simultaneous with the EEG recording. Absence of an epileptiform pattern during an ictal event strongly suggests that the questionable behavior is not epileptic in origin and probably will

not improve with antiepileptic medications. On the other hand, presence of an epileptic pattern supports the diagnosis of epilepsy. As mentioned previously, encephalographic recording of an ictal event is a rare occurrence, and diagnoses usually have to be made with interictal EEG findings. Several factors contribute to this situation. Epileptic seizures are, in many cases, not so frequent as to appear at the time of an EEG recording, because the standard EEG records only about 1 hour of brain activity. Besides, the standard EEG does not allow much freedom of movement—the patient is usually restricted to a bed. Sedation, which is indicated for the standard EEG, is not very useful in this situation because it may suppress the behavior in question. Recent technical advances that allow for long-term EEG monitoring in a free environment have helped to overcome some of these problems.

Two of these methods, portable cassette recordings[62] and radiotelemetry,[54] will be discussed here. With the portable cassette recording system the EEG is recorded on a standard C-120 audio cassette that is carried by the patient, with amplifiers small enough to be hidden under the hair. This system is suitable for long-term EEG recording at home, work, or school without disrupting everyday activities. With this method the clinical correlation of behavior and the EEG is done through behavioral descriptions obtained from relatives, friends, teachers, and the patient. This method is limited in that the temporal correlation might not be accurate; also, it may be difficult to use the cassette recording system with some individuals who are mentally retarded.

Electroencephalography by radiotelemetry, when combined with video recording, provides a composite record of the patient's image and a simultaneous EEG tracing that can be stored for later analysis.[6] With this technique we have been able to evaluate even persons with profound mental retardation for several hours. This method has the advantage that activities or situations that are associated with the behavior under evaluation can be replicated in the laboratory. It is also possible to have a good temporal correlation between the EEG and the behaviors under evaluation. We have found this technique useful in documenting the presence of pseudoepileptic behavior in mentally retarded persons, often in association with real epileptic seizures.[52] The EEG evaluation can be complemented by other physiologic measurements such as respiration or heart rate.

Despite these advances, electroencephalography has its limitations. The presence of epileptiform patterns in the interictal EEG is suggestive but not diagnostic of epilepsy, and even when the child has epilepsy, all his unexplained behaviors are not necessarily epileptic in origin. In fact, epileptics who have mental retardation do have frequent behaviors that are erroneously considered epileptic and treated as such. In these children, good clinical judgment is very important.

A somewhat different situation is presented when the EEG is persistently normal. In this case the behaviors are probably not epileptic.

Positron emission tomography (PET) can compliment the EEG by showing hypometabolic areas in suspected epileptic regions. Presently the availability is limited, which limits the clinical experience, but the studies already published[18,21] suggest that PET may be important in the diagnosis, therapy, and management of epileptic individuals, as well as in other neurologic disorders.[44]

Treatment

Drug Therapy

Some antiepileptic drugs are seizure-type specific, i.e., a drug that is effective in one type of seizure may be ineffective in another. In addition, individuals vary in their reactions to antiepileptic drugs: a medication effective in one type of seizure in one patient might be ineffective for the same type of seizure in a different person.

There is some degree of personal preference in choosing antiepileptic drugs, but epileptologists generally agree on the indications for the most common antiepileptic medications.

Phenytoin, phenobarbital, primidone, and carbamazepine are the major drugs for the treatment of the most common types of epileptic disorders. They are all effective for generalized tonic, tonic-clonic, and partial seizures; it is not clear whether one is superior to the others in the treatment of any particular type of seizure.

The benzodiazepines (e.g., diazepam, clonazepam, and clorazepate dipotassium) have similar actions. Clonazepam is more commonly used for chronic treatment, whereas diazepam is mostly reserved for medical emergencies. These medications can be useful in children with myoclonic, akinetic seizures, and in typical and atypical absences. The clinical results are more contradictory in the case of tonic-clonic, simple partial, and complex partial seizures, where some studies with clorazepate have shown some improvement.

Ethosuximide is particularly effective in treatment of typical absence (petit mal) seizures and is still considered the drug of first choice. It is also highly effective in myoclonic, akinetic, and atonic seizures, but it is not as useful in focal, tonic, or tonic-clonic seizures.

Valproic acid is as effective as ethosuximide for the same type of seizures, and it is also effective in patients with primary generalized tonic-clonic seizures and in patients with photoconvulsive epilepsy. Its effects are much less impressive with other types of seizures.

Acetazolamide, an inhibitor of carbonic anhydrase in the brain, is effective in treatment of absence seizures. Because the effect of the drug disappears after a few months to 2 years of continuous therapy, its use as a primary medication is limited. It is also used as an adjuvant in tonic-clonic seizures. Acetazolamide is much less effective in atonic and myoclonic seizures, and it is not effective in simple or partial complex seizures. The tolerance for the drug is very good.

Other less-known drugs, which have only limited use in refractory cases (paraldehyde, trimethadione, paramethadione, phenacemide, and ACTH) will not be discussed here.

METABOLISM OF ANTIEPILEPTIC DRUGS

Rational use of antiepileptic medications requires a basic knowledge of the pharmacology, biotransformation, and pharmacokinetics of these drugs. Some of this information is summarized in Table 8-8.[8,19] Some important concepts will be discussed briefly.

Elimination half-life refers to the time it takes for the concentration of the drug to be decreased by 50%. Drugs with a longer half-life require less-frequent doses and produce more stable blood levels.

At the steady state the same amount of medication that is administered is biotransformed and eliminated. Before the steady state is reached, the concentration of the medication continuously increases. After that, a given dose will produce a steady plasma level. It is at this moment that a given dose has its maximum therapeutic effect. This is also the time at which it is recommended to measure the plasma level. The time it takes to achieve the steady state is 4 to 5 times the half-life of the medication.

The therapeutic range of serum concentration consists of a low value, usually defined as the serum concentration, below which the therapeutic effect is minimal, and a high value, usually defined as the serum concentration above which side effects are observed or outweigh the

Table 8-8. *Pharmacological Data on Antiepileptic Drugs*

Drug Name	Dosage mg/kg	Dosage mg/day	Average Expected Serum Concentration (μg/ml)	Therapeutic Range of Serum Concentration (μg/ml)	Elimination Half-Life (hours) Adults	Elimination Half-Life (hours) Children	Time to Reach Steady State (days)	Protein Binding (%)
Phenytoin	5	300–400	15	10–20	10–34	5–14	7–28	69–96
Phenobarbital	2	120–180	20	15–40	46–136	37–73	14–21	40–60
Primidone	10	750–1000	6	5–12	6–18	5–11	4–7	0
Carbamazepine	15	1000–1200	6	4–12	14–27		3–4	66–89
Ethosuximide	15	1000–1250	60	40–100	20–60		7–10	0
Valproic acid	45	1500–2500	80	40–150	6–15		1–2	80–95
Clonazepam	0.03–0.1	2–7	Highly variable	0.005–0.07	20–40		—	47
Acetazolamide	10–20	1000–1500	—	10–14	Rapid phase 1½ Slow phase 10–15		—	83–95

Modified from Browne, T.R., and Feldman, R.G.: Epilepsy—Diagnosis and Management. Boston, Little, Brown, 1983; and Dreifuss, F.E.: Pediatric Epileptology. Classification and Management of Seizures in Childhood. Boston, John Wright PSG, 1983.

therapeutic benefits. These values should be used as a rough guideline. The main task is to define the optimum value for each individual, that is, the point of maximum therapeutic efficacy with a minimum of side effects. This can usually be done after several months of treatment. Since the plasma level varies in relation to the time of administration of the medication, it is recommended that blood be drawn at the same time in relation to administration of medication. We prefer to draw blood in the morning, withholding the medications. We obtain the "trough" level, that is, the lowest level for that dosage. Occasionally it is necessary to know the peak level, and in this case a second sample is obtained 2 to 3 hours after administration of the medication. Serum blood levels of the antiepileptic medications are part of the routine evaluation of epileptic patients. Frequency of measurement depends on the severity of the clinical picture, varying from once a year in well-controlled cases to weekly in poorly controlled individuals. Measurement of plasma levels is the best available method to measure the biotransformation and drug interactions of antiepileptic medications and to monitor patient compliance.

Protein binding refers to the amount of a substance bound to plasma proteins, mostly albumin. This has important implications because only the nonbound or "free" fraction of a drug is therapeutically active. The concentration of the free fraction changes following changes in the concentration of albumin or because of the presence of other drugs with stronger binding affinity. Increase in the free fraction does not necessarily change the total concentration of the drug. If the free fraction is higher than usual, toxic effects can be observed even though the total concentration is within the normal therapeutic range. Most laboratories measure the total concentration and not the free concentration of the drug, unless this is specifically requested. This consideration is especially important when phenytoin is combined with valproic acid.

Table 8-8 also shows the expected serum concentration for a given dose when the steady state is reached. If these values are not obtained, several possibilities should be considered. The most common situation is poor compliance. Compliance is not a common problem in institutionalized patients[2] or in those under close observation. Occasionally, poor compliance is observed in patients with serious behavior or psychiatric disorders. Poor compliance is most commonly seen in the outpatient clinic and in self-medicated mildly retarded persons under poor supervision. We have seen a few ruminators or chronic regurgitators who can keep medications in their mouths and spit them out later on. When this problem is isolated, one dose can be omitted or given parenterally. If the episodes are frequent, such patients should be kept either on medications that can be given parenterally or on oral medications with long half-lives, which can be administered less frequently.

Poor intestinal absorption is a possible cause of serum concentrations that are lower than expected and has been described for phenytoin. Low serum concentrations can be caused by an increased rate of metabolization (sometimes the result of enzymatic induction by the same antiepileptic medication), drug interactions, and the use of different drug formulations. Higher concentrations than expected have been described in relation to excessive intake, patients on the wrong dosage, individual variability, drug interactions, and hepatic diseases. Laboratory errors should be considered in both cases.

INDICATIONS FOR ANTIEPILEPTIC MEDICATION

The general principles already described are also valid for the mentally retarded epileptic, but some points deserve to be expanded.

There is no evidence that antiepileptics are useful in patients with brain damage if they are free of epileptic seizures, even in those with abnormal EEGs. It might be tempting to treat patients who have abnormal EEGs, but at present there is general agreement that antiepileptic treatment should be started only after clinical epileptic seizures have become evident.

It may be argued that antiepileptic medication might be useful in patients with difficult diagnostic problems or abnormal EEGs even if obvious seizures cannot be confirmed. I do not support the use of antiepileptic medication in these cases because of the difficulties inherent in the evaluation of the treatment and the dangers of polypharmacy. Electroencephalography is good for the diagnosis of epilepsy, but it is not so good for the evaluation of antiepileptic treatment. In a few exceptional cases, e.g., patients with sudden unexplained changes in behavior and abnormal EEGs, a trial of antiepileptic medication might be attempted, but this should be done under strict medical supervision, with a good baseline and quantification of the episodes that motivated the treatment. It is also recommended that the length of the treatment be determined at the outset; otherwise the medication could be prolonged unnecessarily. If possible, a placebo should be tried.

There is also a tendency to use antiepileptic medications because they have sedative and hypnotic effects, but this is an inappropriate use of these drugs. If such effects are needed, more appropriate medications are preferable.

In summary, the only valid indication for the chronic use of antiepileptic medications in mentally retarded persons with brain damage, with or without EEG abnormalities, is the presence of epileptic seizures.

BEGINNING OF ANTIEPILEPTIC DRUG THERAPY

It is not mandatory to start antiepileptic medications immediately after the first epileptic crisis. In many instances crises may be sporadic, isolated events, followed by long periods of remission that might last for months or even years. The potential risks of antiepileptic medications may outweigh the advantages, and the balance should always be evaluated.

Our goal is to limit the use of antiepileptic medications as much as possible. With the exception of patients in whom status epilepticus is the first manifestation of an epileptic disorder, we do not recommend starting antiepileptic treatment after the first attack. We consider treatment only after the second crisis, and then we reflect on several variables: the length of the seizure, the interval between the first and second seizure, and the presence or absence of EEG abnormalities. We recommend treatment in every case after the third convulsive crisis.

CHOICE OF ANTIEPILEPTIC MEDICATION

The epileptic crisis in the patient with mental retardation will probably be of the focal or multifocal type with secondary generalization; the primary (mostly genetic) form of epilepsy will be less frequent.

There is some disagreement among epileptologists about what drug should be used first. For some, carbamazepine has preference over phenytoin, and this over phenobarbitol. There is also no agreement about whether valproic acid should have preference over ethosuximide in cases of primary generalized epilepsy. At present there is little evidence to prove the superiority of one drug over the others, although there is enough evidence to prove that patients who fail on one of them might improve with one of the others.[56,58] A good deal of the decision about the drug to be used depends on the side effects. There are some suggestions that side effects are more common in children with brain damage, but some side effects, mostly those in the intellectual area, are so subtle[57] that they may not be relevant when dealing with persons with severe to profound mental retardation.

Table 8-9 shows the use of antiepileptic drugs at an institution for mentally retarded persons at the time of our first survey.[3] There is a predominance of patients on phenobarbitol and/or phenytoin. Most of these patients were started in antiepileptics many years ago, before new medications such as carbamazepine and valproic acid were introduced, and there was no need to

Table 8-9. *The Most Commonly Used Antiepileptic Drugs*

	Number of Patients	
Drug Name	July 1976	December 1980
Phenobarbital	47	73
Phenytoin	35	39
Primidone	10	17
Phenobarbital-phenytoin	50	28
Primidone-phenytoin	10	7
Phenytoin-diazepam	16	0
Phenobarbital-diazepam	11	0
Phenobarbital-phenytoin-diazepam	15	1
Total	189	167

From Alvarez, N., and Hazlett, J.: Seizure management with minimal medications in institutionalized mentally retarded epileptics. A prospective study: First report after $4\frac{1}{2}$ years of follow-up. Clin. Electroencephalogr., *14*:164, 1983.

change them. Besides, there are some advantages in the use of phenobarbitol and phenytoin as first-line drugs. Both have long half-lives (see Table 8-8), which makes it possible to use only one or two daily doses, improves compliance, and minimizes fluctuations in serum levels if omissions in administration of the medication occur. In addition, both medications can be given parenterally. Another factor to be considered is that phenobarbitol and phenytoin are relatively inexpensive (see Table 8-10).

MONOTHERAPY VERSUS POLYTHERAPY

Most patients with only one type of epileptic crisis can be controlled with one medication. In fact, in institutionalized individuals, there was improvement in psychomotor behavior and attention when the antiepileptic medications were decreased.[24,49] Two medications might be needed in children with more than one type of seizure, as could be the case in absence seizures and generalized tonic-clonic seizures.

It is recommended that treatment be started with only one antiepileptic medication, in a dose that is $\frac{1}{3}$ to $\frac{1}{4}$ of the total dose, which is increased every 3 to 4 days until the total dose is achieved. We routinely measure plasma levels when the medications have achieved the steady state, and we try to keep the patient within the therapeutic range. The number of epileptic crises is the only element we consider in evaluation of the therapeutic effect of the medication. A

Table 8-10. *Costs of Antiepileptic Medications in 1985*

Drug Name and Size of Capsule or Tablet	Cost per Thousand in U.S. Dollars
Phenobarbital 60 mg	7
Phenobarbital 100 mg	10
Primidone 250 mg	43
Phenytoin 50 mg	57
Phenytoin 100 mg	57
Acetazolamide 250 mg	56
Clonazepam 1 mg	180
Carbamazepine 200 mg	211
Ethosuximide 250 mg	202
Valproic acid 250 mg	230
Valproic acid 500 mg	435

second medication is started only if the patient shows toxic effects or no improvement with high levels of the first medication. If the second medication proves to be effective, the patient is kept on 2 medications for 6 months to 1 year, and after that the first medication is reduced. In 31 adult patients who developed epilepsy after admission to an institution, only 2 required 2 medications for a short period of time; one medication was enough to keep the other 29 patients seizure-free.

Table 8-11 shows our results in the reduction of polypharmacy between July 1976 and December 1980.[3] At the beginning of the study, 247 persons received 454 antiepileptic medications (mean 1.8 per patient). At the end, only 204 patients were taking antiepileptics and the mean was only 1.2 antiepileptic medications per patient. Our experience, which is consistent with the experience of others,[24,49,63] shows that it is possible to decrease the number of medications without detriment to the patient. Only a small number of patients needed 3 or more medications. In some, even massive doses of medications do not control the seizures. In these patients it is always necessary to confirm that one is dealing with epileptic seizures instead of pseudoseizures, that the blood levels of the medications are appropriate, and that side effects are carefully monitored.

In some cases it may be better to accept that the patient is beyond the reach of the available antiepileptic medications and that total control of the seizures is unobtainable, and then to limit the therapy to a realistic goal, e.g., total control of the grand mal generalized tonic-clonic seizures. There is no scientific evidence that patients who do not improve with three medications

Table 8-11. *Medications per Patient July 1976 to December 1980 (247 Patients)*

Number of Medications per Patient	July 1976	Dec. 1976	July 1977	Dec. 1977	July 1978	Dec. 1978	July 1979	Dec. 1979	July 1980	Dec. 1980
0	0	4	7	16	27	40	47	46	50	43
1	98	113	121	120	115	111	108	118	126	136
2	99	80	78	76	76	74	68	62	51	47
3	42	43	36	32	25	20	21	17	18	20
4	8	7	5	3	4	2	3	4	2	1
Mean	1.8	1.7	1.6	1.5	1.4	1.3	1.3	1.3	1.2	1.2

Modified from Alvarez, N., and Hazlett, J.: Seizure management with minimal medications in institutionalized mentally retarded epileptics. A prospective study: First report after 4½ years of follow-up. Clin. Electroencephalogr., *14:*164, 1983.

will be better with four or five medications, but there is evidence that there is an increase in side effects[57] and that reduction of polypharmacy might be associated with improvement of the seizure disorder.[63] This type of information should be transmitted to parents, teachers, and other members of the interdisciplinary team responsible for the patient's welfare. (Peer pressure on the primary care physician is one of the factors identified as leading to polypharmacy.[2,63])

WHEN TO SUSPEND ANTIEPILEPTIC MEDICATIONS

It is not clear whether epileptics with mental retardation should be kept on antiepileptics for the rest of their lives.

We have established the rule that, independent of the degree of mental retardation, psychomotor deficit, or EEG findings, antiepileptics are discontinued when the patient has completed a cycle of 5 years without any reported seizure. In these patients the medication is reduced at a rate of $\frac{1}{3}$ to $\frac{1}{4}$ of the total dosage every 3 to 4 months until total discontinuation in 9 months to 1 year. A long weaning period was elected to avoid withdrawal seizures. If the patient is on more than 1 medication, 1 drug is targeted at a time. When this is discontinued, a second medication is reduced, and so on, until all medications are stopped. If the patient develops seizures on only 1 medication, that medication is increased to previous levels and the attempt to discontinue the drug is terminated. If seizures occur while the patient is still on more than 1 medication, 1 of the medications not considered for discontinuation is increased, and the program proceeds as previously planned.

In the first 6 years of the implementation of this protocol, 70 patients were included. Fifty percent showed recurrence of seizures and were kept or restarted on antiepileptic medications. There were more recurrences among patients

with higher degrees of mental retardation and motor deficits, in those with EEG abnormalities, and among those with myoclonic seizures. Those in whom the diagnosis of seizure was never well confirmed (probably some who had pseudoseizures) predominated among the patients who remained seizure-free. Several of the patients whose seizures recurred had gone without medication for several years, and in most of those requiring medication, monotherapy in the lower therapeutic range was enough. More studies are needed in this area, but we still consider that the attempt to discontinue antiepileptic medications is justified in selected cases.

Both frequency and severity of seizures can increase when antiepileptic medications are decreased, particularly when this is done rapidly. The occurrence of withdrawal seizures is also observed in patients with poor compliance and is independent of the efficacy of the medications. Lack of recognition of this paradoxical effect leads to the perpetuation of polypharmacy. All the antiepileptic medications can present some withdrawal symptoms, but in our experience withdrawal seizures were observed most frequently with phenobarbitol and the benzodiazepines, and occasionally with valproic acid.

SIDE EFFECTS

There is a long and growing list of side effects associated with antiepileptic medications. Some are dose-related, some are the results of idiosyncratic reactions, and others are the consequence of chronic use.

In general most side effects are seen at the beginning of therapy and may improve spontaneously with time. Polytherapy potentiates side effects. Some side effects, like leukopenia, might improve spontaneously and do not necessarily require discontinuation. In other situations, as in the case of folic acid deficiency associated with phenytoin, there is a treatment but it is controversial. Other side effects do not have major clinical implications, e.g., hyperammonemia with valproic acid or increased alkaline phosphatase with phenobarbitol, or thyroid function test changes with phenytoin therapy, and merely require monitoring.

The following side effects are probably the results of idiosyncratic reactions: rashes, dermatitis, exfoliative dermatitis (Stevens-Johnson syndrome), leukopenia, plaquetopenia, pancytopenia, lupus erythematosus, pancreatitis, and acute hepatitis. These side effects are difficult to predict, most occurring at the beginning of therapy. When the reactions are severe the antiepileptic drug should be changed. Sometimes the idiosyncratic reaction is seen in the same patient with more than one drug.

Among the dose-related side effects, the most commonly found are drowsiness, somnolence, acute and chronic sedation, nystagmus, cerebellar syndromes, abnormal movement disorders (chorea, dyskinesis, tremors), dizziness, irritability, and other behavioral changes. These side effects can be controlled with adjustments of the dosage and do not necessarily require one to discontinue the medication.

Recently there has been a growing awareness and concern about side effects related to the chronic use of antiepileptic medications. The list, probably still incomplete, includes gingival hyperplasia, development of coarse facial features, hypocalcemia, osteomalacia, osteoporosis, macrocytosis, folic acid deficiency, hyperactivity, sleep disorders, chronic neuropathy and polyneuropathies, and diminished intellectual performance.

The most common side effects we have found have been gingival hyperplasia, secondary to phenytoin, and drowsiness and somnolence, usually associated with phenobarbitol alone or in combinations. Occasionally persistent leukopenia is recorded, although transitory changes in the complete blood count are much more frequent. Persistent hypocalcemia was observed in several patients on phenobarbitol and/or phenytoin. Asymptomatic hyperammonemia was observed in most of the patients on valproic acid therapy. Hyponatremia, most of the times asymptomatic, was observed in patients on carbamazepine. A syndrome of inappropriate antidiuretic hormone secretion was observed in one patient on carbamazepine and phenytoin.

In seven years we have not had any life-threatening side effect, and very rarely have the side effects been of such magnitude as to make it necessary to stop the medications. Our workup includes a clinical evaluation by a neurologist at least every 6 months, with more frequent clinical evaluations by the primary care medical team. Hematologic and biochemical profile, urinalysis, and serum concentrations of antiepileptic medications are done at least once a year.

It is not possible to discuss in detail all the side effects of the antiepileptic medications, but some will be discussed here because they are particularly interesting for practitioners working with persons with mental retardation.

Changes in Bone Metabolism, Rickets, and Fractures. This problem was first presented by Kruse,[43] who described bone changes in persons on chronic antiepileptic therapy. Later biochemical changes compatible with rickets (increased serum levels of alkaline phosphatase, low serum calcium levels, and high phosphorus levels), as well as alteration in the metabolism of vitamin D, were also described in association with a higher incidence of fractures. These changes have been described almost exclusively in mentally retarded persons with epilepsy living in institutions, most of them medicated with phenytoin and/or phenobarbitol.[4,45]

Because of these reports, it was suggested that high doses of vitamin D be added to the therapeutic plan.[32] However, the problem is not so simple. Some of the original papers failed to notice that phenobarbitol is a potent enzymatic inductor and can selectively induce production of the hepatic fraction of alkaline phosphatase, with resultant elevation of the total alkaline phosphatase. We also found high levels of alkaline phosphatase, but in 14 patients in whom the isoenzymes were measured we found that only the hepatic isoenzyme was elevated. Even though some of the intermediate metabolites of vitamin D were low, the active form of vitamin D, 1-25 dihydroxy vitamin D, was found to be normal.[40] The calcium content of the bones was found to be low by some[10] but not by others.[10,71] We also found low levels of calcium in the blood (see Table 8-12).[3] Recently a nutritional survey in the institution showed the diet to be appropriate in content of vitamin D, and an evaluation of all fractures that occurred in two years (1981 and 1983) showed no significant differences between epileptics and nonepileptics. Besides, recent research points to vitamin-K-dependent factors as possibly involved in this problem.[41]

Bone change is still a controversial issue. Our practice is to ensure that the patients on antiepileptic medications are receiving adequate amounts of vitamin D in the diet; we do not encourage the

Table 8-12. *Calcium Blood Levels and Anticonvulsants*

Patient Group	Calcium Blood Level (mg/ml)				
	8–9	9–10	10–11	>11	All
No anticonvulsant					
Number	31	415	195	9	650
Percent	4.7	63.8	30	1.4	99.9*
Anticonvulsant					
Number	12	124	34	2	172
Percent	7	72.1	19.8	1.2	100.1*

From Alvarez, N., and Hazlett, J.: Seizure management with minimal medications in institutionalized mentally retarded epileptics. A prospective study: First report after $4\frac{1}{2}$ years of follow-up. Clin. Electroencephalogr., 14:164, 1983.

* Percentages do not add to 100 due to rounding.

There is an increased incidence of values on the lower side of the spectrum for those patients on anticonvulsants than for those not taking anticonvulsants. $\chi^2 = 7.843$, DF^3, $p < 0.02$.

use of extra vitamin D in these patients, and we oppose massive doses.

Neurologic and Intellectual Changes. Changes associated with high levels of antiepileptic medications are easily identifiable, but it is difficult to identify the side effects secondary to chronic use of antiepileptics when they occur within the so-called therapeutic range.

Trimble and Corbet,[68] in a study that evaluated 312 institutionalized epileptic children, found that the IQ dropped 10 to 40% even though the blood levels of antiepileptic drugs were in the therapeutic range. Children and adults with mental retardation and brain damage have a predisposition to phenytoin encephalopathy that can present without the classical signs of phenytoin intoxication and with serum levels within the normal limits.[46] Similar clinical pictures have been described with valproic acid, and a few cases of psychiatric and behavior disorders produced by carbamazepine have also been described in persons with brain damage.[14] Fortunately, these disorders have been both rare and reversible, and they should not present a serious problem in the management of these patients.

Behavioral Techniques

There are abundant data suggesting that behavioral methods might improve some epileptic disorders, but the data are not always clear.

The work of Foster and associates is definite about the effectiveness of these techniques in the reflex epilepsies.[7,26,27] In these forms of epi-

lepsy, a particular, well-defined stimulus is the trigger for the epileptic event. The most common recognized trigger is light (photoconvulsive epilepsy), but others, like sound, music, somatosensory stimulation, and reading, have also been identified. In this group of epilepsies, once the characteristics of the trigger have been identified, desensitization techniques can be effective. A variation of the theme is presented by children who have learned how to trigger their reflex epilepsy, for example by waving a hand in front of their eyes or by closing the eyes. In these situations aversive techniques can be effective.

Behavioral techniques might also be useful in patients in whom there is a clear aura that precedes the seizures. A good example is reported by Efrom,[20] in a patient with complex partial seizures of the uncinate type, who, after training, was able to stop the spread of the seizure after the aura.

A different situation, although superficially similar, is presented by patients with serious emotional conflicts. In these patients too the seizures can be preceded by an identifiable event, but in this case the "trigger" is not directly the cause of the seizure, as in the reflex epilepsies, nor is it the beginning or the aura of the seizure, as in the case of complex partial seizures. In this situation the behaviors are the expression of unresolved emotional problems, and psychotherapy could be a better approach. In this area there is not much information on epileptics with developmental disabilities, but there is no reason to believe that the stress of emotional problems that can activate seizures in persons with normal intelligence does not affect individuals with mental retardation. This area needs more research.

If the antecedent event is predominantly anxiety or tension, relaxation techniques can be used as adjuvants to other therapies.

Abnormal behaviors (hyperventilation, rocking, head banging, and others) are not unusual in epileptics with developmental disabilities. At times they precede seizures or seizure-like behaviors. In these situations, behavior modification techniques that ignore negative behaviors and/or encourage positive ones have been reported as useful.[5,9]

A different approach in the behavioral sphere was pioneered by Sterman and Friar,[66] who attempted to decrease the number of seizures through modification of the EEG. In this technique EEG information is biofeedback to the patient, assuming that a favorable change (e.g., an inhibitory phenomenon) in a particular area of the brain will generalize to the whole brain and raise the threshold for seizures. The original approach consisted in increasing the occurrence of 12–14 cps activity found over the Rolandic area, the sensorimotor rhythm (SMR), which prior work in animals showed to be associated with motor inhibition. Subsequent research suggested that other frequencies besides SMR can also raise the seizure threshold.[48] Approximately half of the patients who participate in EEG biofeedback studies show some improvement, but biofeedback is not free from criticism, based mainly on the small number of patients studied, the difficulties in ruling out the placebo effect, and the statistical insignificance of the results of some studies.

The use of any of these behavioral techniques broadens the therapeutic possibilities in the management of developmentally disabled children and adults with epilepsy. However, before being very enthusiastic and committing patients to lengthy procedures, the reader should be aware of some problems that permeate the literature and could explain some of the contradictions frequently found in this area.

One of the most important problems is to document that the behaviors targeted as seizures are true epileptic seizures. This may not be a simple task, because, as mentioned earlier, epileptic seizures can be indistinguishable from nonepileptic behaviors and because both epileptic and nonepileptic seizures can occur in the same individual. Unfortunately, lack of documentation of the true nature of the target behavior is a consistent problem in the evaluation of behavioral techniques in epileptic disorders.

The nature of the true epileptic seizure in itself, which changes with the individual and with environmental changes, is another problem to be considered. Some seizures are more often seen in the early hours of the day, and others are more often seen when the patient is sleeping or drowsy. Some seizures are more frequent when the patient is quiet and resting and may decrease in frequency when the patient is active, even though the true nature of the disorder has not changed. In these patients, fewer seizures during behavioral treatment might be a nonspecific effect, the consequence of keeping the patient involved in some form of activity. This effect will not last long and will not become generalized. The lack of mention of these factors makes it difficult to interpret some studies.

Another frequent pitfall is poor documentation of the plasma levels of the antiepileptic medications during the treatment period. Poor compliance, a frequent cause of intractable seizures, can improve with any of the behavioral techniques discussed, because they all imply frequent interviews and intensive contacts with few persons.

Because of these limitations, when behavioral techniques are considered in the therapeutic plans for persons with developmental disabilities, the causes of pitfalls should be reduced to a minimum. A careful approach will result in benefit for the patient and in understanding of the behavioral techniques.

Surgical Treatment

Surgical procedures have a well-defined role in the treatment of the nonretarded epileptic patient, but there is not much experience in the developmentally disabled population. In fact, in many surgical centers, mental retardation and psychosis are criteria for exclusion from surgery. These criteria may sound inappropriate because the quality of life of many mentally retarded children would improve with better seizure control.

This position, however, should be evaluated in perspective: there are only a few specialized centers for epileptic-oriented neurosurgery, there are many potential candidates for surgery (estimated at 30,000 to 40,000 in the U.S.), and few operations are actually performed (under 200 operations a year in the U.S.). The preoperative evaluation involves lengthy diagnostic procedures that in many cases require intensive cooperation from the patient. Besides, the best candidates for successful operations are those with focal cortical lesions, which is rarely the case in children with developmental disabilities and intractable epilepsy. Hence it is not surprising that high priority for surgery is given to patients with accessible focal lesions, normal intelligence, strong motivation, and high potential for successful socioeconomic rehabilitation.

Even with these limits, some children with seizures and developmental disabilities should be considered for surgery. For example, children with intractable seizures and Sturge-Weber syndrome have improved after hemispherectomy. This improvement extended also to the behavioral and intellectual area. Similar improvement can also be seen in children with infantile hemiplegia and intractable seizures. Children with tuberous sclerosis can improve with the removal of slow-growing brain tumors.

REFERENCES

1. Ajmone-Marsan, C., and Gumnit, R.J.: Neurophysiological aspects of epilepsy. In Handbook of Clinical Neurology, Vol. 15. The Epilepsies. Edited by P.J. Vinken and G.W. Bruyn. Amsterdam, Elsevier, 1974.
2. Alvarez, N.: Compliance for antiepileptic medication in an institution for the mentally retarded. Clin. Electroencephalogr., 13:103, 1982.
3. Alvarez, N., and Hazlett, J.: Seizure management with minimal medications in institutionalized mentally retarded epileptics. A prospective study: First report after 4½ years of follow-up. Clin. Electroencephalogr., 14:164, 1983.
4. Anast, C.: Anticonvulsant drugs and calcium metabolism. Editorial. New Engl. J. Med., 292:587, 1975.
5. Balaschak, B.A.: Teacher implemented behavior modification in a case of organically based epilepsy. J. Consult. Clin. Psychol., 44:218, 1976.
6. Binnie, C.D., et al.: Telemetric EEG and video monitoring in epilepsy. Neurology, 31:298, 1981.
7. Booker, H.E., Foster, F.M., and Klive, H.: Extinction factors in startle (acousticomotor) seizures. Neurology, 15:1095, 1965.
8. Browne, T.R., and Feldman, R.G.: Epilepsy—Diagnosis and Management. Boston, Little, Brown, 1983.
9. Cautela, J.R., and Flannery, R.B.: Seizures: Controlling the uncontrollable. J. Rehabil., 39:34, 1973.
10. Christiansen, C., Rodbro, P., and Lund, M.: Osteomalacia in epileptic patients treated with anticonvulsants. Br. Med. J., 3:738, 1972.
11. Commission on Classification and Terminology of the International League Against Epilepsy. Proposal for revised clinical and electroencephalographic classification of epileptic seizures. Epilepsy, 22:489, 1981.
12. Corbett, J.A., Harris, R., and Robinson, R.G.: Epilepsy. In Mental Retardation and Developmental Disabilities, Vol. VIII. Edited by J. Wortis. New York, Brumer Mazel, 1975.
13. Crothers, B., and Paine, R.S.: Seizures and electroencephalography. The incidence of seizures among patients with cerebral palsy. In The Natural History of Cerebral Palsy. Edited by B. Crothers, and R.S. Paine. Cambridge, Harvard University Press, 1959.
14. Dalby, M.A.: Behavioral effects of carbamazepine. In Complex Partial Seizures and Their Treatment. Advances in Neurology, Vol. 11. Edited by J.K. Penry, and D.D. Daly. New York, Raven Press, 1975.
15. Davis, J., and Cole, J.: Organic therapies. In Comprehensive Textbook of Psychiatry, Vol. II. Edited by A. Freeman, M. Kaplan, and B. Sadock. Baltimore, Williams & Wilkins, 1975.
16. Delgado-Escueta, A.V., Eurile Bacsal, F., and Treiman, D.M.: Complex partial seizures on closed-circuit television and EEG. Study of 691 attacks in 79 patients. Ann. Neurol., 11:292, 1982.
17. Dickmen, S., and Matthews, C.G.: Effect of major motor seizure frequency upon cognitive intellectual functions in adults. Epilepsy, 18:21, 1977.
18. Di Chiro, G., et al.: F-2 Fluoro-2-deoxy-glucose positron tomography of human cerebral gliomas. J. Comput. Assist. Tomogr., 5:937, 1981.
19. Dreifuss, F.E.: Pediatric Epileptology: Classification and Management of Seizures in the Child. Boston, PSG Publishing Co., 1983.
20. Efrom, R.: The conditioned inhibition of uncinate fits. Brain, 80:251, 1957.
21. Engels, J., et al.: Comparative localization of epileptic foci in partial epilepsy by PET and EEG. Ann. Neurol., 12:529, 1982.
22. Eyman, R.K., Caper, L., Moore, B.C., and Zachofsky, T.: Maladaptive behaviors of institutionalized retardates with seizures. Am. J. Ment. Defic., 74:651, 1969.
23. Feldman, R.G., Paul, N.L., and Cummins-Ducharme, J.C.: Videotape recording in epilepsy and pseudoseizures. In Pseudoseizures. Edited by F.L. Riley and A. Roy. Baltimore, Williams & Wilkins, 1982, pp. 122-131.
24. Fischbacher, E.: Effects of reduction of anticonvulsants on well being. Br. Med. J., 285:425, 1982.
25. Floyer, E.B.: A Psychological Study of a City's Cerebral Palsied Children. Manchester, British Council for the Welfare of the Spastics, 1955.
26. Foster, F.M.: Reflex Epilepsy, Conditional Reflexes and Behavioral Treatment. Springfield, Charles C Thomas, 1975.
27. Foster, F.M.: Reading epilepsy, musicogenic epilepsy and related disorders. In Progress in Learning Disabilities. Edited by H.R. Mykleburst. New York, Grune & Stratton, 1975.
28. Gastaut, H., et al.: Childhood epileptic encephalopathy with diffuse slow spike-waves (otherwise known as "petit mal variant") or Lennox Syndrome. Epilepsy, 7:139, 1966.
29. Gibbs, F.A., and Gibbs, E.L.: Atlas of Electroencephalography, Vol. 2. Cambridge, Addison-Wesley, 1952.
30. Graham, P., and Rutter, M.: Organic brain dysfunction and child psychiatric disorder. Br. Med. J., 3:695, 1968.
31. Gruenberg, E.M.: Epidemiology. In Mental Retardation: A Review of Research. Edited by H.A. Stevens, and R. Heber. Chicago, University of Chicago Press, 1964.
32. Hahn, T.J., Mendin, B.A., and Scharp, C.R.: Effects of chronic anticonvulsant therapy on serum 25 hydroxycalciferol levels in adults. New Engl. J. Med., 287:900, 1972.
33. Hauser, W.A.: Epidemiology of epilepsy. In Advances in Neurology, Vol. 19. Edited by B.S. Schoenberg. New York, Raven Press, 1978.
34. Herman, B.P., Dikmen, S., and Wilensky, A.J.: Increased psychopathology associated with multiple seizure types: Fact or artifact? Epilepsia, 23:587, 1982.
35. Hilliard, L.T., and Kirman, B.H.: Mental Deficiency. London, Churchill Livingstone, 1957.
36. Holmes, G.L., McKeever, M., and Russman, B.S.: Abnormal behavior or epilepsy? Use of long term EEG monitoring with severely to profoundly mentally retarded patients with seizures. Am. J. Ment. Defic., 87:456, 1983.
37. Hunt, A.: Tuberous sclerosis: A survey of 97 cases I: Seizures, pertussis immunization, and handicap. Dev. Med. Child Neurol., 25:346, 1983.
38. Ingram, T.T.S., Jameson, S., Errington, J., and Mitchell, R.G.: Living with cerebral palsy. In Clinics in Developmental Medicine, Vol. 14. London, William Heinemann, 1964.
39. Jackson, J.H.: Lectures on the diagnosis of epilepsy. In Selected Writings of John Hughlings Jackson, Vol. 1. Edited by J. Taylor. New York, Basic Books, 1931.
40. Jubiz, W., Haussler, M.R., McCann, T., and Tolman, K.G.: Plasma 1-25 dihydroxyvitamin D levels in patients receiving anticonvulsant drugs. J. Clin. Endocrinol. Metab., 44:617, 1977.
41. Keith, D., et al.: Vitamin K-dependent proteins and anticonvulsant medications. Clin. Pharmacol. Ther., 34:529, 1980.

42. Kirman, B.H.: Epilepsy and cerebral palsy. Arch. Dis. Child., *31*:1, 1956.

43. Kruse, R.: Osteopathien bei Antiepileptischer Lang-Zeittherapic Monatsschr. Kinderheilk, *116*:378, 1968.

44. Lenzi, G.L., and Pantano, P.: Neurological applications of PET. *In* Neurologic Clinic, Vol. 2. Neuroimaging. Edited by F. Buonanno. Philadelphia, W.B. Saunders, 1984.

45. Lifshitz, F., Maclaren, N.K.: Vitamin D dependent rickets in institutionalized mentally retarded children receiving long term anticonvulsant therapy. I. A survey of 288 patients. J. Pediatr., 83:612, 1978.

46. Logan, W.J., and Freeman, J.M.: Pseudodegenerative disease due to diphenylhydantoin intoxication. Arch. Neurol., *21*:631, 1969.

47. Lombroso, C.T.: Differentiation of seizures in the newborn and in early infancy. *In* Antiepileptic Drug Therapy in Pediatrics. Edited by P.L. Morselli, C.E. Pippenger, and J.K. Penry. New York, Raven Press, 1983.

48. Lubar, J.F., and Bawler, W.W.: Behavioral management of epileptic seizures following EEG biofeedback training of the sensorimotor rhythm. J. Biofeedback Self Regul., *1*:77, 1976.

49. Milano Collaborative Group for Studies on Epilepsy: Long term monitoring in the difficult patients. *In* Antiepileptic Drug Monitoring. Edited by C. Gardner-Thorpe, D. Janz, H. Meihardi, and C.E. Pippinger. Tunbridge Wells, England, Pitman, 1977, pp. 197-213.

50. Miniszek, N.A.: Development of Alzheimer's Disease in Down syndrome individuals. Am. J. Ment. Defic., 87:377, 1983.

51. Niedermeyer, E.: Abnormal EEG patterns (epileptics and paroxysmal). *In* Electroencephalography, Basic Principles, Clinical Applications and Related Fields. Edited by E. Niedermeyer and F. Lopes da Silva. Baltimore, Urban & Schwarzenberg, 1982.

52. Neill, J., Alvarez, N., and Courcelle, R.: Diagnosis of pseudoepilepsy in a mentally retarded population. Proceedings of the 35th Annual Meeting of the Eastern Psychological Association, Washington, DC, 1983.

53. Payne, D., Johnson, R.E., and Abelson, R.B.: A comprehensive description of institutionalized retardates in the Western United States. Boulder, CO, Western Interstate Commission for Higher Education, 1969.

54. Porter, R.J.: Methodology of continuing monitoring with videotape recording and electroencephalography. *In* Advances in Epileptology. The Tenth Epilepsy International Symposium. Edited by J.A. Wada and J.K. Penry. New York, Raven Press, 1980.

55. Pueschel, S.M., and Rynders, J.E.: Down Syndrome: Advances in Biomedicine and the Behavioral Sciences. Cambridge, Ware Press, 1982.

56. Ramsey, R.E., Wilder, B.J., Berger, J.R., and Brum, J.: A double blind study comparing carbamazepine with phenytoin as initial seizure therapy in adults. Neurology, 33:904, 1983.

57. Reynolds, E.H.: Mental effects of antiepileptic medications: A review. Epilepsia, 24:585, 1983.

58. Reynolds, E.H., and Shorvon, S.D.: Monotherapy or polytherapy for epilepsy? Epilepsia, 22:1, 1981.

59. Richardson, S.L., Koller, H., Katz, M., and McLaren, J.: Seizures and epilepsy in a mentally retarded population over the first 22 years of life. Appl. Res. Ment. Retard., *1*:123, 1980.

60. Rutter, M.: Sex differences in children's responses to family stress. *In* International Yearbook in Child Psychiatry, Vol. 1, The Child and His Family. Edited by E.J. Anthony and C. Koupernik. New York, John Wiley, 1970.

61. Rutter, M., Tizard, J., and Whitmore, K.: Education, Health and Behavior. New York, John Wiley, 1970.

62. Sato, S., Penry, K.F., and Dreifuss, F.E.: Electroencephalographic monitoring of generalized spike wave paroxysm in the hospital and at home. *In* Quantitative Analysis Studies in Epilepsy. Edited by P. Kellaway and I. Petersen. New York, Raven Press, 1976.

63. Shorvon, S.P., and Reynolds, E.H.: Reduction of polypharmacy for epilepsia. Br. Med. J., 2:1023, 1979.

64. Skatvedt, M.: Cerebral palsy. A clinical study of 370 cases. Acta Paediatr. Scand., *46* (Suppl. 111), 1958.

65. Stephen, E., and Hawks, G.: Cerebral palsy and mental subnormality. *In* Mental Deficiency: The Changing Outlook. Edited by A.M. Clarke, and D.B. Clarke. New York, Macmillan, 1975.

66. Sterman, M.B., and Friar, L.: Suppression of seizures in an epileptic following sensorimotor EEG feedback training. Electroencephalogr. Clin. Neurophysiol., *33*:89, 1972.

67. Tizard, J., and Grad, J.C.: The Mentally Handicapped and Their Families. London, Oxford University Press, 1961.

68. Trimble, M.R., and Corbet, J.A.: Behavioral and cognitive disturbance in epileptic children. Ir. Med. J., *73* (Suppl.):21, 1980.

69. Waxman, S.G., and Gerschwind, N.: The interictal behavior syndrome of temporal lobe epilepsy. Arch. Gen. Psychiatry, *32*:1580, 1975.

70. Woods, G.E.: Cerebral Palsy in Childhood. Bristol, England, Wright, 1957.

71. Zanzi, I., Roginsky, M., Rosen, A., and Cohen, S.: Skeletal mass in patients receiving chronic anticonvulsant therapy. Miner. Electrolyte Metab., 5:240, 1981.

OTHER NEUROLOGIC DISORDERS

NEUROLOGIC BASIS OF CLINICAL EVALUATION

The physical examination of children or adults with severe to profound developmental disabilities can be difficult.

A detailed description of the neurologic examination was presented elsewhere.[1] Here I will address some of the problems encountered when examining an uncooperative patient.

General Observation

A physician should be able to obtain some valuable data even under the most difficult circumstances. A child who runs away or who pushes the examiner away or slaps his face has already given a good deal of information about his gross motor system, his coordination, and his cerebellar system as well as his style of social interaction.

In the case of a child who is moving around the examining room playing with small toys, apparently unaware of his surroundings and the examiner's presence, it is possible, by observation alone, to assess his gait, stance, presence or absence of abnormal movements, the degree of fine and gross motor coordination, the cerebellar system, the muscle trophism, and probably the strength of the muscles. A good deal of the cranial nerve examination can also be done. The proximity of the objects to the eyes, the ability to pick up small objects, or the preference for one eye can give one an idea of the child's visual acuity. Offering toys outside the direct field of vision might help to evaluate the peripheral visual fields. Eye movements can be evaluated by moving objects around the patient while gently holding the head. Abnormal eye movements, e.g., nystagmus, can be seen easily. Offering a penlight to the child and directing it to the face is a simple technique that helps in evaluation of the pupillary reflexes. The eye examination can be completed with the optokinetic drum, which does not need much cooperation. Observation of facial gestures may be sufficient to evaluate the motor components of the 7th nerve. Hearing evaluation is more appropriately performed by the audiologist, but a gross evaluation can be achieved by observing the reaction to noise, which might be limited to changes in behaviors or just changes in respiratory pattern. Presence or absence of drooling, as well as behavior elicited by offering a glass of water or an edible treat, will allow evaluation of complex functions such as chewing, sucking and swallowing, which depend on the integrity of several cranial nerve nuclei located in the brain stem (principally the 9th, 10th, and 12th, but also the 5th and 7th) and the cortical centers involved with these functions. Observing the posture of the head and asking the child to look to the sides is a good way to evaluate the sternocleidomastoid muscle (11th nerve). Keeping the child partially undressed allows for evaluation of the bulk of the muscles and the presence of muscle atrophy. Playing with the child and wrestling with the child for toys gives some measure of muscle strength.

Holding the head steady for a few seconds should allow enough time to measure the head circumference. Undressing the child permits observation of the skin and early detection of lesions that can be part of neurocutaneous syndromes (see Chap. 18).

Even with all these strategies a neurologic exam can be incomplete, especially in children with severe behavior problems, and it may be necessary to repeat the examination. For some procedures, e.g., funduscopy, heavy sedation, or even anesthesia might be necessary. Some other tests, for example, evaluation of the mus-

cle tone, and deep tendon reflexes might be difficult to elicit in uncooperative children who do not relax enough during the examination.

Associated Sensory Deficits

It is important to establish the degree of associated sensory deficits. Visual and auditory impairment is common in children with brain damage, and when impairment is not detected it may aggravate the developmental delay.[44] The clinical examination may not be optimal, and children or adults with developmental disabilities should periodically have ophthalmologic and audiologic evaluations. Some of these patients may benefit from neurophysiologic techniques such as evoked potentials, which do not require much cooperation.

Clinical evaluation of the somatosensory system requires good understanding and cooperation from the patient. Touching or stimulating the patient with a pin gives some information, but a more delicate examination to determine areas of hyposensitivity or sensory levels can be almost impossible. Unfortunately there are no good objective clinical methods to obtain this information in uncooperative patients, but recent reports suggest some role for somatosensory evoked potentials.[4]

Special Investigations

Investigations oriented to obtain an etiological diagnosis (e.g., chromosomal analysis, metabolic and endocrine tests) are discussed elsewhere[33,37] (see also Chaps. 2, 6, and 7). Those oriented towards assessing present clinical status are presented here.

Brain Imaging

Conventional Roentgenography. Conventional roentgenograms of the skull are of limited use since the advent of computerized tomography. They are still valuable, however, in conditions in which primary skull bone disorders are associated with neurologic impairment (e.g., craniosinostosis syndromes), in abnormalities of the cranial base (e.g., basilar impression[17]), and in the diagnosis of skull fractures.

Roentgenograms of the cervical spine are indicated in evaluation of malformations of the cervical bones, especially in persons with Down syndrome, who have a high incidence of subluxation of the cervical spine. They are also indicated in the evaluation of adult patients with the dystonic-choreic form of cerebral palsy, in whom the cervical vertebrae may undergo accelerated osteoarthritic changes. Roentgenograms of the thoracolumbar spine are also indicated for evaluation of other bone disorders such as spina bifida and scoliosis and can be of help in metabolic disorders.

Echoencephalography. Echoencephalography is still useful for evaluations of newborns and also for intrauterine diagnosis of intracranial abnormalities.

Myelography. Myelography has limited indications specific to intraspinal abnormalities such as spinal dysraphism, severe kyphoscoliosis, spinal cord compression, and Down syndrome with cervical subluxation.

Computerized Tomography. Computerized tomography (CT) scans are invaluable in evaluation of the anatomic structure of the brain (malformations, ventricular dilatations, tumors, etc.). Normal CT scans are not unusual, however, even in children with severe developmental disabilities such as polymicrogyria, neuronal heterotopias, or sequelae of mild ischemic-hypoxic insults, which produce changes at the microscopic level.

Neurophysiologic Techniques

Electroencephalography. Encephalograms (EEGs) are widely used for the diagnosis of epilepsy, and they can also be useful in the presence of structural lesions and in evaluation of behavioral problems. As with the CT scan, normal EEGs are not unusual even in the presence of profound mental retardation. The diagnostic capabilities of the EEG have been enhanced by the use of long-term monitoring by portable cassette recorders and by radiotransmission with simultaneous TV recording. This last technique is extremely helpful in differentiating between epilepsy and pseudoepilepsy.[23]

Evoked Potentials. Evoked potentials[6] allows for an objective, replicable evaluation of the auditory and visual pathways.

The early components of the auditory evoked potentials reflect activity originating in the 8th nerve and in the brain stem. This test is used to determine hearing and hearing threshold. Because it does not require the patient's cooperation, and the results are not distorted by heavy sedation, it is very useful in uncooperative patients and in small infants[35, 36, 38] (see also Chap. 5). Brain stem evoked potentials can also help in selection of hearing aids.

Absence of cortical visual evoked potentials is a reliable sign of blindness, but the presence of a normal response is not a guarantee of good vision. Responses can be obtained even in the presence of serious loss of visual acuity or cortical damage.[11] These responses can also be present in children who qualify as legally blind.

Somatosensory evoked potentials are used to explore the posterior tracts of the spinal cord and also the central connections of the somatosensory system. In spite of recent advances,[4] this test is not as useful as visual or auditory evoked potentials.

Testing of evoked potentials is also indicated in patients with neurofibromatosis, who may develop tumors of the 8th cranial nerve[28] or gliomas of the optic nerve. Serial evoked potentials that show increased degree of abnormalities could be an index of organicity in patients with progressive behavior deterioration, as can be the case with Alzheimer-type degeneration in patients with Down syndrome. Somatosensory evoked potentials can be useful in evaluation of anatomic disorders of the spinal cord. In my experience, these potentials have been abnormal in patients with Down syndrome and spinal cord compression caused by subluxation of the cervical spine.

COMMON NEUROLOGIC DISORDERS ASSOCIATED WITH DEVELOPMENTAL DISABILITIES

Progressive Neurologic Disorders

There is a group of neurologic disorders characterized by progressive deterioration. This deterioration can be the consequence of pathology that primarily affects the peripheral nervous system, e.g., the muscular dystrophies or the peripheral neuropathies, without major involvement of the central nervous system, or it can be the consequence of lesions that primarily affect the brain.

Because of the nature of these disorders, these patients will be referred to the pediatrician at some point. The reason for the referral will depend on the primary disorder and the age at which the symptoms began. The diagnostic clue that should make the physician suspicious of a progressive neurologic disorder is the loss of functions already mastered. These syndromes should also be suspected in infants with a positive family history, particularly if the symptoms are similar to those of the other affected members, and in children with developmental disabilities in the absence of congenital anomalies.[21]

Most of the causes are associated with metabolic abnormalities. These are rare disorders, and the practical approach is to become familiar with specialized diagnostic centers where patients can be sent for evaluation.

Table 8-13.   *Most Common Storage Disorders*

Disease	Most Common Clinical Features	Enzyme Deficiency
Sphingolipidosis		
Niemann-Pick	Several forms are recognized (A,B,C,D), differing in age at onset and severity of symptoms. Foamy histiocytes in bone marrow, hepatosplenomegaly, cherry red macula, motor and intellectual deterioration. Some forms without CNS involvement. Autosomal recessive	Sphingomyelinase or activator
Gaucher	Two forms: adult (chronic-nonneuropathic) and infantile (acute neuropathic). Hepatosplenomegaly, anemia, Gaucher cells, CNS involvement, and death in first year in the infantile form, elevated acid phosphatase. Autosomal recessive	β-Glucosidase
Krabbe	Several forms that differ in age at onset and severity of symptoms. CNS involvement with globoid cells, spasticity, quadriparesis. Elevated CSF protein. Autosomal recessive	β-Galactosidase
Metachromatic leukodystrophy	Several disorders. Onset from 1 year to adulthood. Peripheral neuropathy, pain, gait disorder, absent DTRs, dementia. Autosomal recessive	Aryl-sulfatase-A
Fabry	Pain in extremities, angiokeratoma in buttocks and navel, dilated retinal and conjunctival venules. Hypertension. X-linked	α-Galactosidase-A
GM2 gangliosidosis Tay-Sachs and variants	Early psychomotor deterioration, deafness, blindness, startle response, red macula. Autosomal recessive	β-N-Acetyl-glucosaminidase-A Also A and B
GM1 gangliosidosis	Severe CNS involvement, seizures, spasticity, dysostosis. Autosomal recessive	β-Galactosidase
Mucopolysaccharidosis		
Hurler (MPS I)	Early onset of developmental delay. Coarse facies, dwarfism, corneal opacities, gingival hyperplasia, dysostosis, organomegaly. Autosomal recessive	Iduronidase
Scheie syndrome (MPS Ia)	Mild form of Hurler. Mild or no MR. Autosomal recessive	Iduronidase
Hunter (MPS II)	Similar to Hurler, but MR more severe. No corneal clouding and longer life span. X-linked	Iduronate sulfatase
Sanfilippo (MPS III a and b)	Severe MR with minimal connective tissue disorder. Hirsutism. Autosomal recessive	Heparan N-sulfatase or α-N-Acetyl-glucosaminidase
Morquio (MPS IV)	Normal IQ. Marked skeletal abnormalities. Autosomal recessive	Galactosamine sulfatase
Maroteaux-Lamy (MPS VI)	Normal IQ. Marked skeletal abnormalities. Autosomal recessive	Arylsulfatase
Glucuronidase deficiency (MPS VII)	Mild MR. Coarse facial features. Organomegaly. Autosomal recessive	β-Glucuronidase

Disease	Most Common Clinical Features	Enzyme Deficiency
Others Fucosidosis	"Hurler-like." Autosomal recessive	α-Fucosidase
Mannosidosis	Psychomotor retardation, deafness, hepatosplenomegaly, bone changes. Autosomal recessive	α-Mannosidase
Mucolipidosis I	Several forms. Red macula, bone changes, MR in infantile form. Autosomal recessive	Neuraminidase
II	Early onset of "Hurler-like" syndrome. Autosomal recessive	Lysosomal enzymes extremely elevated in these 2 disorders. Generalized enzyme deficiency
III	Mild variant of II, slowly progressive "Hurler-like" features. Autosomal recessive	

Modified from O'Brien, J.F.: The lysosomal storage diseases. Mayo Clin. Proc., 57:192, 1982.

There is a distinctive group of diseases that are the consequence of hereditary deficiencies in lysosomal enzymes (see Table 8-13 and Chap. 2).

Other developmental disorders associated with inherited metabolic disorders are presented in Table 8-14.[22]

Rett's syndrome is a progressive deteriorating condition that has been described only in girls. After an uneventful pregnancy and delivery, these infants develop normally in the first 7 to 12 months after birth. Then a slowly progressive deterioration begins, characterized by delays in motor development, arrest of gait, sometimes nonambulation, truncal ataxia, spasticity, and acquired microcephaly. The girls also show changes in behavior and affect and develop an autism-like syndrome, although the presence of an expressive look differentiates them from autistic children. Stereotypic movements in hands, described as "hand washing" or "hand wringing" have been a constant finding. After a rapid period of deterioration the disease stabilizes, and from then on the prognosis, in terms of life expectancy, depends on the care provided. The cause of this syndrome is unknown, but since it is seen exclusively in girls it could be the consequence of a dominant mutation of an X chromosome, lethal in males. Because the syndrome has been described only recently, however, the possibility of contributing environmental factors cannot be ruled out.[16]

Specific diagnosis is of utmost importance for genetic counseling and for appropriate management (see Chap. 7).

Nonprogressive Neurologic Disorders

Cerebral Palsy

The term cerebral palsy is usually applied to a number of disabilities, the consequence of developmental injuries or perinatal damage to the central nervous system[10] (see also Chaps. 2 and 5). The term refers to a nonprogressive condition that is clinically characterized by abnormalities of motor function and posture and/or an aberrant movement disorder. The definition excludes progressive neurological disorders and also some conditions with identifiable etiologies, e.g., chromosome abnormalities and metabolic derangements like phenylketonuria. Because the definition is not very precise the prevalence of cerebral palsy varies in different studies.[7–14,18,24,32]

Cerebral palsy is an end point of several etiologies as shown in Table 8-15. More than one cause may affect the same child.[8–13] Some developmental disorders can be familial, but most are commonly seen as isolated events. These developmental anomalies represent alteration in the development of the central nervous system. The most common developmental defect is the arrest in migration of neurons, which produces heterotopias[5,22] (see also Chaps. 2, 5, 6, and 7).

Even though children with cerebral palsy have multiple dysfunctions,[34] they are usually classified by the characteristics of the motor syndrome, as shown in Table 8-16 (see also Chaps. 2, 5, and 23).

It is not unusual to find signs of intellectual or physical deterioration in persons with developmental disabilities. Persons with developmental

Table 8-14.   *Inherited Metabolic Disorders Associated with Developmental Disabilities*

Disease	Clinical Symptoms	Metabolic Disorder
Phenylketonuria	Normal at birth. First 2 months: vomiting and irritability followed by developmental delay. Seizures, sometimes infantile spasms, microcephaly. Blonde hair	Phenylalanine hydroxylase
Maple-syrup-urine disease	Urine with sweet maple-syrup-like odor. Symptoms in the first week of life. Opistotonus, increased muscle tone, respiratory irregularities, followed by rapid deterioration and early death, or survival with severe deficit	Accumulation of branched-chain ketoacids
Urea cycle deficiencies	Several clinical entities. Common clinical features are: recurrent episodes of lethargy, vomiting, seizures. Moderate to severe MR, intolerance to protein-containing food. Chronic hyperammonemia	Incomplete urea cycle. Different enzyme deficiencies
Homocystinuria	Normal at birth and early development. Symptoms begin at 5–9 months with delay, seizures. Also ectopia lensis, glaucoma, cataracts, thromboembolic episodes, cerebrovascular accidents. Hair sparse, blonde, and brittle. Erythematous blotches over the skin	Error in methionine metabolism
Hartnup's disease	Developmental delay, photosensitive dermatitis, cerebellar ataxia	Defective intestinal and tubular transport of tryptophan and other amino acids
Galactosemia	Normal at birth. First week vomiting, diarrhea, irritability, failure to gain weight. Jaundice. Hepatosplenomegaly, cataracts, hypotonia. Pseudotumor cerebri. Moderate IQ deficiency	Galacto-1-phosphate uridil transferase
Glycogen storage disease (glycogenosis)	There are several clinical forms, the consequence of different enzymatic deficiencies in metabolization of glycogen. Common symptoms are: muscle weakness and hypotonia, hypoglycemia. Cardiac failure, seizures, intellectual impairment	
Lesch-Nyhan syndrome	Normal at birth. Psychomotor delay in first year. Extrapyramidal movements in 2nd year. Spasticity. Self-destructive biting of fingers, arms, and lips. Hematuria, renal insufficiency. Some individuals might have normal IQ. Elevated serum uric acid	Hypoxanthine guanine phosphoribosyl-transferase

Modified from Menkes, J.H.: Metabolic disorders of the central nervous system. *In* Textbook of Child Neurology. 2nd Ed. Philadelphia, Lea & Febiger, 1980.

disabilities develop multiple sclerosis, Parkinson disease, tumors, and other neurologic disorders as frequently as individuals who do not suffer from such disabilities. Occasionally the origin of this deterioration can be traced to an acute medical problem, e.g., infections, or to chronic medical problems that force the patients into prolonged periods of inactivity. In other cases organic causes, such as peripheral neuropathies or pain related to arthritis, nerve root compressions, or disc herniation, usually explain the clinical deterioration. Only in a few instances

is some rare progressive neurologic disorder involved.

Nevertheless, progressive clinical deterioration can be observed without any demonstrable superimposed disease. It is not clear whether this deterioration is the consequence of an accelerated aging process, institutionalization or social deprivation, or chronic use of medications.

The Floppy Infant

The neurologist is often confronted with the evaluation of an infant or child whose muscle

Table 8-15. *Etiologic Classification of Cerebral Palsy*

Developmental abnormalities
  Disorders of neural migration
    Schizencephaly

Intrauterine factors
  Infections (TORCH)
  Toxic
  Risk factors in pregnancy

Perinatal factors
  Related to delivery
    Mid-forceps
    Breech presentation
    Premature delivery
    Fetal distress

Hypoxic-ischemic encephalopathy

Intracerebral hemorrhage
  Intraventricular
  Subarachnoid
  Subdural
  Intracerebellar

Infection
  Bacterial meningitis
  Herpes simplex

Metabolic factors
  Hypoxia
  Acidosis
  Hypoglycemia

Kernicterus

From O'Reilly, D.E., and Walentynowicsz, J.E.: Etiological factors in cerebral palsy: An historical review. Dev. Med. Child. Neurol., 23:633, 1981.

Table 8-16. *Clinical Classification of Cerebral Palsy*

Symptom	Percentage
Hemiplegia	25–40
Spastic diplegia	10–33
Spastic quadriplegia	9–43
Extrapyramidal (including athetoid, ataxic, and dystonic forms)	9–22
Mixed	9–22

From Nelson, K.B., and Ellenberg, J.H.: Epidemiology of cerebral palsy. Adv. Neurol., *19*:421, 1978.

muscle disorder, because these newborns also have a high incidence of poor deliveries. Hence it is possible to have cerebral palsy superimposed on a primary muscle disorder. In these situations, the presence of associated symptoms (e.g., poor response to environmental changes or to visual or auditory stimulation; delays in language or social development; abnormal head circumference; presence of movement disorders such as athetosis or ataxia; and signs of upper motor neuron disorder such as clonus, increased deep tendon reflexes, or Babinski sign) are strongly suggestive of cerebral palsy or other causes with central nervous system involvement.

Marked muscle weakness, muscle atrophies or hypotrophies, and fibrillations in children with good language and social development and

Table 8-17. *Floppy Infant: Classification and Differential Diagnosis*

Muscle weakness with incidental hypotonia
  Hereditary infantile spinal muscle atrophies
    Werdnig-Hoffmann disease
    Benign variants
  Congenital myopathies

Disorders affecting the central nervous system
  Nonspecific mental deficiency
  Hypotonic cerebral palsy
  Birth trauma
  Chromosomal disorders; Down syndrome
  Metabolic disorders: aminoacidurias, organic acidurias, sphingolipidosis (leukodystrophies)

Connective-tissue disorders
  Marfan syndrome
  Mucopolysaccharidosis

Prader-Willi syndrome

Metabolic, nutritional, endocrine, rickets, hypothyroidism

Benign congenital hypotonia

Modified from Dubowitz, V.: The Floppy Infant. 2nd Ed. Clinics in Developmental Medicine, Vol. 76. Philadelphia, J.B. Lippincott, 1980, p. 16.

tone is decreased. In many cases these patients are referred to the neurologist because of slow motor development, abnormal movement, or aberrant posturing. In other cases decreased muscle tone is a finding in a more complex clinical picture. The term "floppy infant" is commonly used to refer to infants and children who present with muscle hypotonia as the predominant feature.

Normal muscle tone is maintained by a complex neurophysiological system, and tone can be affected by many causes. Table 8-17 is a list of the most important causes of hypotonia.[9]

Diagnostic Differentiation between Floppy Infant Condition and Cerebral Palsy. Because developmental motor delay is a common presentation, the differential diagnosis with cerebral palsy can be difficult. Besides, there are forms of cerebral palsy that are associated with hypotonia, and even the hypertonic forms of cerebral palsy also have a hypotonic phase. The antecedent of a poor delivery, with asphyxia or hypoxia, even though suggestive of brain damage as the cause of the hypotonia, does not exclude primary

Table 8-18. *Causes of Macrocephaly*

Mass lesions
  Intraventricular and posterior fossa tumors
  Arachnoid cysts
  Aneurysms of the vein of Galen
  Subdural hematomas

Megalencephaly (brain of abnormal excessive weight)
  Congenital malformations
  Achondroplasia
  Cerebral gigantism
  Certain degenerative disorders
    Tay-Sachs disease
    Canavan's degeneration
    Alexander's disease
  Familial form

Hydrocephalus
  Noncommunicating
    Aqueductal abnormalities, stenosis, forking, gliosis
    Obstructions due to mass lesions, exudate,
      hemorrhage, parasites
    Obstruction of the 4th ventricle outlet foramina
    Dandy-Walker, arachnoiditis,
      Arnold-Chiari malformation, Vein of Galen
      aneurysm
  Communicating
    Postinfectious, posthemorrhagic, arachnoid villi
      obstructions
    Arnold Chiari malformation
  Excessive production of CSF
    Choroid plexus papilloma

From Swaiman, K.: Mental retardation. *In* The Practice of
Pediatric Neurology. Edited by K. Swaiman and F. Wright.
St. Louis, C.V. Mosby, 1975.

marked motor delay are probably due to peripheral problems, e.g., myopathies or neuropathies.
In these children electromyography, nerve conduction studies, enzyme studies, and muscle biopsies might help in the differential diagnosis.

In the newborn period hypotonia is usually
associated with acute brain damage secondary to
perinatal stress. In most instances the hypotonia
is transitory, but sometimes it evolves later on
into a clear picture of spastic cerebral palsy.

Some chromosome abnormalities, like Down
syndrome and some specific connective tissue
disorders, can also cause both hypotonia and
mental retardation.

The Prader-Willi syndrome is a rare condition
characterized by hypotonia, mental retardation,
obesity, delayed motor development, and hypogonadism. The IQ is usually low, between 40
and 80.

Changes in Head Circumference

Head circumference growth above or below
accepted standards for age should always alert
the physician to the possibility of intracranial
pathology. In general, any measurement more

than 2 standard deviations from the mean should
be considered abnormal. Sudden changes should
also be considered abnormal even though the
head circumference is still within the normal
range.

Macrocephaly

The most frequent causes of macrocephaly are
mass lesions, megalencephaly, and hydrocephalus
(Table 8-18).

Mass Lesions. Different mass lesions can
produce an increase in head circumference either
directly by increasing the intracranial volume or
indirectly by obstructing the normal flow of
cerebrospinal fluid.

Megalencephaly. Megalencephaly is a descriptive term that refers to a brain of excessive
weight. Megalencephaly has been found as an
isolated event, associated with other medical
problems, and as a familial trait. Most children
with megalencephaly have medical problems
such as developmental delay, epilepsy, and other
neurological conditions. It is therefore useful to
measure patient's head circumference. Excessive brain weight does not necessarily correlate
with intellectual deficiencies, however. In some
cases megalencephaly is found as a familial trait
not associated with any other deficiencies.

Hydrocephalus. Hydrocephalus refers to conditions associated with ventricular enlargement
which, in most instances, is secondary to obstruction of the normal egress and flow of cerebrospinal fluid. In rare instances ventricular
enlargement is the result of excessive production
of cerebrospinal fluid.

Communicating and noncommunicating hydrocephalus are both obstructive, in the sense
that there is an interference in the flow of cerebrospinal fluid in both situations. In the noncommunicating type the obstruction, usually the
consequence of abnormalities in areas where the
pathways are narrow, is more obvious. In the
communicating type, the problem is not so
much in the intraventricular flow as in the absorption of cerebrospinal fluid. No obvious anatomical lesions are evident on roentgenograms
or CT scans, but lesions can be found at the
microscopic level. In most instances the etiology
of hydrocephalus remains unknown.

The most common site of ventricular obstruction in noncommunicating cases is within the
lumen of the aqueduct. These obstructions are
mostly congenital anomalies, e.g., stenosis, fork-
ing, and gliosis. Some of these lesions are isolated, and others are found in association with
other congenital abnormalities like meningo-

myelocele or encephalocele. Most newborns with myelomeningocele eventually develop hydrocephalus (see also Chaps. 2 and 6). In a few cases hydrocephalus is caused by tumors or other compressive lesions, prenatal infections, or postnatal infections. A few sex-linked recessive cases have been described.

The Dandy-Walker syndrome consists of a cystic dilatation of the 4th ventricle, attributed to atresia of the foramina of Magendie and Luschka, although it could be the result of a primary developmental abnormality of the cerebellum. The cerebellar hemispheres are small and displaced upward, and the vermis is hypoplastic. The aqueduct of Sylvius and the 3rd and lateral ventricles are usually enlarged. The foramen of Magendie is absent, and one or both foramina of Luschka have failed to develop. The syndrome might manifest early in life, with increased head circumference and occipital bulging, in an infant with normal developmental or only mildly delayed motor development.

Communicating hydrocephalus is frequently found in premature infants who had intraventricular hemorrhage. In these infants the ventricular dilatation might occur well before the increase in head size becomes clinically evident.[40,41] The pathogenesis in these cases is probably related to an obliterative arachnoiditis. A similar pathogenesis may explain postinfectious hydrocephalus.

There are four variations of the Arnold-Chiari malformation, but Type 2 is the most common, and the one that is usually associated with the eponym. It consists of a protrusion of the inferior cerebellar vermis into the spinal canal, with elongation and distortion of the medulla oblongata. The cervical cord is often small and deformed, with the cervical roots directed upward. This syndrome is virtually always associated with myelomeningocele. Other associated malformations are the narrowing of the aqueduct of Sylvius and anomalies of the cerebral cortex, e.g., microgyria and heterotopias.

Computerized tomography is the procedure of choice in the differential diagnosis of megalencephaly. The therapeutic options available are limited and usually in the hands of the neurosurgeon. Removal of the tumors, if present, and/or placement of shunts are the procedures most commonly indicated.

Microcephaly

Microcephaly is associated with a variety of neurological disorders. The clinical manifestations and the degree of CNS dysfunction vary, but there is a correlation between the severity of the microcephaly and the degree of mental retardation.[29] Almost 90% of children with microcephaly will have mental retardation even if they do not show other neurological deficits.[20]

LESSON FROM AN OUTPATIENT NEUROLOGY CLINIC FOR ADULTS WITH MENTAL RETARDATION.

Table 8-19 is a summary of 124 consecutive referrals to an outpatient clinic for adults with mental retardation. These referrals covered a span of approximately 1 year. All the patients were screened by a multidisciplinary team before referral to the clinic. Patients with epilepsy are not included in this review.

The most common referrals were in relation to persons with Down syndrome, which will be discussed later in more detail.

The second most common category, referred to as movement disorders, is probably underrepresented here because the screening team included a psychiatrist, and the patients whose movement disorders were related to psychotropic medications were not routinely referred to the

Table 8-19. *114 Consecutive Referrals to the Outpatient Neurology Clinic**

Diagnosis		No. of Patients
Down syndrome		27
Early dementia	18	
Atlanto-axial instability	9	
Movement disorders		21
Tremors	8	
Parkinson disease	4	
Medication-related	8	
Dystonia	1	
Gait disorders		15
Behavior changes		16
Peripheral nerve disorders		9
Compressive neuropathies	6	
Peripheral neuropathies	2	
Traumatic neuropathy	1	
Cerebrovascular accidents		5
Stroke	3	
Transient ischemic attack	1	
Intraventricular bleeding	1	
Sleep disorders		4
Syncopal attacks		3
Visual problems		3
Shunt malfunctions		2
Headaches		2
Miscellaneous		7

*Note: Seizure disorders are not included here.

neurology clinic. Two well-recognized movement disorders are associated with the chronic use of psychotropic medications. One is a Parkinson-like syndrome, which is dose-related and reversible when the medications are reduced or discontinued, and the other is a more severe disorder referred to as tardive dyskinesia. This is an involuntary movement disorder, observed mostly in the face, predominantly in the buccolingual area, although the limbs and trunk are also involved. The symptoms might be masked by the same psychotropic medications and are usually seen either when the medications are discontinued or within the following months. Tardive dyskinesia can be irreversible.

Gait disorders that start late in life, probably constitute another underrepresented category in the neurology clinic referrals, given the special expertise of the physical therapy and orthopedics departments, which handle most of these cases.

Behavior problems, a common disorder, will be discussed later.

The table also shows a series of clinical problems that can be expected in any general neurology practice: sleep disorders, syncopal attacks, visual problems, and headaches. However, there are some interesting differences, e.g., the infrequency of certain problems frequently seen in the neurology office like headaches and migraine, and the absence of dizziness or pain syndromes. The subjective nature of these disorders probably makes the diagnosis difficult. For example, migraine is a frequent complaint in any neurology practice and should be as frequent in the mentally retarded as in other persons. In light of recent reports about the benefits obtained with propanolol (an excellent antimigraine medication) in some forms of behavior problems,[43] some frequent but rarely diagnosed disorders in the mentally retarded should be reassessed.

Organic versus Nonorganic Behavior Disorders

Behavior deterioration was a frequent cause of referrals. Most of these consultations were motivated because of the possibility of a structural lesion (e.g., brain tumor, subdural collections) or functional disorders such as epilepsy. Excluding patients with Down syndrome and a few others, a complete neurologic workup commonly failed to show neurologic pathology that could be treated or could explain the abnormal behavior. Of the 18 patients referred for behavior changes, only 3 displayed abnormal pathology. Two were found to have shunt malfunctions, and the third,

who was referred for self-abusive behavior in which he would hit a wall head-on, was found to have acute intraventricular bleeding.

This is not to say that the neurologic workups are normal, but that it is difficult to correlate chronic abnormal behaviors or acute deterioration in behavior with the abnormal findings. Most of the clinical experience that helps to define the neurobehavioral syndromes associated with focal brain lesions is the result of research done in previously normal individuals who had discrete brain lesions (usually the consequence of strokes; sometimes tumors, or accidents with brain damage). In most of the patients with brain damage and mental retardation, however, the brain damage is usually diffuse. These patients might have long histories of institutionalization. For example, in this situation, one might be mistaken in attributing a particular perseverative behavior to frontal lobe lesions seen in CT scans. Besides, focusing attention on the "organic component" can lead to the extensive use of polypharmacy in preference to behavioral techniques, which can be more effective in the prevention and treatment of these disorders.

In many instances the explanation for behavioral changes can be found outside the central nervous system. Endocrine disorders (e.g., hypothyroidism, menarche, and menopause), occult infections, gastrointestinal reflux, undiagnosed fractures, and excessive medications can all cause behavioral deterioration. Therefore a thorough clinical history and examination are mandatory.

Peripheral Nerve Disorders

Peripheral nerve disorders have been overlooked in the developmentally disabled population. In 13 persons with dystonic athetotic syndrome we found 7 with carpal tunnel syndrome (median nerve compression) and 2 with ulnar nerve compression at the elbow. The same group of patients showed signs of acute and chronic denervation in several muscles belonging to different cervical roots. We speculate that these patients might have root and/or peripheral nerve damage as a consequence of the persistent abnormal posturing that continuously traumatizes the root and nerves in the cervical area and in the bony canals in the arms.[2] Such nerve damage is a preventable complication, but if it is not detected it will produce muscle atrophy. Unfortunately, even in patients with relatively high IQ, this disorder is mostly asymptomatic, or the patients fail to report the symptoms until the muscle atrophy is obvious.

In cases of entrapment neuropathies an operation to liberate the nerve is indicated. The situation is more complex in cases of cervical root compression. The possibility of improvement with surgery in the cervical spine is not well proven. Besides, the persistence of the movement disorder makes the postoperative period very painful and difficult for these patients.

Chronic polyneuropathies should also be suspected in persons with cerebral palsy and gait deterioration. Chronic neuropathies are responsible for impairment in proprioception, and this impairment could aggravate an already poor gait.

Sleep Disorders

There is not much experience with the new polysomnographic techniques in persons with developmental disabilities.

Our clinical experience is limited to 23 patients. In 12 of these 23, the study showed frequent epileptiform discharges, in many cases with clinical seizures and marked distortion of the sleep cycle. In 6 other patients the study showed obstructive or central apnea. These patients were referred for daytime sleepiness of unknown cause. In 3 other cases, referred for similar symptoms, the polysomnogram showed very poor sleep patterns, with frequent spontaneous arousal and short effective sleep time. One of these patients was an avid consumer of coffee. In one other case, with probable nocturnal myoclonic seizures, the study was compatible with restless leg syndrome, and epilepsy was ruled out as a cause of the disorder. The last patient of the group was referred because of "sudden, unexplained, uncontrollable behavior during the night" in an otherwise quiet person during the daytime. In this patient the sleep study was compatible with night terrors. There was a marked improvement after the patient was medicated with benzodiazepines.

Polysomnographic studies might therefore prove to be useful in the evaluation of behavior changes in individuals with developmental disabilities.

Problems Associated with Down Syndrome

Two medical problems associated with Down syndrome are important from the point of view of the neurologist: atlantoaxial instability (AAI), which can produce serious spinal cord damage, and the behavioral deterioration that is observed in older individuals with Down syndrome and which strongly resembles Alzheimer's dementia.

Atlantoaxial Subluxation

It is estimated that 25 to 30% of the persons with Down syndrome will show radiologic signs of AAI.[30] In a population of 130 adults with Down syndrome, we found that 13 (10%) had radiologic features that suggested high risk for spinal cord compression and that 38 (29%) were at intermediate risk. Among these patients we also found 8 with serious complications (1 with acute torticollis and the other 7 with different degrees of spinal cord compression) who required corrective surgery.[3] Similar findings have been reported for children with Down syndrome.[30] Because of these findings, it is recommended that cervical roentgenograms be obtained for all patients with Down syndrome. The screening and diagnosis are best made with lateral roentgenograms of the upper cervical spine in 3 positions, neutral, flexion, and extension. If the atlanto-odontoid distance is more than 5 mm in flexion, a patient is at high risk for neurologic complications, and when the distance is between 3 and 5 mm the risk is considered intermediate. In these patients certain restrictions in physical activities[12] and close follow-up are recommended. From our cases and the review of the literature the following clinical picture seems to emerge in patients with complications: female predominance, no age preference, and predominance of motor symptoms caused by compression of the spinal cord. Most of the time the symptoms consist of spasticity that starts in the legs; the spasticity can progress to a complete quadriplegia. The motor symptoms are rarely acute, and sometimes the acute presentation consists in torticollis. AAI is a serious condition, but, fortunately, with available treatment the progression of the symptoms can be arrested and in many instances there can be full recovery.

There are not yet clear rules for follow-up of patients with abnormal roentgenograms and no neurologic signs suggesting cord compression. Until more information becomes available, periodic roentgenograms are recommended for these patients. The presence of any one of the symptoms mentioned should also motivate a more complete evaluation.

Alzheimer's Disease

The second common problem consists of a clinical picture of early progressive dementia that clinically and pathologically closely resembles the Alzheimer's dementia of the non-Down population.

Clinical Problems

The early stage is characterized by subtle memory impairment, mostly in the form of forgetfulness and difficulties in learning new information. Later, other intellectual deficits in the areas of attention, language, spatial orientation, reasoning, and personality become the predominant clinical picture. These intellectual and behavioral changes have a profound effect on the ability to lead an independent life. This deterioration occurs early in the life of individuals with Down syndrome. Wisniewski et al.,[42] in 50 unselected institutionalized patients with Down syndrome, found significant neurologic and psychiatric abnormalities and mental deterioration in patients above age 35.

This progressive clinical deterioration is paralleled by changes in the anatomy of the brain. These changes, which include neurofibrillary tangles, neurovacuolar degeneration, and senile plaques, are highly characteristic although not specific to Alzheimer's disease. Malamud[19] reported finding such changes consistently present in the brains of individuals with Down syndrome over 40 years. Others have found the neuropathologic changes of Alzheimer's disease in all their cases of Down syndrome.[26]

Recently Heyman et al.[15] reported a high incidence of Alzheimer's disease and an increased incidence of Down syndrome among relatives of individuals affected by Alzheimer's disease. This finding suggests a common genetic base for this disorder. However, and even after long lives, individuals with Down syndrome and the neuropathologic changes of Alzheimer's disease do not necessarily develop the clinical picture of Alzheimer's disease before death,[31] suggesting that other factors might be operating. Similar observations have been reported in 51 non-Down syndrome individuals, who showed a high incidence of neurofibrillary tangles and senile plaques and no clinical signs of Alzheimer's disease.[39] Further studies of this condition in persons with Down syndrome could be of importance for the understanding of Alzheimer's disease in both the Down syndrome and non-Down syndrome patients.

In summary, the information presently available suggests that there is a high probability for persons with Down syndrome to develop a slowly progressive deterioration of intellectual function as they grow older. Because this picture has many common grounds with Alzheimer's disease as seen in non-Down syndrome individuals, it is presumed, although not yet proven, that these entities are similar. However, more research is needed to know how often persons with Down syndrome will develop Alzheimer's disease, and the associated factors that precipitate the disease. Because there are no specific diagnostic tests for this disorder, premature labeling should be avoided. It is not presently valid to say that all persons with Down syndrome will develop Alzheimer's disease, because this is not supported by available clinical follow-up.

REFERENCES

1. Alvarez, N.: The neurologic examination. *In* Comprehensive Management of Cerebral Palsy. Edited by G.H. Thompson, I.L. Rubin, and R.M. Bilenker. New York, Grune & Stratton, 1983.
2. Alvarez, N., Larkin, C., and Roxborough, J.: Carpal tunnel syndrome in dystonic athetoid cerebral palsy. Arch. Neurol., *11*:311, 1982.
3. Alvarez, N., and Rubin, I.L.: Atlanto-axial Instability in adults with Down syndrome: A clinical and radiological survey. Appl. Res. Ment. Ret., 7:67, 1986.
4. Angel, R.W., Boylls, C.C., and Weinrich, M.: Cerebral evoked potentials and somatosensory perception. Neurology, *34*:123, 1984.
5. Banker, B.Q., and Bruce-Gregorios, J.: Neuropathology. *In* Comprehensive Management of Cerebral Palsy. Edited by G.H. Thompson, I.L. Rubin, and R.M. Bilenker. New York, Grune & Stratton, 1983.
6. Chiappa, K.H.: Evoked Potentials in Clinical Medicine. New York, Raven Press, 1983.
7. Dale, A., and Stanley, F.G.: An epidemiological study of cerebral palsy in western Australia 1956-1975. II. Spastic cerebral palsy and perinatal factors. Dev. Med. Child Neurol., *22*:13, 1980.
8. Dieker, L.J., and Hertz, R.: Intrapartum prevention of brain damage. *In* Comprehensive Management of Cerebral Palsy. Edited by G.H. Thompson, I.L. Rubin, and R.M. Bilenker. New York, Grune & Stratton, 1983.
9. Dubowitz, V.: The Floppy Infant. 2nd Ed. Clinics in Developmental Medicine, Vol. 76. Philadelphia, J.B. Lippincott, 1982.
10. Eiben, R.M., and Crocker, A.C.: Cerebral palsy within the spectrum of developmental disabilities. *In* Comprehensive Management of Cerebral Palsy. Edited by G.H. Thompson, I.L. Rubin, and R.M. Bilenker. New York, Grune & Stratton, 1983.
11. Frank, Y., and Torres, F.: Visual evoked potentials in the evaluation of "cortical blindness" in children. Ann. Neurol., *6*:126, 1978.
12. Goldberg, M.: Statement on athletic participation for patients with Down syndrome (Trisomy 21). Massachusetts Special Olympics. Boston, Tufts University School of Medicine, 1983.
13. Golden, N., and Rubin, I.L.: Intrauterine factors and the risk of development of cerebral palsy. *In* Comprehensive Management of Cerebral Palsy. Edited by G.H. Thompson, I.L. Rubin, and R.M. Bilenker. New York, Grune & Stratton, 1983.
14. Hagberg, B.: Epidemiological and preventive aspects of cerebral palsy and severe mental retardation in Sweden. Eur. J. Pediatr., *130*:71, 1979.
15. Heyman, A., et al.: Alzheimer's disease: A study of epidemiological aspects. Ann. Neurol., *15*:335, 1984.
16. Holm, V.A.: Rett's syndrome: A progressive developmental disability in girls. Dev. Beh. Pediatr., 6:32, 1985.

17. Jacobson, R.I.: Abnormalities of the skull in children. *In* Neurologic Clinics, Vol. 3. Edited by K. Swaiman. Philadelphia, W.B. Saunders, 1985.

18. Kieley, J.L., et al.: Cerebral palsy and newborn care. II. Mortality and neurological impairment in low birthweight infants. Dev. Med. Child Neurol., 23:650, 1981.

19. Malamud, N.: Neuropathology of organic brain syndrome associated with aging. *In* Aging and the Brain. Edited by C.M. Gaitz. New York, Plenum Press, 1972.

20. Martin, H.P.: Microcephaly and mental retardation. Am. J. Dis. Child., 119:128, 1970.

21. Menkes, J.H.: Metabolic disorders of the central nervous system. *In* Textbook of Child Neurology. 2nd Ed. Edited by J.H. Menkes. Philadelphia, Lea & Febiger, 1980.

22. Menkes, J.H.: Malformations of the central nervous system. *In* Textbook of Child Neurology. 2nd Ed. Edited by J.H. Menkes. Philadelphia, Lea & Febiger, 1980.

23. Neil, J., and Alvarez, N.: Differential diagnosis of epileptic and pseudoepileptic seizures in developmentally disabled persons. Appl. Res. Ment. Retard., 7:285, 1986.

24. Nelson, K.B., and Ellenberg, J.H.: Epidemiology of cerebral palsy. Adv. Neurol., 19:421, 1978.

25. O'Brien, J.F.: The lysosomal storage diseases. Mayo Clin. Proc., 57:192, 1982.

26. Olsen, M.I., and Shaw, C.M.: Presenile dementia and Alzheimer's disease in mongolism. Brain, 92:147, 1969.

27. O'Reilly, D.E., and Walentynowicsz, J.E.: Etiological factors in cerebral palsy: An historical review. Dev. Med. Child Neurol., 23:633, 1981.

28. Parker, S.W., Chiappa, K.H., and Brooks, E.B.: Brainstem auditory evoked responses in patients with acoustic neuromas and cerebello-pontine angle meningioma. Neurology, 30:413, 1980.

29. Pryor, H.B., and Thielander, H.: Abnormally small head size and intellect in children. J. Pediatr., 73:593, 1968.

30. Pueschel, S.M., et al.: Symptomatic atlanto-axial subluxation in persons with Down syndrome. J. Pediatr. Orthop., 4:682, 1984.

31. Roper, A.H., and Williams, R.S.: Relationship between plaques, tangles and dementia in Down syndrome. Neurology, 30:639, 1980.

32. Rubin, I.L.: Perinatal factors. *In* Comprehensive Management of Cerebral Palsy. Edited by G.H. Thompson, I.L. Rubin, and R.M. Bilenker. New York, Grune & Stratton, 1983.

33. Schafer, I.A.: Genetics of mental retardation. *In* Comprehensive Management of Cerebral Palsy. Edited by G.H. Thompson, I.L. Rubin, and R.M. Bilenker. New York, Grune & Stratton, 1983.

34. Shapiro, B.K., Wachtel, R.C., Palmer, F.B., and Capute, A.J.: Associated dysfunctions. *In* Comprehensive Management of Cerebral Palsy. Edited by G.H. Thompson, I.L. Rubin, and R.M. Bilenker. New York, Grune & Stratton, 1983.

35. Shomer, H., and Student, M.: Auditory nerve and brainstem evoked responses in normal, autistics, minimal brain dysfunction and psychomotor retarded children. Electroencephalogr. Clin. Neurophysiol., 39:174, 1978.

36. Squires, N., et al.: Auditory brainstem response abnormalities in severely and profoundly retarded adults. Electroencephalogr. Clin. Neurophysiol., 50:761, 1980.

37. Swaiman, K.: Mental retardation. *In* The Practice of Pediatric Neurology. Edited by K. Swaiman, and F. Wright. St. Louis, C.V. Mosby, 1975.

38. Tanguay, P.E., et al.: Auditory brainstem evoked responses in autistic children. Arch. Gen. Psychiatry, 39:174, 1982.

39. Ulrich, J.: Alzheimer changes in non-demented patients younger than sixty-five: Possible early stages of Alzheimer's Disease and senile dementia of the Alzheimer's type. Ann. Neurol., 17:273, 1985.

40. Volpe, J.J.: Observing the infant in the early hours after asphyxia. *In* Intrauterine Asphyxia and the Developing Fetal Brain. Edited by L. Gluck. Chicago, Year Book Medical Publishers, 1977.

41. Volpe, J.J., Pasternak, J.P., and Allen, W.C.: Ventricular dilation preceding rapid head growth following neonatal intracranial hemorrhage. Am. J. Dis. Child., 131:1212, 1977.

42. Wisniewski, K., Howe, J., Williams, D.G., and Wisniewski, H.M.: Precocious aging and dementia in patients with Down's syndrome. Biol. Psychiatry, 13:619, 1978.

43. Yudofsky, S., Williams, D., and Gorman, J.: Propanolol in the treatment of rage and violent behavior in patients with chronic brain syndromes. Am. J. Psychiatry, 138:218, 1981.

44. Zinkin, P.M.: The effect of visual handicaps in early development. Clinics in Developmental Medicine, Vol. 73. Philadelphia, J.B. Lippincott, 1979.

9

ORTHOPEDICS: A FUNCTIONAL APPROACH TO PROBLEM-SOLVING

Sharon R. Menkveld, M.D.

In patients with developmental disabilities, there is a higher prevalence of CNS dysfunction, genetic syndromes, and congenital anomalies, many of which may be associated with specific musculoskeletal problems. The primary diagnosis of developmental disability implies a different set of psychosocial considerations, a different natural history of disease and treatment, and a different process for decision-making about the orthopedic disorders. This chapter describes orthopedic disorders, the distinctive functional approach applied in orthopedics, and the process of decision-making about orthopedic treatment.

Although orthopedic disorders are specifically discussed, this chapter presents a basis for a general discussion of medical care for children and adults when decisions on an appropriate form of intervention require considerations beyond defining of risks and complications of treatment. My goal in identifying important aspects and following the process of orthopedic decision-making is to raise these issues in the context of models for the delivery of medical care, not to postulate ideal solutions. In every aspect of medical decision-making and in value judgments, more factors are involved than I present here. I have selected those factors that are of greatest importance for patients with developmental disabilities.

ORTHOPEDIC DISORDERS

Spasticity and hypotonia are the two most common patterns of musculoskeletal disability. Therefore I will focus first on specific orthopedic problems associated with spastic and hypotonic conditions as typified by cerebral palsy and myelomeningocele. Cerebral palsy is the most common diagnosis in patients with developmental disabilities for which significant orthopedic input is expected. Cerebral palsy is a nonprogressive disorder of the central nervous system that causes delay in acquisition of gross and fine motor skills and has multiple congenital, perinatal, and early-childhood causes. Mental retardation is frequently an associated finding, and variability of involvement is the hallmark of cerebral palsy. Spasticity, however, is the stereotyped presentation of cerebral palsy. Cerebral palsy is discussed in detail because it is common and can be generalized to other patients with developmental disabilities.

Spina bifida causes both upper and lower motor neuron compromise of the spinal cord and conus. This results in motor abnormalities and anesthetic skin. The expected level of functioning is predicted by the level of intact innervation. Spina bifida is presented as hypotonia for contrast and comparison to the spasticity commonly seen with cerebral palsy. Ataxia is presented separately. Other syndromes that are characterized by developmental disabilities and musculoskeletal anomalies are also described here.

Spasticity

Several of the causes of spasticity may be associated with dysfunction. Perinatal insults are a common cause of spasticity in patients with developmental disabilities, but spasticity is also associated with intracranial or intraspinal tumors, diastematomyelia, cervical and thoracic spina bifida, Rud's syndrome, Sjogren-Larsson's syndrome, Bloch-Sulzberger's syndrome, and Sturge-Weber-Dimitri disease. The orthopedic disorders associated with spasticity are grouped below according to anatomic regions.

Ankle and Foot

A toe-toe gait pattern is the most common presenting complaint in patients with neuromuscular disease who are referred to the orthopedist. It is caused by equinus deformity of the ankle resulting from triceps surae spasticity and from an exaggerated stretch reflex of the muscle. Frequently, heel valgus, pes planus, and hyperextension of the knee are secondary deformities. Equinovarus deformity of the foot and ankle is less common, but is seen in some patients with cerebral palsy.

Knee

In patients with spasticity, flexors and extensors of the knee are frequently unbalanced, and either may cause contracture. Flexion deformities can be primary because of spastic hamstrings, secondary because of compensation for hip and ankle deformities, or functional because they lower the center of gravity. Each of these may be evidenced by a "crouch" gait.

Genu recurvatum usually results from a spastic quadriceps or equinus deformity at the ankle. Patients have "back-kneeing," i.e., hyperextension of the knee, during walking.

Hip

Adduction, flexion, and internal rotation of the hip are the most common spastic deforming forces at the hip (Fig. 9-1). These can lead to malrotation of the femur, acetabular dysplasia, and subluxation and dislocation of the joint. Adduction spasticity can lead to difficulty with perineal care and a "scissoring" gait. Flexion deformities of the hip also contribute to a "crouch" gait.

Leg

Leg length discrepancy is characteristic of hemiplegia, but is also seen in di- and quadriplegia. A short-leg limp during walking can also cause scoliosis.

Spine

Scoliosis occurs in 15 to 30% of patients with spasticity. Causes include muscle imbalance, associated congenital vertebral anomalies, and pelvic obliquity. Scoliosis comes to medical attention in several ways: because of back or rib deformity, shoulder or pelvic asymmetry, truncal imbalance in walking or sitting, inability to be positioned in a wheelchair, and, rarely, cardiac or pulmonary problems.

Hand

Spasticity in the adductor pollicis or thumb flexors can result in a thumb-in-palm position. Patients with this deformity lose the pinch capability and are blocked from holding objects in the palm (Fig. 9-2). Finger flexors may also be spastic. This condition is usually accompanied by spasticity in the wrist flexors; thus, extension at the wrist worsens the deformity. Release of objects is thereby inhibited.

Wrist

A flexion deformity of the wrist puts the hands in a dysfunctional position and may be cosmetically disfiguring. A pronation deformity may exist concomitantly or separately and leads to similar dysfunctional positioning of the hand.

Elbow and Shoulder

Flexor spasticity at the elbow may result in positioning difficulty for reaching with the hand; and posturing with the arm and hand during walking can cause loss of balance. Internal rotation, adduction, or the less common abduction deformity of the shoulder can cause functional problems in rare cases.

Hypotonia

Hypotonia defines the functional problems in patients with developmental disabilities who have spina bifida, but it may also be seen in patients with cerebral palsy, CNS tumors, Friedreich's ataxia, Werdnig-Hoffmann syndrome, diastematomyelia, hypertrophic interstitial neuritis, muscular dystrophy (Duchenne's, congenital, or infantile), and congenital myotonia. In a manner parallel to that in spasticity, hypotonia may be present with the following orthopedic

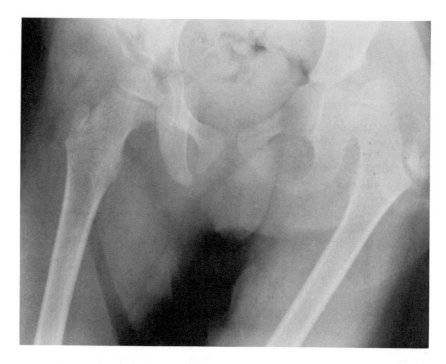

FIG. 9-1. Roentgenogram illustrating how deforming forces of flexion, valgus, and adduction from imbalanced muscle spasticity cause, when present asymmetrically, a "windswept" deformity that can result in dislocation.

problems in various anatomic areas of the musculoskeletal system.

Ankle and Foot

Problems in the foot and ankle are variable in hypotonia and are related to the muscles involved. Imbalance between hypotonic and normally innervated muscles, and the positioning forces in intrauterine and postnatal life and in walking, determine which deformity will result. Equinus, equinovarus, calcaneovarus, pes valgus, calcaneovalgus, pes cavus, and claw toes are most common. All of these are manifested by a nonplantigrade foot, which causes instability for walking and difficulty with shoe fitting (Fig. 9-3). If loss of sensation is also present, ulcers or osteomyelitis may be the reason for seeking consultation.

Knee

Extension or hyperextension deformities are common because the knee has bony and passive ligamentous stability only in full extension. In addition to gait abnormalities, such as back-kneeing, fractures of the femur are common in patients with hypotonia.

Hip

External rotation and abduction as well as flexion deformities are most common when mus-

cles about the hip are hypotonic. Subluxation or dislocation of the hip may result. In dislocated hips, secondary degenerative arthritis can develop early and can become painful. Abduction weakness results in a Trendelenburg lurch, which greatly increases the energy consumed in walking. Patients who have innervation of the trunk musculature with good truncal stability are expected to be able to walk with bracing, at least during childhood.

Spine

Lordosis, kyphosis, and scoliosis are common with hypotonia, and every patient with any of these anomalies should be monitored throughout life.

Upper Extremities

Loss of function rather than a fixed deformity in the upper extremities is observed in patients with hypotonic neuromuscular disease.

Ataxia

Ataxia is distinct from imbalance caused by spastic muscular contraction and may be present independently as very mild CNS dysfunction. The resulting clumsiness and falling can make independent ambulation difficult, and thus the patient with developmental disabilities may first

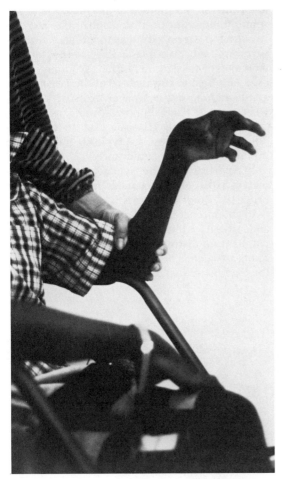

FIG. 9-2. Patient with adduction contracture of the thumb and flexion deformity of the wrist. These conditions decrease the ability to grasp even when active extension is possible.

FIG. 9-3. Patient with flail feet associated with myelomeningocele. Extension contractures of the knee further compromise ambulatory ability of the patient, who requires short leg braces and crutches.

come to the orthopedist for diagnosis. Ataxia may also be the main feature in tumors of the posterior fossa, Hartnup's disease, or Friedreich's ataxia.

Other Anomalies

Many syndromes are characterized by an association of developmental disability with musculoskeletal anomalies. Some, like Klinefelter's syndrome, with dislocation of the radial head, or orofacial-digital myopathy with overlapping short digits, are only of academic interest. Others are associated with anomalies that can be disabling or disfiguring.

The severe neuropathic form of arthrogryposis is seen in patients with developmental disabilities. This disorder is characterized by diminished muscle substance and by a decrease in the active and passive range of motion of all four extremities. Clubbed feet, dislocated knees, and subluxated or dislocated hips are common. The shoulders are internally rotated, forearms pronated, wrists and fingers flexed, and the thumbs adducted into the palms. Maintenance of the functional position of all of these joints will involve the orthopedist in the care of patients with arthrogryposis.

Trisomy 18 (E), one of the abnormal chromosomal configurations in patients with developmental disabilities, is associated with an increased incidence of congenital vertical talus, syndactyly, and arthrogryposis. Trisomy 13-15 (B) has a lesser association with rocker-bottom feet and is characterized by an increased incidence of polydactyly. A rocker-bottom or congenital flat foot is a rigid deformity caused by a vertical talus. The patient walks on the dislocated head of the talus with the forefoot adducted and with a marked hindfoot valgus. Shoe wear and distortion are marked. Pain usually sets in during late adolescence. Patients with Down syndrome (trisomy 21) are typically hypotonic, with increased ligamentous laxity which may lead to recurrent subluxation or dislocation of the patella and shoulder. Hypoplasia of the odontoid process is also noted in Down syndrome and may lead to subluxation of the atlantoaxial joint and to an intermittent neurologic deficit, or to paralysis with even minimal trauma.

Patients with mucopolysaccharidosis type I (Hurler's syndrome) typically develop a gibbous deformity at the thoracolumbar junction of the spine from anterior disk protrusion and the resulting posterior displacement and anterior vertebral-body hypoplasia (Fig. 9-4). The first musculoskeletal signs in Hurler's syndrome, however, are flexion contracture of the large joints, genu valgum, and pes planovalgus with an upright posture. San Filippo syndrome (mucopolysaccharidosis type III) can lead to the same deformities, but these are typically milder, with minimal functional significance.

In Apert's syndrome, syndactyly of the digits, metacarpals, and metatarsals may be complete or partial. Joint synostosis is uncommon.

In chondroectodermal dysplasia, genu valgum and lateral subluxation or dislocation of the patella from distortion of the proximal tibia and fibula are seen. They are a result of shortening of the long bones distal to the femur and humerus,

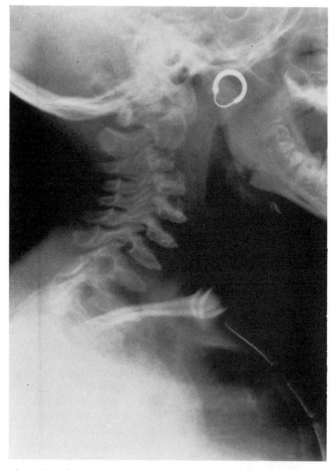

FIG. 9-4. The mucopolysaccharidoses frequently have associated spinal deformities. This roentgenogram of patient with mucopolysaccharidosis shows flattening of vertebral bodies and instability of upper cervical spine, which required operative fusion to prevent neurologic compromise.

which may also cause dislocation of the head of the radius. Polydactyly is another musculoskeletal anomaly associated with this disease.

Gouty arthritis occurs as one of the late complications of toxic nephropathy secondary to lead poisoning.

FUNCTION: AN ORTHOPEDIC APPROACH

In the previous section, the orthopedic disorders have been described in terms of functional disabilities. Orthopedics is a medical and surgical discipline whose basic theme is that of function. Function has become broadly defined to include appearance, which may interfere with a patient's ability to interact successfully with the world, and correction of present deformity to prevent future disability. Function predominates in orthopedics with regard to symptomatology, pathologic definition, investigative technique, and treatment.

A problem is identified by the patient, his family, or various caregivers and is referred to the orthopedist if it involves the musculoskeletal system. During the consultation, the problem will be refined and redefined by the orthopedist in terms of functional deficit. For example, a family may come to the orthopedist because their child with cerebral palsy has a tight heel cord. In this case, gait analysis is performed in a specialized laboratory where muscle firing, joint angular patterns, and force vectors are traced throughout the phases of gait; or a visual analysis is made by the clinician. Active range of motion is ranked above passive range of motion, and testing for fixed contractures is performed. Radiographs are most helpful when taken during weight-bearing or with a limb in a position that increases the risk of joint deformity.

In the medical history-taking and physical examination, the orthopedist will show the family that the problems in the above example are: the child (1) lands on his toes, (2) is unable to get the foot flat and fit into a brace, (3) hyperextends the knee (back-knees) because the ankle cannot bend 90 degrees as the body weight moves forward over the foot, and (4) leans forward and thus is always off balance. Defining the specific problems that the orthopedist will attempt to correct is critical to the subsequent treatment process.

Treatment for specifically defined functional problems is aimed at improving function, not necessarily the deformity. Deformity and disability cannot be clearly separated, however, because there are bidirectional cause-and-effect relationships or feedback loops. Further confusion results when the ultimate cause of both is

cerebral palsy, which is not treated by the orthopedist. Indeed, the orthopedist will choose to address some selected subgroup of the interrelated aspects of spasticity: abnormal stretch reflex, muscle contracture, other soft-tissue contracture, imbalance between muscle groups, lack of voluntary control and separation of muscle groups, increased tone, abnormal reflexes, and bony deformities.

A grouping of orthopedic patients according to their levels of functioning is another data base for orthopedic decision-making.

Patients' Levels of Functioning

For simplicity, levels of function are discussed in terms of the lower and upper extremities, in a sequence of increasingly higher function levels. That is, a given level presupposes fulfillment of the requirements of all lower levels. When a patient with developmental disabilities has reached an appropriate developmental level, it is the task of the orthopedist to ensure that anatomy is not the factor limiting the patient in achieving the corresponding level of functioning. Within each level, therefore, I present the functional requirements grouped by anatomic regions, as in the section on orthopedic disorders.

Locomotion

LYING AND SEMI-ERECT SITTING

For patients who are unable to sit in a wheelchair, a mobile bed cart can be adapted to support them in a semi-erect position. The major requirements are those that allow ease of caretaking by others. Because foot and ankle position can be accommodated by soft footwear, it is rarely a problem. Knee position (most commonly a fixed flexion contracture) requires intervention only when skin breakdown results.

The hips can be a source of two major problems: (1) Adduction contractures can make perineal care difficult. In severely disabled patients perineal care is usually complicated by incontinence, which requires diapers for hygiene. (2) Hip pain during transfers from bed to cart or for bed-changing is caused by arthritis secondary to hip dislocation or subluxation. Improvements in general medical care have lengthened the life span of patients with severe neuromuscular involvement, but over time the secondary complications of arthritis and pain develop. Another common deformity in semi-erect patients is that of "windswept" hips. This spastic deformity is progressive even after skeletal maturity, and it results in late unilateral hip dislocation. A well-accepted guide in orthopedics is that bilaterally dislocated hips should be left dislocated, and unilaterally subluxated or dislocated hips should be repaired in childhood. However, the data that supported the nontreatment of bilateral

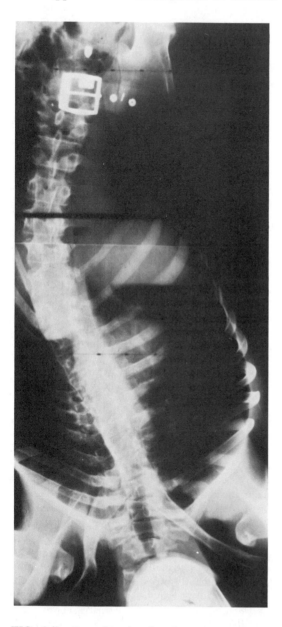

FIG. 9-5. Long "paralytic" scoliosis is one characteristic pattern of both spastic and hypotonic neuromuscular diseases. When curvature has progressed to the degree of severity shown in this roentgenogram, upright sitting posture and balance are compromised. Bracing, wheelchair modifications, and spinal fusion may all be required at different times in the treatment of such curves.

or late unilateral dislocations were based on a shorter life span and should be reviewed for current management recommendations.

Spinal deformities rarely require treatment in semi-erect functional patients, because these patients will not exceed the compromised cardiopulmonary reserve that results from the spinal deformities. Skin breakdown occasionally occurs and is treated locally, rather than with spinal fusion and stabilization. Disuse osteoporosis secondary to the non-weight-bearing of the lower extremity and to minimal anti-gravity stress in the upper extremities leads to an increase of fractures. These pathologic fractures can result from minimal trauma, including routine transfers and bed care, and should be treated conservatively (nonsurgically).

SITTING

Erect sitting in a wheelchair allows an increased range of locomotion and the possibility of independent locomotion. A wheelchair can also increase function in patients who can walk but whose mobility is impaired because of age, systemic disease, obesity, or severe motor disorders of the lower extremities. The position of the feet and ankles must be compatible with wheelchair foot plates, which are set at 90 degrees to the leg extensions. Knees must extend to 90 degrees for stable upright sitting posture. The hips have a greater range of positions because the chair back can be inclined to facilitate sitting. The spine can be supported by the truncal musculature, chair modifications, a spinal orthosis, or spinal fusion and internal fixation (Fig. 9-5). Whatever method is employed, the back must conform to the chair's confines. However, the complications contraindicate surgical intervention when curves have progressed to the severity of causing significant secondary cardiopulmonary compromise.

WALKING

Bipedal ambulation has a strict set of requirements for function. The feet must be plantigrade for weight-bearing, for any necessary bracing, and for upright balance. Stability at the knee for weight acceptance is the primary determinant of the gait pattern. The quadriceps loses effective stabilizing ability as the joint flexes more than 15 degrees. Standing then requires a nonerect posture with the hips flexed so that the centers of mass of the trunk and upper extremities, thighs, and shanks are over the foot. Flexion contractures will lead to a crouched position. External supports, i.e., a walker, braces, or crutches, may be required. The hips must be stable; uneven leg lengths must be equalized. The spine should be maintained in a midline position and with a nonprogressive degree of curvature. Progressive scoliosis can compromise walking through an unbalanced position or inadequate cardiopulmonary capacity. Ataxia must be compensated, usually by external supports. Upper-extremity spastic posturing with walking can cause loss of balance or generalized extensor spasm (Fig. 9-6).

Arm and Hand Functioning

Functioning of the upper extremities requires positioning of the arm in space by the gross motor action of the shoulders and elbows, fine motor hand movements, and appropriate sensory feedback.

GROSS MOTOR POSITIONING

An assistive arm requires only gross motor skills and can be used for holding up large objects (balls) or holding down a flattened object (paper for drawing). Adduction or internal rotation contractures of the shoulder restrict the size of objects that can be held. Flexion contractures or fixed extension of the elbows limits the usefulness of functional positioning of the arm.

FINE MOTOR MANIPULATION

Hand manipulation has two further levels of complexity. Grasp/release allows holding of smaller objects (a glass) and further requires the wrist to be maintained in a neutral position. The tenodesis effect of wrist extension/finger flexion and wrist flexion/finger extension is the passive component of wrist position/finger function. The thumb-in-palm deformity seen with increased spastic tone must be corrected to allow a space for holding objects in the palm. Strength can be increased with muscle transfers to reinforce grasp or release of the digits. This level of functioning can be enhanced or made possible by orthopedic intervention if the developmental stage of the patient is appropriate.

Fine manipulation of still smaller objects requires a complex set of coordinated, balanced musculotendinous contractions as well as extremes of joint range of motion. Except for limited skin syndactyly release, orthopedic intervention is too gross to result in enhancement of the functional level.

Orthopedic Treatment Options

Treatment options for orthopedists include physical therapy, occupational therapy, casting, bracing, use of assistive devices, and surgery,

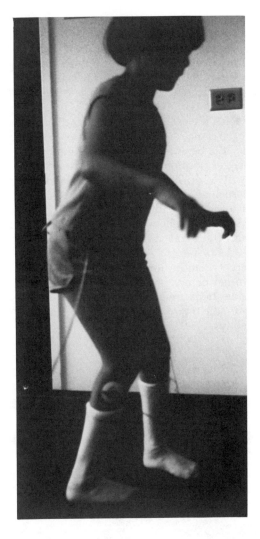

FIG. 9-6. Walking demands positioning and control of feet, ankles, knees, hips, trunk, and upper extremities. Neuromuscular diseases associated with developmental disabilities can cause fixed deformity, disruptive reflex patterning, poor control of separation, and amplitude of muscle contraction, all associated with ataxia.

alone or in combination. These treatment modalities are, to some extent, interchangeable options, depending on the patients' levels of function to determine the aggressiveness of treatment and how strict the definitions of success will be.

Physical and occupational therapy can help to decrease tone, improve position for functioning, decrease soft-tissue contractures and thus increase the range of motion of joints, teach patients patterns of functioning, increase muscle strength, and encourage control of specific muscle groups (Fig. 9-7).

Casting is used for stabilization of body segments to decrease soft-tissue contractures, hold a corrected body position, provide stability after operations or trauma, and allow therapeutic trials of bracing.

Bracing is closely related to casting, but it is a more permanent method of stabilizing body segments, the trunk (spine), or extremities to allow healing or positioning for optimal function.

Assistive devices are aids to increased function, such as a simple strap to hold on to objects, a walker to substitute for truncal balance, a wheelchair to allow independent ambulation, or architectural modifications to provide accessibility.

Surgery can be used when any or all of the above fail or are predicted to fail. The surgical indications are secondary bony deformities, severe soft-tissue contractures, or conjoined structures.

FIG. 9-7. Physical therapy: seeking to optimize function by working with patients and families in schools, workshops, and other community agencies.

A Guide to Referral

Function is the guide for pediatricians and internists as to when patients need to be referred to the orthopedist. Of course, orthopedists should be involved in the initial evaluation of patients for coordinated planning of care when there are significant and ongoing musculoskeletal needs.

Referral to an orthopedist should be for a functional problem, not only for a deformity. For example, "tight heel cords" cause a gait abnormality for ambulators and difficulty in fitting of shoes for nonambulators. If neither problem exists, the orthopedist will have no means of "improving" this patient's condition. An exception may be a progressive bony deformity, specifically, progressive scoliosis/kyphosis, dislocated hips, or hyperextension of the knees (which may be asymptomatic). The orthopedist can be helpful in deciding whether the deformity is a problem, based on the level of functioning expected for a given patient. Orthopedic intervention is enabling intervention; typically, it will be prescribed only if it allows the patient to do something for the first time or to do it better.

The definition of the orthopedist as "the doctor for functional problems" is also well accepted by the specialty. Although speech and language, cognitive skills, or gross or fine motor systems can be involved, the patient or family may first seek medical help for a musculoskeletal problem, and the orthopedist may therefore be the first physician who makes the diagnosis of developmental disability. The orthopedist will routinely refer the patient for primary medical care, which includes the broader issues of developmental disabilities, and retain only the initial musculoskeletal functional complaint on his diagnostic problem list.

THE ORTHOPEDIC DECISION-MAKING PROCESS

The need to examine the decision-making process for medical intervention in cases of developmental disabilities arises because the patient with developmental disability is not an equal partner in the doctor-patient relationship. In ordinary cases, the orthopedic physician presents his formulation of the patient's symptoms, the signs found in the physical examination, and the results of laboratory tests to justify therapeutic recommendations (Fig. 9-8). The goals of treatment are defined, the procedure is explained, and the risks and alternative treatments are identified. The patient then has the opportunity to respond and ask for clarification and fur-

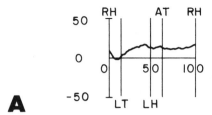

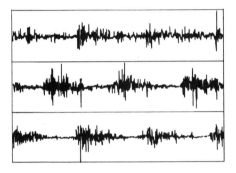

FIG. 9-8. Data from a gait study, a laboratory examination that quantifies (A) joint angular motion, (B) electromyelographic activity of muscles, and (C) position of the body relative to ground reaction forces in order to offer an objective assessment of gait. Information is used by orthopedists to define causes of functional problems and to plan intervention.

ther information, to negotiate the suggested treatment, and to set limits on its implementation. Not all of these contractual rights are exercised by each patient or encouraged by each physician, but the possibility is understood and accepted by both sides in the relationship. In the presence of developmental disabilities, however, even the adult patient is unemancipated; he has an advocate, who may be a family member, guardian, caregiver, or institutional representative, or a group of these. The only member of the decision-making team whose role does not reflect full partnership is the patient. Decisions have to be made, and each step in the decision-making process has to be weighed for the patient rather than by the patient.

In the following pages I will (1) discuss orthopedics as a model for medical decision-making for patients with developmental disabilities, (2) present two case histories that typify the problems presented by patients with developmental disabilities, (3) analyze the elements of decision-making involved in working with developmentally disabled persons, and (4) present a scheme for decision-making based on these elements.

In considering the aspects of decision-making, the psychosocial milieu and the care setting will not be discussed. Each patient with orthopedic needs presents a unique situation that should not be generalized, although the psychosocial milieu and the care setting provide the context for the process of deciding how these needs will be met.

Orthopedics: A Model for Decision-Making

In view of the types of problems it addresses and the approach used, orthopedics is particularly suited to an inquiry into medical decision-making with respect to children and adults with developmental disabilities. Several reasons are given below.

Focus on Function

Often, the problems of patients with developmental disabilities are presented to orthopedists because the patients are unable to carry out some activity, e.g., walking or holding an object. Orthopedists typically treat a deformity not only because it exists, but also because it causes

disability. The focus on function, of course, high-
lights the psychological implications of the diagnosis of developmental disability. It emphasizes
that affected children are slower than normal
children in achieving skill levels, and that adults
reach a developmental plateau at a level below
that of the general population. Thus, patients
with developmental disabilities "cannot do" what
everyone else "can do." In discussing orthopedic
treatment with the family, the physician must
therefore state that cure of the underlying pathologic process is *not the goal,* and that realistic
criteria for the success of treatment must be defined primarily in terms of function. This focus
forces both the family and the health care providers to confront the problem of the disability
or sets of disabilities.

Consent for Surgical Intervention

The act of obtaining consent for orthopedic
surgery from the family of a patient often causes
the family to focus on the entire psychosocial
milieu of the patient, and the family's history of
coping with a member with developmental disabilities is reexamined. The physician opens the
discussion to obtain consent for a planned surgery with the goals, procedure, and risks of the
operation. The family members see operative
intervention as an important focal point of the
decisions they have made in the past, and they
expect the presently planned intervention to be
congruent with the course for care they have
elected for the present and future.

Ambiguity of the Factual Basis
for Decision-Making

The natural history of musculoskeletal neuromuscular disorders in adult populations is not
well characterized, and there is considerable
variation in activity and skill levels in the population with developmental disabilities. This means
that the data for decision-making are ambiguous
and that there is room for the bias of the medical
practitioners. Orthopedic problems in the presence of developmental disabilities differ from
those in the general population only in the physician's greater acknowledgment that the natural
history of the disease or condition, and therefore
the outcome of the proposed treatment, are both
unknown.

Case Histories

The following cases demonstrate some of
the conflicts that are presented to orthopedists who are involved in therapeutic decision-
making.

PATIENT 1

S.J. is a 50-year-old female patient with mild spastic diplegia and moderate DD. She has always lived in the family's
home. After her mother's death, her widowed older sister
moved in and assumed guardianship; she is presently 67
years old. S.J. underwent femoral and pelvic osteotomies for
a subluxating right hip at age 17. She subsequently did well
for 25 years, but then degenerative arthritis developed in
that hip. Nonsteroidal anti-inflammatory agents gave her
symptomatic relief for an additional 5 years, but over the last
2 years her condition has progressively worsened. She cannot rise from a chair without assistance, cannot put on her
own shoes and socks, and occasionally is incontinent of urine
because it is too painful to walk to the toilet even with a
walker and her sister's help. A home health aide comes in
each morning to assist with dressing, bathing, and moving
S.J. to the living room couch, where she spends the day
because it is too painful to get up and move elsewhere. Her
sister is in fair health with mild diabetes and hypertension,
but is unable to lift the patient without assistance, and she
worries about the strain on her heart.

They live in the third-story walk-up apartment where S.J.
has always resided, but she has not been out of the house
since her last visit to her physician. In the past she enjoyed
church services and social activities, shopped daily in the
neighborhood, and watched two generations of children
grow up by seeing them at play in the schoolyard across from
the nearby city park. The sisters argue more now because of
their confinement to the apartment, lack of daily topics for
conversation, and fear of the future. They seek orthopedic
consultation because S.J. has a decubitus on her buttocks
that has been slow in healing because S.J. frequently sits in
her urine when she is incontinent.

The physician arranges hospitalization to care for the
decubitus and tells the sisters to plan on approximately 3
weeks of acute treatment for S.J. Next, he raises the issue of
planning for future placement. Generally, degenerative disease in a single joint can be cured effectively by total joint
replacement, but spasticity is a contraindication to this operation. A wheelchair would allow S.J. much greater mobility
and could be modified to allow toileting. However, this
would require moving from the home S.J. has always lived in
because the doorways and halls are too narrow for wheelchair
passage. The sister predicts that she will be the first to
die and so expects that S.J. will then require placement
elsewhere.

When asked, S.J. is excited about the wheelchair and
about resuming her former life, but is adamant about not
wanting to leave home or go to the hospital. She knows that
her sister will go away as her parents did. She repeats all of
this each time the topic comes up, but is unable to relate
these factors to each other or express what she wants most to
happen.

PATIENT 2

M.F. is a 15-year-old boy with high thoracic diastematomyelia. He has lived in a state-funded institution for the
severely handicapped since the age of 8 years and has had no
serious complications of his condition since neurosurgical
closure was performed at birth. He communicates with a
wide array of vocalizations and enjoys drawing and feeding
himself finger foods.

On the family's last visit 2 years ago, M.F. fell out of his
wheelchair when they walked into the room. As he was being
repositioned in his chair, the family noted that he had difficulty with seating, and they requested medical consultation.
A thoracolumbosacral orthosis had been prescribed at the

time of his admission for control of his kyphoscoliosis, which has progressed to 107 degrees. He can no longer fit in his adaptive wheelchair because of the rigidity of his curvature. Earlier intervention in the progression of his spinal deformity was not indicated because of his unknown life expectancy, which now appears to be of considerable length because of his medical history to date, particularly if the scoliosis is corrected.

The option of posterior spinal fusion with instrumentation is suggested by the orthopedist as the only effective means of partial correction and control of future progression of the kyphoscoliosis. A team meeting of M.F.'s caretakers, unit nursing director, occupational therapist, teacher, and primary-care physician is called. The team members do not consider that the risks of the procedure are warranted to allow M.F.'s continued upright posture in the wheelchair instead of his using a portable reclining bed chair. However, they recommend a conference with the patient's family, because the family has never legally given up custody of the son to the state and has visited him occasionally.

Elements of Decision-Making

I will consider the groups of orthopedic problems encountered and the psychological motivations for their solution, and I will give reasons for the orthopedist's intervention with the patient. Next, I will discuss the roles of persons involved in the orthopedic decision-making process, and their approach to that process. Ethical issues are important considerations in decision-making. I assume here that the individuals who make the decisions for patients with developmental disabilities are persons with good intentions.

For each of the above aspects—medical, psychological, reasons for intervention, roles, and ethics—I have selected those issues that are of greatest importance to patients with developmental disabilities.

The Disease Itself

The elements that should be considered in decision-making concerning orthopedic treatment start with the medical problems presented to the orthopedist. These can be placed in three groups:

ACUTE NEEDS

These are problems that arise suddenly, are usually accompanied by pain, and frequently have a clearcut cause or precipitating event, such as a fracture.

PROGRESSIVE DISEASE

A cornerstone of orthopedic care is the progressive nature of some orthopedic diseases. For example, orthopedists correct deformities in the present to prevent future disability. Secondary degenerative joint disease is a common final pathway for many types of original joint disorders, and orthopedic goal-setting for pediatric patients is based on the outcome at skeletal maturity.

STABLE PROBLEMS

Some orthopedic problems are stable, but continue to require treatment. An example is toe-walking in patients with spastic triceps surae muscles.

Psychological Motivation for Treatment

Disease engenders a set of psychological motivations for solving a patient's medical problems for all individuals involved in his care.

CRISIS INTERVENTION

A crisis is a powerful psychological motivator because the orthopedic problem to be solved is immediate and is understandable in both lay and medical terms, and because the solution is expected to require a limited time. In other words, the orthopedist can say, if we get going we can solve this problem now. Resolution of the crisis brings satisfaction at the end of the procedure.

PLANNING FOR THE FUTURE

Looking ahead and anticipating outcomes, consequences, and implications of present actions is, of course, a motivational aspect of any decision.

ONGOING MAINTENANCE

Patients with chronic disease have multiple health care needs that they learn to depend on having met. Therefore, patients and caretakers are strongly motivated to use the technology and support services these patients require for daily life.

Reasons for Orthopedic Intervention

The following reasons explain why the physician should intervene in the natural history of a disease:

RESTORATION OF HOMEOSTASIS

Returning patients to a baseline condition of functioning, or getting them back to their normal life, is one reason why a doctor-patient relationship is contractually formed.

ENABLING INTERVENTION

The orthopedist seeks to allow patients greater function by substituting for, or repairing, a dysfunctional body segment.

"HOUSEKEEPING"

Attention to preventive health maintenance and ongoing medical needs marks a careful physician. In addition, the medical system requires physician input for certifying the needs for services and prescriptions.

The three factors just mentioned—disease aspects, psychological motivation for treatment, and reasons for intervention—are not arranged hierarchially, but are sometimes parallel. For example, acute needs, determined by pain and sudden loss of function, require crisis intervention for the patient to return to baseline homeostasis. A patient's orthopedic diagnosis, his lifestyle, and his treatment all have natural histories that may be incompletely known. Therefore, planning for the future can be difficult. Maintaining stable pathologic conditions can prevent future acute or progressive problems.

The three sets of aspects can also be interconnected. Acute trauma brings about a manifestation of a previously stable disease whose treatment is aimed at prevention of recurrence; but function must also be maintained in the present for the patient's self-care. Or maintenance therapy for a progressive condition is delayed when the patient develops an acute need, the treatment of which must take precedence. Each of these considerations has the capacity to push the patient's system, which was previously in equilibrium, toward a new direction.

Roles of Participants in the Decision-Making Process

Everyone who has a role in the decision-making process makes his individual behavior congruent with his perception of the appropriate behavior for that role. Patients with developmental disabilities differ in their capacity to participate in making decisions on treatment. Their input is frequently interpreted and translated by other participants, including family members, physicians, and institutional representatives. Any patient may assume a passive role once the doctor-patient relationship has been contracted. For unemancipated persons such as those with developmental disabilities, however, even the contractual obligation is imposed.

The family will generally be guided by their conception of what is best for the patient. Decisions are influenced by cultural and social factors and by family dynamics. Developmental disability as a chronic disorder implies a set of stages of adaptation that families carry into the setting of orthopedic decision-making. There are at least four stages of adaptation for a family member who has any condition that is characterized as a chronic disease. Grief and shock can be followed closely by anxiety, anger, and disbelief when the diagnosis is first presented, then an attempt at coping by intellectualizing, determining to overcome the disability, or seeking help. Acceptance of the diagnosis and its implications can allow family members to redirect their attention to rehabilitation. Family members may remain at any level of this process, which will affect decision-making for orthopedic problems.

Other involved professionals, e.g., physical therapists and nurses, may have daily and prolonged contact with each patient, and therefore their ready availability to the patients, puts them in the position of advocates on behalf of the patient and helping the family adapt to the decision-making process.

Ethical Issues

As stated previously, I am assuming that all participants in the decision-making process are of noble intention.

RIGHT TO TREATMENT

The anomalies common to adults with developmental disabilities who still have a legal guardian, receive reimbursement through government agencies, and are placed in a residential center outside the family home have increased the vociferousness of the defense of the right to treatment. Dearly won rights have an inertia toward being exercised. The legal rights to treatment have been determined, but this does not mean that individuals' conflicts concerning the right to treatment have been resolved.

RIGHT TO SELF-DETERMINATION

A conflict in the right to self-determination by individuals with developmental disabilities arises when they are to be allowed, or forced, to take risks. To force the patient to take the risks inherent in any medical or surgical intervention is conflicting, and yet for another individual to have the power to determine who will make the decisions is paternalistic.

QUALITY OF LIFE

Quality of life is the commonly accepted criterion for justifying medical intervention or nonintervention. The orthopedist conceives of quality of life as function to be gained or lost. There are some guidelines for orthopedic intervention that proceed from social criteria of eligibility for participation in activities. Independent chair-sitting is necessary for wheelchair van transportation. Being able to walk independently, of course, removes all architectural barriers. Energy-efficient ambulation, achieved by any means, widens the physical boundaries within which the patient lives. The long-term solution to the removal of these barriers may be to challenge their validity within the legal system, but these barriers exist today as a factor in determining the quality of life. This criterion of enhancing function places a demand on the patient to pursue that function, even though he did not have a chance to choose the activity imposed on him.

Who, then, speaks for the patient? In ambiguous clinical situations, there is only one accepted standard, i.e., "what is best for the patient." However, the concept of "what is best for the patient" may vary among people of good intention. It is difficult to evaluate the quality of life of a patient who is represented, has his needs translated, or has an advocate.

ALLOCATION OF RESOURCES

Even if "resources" are defined more broadly than in terms of finances, the ethical consideration of allocation of "scarce resources" remains a practical concern. Decisions on medical intervention can involve choosing between alternatives that are truly conflicting. Cost versus benefit cannot be expressed as a ratio, because one frequently compares noncomparable factors.

Ordering Aspects of Decision-Making by Using Value Judgments

The ordering of the above aspects of the decision-making process requires a value judgment. This may reflect the values of a dominant individual, of a team, or of a designated arbiter. One proposed hierarchy of values in decision-making for resolution of conflicts in orthopedic practice is presented as an example. In this hierarchy, stable medical and orthopedic problems are considered to be monitored, and continuous health maintenance is assumed. The primary and secondary justifications for orthopedic intervention are listed, together with the way in which they are supported by the aspects of the decision-making process presented above. The momentum for intervention is guided by the balance of risks and benefits. The momentum associated with clear-cut issues is greater than that for ambiguous issues. It is to be noted that this hierarchical scheme places a high value on patient self-determination.

I. Primary Justifications for Orthopedic Intervention
A. To Relieve Acute Pain
1. Immediacy of pain demands intervention
2. Function is decreased
3. The cause-and-effect relationship is clear
4. Patient input is direct and unambiguous
5. The family is acutely concerned and motivated
6. Treatment presents no ethical conflict
7. The patient has acutely decreased independence with the acute decrease in function
8. Quality of life decreases because of decreased understanding of the world, i.e., why there is pain and why it won't stop
9. The goal is to return to homeostasis
B. To Reestablish Homeostasis
1. The physician accepts as a standard the level of functioning achieved by the patient
2. An opportunity is provided to do things in a new way by using enabling intervention
3. The patient is allowed to take risks
4. The patient is under tension from decreased homeostasis and thus may revise his modes of operating

II. Secondary Justifications for Orthopedic Intervention
A. To Increase Function (Enabling Intervention)
Enabling intervention is not just a pediatric notion; rehabilitation modes can also be enabling in the geriatric population
1. Patient cooperation and input have to be assured so that a contract with the health care team is possible
2. Self-determination is shown by the patient deciding to take a risk
3. Increased function is a goal
4. Quality of life is increased by self-determination and increased function
B. To Prevent Progressive Decrease in Function
1. Progressive decrease in function is separate from acutely decreased function, which is accompanied by acute pain. Progressively decreased function is more likely to be accompanied by chronic baseline pain
2. The causes are more complex than acute loss of function and therefore not as amenable to cure

All benefits and risks of a contemplated intervention are weighted by the values of the persons assigning importance to each issue. A consensus of the value judgments of the team may be attempted, or a dominant individual's values may prevail.

In the existing health care system, obtaining consent for a procedure requires the physician to consider the goals of the procedure and therefore the relative risks and benefits, because he must present them to an increasingly sophisticated forum of family, guardians, and caretakers. The decision to intervene in the natural history of such musculoskeletal disease must always consider appropriate goals for each patient and risks of the treatment options.

CONCLUSION

There are no perfect solutions to the conflicts engendered by medical care in the patients' psychosocial milieus. The process of examining the aspects of decision-making and weighing the values assigned to each aspect is carried out by individuals other than the patient, who want to do what is best for the patient. But their efforts may be bounded by the limitations of the character of the disease, by their role in the decision-making team, and by ethical considerations. Orthopedic problem-solving can be seen as a microcosm of medical decision-making for patients with developmental disabilities, who do not fully participate in the decision-making process.

FURTHER READING

Bleck, E.E.: Orthopedic Management of Cerebral Palsy. Philadelphia, W.B. Saunders, 1979.

Bucholz, R.W., Lippert, F.G. III, Wenger, D.R., and Ezaki, M.B.: Orthopedic Decision Making. Philadelphia, B.C. Decker, 1984.

Drennan, J.C.: Orthopedic Management of Neuromuscular Disorders. Philadelphia, J.B. Lippincott, 1983.

Ferguson, A.B.: Orthopedic Surgery in Infancy and Childhood. Baltimore, Williams & Wilkins, 1981.

Hensinger, R.N., and Jones, E.T.: Neonatal Orthopedics. New York, Grune & Stratton, 1981.

Hoffer, M.M.: Basic considerations and classification of cerebral palsy. Instr. Course Lect., 25:96, 1976.

Hoppenfeld, S.: Orthopedic Neurology: A Diagnostic Guide to Neurologic Levels. Philadelphia, J.B. Lippincott, 1977.

Lovell, W.W., and Winter, R.B.: Pediatric Orthopedics. Vol. 2. Philadelphia, J.B. Lippincott, 1978.

Rang, M., Douglas, G., Bennet, G.C., and Koreska, J.: Seating for children with cerebral palsy. J. Pediatr. Orthop., 1:279, 1981.

Samilson, R.L. (ed.): Orthopedic Aspects of Cerebral Palsy. Lavenham, England, Spastics International Medical Publishers, 1975.

Schafer, M.F., and Dias, L.S.: Myelomeningocele: Orthopedic Treatment. Baltimore, Williams & Wilkins, 1983.

Swash, M., and Schwarts, M.S.: Neuromuscular Diseases: A Practical Approach to Diagnosis and Management. New York, Springer-Verlag, 1981.

Tachdjian, M.O.: Pediatric Orthopedics. Vols. 1 and 2. Philadelphia, W.B. Saunders, 1972.

Thompson, G.H., Rubin, I.L., and Bilenker, R.M.: Comprehensive Management of Cerebral Palsy. New York, Grune & Stratton, 1983.

10

GASTROENTEROLOGY AND NUTRITION

GASTROINTESTINAL PROBLEMS
Ingram M. Roberts, M.D.

Gastrointestinal and hepatobiliary disorders occur frequently in both adults and children with developmental disabilities, especially in those with severe retardation who live in institutions. The major thrust of this review will be devoted to exploring commonly occurring digestive tract ailments in the developmentally disabled population with particular emphasis on the problems of gastroesophageal reflux and chronic hepatitis—two major conditions that account for a large degree of morbidity and mortality in this group of patients.

CONGENITAL ABNORMALITIES ASSOCIATED WITH DOWN SYNDROME

There is a wide variety of congenital anomalies of the gastrointestinal tract that usually become evident in the neonatal period. Interestingly, patients with Down syndrome (trisomy 21) are more likely to have anomalies, including duodenal atresia or stenosis, annular pancreas, malrotation of the small intestine (with or without Ladd's bands), and Hirschsprung's disease.

Duodenal Atresial Stenosis

In one recent series of 672 cases of duodenal stenosis, 27.5% occurred in patients with Down syndrome.[4] Patients with duodenal atresia often present with vomiting in the immediate neonatal period, and the diagnosis is often suggested by the finding of the "double bubble" sign on abdominal roentgenogram caused by gastric and duodenal gas proximal to the site of atresia. The presence of duodenal atresia is easily confirmed with an upper GI series. The diagnosis of duodenal stenosis may be difficult because the patient may develop obstructive symptoms at a later age; duodenal stenosis has been discovered as late as age 12 years in patients with Down syndrome.[89] Congenital atresias or stenoses can also involve the jejunum or ileum. The treatment of either form of duodenal obstruction in patients of all ages is surgical; end-to-end anastomosis is the preferred procedure. Constipation is another common problem in both children and adults with Down syndrome (see constipation, p. 177). At Wrentham State School, 19% of patients with Down syndrome were noted to have constipation (Chap. 26).

Annular Pancreas

Annular pancreas is a congenital abnormality often associated with Down syndrome. It results from the failure of the left bud of the ventral pancreas to migrate to the right side of the duodenum. Instead the left bud encircles the left side of the duodenum, thereby fusing with the remainder of the normal pancreas. Patients may present with associated duodenal obstruction and concomitant duodenal atresia or stenosis. As in the duodenal developmental abnormalities, surgical intervention is necessary, either bypass duodenoduodenostomy or duodenojejunostomy.

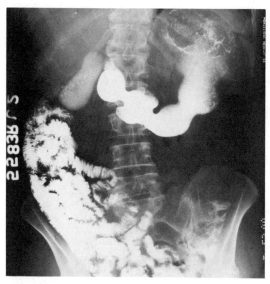

FIG. 10-1. Malrotation of gastrointestinal tract. Note abnormal positioning of jejunal loops in right lower quadrant. (Courtesy of Dr. A. Lawsky.)

The annular pancreas itself is usually not divided because this procedure can induce pancreatitis or duodenal perforation and might not relieve the obstruction.

Malrotation

The developing gastrointestinal tract may undergo malrotation with resultant abnormal positioning of the small intestine and colon (Fig. 10-1). Malrotation may predispose to volvulus of the midgut by twisting about its mesentery. Malrotation most commonly presents in the neonatal period; abnormalities of midgut rotation usually become evident within the first week of life, and 80% are evident by the end of the first month of life.[52] The patient often presents with bilious vomiting and rectal bleeding.[52] "Duodenal beaking" may be seen on upper GI series if a frank midgut volvulus develops.

Ladd's bands are adhesive bands that extend from the right lateral abdominal wall to the cecum and "right colon" (abnormally located in the left upper quadrant). Internal herniation may occur through these bands with obstruction usually involving the descending duodenum.[59] Treatment of malrotation and/or herniation through Ladd's bands requires reduction of the volvulus if possible; if not, resection is necessary.[8] Bands should be lysed if present. Ladd's bands can often be difficult to uncover at laparotomy; the abdomen must be thoroughly explored in order to avoid missing these adhesions. If the volvulized bowel is found to be viable at surgery, results are quite good; if the midgut is ischemic or frankly gangrenous, resection is required. Short-bowel syndrome may develop as a sequela.

Hirschsprung's Disease

Hirschsprung's disease is characterized by constipation or obstipation due to dilated bowel proximal to an area where ganglion cells of Meissner's (submucosal) and Auerbach's (myenteric) plexuses are congenitally absent. This denervated segment (often in rectum or sigmoid colon) results in a functional obstruction. Patients with Down syndrome have a high frequency of Hirschsprung's disease,[75] but only 2% of patients with Hirschsprung's disease have Down syndrome. This association has implicated a possible influence of chromosome 21 on the genetics of Hirschsprung's disease, although a clear-cut pattern of inheritance remains to be elucidated.[21] Many patients with Down syndrome have idiopathic constipation that is not secondary to Hirschsprung's disease or hypothyroidism (another frequent condition associated with Down syndrome). Patients with refractory constipation or obstipation (particularly those with Down syndrome) therefore need to be investigated for the presence of Hirschsprung's disease. Although Hirschsprung's disease usually involves the distal colon, occasionally the entire colon is affected and rarely the small intestine as well. The diagnosis of Hirschsprung's disease may be suggested by evidence of colonic dilatation or megacolon on abdominal flat plate. Subsequent barium enema often shows a narrowed distal rectal segment with proximal dilatation. Digital or proctoscopic examination of the rectum usually yields an absence of stool without evidence of organic obstruction. The definitive diagnosis may be established by full-thickness rectal biopsy. Motility studies can be helpful by diagnostically showing failure of internal sphincter relaxation with rectal distension. Treatment in patients of all ages is surgical; resection of the aganglionic segment should be undertaken, but the bowel proximal to the point of resection should be biopsied to look for the presence of ganglion cells prior to performing the final anastomosis.

OTHER SYNDROMES

Myotonic Dystrophy

Myotonic dystrophy is an autosomal dominant condition with a prevalence in the general population of 5 per 100,000. This disorder affects the gastrointestinal tract predominantly in the esophagus and colon. Myotonic dystrophy causes dysphagia and aspiration by weakening the skeletal muscle of the upper esophageal sphincter, tongue, and pharynx. Atony of the upper esophageal sphincter has been described, along with aperistalsis of the esophageal body.[74] The colon may become dilated and redundant with the development of secondary intestinal pseudo-obstruction.[84a] Myotonic dystrophy often becomes evident by age 10, but occasionally there is involvement at birth.[38] Treatment is often unsatisfactory; there are few data on either the medical or surgical approach to treatment of the gastrointestinal abnormalities in myotonic dystrophy.

Tuberous Sclerosis

Tuberous sclerosis, probably inherited as an autosomal dominant condition, is associated with retardation, seizures, and adenoma sebaceum. The gastrointestinal tract is affected by malrotation with or without Ladd's bands (in similar fashion to Down syndrome patients). A case of tuberous sclerosis presenting with a large postero-lateral diaphragmatic hernia in addition has been described.[72] Treatment requires surgical correction of the anatomic defects.

Cornelia de Lange Syndrome

The Cornelia de Lange syndrome, characterized by mental retardation, hirsutism, microcephaly, and characteristic facies, is occasionally associated with abnormalities of the gastrointestinal tract. In addition to malrotation, aspiration secondary to upper esophageal sphincter dysfunction and esophageal stricture formation secondary to lower esophageal sphincter incompetence with free reflux, have been described.[58] Treatment includes surgical correction of the anatomic abnormalities and vigorous antireflux therapy (see Gastroesophageal Reflux, p. 178).

Sotos Syndrome

Sotos syndrome is an autosomal dominant condition, and manifestations include macrocephaly, mental retardation, accelerated growth, and characteristic facies. It is occasionally associated with melanotic pigmentation of the genitalia and hamartomatous polyps of the small intestine and colon.[84] The pigmentary changes are similar to those found in patients with Peutz-Jeghers syndrome, but the distribution of the pigment appears to be different (Peutz-Jeghers syndrome is usually associated with pigmentation of the oral mucosa). Surgical resection of asymptomatic polyps in Sotos syndrome is not indicated unless complications such as gastrointestinal bleeding, intestinal obstruction, or intussusception occur. Although the hamartomas of the Peutz-Jeghers and Sotos syndrome are associated with a low incidence of malignancy,[14] follow-up of these patients should be performed.

MAJOR ACQUIRED CONDITIONS

Constipation

Developmentally disabled patients commonly suffer from constipation or obstipation. At Wrentham State School, 41% of institutionalized patients with severe developmental disabilities were noted to have constipation (Chap. 26). Management usually involves institution of a high-bulk diet and agents such as bran and commercial psyllium compounds.[41] Other patients may require occasional laxatives, stool softeners, suppositories, enemas, or manual disimpaction (see Chap. 27). Mineral oil should be avoided if possible because of the likelihood of aspiration, which, particularly in these patients, can lead to lipoid pneumonia. Patients with persistent symptoms of constipation need to have a workup to ensure that conditions such as Hirschsprung's disease, pseudo-obstruction, hypothyroidism, or segmental dilatation of the colon[33] are not overlooked.

Many medications used in this patient population may precipitate episodes of constipation. These include the phenothiazines, tricyclic antidepressants, antiparkinsonian drugs, ganglionic blockers, and α-adrenergic agents such as clonidine. If possible these drugs should be discontinued. The etiology of chronic idiopathic constipation in nonretarded patients remains obscure; some patients with constipation have normal colonic transit when measured with radiopaque markers, whereas others have prolonged right colonic transit or prolonged left colon/rectosigmoid transit.[48,99] Cholinergic medications (bethanecol, urecholine) and naloxone, an opioid antagonist,[57] have been empirically instituted in attempts to augment colonic motility and diminish symptoms in nonretarded patients with idiopathic constipation; studies have yet to be performed in the developmentally disabled population with constipation.

Foreign Bodies and Bezoars

Various foreign bodies may be ingested by institutionalized developmentally disabled patients (see section on pica in Chap. 20). Most often small objects such as buttons, pins, or coins

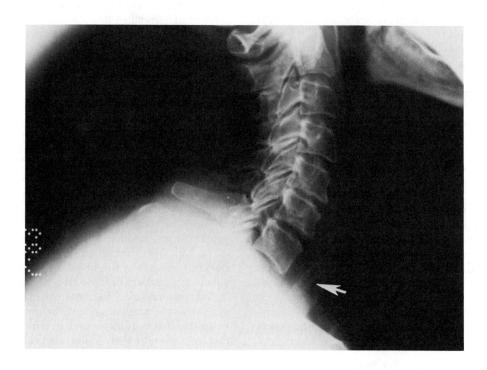

FIG. 10-2. Foreign body ingestion. The arrow indicates the position of a chicken bone lodged in the cervical esophagus. (Courtesy of Dr. A. Lawsky.)

are swallowed (Fig. 10-2). In 80 to 90% of cases the object is asymptomatically passed in the feces.[61,85] In 10 to 20% of patients the object is impacted at the gastroesophageal junction or pylorus and requires nonsurgical removal.[85,100] Large foreign bodies impacted at the gastroesophageal junction can be removed either by an intubation suction technique[55] or by rigid or flexible esophagoscopy. These patients usually present with symptoms of esophageal obstruction (vomiting, dysphagia), and the obstruction is revealed by esophageal contrast study. Meglumine diatrizoate (Gastrograffin) is the medium of choice, particularly if perforation is suspected.[73] Foreign bodies that fail to pass through the stomach within 48 to 72 hours may be removed by the grasp technique with a flexible fiberoptic endoscope.[100] Perforation after foreign body ingestion occurs only about 1% of the time.[32] Fixed points of the gastrointestinal tract may predispose to perforation; the ileocecal area is the most common site, with perforation at the

pylorus or first and second parts of the duodenum occurring less frequently.[85]

Bezoars can occur in the developmentally disabled population and can cause obstruction and perforation. Phytobezoars (vegetable) and trichobezoars (hair) have been found alone and in combination with foreign bodies.[11] These are most often located in the stomach, but the esophagus and small intestine are occasionally involved. Pure phytobezoars can be dissolved by various enzymes (cellulase, etc.) given orally,[27,92] and this therapy should be attempted prior to endoscopic or surgical removal.

Gastroesophageal Reflux

Gastroesophageal reflux accompanied by vomiting, rumination, or upper gastrointestinal bleeding is one of the commonest and potentially most serious pathologic conditions of the gastrointestinal tract in developmentally disabled children and adults. The prevalence of vomiting or regurgitation in developmentally disabled patients has been estimated to be 10 to 15% in several studies.[6,90] Among this group of patients up to 75% have frank gastroesophageal reflux demonstrable through esophageal function testing.[90] Rumination was a presenting symptom of reflux in 25% of patients in one series.[104] Patients with gastroesophageal reflux often present with frank hematemesis, guaiac-positive stool, and/or iron deficiency anemia. Investigators in separate series have found anemia in 25 to 50% of developmentally disabled patients with reflux and gastrointestinal blood loss in 33 to 50%.[17,90,91,104] All patients developing vomiting, rumination, iron-deficiency anemia, or upper gastrointestinal bleeding should therefore be investigated for the presence of gastroesophageal reflux.

Pathogenesis

The pathogenesis of gastroesophageal reflux is thought to be multifactorial. A variety of abnormalities in esophageal function may contribute to reflux. These include abnormalities of the anti-reflux mechanism (lower esophageal sphincter), increases in the toxicity of the refluxed material, deficiencies in esophageal clearance of refluxed secretions, and diminished resistance of esophageal tissue to the refluxed material.[29,82]

In retarded patients the factors contributing to gastroesophageal reflux can be summarized as follows:

1. Abnormal anti-reflux mechanism
   Decrease in lower esophageal sphincter pressures
   Inappropriate relaxation of the lower esophageal sphincter
   Recumbent positioning
   Drugs that affect the lower esophageal sphincter: theophylline, anticholinergics, etc.
2. Increases in volume of refluxed material
   Decreased gastric emptying
   Increased output of acid
3. Toxicity of refluxed materials
   Acid
   Pepsin
   Bile salts
4. Diminished tissue resistance
   Role of prostaglandins
5. Decreased clearing mechanisms
   Low salivary flow
   Impaired esophageal motility

ANTI-REFLUX MECHANISM

The major barrier to gastroesophageal reflux appears to be the pressure generated through the intrinsic tone of the lower esophageal sphincter.[29] Low pressure of the sphincter and/or inappropriate relaxation of the sphincter may both be responsible for episodes of esophageal reflux.[30] One recent study of developmentally disabled patients with reflux revealed that lower esophageal sphincter pressures were significantly lower (12.5 ± 3.2 mm Hg) than those of developmentally disabled control patients without reflux (29.0 ± 4.6 mm Hg, $p < 0.01$).[90] In another series of developmentally disabled patients with reflux, 68% of patients evaluated with manometry had lower esophageal sphincter pressures below 11 mm Hg.[104]

GASTRIC VOLUME FACTORS

Delayed emptying of gastric contents has been demonstrated in certain patients with gastroesophageal reflux.[47] Institutionalized severely retarded patients in whom gastrostomy is being contemplated need to have investigatory studies for gastroesophageal reflux prior to surgery; a recent study found that 4 of 30 developmentally disabled patients who underwent gastrostomy died from aspiration pneumonia within the first year after surgery.[78] Presence of gastroesophageal reflux therefore appears to be a relative contraindication to feeding gastrostomy unless specific anti-reflux surgery (i.e., fundoplication) accompanies the gastrostomy.[19, 103]

TOXICITY OF REFLUXED FLUID AND TISSUE RESISTANCE

Animal studies have revealed that hydrochloric acid, pepsin, bile salts, and even prostaglandins may play an important role in the development of esophagitis.[29, 31] Detailed studies on the contributions of these factors to the development of reflux esophagitis in humans are presently lacking.

INTRINSIC ESOPHAGEAL CLEARING MECHANISMS

In addition to the potency or toxicity of the refluxed material, the more prolonged the contact of fluid with the esophageal mucosa, the greater the predisposition there is to the development of esophagitis. A recent study in normal nonretarded patients that directly measured esophageal acid clearance through pH probe monitoring found that if saliva was aspirated from the oral cavity, esophageal acid clearance was markedly impaired.[43] Although the differences were not statistically significant, acid clearance was diminished when patients were moved from a sitting to a recumbent position.[43] The esophageal clearing mechanism in normal patients is in itself multifactorial: position, esophageal motility, and salivary flow all appear to participate. There are no current investigations of the clearing mechanism in the developmentally disabled population, but a recent series revealed that 19 of 21 developmentally disabled patients with vomiting and histologic evidence of reflux esophagitis were nonambulatory.[18] This high prevalence suggests that the effect of position may be a major determinant of reflux in the severely retarded and developmentally disabled patient who is confined to bed.

Diagnosis

A number of currently available tests can be used to document gastroesophageal reflux; unfortunately, a single "gold standard" test with complete sensitivity and specificity currently does not exist.

BARIUM SWALLOW

Barium can be seen to reflux from stomach to esophagus during the course of fluoroscopy. This test has been shown to have a sensitivity of only 30 to 40%,[82] but it is easily performed in the developmentally disabled patient: only minimal cooperation is needed from the patient, and a great deal of sophisticated or expensive equipment is not required.

Occasionally a "mega-aeroesophagus" (dilated, air-filled esophagus) is seen on a plain chest roentgenogram, suggesting the diagnosis of gastroesophageal reflux.[94]

MOTILITY STUDIES

Esophageal manometry can be used to detect a hypotonic lower esophageal sphincter, but this test is unsuitable for most developmentally disabled patients because it cannot document actual presence of reflux (only pressures are recorded) and the patient must be able to cooperate. The equipment is also costly.

pH TESTING OR MONITORING

Tests of esophageal pH have the highest sensitivity (40 to 88%) and specificity (83 to 99%) for the diagnosis of gastroesophageal reflux.[82] Esophageal pH is monitored with an electrode positioned proximal to the lower esophageal sphincter, either acutely after provocative maneuvers or over a prolonged period as in Holter cardiac monitoring.[34] pH monitoring tests are difficult to perform in the developmentally disabled because patient cooperation is paramount for reliable results.

ENDOSCOPY

Flexible fiber-optic endoscopy can be extremely useful for histologic confirmation of the diagnosis of reflux esophagitis. Although endoscopic examination of patients with reflux may uncover gross abnormalities such as erythema, friability, and ulceration, the correlation of mucosal appearance through the endoscope with the actual histology found on biopsy is in fact quite poor.[10] It is therefore essential to take biopsies during all endoscopic procedures when gastroesophageal reflux is suspected. Most pathologists accept the classical criteria for esophagitis (basal cell hyperplasia, papillary lengthening),[49] but it has been reported in a recent study that the presence of intraepithelial eosinophils is 94% specific for reflux esophagitis and correlates well with other tests for gastroesophageal reflux.[107] Although endoscopy is an invasive and expensive procedure, it serves an important role in evaluating patients with refractory reflux symptoms and makes it possible to accurately evaluate those patients with complications of reflux (e.g., stricture, Barrett's esophagus).

Treatment

MEDICAL THERAPY

The therapy of gastroesophageal reflux in children and adults is aimed at strengthening antireflux mechanisms and decreasing the toxicity of the refluxed material. Initial treatment measures include elevation of the head of the bed, avoidance of foods such as chocolate, juices, and coffee that can exacerbate reflux, and, if possible, elimination of medications (e.g., theophylline, anticholinergics, diazepam) that can diminish lower esophageal sphincter pressure. Medications can be a particular problem in developmentally disabled patients, who are often maintained on assorted neuroleptics. Antacids are often given 1 and 3 hours after meals and at bedtime in an attempt to neutralize gastric acidity. On this regimen 6 of 9 developmentally disabled patients with reflux had improvement.[90] Alginic acid, which forms a solution of high viscosity that floats on the pool of gastric secretions as a barrier to reflux, may also be promising. Presently, however, double-blind studies have not definitively demonstrated whether antacids or alginic acid reduce reflux symptoms in nonretarded patients through a true pharmacologic effect.[40,50]

Several other agents may be added to the treatment regimen of patients who do not respond to the above measures. These include

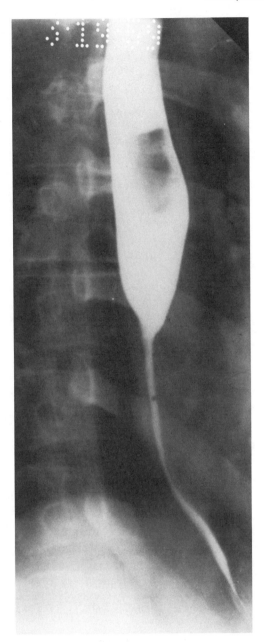

FIG. 10-3. Esophageal stricture. A long, tapering stricture in the lower esophagus, a consequence of long-standing gastroesophageal reflux. Note dilatation of the esophageal lumen proximal to the stricture. (Courtesy of Dr. A. Lawsky.)

H_2-receptor antagonists such as cimetidine, cholinomimetic drugs such as bethanechol, or the dopamine antagonist, metoclopramide. Bethanechol is thought to diminish reflux by increasing the tone of the lower esophageal sphincter. Double-blind trials with nonretarded patients given 25 mg bethanecol 4 times daily have shown statistically significant improvement in

symptoms and endoscopically documented healing of esophagitis.[96,97]

Cimetidine diminishes reflux by blocking the histamine-mediated production of gastric acid through its interaction with the H_2 receptors of the parietal cells. In double-blind studies, cimetidine given in a dose of 400 mg 4 times daily has also been shown to improve symptoms and endoscopic healing in statistically significant fashion.[36,102]

Metoclopramide is thought to increase the tone of the lower esophageal sphincter and to increase gastric emptying. This combination of actions suggests that it might be a particularly efficacious agent for the treatment of reflux esophagitis. Metoclopramide has been documented to speed gastric emptying in patients with delayed emptying and reflux.[65] Double-blind studies with metoclopramide have demonstrated only symptomatic improvement (no data on histology) in patients with reflux, and further controlled trials need to be performed to discover whether metoclopramide will prove to be a valuable therapeutic option.[2]

Patients who are refractory to medical treatment for gastroesophageal reflux or who develop complications should be considered for surgical therapy.

COMPLICATIONS AND SURGICAL THERAPY

Only 5 to 10% of nonretarded children and adults fail to respond to medical management, but the failure rate of medical therapy appears to be much higher in the retarded population.[62,82] A recent study with severely retarded children reported complete or partial response to medical therapy in only 26% of patients.[104] Complications such as aspiration pneumonia, persistent anemia, and/or upper gastrointestinal bleeding appear to be relative indications for surgical treatment. In one study in which 28 developmentally disabled patients with documented reflux were identified, there were 39 episodes of pneumonia and 39 episodes of gastrointestinal bleeding over a $2\frac{1}{2}$-year period.[17] Esophageal stricture (Fig. 10-3) has been noted to develop in 13% of developmentally disabled patients with reflux.[104] This complication may be managed by esophageal dilation with bougies, thereby stretching the scarred esophagus to an adequate luminal diameter to prevent dysphagia.[62] Refractory strictures, however, may require correction with esophagectomy and cervical esophagogastrostomy.[91]

The most popular anti-reflux operation currently performed in the developmentally dis-

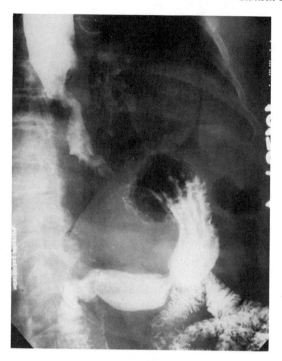

FIG. 10-4. Carcinoma of the esophagus. The distal portion of the esophagus is involved with a circumferential ulcerating mass. Adenocarcinoma of the esophagus is commonly seen in association with Barrett's esophagus. (Courtesy of Dr. A. Lawsky.)

abled population is the Nissen fundoplication.[17,90,91,104] In this procedure a transabdominal approach is taken, and the fundus of the stomach is wrapped around the gastroesophageal junction in order to strengthen the barrier to reflux.[37] Nissen fundoplication led to a marked improvement in 12 of 14 patients who had failed medical therapy in one series[104] and cessation of upper gastrointestinal bleeding, vomiting, and pneumonia in 21 of 22 patients unresponsive to medical therapy in another study.[17]

Other anti-reflux operations such as the Belsey and Hill procedures have not enjoyed high popularity, but results appear to be good.[45] A new device, the Angelchik prosthesis, is a C-shaped ring that is tied around the gastroesophageal junction subdiaphragmatically to provide a reflux barrier.[7,56] The efficacy of the Angelchik prosthesis remains to be critically determined.

A complication of gastroesophageal reflux that was first described in 1950 by Barrett[6a] is replacement of the normal squamous esophageal epithelium by several varieties of columnar epithelium.[76,87] The clinical relevance of this reflux-induced acquired metaplasia is that there

appears to be an increased incidence of adenocarcinoma of the esophagus in these patients (Fig. 10-4).

Investigators have observed incidence rates of adenocarcinoma in patients with Barrett's esophagus from 2.5% to 46%.[69,87,88] The overall prevalence of Barrett's esophagus in endoscopic series ranges from 0.6% to 13%.[26]

The prevalence of Barrett's esophagus in the retarded population is not known, but in a series of 27 developmentally disabled patients who underwent endoscopy for evaluation of upper gastrointestinal bleeding, iron deficiency anemia, and/or reflux symptoms, 7 cases (26%) of Barrett's esophagus were discovered.[82a] Treatment of this complication of reflux appears problematic; one study of Barrett's esophagitis treated with cimetidine showed healing of ulcerations, but no regression of columnar epithelium to squamous epithelium.[54] There has been a report of reversion to squamous epithelium after Nissen fundoplication, but this has not been found with any consistency after anti-reflux surgery.[13] Most gastroenterologists agree that periodic endoscopy with biopsy is beneficial for cancer surveillance in patients with Barrett's esophagus, but a uniform protocol for the serial timing of such procedures does not exist.[87]

GASTROINTESTINAL AND HEPATOBILIARY INFECTIONS

Parasitic Infestation

Institutionalized developmentally disabled patients are predisposed to oral-fecal transmission of assorted gastrointestinal pathogens. Hygiene may be suboptimal and toilet training extremely difficult in such facilities. These problems were greater in the past, when the ratio of institutionalized patients to staff was much higher, but institutional populations still experience occasional outbreaks of bacterial infectious diarrhea (salmonella, shigella, etc.) (Chap. 30).

A survey of a residential school for the retarded in Manitoba recently revealed an overall rate of giardiasis and other parasitic infection near 50%.[70] The diagnosis of giardiasis is sometimes difficult to make because stool examination may be negative in 30 to 50% of patients.[16] In these cases aspiration of duodenal fluid is essential in finding the trophozoites.[83] New diagnostic tests have been developed (counter immunoelectrophoresis to detect Giardia antigen in feces, immunofluorescence to detect serum antibodies to Giardia), but these are not yet routinely available.[23,98]

Giardiasis may be treated with quinacrine hydrochloride, metronidazole, or furazolidone.

All have been found effective in the treatment of giardiasis.[22,108] Patients who fail to respond need to be investigated for IgA deficiency, which is associated with an increased incidence of gastrointestinal infections.[15] Developmentally disabled patients admitted to institutions should have routine stool screenings for parasites, pathogens should be vigorously treated, and parasitic infection should always be considered a possibility in the differential diagnosis of diarrhea.[70]

Infectious Hepatitis

The characteristics of the three forms of infectious hepatitis are shown in Table 10-1. (See also Chap. 30.)

Hepatitis A

In the U.S. approximately 40% of adults have IgG antibody to hepatitis A in their serum, indicating previous exposure to the virus.[35] Hepatitis A is a 27-nm RNA-containing particle that resembles an enterovirus.[110] One large study (979 patients) revealed a 74.8% prevalence of antibody to hepatitis A in institutionalized retarded patients, considerably higher than that of the normal population, indicating extensive exposure to the virus.[106] Hepatitis A is easily spread by the fecal-oral route among residents in an institution, and to staff personnel through contact with infected patients.[12,39,44]

Fortunately, infection with hepatitis A virus is usually a benign process, with fulminant hepatic necrosis occurring in less than 0.1% of cases in epidemics.[64] One series has suggested that up to 14% of patients with fulminant necrosis might have hepatitis A as an etiologic agent.[77] The vast majority of patients recover completely without development of sequelae (e.g., chronic hepatitis or carrier states).[24]

The diagnostic test of choice for acute infection with hepatitis A is detection of IgM antibody to the virus in the serum. This test has a much higher specificity (99%) than conventional assays, which measure only total antibody or IgG antibody to hepatitis.[35,93] Protection from clinical infection with hepatitis A is afforded by Immune Serum Globulin (ISG) intramuscularly, if administered within 1 to 2 weeks after exposure in both adults and children.[110] Patients and institutional staff should both receive ISG should an outbreak of hepatitis A occur.

Hepatitis B

The intact hepatitis B virus is a 42-nm DNA-containing particle.[110] This virus contains several distinct antigens that are immunogenic: surface antigen (HB_sAg), core antigen (HB_cAg), and "e" antigen (HB_eAg). HB_sAg is found on the external coat of the virus, and HB_cAg is found on the nucleocapsid core. HB_eAg is a protein also associated with the inner core of the virus and presumably with DNA polymerase activity (e.g., active viral replication and infectivity).[24]

Antibody to hepatitis B surface antigen (Anti-HB_s) confers protective immunity, whereas antibodies to core or "e" antigens (Anti-HB_c and Anti-HB_e) serve only as serologic markers and are not in themselves immunoprotective.[24,61] In the general U.S. population the prevalence of Anti-HB_s is estimated to be 5 to 11%,[24,68] but in the developmentally disabled institutionalized population anti-HB_s has been found in 32 to 66.3% of patients, indicating extensive exposure to the hepatitis B virus.[5,105,106] Patients with Down syndrome appear to have an unusually

Table 10-1. *Infectious Hepatitis*

	Hepatitis A	Hepatitis B	Non-A, Non-B Hepatitis
Transmission	Fecal-oral	Parenteral, venereal, other body fluids	Parenteral
Virus	27-nm RNA virus	42-nm DNA virus	Yet to be identified
Incubation	2 to 6 weeks	6 weeks to 6 months	2 weeks to 6 months (?)
Chronic infection	No	Yes, up to 30% of patients who remain HB_sAg +	Yes, up to 45% of patients
Carrier state	No	Yes, up to 5% of patients	Yes (?)
Serologic markers	IgG and IgM antibody to hepatitis A	HB_sAg, Anti-HB_s HB_cAg, Anti-HB_c HB_eAg, Anti-HB_e	Yet to be identified

high carrier rate of hepatitis B, for unclear reasons.[42]

The clinical diagnosis of hepatitis B infection (elevated liver function tests, hepatomegaly, jaundice, etc.) can be confirmed by the presence of $HB_s Ag$ in the serum; anti-HB_s and anti-HB_c are other markers that may be helpful diagnostically. Anti-HB_c may be present in the "window" period when $HB_s Ag$ has been cleared from the serum and before anti-HB_s is detectable.[24] The existence of anti-HB_s normally indicates resolution of infection and the presence of immunity. Blood and body fluids of patients with $HB_s Ag$ often also contain $HB_e Ag$ and should be considered infectious and necessary disposal precautions should be undertaken.[101] Although hepatitis B is usually transmitted parenterally, infectious patients may excrete virus in saliva, semen, and urine. Horizontal transmission through oral secretions has been documented.[63] This source may be a major route of transmission in the institutionalized retarded population.

In contrast to patients with hepatitis A, patients with hepatitis B frequently develop long-term complications. Over 90% of patients with acute hepatitis B recover uneventfully within 3 to 6 months after infection, but fulminant hepatic necrosis and death occur in 1 to 5% of patients.[79] A chronic $HB_s Ag$ carrier state ensues in 1 to 5% of patients after hepatitis B infection.[71,86] Chronic active hepatitis may develop in 30% of patients who remain $HB_s Ag$ positive and may eventually progress to cirrhosis.[79] Another complication is the striking association between persistent $HB_s Ag$ and the subsequent development of hepatocellular carcinoma years later.[3,46,51]

Several series have revealed that 7 to 44% of institutionalized retarded patients have persistence of $HB_s Ag$, which is a rate far in excess of the population at large (<0.5%).[5,42,105,106] Indeed, a 44% carrier rate has been found in Down syndrome patients at Wrentham State School (Chap. 26). Hepatitis B probably represents the etiologic agent responsible for the majority of cases of chronic active hepatitis and cirrhosis in the developmentally disabled population, although the exact rate of association is unknown. Liver biopsy is the only means to histologically identify these patients and distinguish them from patients with chronic persistent hepatitis, a benign condition not requiring therapy. The presence of elevated hepatic transaminases (SGPT, SGOT) for greater than 6 months is considered an indication for liver biopsy. Unfortunately, trials of immunosuppressive therapy (steroids and/or azathioprine) in patients with

$HB_s Ag$-positive chronic active hepatitis have been disappointing.[25,60,80,81,109]

A major advance in the struggle to eradicate $HB_s Ag$-induced liver disease has come through the recent development of a hepatitis B vaccine. The vaccine is safe, efficacious, and highly immunogenic; over 90% of patients produce Anti-HB_s after receiving the series of 3 injections.[20,28,67,95] All staff and patients in institutions for the mentally retarded who do not already have Anti-HB_s should routinely receive the vaccine.

Chronic Liver Disease

Non-A, non-B hepatitis accounts for over 90% of posttransfusion hepatitis in children and adults and has been estimated to progress to chronic active hepatitis in 20 to 45% of cases.[9,53] The etiologic agent for this parenterally transmitted condition remains to be identified, and there is no diagnostic serologic test (the diagnosis is therefore one of exclusion). Many patients are asymptomatic, and data regarding treatment of chronic active heptatitis secondary to non-A, non-B hepatitis are sparse. Although progression to cirrhosis occasionally occurs, disease activity is low and prognosis is often good. Steroid therapy has been tried empirically to control disease activity in symptomatic, progressive cases. There appears to be evidence that posttransfusion transmission of non-A, non-B hepatitis can be prevented by screening donor blood for elevated transaminases.[1]

Other uncommon etiologies of chronic active hepatitis such as Wilson's disease, drugs, and alpha$_1$-anti trypsin deficiency should always be considered in the developmentally disabled patient with chronic liver disease, although they are rarely found. Autoimmune or "lupoid" hepatitis, a form of chronic active liver disease of unknown etiology, is occasionally uncovered. This condition is often associated with the presence of "autoimmune" phenomena such as LE cells and various auto antibodies (anti-nuclear, anti-smooth muscle, etc.).[66] Autoimmune hepatitis is important because it can progress rapidly to cirrhosis or subacute hepatic necrosis; however, it is the one form of chronic active hepatitis that responds well to steroids and/or azathioprine therapy.[25]

REFERENCES

1. Aach, R.D., et al.: Serum alanine aminotransferase of donors in relation to the risk of non-A, non-B hepatitis in recipients. N. Engl. J. Med., *304*:989, 1981.
2. Albibi, R., and McCallum, R.W.: Metoclopramide: Pharmacology and clinical application. Ann. Intern. Med., *98*:86, 1983.

3. Alpert, E.: Primary tumors of the liver: Etiologic and diagnostic features. *In* Viewpoints on Digestive Disease, American Gastroenterological Association, 14, 9-12, 1982.

4. Bachmann, K.D.: Die angeborene Duodenalstenose. Dtsch. Med. Wochenschr., 105:1428, 1980.

5. Bakal, C.W., et al.: Deinstitutionalized mentally retarded hepatitis-B surface antigen carriers in public school classes: A descriptive study. Am. J. Public Health, 70:709, 1980.

6. Ball, T.S., Hendrikson, H., and Clayton, J.: A special feeding technique for chronic regurgitation. Am. J. Ment. Defic., 78:486, 1974.

6a. Barrett, N.R.: Chronic peptic ulcer of the oesophagus and oesophagitis. Br. J. Surg., 38:175, 1950.

7. Benjamin, S.B., et al.: The angelchik antireflux prosthesis: Effects on the lower esophageal sphincter of primates. Ann. Surg., 197:63, 1983.

8. Berardi, R.S.: Anomalies of midgut rotation in the adult. Surg. Gynecol. Obstet., 151:113, 1980.

9. Berman, M., et al.: The chronic sequelae of non-A, non-B hepatitis. Ann. Intern. Med., 91:1, 1979.

10. Biller, J.A., Winter, H.S., Grand, R.J., and Allred, E.N.: Are endoscopic changes predictive of histologic esophagitis in children? J. Pediatr., 103:215, 1983.

11. Bitar, D.E., and Holmes, T.W.: Polybezoar and gastrointestinal foreign bodies in the mentally retarded. Am. Surg., 41:497, 1975.

12. Boughton, C.R., Hawkes, R.A., Lehmann, N.I., and Grohmann, G.S.: Hepatitis A outbreak in a residential school. Aust. N.Z. J. Med., 10:4, 1980.

13. Brand, D.L., Ylvisaker, J.T., Gelfand, M., and Pope, C.E.: Regression of columnar esophageal (Barrett's) epithelium after anti-reflux surgery. N. Engl. J. Med., 302:844, 1980.

14. Burdick, D., and Prior, J.T.: Peutz-Jeghers syndrome: A clinicopathologic study of a large family with a 27-year follow-up. Cancer, 50:2139, 1982.

15. Burgio, G.R., et al.: Selective IgA deficiency: Clinical and immunological evaluation of 50 pediatric patients. Eur. J. Pediatr., 133:101, 1980.

16. Burke, J.A.: Giardiasis in childhood. Am. J. Dis. Child., 129:1304, 1975.

17. Byrne, W.J., et al.: Gastroesophageal reflux in the severely retarded who vomit: Criteria for and results of surgical intervention in twenty-two patients. Surgery 91:95, 1982.

18. Byrne, W.J., et al.: A diagnostic approach to vomiting in severely retarded patients. Am. J. Dis. Child., 137:259, 1983.

19. Carson, J.A., Tunell, W.P., and Smith, E.I.: Pediatric gastroesophageal reflux: Age-specific indications for operation. Am. J. Surg., 140:768, 1980.

20. Centers for Disease Control: Inactivated hepatitis B virus vaccine: Recommendation of the immunization practices advisory committee. Ann. Intern. Med., 97:379, 1982.

21. Cohen, I.T., and Gadd, M.A.: Hirschsprung's disease in a kindred: A possible clue to the genetics of the disease. J. Pediatr. Surg., 17:632, 1982.

22. Craft, J.C., Murphy, T., and Nelson, J.D.: Furazolidone and quinacrine: Comparative study of therapy for giardiasis in children. Am. J. Dis. Child., 135:164, 1981.

23. Craft, J.C., and Nelson, J.D.: Diagnosis of giardiasis by counter-immunoelectrophoresis of feces. J. Infect. Dis., 145:499, 1982.

24. Czaja, A.J.: Serologic markers of hepatitis A and B in acute and chronic liver disease. Mayo Clin. Proc., 54:721, 1979.

25. Czaja, A.J.: Current problems in the diagnosis and management of chronic active hepatitis. Mayo Clin. Proc., 56:311, 1981.

26. Dahms, B.B., and Rothstein, F.C.: Barrett's esophagus in children: A consequence of chronic gastroesophageal reflux. Gastroenterology, 86:318, 1984.

27. Deal, D.R., Vitale, P., and Raffin, S.B.: Dissolution of a postgastrectomy bezoar by cellulase: A rapid, noninterventive technique. Gastroenterology, 64:647, 1973.

28. Dienstag, J.L.: Toward the control of hepatitis B. N. Engl. J. Med., 303:875, 1980.

29. Dodds, W.J., Hogan, W.J., Helm, J.F., and Dent, J.: Pathogenesis of reflux esophagitis. Gastroenterology, 81:376, 1981.

30. Dodds, W.J., et al.: Mechanisms of gastroesophageal reflux in patients with reflux esophagitis. N. Engl. J. Med., 307:1547, 1982.

31. Eastwood, G.L., et al.: Beneficial effect of indomethacin on acid-induced esophagitis in cats. Dig. Dis. Sci., 26:601, 1981.

32. Eldridge, W.W., Jr.: Foreign bodies in the gastrointestinal tract. JAMA, 178:665, 1961.

33. Etzioni, A., Benderly, A., and Bar-Maor, J.A.: Segmental dilatation of the colon, another cause of chronic constipation. Dis. Colon Rectum, 23:580, 1980.

34. Euler, A.R., and Byrne, W.J.: Twenty-four hour esophageal intraluminal pH probe testing: A comparative analysis. Gastroenterology, 80:957, 1981.

35. Feinstone, S.M., and Purcell, R.H.: New methods for the serodiagnosis of hepatitis A. Gastroenterology, 78:1092, 1980.

36. Fiasse, R., et al.: Controlled trial of cimetidine in reflux esophagitis. Dig. Dis. Sci., 25:750, 1980.

37. Foglia, R.P., et al.: Gastroesophageal fundoplication for the management of chronic pulmonary disease in children. Am. J. Surg., 140:72, 1980.

38. Gardner-Medwin, D.: Clinical features and classification of the muscular dystrophies. Br. Med. Bull., 36:109, 1980.

39. Goodman, R.A., et al.: Nosocomial hepatitis A transmission by an adult patient with diarrhea. Am. J. Med., 73:220, 1982.

40. Graham, D.Y., and Patterson, D.J.: Double-blind comparison of liquid antacid and placebo in the treatment of symptomatic reflux esophagitis. Dig. Dis. Sci., 28:559, 1983.

41. Graham, D.Y., Moser, S.E., and Estes, M.K.: The effect of bran on bowel function in constipation. Am. J. Gastroenterol., 77:599, 1982.

42. Hawkes, R.A., et al.: Hepatitis B infection in institutionalized Down's Syndrome inmates: A longitudinal study with five hepatitis B virus markers. Clin. Exp. Immunol., 40:478, 1980.

43. Helm, J.F., et al.: Determinants of esophageal acid clearance in normal subjects. Gastroenterology, 85:607, 1983.

44. Helmsing, P.J., Duermeyer, W., vanHattem, G.C.A.M., and Wielaerd, F.: An outbreak of hepatitis A in an institution for the mentally retarded. J. Med. Virol., 5:143, 1980.

45. Hermreck, A.S., and Coates, N.R.: Results of the Hill antireflux operation. Am. J. Surg., 140:764, 1980.

46. Heyward, W.L., et al.: Serological markers of hepatitis B virus and alpha-fetoprotein levels preceding hepatocellular carcinoma in Alaskan Eskimos. Lancet, ii:889, 1982.

47. Hillemeier, A.C., et al.: Delayed gastric emptying in infants with gastroesophageal reflux. J. Pediatr., 98: 190, 1981.

48. Hinton, J.M., Lennard-Jones, J.E., and Yoring, A.C.: A new method for studying gut transit times using radiopaque markers. Gut, 10:842, 1969.

49. Ismail-Beigi, F., Horton, P.F., and Pope, C.E.: Histological consequences of gastroesophageal reflux in man. Gastroenterology, 58:163, 1970.

50. Johnson, L.F., and DeMeester, T.R.: Evaluation of elevation of head of the bed, bethanechol, and antacid foam tablets on gastroesophageal reflux. Dig. Dis. Sci., 26:673, 1981.

51. Keshgegian, A.A., and Ochs, R.H.: Orcein-positive hepatitis B surface antigen and liver carcinoma: Their association in an eastern U.S. population. Arch. Pathol. Lab. Med., 105:190, 1981.

52. Kiesewetter, W.B., and Smith, J.W.: Malrotation of midgut in infancy and childhood. Arch. Surg., 77:483, 1958.

53. Koretz, R.L., Stone, O., and Gitnick, G.L.: The longterm course of non-A, non-B post-transfusion hepatitis. Gastroenterology, 79:893, 1980.

54. Kothari, T., Mangla, J.C., and Kalra, T.M.S.: Barrett's ulcer and treatment with cimetidine. Arch. Intern. Med., 140:475, 1980.

55. Kozarek, R.A., and Sanowski, R.A.: Esophageal food impaction—description of a new method for bolus removal. Dig. Dis. Sci., 25:100, 1980.

56. Kozarek, R.A., et al.: An anti-reflux prosthesis in the treatment of gastroesophageal reflux. Ann. Intern. Med., 98:310, 1983.

57. Kreek, M.J., Hahn, E.F., Schaefer, R.A., and Fishman, J.: Naloxone, a specific opioid antagonist, reverses chronic idiopathic constipation. Lancet, i:261, 1983.

58. Lachman, R., Funamura, J., and Szalay, G.: Gastrointestinal abnormalities in the Cornelia de Lange Syndrome. Mt. Sinai J. Med. (NY), 48:236, 1981.

59. Ladd, W.E.: Congenital obstruction of the duodenum. N. Engl. J. Med., 206:277, 1932.

60. Lam, K.C., Lai, C.L., Trepo, C., and Wu, P.C.: Deleterious effect of prednisolone in HB$_s$Ag-positive chronic active hepatitis. N. Engl. J. Med., 304:380, 1981.

61. Lander, J.J., Giles, J.P., Purcell, R.H., and Krugman, S.: Viral hepatitis, type B (MS-2 strain): Detection of antibody after primary infection. N. Engl. J. Med., 285:303, 1971.

62. Leape, L.L., and Ramenofsky, M.L.: Surgical treatment of gastroesophageal reflux in children. Am. J. Dis. Child., 134:935, 1980.

63. Leichtner, A., et al.: Horizontal non parenteral spread of hepatitis B among children. Ann. Intern. Med., 94:346, 1981.

64. Lucke, B.: The pathology of fatal epidemic hepatitis. Am. J. Pathol., 20:471, 1944.

65. McCallum, R.W., Fink, S.M., Lerner, E., and Berkowitz, D.M.: Effects of metoclopramide and bethanechol on delayed gastric emptying present in gastroesophageal reflux patients. Gastroenterology, 84:1573, 1983.

66. McKay, I.R., Taft, L.I., and Cowling, D.C.: Lupoid hepatitis. Lancet, i:1323, 1956.

67. Maynard, J.E.: Prevention of hepatitis B through the use of vaccine. Ann. Intern. Med., 97:442, 1982.

68. Miller, D.J.: Seroepidemiology of viral hepatitis. Postgrad. Med., 68:137, 1980.

69. Naef, A.P., Savary, M., and Ozzello, L.: Columnar lined lower esophagus: An acquired lesion with malignant predisposition. J. Thorac. Cardiovasc. Surg., 70:826, 1975.

70. Naiman, H.L., Sekla, L., and Albritton, W.L.: Giardiasis and other intestinal parasitic infections in a Manitoba residential school for the mentally retarded. Can. Med. Assoc. J., 122:185, 1980.

71. Nielsen, J.O., Dietrichson, O., Elling, P.L., and Christoffersen, P.: Incidence and meaning of persistence of Australia antigen in patients with acute viral hepatitis: Development of chronic hepatitis. N. Engl. J. Med., 285:1157, 1971.

72. Ohri, G.L., DeVenecia, R., and Acs, H.: Tuberous sclerosis presenting as diaphragmatic hernia in newborn. Dev. Med. Child Neurol., 22:509, 1980.

73. Ott, D.J., and Gelfand, D.W.: Gastrointestinal contrast agents: Indications, uses, and risks. JAMA, 249:2380, 1983.

74. Palmer, E.D.: Disorder of the cricopharyngeus muscle: A review. Gastroenterology, 71:510, 1976.

75. Passarge, E.: The genetics of Hirschsprung's Disease. N. Engl. J. Med., 276:138, 1967.

76. Paull, A., et al.: The histologic spectrum of Barrett's esophagus. N. Engl. J. Med., 295:476, 1976.

77. Rakela, J.R., et al.: Hepatitis A virus infection in fulminant hepatitis and chronic active hepatitis. Gastroenterology, 74:879, 1978.

78. Raventos, J.M., Kralemann, H., and Gray, D.B.: Mortality risks of mentally retarded and mentally ill patients after a feeding gastrostomy. Am. J. Ment. Defic., 86:439, 1982.

79. Redeker, A.G.: Viral hepatitis: Clinical aspects. Am. J. Med. Sci., 270:9, 1975.

80. Redeker, A.G.: Treatment of chronic active hepatitis: Good news and bad news. N. Engl. J. Med., 304:420, 1981.

81. Reynolds, T.B.: Chronic hepatitis: Current dilemmas. Am. J. Med., 69:485, 1980.

82. Richter, J.E., and Castell, D.O.: Gastroesophageal reflux: Pathogenesis, diagnosis and therapy. Ann. Intern. Med., 97:93, 1982.

82a. Roberts, I.M., Curtis, R.L., and Madara, J.L.: Gastroesophageal reflux and Barrett's esophagus in developmentally disabled patients. Am. J. Gastroenterol., 81:519, 1986.

83. Rosenthal, P., Liebman, W.M.: Comparative study of stool examinations, duodenal aspiration and pediatric entero-test for giardiasis in children. J. Pediatr., 96:278, 1980.

84. Ruvalcaba, R.H.A., Myhre, S., and Smith, D.W.: Sotos syndrome with intestinal polyposis and pigmentary changes of the genitalia. Clin. Genet., 18:413, 1980.

84a. Schuffler, M.D., et al.: Chronic intestinal pseudoobstruction (a report of 27 cases and a review of the literature). Medicine, 60:173, 1981.

85. Schwartz, G.F., and Polsky, H.S.: Ingested foreign bodies of the gastrointestinal tract. Am. Surg., 42:236, 1976.

86. Shulman, N.R., Hirschman, R.J., and Barker, L.F.: Viral hepatitis. Ann. Intern. Med., 72:257, 1970.

87. Sjogren, R.W., and Johnson, L.F.: Barrett's esophagus: A review. Am. J. Med., 74:313, 1983.

88. Skinner, D.B., et al.: Barrett's esophagus, comparison of benign and malignant cases. Ann. Surg., 198:554, 1983.

89. Smith, G.V., and Teele, R.L.: Delayed diagnosis of duodenal obstruction in Down's Syndrome. Am. J. Roentgenol., 134:937, 1980.

90. Sondheimer, J.M., and Morris, B.A.: Gastroesophageal reflux among several retarded children. J. Pediatr., 94:710, 1979.

91. Spitz, L.: Surgical treatment of gastroesophageal reflux in severely mentally retarded children. J. R. Soc. Med., 75:525, 1982.

92. Stanten, A., and Peters, H.E.: Enzymatic dissolution of phytobezoars. Am. J. Surg., *130:*259, 1975.

93. Storch, G.A., et al.: Use of conventional and IgM-specific radioimmunoassays for anti-hepatitis A antibody in an outbreak of hepatitis A. Am. J. Med., 73:663, 1982.

94. Swischuk, L.E., Hayden, C.K., Jr., and van Caillie, B.D.: Mega-aeroesophagus in children: A sign of gastroesophageal reflux. Radiology, *141:*73, 1981.

95. Szmuness, W., et al.: Hepatitis B vaccine: Demonstration of efficacy in a controlled clinical trial in a high-risk population in the United States. N. Engl. J. Med., *303:*833, 1980.

96. Thanik, K.D., Chey, W.Y., Shah, A.N., and Gutierrez, J.G.: Reflux esophagitis: Effect of oral bethanechol on symptoms and endoscopic findings. Ann. Intern. Med., 93:805, 1980.

97. Thanik, K.D., et al.: Bethanecol or cimetidine in the treatment of symptomatic reflux esophagitis, a double-blind control study. Arch. Intern. Med., *142:*1479, 1982.

98. Visvesvara, G.S., Smith, P.D., Healy, G.R., and Brown, W.R.: An immunofluorescence test to detect serum antibodies to Giardia Lamblia. Ann. Intern. Med., 93:802, 1980.

99. Wald, A.: Colonic transit time and anorectal manometry in chronic idiopathic constipation. Arch. Intern. Med., *146:*1713, 1986.

100. Waye, J.D.: Removal of foreign bodies from the upper intestinal tract with fiberoptic instruments. Am. J. Gastroenterol., 65:557, 1976.

101. Werner, B.G., and Grady, G.F.: Accidental hepatitis-B-surface-antigen-positive inoculations: Use of e antigen to estimate infectivity. Ann. Intern. Med., 97:367, 1982.

102. Wesdorp, E., et al.: Oral cimetidine in reflux esophagitis: A double blind controlled trial. Gastroenterology, 74:821, 1978.

103. Wesley, J.R., et al.: The need for evaluation of gastroesophageal reflux in brain-damaged children referred for feeding gastrostomy. J. Pediatr. Surg., *16:*866, 1981.

104. Wilkinson, J.D., Dudgeon, D.L., and Sondheimer, J.M.: Comparison of medical and surgical treatment of gastroesophageal reflux in severely retarded children. J. Pediatr., 99:202, 1981.

105. Williams, C., Weber, F.T., Cullen, J., and Kane, M.: Hepatitis B transmission in school contacts of retarded HB$_s$Ag carrier students. J. Pediatr., *103:*192, 1983.

106. Williamson, H.G., et al.: A longitudinal study of hepatitis infection in an institution for the mentally retarded. Aust. N.Z. J. Med., *12:*30, 1982.

107. Winter, H.S., et al.: Intraepithelial eosinophils: A new diagnostic criterion for reflux esophagitis. Gastroenterology, 83:818, 1982.

108. Wolfe, M.E.: Current concept in parasitology: Giardiasis. N. Engl. J. Med., 298:319, 1978.

109. Wright, E.C., et al.: Treatment of chronic active hepatitis: An analysis of three controlled trials. Gastroenterology, 73:1422, 1977.

110. Wright, R., and Millward-Sadler, G.H.: Acute viral hepatitis. *In* Liver and Biliary Disease. Edited by R. Wright, K.G.M.M. Alberti, S. Karran, and G.H. Millward-Sadler. Philadelphia, W.B. Saunders, 1979, pp. 585-646.

FEEDING DISORDERS

Eunice Shishmanian, R.N., M.S.
Holly Tomlinson, R.P.T.

Problems of eating and feeding have significant nutritional, developmental, and psychological implications. Feeding is the process of nourishing the body by providing nutrients and energy for growth and health maintenance. Palmer and Ekvall[4] define a feeding problem as "the inability or refusal to eat certain foods because of neuromuscular dysfunction, obstructive lesions or psychological factors which interfere with eating, or a combination of two or more of these. By this definition, it should be clarified that a feeding problem is a clinical entity rather than a specific disease."

Recognition of the impact of feeding difficulties on children and adults with developmental disabilities has been fueled by societal changes. Legislation has progressively mandated more encompassing therapy, education, and services to the handicapped population. While advances in medical care and technology have increased the rate of survival of many infants with major neurologic, respiratory, and cardiac difficulties, they have resulted in increased problems with growth, nutrition, and feeding. At the same time, approaches for assessment and intervention addressing sensory and physical impairments that interfere with feeding and oral motor function have been developed. In addition, medical regimens for providing adequate nutrition use alternative feeding measures where necessary (i.e., hyperalimentation or tube feedings), with introduction of oral feedings at the same time or later if possible.

NORMAL INTERACTION AND DEVELOPMENT

Normally, the feeding experience provides significant opportunities for interaction between parent and child in the process of development.

Infants get to know their parents during feeding times when they are afforded an opportunity to interact in a meaningful relationship. Responses are usually those of warmth, satisfaction, and mutually gratifying communications. The infant is usually held in close bodily contact with the mother in a manner conducive to total involvement of the two participants. In the optimal situation, this is a pleasant, physically relaxing time for the mother who feels comfortable with her baby. These early seeds of sociability eventually lead to the companionship at mealtimes that one associates with pleasant conversation.

Feeding provides a rich learning environment. The infant learns about the physical and social world through sensory input—listening to mother's voice, seeing her face, smelling her, and feeling the tensions of her body as well as her touches and strokes. The mouth is important in helping the infant feel, taste, smell, and even hear (squeal, crunch, slurp). Foods add color, shape, and interesting experiences. In addition, the infant is learning how to use the many complicated parts of his mouth and pharynx; oral motor development takes place in the processes of sucking, swallowing, and moving the tongue. The same parts and muscles that form sounds will later form words. Adults learn to read such cues as pleasure, annoyance, difficulty, amusement, hunger, and satiety while watching infants eat.

The developmental sequence of feeding in the infant follows the development of voluntary movement. The infant concomitantly moves from discovery to self-mastery, independence, and finally separation from the mother. Each stage prepares the child for the one to follow. Both parent and infant work at accomplishing these changes. The infant who attempts to establish increasing autonomy must give up some dependence. Likewise the parent who promotes independence must accept a loss of control. Growth progresses by fits and starts, practice providing nature's way of working.

FEEDING AND THE CHILD WITH A DEVELOPMENTAL DISABILITY

Parents anticipate the birth of a healthy infant throughout a pregnancy, and a crisis results at the birth of an infant with a disability. They grieve for the desired healthy infant, and yet they must come to know their infant. The opportunity for developing closeness and relatedness described as bonding can be impeded by these uncomfortable feelings. In addition, the pattern of mutual interaction between mother and infant that normally develops during feeding is altered when a child has a developmental disability. Mother and infant may be separated if the infant requires specialized medical care such as that provided in a neonatal intensive care unit.

Parental nurturance in the usual manner is interrupted.

Recently the parent-infant system has come to be viewed as one in which both participants are mutually dependent. Each of the participants brings individual patterns or tendencies to the interactive process. Infants with disabilities may not be able to produce clear cues. Their parents may be confused by their behavior and have difficulty responding appropriately.

Parents take for granted that feeding skills will develop with little effort or instruction, and they feel responsible for feeding their children. They equate feeding with providing loving care and view difficulties or problems in this area as a reflection of their incompetence. Feelings of self-doubt may emerge if the infant does not feed well or fails to gain weight. The problem may actually be exaggerated by attempts to feed more frequently, trial of a wide variety of foods, or following advice of trusted and experienced resources. Strong feelings of failure, helplessness, and inadequacy prevail. Positive interactions in the form of touching, talking and looking may be subverted as the focus of the feeding experience becomes task-oriented with emphasis on adequate intake.

The communicative interaction between mother and infant carries confusing messages to the infant as well. Body tension, anxiety and frustration in the voice, and facial expressions tell the infant that things are not okay.

CAUSES OF FEEDING PROBLEMS

Infants with developmental disabilities may have any of several types of feeding problems, the causes of which can be congenital structural deformities, neurological dysfunction, systemic illness, or prematurity with a developmental focus. Feeding concerns in any of the suggested categories may have a primary or secondary behavioral or emotional component. These may be manifested as bizarre food habits, mealtime tantrums, a dislike for many foods, rumination, and altered intake.

Congenital Structural Deformities

Anatomic defects of the oral structures impose mechanical impediments on the feeding experience. Children with structural defects commonly exhibit intact neurologic systems with normal ability to suck and swallow. Anatomic formation of the oral structures, however, may prevent effective use of them. The infant with cleft lip or palate cannot form an adequate seal to accomplish effective sucking. Specialized feeding techniques such as a cleft palate feeder and proper positioning may be required until the defect can be corrected surgically. However, once the anatomic defect is repaired, normal progression of feeding skills is usually possible. Until surgical correction occurs, primary goals must be to maintain adequate oral intake and to encourage development of a comfortable, mutually beneficial feeding interaction between parent and child.

Neurologic Dysfunction

The child with neurologic dysfunction frequently displays compromised oral motor ability. Abnormal muscle tone, whether hypertonia or hypotonia, can have significant impact on motor development, including feeding skills. For many children with neurologic dysfunction, oral function reflects the general pattern of neuromuscular dysfunction. Hypotonia may prevent a child from supporting himself against gravity. Orally, this is often manifested as an open mouth with tongue resting forward, or in excessive drooling. Children with hypertonia often retain primitive reflexes and exhibit abnormal patterns in both gross and oral motor movements. As a result of tone abnormalities, these children may manifest a variety of feeding problems including weak and ineffective lip and tongue movements, poor swallowing ability, delayed development of feeding abilities, and inability to progress to independent feeding skills.

Systemic Illness

Medical conditions may cause stress to the human organism which can be either acute or chronic. Disease in any system of the body affects the total system. Therefore it is common that children with a variety of disease conditions have eating problems.

Cardiac or pulmonary dysfunction can cause increased cardiac and respiratory rates, color changes, and fatigue. Increased secretions limit functional abilities and often induce choking. There is inability to manage the functions of eating and breathing simultaneously as well as tolerating the volume of a feeding. Gastrointestinal dysfunctions may make the ingestion of food unpleasant or increasingly difficult. Vomiting, regurgitation, and esophagitis are strong deterrents to eating. Providing adequate nutrition for children with illnesses causes problems in feeding evidenced in crying, fussiness, altered sleep, slow weight gain, and failure to thrive. Adequate nutrition must be provided through alternative methods such as intravenous, central lines, naso-

gastric tubes, or gastrostomy tubes (see section in this chapter on alternative feeding methods). Oral activities should be maintained at whatever level possible such as by the use of a pacifier or taste treats. Parents will need emotional support, education and assistance in understanding the reasons for the choice of treatments as well as the attention needed to continue to provide for developmental and psychological needs.

CLINICAL VIGNETTES

Amy. Now six months of age, Amy is considered a poor feeder by her mother. Feedings are stressful; she gulps formula from a large hole in the nipple, choking and sputtering frequently. She is difficult to hold, arching backwards during choking spells. Distressful feedings and poor weight gain are the presenting concerns.

Jared. Jared had a gastrostomy tube placed during his first week of life; the history indicates that he exhibited a weak suck at that time. He is a reasonably well-nourished 12-month-old who appears to enjoy his mealtimes of tube feedings. He points to his feeding apparatus and holds the tube while his mother adjusts the equipment for administration. His parents are frustrated in their attempts to get Jared to take any type of solid food, though he will occasionally accept teaspoons of apple juice or suck on a lollipop.

Mary Beth. Mary Beth is 10 years old, small for her age, with a diagnosis of cerebral palsy. She exhibits extensor posturing throughout her body, has no sitting balance, and has limited use of her hands. She cannot feed herself and is fed in a reclining position in her wheelchair. Though Mary Beth appears to enjoy foods, presenting concerns are that she is a very slow feeder, is messy at feeding, and has difficulty maintaining weight. Much of the food is pushed out of her mouth by her tongue, and she has particular difficulty ingesting liquids.

ASSESSMENT OF FEEDING PROBLEMS

Feeding problems are generally complex, and many areas of development can be involved. Therefore, for the purposes of understanding, interpreting, and as a guide for management, assessment requires a comprehensive multidisciplinary appraisal. A sound understanding of normal child development is essential, not only of feeding but in all areas of development including gross and fine motor skills, speech, cognition, and social interaction.

Particularly in problematic cases, comprehensive evaluation by an interdisciplinary team is necessary to provide a composite picture of the problem for establishment of the most effective program. Nutritionist, nurse, physician, physical therapist, occupational therapist, speech pathologist, psychologist, and dentist all provide information relevant to the evaluation process. Each looks at the problem from a different perspective; the team approach assures that all relevant and significant aspects will be considered.

Health History and Physical Examination

Assessment of health status requires a careful medical history to determine factors that may be contributing to the feeding problem.

Respiratory status can have a major impact on feeding abilities. This is particularly true for infants with bronchopulmonary dysplasia or aspiration syndrome (Chap. 11), but there may also be other factors. For example, children with abnormal muscle tone may have irregular and inefficient breathing patterns that make coordination of breathing and swallowing difficult. The distress these children experience when they try to coordinate sucking, swallowing, and breathing makes them instinctively reluctant to feed in order to protect the airway. Persistent chronic upper airway congestion may be an indication of swallowing dysfunction and the inability to manage oral secretions. Fluoroscopic studies of the swallowing mechanism may be indicated to determine if aspiration is occurring.

Medication regimens should be reviewed thoroughly. Single medications, combinations of drugs, and the times of administration can significantly affect appetite, taste, gastrointestinal functioning, and the individual's temperament, behaviors, and state of alertness.

The physical examination is a component of a complete evaluation of health status. Attention should be directed to the status of the oral structures, noting the health of the oral mucosa, structures of the palate, eruption, position and condition of the teeth, and occlusion of the jaws. Dental caries can often produce foul breath, pain, and alteration in food tastes. Malocclusion hampers chewing and may be exhibited in inability to handle fibrous foods.

Growth and Nutrition Assessment

Accurate measurements of growth should be accomplished using standard guidelines. Measurements should be consistent and should be done by trained examiners with appropriate equipment. Special equipment may be required for the disabled population, such as a scale with a lift or one adapted for a wheelchair.

Measurements obtained of growth parameters should be plotted on representative growth charts. Such graphs are those of the National Center for Health Statistics published in 1976 which were developed from a cross section of the United States population.[3] These charts show curves for the 5th through the 95th percentiles, plotting the size of children by percentile level at consecutive ages. Serial recordings of a child's growth rather than a single measurement at one point in time provide a more reliable assessment of the pattern of growth. The relationship between height and weight should also be plotted. Unfortunately, there are no standard growth charts for handicapped children.

A feeding history provides information on changes in feeding behaviors over time and on the successful and unsuccessful interventions that have been attempted. It also allows the primary caregivers to express their perceptions of the problem and offers insight into environmental influences on feeding. One needs to consider the number of persons involved in feeding and their attitudes about feeding. These factors are particularly relevant for the child or adult in an institution or community residence. Often there may be conflicting opinions on the way a child should be fed, a lack of consistency in feeding approaches, and a variance in the way the child may eat for different persons. Information should be obtained about mealtimes, e.g., the location, the people usually present, and the child's response to the environment. Children generally learn improved feeding behaviors from family members and/or peers, but some children may require a setting in which there are fewer distractions. The frequency of feedings and length of each session should also be considered. For example, in an effort to ensure adequate caloric intake the feeder may feel pressured to extend mealtimes for lengthy periods (up to 2 hours) or to give more frequent feedings, thus spending most of each day on feeding activities.

Dietary pattern is an integral part of the total nutritional picture. Food records should describe the quality and quantity of food intake for a period of time. One is cautioned to consider the validity of each record on the basis of the motivation and abilities of the recorder.

A 24-hour recall of food intake can provide a rapid overview of data for a single time period, but it may not illustrate typical patterns. A record of food taken over 3 or more days affords more precise information about amounts and types of food. Cooperation of the caregiver is essential in accomplishing this time-consuming task. Food intake data allows one not only to calculate average daily intake of calories but to determine intake of specific or total nutrients as well.

Oral-Motor Evaluation

Part of any accurate assessment of oral-motor abilities depends on a comprehensive motor evaluation, preferably prior to the feeding observation. Head control contributes significantly to oral motor ability, and independent sitting balance and fine motor abilities are both prerequisites for development of independent feeding skills.[1] The position of the child's body during feeding is the key to improved oral motor function. Many children with feeding problems, particularly those with neurologic impairments, are fed in a reclining position, or in a semireclining position in which gravity assists movement of the food. These positions promote passive rather than active feeding, result in abnormal posturing and oral movement, and place the child at high risk for aspiration. The optimal position for facilitation of feeding consists of sitting with the head upright, shoulders and hips in alignment, arms in toward midline, hips and knees flexed to 90°, and feet fully supported on a stable base. A stable, upright, symmetrical posture, whether in a parent's arms or in an appropriate seating device, should be encouraged for any child, but it is particularly relevant for the child with central nervous system dysfunction.

The upright position promotes coordination of breathing and swallowing and the handling of oral secretions. It is the basis for improvement of body tone, and it promotes opportunity for exploration of the environment and practice of both gross and fine motor skills. For many children, simple correction of their sitting position can be a major element in remediation of feeding difficulties.

Assessment of oral-motor function requires an understanding of normal and abnormal movement patterns. Evans-Morris[1] has suggested a classification of oral motor patterns that includes normal, primitive, and abnormal. Normal patterns are those observed in normal progression from infancy to adulthood, e.g., sucking, tongue lateralization, and chewing. Primitive patterns are those observed in infancy but which normally do not persist in the older child or adult. For example, root and suck/swallow reflexes are frequently seen in the individual with central nervous system dysfunction. Abnormal movement patterns are not seen at any time in the normal course of feeding development (e.g.,

tongue thrust, jaw thrust, lip retraction, and passive or inactive swallowing). These are patterns often seen in spastic cerebral palsy with pseudobulbar involvement.

Inadequate nutritional intake often results from poor oral motor function. There may be loss of food from the mouth before it can be swallowed. Parents may report that the child takes in adequate amounts of food but does not gain weight. Due to abnormal muscle tone and/or other medical problems, caloric requirements may differ. In such situations it can be helpful to suggest appropriate food textures, appropriate amounts of food, and ways to add supplemental calories without increasing food quantity.

Feeding Observation

Medical and feeding histories provide valuable information, but the most crucial component of a feeding assessment is observation of a feeding session. This is best done by approximating the normal feeding environment. All efforts should be made to provide familiar surroundings such as the child's usual seating device feeding utensils, and to use familiar foods. Observations at this time allow for assessment of interactions during feeding as well as the child's responses to food and abilities to handle it.

Through observation of the intake of food one obtains information about oral movements and ability to manage food of different textures. Assessment should include the following: coordination of suck, swallowing, and breathing; strength, rhythm, and endurance of sucking; and tongue mobility and lip movements. Inability to manage particular food textures can result in gagging, choking, or loss of food, such as when the effort to move food to the back of the mouth results in tongue thrusting that pushes the food out of the mouth. One of the most frequently observed problems among the developmentally disabled population is that of inappropriate food textures for the child's oral motor abilities.

Observation of oral movements when food is presented is part of the sensory evaluation. Abnormal sensory response may be manifested as hyposensitivity or hypersensitivity. Hyposensitivity is frequently seen in the child with hypotonia and delayed reaction responses. Orally, one may note a depressed gag reflex with apparent lack of awareness of the presence or location of food in the mouth. Hypersensitivity may be seen with increased muscle tone and abnormal patterns of movement resulting from stimuli that are overwhelming. Individuals may demonstrate total body hypersensitivity with strong oral manifestations or may exhibit a combination of responses such as hypersensitivity intraorally and decreased sensation extraorally. Sensory responses may be triggered not only by tactile cues such as food textures, but also by smell, sight, taste, and sound. It is important to be able to determine whether the response is actual dislike of a stimulus or an inability to modify emotional responses such as excitement or fear. The latter response is frequently observed when the increased muscle tone results in an overflow of tone with motor disorganization.

Liquids pose a problem for individuals with central nervous system impairments. Decreased sensation or inefficient lip and tongue movements prevent coordination of rapid swallowing of liquid and result in some loss from the corners of the mouth. The sudden rush of liquid to the back of the throat poses a threat to the airway that can be frightening. The instinct to protect the airway may result in even more abnormal patterns of movement or complete refusal to take liquids. Simple remediation can often be accomplished by thickening the liquids. This reduces the rate of flow, gives the child more time to control and swallow the liquid, and allows for development of a more normal swallowing pattern.

Progression in the development of independent feeding skills should also be assessed—for example, finger feeding, spoon feeding, cup drinking, and willingness to participate in self-feeding. Gesell and Ilg[2] have established developmental norms for feeding skills that can be used as guidelines.

MANAGEMENT OF FEEDING PROBLEMS

Intervention should be initiated as soon as a feeding problem is recognized. Remediation is facilitated if it is begun before abnormal patterns of movement and habits have become well established or nutritional intake has been compromised. Secondary emotional and behavioral factors can complicate what was initially a purely organic problem.

Unfortunately, treatment is frequently delayed for a variety of reasons. Medical issues may take precedence, or the feeding problem may be expected to resolve spontaneously. Parents may not know where to seek guidance. Numerous attempts at solutions may be tried and then discarded when immediate success is not achieved.

Most feeding problems are chronic and complex. Retraining is generally a slow process requiring a great deal of patience and investment of time. Management requires thorough assess-

ment by a "feeding team" and a well-designed, consistent approach with much support to parents.

Treatment goals include two objectives. The first is to provide optimal caloric and fluid intake. The second is to maximize active participation in the feeding process with a program directed toward progressive learning of more normal feeding patterns and promoting a positive attitude around mealtimes. Components of a remedial program should be individually designed on the basis of findings from the feeding evaluation.

Intervention strategies should be based on the individual's developmental level, encouraging as much active participation as possible. Allowing some control over the feeding situation fosters independence and allows food and feeding times to be viewed as more positive and enjoyable experiences.

A relaxed, nonintrusive approach to mealtimes that encourages eye contact and verbal reinforcement aids in a mutually beneficial interaction. Consistency is important in remediation of abnormal patterns and development of more efficient behaviors and should include feeding personnel, feeding techniques, mealtimes, and environment. Feedings should progress at the child's pace and be confined to reasonable time frames in order to avoid fatigue and frustration.

The fundamentals for improvement of oral motor function are positioning, normalization of body tone and movement, and encouragement of appropriate responses to sensory stimuli. Upright positioning in an age-appropriate seating device forms the basis for initiation of the feeding program. Wheelchairs and feeding seats may require adaptations in order to provide an appropriately stable and comfortable position.

Therapeutic techniques, prior to and during the feeding session, may be required in order to obtain relaxation or enhancement of body and oral muscle tone, and should be carried out under the direction of a trained professional.

Oral stimulation consists of tactile input to the oral and facial area using a variety of textures that can be tolerated. This results in improvement in response to sensory stimulation in the oral area. It may also aid in inhibition of primitive reflexes, drooling and improve swallowing ability. Stimulation can be provided by the child's own hand-to-mouth behavior, toys to mouth, tooth brushing, or by the feeder. Food can also provide sensory stimulation through variation in temperature, increments in texture, and varied tastes and smells. For those on enteral feeding programs, maintenance of oral stimulation or some form of daily oral intake appears to provide an important foundation for eventual reintroduction of oral feedings.

The sensory cues provided by the tactile input will also help improve oral movements such as lip closure and tongue mobility. When abnormal muscle tone prevents intrinsic jaw stability, external stability can be provided through jaw control by the feeder. When used correctly it can provide stability for improved bottle drinking, cup drinking, and spoon feeding.

Adaptive equipment (e.g., special nipples, Teflon-coated spoons, flattened bowls of varied sizes, cut-out cups, and spoons with built-up handles) is available to aid in facilitating feeding. The goal is to use the least amount of equipment while allowing the individual to be as efficient and independent as possible. Adaptive feeding techniques and equipment for use at home should be initiated by a trained professional in the context of a program of ongoing parental education.

Sensitivity toward parental abilities is essential in carrying out a feeding program. Understanding of the rationale behind the use of special techniques and agreement on goals for feeding will facilitate follow-through. Parents experience success for their efforts through their child's progress in feeding and a more relaxed and social mealtime environment. This ensures optimal growth and nutrition as well as encouraging development and psychosocial awareness.

REFERENCES

1. Evans-Morris, S.: Oral-motor development: Normal and abnormal. *In* Oral-Motor Function and Dysfunction in Children. Edited by J. Wilson. Chapel Hill, University of North Carolina, 1977, pp. 156-162.
2. Gesell, A., and Amatruda, C.: Developmental Diagnosis. 3rd Ed. Edited by H. Knoblock and B. Pasamanick. New York, Harper and Row, 1974, pp. 34-99.
3. National Center for Health Statistics, U.S. Department of Health, Education and Welfare. NCHS Growth Curves for Children: Birth to 18 Years. Series 11, No. 165, DHEW Publication No. (PHS)78-1650. Washington, DC, U.S. Government Printing Office, 1977.
4. Palmer, S., and Ekvall, S.: Pediatric Nutrition in Developmental Disorders. Springfield, IL, Charles C Thomas, 1978, p. 107.

BIBLIOGRAPHY

Howard, R., and Winter, H. (eds.): Nutrition and Feeding of Infant and Toddlers. Boston, Little, Brown, 1984.
Mueller, H.A.: Facilitating feeding and prespeech. *In* Physical Therapy Services in the Developmental Disabilities. Edited by P.H. Pearson, and C.E. Williams. Springfield, IL, Charles C Thomas, 1980.
Pipes, P.L.: Nutrition in Infancy and Childhood. 3rd Ed. St. Louis, C.V. Mosby, 1985.
Zelle, R., and Coyner, A.: Developmentally Disabled Infants and Toddlers: Assessment and Intervention. Philadelphia, F.A. Davis, 1983.

ALTERNATIVE FEEDING METHODS

Carol A. Walsh, R.N.-C., B.S.N., M.P.H.
Theodor Feigelman, M.D.

The nutritional problems of individuals with developmental disabilities can arise from multiple causes. They are often attributed to poorly characterized associations of the developmental disorder itself. It may not be appreciated that the patient with recurrent vomiting, aspiration pneumonia, and failure to thrive may be suffering from a treatable disorder. Unfortunately, it is often difficult to diagnose the underlying factors, which can include swallowing disorders, gastroesophageal reflux (GER), or a combination of both. Clinical awareness of these syndromes can lead to appropriate investigative procedures, diagnosis, and treatment. In older children and adults, lack of compliance and inability to understand even simple diagnostic procedures requires creative effort to design a workup, and some procedures may be difficult to perform.

In some situations, medical intervention can result in resolution of the presenting problem, whereas in others, surgical intervention may be required to establish alternative methods of feeding. Feeding tubes have undergone constant improvement, and the currently available products are acceptable to both the patient and care providers.

Regardless of the intervention, suspicion and recognition of a potentially correctable disorder are vital in providing improved health, nutrition, and quality of life for this population.

PROBLEMS CONTRIBUTING TO FEEDING DYSFUNCTION

Oral Problems

Oral motor dysfunction can occur secondary to structural abnormalities, developmental delays, and chronic or progressive central nervous system disease. Structural abnormalities include tracheoesophageal fistula, cleft palate, malocclusion, and macroglossia. These problems can result in recurrent pulmonary aspiration of oral feedings.

Neurologic Abnormalities

Persisting infantile reflexes such as the startle and rooting reflexes, and the phasicbite reflex (munching) can contribute to pharyngeal aspiration. Other manifestations of severe central nervous system disorders include incoordinated jaw and tongue thrusts and retractions, a tonic bite reflex, a hypo- or hyperactive gag reflex, and incoordination of swallowing and breathing. Chronic global degeneration of the central nervous system, as produced by Tay-Sachs disease, mucopolysaccharidoses, mucolipidoses, Alzheimer's disease, and cerebrovascular insufficiency syndromes, can contribute to any of these conditions, thus causing feeding dysfunction. Similarly, acute cerebrovascular accidents involving the lower nuclei can contribute to dysphagia.

Psychiatric Disorders

Psychiatric disturbances can result in a host of feeding difficulties.[9] (See Chap. 20, sections 1 and 2.) Syndromes similar to anorexia nervosa may result in refusal of oral intake with no demonstrable organic pathology. Behavioral aberrations may preclude the ability to sit at a table to eat. Unfortunately, in this population, these changes in behavior are nonspecific and may require extensive investigation in the search for organic disease, a process that by itself can be disturbing to the unaware individual and further aggravate food refusal.

Gastroesophageal Reflux

In retarded pediatric groups, GER has been implicated as a cause of developmental delay.[5] Regurgitation of feedings (and their occasional aspiration) contributes to malnutrition and the symptom of "failure to thrive."

GER should be considered in the differential diagnostic workup of feeding and nutritional disorders in patients with CNS dysfunction. In adults, the presence of growth retardation (or failure to thrive), sexual immaturity, and chronic pulmonary disease are often part of the constellation of symptoms found in GER-induced malnutrition.[17] The individual with severe impairment cannot adequately communicate chest discomfort, which may allow the symptoms of GER to go unnoticed.[43] Significant esophageal pathology, including Barrett's esophagus, has been found in adults who presented only with recurrent aspiration, feeding difficulties, and malnutrition.

The prevalence of GER in normal and retarded populations has been well described.[42] (See also section in this chapter on gastrointestinal problems.) The association between the presence of GER and severe central nervous system dysfunction in pediatric populations was noted in the early 1970s.[1,29] In a series of 74 infants and children who were operated on for GER, 20 (27.0%) had failure to thrive, 18 (24.3%) had repeated pneumonias, 5 (6.8%) had asthma, and 14 (18.9%) had a neurologic disorder. The patients with neurologic disorders included 3 with Down syndrome, 3 with a history of perinatal cerebral trauma, 3 with cerebral palsy, 4 with no known diagnosis, and 1 with systemic dysmyotonia.[18] Analysis of another series of 83 infants and children with GER revealed that 54 (65%) had "coexistent brain damage."[44]

Cadman, Richards, and Feldman[8] reported finding eight severely retarded children with chronic vomiting, anemia, and chest disease, presumably caused by GER. These children all had acquired brain damage, either from trauma, anoxia, or infection.

Sondheimer and Morris[45] studied GER in a retarded pediatric population with recurrent vomiting. With the use of esophageal radiographs, acid reflux testing, and upper gastrointestinal endoscopy, GER was demonstrated in 75% of those with chronic vomiting and esophagitis in 71% of those with GER. Most of the patients with GER were recumbent, and an extensive investigation of an ambulatory group was not done. In most of the patients in whom rumination and vomiting appeared to be behaviorally induced, organic pathophysiology was almost always demonstrable.

The relationship between the increased frequency of GER and severe CNS dysfunction has not been satisfactorily explained. Sondheimer and Morris note:

> The relatively late age of onset of symptoms in these patients in contrast to children of normal intelligence with GER, in whom symptoms usually appear during the first months of life, suggests that gastroesophageal reflux might be an acquired lesion resulting from some environmental or physical factor peculiar to the handicapped child. It has been speculated that prolonged supine positioning may predispose to the development of GER, or that abdominal compression resulting from scoliosis or spasticity of abdominal musculature might produce reflux by elevating intragastric pressure over that of the LES.[45]

In experiments with cats, it has been shown that acid perfusion and subsequent inflammation of the esophagus contributes to diminished lower esophageal sphincter (LES) pressure, with restoration of normal pressure on healing.[27] It is therefore possible that the reduced LES tone seen in retarded pediatric patients is secondary to chronic GER and inflammation.[45]

Other Causes

Severe musculoskeletal deformities can inhibit self-feeding or result in positioning that causes pharyngeal aspiration. Chronic rumination with regurgitation can result in weight loss and poor nutritional status.

Upright positioning in the face of severe neuromuscular or musculoskeletal impairment can be mechanically difficult. It has been suggested recently that upright positioning for infants with GER may even be detrimental, actually making the GER worse.[38] This further underscores the pathophysiologic complexity of this clinical entity.

MANAGEMENT ALTERNATIVES

Management of feeding dysfunction depends on the cause and may include the use of muscle relaxants, surgical correction of structural abnormalities, and introduction of dietary modifications such as high-calorie special-texture diets and specific feeding techniques. Use of adapted equipment (e.g., spoons, plates, and positioning devices) allows more normal feeding patterns. Appropriate education of parents and caregivers regarding equipment, body positioning, and the minimizing of environmental stimuli often brings positive results. Aversive reinforcement, although not commonly practiced, has been successfully used to control gastrointestinal bleeding associated with regurgitant behavior.[48]

When conservative measures are unsuccessful, further diagnostic evaluation, alternative feeding devices and/or surgery are indicated.

IDENTIFICATION OF CANDIDATES FOR ALTERNATIVE FEEDING METHODS

Guidelines for the establishment of short- and long-term enteral alimentation are described by Dobie and colleagues[12,13] and are well defined by Heymsfield et al.[26] and Heitkemper et al.[25]

Acute Indications

Acute dehydration can be treated either by enteral or parenteral (intravenous) rehydration. Oral electrolyte solutions are beneficial for acutely dehydrated pediatric patients.[40] Similarly, retarded adults with acute dehydration and limited intravenous access can benefit from these oral preparations. If the patient is too ill, or incapable of understanding and cooperating with an increase in oral intake, rehydration can be accomplished via intravenous or enteral alimentation using a tube.

Intravenous access can be difficult to attain and maintain. Patients with spastic muscle disease may accidentally dislodge an IV catheter, and continuous restarting of such catheters can be uncomfortable. Furthermore, infusion rates vary widely depending on the degree of muscle spasm.

Introduction of a nasoenteral feeding tube with appropriate electrolyte solutions can be a life-saving intervention. Maintenance can continue with a gradual increase in protein and calorie intake until the patient has been resuscitated to the point of being able to resume oral intake. A similar situation exists for the individual who has been unable to eat because of an acute debilitating illness such as pneumonia.

Chronic Indications

Patients who can benefit from long-term alternative feeding methods include those with recurrent symptoms that may not have initially been attributed to feeding dysfunction. These symptoms include:

1. growth retardation with chronic inanition (failure to thrive)
2. recurrent, direct pharyngeal aspiration
3. recurrent pneumonia or bronchiectasis
4. acute asthma, not necessarily associated with atopic disease or obvious aspiration
5. chronic or intermittent upper gastrointestinal bleeding
6. combination of reflux esophagitis and bronchospastic disease

Patients who have the above symptoms fall into three categories: "pure aspirators," "pure refluxers," and combination "refluxer-aspirators."

Pure aspirators are those patients who have oral motor dysfunction resulting in recurrent pulmonary aspiration. Symptoms include dehydration, failure to thrive, dysphagia, choking, recurrent pneumonia, bronchospasm masquerading as atopic asthma, and eventually chronic obstructive pulmonary disease.

Pure refluxers show symptomatology similar to the aspirators. They can also exhibit rumination, intermittent vomiting, subtle gastrointestinal bleeding, or frank hematemesis, all caused by GER.

Combination refluxer-aspirators have oral motor dysfunction with pharyngeal aspiration as well as GER and may exhibit any or all of the symptoms mentioned above. This category probably represents the most common cause of feeding dysfunction and failure to thrive in the developmentally disabled population.

Diagnosing the combination refluxer-aspirator is most difficult. For instance, when the clinical signs of GER are predominant, a patient with pervasive developmental disabilities may still have a swallowing disorder. Conversely, there should be a high index of suspicion for GER in the pure aspirator. Thus, the diagnoses of pure aspiration and pure GER may not be mutually exclusive, and the diagnostic workup for one must include appropriate studies to rule out the other.

Clinical Evaluation

Clues to the diagnosis of feeding or oral motor dysfunction can be suggested by symptoms that parents or caregivers might not recognize as being directly related to feeding. In older patients, reliable historical information is often not available. The clinician should be alert to certain historical factors.

History

The etiology of the developmental disorder can be critical in determining the etiology of a nutrition disorder. For example, the appropriate diagnosis for a patient with spastic quadriplegia and intermittent bronchospasm might not be extrinsic asthma. In the face of this developmental disorder, pulmonary aspiration becomes a likely possibility.

Presenting symptoms of physical immaturity, low-weight-for-age, failure to thrive, primary amenorrhea, delayed menarche, and delayed development of secondary sex characteristics suggest subclinical chronic malnutrition.[19,40]

Unexplained behaviors and symptoms including difficult feeding, frequent rumination or vomiting, heme-positive stools, recurrent aspiration pneumonias, bronchitis, and bronchiectasis can all be the result of a patulous lower esophageal sphincter.

Descriptions of chronic rumination, regurgitation or vomiting, and chronic or recurrent gastrointestinal bleeding or anemia suggest GER.

A history of chronic bronchitis, bronchiectasis, asthma, or recurrent pneumonia can suggest severe feeding dysfunction caused by aspiration.

Physical Examination

The most pertinent portion of the physical examination relates to the growth and development of the individual.

General appearance, height- and weight-for-age, and assessment of affect are important in determining the adequacy of nutritional intake. Initial anthropometric assessment is essential to establish a growth baseline. Individual longitudinal measurements of growth are required because the patient with severe musculoskeletal impairment cannot be compared with established standards.

Patients with spasticity frequently cannot coordinate hand-to-mouth movements, and swallowing may be impaired. Patients with flaccid muscle disease cannot initiate or coordinate feedings. It is important to check the gag reflex and tongue movements and to observe feedings directly.

The presence of major skeletal deformities is probably a significant contributor to GER.[32] A patient who can sit erect will be able to eat in a more physiologic manner than a patient who is fed in a supine position.[24]

Signs of dehydration should be sought. Thin skin or skin without subcutaneous fat suggest chronic undernutrition. Thin hair is common. Patients with sexual immaturity may lack pubertal hair and have underdeveloped genitalia and breasts caused by deficiencies of sex steroids.[19]

Auscultation of the chest often reveals signs of chronic pulmonary disease. Coarse rhonchi or wheezes and an increase in pulmonary secretions may appear after meals.

Rectal examination may reveal occult blood in the stool if esophageal or gastric bleeding is present.

Laboratory Studies

Basic laboratory studies include a complete blood count with differential and routine serum chemistries. The hematocrit may be surprisingly normal in patients with chronic upper gastrointestinal bleeding, because of chronic duodenal reabsorption of iron and chronic volume contraction. Red blood cells can be normochromic or hypochromic, depending on the amount and severity of gastrointestinal blood loss, and usually fit the nonspecific pattern of the anemia of chronic disease. The white blood cell count may be elevated during periods of acute stress or infection. Some patients with chronic malnutrition may show severe leukopenia during periods of severe stress or sepsis.

Despite reports to the contrary, serum albumin appears to be in or near the normal range. We have found that a more accurate reflection of protein metabolism is a measurement of the blood urea nitrogen, which is usually less than 10 mg/dl in chronically undernourished patients in the absence of renal disease. Serum alkaline phosphatase may occasionally be mildly elevated, possibly due to parathyroid hormone (PTH) demand on bone for calcium that is not being supplied by dietary intake.

Endocrine studies should include thyroid function to rule out hypothyroidism as a cause of anorexia and hyperthyroidism as a cause of weight loss, asthenia, and anorexia. Males usually manifest subnormal free and total testosterone levels with normal gonadotropins and cortisol reserve.

Insulin and somatomedin levels may be reduced, with elevated growth hormone levels in malnourished patients. The elevation in growth hormone may result from defects in secretory functions in the hypothalamic-pituitary axis. Females usually show low circulating estrogen levels with normal gonadotropins and are usually anovulatory.

Arterial blood gases may show a chronically decreased pO_2 and increased pCO_2, depending on the severity of the lung disease. If the reflux and/or aspiration have progressed to a point where the pCO_2 is elevated and the clinical diagnosis includes chronic obstructive lung disease, then feeding tube placement or surgical intervention becomes imperative.

Radiologic Studies

Parenchymal changes in the lungs can be seen either on an acute or a chronic basis. The acute presentations may show as lobar pneumonias (see Fig. 10-5). Chronic findings may be nonspecific or consistent with bronchiectatic changes. An upright chest radiograph may show the surprising finding of an air fluid level or dilated esophagus in the mid-chest (Fig. 10-6). This may be consistent with a large hiatal hernia.

In patients with oral motor dysfunction, a cinematographic swallowing study under fluoroscopy with careful otolaryngologic and dental examination is required. Usually these patients exhibit spasticity or incoordination of skeletal musculature elsewhere (see Chap. 11, Recurrent Aspiration Syndrome). An upper GI series may confirm the diagnosis of a hiatal hernia but may not confirm the presence of reflux esophagitis. The study must be done carefully because of the occasional direct pulmonary aspiration of barium. Fluoroscopy can disclose disordered esophageal motility and strictures. The upper GI radiograph itself can explain or indicate other potential causes for upper GI bleeding such as ulcer disease or tumors (see section in this chapter on gastrointestinal problems).

Byrne et al.[6] have recently derived a diagnostic algorithm for severely retarded children and young adult patients (to age 25) who vomit, have GI tract blood loss, have recurrent pneumonias, and who carry the diagnosis of failure to thrive. In these patients, upper GI radiography, endoscopy, and biopsy are of paramount importance for the diagnosis of GER. The use of gradation of GER on the upper GI series eliminates many false positives. Reflux into the cervical esophagus, gross esophagitis or esophageal ulcers, or

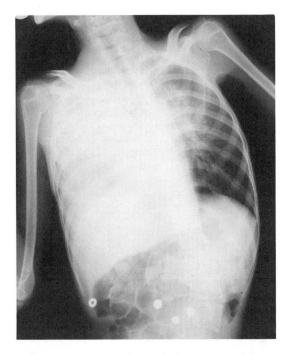

FIG. 10-5. Chest radiograph showing consolidation in right chest of 30-year-old female who had recurrent "asthma" and pneumonias. After diagnostic evaluation showed no gastroesophageal reflux, a feeding gastrostomy was placed. The result has been complete radiologic resolution with no further respiratory problems in the 3 years following placement of gastrostomy tube.

microscopic evidence of esophagitis provides indications for aggressive treatment.[7,10]

Other tests suggested in the workup of GER but which may be difficult in the uncooperative patient include radionuclide gastric reflux study, the Bernstein acid-perfusion test, esophageal manometry, and prolonged pH monitoring of the esophagus.[42] (Also see section in this chapter on gastrointestinal problems.)

Upper Gastrointestinal Endoscopy

A patient with recent episodes of upper gastrointestinal bleeding without a definite diagnosis warrants endoscopy. Upper gastrointestinal bleeding occurs more frequently from esophagitis than might be expected (see Chap. 28, Infirmary Unit). Because many of the patients are not able to express the source of what must be a painful experience, consideration must be given to this diagnosis. Upper GI bleeding is occasionally severe, but it is not usually life-threatening.

The liberal use of diagnostic procedures to investigate for reflux esophagitis in children with central nervous system disease is well-supported,[5]

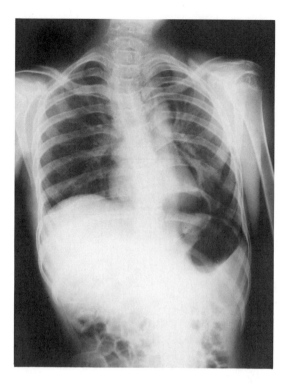

FIG. 10-6. Chest radiograph of a 28-year-old male with severe upper gastrointestinal bleeding and recurrent pneumonias shows large dilated esophagus and hiatal hernia. After Nissen fundoplication and a feeding jejunostomy, bleeding and pneumonias ceased.

but a less aggressive approach is suggested for children without central nervous system disease.[2] No studies have addressed the problems of adults with these physiologic disorders, but a suspicion of reflux esophagitis by history justifies endoscopy and biopsy.

We have had many surprises revealing significant esophageal pathology in retarded adults who had few of the classic symptoms of GER. The presence of growth retardation, sexual immaturity, chronic pulmonary disease, and the symptom of failure to thrive can all be due to GER-induced chronic malnutrition.

Therefore, a patient with any one of the aforementioned symptoms should be considered a candidate for upper GI endoscopy and biopsy because these are the most definitive techniques for the diagnosis of esophagitis.[42]

Preparation for endoscopy should include generous doses of anxiolytic medication prior to and during the procedure. The most important aspect of the endoscopy is the tissue diagnosis; serial mucosal biopsies should be taken from the esophagus regardless of the gross mucosal appearance. Esophageal histology is the most sen-

sitive and specific indicator of gastroesophageal reflux. We have had several instances of normal-appearing esophageal mucosa that showed changes typical of esophagitis on microscopic inspection. This may have been due to quiescent bleeding with some superficial mucosal healing. The tissue must be examined for intraepithelial inflammatory cells and evidence of metaplastic change (Barrett's esophagus) by a pathologist well versed in the difficulties associated with interpreting esophageal biopsies.[4] (See also section in this chapter on gastrointestinal problems)

SELECTION OF APPROPRIATE FEEDING TUBES

Historically, large-bore rubber nasogastric tubes were used for feedings in institutionalized individuals. The association of these tubes with "forced feeding" has made many clinicians reluctant to use feeding tubes for nutritional sustenance. Maintenance of feeding tubes can be difficult, but it is possible when their benefits are appreciated. Other feeding tubes include naso-duodenal tubes, gastrostomy tubes, and jejunostomy tubes. The type of tube used is determined by the underlying problem.

Traditional gastrostomy and jejunostomy feeding tubes are familiar to most clinicians, but recent advances in nasoenteral feeding are noteworthy. New commercial feeding preparations have been introduced, which allow administration of nutrients through small-bore feeding tubes. The first small-bore tubes were made of polyvinyl chloride (PVC), which tended to stiffen in the acidic gastric environment and required frequent replacement.[21] Silicone and polyurethane tubes have since been developed. These tubes are metabolically inert and can be left in place for longer periods of time. The nasoduodenal tubes have weighted tips that facilitate passage past the pylorus.

These small-diameter tubes appear to cause minimal, if any, discomfort of the patient. The Duo-Tube system (Argyle-Quest, St. Louis) allows for easy insertion. An outer tube of PVC is inserted first, and then a jet of water is used to propel the inner silicone tube into position. The outer tube is then withdrawn, and the silicone tube is taped in place. Other tubes, placed with the aid of a stylet, are also available.

Because of their small size, these tubes can be easily coughed out or dislodged accidentally during normal activities. In many situations the tube can be replaced by encouraging the patient to swallow a small amount of fluid or by promoting the sucking reflex.

Nasogastric Tubes

For the patient with a swallowing disorder that precludes continued oral feedings because of recurrent pulmonary aspiration, nasogastric tubes are indicated. It is not necessary to perform radiographic studies for tube placement because the pharynx is bypassed. However, the presence of GER must be ruled out before the decision to use nasogastric feedings is made.

Nasoduodenal Tubes

In cases in which GER has been diagnosed and nasoenteral feedings are to be introduced, the nasoduodenal route must be used. These feedings can be given either on a long-term basis or for preoperative repletion prior to surgical correction for GER. Radiographic confirmation of the tube's passage past the pylorus is mandatory prior to the introduction of feedings (Fig. 10-7).

Gastrostomy Tubes

Gastrostomy tubes[14] are indicated for the patient with pure aspiration for whom oral feedings are contraindicated, and whose lifestyle would be affected by the presence of a nasal tube. The tube can be kept hidden under the clothes and out of the patient's reach. The advent of percutaneous gastrostomy tube placement with upper gastrointestinal endoscopy[33] eliminates the need for an open abdominal procedure in some instances.

Gastrostomy tube placement is also indicated for the patient with failure to thrive in whom no organic basis for food refusal can be found. Gastrostomy catheters allow for provision of adequate nutrition while oral feedings are slowly reintroduced.

Intraoperative gastrostomy placement may be undertaken during an anti-reflux procedure to prevent postoperative gas-bloating syndromes.[6] The gastrostomy catheter can also be used for postoperative feeding if there are any problems with tolerance to oral feedings. A gastrostomy catheter may be necessary for the patient with a previously undiagnosed aspiration syndrome who continues to present with aspiration pneumonia despite a successful anti-reflux procedure.

The mortality risks of simple gastrostomy in the presence of gastroesophageal reflux have been reported as high as 10% due to pulmonary aspiration. Therefore, prior to insertion of a gastrostomy tube, preliminary investigation with endoscopy and mucosal biopsies is indicated to rule out GER.[41]

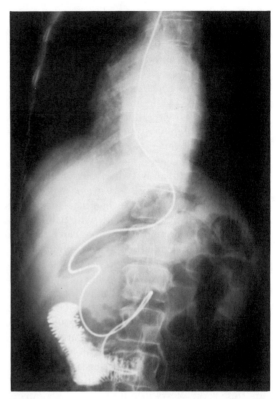

FIG. 10-7. Abdominal radiograph with Gastrografin injection, confirming placement of nasoduodenal feeding tube in small bowel of patient with severe gastroesophageal reflux.

Jejunostomy Tubes

Careful selection of candidates for jejunostomy tube placement is required. These include patients for whom an anti-reflux procedure is contraindicated. Only patients with a mature jejunum who can tolerate lower-osmolar constant-infusion feedings should be considered.

SCHEDULES AND MAINTENANCE OF FEEDING APPARATUS

Feedings can be given either by bolus or by constant infusion. Several infusion pumps are commercially available. Some are portable, allowing for increased patient mobility. Many have alarms and other safeguards to alert the care provider of any problems. Formula containers and infusion sets are also widely available.

Alternative feedings by any of the above routes are best established with continuous infusion of low-osmolar formula to establish patient tolerance. Feedings can then be advanced to solutions of higher concentration, and the bolus technique introduced for the nasogastric, nasoduodenal, and gastrostomy tubes. Bolus feedings allow for normal patient activity between feedings, as well as obviating the need for an infusion pump. Unfortunately, because of volume limitations, the jejunum can rarely accept bolus feedings and usually requires constant infusion.

Maintenance of the above tubes can be difficult in patients with limited understanding or behavior problems, especially in those whose mobility and movement are not limited. Creative problem-solving is necessary to keep the tube out of reach. Unfortunately, when provision of adequate nutrition is a priority, restraint may be necessary, such as mitts on the hands. Usually such restraints can be discontinued with habituation. Gastrostomy and jejunostomy tubes can be hidden under dressings and clothing. Gastrostomy stomas can be constructed so that a permanent indwelling catheter is not required. A permanent stoma with a muscular valve can be created, allowing for intubation only at feeding time.

Introduction of alternative feeding methods can cause concern among parents and care providers who are not familiar with these techniques, and thoughtful explanation and discussion are necessary. However, familiarity with the use of a feeding tube soon allows it to be viewed as a normal part of the patient's life.

MANAGEMENT OF ASPIRATION

When oral motor dysfunction and pulmonary aspiration are the only problems, a long polyurethane or silicone nasoduodenal or nasogastric feeding tube is the most conservative treatment. Patients with these tubes can receive intermittent bolus feedings, remaining free of infusion apparatus and attendants between feedings. No further treatment is needed for patients who can tolerate a tube through the naris, but they will usually do better with a permanently anchored gastrostomy tube.

Surgical gastrostomy is a relatively safe and simple procedure,[14] and in some instances percutaneous gastrostomy tubes can be used.[33] More involved surgery may be required, such as cleft-palate repair[15] or cricopharyngeal myotomy,[3,15] depending on the reason for aspiration.

MANAGEMENT OF GASTROESOPHAGEAL REFLUX

Medical

The conservative approaches to controlling the symptoms of GER have been outlined in this chapter (Gastrointestinal Problems) and elsewhere.[42] (See also Chap. 11, Recurrent Aspiration Syndrome.) These include small, frequent meals, upright positioning after meals, elevation of the head of the bed, and avoidance of chocolate, caffeine, nicotine, and late evening snacks. Medications such as theophylline and the phenothiazines, which may decrease lower esophageal sphincter pressure, should also be avoided. Indefinite treatment with antacids, H_2-receptor-blockers such as ranitidine and cimetidine, or bethanechol (which helps to stimulate the lower esophageal sphincter) is indicated.[16,23,47] Metoclopramide, which increases lower esophageal sphincter pressure and improves the rate of gastric emptying, may also be useful.[20,35,36] Bethanechol-associated hypothermia[22] and metoclopramide-associated dyskinesia should be considered in a population with compromised nervous systems.

If medical therapy is unsuccessful after a reasonable amount of time, surgical consultation for an anti-reflux procedure is recommended.[6,31,34,46]

Surgical

Conventional medical therapy for gastroesophageal reflux has been less successful in children with central nervous system dysfunction than in the normal population, with only a 26% response rate.[49] Accordingly, there has been a more aggressive approach to anti-reflux surgery in these children. With the recent advances in the medical treatment of GER, however, a prolonged medical trial may still be warranted. A child with an LES tone of less than 10 mm Hg probably will not respond to medical therapy[45] and should receive surgery. Patients with GER of Grade III or higher,[10] those with a recurrent problem attributable to GER within 1 year, and those with failure to thrive plus one problem attributable to GER are considered the most likely to respond to surgery.[6]

Unfortunately, the results of surgery are not as satisfactory in children with central nervous system disorders as in normal children. It is likely that the subtle swallowing disorders in patients with associated CNS disease still contribute to pulmonary aspiration despite successful anti-reflux procedures. In a study of patients with GER as the only problem, 97% of normal patients showed complete resolution of respiratory symptoms with surgery, but only 58% of patients with associated CNS disorders showed complete resolution.[31] However, since at least partial resolution was attained in 84% of the patients with CNS disease, one should still consider surgery as a viable, albeit possibly limited, alternative. Further optimistic surgical reports have indicated excellent long-term improvement in constitutional symptoms, increased ease of care, and reversal of failure-to-thrive states, vomiting, gastrointestinal bleeding, and pneumonias.[6,46]

The anti-reflux surgery of choice in both children and adults is Nissen fundoplication.[11,30,37] Postoperative increases in LES tone in the normal population have been attributed to improvement in the function of the lower esophageal smooth muscle rather than direct mechanical effects of the surgical gastric wrap itself.[28]

NUTRITIONAL MAINTENANCE IN ENTERAL FEEDING

There is only limited information available regarding caloric requirements for individuals with severe musculoskeletal deformity and neurologic disorders (J. Haley, T. Feigelman, and R. Converse, unpublished data). Anthropometric parameters for calculation of ideal body weight in the severely physically impaired cannot be standardized, making utilization of tables (e.g., Metropolitan Height and Weight Tables) inappropriate. Energy requirements and ideal body weight must be assessed through analysis of the patient's physical status, motor activity, and severity of neurologic impairment (presence of spasticity or flaccidity). In some adult cases, correlation with pediatric standards can be used. For instance, a prepubertal 20-year-old with growth retardation can be compared with the standards for a normal 10-year-old.

Patients with severe skeletal and neurologic infirmity present unique problems. Ideal body weights may be impossible to calculate, but parameters can be defined. Calculations for such individuals could be made from baseline anthropometric studies with subsequent reevaluation on an individual longitudinal basis.

Nutritional consultation is mandatory in defining caloric and nutritional needs prior to and during enteral nutrition. A nutritional support team can provide valuable recommendations.

The desired weight must be determined on an individual basis. It must be cautioned that "too fat" can be as detrimental as "too thin." Preexisting conditions such as scoliosis can be aggravated, especially in the individual who reaches puberty through improved nutrition.[17] A slow, steady weight gain is more physiologically acceptable to the patient. Modifications of adaptive equipment (wheelchairs, mobility devices) can be difficult when a rapid weight gain occurs.

Daily caloric requirements for adults can be estimated with the standards shown in Table 10-2. The figures in this table should be used only for patients whose physical status and activity can be correlated with those of the normal adult. Patients with growth retardation can be assessed with other parameters, such as degree of muscle spasticity. Caloric requirements for the more severely impaired can be correlated with amount of motor activity. Individuals with spasticity may need up to 50 or 60 cal/kg/day, whereas those with hypotonia may need as little as 17 cal/kg/day (J. Haley, T. Feigelman, and R. Converse, unpublished data).

Weights must be checked frequently during the early period of enteral feeding. Subsequent adjustments in caloric intake can then be made as necessary.

The need for vitamin and mineral supplementation remains unclear. One may routinely prescribe a daily multivitamin and mineral supplement. The need to follow biochemical parameters (complete blood count, routine chemistries) is decided on an individual basis depending on concurrent medical problems and type of feeding.

In summary, indications for feeding intervention include acute dehydration, chronic inanition, and perioperative nutrition. Successful resolution of recurrent pneumonias, apparent extrinsic asthma (even associated with eosinophilia), and growth retardation can be achieved with alternative methods of feeding.

Syndromes that involve only aspiration can be treated with nasogastric or gastrostomy tube feedings. Patients with gastroesophageal reflux and esophagitis as the only problems, and for whom conservative medical therapy has failed, require anti-reflux surgery. Patients with combination disease may require both permanent bypass of the swallowing mechanism and an anti-reflux procedure.

Caloric requirements must be established on a case-by-case basis, using standards developed for the general population and then individually tailoring caloric intake to the needs of the patient.

Table 10-2. *Daily Caloric Requirements*

Desired Outcome	Sedentary	Moderately Active
Weight gain	35 cal/kg	40 cal/kg
Weight maintenance	30 cal/kg	35 cal/kg
Weight loss	20–25 cal/kg	30 cal/kg

REFERENCES

1. Abrahams, P., and Burkitt, B.F.E.: Hiatus hernia and gastroesophageal reflux in children and adolescents with cerebral palsy. Aust. Paediatr. J., 6:41, 1970.
2. Balistreri, W.F., and Farrell, M.K.: Gastroesophageal reflux in infants. N. Engl. J. Med., 309:790, 1983.
3. Blakeley, W.R., Garety, E.J., and Smith, D.E.: Section of the cricopharyngeus muscle for dysphagia. Arch. Surg., 96:745, 1968.
4. Bozymski, E.M., Herlihy, K.J., and Orlando, R.C.: Barrett's esophagus. Ann. Intern. Med., 97:103, 1982.
5. Bray, P.F., et al.: Childhood gastroesophageal reflux: Neurologic and psychiatric syndromes mimicked. J.A.M.A., 237:1342, 1977.
6. Byrne, W.J., et al.: Gastroesophageal reflux in the severely retarded who vomit: Criteria for and results of surgical intervention in twenty-two patients. Surgery, 91:95, 1982.
7. Byrne, W.J., et al.: A diagnostic approach to vomiting in severely retarded patients. Am. J. Dis. Child., 137:259, 1983.
8. Cadman, D., Richards, J., and Feldman, W.: Gastroesophageal reflux in severely retarded children. Dev. Med. Child. Neurol., 20:95, 1978.
9. Clouse, R.E., and Lustman, P.J.: Psychiatric illness and contraction abnormalities of the esophagus. N. Engl. J. Med., 309:1337, 1983.
10. Darling, D.B., McCauley, R.G.K., Leonides, J.C., and Schwartz, A.M.: Gastroesophageal reflux in infants and children. Correlation of radiologic severity, grade and pulmonary pathology. Radiology, 127:735, 1978.
11. Demeester, T.R., Johnson, L.F., and Kent, A.: Evaluation of current operations for the prevention of gastroesophageal reflux. Ann. Surg., 180:511, 1974.
12. Dobie, R.P., and Butterick, O.D., Jr.: Continuous pump/tube enteric hyperalimentation—use in esophageal disease. JPEN, 1:100, 1977.
13. Dobie, R.P., and Hoffmeister, J.A.: Continuous pump/tube enteric hyperalimentation. Surg. Gynecol. Obstet., 143:273, 1977.
14. Dozos, R.R., and Lewis, D.J.: Gastrostomy: scalpel or scope. Mayo Clin. Proc., 58:138, 1983.
15. Duranceau, A.C., Jamieson, G.G., and Beauchamp, G.: The technique of cricopharyngeal myotomy. Surg. Clin. N. Am., 63:833, 1983.
16. Euler, A.R.: Use of bethanechol for the treatment of gastroesophageal reflux. J. Pediatr., 96:321, 1980.
17. Feigelman, T., et al: Sexual maturation in the third and fourth decades after nutritional rehabilitation by enteral feeding. J. Pediatr., 111:620, 1987.
18. Fonkalsrud, E.W., Ament, M.E., Byrne, W.J., and Rachelefsky, G.S.: Gastroesophageal fundoplication for the management of reflux in infants and children. J. Thorac. Cardiovasc. Surg., 76:655, 1978.
19. Frisch, R.E.: Weight at menarche: Similarity for well-nourished and undernourished girls at differing ages, and evidence for historical constancy. Pediatrics, 50:445, 1972.
20. Fuchs, B., and Bartolomeo, R.S.: Prevention of meal-induced heartburn and regurgitation with metoclopramide in patients with gastroesophageal reflux. Clin. Ther., 5:179, 1982.
21. Goldfarb, I.W., DeCourcy, M., and Eyman, L.: Enteral feeding with the Argyle-Quest Duo-Tube. St. Louis, Sherwood Medical Industries, 1981.
22. Guerra, M.F., and Ives, T.J.: Bethanechol and hypothermia. Ann. Intern. Med., 99:279, 1982.
23. Guslandi, M., et al.: Ranitidine versus metoclopramide in the medical treatment of reflux esophagitis. Hepatogastroenterology, 30:96, 1983.
24. Guttman, F.M.: On the incidence of hiatal hernia in infants. Pediatrics, 50:325, 1972.
25. Heitkemper, M.E., et al.: Rate and volume of intermittent enteral feeding. J. Parenter. Ent. Nutr., 5:125, 1981.
26. Heymsfield, S.B., et al.: Enteral hyperalimentation: An alternative to central venous hyperalimentation. Ann. Intern. Med., 90:63, 1979.
27. Higgs, R.H., Castell, D.O., and Eastwood, G.L.: Studies on the mechanism of esophagitis-induced lower esophageal sphincter hypotension in cats. Gastroenterology, 71:51, 1976.
28. Higgs, R.H., Castell, D.O., and Farrell, R.L.: Evaluation of the effect of fundoplication on the incompetent lower esophageal sphincter. Surg. Gynecol. Obstet., 141:571, 1975.
29. Holmes, T.W., Jr.: Chalasia, peptic esophagitis and hiatal hernia: A common syndrome in patients with central nervous system disease. Chest, 60:441, 1971.
30. Johnson, D.G., Herbst, J.J., Oliveros, M.A., and Steward, D.R.: Evaluation of gastroesophageal reflux surgery in children. Pediatrics, 59:62, 1977.
31. Jolley, S.G., et al.: Surgery in children with gastroesophageal reflux and respiratory symptoms. J. Pediatr., 96:194, 1980.
32. Kassem, N.Y., Groen, J.J., and Fraenkel, M.: Spinal deformities and esophageal hiatus hernia. Lancet, 1:887, 1965.
33. Larson, D.E., Fleming, C.R., Ott, B.J., and Schroeder, K.W.: Percutaneous endoscopic gastrostomy—simplified access for enteral nutrition. Mayo Clin. Proc., 58:103, 1983.
34. Leape, L.L., and Ramenofsky, M.L.: Surgical treatment of gastroesophageal reflux in children. Am. J. Dis. Child., 134:935, 1980.
35. McCallum, R.W., Fink, S.M., Lerner, E., and Berkowitz, D.M.: Effects of metoclopramide and bethanechol on delayed gastric emptying present in gastroesophageal reflux patients. Gastroenterology, 84:1573, 1983.
36. McCallum, R.W., et al.: Metoclopramide in gastroesophageal reflux disease: Rationale for its use and results of a double-blind trial. Am. J. Gastroenterol., 79:165, 1984.
37. Nissen, R.: :Gastropexy and "fundoplication" in surgical treatment of hiatus hernia. Am. J. Dig. Dis., 6:954, 1961.
38. Orenstein, S.R., Whitington, P.F., and Orenstein, D.M.: The infant seat as treatment for gastroesophageal reflux. N. Engl. J. Med., 309:760, 1983.
39. Osler, D.C., and Crawford, J.D.: Examination of the hypothesis of a critical weight at menarche in ambulatory and bedridden mentally retarded girls. Pediatrics, 51:675, 1973.
40. Pizarro, D., et al.: Oral rehydration in hypernatremic and hyponatremic diarrheal dehydration. Am. J. Dis. Child., 137:730, 1983.
41. Raventos, J.M., Kralemann, H., and Gray, D.B.: Mortality risks of mentally retarded and mentally ill patients after a feeding gastrostomy. Am. J. Ment. Def., 86:439, 1982.
42. Richter, J.E., and Castell, D.O.: Gastroesophageal reflux: Pathogenesis, diagnosis and therapy. Ann. Intern. Med., 97:93, 1982.
43. Roberts, I.M., Curtis, R.L., and Madara, J.L.: Gastroesophageal reflux and Barrett's esophagus in developmentally disabled patients. Am. J. Gastroenterol., 81:519, 1986.

44. Schatzlein, M.H., et al.: Gastroesophageal reflux in infants and children—diagnosis and management. Arch. Surg., *114*:505, 1979.
45. Sondheimer, J.M., and Morris, B.A.: Gastroesophageal reflux among severely retarded children. J. Pediatr., *94*:710, 1979.
46. Spitz, L.: Surgical treatment of gastroesophageal reflux in severely mentally retarded children. J. R. Soc. Med., 75:526, 1982.
47. Thanik, K.D., Chey, W.Y., Shah, A.N., and Gutierrez, J.G.: Reflux esophagitis: Effect of bethanechol on symptoms and endoscopic findings. Ann. Intern. Med., 98:805, 1980.
48. Van Heuven, P.F., and Smeets, P.M.: Behavioral control of chronic hiccupping associated with gastrointestinal bleeding in a retarded epileptic male. J. Behav. Ther. Exp. Psychiatry, *12*:341, 1981.
49. Wilkinson, J.D., Dudgeon, D.L., and Sondheimer, J.M.: A comparison of medical and surgical treatment of gastroesophageal reflux in severely retarded children. J. Pediatr., 99:202, 1981.

OBESITY

Robert Wharton, M.D.

Obesity is a serious health care problem for individuals with developmental disabilities in that it is an extremely common coincidental problem, it has prominent medical and psychosocial morbidity often exceeding that of the primary disorder, and it is quite resistant to therapy. In spite of its significance, however, little is known about obesity in this population because medical and epidemiologic research is only in its incipient stages. For this discussion, obesity will be classified in terms of syndromes in which it is a cardinal or primary feature, as represented by Prader-Willi syndrome (PWS), and in developmental disabilities in general, in which it can be viewed as a prominent secondary feature.

Although existing in both primary and secondary roles in various developmental disabilities, obesity should neither be considered essential for the diagnosis of PWS nor inevitable in its occurrence in other disabilities. In addition, its occurrence should not be marked with resignation and passive acceptance. Instead, obesity must be considered preventable in situations in which patients are at high risk to develop the complication, and treatable once it has occurred. Only by assuming an active and aggressive stance can physicians hope to manage this disturbingly common and refractory disorder.

PRIMARY OBESITY

Obesity can be considered a primary or necessary feature in the diagnosis of several syndromes, each of which is quite rare. The disorders do share several characteristics but can often be differentiated by close observation of physical characteristics and family history (see Table 10-3). In syndromes in which obesity is a primary feature, Prader-Willi syndrome is the most common and will therefore occupy the majority of the discussion.

PRADER-WILLI SYNDROME

Prevalence

Prader, Labhart, and Willi in 1956 described 9 patients, 5 males and 4 females, with obesity, short stature, cryptorchidism, mental retardation, and lack of muscle tone in infancy.[30] Although the disorder has been referred to as the HHHO syndrome (hypotonia, hypogonadism, hypomentia, and obesity),[39] its current designation as PWS is far superior because it does not carry the implication that obesity is an unavoidable feature.

With increasing awareness of the syndrome and with the recent discovery of genetic markers that can support or confirm the diagnosis, the reported incidence of the syndrome continues to undergo revisions from early estimates of 1:170,000 to the recent estimate of 1:5,000 to 1:10,000,[4,7] the latter comparable to that for phenylketonuria. Although the figure of 1:10,000 may be misleadingly elevated, the true incidence of PWS is difficult to determine because mild cases may not present with either significant obesity or mental retardation. Evaluation of the true incidence of the disorder will have to await improved screening techniques and better diagnostic tools.

Diagnosis

In spite of the emergence of new sophisticated laboratory techniques to assist in identifying the chromosomal defect in PWS patients, establishing the diagnosis of PWS remains a clinical problem. In order to recognize the syndrome more quickly and to diagnose mild cases, the clinician must be aware of the features that are considered necessary for a diagnosis and how these features evolve over time. Diagnostic guidelines will be placed within the framework of developmental stages from the prenatal period through adulthood (Table 10-4).

Prenatal Period

The most significant feature of the PWS child in utero is profound hypotonia. Mothers, particularly those with previous normal pregnancies, generally describe the child as quiet and

Table 10-3. *Congenital Syndromes with Obesity a Primary Feature*

		Syndrome			
	Prader-Willi	Laurence-Moon-Biedl-Bardet	Cohen	Weiss	Biemond II
Obesity	+	+	+	+	+
Short stature	+	+	−	+	+
Hypogonadism	+	+	+	+	+
Polydactyly	−	+	−	−	+
Retinitis pigmentosa	−	+	−	−	−
Mental retardation	+	+	+	+	+
Renal involvement	−	+	−	−	−
Dysmorphism	+	−	+	−	−
Autosomal recessive	−	+	+	−	−

inactive and frequently voice their concerns to their obstetricians during pregnancy. Delivery of the PWS child is often complicated by breech or transverses lies—common presentations of the hypotonic infant.

Early Childhood (from Birth to 2 Years)

Four clinical features are essential for diagnosis and appear in more than 90% of cases. They are central hypotonia, severe feeding difficulties and poor weight gain, hypogonadism (more easily recognized in males), and the following dysmorphic features:

Major features
  Narrow bifrontal diameter
  Almond-shaped eyes
  Upslanting palpebral fissures
  Triangular shaped mouth

Table 10-4. *Developmental Stages of Patients with Prader-Willi Syndrome*

Stage	Physical Characteristics	Behavioral Characteristics	Cognitive Features
Prenatal	Abnormal position in utero Decreased fetal movements		
Under 2 yrs	Hypotonia* Feeding problems* Hypogonadism* Dysmorphism*	Friendly Loving Pleasant	Delayed motor milestones Sit 12 months Walk 24 months
2 to 6 yrs	Obesity (truncal) Small hands/feet Short stature	Tantrums Obstinacy Hyperphagia* Impulsivity Repetition	Speech delay Mental retardation diagnosed Dysarthria
6 to 12 yrs	Scoliosis Abnormal pubertal development Skin sores	Social blunting Disinhibition Poor impulse control	School problems
12 to 17 yrs	Sleep apnea Pulmonary hypoventilation	Aggression Hallucinations Poor self esteem Depression	School problems
17 and over	Morbid obesity Cor pulmonale Pulmonary hypertension Premature death		Possible cognitive deterioration

* Necessary for diagnosis

Minor features
  Fair skin
  High palate
  Strabismus

If these findings are present and they are supported by chromosome analysis demonstrating the deletion of 15q11.2 as found in at least 50% of the cases, the diagnosis can be firmly established.

HYPOTONIA

Hypotonia is the most impressive early clinical feature of PWS. It is essential for diagnosis and is present in 100% of PWS in neonates and infants. The main physical impact of hypotonia is the weak suck of the infant, which results in feeding difficulties. Infants with PWS are rarely capable of breastfeeding and characteristically require either gavage feedings or special nipples in order to avoid severe growth retardation and failure to thrive. It is not uncommon for parents to talk about feeding their children with medicine droppers for the first few months.

Attempts to determine the pathogenesis of the hypotonia have been consistently unrewarding because evaluations of creatine phosphokinase, aldolase, nerve conduction velocity, and electromyography have generally been normal.[1] Electron microscopic studies have shown nonspecific findings similar to those seen in neurogenic atrophy, essential hypotonia, and disuse,[1,7,13] and are not thought to be a result of an essential myopathy or neuropathy.

HYPOGONADISM

The second major clinical feature of infants with PWS necessary for diagnosis is hypogonadism represented by genital hypoplasia.[37] The genital hypoplasia is more easily recognized in males, who present with cryptorchidism, underdeveloped scrotum, and small penis. The testes are generally small and soft and either in the inguinal canal or the scrotal sac and not intraabdominal.[7,37] The penis, although small, is only rarely a micropenis. The relatively small size of the penis becomes more apparent with time and lack of significant continued growth.[35] In females, hypogonadism is represented by a small clitoris and hypoplastic labia. These differentiations in the female are difficult to establish, however, and frequently go undetermined.

DYSMORPHISM

Infants and young children typically have a narrow bifrontal diameter, almond-shaped eyes, upslanting palpebral fissures, and a triangular mouth with a thin down-turned upper lip. Skin and hair coloring is generally fair, especially when compared to that of parents and siblings. Additional features that may be present at this time include strabismus and high arched palate. Attempts to clarify distinguishable features, including detailed analysis of dermatoglyphics[18,32,34] and ophthalmologic studies, have been unrewarding except in a few patients.[15]

BEHAVIOR AND COGNITION

Infants and toddlers have been described as happy, affectionate, pleasant, and friendly.[7] The impression that one gets is that the infant with PWS is in some measure unusual and is indiscriminant in placing affections.

MOTOR DEVELOPMENT

Significant motor delay is a consistent finding in children with PWS. Although most data have been obtained through retrospective analysis, the average ages for sitting and walking are approximately 12 months and 24 months, respectively. Indeed, this motor delay, coupled with central hypotonia, frequently leads to the misdiagnosis of cerebral palsy in infants with PWS. One can hope that early diagnosis and testing will provide more information about PWS in this time period.

In summary, the infant with PWS presents with profound central hypotonia leading to poor suck, and growth problems, hypogonadism, and characteristic dysmorphic features. In addition, delayed motor milestones are characteristically apparent. Unfortunately, unless they can be substantiated by chromosome analysis, these clinical observations are insufficient to establish the diagnosis of PWS. Hyperphagia and obesity are also considered necessary for definitive diagnosis, and although obesity has been seen as early as 6 months, it usually develops later.

On the other hand, tentative diagnosis of PWS should not await the development of hyperphagia. Any child with at least three features from this constellation of findings, in spite of a lack of other distinguishable characteristics, should be followed closely for the development of hyperphagia and obesity. Too often, intervention and dietary management await a definitive diagnosis, as attested to by parents of children with PWS who routinely hear, "We really don't know what the problem is."[38] This statement is not entirely accurate in that the problem is known; it is the name that is given to the disorder associated with the problem that is not known.

Early Childhood (2 to 6 Years)

The transition from infancy and early childhood to later childhood is one of profound confusion and disappointment for parents of children with PWS. Apparent recovery from hypotonia is now followed by unexplained deteriorating behavior manifested by hyperphagia and its resultant obesity.

PHYSICAL CHARACTERISTICS

It is during early childhood that obesity, considered the cardinal feature of PWS, begins to appear. A child previously underweight slowly develops increased weight, with fat most prominently distributed centrally over the trunk, buttocks, and thighs but sparing the hands and feet. Athough individuals with PWS appear to have decreased caloric requirements as compared with normal controls,[16] their obesity develops solely on account of excess caloric intake. It has been documented that individuals with PWS left without food restriction will eat in excess of 5,000 calories per day.[3] Initial excess caloric consumption may not involve inappropriate food behaviors but may simply represent a young child finishing portions that are in excess of need. It is neither inappropriate for a child to be told to "clean his plate" nor unexpected that a parent formerly concerned with undernutrition provides excess food at mealtimes to ensure adequate intake. In this manner, the force-feeding that was so necessary in infancy is replaced by overfeeding in early childhood. This overfeeding can lead to obesity and therefore precedes the inappropriate appetitive behavior that eventually appears.

In addition to obesity, other physical characteristics that appear during early childhood are small hands and feet and short stature. The etiology of the short stature, present in greater than 90% of individuals with PWS and also seen in genetically obese animals,[5] has similarly proved elusive. Attempts to characterize the short stature in patients with PWS have focused almost exclusively on studies with growth hormone[20] and have failed to find a distinct lesion specific to the syndrome. Results in these studies have been typical of obese populations in general, i.e., normal growth hormone with blunted or impaired rise from insulin-induced hypoglycemia.

BEHAVIOR

It is ironic that the behavior that will prove to be the most difficult to manage in the syndrome, the behavior that denies to individuals with PSW the ability to live unsupervised lives, and the behavior that forces parents to request residential care for the children, is first seen as a welcome sign of recovery for children who until this point had not only failed to thrive but who had never appeared to have any significant appetite.

Although the hyperphagia is well described[4,7,13,18,39] and may consist of eating inedibles, taking food from siblings, taking food from cabinets and refrigerators, foraging for food, and excessive tantrums when attempts are made to restrict intake, the etiology of the hyperphagia is poorly understood and the subject of intense speculation. Studies of the etiology of the hyperphagia have treated PWS as a hypothalamic disorder with an undefined "lesion" interfering with the ability to experience satiety, as an altered "set point" not involving the hypothalamus; and, as a disorder of appetite secondary to fat cell hypertrophy and abnormally elevated levels of lipoprotein lipase (a rate-limiting enzyme of lipolysis and fat storage). Of these various concepts, the most compelling is that of PWS as a hypothalamic disorder manifested by lack of appetite control, hypothalamic hypogonadism, decreased sensitivity to pain, various skin disorders, and abnormal response to cold.

In addition to the hyperphagia, temper tantrums and other demonstrations of transient loss of control appear during this period. The tantrums appear to be more severe and more unpredictable than those normally seen in early childhood. It is thought that these outbursts represent a disorder of hypothalamic control mechanisms that result in disinhibition of central regulation. This disinhibition becomes more prevalent as a behavior manifestation in succeeding years.

COGNITION

There is a heterogeneity of cognitive function in children with PWS. Although most will function within a mild to moderately retarded range, some, between 5 and 10%, demonstrate borderline or normal IQs. Lack of retardation should not eliminate the possibility of PWS. When specific learning disabilities are found in testing, they appear to demonstrate deficits in the areas of visual processing and visual short-term memory. The flaws in these findings lie in the fact that there are no comprehensive studies evaluating individuals with PWS from before diagnosis through childhood and the later years. In addition, too few non-obese children with PWS have been prospectively evaluated using standard educational measures. It is important to document intellectual functioning in PWS especially as it relates to obesity, because there is some suggestion that intellectual function may be preserved with maintenance of ideal body weight.[8]

Middle Childhood (6 to 12 Years)

PHYSICAL CHARACTERISTICS

The most prominent physical characteristics to appear at this time are scoliosis and abnormal pubertal development. Although scoliosis is not a routine finding in obese adolescents, it is reasonably common in individuals with PWS. Indeed, in one study of 37 patients,[23] 86% were found to have a significant structural deformity. The likelihood of scoliosis increases with age; one study has reported the presence of scoliosis in over 95% of adults.[17] Moreover, because the curvature may require active intervention such as a brace or surgery, all individuals must be monitored closely. Other orthopedic problems such as hip dysplasias are also not uncommon and should be evaluated in routine examinations.

The second major feature during this period is the continuation of hypogonadism. As stated earlier, the hypogonadism associated with PWS is centered in the hypothalamus. Evaluation of the pituitary-gonadal system has demonstrated basal testosterone and estradiol to be borderline or low and luteinizing hormone (LH) and follicle-stimulating hormone (FSH) to be either low or inappropriately within the normal range. After injection of gonadotropin-releasing hormone (Gn-RH) there is only a blunted response of LH and FSH due to reduced gonadotropin reserves secondary to longstanding Gn-RH deficiency.[4,5,19] In spite of this documented deficiency, reports of sexual maturation in patients with PWS include menarche, and menstruation. In addition, precocious puberty has been reported from several clinics. When assessing these cases it is vital to have information on complete physical evaluation as well as laboratory findings to ensure that the precocious puberty is not a premature adrenarche, which is not dependent on the hypothalamic-pituitary axis and therefore not outside the realm of the normal, and that the menarche and menstruation are not the result of breakthrough bleeding secondary to estrogen production and estrogenization from peripheral (fat) conversions of adrenal steroids into estrogen.

An additional factor that must be considered is the individual's desire to have normal hormonal function. A female who insists that she is menstruating may be misinterpreting breakthrough bleeding. It is incumbent on the health care provider to explain the basis of the hormonal changes to the patient without discrediting her feelings.

BEHAVIOR

The main behavior characteristics in middle childhood are extensions of features seen earlier in childhood. However, now that the child is in school and other social settings, the impulsiveness and obstinacy that were previously noted are now labeled as poor impulse control, social blunting, and disinhibition. The described behavior is not new behavior, but rather a continuation and developmental progression and expansion of characteristics previously noted, a "maturing process" of abnormal behavior.

Adolescence (12 to 17 Years)

PHYSICAL CHARACTERISTICS

For the untreated individual with PWS the physical characteristics and problems are the direct result of obesity. Problems that begin to appear are sleep apnea, which can progress to the pickwickian syndrome, and alveolar hypoventilation. Important symptoms and signs for the presence of sleep apnea are prominent snoring, restless sleep, episodes of cessation of chest wall movement during sleep, nocturnal enuresis, diaphoresis, early morning headaches and lethargy, and finally daytime somnolence. Because the differential diagnosis for this symptom complex includes hypothyroidism (which by itself can cause sleep apnea), metabolic disorders, depression, and primary sleep disorders, to name a few, a careful history should be taken at this time. Sleep apnea in the presence of morbid obesity has a high mortality rate if left untreated; therefore investigation should proceed vigorously to confirm the diagnosis, and appropriate intervention should be initiated immediately. In addition to sleep apnea, scoliosis and abnormal pubertal development persist during this period and may require treatment.

BEHAVIOR

The behavioral consequences of the syndrome continue to accelerate during the adolescent years. The teen with PWS demonstrates significant problems with self-esteem, sadness, and depression. In addition, this is a time when runaway behavior may begin, either in search of food or as an attempt to deal with poorly understood rage. A third new feature that may manifest itself at this time is the development of auditory hallucinations that are generally short-lived and associated with rage reactions.

Adulthood

PHYSICAL CHARACTERISTICS

Physical problems in adults with PWS depend on the presence of obesity. If obese, and especially if morbidly obese (>200% of ideal body weight), the patient with PWS has a significantly decreased life expectancy and will most likely suffer from sleep apnea, pickwickian syndrome, pulmonary hypertension, cor pulmonale, advanced arteriosclerotic heart disease, and type II diabetes. It must be stressed that these problems are totally dependent on the presence of morbid obesity and are therefore potentially avoidable.

BEHAVIOR

The adult with PWS will not assume additional behavioral characteristics but will rather stabilize. Adults who developed significant tantrums and foraging behavior as children will most likely continue with these behaviors but perhaps with some additional control. Similarly, those who had significant social blunting and poor impulse control as children will likely continue with those behaviors. The most consistent picture of adults is one of sadness, poor self-esteem, and depression.

COGNITION

Cognitive function may decline during adulthood, especially if the morbid obesity remains unchecked.

CHROMOSOMES

Twenty years following the identification of a constellation of findings by Prader, Labhart, and Willi, Hawkey and Smithies described a patient with the syndrome who had an abnormal karyotype showing a 15:15 Robertsonian translocation.[14] Five years later Ledbetter et al.,[24] looking closely at chromosome 15 with G-banding analysis, found small deletions in chromosome 15 with breakpoints in bands q11 and q13 in 4 of 5 patients with PWS. Most studies demonstrate that approximately 50% of patients with well-documented PWS have the chromosomal deletion 15q11.2 identified by Ledbetter. However, in addition to the chromosome-15 deletion thought to be characteristic of the disorder, other reported abnormalities include balanced and unbalanced translocations involving chromosome 15, extra isochromosome of 15p, and pericentric inversion of chromosome 15.[25] All patients being evaluated for PWS should have chromosomal studies utilizing prophase banding techniques to look for the deletion, but absence of an identified deletion should not exclude the diagnosis.

Evaluation and Treatment

Treatment of individuals with PWS must be based on the comprehensive treatment of a disease rather than on isolated treatment of one symptom. The most obvious and important factor related to obesity is prevention by early recognition of disease. Problems with early diagnosis center around the fact that most clinicians are reluctant to diagnose PWS unless obesity is present. However, as stressed earlier, although there is often not sufficient evidence early in the course of the disease to diagnose PWS, there is sufficient information to suspect the diagnosis and therefore embark on early surveillance for the development of inappropriate food behavior, hyperphagia, or obesity. Table 10-3 should serve as a guide when evaluating patients suspected of having a congenitally based obesity.

Diet Therapy

Dietary intervention, the key to weight-related problems, must depend on the age, weight, and developmental level of the child. Parents of children with PWS must constantly maintain strict dietary vigilance over their children from the first day of diagnosis.

For children diagnosed prior to the onset of obesity, the obvious goal must be weight regulation. No child will gain weight unless caloric intake exceeds energy requirements; therefore the child with PWS should be given regular, balanced calorie meals at a caloric intake that will ensure that the child maintains the proper weight for height. Because the individual with PWS tends to require a limited amount of calories for weight maintenance, caloric intake may be reduced compared to siblings, peers, and family members. In the first 5 years of life the child may experience loss of stature unassociated with caloric reduction, and an early acceleration of weight for height must be monitored by frequent measurements. Adequate calories for growth need to be maintained.

Once the child begins to gain excess weight, diet will depend on degree of obesity, age, and support. The young growing child should be placed on a balanced calorie-deficit diet aimed at reduction of excess calories as represented by fats and unlimited fluids. Children should experience no problems with growth on this regimen. Older, more significantly obese children (>170% of ideal body weight) require a more restrictive diet. In these instances one can either use a severely calorie-restricted diet based on anticipated calorie requirements for patients with PWS ($\sim$11 to 20 kcal/kg for weight maintenance)[7] or the protein-sparing modified fast.[2] The key to either of these diets is enforcement, and one must anticipate the behavioral consequences of limiting intake when suggesting any intervention.

The protein-sparing modified fast has been studied in several settings, with conflicting results. The claimed benefits for the diet are its anorexic effect,[2] improved general behavior, ability to monitor compliance by testing for ketosis, and rapid and consistent weight loss through increased mobilization of fat stores. However, others deny its anorexic effect and do not see the benefit over simpler diets. In addition, by restricting the diet to small amounts of a limited number of choices, it can intensify the burden for families. We have used this fast in selected obese adolescents and adults living at home whose parents can mobilize themselves for short bursts of intensive intervention. We find that individuals with PWS react enthusiastically and take pride in their efforts, and parents are struck by the improved behavior and "intellect" demonstrated by their children during these "diet bursts." Although this method may not result in dramatic long-term weight loss, it is effective for moderate weight reduction. In general, as the key to any dietary intervention is compliance, the potential for disruption vs. success in the home setting must be carefully weighed before any approach is suggested.

Behavior Therapy

It is important that the family be able to anticipate future behavior and intercede with appropriate guidelines. The early years are difficult for parents in that the child with PWS appears to improve by about 2 years of age, and parents who have been concerned with hypotonia, delayed motor development, and poor weight gain are now faced with children who begin to walk and begin to want to eat. Parents can in no way be prepared for this paradoxical turn of events that makes these apparent features of improvement the centerpiece of future difficulties. Families therefore need to be educated in appropriate food behavior. The first guideline is that extra food should not be available to children. Although this guideline may appear straightforward, it can be difficult to follow in large families with other young children and multiple family caregivers. Children with PWS need to be provided limited, designed portions and

should not be offered incentives to finish their meals. In addition, they should not be able to finish the meals of other family members. Food must never be used as a reward, reinforcer, bribe, incentive, or pacifier. The guidelines that are made when the child with PWS is young will always be necessary because developmental age as it relates to food may never alter.

Children with PWS may search for food. For the young child, this means that food should be placed out of reach and where it is not visible. When children begin to take food from the refrigerator, families need to consider using locks to prevent unsupervised eating. Although this may be a psychological and practical inconvenience to families, it must be seriously considered, especially if the child is taking food and gaining weight. Because inappropriate food behavior is no more a manifestation of bad behavior than excessive thirst in a child with out-of-control diabetes, it should not be reacted to with excess punishment. Instead, families must react by praising good behavior and trying to limit access, which will predictably produce problems. Tantrums over denial of food need to be treated in the same supportive, firm, and controlling way that the parents would use to handle a child who is out of control for any other reason.

Gastric Bypass Surgery

A more drastic intervention for the morbidly obese individual is gastric bypass surgery involving a gastric stapling procedure. This procedure should only be considered for the morbidly obese patient with life-threatening consequences of obesity, such as severe diabetes or pickwickian syndrome. Although no study has shown permanent weight loss in this population with this measure, it can, at least in the short term, benefit a patient who can be carefully monitored and who may die without drastic intervention.

Medication

Various attempts have been made to restrict appetite through medication, with little success. One avenue of thought has been to interfere with the natural effect of serotonin on the control of appetite.[4] Tryptophan, a precursor of serotonin and an essential amino acid associated with a reduction in appetite, was added in varying concentrations to liquid-formula diets given to a group of hospitalized patients with PWS. Neither increased nor decreased levels had any noticeable effect on appetite, however. In another trial, fenfluramine, a serotonin agonist, was given to a small number of patients with PWS (personal communication), again without success.

The other direction medication has undergone is to interfere with the endorphin system, blocking the actions of endogenous opioids with naloxone.[21,25,27] These trials are based on the existence of congenitally obese mice (ob/ob) with a hyperendorphin syndrome that can be blocked with naloxone. Attempts to control appetite in patients with PWS with naloxone have not consistently demonstrated a significant anorexic effect.[22,27,36]

In general, therefore, for the present, weight loss must be based on significant caloric restriction achieved through rigid surveillance and control. Most patients with PWS are currently not considered suitable candidates for independent living, and permanent parental supervision may have only limited applicability. The current recommendation from centers dealing with this population is that effective weight management is best attained by the strict supervision available in residential treatment centers, which can provide careful monitoring and have structured behavioral programs. Because of the lack of standard findings, the role of causality cannot be entertained at this time. More work on a submicroscopic level is needed to clarify this interesting and important concern.

SECONDARY OBESITY

Although primary or congenital syndromes of obesity have occupied most of this chapter, secondary obesity is in fact a considerably more common problem. Indeed, in mental retardation in general and Down syndrome specifically, obesity can often be considered a coexisting partner of the primary disorder. Other conditions in which obesity is secondary to the primary disorder are Carpenter syndrome, Albright hereditary osteodystrophy, XO (Turner) syndrome, XXXXY syndrome, and XXY (Klinefelter) syndrome.

Prevalence

In the general population, the prevalence of obesity in childhood is between 15 and 25%.[9] In adults the prevalence is between 10 and 20%. Obesity in patients with mental retardation is less well documented. Although data indicate that prevalence is about the same as for the general population,[12] some persons working with this population feel that the prevalence is probably considerably higher. Within the childhood population, obesity proceeds in general in a linear fashion except for the period of early adoles-

cence, when there is an increased incidence of obesity in females. It would appear that the peak age for accelerated weight gain is earlier in some mentally retarded children than in the population in general. When the data are closely examined, it is found that children with Down syndrome develop significant weight gains at around 2 to 3 years of age.[29]

Diagnosis

Obesity may be diagnosed visually, by a weight for height greater than 120% of ideal body weight (IBW) on the basis of appropriately standardized growth charts, or by a triceps skin-fold thickness greater than the 85th percentile. Although skin-fold thickness has the highest correlation with total body fat measured by underwater weighing, K^+ counting, or total body water,[9] few physicians have the calipers or training necessary to obtain accurate measurements, and in fact visual assessment is a valid and reliable tool for diagnosis. If a person appears obese, he or she generally *is* obese.

When using growth charts to plot height and weight, care should be taken to use standardized curves for the population in question. For children with Down syndrome, appropriate growth curves should be used so that the diagnosis of obesity is not delayed. If there is uncertainty in clinical data or visual assessment, one can obtain skin-fold measurements to secure a diagnosis.

Etiology

Three factors are involved in weight regulation: energy intake, energy storage, and energy expenditure. The known causes of obesity in the population under discussion are not significantly different from the causes of obesity in the general population; in either group, obesity is caused by an excess of calories consumed over calories expended. There is practically no research in this area with respect to individuals with developmental disabilities; therefore relative contributions toward obesity of differences in metabolic rate, cold- and exercise-induced thermogenesis, and brown-fat distribution have not yet been determined. Although there may be factors in certain populations, such as decreased lean body mass in individuals with Down syndrome and PWS, that contribute to decreased metabolic rate and therefore decreased energy expenditure, these factors only cause an increase in susceptibility, which would not cause obesity without excess intake. This discussion will focus on the premise that the main contributions to energy imbalance are environmentally based.

Environmental Factors

The first period of concern for children with developmental disabilities, particularly for children with Down syndrome, is in infancy. When infants demonstrate poor weight gain, limited interaction with parents, and poor motor development, visible weight gain may be taken as the first sign of successful parenting. This should not be viewed by professionals as abnormal behavior in parents. The concern at this period is that food intake can become the common denominator for future successful parenting and that an issue that should serve as merely a component of a child's health becomes instead the dominant criterion of well-being. In this setting obesity not only develops readily but persists for as long as misperceptions about the role of food vis-à-vis parenting persist (see section in this chapter on feeding disorders).

For the young child with developmental disabilities, the second period for concern is when food is used inappropriately for appeasement and reinforcement. These children may have difficulty managing their behavior, and promises of treats often accomplish what discipline has failed to do. Unfortunately for some patients, this inappropriate use of food not only leads to excess weight but to the situation in which food becomes a necessity for continued behavioral management. What frequently results is that behavior problems accelerate as children tend to lose control when they merely anticipate the forthcoming food reward. The food rewards then obviously lose their effectiveness, and general behavior deteriorates. In addition, even when behavior modification with food rewards is successful, obesity may result from the high caloric content of the foods used as rewards.

As the child becomes older, schools and residential treatment centers become the new environments in which excess calories may be consumed in behavior modification regimens. Although these settings may be more effective than families at designing and adhering to effective behavior modification programs using food as reinforcement, their success in behavior management is a liability in terms of weight gain. In these situations, the more successful a program is in managing behavior, the more rewards the person will receive and consequently the more weight the person will gain. For a particular individual, this weight gain will more than negatively offset the improvements achieved by the group at large.

In addition to the active use of food as a reinforcer, excess food intake is also the result of increased access to food in situations in which individuals are more likely to be bored, sad, lonely, isolated, or in other ways chronically understimulated.

Food also serves as a source of independence and autonomy for a group that may be without significant freedom. Individuals may enjoy the autonomy of being able to make decisions about when, what, and how much to eat. Therefore, in order to restrict the use of food to influence behavior, one needs to create other channels that will provide opportunities for choices and decision-making.

The use of food as a source of parental satisfaction, pacifier, reward, reinforcer, and general behavior modifier clearly leads to excess weight. The morbidity caused by food used in this way is twofold: first, development of medical complications of obesity, and second, development of inappropriate use of food, which results in deterioration of behavior and further social isolation.

In addition to increased caloric consumption, decreased caloric expenditure due to lack of exercise is a frequent problem for individuals with developmental disabilities. Reasons for decreased activity may include physical problems that may accompany the mental retardation, limited opportunities, decreased expectations, and other situational difficulties. Furthermore, should obesity develop, exercise will be even further decreased, with an even greater increase in the difference between caloric intake and expenditure.

Medication

Children and adults with difficult behavioral problems, in addition to receiving food as a source of behavior management, are also likely to be inadvertently placed on appetite-inducing medication for behavior management and for control of depression, hyperactivity, agitation, and thought disorders.

The most commonly used medications are the neuroleptic and antipsychotic drugs, the two worst offenders being thioridazine (Mellaril) and chlorpromazine (Thorazine). A not unusual consequence of Mellaril therapy is improvement in behavior followed by rapid weight gain as illustrated in Figure 10-8. This figure shows the weight problems encountered by a moderately retarded male given Mellaril for behavior control when he was 15 years old. At the time he began taking the medication he was at his ideal body weight (based on weight for height). Shortly after starting Mellaril his behavior improved and he became easier to manage. However, he also developed increased inappropriate food behav-

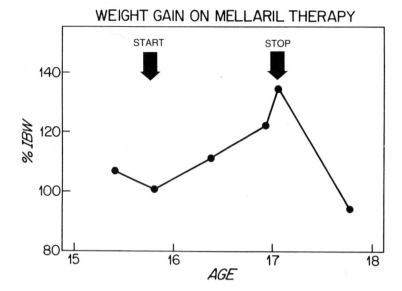

FIG. 10-8. Weight gain on Mellaril therapy showing increase in ideal body weight while drug was used and decrease when it was discontinued.

ior including stealing food, foraging for food, and eating occasional nonfood substances. Because of his behavior change the dosage of Mellaril was increased for additional control. Fifteen months following his starting on Mellaril, his weight was 120% of his ideal body weight. When his weight reached 140% of his ideal body weight, the Mellaril was discontinued, and within 1 year he lost 21 pounds and returned to his ideal body weight. This patient's experience represents a not atypical scenario for the weight effects of both Mellaril and Thorazine. Antidepressants can also lead to appetite stimulation. In this group of agents, imipramine is the leading offender.

When faced with the dilemma of medication being essential not only for a patient's well-being but for the sake of the community in which that patient is residing, one must judge the risk of continuing obesity and its consequences against the effects of continued behavioral disruption. If behavior management is of primary importance, one can try changing the medication to one that is less of an appetite stimulant. For the patient in whom the drugs are not effective, the options are straightforward, and cessation of the medication is indicated.

Disease-Related Factors

In any person in whom there is a change in eating behavior, with or without a change in weight, physicians should always be concerned that the change might be a complication of medical problems. In the population under discussion

two common medical conditions are hypothyroidism (see Chap. 15), particularly in Down syndrome,[35] and depression (see Chap. 20). As these entities are thoroughly discussed elsewhere, I will only refer to them here. Of the two conditions, it would appear that depression is the more frequently underdiagnosed disorder and that, in addition to weight gain leading to a more sedentary and passive behavior, depression can also lead to overeating, which will then result in obesity and decreased mobility and interaction. It is important in this setting that the primary disease be recognized and treated effectively before embarking on inappropriate behavioral strategies.

Complications

Obesity, rather than being viewed as a disorder leading to increased fat cell deposition, should instead be seen, especially in the older population, as a multisystem disease involving respiratory, cardiovascular, endocrine, and musculoskeletal systems.

For young children, particularly those who are not morbidly obese, the initial complications of obesity are predominantly psychosocial. However, increasing age and severity of obesity will lead to medical complications within a short period of time, cardiovascular complications being among the most common. Hypertension in the young obese patient is disturbingly common, affecting no less than 25% of patients seen in weight-control programs. Although the precise etiology of the hypertension is unclear, mild high blood pressure does usually improve with weight loss. Other complications of childhood obesity include musculoskeletal disorders such as Blount's disease and slipped capital femoral epiphysis, and respiratory disorders as seen in sleep apnea and the pickwickian syndrome.

As obesity persists into adulthood, the likelihood of complications increases. Diabetes mellitus is the most prevalent complication in adults. Other complications include hyperlipidemia, coronary artery disease, and even enuresis. In addition to these medical complications it is well known that obese children suffer from decreased self-esteem and are considered lazy, stupid, and less likeable by their non-obese peers and are therefore subject to considerable peer abuse and resultant psychological handicaps.

Prevention and Treatment

In most discussions of management of patients with obesity, directives for intervention begin only after the problem has been identified. Thus parents and health care workers are not faced with the task of preventing obesity but with the more difficult challenge of curing persisting obesity. The most effective treatment for obesity, however, needs to be anticipation, inasmuch as it is generally held that weight loss and then maintenance of that loss is successful in less than 5% of obese individuals.[6]

Environment

As developmentally disabled individuals cannot be considered to be a homogenous group in terms of their environment, there cannot be a single treatment plan that will be indicated for all clients.

It is essential to identify environmental risk factors at an early stage. Health care providers need to be aware of parents' response to their disabled child and the impact of the child's disability on their feeding practices. Feeding techniques and eating habits, appropriate and inappropriate food utilization, and the likelihood for obesity to develop without intervention are all factors that need to be addressed with parents. If one can help parents anticipate the development of obesity, one can significantly aid in its prevention. In an important study on feeding behavior in children with Down syndrome,[31] it was demonstrated that the prevalence of obesity in this extremely high-risk population could be significantly reduced through a structured program of intervention. The value of this study lies in the demonstration that the etiology of the de-

velopment of obesity and the etiology of persistent obesity may in fact be quite different and may therefore require different therapies and have different prognoses. For the former, obesity may develop due to increased susceptibility that exists with respect to certain genetic, metabolic, and environmental factors. With increased understanding of these factors, modification of the behavior of those in positions of responsibility may be the single most important factor in preventing obesity. For the latter group, with obesity that persists despite what appears to be adequate education and behavior modification, other factors need to be explored. One area of difficulty for parents of disabled children is the degree to which they infantalize their children regardless of the child's chronological age. Parents may have problems with limit-setting and restricting instant gratification and may use treats and rewards to avoid guilt. Additional difficulties are presented when parents differ in their acceptance of the child's disability and are therefore unable to follow a consistent approach to problem-solving.

Parents who are having difficulties in accepting their child's disability and who cannot resolve their own conflicts about their child may need family counseling before they can be effective in limit-setting with their children. Caring for disabled children can be disruptive and can generate turmoil even in the most stable household. Health care providers need to be sensitive to the family stresses that may exist and to what extent they interfere with the resolution of feeding disorders.

As the disabled individual ages, the environments in which he interacts will include schools, workshops, group homes, residential centers, and other community residences. In each of these environments, supervision and support will receive different amounts of emphasis and reliability. However, personnel within the framework of each environment need to explore ways in which intervention can be initiated to prevent obesity as well as means to structure environments and their supports in order to assist with weight reduction.

Behavior Management

With the advent of more comprehensive care for the disabled, there is considerable interest in developing weight-loss programs for mentally retarded children and adults.[33] Although these programs vary in organization, implementation, and structure, they tend to investigate the impact of behavior modification and the use of support systems, the most common behavior modification techniques explored having been in relation to parental and child education and modification of eating techniques (e.g., alteration of eating speed, bite size, food left on plate). Most studies designed to explore potential for weight loss have in fact demonstrated that with behavioral techniques, together with the structured implementation and enforcement of these techniques by parents or others in a supportive position, weight reduction does occur.[11,25,26,30] However, only when the support and supervision are maintained does the weight loss persist. Therefore, behavior programs should be a part of weight control, but their main effectiveness is when external structure and supervision can work in parallel with behavior modification.

Diet

Decreased caloric intake must be the cornerstone of any successful weight-loss program. As this has already been discussed in relation to weight loss in patients with PWS, it will not be repeated in this section. However, it is noteworthy that eating behavior and caloric consumption *during meals* has been documented to be relatively similar in the retarded and nonretarded population,[11] emphasizing that diet manipulation depends more on decreased consumption between meals than during the meals themselves.

Without eliminating the effectiveness of a reinforcement program, a change of rewards from calorically dense items such as candies and other foods high in fat, to fat-free, sugar-free, and other specific "diet" treats can often prevent inappropriate weight gain. Therefore the key to effective dietary intervention is the restriction of the excess calories consumed as snacks. A special effort should be aimed at controlling caloric intake of food used for reinforcement.

Regardless of the setting, if free access to food and inappropriate food rewards persist, no diet will be successful. Success demands an alteration in all foods consumed during a 24-hour period, a prospect that requires not only appropriate nutritional information but close supervision and support as well. It is only with the knowledge that supervision is available that a nutritional plan can be initiated.

Exercise

Exercise should play a prominent role in all weight-reduction and weight-maintenance programs.[10] Although the activities scheduled must be appropriate for the abilities of the partici-

pants, a program should aim for activities that generate a sustained increase in heart rate for at least 15 to 20 minutes at a time. This may involve riding stationary bicycles, walking, or exercises. Group activities and sports can frequently be quite successful not only in developing fitness and calorie expenditure but also in promoting an increased sense of the importance of the problem and pride in achievement. Events should be arranged so that all individuals can successfully participate at their own levels, with the recognition that for some individuals pleasure derived from participation will outweigh the caloric expenditure.

Obesity is currently a major health problem in the United States, for both children and adults. It is a particular problem for the developmentally disabled, who frequently undergo late diagnosis and considerable resistance to sustained weight reduction. In order to facilitate success in this field, efforts need to be directed at increasing knowledge about the epidemiology of obesity and at improved screening techniques and methods of prevention.

Health care workers at all levels involved with the developmentally disabled individual and that individual's family should use their times of contact to emphasize the importance of maintaining ideal body weight and should offer concrete suggestions and appropriate referrals at the earliest suggestion of weight problems.

ACKNOWLEDGMENTS

I would like to thank William Mitchell, Ph.D., and the other members of the Prader-Willi team at Children's Hospital, Boston. In addition, I owe special appreciation to the late Aaron Feder, M.D.

REFERENCES

1. Afifi, A.R., and Zellweger, H.: Pathology of muscle hypotonia in the Prader Willi Syndrome, light and electronmicroscopic study. J. Neurol. Sci., 9:49, 1969.
2. Bistrian, B.R., Blackburn, G.L., and Stanbury, J.B.: Metabolic aspects of a protein-sparing modified fast in the dietary management of Prader Willi obesity. N. Engl. J. Med., 296:774, 1979.
3. Bray, G.A.: The Obese Patient. Philadelphia, W.B. Saunders, 1976.
4. Bray, G.A., et al.: The Prader Willi syndrome: A study of 40 patients and a review of the literature. Medicine, 62:59, 1983.
5. Bray, G.A., and York, D.A.: Hypothalamus and genetic obesity in experimental animals: An autonomic and endocrine hypothesis. Physiol. Rev., 59:719, 1979.
6. Brownell, K.D.: The psychology and physiology of obesity: Implications for screening and treatment. J. Am. Diet. Assoc., 84:406, 1984.
7. Cassidy, S.B.: Prader Willi syndrome. Curr. Probl. Pediatr., 14:1, 1984.
8. Crnick, A., Sulzbacher, S., Snow, J., and Holm, V.A.: Preventing mental retardation associated with gross

obesity in the Prader Willi Syndrome. Pediatrics, *66:* 787, 1980.

9. Dietz, W.: Childhood obesity, susceptibility, cause and management. J. Pediatr., *103:*676, 1983.
10. Fox, R., Burkhard, J.E., and Rotatori, F.: Physical fitness and personality characteristics of obese and non-obese retarded adults. Int. J. Obes., *8:*61, 1984.
11. Fox, R.A., Hancoter, H., and Rotatori, A.: A streamlined weight loss program for moderately retarded adults in a sheltered workshop setting. Appl. Res. Ment. Retard., *5:*69, 1984.
12. Fox, R., and Rotatori, A.F.: Prevalence of obesity in mentally retarded adults. Am. J. Ment. Defic., *87:*228, 1982.
13. Hall, B., and Smith, D.: Prader Willi Syndrome: A resume of 32 cases. J. Pediatr., *81:*286, 1972.
14. Hawkey, C.J., and Smithies, A.: The Prader-Willi syndrome with a 15/15 translocation: Case report and review of the literature. J. Med. Genet., *13:*152, 1976.
15. Hittner, H.M., et al.: Oculocutaneous albinoidism as a manifestation of reduced neural crest derivatives in the Prader-Willi syndrome. Am. J. Ophthalmol., *94:*328, 1982.
16. Holm, V.A.: Prader-Willi Syndrome. Baltimore, University Park Press, 1981.
17. Holm, V.A., and Laureen, E.L.: Prader-Willi syndrome and scoliosis. Develop. Med. Child Neurol., *23:*192, 1981.
18. Holt, S.B.: Dermatoglyphics in Prader-Willi syndrome. J. Ment. Defic. Res., *19:*245, 1975.
19. Jackson, H.J., and Thorbeche, P.J.: Treating obesity of mentally retarded adolescents and adults: An exploratory program. Am. J. Ment. Defic., *87:*302, 1982.
20. Jeffcoate, U.T., Laurance, B.W., Edwards, C.R.W., and Besser, G.M.: Endocrine function in the Prader-Willi syndrome. Clin. Endocrinol., *12:*81, 1980.
21. Krotkiewski, M., Fagerberg, B., Bjorntorp, P., and Terenius, L.: Endorphins in genetic human obesity. Int. J. Obes., *7:*597, 1983.
22. Kyriakides, M., Silverstone, T., Jeffcoate, W., and Laurance, B.: Effect of naloxone on hyperphagia in Prader-Willi syndrome. Lancet, *i:*876, 1980.
23. Laurance, B.M., Brito, A., and Wilkinson, T.: Prader-Willi syndrome after age 15 years. Arch. Dis. Child., *56:*181, 1981.

24. Ledbetter, D.H., et al.: Deletions of chromosome 15 as a cause of the Prader-Willi syndrome. N. Engl. J. Med., *304:*325, 1981.
25. McCarran, M.S., and Andrasik, F.: A behavioral weight loss program for mentally retarded adults. Porter Presentation at Annual Meeting of Association for the Advancement of Behavior Therapy, 1984.
26. McCloy, R.F., and McCloy, J.: Encephalins, hunger and obesity. Lancet, *ii:*793, 1979.
27. McCloy, R.F., and McCloy, J.: Naloxone and Prader-Willi syndrome. Lancet, *i:*1418, 1980.
28. Margules, D.L., et al.: ß-endorphin is associated with overeating in genetically obese mice and rats. Science, *202:*988, 1978.
29. Pipes, P.L., and Holm, C.A.: Feeding children with Down Syndrome. J. Am. Diet. Assoc., *77:*277, 1980.
30. Prader, A., Labhart, A., and Willi, H.: Ein Syndrom von Adipositas, Kleinwuchs, Kryptorchismus und Oligophrenie nach Myotonicartigem zustand in Neugeborenalter. Schweiz. Med. Wochenschr., *86:*1260, 1956.
31. Pueschel, S.M., and Rynders, J.C.: Down Syndrome. Cambridge, MA, Academic Guild, 1982, p. 273.
32. Reed, T., and Butler, M.G.: Dermatoglyphic features in Prader-Willis syndrome with respect to chromosomal findings. Clin. Genet., *25:*341, 1984.
33. Rotatori, A.F., Fox, R., and Srotsky, H.: Multicomponent weight reduction program for achieving weight loss in the adult retarded. Ment. Retard., *118:*31, 1980.
34. Smith, A., and Simpson, B.: Dermatoglyphic analysis of 24 individuals with Prader-Willi syndrome. J. Ment. Defic. Res., *26:*91, 1982.
35. Stephenson, J.B.P.: Prader-Willi syndrome: Neonatal presentation and later development. Dev. Med. Child Neurol., *22:*792, 1980.
36. Sullivan, S.: Naloxone and Prader-Willi syndrome. Lancet, *i:*1140, 1980.
37. Uehling, D.: Cryptorchidism in Prader-Willi syndrome. J. Urology, *124:*103, 1980.
38. Witt, R.J.: Prader-Willi syndrome. The disabled child. N. C. Med. J., *44:*499, 1983.
39. Zellweger, H., and Schneider, H.J.: Syndrome of hypomentia-hypogonadism-obesity (HHHO) or Prader Willi syndrome. Am. J. Dis. Child., *115:*588, 1968.

11

PULMONARY DISORDERS

RECURRENT ASPIRATION SYNDROME

Noam Gavriely, M.D., D.Sc.

Repeated aspiration of food or gastric content into the lung, the recurrent aspiration syndrome, produces a spectrum of chronic lung diseases. These include recurrent aspiration pneumonia and its consequences, such as parenchymal injury, or hyperreactive airways manifested as asthma. A definitive diagnosis of recurrent aspiration syndrome can be made when stage V gastroesophageal reflux[15] is demonstrated by radiologic evidence of refluxed contrast material in the lung. However, in the majority of cases the diagnosis is based on the coexistence of chronic or recurrent lung disease and an opportunity for aspiration. Although it is often difficult to establish the causative relationships between swallowing dysfunction, vomiting, gastroesophageal reflux, and recurrent aspiration syndrome, there are sufficient data to justify such a notion in severely retarded patients[2,18] as well as in the general pediatric population.[4,6,7,12,16]

Only a scant amount of data is available on the natural history of recurrent aspiration, and there have been no experimental studies of repeated aspiration in animal models. The sequence of events and the pathophysiology of repeated lung injury are not known. Without corrective intervention, there is a cumulative loss of lung parenchyma and fibrosis of the lung or, in some patients, chronic obstructive lung disease. The latter may also be the consequence of asthma that is induced by frequent recurrent aspiration.[7] The degree of reversibility of aspiration-induced lung diseases is unclear, although appropriate treatment (see below) of the underlying gastroesophageal problem does arrest further progression of the diseases.[9]

The prevalence of recurrent aspiration syndrome in the general pediatric population is not known. Recent studies suggest that many patients with chronic pulmonary disorders, such as recurrent pneumonia or asthma, are actually suffering from recurrent aspiration syndrome.[4,6,7,9,10,12] Among selected groups of patients with chronic pulmonary disorders, as many as two-thirds have been found to have gastroesophageal reflux when studied carefully.[7] Despite the uncertainty regarding the causative relationship between gastroesophageal reflux and recurrent aspiration syndrome, it is possible that the prevalence of recurrent aspiration syndrome is proportional to that of "intrinsic" chronic pulmonary diseases in the pediatric age group.

The prevalence of recurrent aspiration pneumonia in severely retarded patients is proportional to the prevalence of gastroesophageal reflux. Sondheimer and Morris[18] report a prevalence of recurrent aspiration syndrome of 40% in children with gastrointestinal reflux. Byrne and co-workers[2] report a similar prevalence (43%). In these studies 12.6 to 15% of the total patient population had frequent vomiting, of which two-thirds to three-fourths had gastroesophageal reflux. From these data one can calculate that the prevalence of recurrent aspiration syndrome is approximately 4% in severely retarded patients. As a group these patients require frequent, skilled medical attention, with chronic medication and frequent hospitalizations. They represent a greater-than-average burden on health care available for the retarded. All effort should be taken to identify the population at risk, in view of the relative simplicity and success of preventive measures.

PREDISPOSING FACTORS

Patients with severe retardation and disabilities have an increased risk of developing recurrent aspiration syndrome, because of the high frequency of predisposing factors. These predisposing factors can be subdivided into three major groups: (1) abnormalities of gastrointestinal function, (2) neurologic and neuromuscular disorders, and (3) behavioral and situational problems. Chronic gastroesophageal reflux is found in approximately one-tenth of retarded patients[2,18] and is by far the most important predisposing factor. The pathophysiology, diagnosis, and details of treatment of gastroesophageal reflux are discussed in detail in Chapter 10. In addition to their high rate of esophageal motility disorders, such as hiatal hernia with reflux, achalasia, and diffuse esophageal spasm, many disabled patients have delayed emptying of the stomach, with chronic constipation and elevated intra-abdominal pressure. These gastrointestinal disorders are associated with a high frequency of vomiting and regurgitation, with frequent aspiration of gastric content and the development of recurrent aspiration syndrome. Another gastrointestinal risk factor that is more prevalent in the disabled than in the general population is associated with the frequent use of nasogastric or nasoduodenal feeding tubes. These tubes, even if they are of small bore and made of biocompatible materials, create a partial incompetence of the esophageal sphincters and result in an increased incidence of reflux and aspiration.

Coordination of the swallowing function is often impaired in the patient with severe disabilities. An absent or hyperactive gag reflex interferes with the passage of a bolus of food or liquid from the oral cavity into the esophagus. This causes frequent aspiration while eating and many coughing spells during the course of a meal. Poor oral hygiene is another important predisposing factor. Aspiration of saliva made infectious by tooth decay constitutes a risk for the development of recurrent aspiration syndrome.

An abnormal neurologic status is often associated with vomiting and aspiration. Seizure disorders, especially of the grand-mal type, constitute an important predisposing factor. Severe mental retardation with dependency on caretakers for feeding and body manipulation renders the patient susceptible to aspiration during mealtimes or between meals while being repositioned. An impaired cough reflex, caused by a general decrease in the level of consciousness or by specific lesions in the sensory or motor pathways of the cough reflex arc, is often found in disabled patients. Because cough is the primary mechanism for clearing of aspirated material from the airways, its absence often leads to development of recurrent aspiration syndrome.

Increased intra-abdominal pressure is an important risk factor for vomiting and gastroesophageal reflux. Patients with severe retardation and disabilities are often afflicted with moderate to severe spinal deformities. These deformities are frequently associated with reduced abdominal space and an increase in intra-abdominal pressure. This can cause increased gastric pressure and gastroesophageal reflux, especially in conjunction with insufficiency of the cardioesophageal sphincter. Kassem, Groen, and Fraenkel[13] found spinal deformities, primarily kyphosis and scoliosis, in 59% of patients with hiatal hernia as compared to 19% among a control group of ulcer patients. They suggested that the increased abdominal pressure secondary to deformation of the spinal column was the predisposing factor for the hiatal hernia. Orthopedic corsets that are prescribed for kyphoscoliosis or prolapsed intervertebral disc also create increased intra-abdominal pressure and increase the risk of reflux and recurrent aspiration syndrome.

Behavioral problems are often related to the oropharynx and gastrointestinal tract. Aerophagia leads to increased abdominal pressure and vomiting. Regurgitation of gastric content can be an expression of a behavioral problem or of stress with the ensuing risk of aspiration. Finally, pica activity, with ingestion of foreign materials, is sometimes complicated by aspiration. Particular attention should be paid to the pulmonary consequences that can follow the ingestion of hydrocarbon derivatives.

CLINICAL PRESENTATION AND DIAGNOSIS

Recurrent pneumonia, asthma, chronic obstructive pulmonary disease, night cough, cough during meals, bronchiectasis, and lung fibrosis can all be manifestations of recurrent aspiration.

Why a specific lung disorder develops in any given patient is seldom understood. Summaries of clinical data from disabled patients and from normal subjects show little correlation between the nature of the gastrointestinal problem and the resulting pulmonary disorder. Frequent vomiting is more often associated with aspiration pneumonia, whereas nocturnal gastroesophageal reflux is believed to be related to night cough and asthma. Difficulty in swallowing and severe deformities of the oropharyngeal cavity are often linked to aspiration of food during meals and frequent coughing spells.

The diagnosis of recurrent aspiration syndrome should be considered whenever a chronic or recurrent lung disorder is associated with any of the predisposing factors listed earlier. One should document the presence of aspiration, before the diagnosis of recurrent aspiration syndrome can be definitely established, by finding contrast material in the lung via radiologic examination, demonstration of gamma activity in the lung after a swallow of radioactively labeled meal, demonstration of food or gastric content in material aspirated by nasotracheal suction, or when a reliable description is given by a medical worker who witnessed the acute event. A tentative diagnosis of recurrent aspiration syndrome can be made when recurrent pulmonary disease, not explained by alternative causes, is associated with gastroesophageal reflux, reduced state of consciousness, seizure disorder, or other predisposing factors. The diagnosis can be confirmed if a therapeutic trial of measures to prevent aspiration of injurious material into the lung is successful.

Methods for the diagnosis of gastroesophageal reflux are described in Chapter 10. For many years, radiologic demonstration of previously swallowed contrast material in the airways was the only available method for the diagnosis of aspiration.[15] The limitations of radiologic studies are related to the need for repeated exposures and radiation. Also, each acute aspiration event causes symptoms and signs that are related to the extent of lung injury. This, in turn, is a function of the volume and chemical composition of the aspirate and the integrity of pulmonary defense and clearance mechanisms. Aspiration is initially followed by cough, wheezing, bronchospasm, and cyanosis. Airway occlusion with large food particles should be cleared promptly, or asphyxia may result. In the next hour signs develop that reflect the maldistribution of ventilation and perfusion and a massive loss of fluid into the lung interstitium. Hypoxia, with a wide al-

veolar-arterial oxygen difference, is the main finding when arterial blood gases are measured. Hypovolemic shock with poor tissue perfusion can also contribute to the hypoxia and to metabolic acidosis. If CO_2 retention is observed, the aspirate is more likely to have particles in it. Roentgenogram of the chest may reveal interstitial and alveolar edema. The infiltrates are diffuse, with some localized areas affected more than others. Improvement starts in two to three days. Resolution of the radiologic findings and a decrease of the alveolar-arterial oxygen gradient are the usual indicators of improvement. Infection can be a problem in early recovery, with an ever-present risk of empyema and lung abscess. Roentgenograms of the chest may show localized fibrous strands for a few months following aspiration. This is associated with local replacement of lung parenchyma with scar tissue. In patients with recurrent aspiration syndrome, radiographic signs of prior aspirations may be visible on chest roentgenograms that show acute aspiration pneumonia.

THERAPY

The goal of treatment of recurrent aspiration syndrome is to prevent the aspiration of injurious material. Successful prevention of further aspiration diminishes or eliminates pulmonary symptoms in virtually all recurrent aspiration syndrome patients. By contrast, treatment of the pulmonary problems alone is difficult and disappointing and may be associated with further complications. For example, aminophylline, used as a bronchodilator when airway constriction is present, reduces gastroesophageal sphincter pressure,[3] thus inducing more reflux and possible aspiration. Another example is chest physical therapy, an important adjuvant in the treatment of pneumonia, atelectasis, and bronchiectasis. This treatment involves positioning the patient at various angles and use of vigorous physical manipulations. These are likely to induce or facilitate further gastroesophageal reflux and aspiration. The benefits of aminophylline and related bronchodilators and of chest physical therapy in patients with recurrent aspiration syndrome should be carefully weighed against the risks described. Furthermore, should chest physical therapy be prescribed, the therapist should be alerted to the need to limit therapy to the upright and semi-upright positions. These warnings are unnecessary in intubated patients with a cuffed endotracheal tube. Specific measures for treatment of an acute aspiration event are noted below, but one cannot overemphasize the importance of preventing aspiration as the ultimate therapeutic goal.

Gastroesophageal reflux is the most prevalent basis for recurrent aspiration; therefore effective treatment should be initiated promptly to prevent further aspiration. The available medical and surgical measures for treating gastroesophageal reflux are described in Chapter 10. The decision on what regime to use depends on the patient's status, prognosis, and the extent of disease. In mild cases with infrequent pneumonia, intensive medical therapy may be initiated and continued for approximately six weeks. If reflux of injurious material does not cease within this period, strong consideration should be given to surgical intervention.[14] This is particularly true in the population with severe retardation, in whom the rate of long-term success of medical treatment is low and the likelihood of spontaneous resolution is small. In recent years the rate of success of surgical anti-reflux procedures, in particular the Nissen fundoplication, has improved substantially (Chap. 10). The exact criteria for surgical intervention are unclear, but in defense of their lungs retarded patients with documented gastrointestinal reflux should be considered as surgical candidates before irreversible, life-threatening pulmonary damage develops.

Recurrent aspiration syndrome may be related to other etiologies. Better control of seizure disorders may also minimize pulmonary damage if it is related to aspiration during seizure activity. When aspiration is due to poor or absent coordination of the swallowing mechanism or to laryngeal incompetence, alternative management should be utilized. If reversibility of the impairment is expected within a short period of time, temporary measures to bypass the pharyngeal cavity may be used. These include a narrow Silastic nasoduodenal feeding tube or a feeding gastrostomy. These methods have several disadvantages: aspiration can still occur if gastroesophageal reflux develops, aspiration of saliva with oral flora is not prevented, and there is deprivation of the satisfaction associated with eating even when mental deficiency is severe. The use of feeding tubes or gastrostomy is associated with substantial cost because of the intense, prolonged intensive care that is often required. In selected patients an alternative is tracheostomy with laryngotracheal closure. Several procedures have been proposed to separate the upper airway from the digestive tract.[14] The simplicity and potential reversibility of these procedures offer significant advantages. It should be

emphasized that tracheostomy alone does not prevent aspiration, and in many cases may be associated with increased frequency of aspiration. This is due to the collection of food or secretions above the cuff and to leakage into the trachea during manipulations of the tracheostomy tube. The various surgical procedures are simple and provide a high rate of success in controlling aspiration. Their major shortcoming is the interruption of phonation, but in nonverbal retarded patients this is much less of a problem than in verbal-communicative patients.

In all recurrent-aspiration patients special care should be taken to avoid body positions and manipulations that predispose to aspiration. In general, upright or semi-upright positions should always be maintained. Frequent, small meals are better than three large ones. Soft or semisolid food is often tolerated better than liquids. Many patients will have little difficulty with their fluid intake if it is given as gelatin or in other semisolid forms, but will aspirate liquids and suffer massive coughing spells. Solid food should be avoided because aspiration of an unchewed chunk can be lethal. Particular care should be taken with patients who require assistance during feeding. Personnel must be aware of the patient's condition, and adequate time should be allowed for each meal.

Other general measures can at times be helpful in the management of recurrent aspiration. Orthopedic devices are often associated with increased intra-abdominal pressure and should be avoided in patients subject to recurrent aspiration syndrome.[13] Surgical procedures for elective treatment of kyphoscoliosis that involve prolonged body casts postoperatively are generally contraindicated in patients with recurrent aspiration syndrome. If such a procedure is essential, definitive correction of the predisposing factors for recurrent aspiration syndrome should be completed prior to the orthopedic procedure.

Oral hygiene is an essential factor in the prevention of aspiration of infected material. Regular, complete dental care must be provided. At times, dental extraction may be the only solution for recurrent inoculation of the tracheobronchial tree with infected salivary secretions.

In some patients with mental retardation, behavioral problems predispose to aspiration. In particular, aerophagia causes increased intragastric pressure from the swallowed air, and the elevated pressure can cause vomiting and aspiration. In some patients relief of the underlying physical problem by fundoplication, bougie, or other measures may improve the behavioral problems. However, behavioral control may sometimes minimize aerophagia when the latter is not associated with definite signs of physical disorder.

PATHOPHYSIOLOGY

Lung injury following pulmonary aspiration results from the effects of food material, gastric contents, or acid secretions on the respiratory epithelium and the pulmonary capillary endothelium. The consequences of repeated aspiration are not known, and it is assumed that each aspiration event produces an injury that is independent of any previous event. The well-studied pathophysiology of acute (nonrecurrent) aspiration is thought to be applicable to recurrent aspiration syndrome, but it fails to account for the additive effect of recurrent lesions that lead to the development of chronic lung impairment, and it does not explain the hyperreactive airway disease associated with gastroesophageal reflux and recurrent aspiration syndrome. Additional basic and clinical research is needed to explain the pathophysiological mechanisms of recurrent aspiration syndrome-related chronic pulmonary disease.

The nature of lung injury due to aspiration is closely related to the volume and acidity of the aspirate, and to the amount and type of food material in the aspirate.[11,17,20] All types of aspirates impose some degree of mechanical airway obstruction, with impaired distribution of ventilation in the acute phase immediately following the aspiration event. The extent, duration, and nature of subsequent lung injury are specific for each type of aspirate. Acid aspiration causes significant injury in experimental animals when the pH is below 2.5.[17] Pathophysiological changes are similar following instillation of exogenous acid or clear gastric secretions. An acute chemical "burn" is the main histologic response of the airway to intrabronchial acid instillation. There are both epithelial and endothelial damage, leading to alveolar hemorrhage and pulmonary edema immediately after aspiration. Only part of the ensuing damage is due to the direct action of acid. Circulating substances are released from the primary site of the chemical burn. The vasoactive substances, in particular thromboxane, trigger an avalanche of detrimental histologic and functional responses. Increased permeability of pulmonary capillary endothelial cells causes leakage of plasma into the interstitial space and into the alveoli. The colloid osmotic pressure of the plasma proteins, which is normally sufficient to prevent transudation, becomes inadequate. Three factors contribute to the severe shift of

fluids: (1) increased pulmonary vascular hydrostatic pressure due to vasospasm and external pressure of edematous fluid on pulmonary capillaries[1]—this increased pressure contributes to the driving force for transudation and exudation; (2) increased permeability of endothelial cells to proteins, resulting in a rise in colloid osmotic pressure in the perivascular, interstitial, and alveolar spaces; and (3) overload of the limited capacity of the pulmonary lymphatics. A contributing factor is the destruction of type II surfactant-producing alveolar cells. An increased alveolar surface tension with a tendency for alveolar closure also acts to increase capillary transmural pressure and fluid transudation. Surfactant deficiency and flooding of the alveolar spaces with edematous fluid induce alveolar closure and atelectasis.

Most of the pathophysiological changes that occur following aspiration are the result of fluid exudation and an increased lung water content. Lung compliance is reduced due to increased mass and surface tension. This increases the work of breathing and O_2 consumption. Pulmonary gas exchange deteriorates because of maldistribution of ventilation and blood flow on the one hand and increased diffusion barrier on the other. The resulting hypoxemia and increased alveolar-arterial oxygen difference ($AaDo_2$) can be determined from arterial blood gas measurements. Volume loss into the lung parenchyma can be substantial. Circulatory hypovolemia and shock are frequent complications of the acute event. The combination of circulatory failure and hypoxemia is especially detrimental because the ensuing tissue hypoxia creates a metabolic acidosis. The pulmonary vascular response to hypoxia, with vasoconstriction and mechanical capillary resistance caused by the engorged interstitium, leads to increased pulmonary arterial pressure.[1] On the other hand, left atrial filling pressure is reduced due to the hypovolemia. These events can and should be closely monitored with a balloon-directed catheter (Swan-Ganz). A common finding in acute severe aspiration is an increase in the pulmonary artery pressure, with normal or reduced wedge pressures reflecting the pathophysiologic changes described above.

In addition to the loss of water into the lung, erythrocytes, fibrin and other plasma proteins, and polymorphonuclear leukocytes are deposited in the alveolar spaces. The time course of the pathologic changes that follow acute aspiration of acid has been studied in a few animal models. Intrabronchial instillation of 2 to 4 ml/kg of hydrochloric acid, pH < 1.5, is the customary model for the study of acute aspiration. The distribution of the aspirate in the airways and alveolar spaces is rapid (<20 sec) and widespread. In addition, mediators such as thromboxane are released following a localized instillation of hydrochloric acid, spread through the bloodstream, and cause vasoconstriction, aggregation of thrombocytes, and exudation in remote lung regions not directly affected by the initial acid burn. Areas of atelectasis appear shortly after instillation. These are probably due to increased bronchial tone, because the bronchial epithelium is generally intact when examined microscopically 1 hour after instillation. The most striking findings at that time are related to the vascular congestion with interstitial edema of the alveolar walls. Localized areas of hemorrhage into the alveolar spaces can also be observed.

A few hours after acid instillation, vascular changes predominate and are accompanied by signs of damage to the bronchial epithelium. The submucosa is infiltrated with polymorphonuclear leukocytes, and degenerated epithelial cells fill the bronchial lumen. This inflammatory process is particularly severe in the bronchioles. The alveolar spaces fill with fluid, erythrocytes, and polymorphonuclear leukocytes. Surfactant-producing alveolar (type II) cells and some structural (type I) cells also detach from the basement membrane into the alveolar space. If the animal survives, within the subsequent two days there is an increased polymorphonuclear leukocytic infiltrate with consolidation of the lung parenchyma. Forty-eight hours after the aspiration, hyaline membranes form. Initial signs of resolution and of regeneration of bronchial epithelium are seen as early as on the third day. Three weeks following the acute event, the lungs of experimental animals regain much of their structural integrity. The only residua are some increase in weight and focal parenchymal mass, and bronchiolitis obliterans.[19] The improvement in physiologic parameters follows the course of healing, as shown by histologic studies. Gas exchange, pulmonary function tests, and pulmonary hemodynamics return to normal following acute aspiration pneumonia.

Alternative models of aspiration have been developed to study the consequences of aspiration of gastric fluid with a higher pH containing some food particles. This is more frequent than the aspiration of very-low-pH gastric fluid. The acute stages immediately following aspiration are similar to very-low-pH acid aspiration, but a remarkable difference is the subsequent development of alveolar hypoventilation, with CO_2 retention and hypercapnia. Mechanical obstruction by food particles and bronchial epithelial cells may explain a portion of this difference, but not all. Other unknown factors may contribute to the airway closure, because filtered gastric content at a normal pH can also induce hypercapnia. Hemorrhagic pulmonary edema, peribronchial alveolitis, and local arterial thrombosis also occur following nonacidic gastric fluid aspiration when food particles are present. After 48 hours the initial polymorphonuclear infiltrate changes to a mononuclear cell population. Foreign body reaction is the predominant picture over the next few days, resolution beginning after 7 days. The time course, extent, and completeness of resolution are largely related to the nature and source of the aspirated particles.

Specific forms of pneumonitis occur following aspiration of lipid (lipoid pneumonia) and repeated aspiration of leguminous seeds. Peanuts, beans, lentils, and peas produce nodular granulomas around the cellulose component of the seed. The latter conditions are rarely diagnosed ante mortem or without surgery, but should be suspected in severely retarded and debilitated patients with poorly resolving radiologic findings.

TREATMENT OF AN ACUTE ASPIRATION EVENT

Acute aspiration is a potentially lethal event and should be treated promptly by skilled medical personnel. Aspiration may often escape notice in severely retarded patients. If, however, the acute event is witnessed or discovered promptly, measures should be taken to minimize the volume and extent of distribution of aspirate in the lung. A head-down position is used, with the patient lying on his side to decrease the number of lobes involved. The Heimlich maneuver[8] should be used repeatedly if cough is ineffective or absent, even if the aspirate is a nonparticulate liquid. Suctioning via an endotracheal tube is useful, particularly if it is coordinated with a chest-compression maneuver. If signs of asphyxia or severe hypoventilation exist, emergency bronchoscopy is indicated to remove large particles from the airways. However, if the aspirate is only liquid, bronchoscopy contributes little beyond what can be achieved by suctioning. There is no role in the treatment of acute aspiration for broncho-alveolar lavage with saline or any other solution.

Once mechanical clearing of the airways has been completed, an estimate of the extent of lung injury should be made. It is useful to plan treatment in anticipation of forthcoming pathophysiological events, and it is wise to err towards a more severe estimation of damage than might at first seem justified. If aspiration volume is estimated to be more than minimal, or when acidic or particulate gastric content is inhaled, severe lung injury should be anticipated. As described previously, transudation and exudation into the peribronchial and interstitial spaces are the immediate events associated with lung injury.[1] Treatment should therefore be directed towards reducing the rate of exudation, replacing lost intravascular fluids, and combating the resulting hypoxia. Endotracheal intubation, mechanical ventilation, and positive end-expiratory pressure (PEEP) should be initiated earlier than they would be indicated from the arterial blood gas composition.[5] Adequate alveolar ventilation with sufficient oxygenation prevents hypoxic pulmonary vasoconstriction and the ensuing increase in pulmonary vascular pressures. Minimizing the increase in pulmonary arterial pressure helps to reduce the hydrostatic pressure gradient and leakage across the capillary endothelial membrane. PEEP serves a similar purpose from the alveolar side of the hydrostatic gradient.[1]

Intravenous fluid is needed to maintain appropriate intravascular volume. The rate of fluid administration is best judged from changes in multiple hemodynamic parameters such as pulmonary arterial pressure, central venous pressure, cardiac output, and arterial blood pressure. The therapeutic goals are adequate cardiac output, a mixed venous oxygen near 40 torr, and a near normal mean pulmonary pressure. The particular fluid that should be used is debatable, some advocating colloid solutions over crystalloids.[20]

The role of vasoactive drugs in the treatment of acute aspiration is still under investigation. Pulmonary vasodilation with sodium nitroprusside has been found useful in a study of excised dog lobes.[1] Although an attractive and reasonable hypothesis underlies this treatment, further animal and clinical experiments are needed before adopting pulmonary vasodilation into clinical practice.

The role of steroids is still being debated, with most authorities unconvinced of their usefulness. Similar views exist regarding the use of antibiotics at the time of the acute event. It seems better to give antibiotics only when signs of infection with an identified organism are present.

Recurrent aspiration syndrome is a multifactorial problem that is sometimes life-threatening. If aspiration is not controlled, the lungs eventually become permanently damaged to the extent that fatal respiratory failure occurs. On the other hand, timely and successful treatment of predisposing factors can bring rapid and dramatic improvement in pulmonary status and a sense of well-being to the individual. Basic studies of the degree of reversibility of lung injury following multiple aspiration episodes are not yet available. Such data are important for both medical and economic reasons, given the substantially higher-than-average cost of medical treatment of those 4% of severely mentally retarded patients who are afflicted with recurrent aspiration syndrome.

REFERENCES

1. Broe, J.B., Toung, T.J.K., Permutt, S., and Cameron, J.L.: Aspiration pneumonia: Treatment with pulmonary vasodilators. Surgery, *94*:95, 1983.
2. Byrne, W.J., et al.: A diagnostic approach to vomiting in severely retarded patients. Am. J. Dis. Child., *137*:259, 1983.
3. Cohen, S.E.: The aspiration syndrome. Clin. Obstet. Gynecol., *9*:235, 1982.
4. Darling, D.B., McCauley, G.K., Leonidas, J.C., and Schwartz, A.M.: Gastroesophageal reflux in infants and children: Correlation of radiological severity and pulmonary pathology. Radiology, *127*:735, 1978.
5. East, T.D., IV, Pace, N.L., and Westenskow, D.R.: Synchronous versus asynchronous differential lung ventilation with PEEP after unilateral acid aspiration in the dog. Crit. Care Med., *11*:441, 1983.
6. Euler, A.R., and Byrne, W.J.: Twenty-four-hour esophageal intraluminal pH probe testing: A comparative analysis. Gastroenterology, *80*:957, 1981.
7. Euler, A.R., et al.: Recurrent pulmonary disease in children: A complication of gastroesophageal reflux. Pediatrics, *63*:47, 1979.
8. Heimlich, H.J.: A life-saving maneuver to prevent foodchoking. J.A.M.A., *234*:398, 1975.
9. Herbst, J.J.: Gastroesophageal reflux. J. Pediatr., *98*:859, 1981.
10. Heyman, S., Kirkpatrick, J.A., Winter, H.S., and Treves, S.: An improved radionuclide method for the diagnosis of gastroesophageal reflux and aspiration in children (milk scan). Radiology, *131*:479, 1979.
11. James, C.F., et al.: Pulmonary aspiration: Effects of volume and pH in the rat. Anesth. Analg., *63*:665, 1984.
12. Jolley, S.G., et al.: Esophageal pH monitoring during sleep identifies children with respiratory symptoms from gastroesophageal reflux. Gastroenterology, *80*:1501, 1981.
13. Kassem, N.Y., Groen, J.J., and Fraenkel, M.: Spinal deformities and oesophageal hiatus hernia. Lancet, *i*:887, 1965.
14. Kirchner, J.C., and Sasaki, C.T.: Surgery for aspiration. Otolaryngol. Clin. N. Am., *17*:49, 1984.
15. McCauley, R.G.K., Darling, D.B., Leonidas, J.C., and Schwartz, A.M.: Gastroesophageal reflux in infants and children: A useful classification and reliable physiologic technique for its demonstration. Am. J. Roentgenol., *130*:47, 1978.

16. MacFadyen, U.M., Hendry, G.M.A., and Simpson, H.: Gastro-esophageal reflux in near-miss sudden infant death syndrome or suspected recurrent aspiration. Arc. Dis. Child., *58*:87, 1983.
17. Mendelson, C.L.: The aspiration of stomach contents into the lungs during obstetric anesthesia. Am. J. Obstet. Gynecol., *52*:191, 1946.
18. Sondheimer, J.M., and Morris, B.A.: Gastroesophageal reflux among severely retarded children. J. Pediatr., *94*:710, 1979.
19. Stewardson, R.H., and Nyhus, L.M.: Pulmonary aspiration: An update. Arch. Surg., *112*:1192, 1977.
20. Wynne, J.W.: Aspiration pneumonitis: Correlation of experimental models with clinical disease. Clin. Chest Med., *3*:25, 1982.

BRONCHOPULMONARY DYSPLASIA
Elizabeth R. Brown, M.D.

The term bronchopulmonary dysplasia (BPD) was coined by Northway, Rosan, and Porter in 1967.[8] They described the chronic lung changes seen in 32 infants with respiratory distress syndrome who required more than 24 hours of a high inspired-oxygen concentration delivered by positive-pressure ventilation. They identified four stages of the disease process on the basis of both clinical and radiographic abnormalities

Table 11-1. *Stages of Bronchopulmonary Dysplasia*

Evidence of Abnormality	Stage			
	I **Acute Respiratory Distress Syndrome** **(0–3 Days of Age)**	**II** **Regeneration** **(4–10 Days of Age)**	**III** **Transition to Chronic Disease** **(10–20 Days of Age)**	**IV** **Chronic Disease** **(>30 Days of Age)**
Radiographic	Granular reticular pattern Air bronchograms	Opacification	Small rounded radiolucent areas Areas of irregular density "Sponge like"	Enlargement of lucent areas Strands of radiodensity
Pathologic	Hyaline membranes	Persisting hyaline membranes	Decreased hyaline membranes	
	Atelectasis	Emphysematous coalescence of alveoli	Emphysematous alveoli with atelectasis of surrounding alveoli	Emphysematous alveoli associated with tributary bronchioles having hypertrophy of peribronchiolar smooth muscle Atelectasis
	Lymphatic dilatation		Interstitial edema	Tortous lymphatics
	Metaplasia and necrosis of bronchiolar mucosa	Increased patchy squamous metaplasia Increased bronchiolar necrosis	Increased mucosal metaplasia and hyperplasia	Perimucosal fibrosis
	Patchy loss of ciliated cells	Necrosis and repair of alveolar epithelium	Fine strands of interstitial collagen	Increased number of macrophages, histiocytes, and foam cells
	Hyperemia	Focal thickening of capillary basement membrane	Focal thickening of basement membrane	Focal thickening of basement membrane with marked separation of capillaries from alveolar epithelium Fine collagen fibrils Increased reticulum Elastin in fibers in septal walls Vascular lesions of the pulmonary hypertensive type

(Table 11-1). The initial stage (days 0–3) was that of acute respiratory distress syndrome (RDS). This was followed by a period of lung regeneration (days 4–10), during which time chest radiographs showed opacification of the lung fields. At the end of 10 days, the changes either resolved or progressed to a period of transition to chronic disease characterized radiologically by rounded areas of radiolucency resembling bullae (Fig. 11-1). The fourth stage, that of chronic disease, involved persistence of these changes beyond 1 month of age. The period of chronic disease is characterized by a chest radiograph showing round lucent areas in the lungs alternating with thin strands of radiodensity, i.e., areas of emphysema surrounded by areas of atelectasis and fibrosis (Fig. 11-2).

For the purposes of the present discussion, an infant is considered to have BPD if oxygen and respirator therapy were required on the first day of life, oxygen therapy was continued beyond 1 month of age, and the infant has radiologic changes consistent with those described by Northway, Rosan, and Porter. I will review what is known about the etiopathogenesis of the disease, the acute and chronic pulmonary changes, the long-term medical management and neurologic outcomes for these high-risk infants, and the psychosocial manifestations of the stress experienced in caring for them.

ETIOPATHOGENESIS

Although there is considerable controversy about the etiopathogenesis of BPD, the sine qua non of the disease is exposure to increased oxygen concentrations delivered with positive-pressure ventilation. Other factors including lung immaturity and genetic predisposition have also been implicated.

Bronchopulmonary dysplasia occurs in 16 to 21% of infants who require assisted ventilation. The degree of immaturity of the infant correlates with the likelihood of development of chronic lung disease: in infants less than 1,000 grams birth weight, the incidence may be as high as 40%. In recent years, the survival of such infants has dramatically increased (Table 11-2). This increase in survival may be related to advances in perinatal care, which include fetal monitoring, maternal transport to a perinatal center for delivery of a preterm infant, and improved neonatal intensive care unit management of respiratory support, metabolic balance, and intravenous nutrition. The price of survival for these very tiny infants is often high: chronic lung disease with or without neurologic compromise.

Oxygen Toxicity

There appears to be a dose-response relationship between oxygen exposure and development

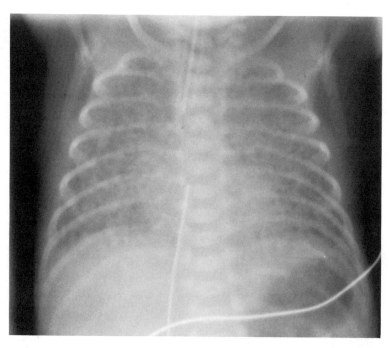

FIG. 11-1. Bronchopulmonary dysplasia at 11 days of age (transition stage).

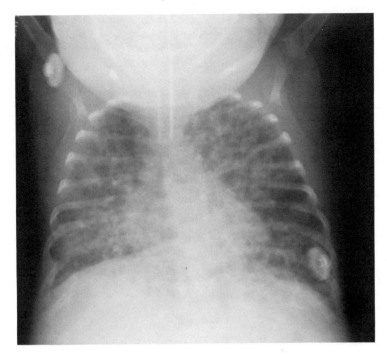

FIG. 11-2. Chronic bronchopulmonary dysplasia at 3 months of age.

of BPD. In a study of 299 infants reported by Edwards and his colleagues,[2] infants who were exposed to an $F_{I_{O_2}}$ of 0.8 to 1.0 for 6 days, 0.4 to 0.79 for 18 days, or 0.22 to 0.39 for 53 days had increased risk of either dying or developing chronic lung disease. Thus, high oxygen concentrations for a short time or lower oxygen concentrations for a longer time are both associated with risk of developing BPD.

Barotrauma

Mechanical trauma from positive-pressure ventilators has also been implicated as a cause of BPD. Virtually all infants with BPD have been treated with respiratory support. Taghizadeh

Table 11-2. *Characteristics of Infants with Bronchopulmonary Dysplasia*

	1978	1979	1980	1981
Percent survival <1000 g (to NICU discharge)	40	38	57	58
Number with BPD	31	48	46	62
Number <1000 g	15	28	26	41
Mean birth weight (kg)	1.20	1.10	1.05	1.01

Data from the Joint Program in Neonatology (Brigham and Women's Hospital, The Children's Hospital, and Beth Israel Hospital), Boston.

and Reynolds[12] reported that all infants in their center who died with lung changes consistent with BPD had been exposed to peak inspiratory pressures of greater than 35 cm H_2O and peak respiratory rates of greater than 30 breaths per minute. They reported a decreased incidence of BPD with changes in respiratory management toward lower peak inspiratory pressures, lower respiratory rates, and longer inspiratory times.[9] This type of ventilation has been called a "square wave pattern."

Family History of Asthma

Family history may be important in determining which children are at highest risk. Nickerson and Taussig[6] reported a relationship between family history of allergic disease and the risk of BPD in a group of infants with RDS. In that study, 33% of infants with RDS who did not get BPD had a family history of asthma compared with 77% of infants who did develop BPD. This finding needs further investigation in a larger epidemiologic study; however, the results do suggest that the underlying genetic susceptibility on which the toxic insult acts may be a major determinant of the degree of lung injury. Thus, the risk of BPD is really a function of gestational age × oxygen exposure × peak inspiratory pressure on the respirator × family history.

MORTALITY

The first year of life for infants with BPD is characterized by a high rate of both mortality and morbidity. The mortality rate for infants with BPD in the first year of life has remained at about 20% over the last decade. About 12% die in the neonatal intensive care unit. The remaining 8% die after NICU discharge. The major causes of death are (1) progressive respiratory failure, often complicated by cor pulmonale; (2) lower respiratory tract infection, and (3) sudden unexplained death with a history similar to what has been described as the sudden infant death syndrome (SIDS).

Progressive Respiratory Failure Complicated by Cor Pulmonale

The right-sided heart failure seen in these infants is best followed by serial EKGs and echocardiogram. The EKG will show an increased P wave in lead II along with changes compatible with right ventricular hypertrophy. The echocardiogram will show prolonged right ventricular systolic ejection times. The development of cor pulmonale might be related to the repeated hypoxic insults these infants have suffered. This may be critical because the pulmonary artery pressure rises when the Po_2 drops below 50 torr. Moreover, Unger and his colleagues, using the newborn dog model, showed that repeated intermittent drops in Po_2 resulted in a progressively increased pulmonary artery pressure.[13] This mechanism could explain the right-sided heart changes seen so commonly in infants with BPD. The incidence of cor pulmonale has decreased in recent years, during which time stricter attention has been paid to maintenance Po_2 values. Oxygen has been delivered by nasal canula to minimize fluctuations in Po_2. The use of the nasal canula for administration of oxygen has enabled caretakers to provide an uninterrupted supply of oxygen and thereby lessen the number of hypoxic episodes.

Lower Respiratory Tract Infection

Lower respiratory tract infections in the first 2 years of life are more common in low-birth-weight infants than in those born at term, but the highest risk group are low-birth-weight infants whose course was complicated by BPD (Table 11-3). As many as 50 to 85% of infants with BPD develop bronchiolitis or pneumonia in the first 2 years of life.[3,5,14] The incidence is lower in the second year of life compared to the first. The major cause of death with these infections is respiratory failure, and the most common organism associated with death in this setting is respiratory syncytial virus (RSV). Care should be taken with BPD infants to minimize exposure to infections, particularly viral infection in the winter months.

Sudden Death

In recent years, a number of infants between the ages of 4 and 12 months who seemed to have recovered from their BPD died suddenly and unexpectedly in a manner similar to that described for infants with SIDS, i.e., they were found dead in their cribs, usually in the morning, without crying out and without any indication of illness. When 53 infants with BPD were compared with 65 infants less than 1,000 grams birthweight who did not have BPD, there was a much greater incidence of unexplained sudden death in the infants with BPD (6 with BPD versus 1 without BPD).[16] There were no significant differences in factors that have been associated with a higher risk of SIDS such as gestational age, socioeconomic status, multiple birth, apnea, or birth asphyxia. Whether this indeed represents a subset of infants with SIDS remains to be established.

EARLY CHILDHOOD MORBIDITY

The outcomes at 2 years of age for infants with bronchopulmonary dysplasia are shown in Table 11-4.

Table 11-3. *Lower Respiratory Tract Infections in Infants with Bronchopulmonary Dysplasia*

Author	Population	n	# LRT Infections		
			Year 1	Year 2	Year 0–2
Markestad and Fitzhardinge[5]	BPD	20	17	10	
Vohr, Bell, and Oh[14]	BPD	26	13	6	
Hack et al.[3]	<1500 gm	86			10
Pape et al.[7]	<1000 gm	43			15

Table 11-4. *Outcomes for Infants with Bronchopulmonary Dysplasia*
(n = 33 of 40 Surviving Infants Born in 1980)

Condition at 2 Years of Age	Number	Percent
Cognitively and neurologically normal	20	61
Abnormalities		
Lung		
Persistent wheezing	3	9
Lower respiratory tract infection	10	30
Mechanical airway trauma from prolonged intubation	4	12
Retrolental fibroplasia		
Mild	7	21
Severe	3	9
Cerebral palsy	3	9
Developmental delay	10	30
Growth delay	15	45

Data from the Joint Program in Neonatology, Boston.

Pulmonary Problems

Local airway problems included those secondary to the respirator or endotracheal tube, e.g., laryngeal cysts, tracheal stenosis, hematomas on the vocal cords, and vocal cord damage resulting in hoarseness. Nine percent of the infants had persistent wheezing unassociated with respiratory infections. The majority of the infants with BPD had wheezing with acute respiratory infections. Bronchiolitis or pneumonia was seen in 30% of the infants, and 70% of those infants required hospitalization for their illness. The majority of infants with bronchiolitis had their disease secondary to RSV infection.

Central Nervous System

The neurologic outcomes for these infants did not differ significantly from those of infants of similar birth weight and gestational age who did not have BPD. The most common clinical presentation was a spastic diplegia, which is also the most common form of cerebral palsy seen in infants born prematurely. These motor manifestations of cerebral palsy usually occur secondary to an intraventricular hemorrhage with associated periventricular leukomalacia. Intraventricular hemorrhage is seen in about 40% of infants less than 1,500 grams birth weight. Hydrocephalus occurs in 25% of infants with intraventricular hemorrhage.

Growth and Nutrition

Growth delay is a significant problem in infants with BPD. Only 7% of infants with BPD had a weight or height measurement over the 50th percentile at 2 years of age. This is consistent with the growth data reported by Markestad and Fitzhardinge.[5] Part of this growth failure may be accounted for by increased caloric need. Weinstein and Oh[15] demonstrated that infants with BPD had a 25% higher resting oxygen consumption than control infants matched for birth weight and both gestational and chronologic age. Thus, these infants have both a greater energy expenditure and a need for a higher caloric intake. This is often difficult to provide since fluid restriction is often imposed because of the risk of cor pulmonale. Infants with BPD benefit from diuretic therapy with careful management of fluid and caloric intake. Nutritional counseling is an important component of management.

Methods for increasing caloric intake in the face of a fluid restriction include concentration of the formula to 24 to 34 calories per ounce, addition of caloric supplements such as medium-chain triglycerides or polycose to the formula, and the use of frequent small feedings. Feeding is a demanding exercise for these infants and may be compared to walking up a flight of stairs for an adult. Infants with BPD can become short of breath with feeding, and their intake can be compromised. Often, 1 to 2 ounces per feed is all the baby is able to take before becoming exhausted. In spite of the challenge in providing adequate nutrition, it is critical to solve the problem, because without adequate growth there is no lung growth, and without lung growth there can be no resolution of the chronic lung changes. As lung volumes increase with an increase in the infant's size, alveoli can grow both in number and in size. There is also an increase in airway diameter with increasing lung size. Growth of both airways and alveoli result in improved ventilation and improved gas exchange.

Pulmonary function

Few long-term pulmonary function studies have been reported for infants with BPD. Most studies report assessments done in the early years of life. Bryan and co-workers showed that infants who required ventilatory support had a lower arterial oxygen tension level than infants with RDS who did not require ventilator therapy; however, by 6 to 12 months of age, only those infants who developed BPD had residual abnormalities including increased functional residual capacity (FRC) and decreased dynamic compliance.[1] Stocks and Godfrey[11] reported that infants who required mechanical ventilation had increased airway resistance at 4 and 11 months of age when compared with infants treated with oxygen alone or with oxygen and continuous positive airway pressure. Lamarre et al.[4] found that when infants with BPD grew, these changes were no longer found. There is growing evidence, however, that ventilated infants who develop BPD do not recover completely. Smyth and co-workers[10] reported that 6 of 8 infants with severe BPD as neonates had bronchial hyperreactivity at a mean age of 8.4 years. Wheeler et al.[17] recently reported that FRC and maximum mid-expiratory flow rates were increased in a group of 7-to-9-year-old children with a history of BPD compared to other preterm or term infants. Thus, although the long-term pulmonary outcome for infants who required respiratory support is good, the subgroup of infants who develop chronic lung changes of BPD continue to show signs of ongoing pulmonary abnormalities associated with obstructive airway disease. Most of these children are functionally normal in spite of the pulmonary function test abnormalities, but further studies are required to follow them through into adulthood before the full impact of the disease process can be evaluated and understood.

PSYCHOSOCIAL PROBLEMS

Bronchopulmonary dysplasia places a tremendous strain on the infant's family. The physical effort of caring for the child is considerable. The infant is on home oxygen therapy and must be consistently monitored, is usually on several medications including diuretics (furosamide, aldactone, diuril), bronchodilators (theophylline, orseprenaline), and nutritional supplements (vitamins, iron, caloric supplements, and mineral supplements). The infant can be difficult to care for because of irritability secondary to hypoxia and poor feeding, and care can be frustrating because of his slow progress in growth and development.

Parents also experience tension and anxiety about long-term outcome, both pulmonary and neurologic. The time commitment for a single family member, often the mother, can result in disturbed family relationships between parents and among siblings. Therapy for infants with BPD requires close monitoring of the entire family unit.

Many services are available to help families with chronically ill children. Visiting nurse associations can provide at-home medical help, counseling, and support for the child's primary caretaker. Homemaking services should be provided where possible because family members may be forced to neglect housekeeping in order to meet the child's medical needs. Respite services are needed to give parents some free time to spend either alone or with other family members. Without such support systems some mothers cannot leave their infants for long periods of time.

Early Intervention Programs play an important role in following the developmental progress of these infants as well as in providing ongoing family support. Such programs can often provide physical therapy, developmental evaluation and infant stimulation, social service support, and organization of parent groups, and they should be routinely utilized for children with BPD.

PERSPECTIVES FOR THE FUTURE

The long-term outlook for infants with bronchopulmonary dysplasia has changed considerably as NICU management of low-birth-weight infants has improved. In the 1970s the mean birth weight of infants who developed BPD was 1,400 grams. Few infants of this birth weight develop BPD now. In the 1980s the disease is seen primarily in infants less than 1,000 gram birth weight. Significant changes in the management of respiratory distress syndrome will be seen in this decade. Several studies are already in progress to assess the effect of artificial surfactant in the treatment of RDS. If successful, this therapy would result in decreased exposure to oxygen and positive-pressure ventilation, which would have a major effect on the incidence of BPD. In addition, new methods of ventilatory support are being explored that would decrease the barotrauma associated with positive-pressure ventilation. In future years, therefore, this disease may all but disappear. For the time being, however, we must help the very tiny infants of this world pay the price of their survival.

REFERENCES

1. Bryan, M.H., Hardie, M.J., Reilly, B.J., and Swyer, P.R.: Pulmonary function studies during the first year of life in infants recovering from the respiratory distress syndrome. Pediatrics, *52*:169, 1973.
2. Edwards, D.K., Dyer, W.M., and Northway, W.H.: Twelve years' experience with bronchopulmonary dysplasia. Pediatrics, *59*:839, 1977.
3. Hack, M., et al.: Rehospitalization of the very-low-birth-weight infant. Am. J. Dis. Child., *135*:263, 1981.
4. Lamarre, A., et al.: Residual pulmonary abnormalities in survivors of idiopathic respiratory distress syndrome. Am. Rev. Resp. Dis., *108*:56, 1973.
5. Markestad, T., and Fitzhardinge, P.M.: Growth and development in children recovering from bronchopulmonary dysplasia. J. Pediatr., *98*:597, 1981.
6. Nickerson, B.G., and Taussig, L.M.: Family history of asthma in infants with bronchopulmonary dysplasia. Pediatrics, *65*:1140, 1980.
7. Pape, K.E., Buncie, R.T., Ashby, S., and Fitzhardinge, P.M.: Status at 2 years of low birthweight infants born in 1974 with birthweight of less than 1,001 gms. J. Pediatr., *92*:253, 1978.
8. Northway, W.H., Rosan, R.C., and Porter, D.Y.: Pulmonary disease following respirator therapy of hyaine membrane disease. N. Engl. J. Med., *276*:357, 1967.
9. Reynolds, E.O.R., and Taghizaded, A.: Improved prognosis of infants mechanically ventilated for hyaline membrane disease. Arch. Dis. Child., *49*:505, 1974.
10. Smyth, J.A., et al.: Pulmonary function and bronchial hyperactivity in long-term survivors of bronchopulmonary dysplasia. Pediatrics, *68*:336, 1981.
11. Stocks, J., and Godfrey, S.: The role of artificial ventilation, oxygen, and cpap in the pathogenesis of lung damage in neonates: Assessment by serial measurements of lung function. Pediatrics, *57*:352, 1976.
12. Taghizadeh, A., and Reynolds, E.O.R.: Pathogenesis of bronchopulmonary dysplasia following hyaline membrane disease. Am. J. Pathol., *82*:241, 1976.
13. Unger, M., Atkins, M., Briscoe, W.A., and King, T.K.C.: Potentiation of pulmonary vasoconstrictor response with repeated intermittent hypoxia. J. Appl. Phys., *43*:662, 1977.
14. Vohr, B.R., Bell, E.F., and Oh, W.: Infants with bronchopulmonary dysplasia: Growth pattern and neurologic and developmental outcome. Am. J. Dis. Child., *136*:443, 1982.
15. Weinstein, M.R., and Oh, W.: Oxygen consumption in infants with bronchopulmonary dysplasia. J. Pediatr., *99*:959, 1981.
16. Werthammer, J., Brown, E.R., Neff, R.K., and Taeusch, H.W.: Sudden infant death syndrome in infants with bronchopulmonary dysplasia. Pediatrics, *69*:301, 1982.
17. Wheeler, W.B., Castile, R.G., Brown, E.R., and Wohl, M.E.: Pulmonary function in survivors of prematurity. Am. Rev. Respir. Dis., *129*:218, 1984.

12

CARDIAC DISORDERS

David R. Fulton, M.D. □ *Samuel Z. Goldhaber, M.D.*

This chapter describes the role of the cardiologist caring for individuals with developmental disabilities. We hope to enable pediatricians, internists, and other health care professionals to make prompt and appropriate referrals so that these patients can gain maximal benefit from recent advances in cardiology.

Regardless of the presence of a developmental disability, most heart disease in children is congenital rather than acquired, whereas in adults, most heart disease is acquired rather than congenital. The frequency of congenital heart disease in the general population is estimated to be 8 per 1,000 live births; approximately half require early intervention. The specific lesions occur with predictable frequency[4,12] and have been well defined (Table 12-1).

ETIOLOGY

Congenital

In children with cardiac disorders, a specific single etiology for the cardiac derangements can be proven in only 10% of all cases, including chromosomal abnormalities in 5%, single mutant genes in 3%, and in 2%, a specific environmental agent to which the fetus was exposed. The remaining 90% of congenital heart disease represent disorders arising from a genetic-environmental interaction that is multifactorial.[17] Abnormal chromosomal states (Table 12-2) are responsible not only for cardiac defects but also other organ system involvement and therefore present as syndromes (see also Chap. 7). Trisomy 21, or Down syndrome is the most frequent chromosomal disorder. It occurs in 1.5 to 1.7 per 1,000 live births[4,18] and is associated with well described heart lesions, mental retardation, and other abnormalities of organogenesis (see also Chap. 2). Other developmental aberrations can occur from deletion, in which a chromosome breaks and causes loss of genetic material, or from translocation, in which a broken fragment of one chromosome is transferred to another chromosome. In asymptomatic infants with recognizable syndromes that coexist frequently with heart disease, careful early cardiac assessment is advisable. Single mutant genes, also responsible for heart disease and developmental disorders, are generally inherited in mendelian fashion as either autosomal dominant (Table 12-3), autosomal recessive (Table 12-4), or X-linked (Table 12-5).[16]

Cardiac teratogens fall into several categories including drugs, infections, and maternal illnesses, some of which are also responsible for damage to other organ systems (Table 12-6). However, primary environmental factors causing heart disease in the absence of a vulnerable genetic substrate are difficult to pinpoint. For example, congenital rubella often causes peripheral pulmonic stenosis, patent ductus arteriosus, or septal defects in addition to mental retardation. Other potential teratogens have been described, but current theory suggests that these environmental agents must interact with a pre-

Table 12-1. *Diagnostic Frequencies of Heart Disease in Infants*

Diagnosis	Infants		1969–1974, n = 2381; no./1000 Live Births	1975–1977, n = 1236; no./1000 Live Births
	No.	%		
Ventricular septal defect	374	(15.7)	0.345	0.462
d-Transposition of great arteries	236	(9.9)	0.218	0.206
Tetralogy of Fallot	212	(8.9)	0.196	0.258
Coarctation of aorta	179	(7.5)	0.165	0.233
Hypoplastic left heart syndrome	177	(7.4)	0.163	0.166
Patent ductus arteriosus	146	(6.1)	0.135	0.141
Endocardial cushion defect	119	(5.0)	0.110	0.137
Heterotaxias (dextro-, meso-, levo-, asplenia)	95	(4.0)	0.088	0.103
Pulmonary stenosis	79	(3.3)	0.073	0.074
Pulmonary atresia with intact ventricular septum	75	(3.1)	0.069	0.074
Atrial septal defect secundum	70	(2.9)	0.065	0.092
Total anomalous pulmonary venous return	63	(2.6)	0.058	0.056
Myocardial disease	61	(2.6)	0.056	0.045
Tricuspid atresia	61	(2.6)	0.056	0.058
Single ventricle	58	(2.4)	0.054	0.103
Aortic stenosis	45	(1.9)	0.041	0.040
Double-outlet right ventricle	35	(1.5)	0.032	0.034
Truncus arteriosus	33	(1.4)	0.030	0.043
l-Transposition of great arteries	16	(0.7)	0.015	0.022
Other heart disease	117	(4.9)	0.108	0.132
No significant heart disease	24	(1.0)	0.022	0.017
Primary pulmonary disease	106	(4.5)	0.097	0.274
Total	2381	(100)		

From Fyler, D.C., et al.: Report of the New England Regional Infant Cardiac Program. Pediatrics, 65(Suppl.):376, 1980. Reproduced by permission of Pediatrics.

disposed gene pool at a vulnerable time period for organogenesis to produce a cardiac malformation.[17]

Acquired

The leading cause of acquired heart disease in association with developmental disability is probably viral disease that produces both encephalitis (or meningoencephalitis) *and* concurrent myocarditis. Another cause of acquired neurologic and cardiac impairment is perinatal asphyxia. Generally the cardiac damage is transient and is manifested as mild to moderate congestive heart failure, often associated with tricuspid insufficiency. However, at times, the myocardial dysfunction from asphyxia can produce right-to-left shunting of blood at the atrial or ductal level, known as persistent fetal circulation.[5] The mortality associated with this abnormality may be higher than 40%, regardless of therapy. Those surviving may experience a residual cardiomyopathy, though clinically apparent cardiac disease is usually not manifested.

Cyanotic heart disease can also cause neurologic impairment. Children with cyanotic heart disease have been shown to be developmentally disabled, as evidenced by intelligence testing, motor skills, and perceptual tasks.[11,19] Recent evidence also indicates that the duration of hypoxemia prior to corrective surgical repair correlates directly with the degree of impairment of cognitive function.[14] Though the underlying cause for the disabilities in these children may be multifactorial, the findings argue for correction of cyanotic heart lesions as early as is practical. These children are susceptible to strokes due to cerebral hypoxia in the presence of anemia. They are also at risk for cerebral infarcts from paradoxical embolism or brain abscesses in the presence of right-to-left shunting. Cardiac catheterization and open heart surgery in the cyanotic child may add risk for neurologic damage due to venous thromboembolism[3] or air embolism.[1] Right-to-left shunting may also exist with pulmonary hypertension at systemic or suprasystemic pressures resulting from large left-to-right shunts (ventricular septal defects, patent ductus arteriosus, atrioventricular canal) that have not been surgically repaired in the first several years of life.

Table 12-2. *Congenital Heart Diseases in Selected Chromosomal Aberrations*

Population Studied	Frequency of CHD (%)	Most Common Lesions		
		1	2	3
General population	1	VSD	PDA	ASD
21 trisomy (Down syndrome)	50	VSD or AV canal	ASD	PDA
18 trisomy	99 +	VSD	PDA	PS
13 trisomy	90	VSD	PDA	Dex
22 trisomy	67	ASD complex	VSD	PDA
22 partial trisomy (cat-eye)	40	TAPVR	VSD	ASD
4p −	40	ASD	VSD	PDA
5p − (cri-du-chat)	20	VSD	PDA	ASD
8 trisomy (mosaic)	50	VSD	ASD	PDA
9 trisomy (mosaic)	50	VSD	COA	DORV
13q −	25	VSD		
+ 14q −	50	PDA	ASD	TOF
18q −	50	VSD		
XO (Turner syndrome)	35	COA	AS	ASD
XXXXY	14	PDA	ASD	ARCA
Fragile-X syndrome				

Abbreviations: ARCA, anomalous right coronary artery originating from pulmonary artery; ASD, atrial septal defect; VSD, ventricular septal defect; AV canal, atrioventricular canal; COA, coarctation of aorta; Dex, dextroversion (right-sided heart with situs solitus of abdominal viscera and atria); DORV, double-outlet right ventricle; PDA, patent ductus arteriosus; PS, pulmonic stenosis; TAPVR, total anomalous pulmonary venous return; TOF, tetralogy of Fallot; 4p −, deletion of short arm of a #4 chromosome; 5p −, deletion of a short arm of a #5 chromosome; 13q −, deletion of a long arm of a #13 chromosome; + 14q −, additional #14 chromosome with deletion of long arm; 18q −, deletion of long arm of a #18 chromosome.

From Nora, J.J., and Nora, A.H.: The evolution of specific genetic and environmental counseling in congenital heart diseases. Circulation, 57:205, 1978. By permission of the American Heart Association.

CLINICAL ASPECTS

Serious congenital heart disease in infancy generally presents as either cyanosis due to too little pulmonary blood flow or congestive heart failure due to excessive pulmonary blood flow. In newborns, cyanotic heart disease is suspected following delivery when supplemental oxygen (100% F_{IO_2}) fails to raise arterial Po_2 to at least 150 mm Hg. These infants may be tachypneic because of profound hypoxemia or metabolic acidosis. The second heart sound may be single (e.g., pulmonary atresia) or narrowly split (e.g., transposition of the great arteries). Murmurs are either absent or of the soft systolic ejection variety. A chest radiograph will show a normal-sized heart with decreased pulmonary blood flow (e.g., pulmonary atresia) or mild cardiac enlargement with increased pulmonary blood flow (e.g., *d*-transposition of the great arteries). The electrocardiogram will usually show predominant right ventricular forces, normal in newborns, but deviations in axis (e.g., tricuspid atresia) or left-sided forces (e.g., pulmonary atresia with intact ventricular septum) may provide clues to the diagnosis.

Infants with lesions producing congestive heart failure (CHF) often present clinically after leaving the nursery. The parents of an infant with CHF will describe persistent diaphoresis, tachypnea, prolonged feeding, decreased intake, or failure to gain weight. On examination, tachycardia and tachypnea are noted; wheezes or rales may be heard over the lung fields. The pulmonic component of the second heart sound may be accentuated in the presence of pulmonary artery hypertension. A harsh holosystolic murmur with a diastolic rumble is heard with moderate-sized ventricular septal defects, whereas a shorter, softer systolic ejection murmur without a diastolic component is present with large septal defects and pulmonary artery hypertension. Hepatomegaly may be present, but peripheral edema is a rare finding. The chest radiograph will show a large heart with increased pulmonary blood flow. Electrocardiographic changes will reflect the degree of left-sided overload (left ventricular hypertrophy) and pulmonary artery hypertension (right ventricular hypertrophy) if present.

In contrast to the infant with heart disease, who is usually symptomatic, the older child or adult with a developmental disability and heart disease will often be asymptomatic when a heart murmur is first discovered. Differentiation of innocent murmurs or venous hums (found in at least 50% of all children) from stenotic lesions of

Table 12-3. *Autosomal Dominant Heart Disease Associated with Neurologic Impairment*

Syndrome	Cardiac Involvement
Apert	VSD, TOF, COA
Multiple lentigenes (leopard)	PS
Neurofibromatosis	PS, pheochromocytoma
Noonan	PS, ASD, cardiomyopathy
Treacher-Collins	VSD, PDA, ASD
Tuberous sclerosis	Rhabdomyoma
Waardenburg	VSD
Williams	Supravalvar AS or PS, PPS

Abbreviations: PS, pulmonic stenosis; ASD, atrial septal defect; VSD, ventricular septal defect; PDA, patent ductus arteriosus; AS, aortic stenosis; COA, coarctation of aorta; TOF, tetralogy of Fallot; PPS, peripheral pulmonic stenosis.

Adapted from Nora, J.J., and Nora, A.H.: The evolution of specific genetic and environmental counseling in congenital heart diseases. Circulation, 57:205, 1978.

Table 12-4. *Autosomal Recessive Heart Disease Associated with Neurologic Impairment*

Syndrome	Cardiac Involvement
Carpenter	PDA, VSD, PS, D-TGA
Chondrodysplasia punctata	VSD, PDA
Ellis-van Creveld	ASD
Fanconi	ASD, PDA
Homocystinuria	AO + PA dilatation, thrombosis
Laurence-Moon-Biedel	VSD
Meckel	VSD, PDA, COA, PS
Mucolipidosis III	AS, AR
Mucopolysaccharidosis I-H, IV	AS, AR
Seckel	VSD, PDA
Smith-Lemli-Opitz	VSD, PDA
Zellweger	PDA, VSD

Abbreviations: PDA, patent ductus arteriosus; VSD, ventricular septal defect; PS, pulmonic stenosis; D-TGA, *d*-transposition of the great arteries; ASD, atrial septal defect; AS, aortic stenosis; AR, aortic regurgitation; AO, aorta; PA, pulmonary artery; COA, coarctation of aorta.

Adapted from Nora, J.J., and Nora, A.H.: The evolution of specific genetic and environmental counseling in congenital heart diseases. Circulation, 57:205, 1978.

the aortic or pulmonic valve, atrial septal defects, small ventricular septal defects, or patent ductus arteriosus is crucial. The pediatric or adult cardiologist may be alerted to a serious organic murmur in the presence of wide, fixed splitting or a diminished pulmonic component of the second heart sound, a mid-diastolic rumble at the left lower sternal border, variable or constant systolic ejection clicks, palpable thrills, or radiation of a systolic murmur into the neck or suprasternal notch. The absence of these signs, especially in the presence of a musical vibratory systolic ejection murmur at the left lower sternal border or at the base, suggests an innocent murmur for which diagnostic tests are not likely to be helpful.[5]

When an organic lesion is thought to be present, referral to a pediatric or adult cardiologist is appropriate. Cardiac signs necessitating further evaluation are as follows:

1. wide, fixed splitting of the second heart sound
2. accentuation of pulmonic component of the second heart sound
3. systolic clicks
4. systolic murmurs (grades III through VI)
5. radiation of systolic murmurs to neck or suprasternal notch
6. diastolic murmurs
7. continuous murmurs unaffected by position change

Prior to physical examination, we ask the parent, guardian, or attendant about the presence of decreased exercise tolerance, increasing fatigue, chest pain, palpitations, syncope, dizziness, and frequent pneumonias. The examination may often be best achieved with the patient seated in the lap of a parent or familiar person. Auscultation, the most critical part of the cardiac assessment, should take place first. The examiner can approach the developmentally disabled child or adult more easily if a chair is pulled slowly toward the patient, the physician remaining seated to avoid frightening the patient. Often the offer of an interesting, brightly colored object holds the patient's attention and permits completion of the examination.

Pediatric Clinical Aspects

For the younger child who begins to cry, a bottle or pacifier can be used. The stethoscope may be placed first on a doll or on the parent, guardian, or attendant. The stethoscope may then be positioned on the child's knee and gradually but strategically advanced to the precordium, where a standard examination of the cardiovascular system is performed as quickly and thoroughly as the child will allow. Frequently, only an abbreviated examination is possible, focusing on the second heart sound, left

Table 12-5. *X-Linked Recessive (R) and Dominant (D) Syndromes with Associated Cardiovascular Abnormalities*

Abnormality	Types (and Risk or Penetrance) of Cardiovascular Disease
Mucopolysaccharidosis type II (Hunter) X-R	Coronary artery disease, valvar disease (100%)
Muscular dystrophy (Duchenne and Dreifuss types) X-R	Myocardiopathy (67%)
Focal dermal hypoplasia X-D	Occasional congenital heart defects, telangiectasis (5–10%)
Incontinentia pigmenti X-D	Patent ductus arteriosus, primary pulmonary hypertension (low)
Fragile-X syndrome	Uncertain

Adapted from Nora, J.J., and Nora, A.H.: The evolution of specific genetic and environmental counseling in congenital heart diseases. Circulation, 57:205, 1978. By permission of the American Heart Association.

lower sternal border, and the upper sternal border bilaterally. The remainder of the physical examination is completed with particular attention to the character, strength, and timing of the pulses in all extremities. Recording upper and lower extremity blood pressures is deferred until the end of the examination but is essential in the child being examined for the first time to exclude coarctation of the aorta.

An electrocardiogram can be taken with the child seated in the lap of a familiar person. For the echocardiogram, required occasionally for more thorough investigation of a suspected lesion, the parent or friend may sit or lie next to the child on the examining table. Turning the lights down but not completely off may alleviate some anxiety. The procedure requires 30 to 45 minutes for an optimal study, so sedation may be imperative for some uncooperative patients. The choice in our laboratory is an appropriate dose of chloral hydrate given orally at least 1 hour prior to starting the study. No attempt should be made to approach the child for this time period to allow for maximal sedative effect.

Adult Clinical Aspects

Physicians who care for adults *without* developmental disabilities are used to following

Table 12-6. *Selection of Potential Cardiovascular (CV) Teratogens*

Potential Teratogens	Frequency of CV Disease (%)	Most Common Malformations
Drugs		
Alcohol	25–30	VSD, PDA, ASD
Amphetamines	5–10	VSD, PDA, ASD, TGA
Anticonvulsants		
Hydantoin	2–3	PS, AS, COA, PDA
Trimethadione	15–30	TGA, TOF, HLH
Lithium	10	Ebstein's anomaly, TA
Sex hormones	2–4	VSD, TGA, TOF
Thalidomide	5–10	TOF, VSD, ASD, TAC
Rubella infection	35	PPAS, PDA, VSD, ASD
Maternal conditions		
Diabetes	3–5	TGA, VSD, COA
	(30–50)	(Cardiomyopathy)
Lupus	Unknown	Heart block
Phenylketonuria	25–50	TOF, VSD, ASD

Abbreviations: VSD, ventricular septal defect; PDA, patent ductus arteriosus; ASD, atrial septal defect; TGA, transposition of the great arteries; PS, pulmonic stenosis; AS, aortic stenosis; COA, coarctation of aorta; TOF, tetralogy of Fallot; HLH, hypoplastic left heart; TA, tricuspid atresia; TAC, truncus arteriosus communis; PPAS, peripheral pulmonary artery stenosis.
Adapted from Nora, J.J., and Nora, A.H.: The evolution of specific genetic and environmental counseling in congenital heart diseases. Circulation, 57:205, 1978. By permission of the American Heart Association.

the conventional sequence of obtaining history, physical examination, and laboratory evaluation prior to formulating an assessment. For developmentally disabled adults with possible cardiac disease, the history may be unobtainable or unreliable. Therefore it is important to review the history with attendants, friends, parents, or guardians. Salient features include the development of chest pain,[9] dyspnea, syncope,[6] or cyanosis. Prior to the initial cardiologic evaluation, it is useful to have obtained a chest radiograph and electrocardiogram. The procedures we use to examine patients and to obtain laboratory tests on developmentally disabled adults are virtually identical to those just described for children.

Cardiac assessment of adults will be facilitated if the cardiologist has a working knowledge of cardiac disorders associated with Down syndrome and other developmental disabilities. Down syndrome patients may have atrial septal defects that need surgical repair or ventricular septal defects that simply require endocarditis prophylaxis prior to dental or surgical procedures. Preliminary observations suggest that asymptomatic patients with Down syndrome may also have two associated but generally unexpected valvular cardiac abnormalities: (1) mitral regurgitation due to mitral valve prolapse or (2) nonrheumatic aortic regurgitation.[10]

Cardiomyopathy is a frequent problem for which developmentally disabled adults are referred to the cardiologist. It is important to exclude surgically correctable causes of cardiomyopathy, such as valvular aortic stenosis. If surgical therapy is not warranted, medical therapy with preload and afterload reducers may be appropriate in addition to treatment with diuretics and possibly digitalis. Arrhythmias, often associated with cardiomyopathy, should be treated aggressively if associated symptoms such as lightheadedness or signs such as syncope persist after treatment of the underlying cardiomyopathy.[20]

When a drug regimen is prescribed, it is important to devise a plan in which the drugs are administered consistently and in which the patient is monitored for potential adverse effects (e.g., hypotension, exacerbation of arrhythmia, and rash). To achieve this goal, it may be prudent to initiate certain drugs such as quinidine, procainamide, captopril, or prazosin in an inpatient setting. For both inpatients and outpatients, judicious use of antiarrhythmic drug blood levels is helpful in optimizing the dosage.[8]

When prescribing cardiac and psychotropic drugs, it is worth remembering that cartain cardiac drugs can cause adverse psychotropic effects and, conversely, that certain psychotropic drugs can cause adverse cardiac effects. For example, propranolol, the prototype of the beta blockers, is useful in treating angina, hypertension, and some arrhythmias. However, side effects of propranolol include fatigue, lethargy, depression, and even nightmares. Conversely, tricyclic antidepressants (such as imipramine) may be effective in treating vegetative depression in developmentally disabled patients but may also cause adverse cardiac effects such as atrioventricular block, intraventricular conduction defects, and, most ominously, arrhythmias such as ventricular tachycardia.

INPATIENT MANAGEMENT

Pediatric Medical

The cyanotic infant should be transferred immediately to a tertiary medical center where two-dimensional echocardiography, cardiac catheterization, and cardiothoracic surgery are available. Prostaglandin E_1, a potent dilator of the ductus arteriosus, can be used to improve pulmonary perfusion in the infant with decreased pulmonary blood flow and metabolic acidosis.[2]

In general, medical management of heart disease in children with developmental disability does not differ from that of other children. The infant or child with congestive heart failure should be admitted to the hospital and started on digitalis (Table 12-7) and adjunctive therapy (Table 12-8). Initially, fluid restriction to daily maintenance requirements may prove helpful, but caloric needs for growth will eventually require liberalization of fluids and, therefore, possible upward adjustment of diuretic dosages. Supplementation of formula to 30 to 35 calories per ounce is beneficial in providing additional calories for a given volume of fluid.

Both the infant with CHF and cyanosis and the older child with hemodynamically significant cardiac disease by non-invasive evaluation will require cardiac catheterization to confirm the diagnosis and to determine appropriate surgical intervention. Advance preparation for both the parents and child is advisable when possible. Many institutions plan group meetings for parents and children in which the procedure and hospital protocol are discussed. A tour of the cardiac catheterization laboratory enables the child to visualize the imposing equipment. Often a cardiologist will describe the procedure in detail, demonstrate examples of cineangiograms, and provide a question-and-answer period. An

Table 12-7. *Dosages for Digitalization and Maintenance*

| | Digoxin (Lanoxin) | |
Age (weight)	Total Digitalizing Dose (IV)	Maintenance (oral)
Newborn–2 wk	25–40 g/kg	10–20 g/kg/day
2 wk–2 yr (13 kg)	40–60 g/kg	10–20 g/kg/day
2 yr–5 yr (13–18 kg)	25–40 g/kg	10–20 g/kg/day
5 yr–12 yr (18–36 kg)	25–35 g/kg	10–14 g/kg/day
12 yr (36 kg)	1.0–1.5 mg total dose	0.125–0.5 mg/day total dose

From Fulton, D.R., and Grodin, M.: Pediatric cardiac emergencies. Emerg. Med. Clin. N. Am., *1*:45, 1983. Philadelphia, W.B. Saunders.

additional approach utilizes puppet therapy to present the basics of the procedure. This interactive approach allows the child to act out feelings that may not be readily verbalized. Finally, a visit to the pediatric floor may be permissible in some hospitals and should be encouraged if possible. Though space limitations may prevent it, arranging for the parent to stay in the child's room and to participate in the clinical care often alleviates anxiety for the family.

Adult Medical

In general, medical inpatient management of heart disease in adults with developmental disability does not differ from that of other adults.

Table 12-8. *Adjunctive Therapy for Congestive Heart Failure*

Digoxin and diuretics	
Oxygen	30 to 40% mist
Cardiac chair	Upright positioning
Fluid restriction	50 to 90 ml/kg/day
Sedation	Morphine, 0.1 to 0.2 mg/kg every 4 to 6 hr
Treatment of precipitating conditions	Infection, fever, anemia, etc.
Correction of electrolyte abnormalities	
Ventilation	With positive end-expiratory pressure
Inotropic agents	Isoproterenol, 0.1 to 1.0 μg/kg/min; Dopamine, 2 to 4 μg/kg/min, may increase to 15 μg/kg/min
Afterload reduction	Sodium nitroprusside, 0.25 μg/kg/min starting dose; may be increased to therapeutic effect or 5 μg/kg/min

From Fulton, D.R., and Grodin, M.: Pediatric cardiac emergencies. Emerg. Med. Clin. N. Am., *1*:45, 1983. Philadelphia, W.B. Saunders.

The most frequent inpatient problems are coronary disease, valvular disease, and arrhythmias. Primary myocardial disease and congenital heart disease such as endocardial cushion defects are less common but by no means rare. We have found that when a developmentally disabled adult is hospitalized in a general hospital, a curious mix of compassion, fear, prejudice, and lack of understanding may exist among some members of the administrative, nursing, and medical staffs. While some feel comfortable caring for developmentally disabled patients, others are wary and fear physical and emotional outbursts. There are those who clearly resent the allocation of financial resources necessary to provide high-quality subspecialty care. Whereas some hospital staff members believe developmentally disabled adults should receive the same treatment as nondisabled patients, others believe that subjecting retarded patients to potentially uncomfortable diagnostic procedures such as cardiac catheterization demonstrates a lack of compassion. Medical and nursing staff may find it difficult to witness painful procedures "inflicted" on patients who are "helpless." They may wonder whether the intended procedure is absolutely necessary for the patient's well-being.[7]

These reactions to developmentally disabled adults are understandable because most medical and nursing schools provide little, if any, exposure to developmentally disabled patients. Furthermore, until recently, developmentally disabled adults were admitted to general hospitals much less frequently. While pediatricians are used to dealing with young patients who do not fully understand the events surrounding hospitalizations, medical staff members who care for adults may find this type of experience discomforting.[7]

Pediatric Surgical

Following catheterization, a decision regarding need for cardiac surgery is made. In cyanotic infants, procedures include palliative shunts between aortic and pulmonary arteries and primary repair of the defect to improve pulmonary blood flow, depending on the underlying anatomy. In acyanotic infants, surgical procedures include primary repair of a left-to-right shunt and, rarely, pulmonary artery banding to decrease pulmonary blood flow. Once surgery is decided on, preparation for the family should follow the same outline as that for cardiac catheterization, with pre-operative teaching and visits to the intensive care unit. Though the role of parents in the care of the child is limited in the early postoperative period, parents should be encouraged to participate actively in care after transfer from the intensive care unit.

Adult Surgical

We have learned that admitting developmentally disabled adults to our postsurgical cardiac intermediate care unit preoperatively can be very helpful. The primary care nurse provides preoperative care and patient teaching, and follows through by caring for the patient postoperatively. The first step in providing care is thorough assessment and documentation of the patient's functional patterns. Assessment of nutritional intake, bowel and bladder habits, usual daily activity, behavior modification techniques, self-care ability, cognitive skills, diversional activities, sensory modes, usual sleep and rest pattern, coping ability, and relationships with staff and others provides an overall profile of the individual. This information can lead to increased understanding and an individualized approach to care. Developing a rapport and a mutually trusting relationship with the patient can be facilitated if an institutional staff member or family member accompanies the patient throughout the hospitalization. The patient can be reassured by observing the staff or family member and nurse working together as a team to ease the burdens of hospitalization. Prior to the operation, we also acquaint patients with the nurses in the cardiac surgical intensive care unit. This helps both the patient and nurses feel more comfortable with each other.[7]

For preoperative teaching, we borrow techniques used in some pediatric hospitals. We use a doll as a means of explaining to the patient what will take place. The doll is made of plain cloth so that a face, heart, and sternum can be drawn on it. Intravenous tubing is used to simulate the endotracheal tube, various monitoring lines, chest tubes, and a Foley catheter. The primary nurse responsible for the preoperative teaching

can insert the various lines into the doll and tell the patient that he or she will have similar experiences. The nurse demonstrates listening to the doll's heart and lungs and administers chest physical therapy with percussion and vibration. The nurse places a bandage on the doll's chest and explains that the doll will be with the patient when he or she awakens in the intensive care unit. Teaching is repeated again on the preoperative evening and is reinforced by the surgeon, surgical resident, and chest physical therapist.[7]

Postoperatively, we have found that pain and sleep medications should be given on a routine schedule rather than as needed, because the patient may not request them. Periods of anxiety or anger are treated with mild sedation and/or behavior modification techniques. Diversional activities such as television, radio, coloring books, and toys are also useful strategies. Resumption of independence in self-care activities begins as soon as the patient is medically stable.[7]

OUTPATIENT MANAGEMENT

Pediatric

Continuing management of these patients on an outpatient basis requires ongoing input from the pediatric cardiologist, pediatrician, nurse practitioner, nutritionist, social worker, and specialists caring for problems relating to other organ system involvement. For children awaiting definitive repair or who have undergone palliative procedures, the primary goal is to optimize growth prior to the next planned procedure. Adequate growth is often achieved only after daily caloric intake reaches 150 kcal/kg. Some children can ingest the required volume of fluid, but others require caloric supplementation to maintain sufficient intake. A number of infants can ingest very limited amounts of fluid, and some cannot feed orally at all. Supplementation, therefore, may be required via nasogastric tube or by gastrostomy. Individuals specialized in infant feeding problems provide invaluable aid in training parents to teach oral feeding to these children. Despite adequate calories, it is well recognized that growth in cyanotic infants is slow relative to that of infants of the same birth weight without heart disease or other organ system involvement. Parents should be apprised of this fact to prevent discouragement. In addition, it is helpful to indicate to the parents that complete surgical repair will not guarantee "catch up" growth because other factors that are uninfluenced by successful surgical procedures can contribute to growth delay.

Other clinical parameters to which health care providers should be alerted are progression of cyanosis, decreasing intensity of shunt murmur, and anemia. An increase in cyanosis, often accompanied by a decrease in the continuous murmur of a shunt between aortic and pulmonary arteries, indicates insufficient pulmonary artery perfusion and signals the need for an additional surgical procedure. Relative anemia in a child with cyanotic heart disease (hematocrit less than 40% and low red cell indices) is an indication for red cell transfusion to minimize risk of a cerebral vascular accident. In contrast, polycythemia (hematocrit greater than 65%) indicates the need for a shunt or surgical repair in the child with cyanotic disease.

Older children and adults with heart disease are at risk for infectious complications. All patients with cyanotic disease, obstructive lesions of the left heart or aorta, prosthetic valves, carditis, or ventricular septal defects must receive bacterial endocarditis prophylaxis prior to dental work or septic surgical procedures. The case for this therapy in mitral valve prolapse is controversial. Prolonged fever, especially following dental manipulation, should prompt further evaluation for occult bacteremia. A child who develops fever, personality change, increasing lethargy, focal neurologic signs, or seizures requires intensive investigation for possible cerebral abscess in a facility with head CT scanning capability and neurosurgical back-up.

Proscription of strenuous exercise is generally not necessary except for the individual with aortic stenosis or hypertrophic cardiomyopathy. Infants and children almost always self-restrict when unable to continue with a given activity. A change in exercise tolerance in an individual with heart disease should prompt referral for cardiac evaluation.

Children who do not have corrective surgery for large left-to-right shunts will develop irreversible pulmonary artery hypertension (i.e., Eisenmenger syndrome) within several years, eventually leading to death from severe right heart failure in late adolescence or early adulthood. When the resistance in the pulmonary arterial bed exceeds that in the systemic arterial bed, right-to-left shunting occurs. The resulting progressive hypoxemia leads to polycythemia, which should be treated by phlebotomy when the hematocrit exceeds 65%. These individuals are at risk for the same complications as those with primary cyanotic heart disease and should be evaluated and treated in a similar fashion. Of additional importance to the clinician is the risk for these individuals when subjected to a surgical procedure requiring general anesthesia. If they are allowed to become hypovolemic or hypoxic, pulmonary vasoconstriction occurs with subsequent increased right-to-left shunting. The ensuing arterial hypoxemia leads to metabolic acidosis aggravating pulmonary vasoconstriction, producing an often fatal cycle. To minimize the likelihood of these events, these patients *must* be well hydrated and oxygenated.

Adult Outpatient

The Wrentham State School in Massachusetts provides an excellent model for comprehensive care of developmentally disabled adults. Cottage-style housing has replaced large dormitories. Some residents have obtained simple but meaningful jobs in sheltered environments. Community-based programs have encouraged deinstitutionalization and placement in foster homes whenever feasible.[13]

Medication regimens for chronic problems are reviewed at least on a monthly basis. The medication orders, labortory results, and problem lists are computerized for easier access to the medical data base. Furthermore, referral services to medical and surgical subspecialists are provided routinely several times per month, and emergency consultation is always available. For example, the Brigham and Women's Hospital sends consultant physicians to the cardiology clinic at Wrentham State School once every two weeks. Each year, the cardiology clinic processes approximately 200 patient visits. This clinic permits nurse practitioners, physician assistants, and staff physicians from Wrentham State School to discuss cardiology-related patient management problems directly with Brigham and Women's Hospital consultants (see also Chap. 26).

The physician, nurse practitioner, or physician's assistant who cares for developmentally disabled patients should not hesitate to refer a patient with a chromosomal disorder to a cardiologist for an initial evaluation. Other developmentally disabled patients with possible organic heart murmurs, cardiomyopathy, arrhythmia, or hypertension should also receive cardiologic assessment. In many instances echocardiography will be obtained, and if a potential surgically correctable lesion is found, the patient may undergo cardiac catheterization. We have discussed strategies that we as cardiologists use to care for developmentally disabled patients with cardiovascular problems. However, the astute primary care clinician's assessment of a particular patient's medical and psychosocial problems is of paramount importance in day-to-day clinical practice.

REFERENCES

1. Adler, D.S.: Nonthrombotic pulmonary embolism. *In* Pulmonary Embolism and Deep Venous Thrombosis. Edited by S.Z. Goldhaber. Philadelphia, W.B. Saunders, 1985, pp. 209-241.
2. Freed, M.D., et al.: Prostaglandin E in infants with ductus arteriosus-dependent cyanotic congenital heart disease. Circulation, *64:*899, 1981.
3. Fulton, D.: Venous thromboembolism in children. *In* Pulmonary Embolism and Deep Venous Thrombosis. Edited by S.Z. Goldhaber. Philadelphia, W.B. Saunders, 1985, pp. 243-257.
4. Fyler, D.C., et al.: Report of the New England Regional Infant Cardiac Program. Pediatrics, *65*(Suppl.): 375, 1980.
5. Gersony, W.M., Duc, G.V., and Sinclair, J.C.: "PFC" syndrome (persistence of the fetal circulation). Circulation, *40:*111, 1969.
6. Goldhaber, S.Z., and Benotti, J.R.: Syncope. *In* Emergency Medicine. Edited by H.L. May. New York, John Wiley, 1984, pp. 181-198.
7. Goldhaber, S.Z., Reardon, F.E., and Goulart, D.T.: Cardiac surgery for adults with severe mental retardation: Dilemmas in management. Am. J. Med., *79:*403, 1985.
8. Goldhaber, S.Z., and Smith, T.W.: Blood tests. *In* Diagnostic Methods in Clinical Cardiology. Edited by R.F. Cohn and J. Wynne. Boston, Little Brown, 1982, pp. 333-365.
9. Goldhaber, S.Z., and Wolf, M.A.: Chest pain. *In* Emergency Medicine. Edited by H.L. May. New York, John Wiley, 1984, pp. 111-127.
10. Goldhaber, S.J., et al.: Valvular heart disease (aortic regurgitation and mitral valve prolapse) among institutionalized adults with Down syndrome. Am. J. Cardiol., *57:*278, 1986.
11. Linde, L.M., Rasof, B., and Dunn, O.J.: Mental development in congenital heart disease. J. Pediatr., *71:*198, 1967.
12. Nadas, A.S., and Fyler, D.C.: Pediatric Cardiology. 3rd Ed. Philadelphia, W.B. Saunders, 1972, p. 294.
13. Nelson, R.P., and Crocker, A.C.: The medical care of mentally retarded persons in public residential facilities. N. Engl. J. Med., *299:*1039, 1978.
14. Newberger, J.W., Silbert, A.R., Buckley, L.P., and Fyler, D.C.: Cognitive function and age at repair of transposition of the great arteries in children. N. Engl. J. Med., *310:*1495, 1984.
15. Newburger, J.W., et al.: Noninvasive tests in the initial evaluation of heart murmurs in children. N. Engl. J. Med., *308:*61, 1983.
16. Nora, J.J.: Etiologic aspects of heart disease. *In* Heart Disease in Infants, Children and Adolescents. 3rd Ed. Edited by A.J. Moss, F.H. Adams, and G.C. Emmanouilides. Baltimore, Williams & Wilkins, 1983.
17. Nora, J.J.: Multifactorial inheritance hypothesis for the etiology of congenital heart diseases: The genetic environmental interaction. Circulation, *38:*604, 1968.
18. Penrose, L.S., and Smith, G.F.: Down's Anomaly. Boston, Little Brown, 1966.
19. Silbert, A., et al.: Cyanotic heart disease and psychological development. Pediatrics, *43:*192, 1969.
20. Wolf, M.A., and Goldhaber, S.Z.: Arrhythmias. *In* Emergency Medicine. Edited by H.L. May. New York, John Wiley, 1984, pp. 129-152.

13

OPHTHALMOLOGIC DISORDERS

Johan Zwaan, M.D.

Because vision is one of the major means for sensory interaction with our environment, a thorough knowledge of the visual potential of persons with mental retardation is an essential component in determining the level of rehabilitation that can be expected. Indeed, mental retardation may be partially due to sensory deprivation: instances are known in which blind children with normal intelligence were considered to be retarded. In those cases correction of the visual problem as far as possible and adoption of special methods, developed for the education of the visually handicapped, can increase functioning ability. The approach to rehabilitation may have to be modified depending on the visual acuity of the patient. Identification of visual problems has often been a stumbling block in development of successful rehabilitation programs. A telling example comes from an institution for the mentally handicapped in Pennsylvania. When an ophthalmologic screening program was first initiated, fewer than 4% of the 1,500 individuals in the institution were found to have visual problems. Ten years later, with experience gained by both staff and ophthalmologist, 20% of the same group of patients were recognized to have significant visual impairment.[7]

Severe visual disorders are much more prevalent among individuals with mental retardation than among the general population. Depending on the character of the group studied (average age, etiology of the mental retardation, etc.) and the types of disorders identified, percentages range from 12 to 52%.[1,3,5,9]

Therefore it should not come as much of a surprise that mental retardation is often associated with visual handicap. Indeed, the eye should really be considered an outpost of the brain, because there are embryologic and histologic reasons to consider the retina as part of the brain. Damaging influences can affect both organs. Second, a large part of the brain is involved with vision, including the processing of the visual impulse from retinal photoreceptor to occipital cortex, visual attention, recognition and memory, and control of eye movements. Almost 40% of the nerve fibers in the central nervous system pass within the optic chiasm, 70% of the brain may be involved with vision and ocular motility.[14] Thus there is a good chance that damage to the brain will involve some part of the visual system. Finally, it is known that inborn errors of metabolism have ocular as well as cerebral manifestations.[6,10]

ROLE OF THE OPHTHALMOLOGIST

In addition to the provision of routine eye care, the ophthalmologist can make significant contributions to the overall care of the patient with mental retardation. The importance of a visual evaluation within the framework of rehabilitation has already been mentioned. At times a careful eye examination can help in solving diagnostic puzzles, e.g., the recognition or exclusion of certain syndromes, thus making it possible to better predict prognosis and help with genetic counseling.

240

A precise description of eye findings helps delineate the extent of the abnormalities associated with certain syndromes. Because multiple possible etiologies are not uncommon, it may be difficult to sort out which physical sign goes with which etiologic factor. For example, a patient with a diagnosis of Seckel's dwarfism was found to have optic atrophy and cortical blindness. Since these conditions have not been described previously as part of the syndrome, it is likely that these findings are related to birth trauma rather than to a syndrome that may have genetic implications. Similarly, cataracts and corneal opacities have been reported to be part of the syndrome caused by phenylketonuria. A recent study showed that these abnormalities are not directly related to the metabolic aberrations in this disease.[15]

POPULATION STUDIED

The experiences reported in this chapter have been gained in part by the ophthalmological examination and management of individuals in an institution over a 6-year period. Due to the process of deinstitutionalization the number of persons diminished from around 1,100 to around 700 during this time period (see Chap. 26). Because most of the less-retarded individuals have been placed in the community, the remaining population is proportionally more handicapped, and this situation may affect the approach to eye care taken with this population, most of whom are adults. Etiologies for their handicaps are diverse. Roughly 15 to 20% of the patients have Down syndrome, and somewhat less than one-third have perinatal or postnatal causes for brain damage. The remainder consists of small numbers of patients with recognized syndromes (tuberous sclerosis, phenylketonuria, etc.) and a large number for whom definitive diagnoses have not been made.

Perhaps another 200 patients have been seen in an outpatient clinic setting. These are primarily children living at home, and some adults living in a community setting.

EYE EXAMINATION

The eye examination of persons with mental retardation is in principle not very different from that used routinely. It may be necessary, however, to modify techniques or to forgo part of the examination.

Visual Acuity

The quality of the vision is the most important information to be gained from the eye examination. Therefore the examination generally begins with an attempt to assess visual acuity. Both subjective and objective methods are valuable, and the choice of method obviously depends on the capabilities of the patient. Ideally, a quantitative measure should be obtained, but this is not always possible. If the patient does not respond at all to standard tests, his behavior may at least allow a determination of the adequacy of vision for daily needs. In this case the impressions of personnel or family in frequent contact with the patient become very important. In particular, deterioration in behavior requiring adequate vision may be the clue that an eye problem exists.

If the patient can respond verbally or by appropriate gestures, a subjective measure of visual acuity can be obtained. Standard Snellen charts can be used only occasionally, and more success is usually met by the use of letter comparison tests, such as the STYCAR test (Screening Test for Young Children and Retardates). In this test letters are shown on a chart placed 20 feet from the patient. The letters then have to be matched with the same letters on flash cards available to the patient. Allen cards show figures, such as a car or a birthday cake, which are calibrated for distance. Thus, if the cards are identified accurately at a distance of 20 feet, the vision is 20/30. In the "E-game," the orientation of various sizes of the letter E has to be indicated with a model E or by pointing with a hand. Sometimes finger-counting at various distances can be used. All these tests have the disadvantage that they use single optotypes, which in cases of amblyopia can lead to an over-estimation of acuity.

Vision should always be measured separately for each eye. If use of an occluder is not feasible, one eye may have to be patched to measure monocular visual acuity. One should be careful to avoid cheating, such as peeking around the occluder. Because the attention span of some patients is short, testing procedures should be brief. Finally, many children and adults with mental retardation find it difficult to concentrate at the normal distance for acuity testing, i.e., 20 feet. More effective testing may then be done at a closer distance, for instance, 10 feet. Testing at a closer distance gives an acceptable measure of visual acuity, except that patients with myopia or astigmatism may see better than they would at 20 feet. The difference in acuity scores is not a major drawback, because these problems can be detected by other means.

If subjective tests are impossible, objective methods may be resorted to. Visual fixation and following of a small object or a penlight and pupillary responses are useful indicators. More quantitative methods are also available. Induction of optokinetic nystagmus (OKN), by passing a pattern of alternating black and white stripes in front of the eyes, can be semiquantitated by adjusting the width of the stripes.[2] One drawback to the use of this method is that the absence of an OKN response may be due to oculomotor problems rather than to a sensory deficit. Moreover, there is some evidence that the OKN response takes place at a subcortical level.[12]

Visually evoked potentials have been used to estimate visual acuity, but the results must be interpreted with caution. A normal VEP can apparently occur even in the absence of functioning visual cortex, area 17. The reverse is also true, particularly for young infants. A negative result does not necessarily preclude the presence, or delayed development, of visual function.[4]

A behavioral test that has been useful in some patients is the forced-choice preferential looking technique.[11] This method is based on the finding that infants prefer to fixate on a pattern rather than on a homogeneous field. The subject is presented with a choice between two stimuli of equal luminance, a screen with a grating of black and white stripes and another screen that is gray. An observer who is not aware of the location of the pattern determines whether the subject fixates on the left or the right screen. Acuity is estimated by determining the smallest stripe width, which is differentially fixated relative to the blank field. A variation, which tests for stereopsis, is also available.[8] The test was originally developed for the determination of visual acuity in preverbal infants, but it has some applicability for the testing of patients with limited abilities. It has some disadvantages in that it is labor-intensive and time-consuming and requires a certain amount of cooperation by the patient.

Refraction

A subjective determination of the refractive state is extremely difficult. One generally has to rely on the use of an objective method such as retinoscopy. This technique gives very accurate results as long as the patient is able to fixate on the light of the instrument. It is most easily done after the use of cycloplegics to dilate the pupil and to neutralize accommodation. Occasionally a patient does not cooperate, and the procedure may have to be done under anesthesia. This is only justified if a more extensive eye examination under anesthesia is required.

The method is relatively simple. One observes the way in which a beam of light entering the eye and reflecting from the retina is being refracted. Lenses can be introduced in the path of the light beam to neutralize the refractive error of the eye being examined.

Visual Field Testing

Formal determination of the visual field is almost never possible in patients with mental retardation, although at times a reasonably reliable confrontation field can be obtained to demonstrate significant deficits, such as hemianopia.

Anatomic Examination

Careful evaluation of both the anterior segment and the fundus of the eye is essential. Patients can experience this examination as quite threatening, and methods have to be adapted to take this into account. A good slit-lamp examination is frequently not well tolerated, but one can also obtain much information by use of the ophthalmoscope (with a +5.00 or +6.00 lens for magnification), either with direct illumination (Fig. 13-1) or with retroillumination (Fig. 13-2). The latter will clearly demonstrate any opacities in the media as dark areas against the red reflection of light from the retina. It is helpful to dilate the pupils for fundus examination with the direct ophthalmoscope, but dilation is essential if the indirect ophthalmoscope is used. Even with poor fixation by the patient, this instrument usually allows the study of most of the fundus because of its wide field. A disadvantage is the low degree of magnification compared to the direct ophthalmoscope, and fine details may be overlooked. It is often difficult to measure intraocular pressure by Schiotz or applanation tonometry, and one may have to be content with a rough estimate based on palpation.

External Aspects

Abnormalities of the orbits, the eyelids, and the size of the eye are associated with several syndromes in which mental retardation occurs. The orbits are very shallow in Apert's syndrome and may be asymmetric in neurofibromatosis. Epicanthal lid folds and a slant of the lid fissure are typical, although not pathognomonic, for Down syndrome. Abnormalities of the skin of the eyelids and the surrounding skin are seen in various phakomatoses, e.g., hemangioma in Sturge-Weber syndrome, neurofibromas or plexiform neuromas in neurofibromatosis,

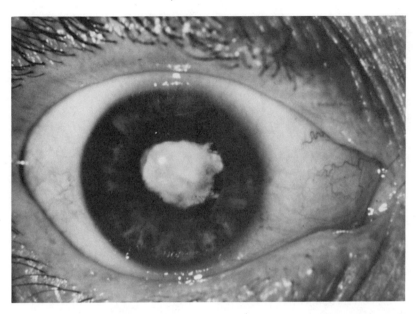

FIG. 13-1. Partially calcified cataract in a patient with trisomy 21. The abnormality is obvious enough to be seen with the naked eye, but details can be appreciated better by use of an ophthalmoscope or, ideally, a slit lamp.

and adenoma sebaceum in tuberous sclerosis. Microphthalmia can be seen in congenital rubella syndrome, fetal alcohol syndrome, and to a severe degree in trisomy 13. An autosomal recessive syndrome has been reported in which hydrocephalus and mental retardation are combined with microphthalmia.[13]

Although dysmorphic findings are helpful diagnostically, the help of the ophthalmologist is more commonly sought for the diagnosis and treatment of routine disorders. Conjunctivitis and blepharitis occur frequently; their treatment is not any different for the mentally retarded patient, and consultation by an ophthalmologist is not essential. If, however, symptoms persist for more than a few days, the possibility of other diagnoses may need to be entertained. Patients diagnosed as having conjunctivitis may in actuality have iritis, keratitis secondary to entropion and rubbing of the cornea by the eyelashes, exposure keratitis due to ectropion (Fig. 13-3), or lens-induced glaucoma.

Some abnormalities may be associated with the use of medications. Allergic reactions to topical eye medications have been described. Several patients in our study population have shown a symptom complex of moderate photophobia, injection of the conjunctiva, and, on slit lamp examination, small granular deposits in the cornea. These findings may be related to the use of phenothiazines.

Ocular Motility

Disorders of ocular motility, such as strabismus and nystagmus, are frequently seen in this population. Congenital motor nystagmus is compatible with good vision, but in sensory nystagmus the vision is usually reduced. Optic atrophy, albinism, and significant congenital cataracts are among the causes of sensory nystagmus. Indeed, any significant reduction of vision early in life can lead to nystagmus.

Strabismus is extremely common, particularly in patients with Down syndrome and cerebral palsy; as many as one-third to one-half of patients with cerebral palsy show misalignment of the eyes.[1,5] Generally the misalignment is not due to any anatomic abnormality of the muscles or to motor nerve paralysis, and one must assume that the control mechanisms are at fault. The most important consideration in strabismus is that it can generate amblyopia. This is, of course, only the case as long as the visual system is still immature. The age at which the visual cortex becomes stabilized varies for different individuals, but it probably occurs between the ages of 7 and 10. If the strabismus ,has not been discovered until later, or if treatment has not been possible, amblyopia treatment is no longer feasible. If strabismus is acquired at a later age, for instance by paralysis of the innervation of the extraocular muscles or by a blow-out fracture of the orbital

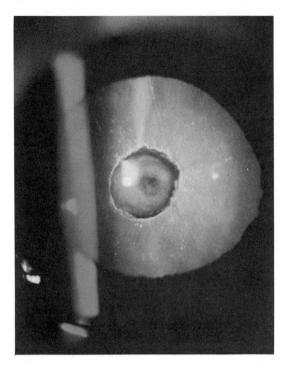

FIG. 13-2. Congenital cataract, seen by retro-illumination as a dark spot against the red background of light reflecting from the fundus.

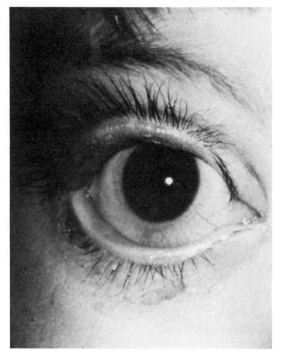

FIG. 13-3. Ectropion (turning out of the eyelids), common in trisomy 21, which can lead to exposure keratitis and keratinization and thickening of the lid margins. The conjunctiva becomes irritated and injected, leading to an erroneous diagnosis of conjunctivitis.

floor (Fig. 13-4), one must assume that diplopia accompanies the nonalignment of the eyes even if the patient is unable to express the problem.

Examination for abnormalities of motility requires a modicum of cooperation, but even in the uncooperative patient it is usually possible to determine if the eyes are properly aligned. The corneal light reflex test is very useful. A small penlight shining on the eyes should be reflected in the center of both pupils if the eyes are aligned in that particular position. If a strabismic deviation exists, the fixing eye will still show the reflection of the light in the pupil, but the deviating one will show the reflection away from the pupil, medially if the eye is exotropic and laterally if an esotropia exists.

Cornea

Acquired corneal problems, such as herpes simplex keratitis, corneal abrasions secondary to trauma, and keratitis sicca, are seen among individuals with retardation with at least the same frequency as in the general population. Some problems, however, definitely have a much higher frequency. Keratoconus is a thinning of the cornea, usually in its central or inferotemporal area, which leads to bulging out of the tissue. In more

advanced stages breaks may develop in Descemet's membrane, leading to accumulation of fluid in the corneal stroma and significant scarring (Fig. 13-5). The astigmatism accompanying the distortion of the cornea and the scarring can lead to significant loss of vision. It is well accepted that keratoconus is frequently found among patients with Down syndrome, but we have come to recognize that the abnormality is seen with almost equal frequency among other retarded patients (J. Zwaan, A.E. Sierra, and H.L. May, unpublished data). The cause of the abnormality is unknown. In more advanced cases the only treatment available is a corneal transplant. This is only justified for patients who are cooperative enough to tolerate frequent and detailed eye examinations and frequent application of topical eye medications.

Another problem rather commonly encountered consists of scarring and vascularization of the cornea secondary to eyelid problems. For instance, if the eyelids turn in and the lashes rub chronically against the cornea, chronic keratitis is the result. Exposure keratitis due to ectropion and "dry eye" can also cause permanent corneal

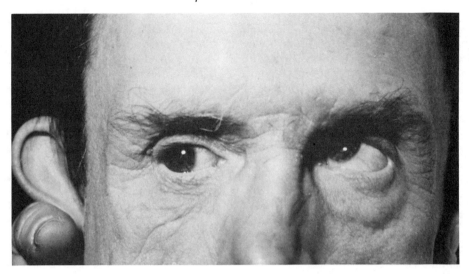

FIG. 13-4. Left esotropia and hypertropia. This patient may have congenital esotropia, but interpretation is complicated by presence of a blow-out fracture of the floor of the right orbit.

damage. Surgery to reposition the eyelids and frequent application of tear substitutes may quiet down the keratitis, but if the condition has existed for a while the secondary corneal changes are usually permanent.

The keratitis secondary to the use of certain medications has already been discussed.

Cloudiness of the cornea is typical of a number of inherited metabolic diseases associated with mental retardation. Typical examples are some of the mucopolysaccharidoses and mucolipidoses. Clouding of the cornea can also occur as a consequence of glaucoma, particularly when the rise in intraocular pressure is acute.

Iris

Various types of mental retardation may be associated with abnormalities of the iris. Brush-

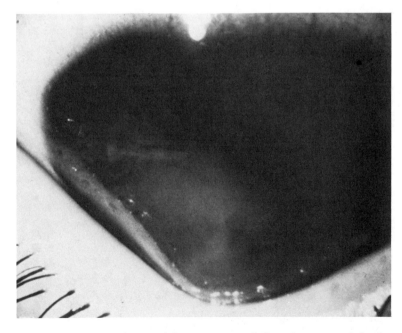

FIG. 13-5. Extensive keratoconus with corneal thinning, particularly at the apex, and cloudiness due to edema and scarring. The patient has severe visual loss.

field spots are well known and are often seen in patients with Down syndrome, although they may also be seen in others. These are small white or tan dots arranged in a circle around the midperiphery of the iris. They are much more common in blue than in brown eyes. Histologically the dots consist of normal iris stroma that stand out because they are surrounded by atrophic areas. Over 90% of adult patients with neurofibromatosis show Lisch nodules of the iris, round nevus-like accumulation of melanocytes. Neither of these two abnormalities causes any problems.

If the iris does not dilate after the use of mydriatics or if adhesions between iris and lens are seen, iritis may be present; iritis is otherwise difficult to diagnose if the patient refuses a slit-lamp examination.

Lens

Clouding of the lens, or cataract, occurs in a number of mental retardation syndromes. Probably the best known example is the maternal rubella syndrome. Galactosemia and Lowe's syndrome are also associated with cataracts. Congenital cataracts are no more frequent in Down syndrome than in the general population, contrary to what is usually thought. It is true, however, that these patients may develop cataracts at a relatively early age. Typically, the lens shows fairly coarse snowflake-like opacities throughout its cortex, often combined with more dense opacities in the visual axis (Fig. 13-6). The lens can also become cataractous from self-abuse such as head-banging and other blunt trauma.

Dislocation of the lens is typical of homocystinuria and sulfite oxidase deficiency. The lens, usually cataractous, may move entirely free in the vitreous cavity. If the lens is displaced into the anterior chamber, glaucoma and corneal decompensation can be the result. An attempt should be made to avoid this complication by chronically constricting the pupils with appropriate medication.

Optic Nerve

Developmentally handicapped patients often show abnormalities of the optic nerve. Optic atrophy, in which the disk has a pale appearance, occurs in a variety of pediatric neurologic disorders, e.g., adreno- and metachromatic leukodystrophy, cranial synostoses, hydrocephalus, porencephaly, and other brain anomalies. In patients with cerebral palsy a partial optic atrophy is often seen, mostly on the temporal side of the disk.

Elevated intracranial pressure, if not recognized and not relieved, can cause papilledema, which in turn can lead to optic atrophy and significant visual loss.

Optic nerve hypoplasia often gives poor vision; the disk appears smaller than normal and is abnormally pigmented. A "bull's eye" appear-

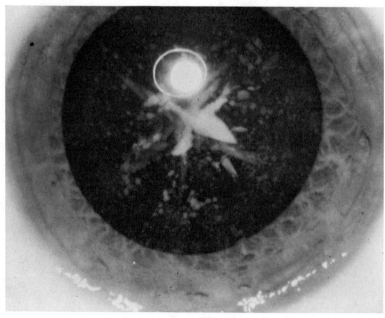

FIG. 13-6. Cataract, typical for trisomy 21, with central opacities in combination with snowflake-like densities in the peripheral cortex.

ance is common. The anomaly may occur by itself, or it may be associated with severe brain malformations such as anencephaly and cerebral midline defects. In tuberous sclerosis a typical finding is a yellowish mulberry-shaped mass emanating from the disk (Fig. 13-7). This is a glial hamartoma. Although it is highly specific for tuberous sclerosis, it is seen only in a small proportion of the patients with this phakomatosis.

If the intraocular pressure cannot be measured, the appearance of the disk is an important consideration in the determination of the possible presence of glaucoma. The cup/disk ratio, localized excavation of the disk toward the rim in any area, and the overall status of the rim of the optic cup should always be noted.

Retina

A number of intrauterine infections can cause both mental retardation and retinal abnormalities. Toxoplasmosis can give severe and destructive inflammation in the retina with secondary involvement of the choroid. When the inflammation eventually subsides, atrophic chorioretinal scars are left behind, in association with significant pigment clumping. However, viable parasites persist, and flare-ups are common. Visual loss is due not only to the retinal damage, but also to damage to the visual pathways by meningoencephalitis. Congenital anomalies such as microphthalmos may be present. Congenital

cytomegalovirus disease can also affect the retina, leaving chorioretinal scars mostly in the periphery and the central nervous system, resulting in damage to the posterior visual pathways. Congenital rubella syndrome includes a retinopathy giving a salt-and-pepper appearance to the fundus (Fig. 13-8). The effect on visual function fortunately is not severe, and the electroretinogram is relatively normal. Significant visual loss may still be present due to glaucoma, cataracts, optic nerve fiber damage, or as a result of the encephalitis. Herpes simplex infection, usually type II, can be acquired during birth and can lead to severe retinitis as well as encephalitis.

Prematurity, which puts a child at risk for central nervous system damage, is also associated with retrolental fibroplasia or retinopathy of prematurity (see Chap. 5). Although the use of oxygen is generally blamed for the occurrence of this problem, several cases have now been reported in which no supplemental oxygen had been given. Thus the precise mechanism leading to the retinopathy is unknown. Obliteration of immature retinal capillaries with consequent retinal hypoxia leads to a proliferation of neovascular tissue. This regresses in most patients, but may be progressive, in which case the vasoproliferative phase is followed by a cicatricial phase. The result can range from induction of high myopia, presence of vitreous membranes, and dragging of the retina, all the way to total retinal detachment.

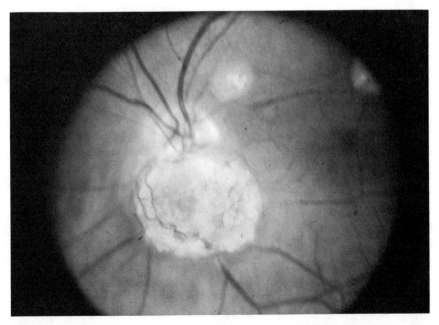

FIG. 13-7.   Mulberry-shaped astrocytoma of the optic disk in tuberous sclerosis. Glial hamartomas are also visible in the retina.

Many inherited metabolic diseases are deleterious for both brain and retina. Retinitis pigmentosa with classical "bone spicules" or with a salt-and-pepper appearance of the retina is present in the Laurence-Moon-Biedl syndrome, in Hallervorden-Spatz disease, and in several of the mucopolysaccharidoses. It can also be seen in mucolipidosis type IV. In advanced cases, optic atrophy and attenuation of the retinal blood vessels are also found. In storage diseases such as Tay-Sachs and Sandhoff disease, the macula typically presents as a cherry-red spot at the time that other signs of the disease such as psychomotor retardation became apparent. It may be seen in generalized gangliosidosis and sometimes in metachromatic leukodystrophy.

In addition to the disk abnormality already mentioned in tuberous sclerosis, more commonly flat whitish glial hamartomas of the retina can be found; these are occasionally found in neurofibromatosis as well. The fundus abnormality in the Sturge-Weber syndrome is a hemangioma of the choroid. In the Aicardi syndrome, peculiar chorioretinal lacunar lesions are combined with absence of the corpus callosum, flexion spasms, and severe retardation.

SPECIAL EXAMINATIONS

At times the information obtainable from the standard eye examination is not adequate for diagnosis or treatment and special examinations need to be employed. Electrophysiological tests such as visual evoked response and electroretinography have been mentioned. Other examples follow.

Conjunctival Biopsy

Biopsy of the conjunctiva is a simple method to allow a tissue diagnosis of metabolic disease, in particular storage diseases such as the mucopolysaccharidoses. After application of topical anesthetic drops a small fragment of the conjunctiva, usually near the superior limbus, is lifted up with fine forceps and snipped off with scissors. The tissue is fixed and processed for electron microscopy and/or histochemistry, including immunochemical methods. Antibiotic drops or ointment is applied to the eye a few times daily until the biopsy site is healed, which takes one to two days. Other than a mild foreign-body sensation there is usually no morbidity. The method can be quite informative, e.g., elucidating the diagnosis of mucolipidosis type IV in two brothers with severe psychomotor retardation, mild corneal clouding, and optic atrophy.[16]

Examination Under Anesthesia

Occasionally a patient is so uncooperative that an adequate eye examination is impossible even after sedation. If any serious eye pathology is suspected, there should be no hesitation to carry out an examination under anesthesia. For a routine examination, however, this approach appears not to be justified. The choice of anesthetic

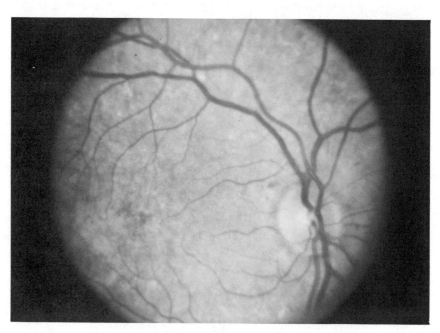

FIG. 13-8.   Salt-and-pepper retinopathy seen in rubella. The macula is also affected.

agent(s) to be used is of course the responsibility of the anesthesiologist, but there should be input from the ophthalmologist because of possible effects of the medication on the eye. Ketamine, for instance, can cause a rise in intraocular pressure, which could make it more difficult to determine whether a patient had glaucoma.

Ultrasonography

The use of ultrasound for diagnosis of orbital problems has to a large extent been superseded by computerized axial tomography. Ultrasonography remains a very useful tool, however, for the diagnosis of certain intraocular problems in the presence of cataracts or other conditions of the media that prevent a view of the retina. Ultrasound allows one to determine whether a retinal detachment or a vitreous hemorrhage is complicating the presence of a cataract. Such a finding has obvious implications for decisions concerning cataract removal.

TREATMENT

Treatment of eye disorders in the developmentally disabled should be guided by the same principles that hold for the general population. Surgical intervention, in particular, requires careful balancing of the expected benefits against the possible risks. Informed consent should always be obtained, if not from the patient, then from parents or legal guardian.

Refractive Errors

Whether refractive error should be corrected by the prescription of glasses depends on the individual patient. A moderate refractive error, such as myopia or astigmatism, often does not interfere at all with a patient's daily activities. Wearing of glasses is then not rewarding to the patient, and the glasses become "lost" or broken. Even patients whose cataracts have been removed often do astonishingly well without correction. Patients who are in their late thirties or forties and who are engaged in close-up work may require reading glasses. Again, the decision should be individualized, and personnel closely involved with the patient should be consulted.

Strabismus

In dealing with a young patient with strabismus, the main concern of treatment should be the prevention of amblyopia. Prescription of glasses, patching, and surgery all have their place in the treatment, and the fact that a child is retarded should be taken into consideration only to the extent that it may bear on the diagnostic or therapeutic considerations. For instance, in cerebral palsy strabismic deviations are common.[1] Both the amount and the direction of the eye turn can be quite variable in this situation, and the surgical decision-making should be very conservative.

Surgery for misalignment of the eyes in adult mentally retarded patients is usually not justified. No visual benefit can be expected from the surgery, and the risks are not negligible. There are some exceptions to this. If the strabismus is acquired at a later age and appears to be causing diplopia, surgery to relieve the latter is indicated. Another good reason for strabismus surgery is the awareness of the patient of the appearance of the deviated eye and of the reaction of others to the strabismus.

Cataract

For a number of reasons cataract removal should also be approached conservatively. The surgical aftercare of patients with mental retardation is more difficult, and the chances for infection or traumatic injury are increased. In addition, cataracts have to be rather advanced before they decrease the vision so much that the daily activities of a patient become inhibited. Again, the input of persons dealing daily with the patient can be very helpful. The principles of the surgical techniques to be used are the same as for the average patient. In younger patients vitrectomy instruments are very helpful. They allow removal of the cataract through a very small opening into the eye, thus decreasing postoperative risks. They also enable one to deal with some complications not infrequently encountered such as adhesions between iris and lens or presence of the vitreous in the anterior segment.

Whether cataract removal should be followed by implantation of an intraocular lens is debatable. The advantage of a more natural optical correction of the aphakia is outweighed by the difficulty in postoperative follow-up. Many patients are difficult to examine by slit lamp, and eye medications are often difficult to apply. These problems increase the risks of the surgery.

ACKNOWLEDGMENTS

Some of the research described in this chapter was supported by Grant No. EY-03158 of the National Eye Institute. I am grateful to Dr. Richard Robb and Dr. Harold May for their encouragement and to Ms. Shirley Richards for her capable assistance in the Eye Clinic at the Wrentham State School.

REFERENCES

1. Black, P.: Visual disorders associated with cerebral palsy. Br. J. Ophthalmol., *66:*46, 1982.
2. Dayton, G.O., et al.: Developmental study of coordinated eye movements in the human infant. 1. Visual acuity in the newborn human: A study based on induced optokinetic nystagmus and electro-oculography. Arch. Ophthalmol., *71:*865, 1964.
3. Hagberg, G.: Severe mental retardation in Swedish children born 1959-1970: Epidemiological panorama and causation factors. *In* Major Mental Handicap: Methods and Costs of Prevention. Edited by K. Elliot and M. O'Connor. Ciba Foundation Symposium 59. Amsterdam, Elsevier, 1978, pp. 29-51.
4. Hoyt, C.S.: The clinical usefulness of the visual evoked response. J. Pediatr. Ophthalmol Strabismus, *21:*231, 1984.
5. Jaeger, E.A.: Ocular findings in Down's syndrome. Trans. Am. Ophthalmol. Soc., *78:*808, 1980.
6. Kenyon, K.R.: Lysosomal disorders affecting the ocular anterior segment. *In* Ocular Pathology Update. Edited by D.H. Nicholson. New York, Masson, 1980, pp. 1-21.
7. Lester, R.L.: The visually handicapped child. *In* Pediatric Ophthalmology. 2nd Ed. Edited by R.D. Harley. Philadelphia, W.B. Saunders, 1983, pp. 1319-1348.
8. Mohindra, I., et al.: Stereopsis in infantile esotropia. Ophthalmology, *92:*691, 1985.
9. Nelson, R.P., and Crocker, A.C.: The medical care of mentally retarded persons in public residential facilities. N. Engl. J. Med., *299:*1039, 1978.
10. Spaeth, G.L., and Auerbach, V.H.: Inborn errors of metabolism affecting the eye. *In* Pediatric Ophthalmology. 2nd Ed. Edited by R.D. Harley. Philadelphia, W.B. Saunders, 1983, pp. 1053-1143.
11. Teller, D.Y., et al.: Visual acuity for vertical and diagonal gratings in human infants. Vision Res., *14:*1433, 1974.
12. Wanger, P., and Tersson, H.E.: Visual evoked responses to pattern-reversal stimulation in childhood amblyopia. Acta. Ophthalmol., *58:*697, 1980.
13. Warburg, M.: Hydrocephaly, congenital retinal nonattachment, and congenital falciform fold. Am. J. Ophthalmol., *85:*88, 1978.
14. Wolintz, A.H.: Essentials of clinical neuro-ophthalmology. Boston, Little Brown, 1976, p. 3.
15. Zwaan, J.: Eye findings in phenylketonuria. Arch. Ophthalmol., *101:*1236, 1983.
16. Zwaan, J., and Kenyon, K.R.: Two brothers with presumed mucolipidosis IV. *In* Genetic Eye Diseases: Retinitis Pigmentosa and Other Inherited Eye Disorders. Edited by E. Cotlier, I.H. Maumenee, and E.R. Berman. New York, Liss, 1982, pp. 381-390.

14

OUTPATIENT OTOLARYNGOLOGIC CARE

Howard G. Smith, M.D. □ *Ellen M. Friedman, M.D., F.A.A.P., F.A.C.F.* □ *Shirley A. Roy, R.N.*

Providing otolaryngologic treatment for developmentally disabled individuals of all ages requires creativity and flexibility in the application of standard examination and treatment techniques. An examiner sensitive to the emotional and intellectual development of the patient will not only provide excellent medical care but will also contribute to the patient's trust of and appreciation for other health care providers.

In this chapter, we detail our experience with the otolaryngologic treatment of developmentally disabled individuals in clinics operated at Children's Hospital, Boston, and at residential schools operated by the Commonwealth of Massachusetts. We review examination techniques and specific management of common disorders that should be useful to otolaryngologists and primary care physicians treating this group of patients in a variety of clinical settings.

PATIENT POPULATION

The information in this chapter is based primarily on experience with a population of developmentally disabled persons residing at two Commonwealth of Massachusetts residential institutions, Walter E. Fernald State School and Paul A. Dever State School. Less than 10% of the clinic population was living in various private residential schools or within the community in private residences.

The demographic features of this patient population are listed in Table 14-1. Males comprised the greater proportion of patients. The patients

were relatively young, with an average and median age in the mid-twenties. The patients represented all age groups from childhood through senescence.

The causes of the developmental disabilities in this population are shown in Table 14-2. Approximately one-third of patients were found to have trisomy 21 or other chromosomal abnormalities, one-third had experienced general pre- or perinatal difficulties including anoxia, and the final one-third of patients could not be classified due to lack of information.

In order to provide information about infants, toddlers, and children under the age of 5 who were not part of the state school population, we have drawn on our experiences at the Children's Hospital general ENT clinics, the Children's Hospital orofacial clinics, and the Massachusetts Eye and Ear Infirmary and pediatric ENT clinics.

STATE SCHOOL CLINIC ORGANIZATION

The physical arrangement and the staffing patterns of our ENT clinic evolved over a number of years by the process of trial and error. The following section describes our current configuration, which has proven the most satisfactory. (See also Chap. 27.)

The otolaryngology clinic is held in a single large room located on the ground floor. This location provides ready access for patients in wheelchairs or stretchers and minimizes the

Table 14-1. *Patient Profile*

Gender	Number
Male	463
Female	250
Both	713

Age 26.8 yr (standard error of mean = 1.7), median age 25.4 yr., range 6–72 yr.

tendency of individuals to wander off while entering or leaving the examination area.

Patients are transported to the clinic by bus or van from their respective institutions. Transportation is coordinated to minimize waiting after arrival at the clinic. Vans are equipped with a wheelchair-stabilizing apparatus and power lifts to facilitate transport of physically handicapped patients.

The clinic is equipped with standard otolaryngologic equipment. There is an ample supply of otoscopic and nasal specula in pediatric and adolescent sizes. There is a hand-held otomicroscope (Hallpike otoscope, Keeler), and we have access to a pediatric-sized fiber-optic pharyngolaryngoscope (Machida, Olympus). Other specialized equipment includes an anesthesia administration machine with cardiovascular monitoring equipment for administering nitrous oxide.

Patients are seen on direct referral by their physicians, nurse practitioners, audiologists, or speech pathologists. Written referrals and residential records accompany each patient in order that sufficient information about the patient's past and current clinical problems be at hand.

The ENT clinic personnel include the pediatric otolaryngologist, the clinic nurse, and the clinic coordinator. In addition, two patient attendants aid in positioning patients during their examinations.

The clinic otolaryngologist and the clinical nurse work together to deliver clinical diagnostic

Table 14-2. *Etiology of Retardation*

Category	Number	Percent
Unknown	223	31.3
Trisomy 21	195	27.3
Prenatal	137	19.2
Perinatal	94	13.2
Other chromosomal	43	6.0
Anoxia	21	2.9
Total	713	99.9

Percentage total does not add to 100 due to rounding.

and therapeutic services to the patients. We consider that services for these individuals should be delivered in a continuing manner by the same team of professionals in order to provide optimal coordination of care and to foster the patients' trust in the providers.

Otolaryngology residents and medical students from participating institutions assist as members of the team. Their participation is important in order that they develop an appreciation of this population's medical needs and learn, from hands-on experience, how to deliver such care. Because residents rotate frequently from service to service, they are preferably not to be used as providers of primary care.

In contrast to the medical personnel, the clinic coordinator is a full-time employee at the state school and is always available to answer questions and contact clinicians for emergencies. This person is responsible for arranging all routine clinic appointments and tracing patients who miss an appointment so that they are not lost to follow-up. This key individual also arranges outside laboratory studies for the patient and distributes clinic reports to referring professionals.

The clinic attendants frequently work with the individuals being examined, and their familiar faces provide a comforting atmosphere for the patients. The attendants are also able to provide clinicians with background information on the patients otherwise available only through time-consuming review of written records. (See also Chap. 27.)

HOSPITAL-BASED CLINIC ORGANIZATION

Developmentally delayed infants and young children are usually evaluated and treated with others of the same chronologic age in general pediatric ENT clinics. Staff otolaryngologists supervise ENT residents and medical students and become closely involved with difficult and continuing cases. Follow-up appointments are arranged so that the child and family see the same group of clinicians on successive visits.

In the general ENT clinic, the outpatient clinic nurse plays a vital role in the delivery of care. In addition to assisting during the examination and performing office procedures such as cerumen removal and dressing changes, this individual supervises family and patient teaching, amplifying and clarifying information presented by other clinicians. The clinic nurse also supervises the flow of patients to the audiology department and clinical laboratories and gathers the data obtained in order to facilitate patient management.

Children with congenital mid-facial abnormalities such as cleft lip and/or cleft palate, Treacher Collins syndrome, and hemifacial microsomia receive ENT care in multidisciplinary orofacial or craniofacial clinics attended by staff otolaryngologists, plastic surgeons, and orthodontists. The clinics are also staffed by a clinic coordinator, clinic nurses, audiologists, speech pathologists, and social workers, all of whom contribute to the timely delivery of quality otolaryngologic care for this group of patients.

THE ENT EXAMINATION

Extent of Examination

Although many practitioners assume that developmentally disabled persons are difficult or nearly impossible to examine thoroughly, this is not our experience. Children under the age of six can always undergo a complete otologic evaluation as well as examination of the anterior nasal cavity, the oral cavity and oropharynx, and the neck. Newborns presenting with airway obstructive problems also undergo calibration of the nasal airways with appropriately sized catheters and examination of the hypopharynx and larynx with a rigid laryngoscope and tracheoscope (Storz) or with a flexible fiber-optic pharyngoscope (Machida, Olympus). Young infants can also be readily examined with the latter instrument after a topical anesthetic is applied to the nasal linings.

The otolaryngologic examination of adult patients is more challenging. In our experience, nearly one-third of the adult patients seen underwent a complete ENT evaluation including otologic examination, examination of the nasal cavity, the nasopharynx, the oral cavity, the oropharynx, the hypopharynx and larynx, and the neck (Table 14-3). An additional 60% of patients seen for an initial visit underwent the same ENT evaluation lacking only the successful completion of mirror examinations of the nasopharynx and hypopharynx. Only 8.3 percent of patients underwent limited examination of either the ear, nasal cavities, or pharynx because of lack of patient cooperation.

Examining Techniques

Effective otolaryngologic examination of developmentally disabled and multiply handicapped patients requires flexibility and sensitivity on the part of the clinic team. In many cases, multiply handicapped patients have minimal or no mental

Table 14-3. *Extent of Initial Examination*

Visit Classification	Number	Percent
Screening examination	429	60.2
Complete examination	225	31.6
Selected site	59	8.3
Total initial visits	713	100.1

Percentage total does not add to 100 due to rounding.

deficiency. They may lack sufficient physical coordination for complete verbal or written expression even though they are very much aware of what is going on. Each should be treated with respect, consideration, and warmth, and should be provided with the opportunity for complete and natural expression.

Certain special considerations that enhance the physician's ability to evaluate these patients deserve discussion. There must be access to the examining facilities and to examining equipment, not only for ambulatory patients but also for those with handicaps requiring the use of wheelchairs or stretchers. A standard examining chair with power elevator and tilt features is used for ambulatory patients. Examination of wheelchair and stretcher patients requires an enlarged area around the main examining chair and the examining-equipment console. Patients can often be examined and treated in their own wheelchairs or on the transporting stretchers rather than transferring them to the examining chair. Initially, a power lift for stretchers was used, but this did not prove to be a useful piece of equipment.

It is necessary to have adequate assistance in carrying out the examination. Many patients are fearful of the examining room and the entire situation. It is helpful to have friends, family, or familiar attendants accompany patients to the examination. Such attendants can be helpful in calming the patient and can provide a helping hand in positioning during the examination.

It is useful to observe the patient briefly before beginning the ENT examination. The patient's skin condition yields useful clues regarding behavior. Scratches, scars, and calluses may indicate self-abusive behavior. Patients with such marks may also be prone to aggressive behavior, and care must be taken.

Many persons with developmental disabilities exhibit relatively uninhibited behavior, and medical personnel should not be surprised by the offer, often insistent, of a hug. Returning the

Table 14-4. *Types of Disease Treated*

Disease Site	Number	Percent
Auricle/temporal bone	1112	87.63
Nose/paranasal sinuses	80	6.30
Larynx/lower throat	61	4.81
Oral cavity/upper throat	16	1.26
Total	1269	100.00

compliment can initiate the bond of trust necessary for the delivery of effective medical care.

If the patient has a known auditory or visual problem, alternative methods of communication such as a gentle touch on the arm or back can be valuable in establishing a relationship. Currently, sign language and gestural communication systems are taught to persons with communication dysfunction, and these techniques can be useful.

The otolaryngologic examining techniques are tailored to patients in the pediatric age range. Developmentally disabled patients respond more predictably if the examiner approaches the patient according to the patient's emotional and intellectual age rather than the patient's physical or chronological age.

Many patients will not sit voluntarily on the examining chair but will permit examinations to be carried out while they are sitting on other chairs around the room. Until the confidence of the patient is won, it is wise to pursue the examination in any position or place where the patient feels comfortable. This approach facilitates rather than interferes with the performance of a complete examination. Time spent and patience demonstrated at the initial contact with the patient are rewarded with an added measure of cooperation in subsequent encounters.

It is worthwhile to show the patient examining instruments prior to their use. Many patients enjoy touching the instruments and handling them. This not only shows them that the instruments are not dangerous, but also transmits a feeling of friendship to them. As with young children, it is often useful to avoid instrumentation that is unfamiliar and somewhat forbidding. For example, it is useful to employ the electric otoscope rather than the nasal speculum for performing an intranasal examination. The former instrument affords an excellent view and is a more familiar object.

The use of sedation is occasionally necessary for agitated patients who cannot otherwise be calmed. The combination of chloral hydrate and diazepam is useful. Many patients seen in the outpatient clinic are receiving anti-seizure medications or tranquilizers. Therefore it is often necessary to increase the administered dose beyond that calculated for the patient's size or weight.

A general anesthetic technique using nitrous oxide, similar to that used in dental offices, has also been successfully used in selected cases. The anesthetic is administered by qualified personnel using a standard anesthesia machine. Patients have nothing to eat (NPO) for 6 to 8 hours prior to the examination. Atropine is routinely administered to prevent bradyarrythmias and excessive secretions. This technique has permitted removal of extensive debris and foreign bodies from ear canals and has afforded an adequate examination of the tympanic membrane and portions of the middle ear that are accessible.

Clinical findings and therapeutic recommendations must be clearly communicated to referring professionals in a timely fashion. The details of a clinic visit are dictated and transcribed, but a summary of diagnostic information and suggested therapy is communicated verbally or in writing on the day of the patient's visit in order to minimize confusion or delay in the initiation of therapy.

It is most important that the examiners and all personnel working in the clinic maintain a sense of humor. All patients respond favorably to a happy atmosphere. Background music in the clinic adds a calming influence.

DISEASES TREATED AND TREATMENT STRATEGIES

Table 14-4 lists the principal diagnoses made at both initial and subsequent clinic evaluations during our clinical experience at the state residential ENT clinics. Nearly 90% of patients were seen for otologic disorders. A significantly smaller proportion of patients were seen for disorders of the nose and paranasal sinuses and for diseases of the throat.

Otologic Disease

The most commonly treated otologic problems were chronic otitis media and cerumen impaction. Together they accounted for 60% of patients seen at the clinic (Table 14-5). Approximately 10% of patients were seen for otitis media with effusion, for tympanic membrane perforation, or for sensorineural hearing loss. Smaller numbers of patients were seen with other isolated disorders. It is of note that isolated cholesteatoma was only detected in 1.6% of patients.

The population seen at this clinic included a high proportion of patients presenting with chronic ear disease potentially requiring surgical intervention. These disorders included chronic otitis media, tympanic membrane perforation, tympanic retraction pocket, cholesteatoma, and canal stenosis.

The population of infants and children under 6 years seen at hospital-based clinics had a similar abundance of otologic problems. Children in this age group had a high incidence of otitis media with effusion and acute recurrent suppurative otitis media. They rarely presented with evidence of chronic or degenerative middle ear disease.

Chronic Middle Ear Disease

The management of chronic suppurative otitis media depends primarily on medical therapy; surgical therapy is reserved for patients failing to respond or for those with demonstrated cholesteatoma or particularly invasive infectious disease. Patients receive topical and systemic antibiotics after appropriate ear canal specimens are sent for bacteriologic cultures.[2] The need to eliminate water from the external canal must be stressed. This is achieved by the use of either custom-made ear molds or cotton plugs impregnated with petrolatum. The majority of patients respond to one or two 3-week courses of such therapy. Resistant infections often respond to the combination of systemic cephalosporin antibiotics such as cephalexin and cefaclor together with topical gentamicin drops, available commercially as an ophthalmic preparation.

Patients with resistant chronic otitis media, cholesteatomas, unstable tympanic membrane retraction pockets, tympanic membrane perforations, and foreign bodies deep in the ear canal require operative intervention under general anesthesia. A detailed report of the otologic surgery on this group of patients is not the subject of this chapter, but some general observations are worthy of note. The developmentally disabled patients with chronic otitis media with or without cholesteatoma do not have more extensive disease, temporal bone destruction, or compromise of vital structures such as the facial nerve when compared with groups of non-developmentally disabled individuals undergoing similar surgical procedures. The patients successfully undergo operative surgery without incident and with rare behavioral problems. The entire experience is more comfortable for patients when familiar attendants accompany them to the hospital

Table 14-5. *Types of Otologic Disease*

Diagnosis	Number	Percent
Chronic otitis media	352	31.65
Cerumen impaction	321	28.87
Otitis media/effusion	130	11.69
Tympanic membrane perforation	116	10.43
Sensorineural hearing loss	101	9.08
Tympanic retraction pocket	35	3.15
Otitis externa	22	1.98
Cholesteatoma	18	1.62
Canal stenosis	5	0.45
Tympanosclerosis	5	0.45
Myringitis	4	0.36
Foreign body	3	0.27
Total	1112	100.00

and stay with them during the perioperative period.

It is essential to use special techniques to assure the integrity of surgical dressings and ear canal packing. An extended mastoid-type pressure dressing incorporating a chin strap will protect the operated ear. During the early postoperative period, the patient may require sedation and restraint. These measures together decrease the incidence of postoperative canal stenosis.

Tests of auditory function are carried out pre- and post-operatively by audiologists familiar with the testing of developmentally disabled patients. Behavioral audiometric techniques yield reliable information in many patients, particularly after behavioral conditioning sessions. Objective audiometry employing the measurement of auditory evoked brainstem potentials provides an accurate assessment of a patient's hearing.[7]

Cerumenosis

Dry, firm impactions of cerumen were the second most common otologic problem seen in the clinic. This condition is particularly common with Down syndrome patients, who have small external auditory canals and eczematoid skin changes.[17] Both conditions contribute to the accumulation of cerumen and squamous debris within the external canal.

Periodic removal of cerumen is important. Cerumen impactions can cause external otitis, vertigo, and conductive hearing loss as well as obscure significant otologic pathology.

Attempts to remove crusty cerumen can produce pain and a negative experience for the patient. For this reason, it is necessary to soften or liquefy the keratin debris prior to removal with the use of a glycerin–hydrogen peroxide otic preparation (Debrox, Murine). Once softened, the cerumen is removed by water irrigation or small suction tips.

Antibiotic-steroid otic preparations (Cortisporin, Coly-Mycin) are also helpful in softening the cerumen. These medications readily penetrate through crusty debris and have the additional advantage of suppressing or treating concomitant external canal infections. More recalcitrant cases of impaction can be treated by alternating the glycerin–hydrogen peroxide or antibiotic-steroid solutions with dioctal sodium sulfosuccinate liquid (Colace). This latter preparation is safe for use within the ear canal and is very effective. Triethanolamine-complex-containing products (Cerumenex) should be avoided because they can induce severe contact dermatitis.

Parents or attendants caring for children and adults with Down syndrome or other patients with recurring cerumen impactions should cleanse the ear canals on a routine basis to prevent the reaccumulation of cerumen debris. Most effective is the biweekly irrigation of the ear canals using warm tap water followed by instillation of an antibiotic-steroid otic suspension. A softening agent should be used prior to irrigation if the cerumen debris is excessively crusty. This procedure should be individualized, and a variety of preparations can be used successfully.

Otitis Media with Effusion

Otitis media with effusion was the third most common disorder treated and occurred most often in children and adolescents.[5] Infants and children with skull base abnormalities such as those associated with Down and Treacher Collins syndromes have a high incidence of middle ear disease due to eustachian tube malformation.[1,11] Children with cleft palates and submucous clefts also frequently have eustachian tube dysfunction.[10]

Children should be monitored closely for development or persistence of middle ear infection and fluid. The conductive hearing loss associated with these conditions can have a serious negative impact on communication skills and behavior patterns in the developmentally disabled individual.[9]

Children with these disorders should be seen initially by age 4 to 6 months. An otologic and careful pharyngeal exam should be followed by a routine test of hearing. Behavioral audiometric techniques should be supplemented if necessary by more objective techniques including auditory evoked brain stem potential measurements and impedance audiometry. If the child is free of otologic disease, an annual return visit should be planned, preferably in the middle or end of the winter months. Children with ongoing middle ear disease are routinely examined every 4 months.

Treatment commences with several courses of systemic antibiotics. Patients with residual middle ear fluid for more than 8 consecutive weeks or patients with significant conductive hearing losses interfering with development of communication skills should be scheduled for insertion of tympanostomy tubes. These tubes are as useful for developmentally disabled children and adults as they are for the general population. Small ear canals do present technical difficulties. Small-profile tubes such as "bobbin" or small "collar button" styles are preferred because they are more easily inserted and collect minimal amounts of debris. Semipermanent tubes such as Goode T-tubes, even if trimmed, tend to attach to canal skin and extrude prematurely.

Sensorineural Hearing Loss

Over 9% of the state school ENT clinic population presented with a primary diagnosis of sensorineural hearing loss (Table 14-5).[15] Many additional patients evaluated for middle ear disease also had cochlear and/or neural hearing losses.

Patients over the age of 3 can be initially evaluated using behavioral audiometry and impedance audiometry. If reliable information is obtained, the patient with a demonstrable loss is given an appropriate otologic evaluation including radiologic imaging of the temporal bone and necessary treatment including amplification. Interval monitoring is carried out.

Infants or patients with unreliable behavioral audiometric data or signs of possible retrocochlear disease should undergo objective audiometric testing by measurement of auditory evoked brain stem potentials and by tympanic membrane impedance testing.[7]

Amplification using conventional hearing aids is an appropriate and useful rehabilitation measure in this population. Patients with previously undiagnosed or progressive hearing losses may show significant behavioral improvement after amplification is introduced.

The decision to insert tympanostomy tubes in patients with mixed hearing losses requiring amplification should be made with caution. An open tympanostomy tube allows moisture from the middle ear space to reach the ear canal. Even a vented ear mold will prevent adequate ventilation of the ear canal, and chronic otitis externa can result.

Auricular Hematoma

Patients with self-abusive behaviors frequently present with auricular hematomas, the antecedents of cauliflower ears. Trauma to the pinna produces bleeding between the cartilage and the overlying perichondrium. Because attendants are sometimes unaware of the need for prompt treatment of this condition, many patients with this problem present to the clinic with other primary diagnoses after irreversible auricular damage has already occurred.

Treatment includes drainage of the blood or serous fluid and application of a pressure dressing in order to prevent reaccumulation. One should incise the skin widely in order to provide a route for continued drainage during the 4 to 5 days necessary for readherance of the perichondrium to the cartilage. During this time, a mastoid-type pressure dressing is applied. The patient is treated with a systemic antistaphylococcal antibiotic, such as dicloxacillin or a cephalosporin.[8] The success of this treatment depends on the completeness of drainage and the creativity used to maintain the dressing.

Nasal and Paranasal Sinus Disease

The most common disorders are rhinitis and blunt nasal trauma (Table 14-6). Nearly 50% of patients presenting to the state school ENT clinic with primary nasal problems were suffering from chronic rhinitis with or without sinusitis. Over 20% of patients with nasal problems had sustained nasal trauma, and nearly 9% had nasal fractures. Recurrent or persistent epistaxis affected over 7% of the 80 patients seen for nasal problems.

Chronic Rhinitis and Sinusitis

Chronic rhinitis is a common and recurring problem in patients with Down syndrome, because these patients have small nasal cavities and somewhat hypoplastic ethmoid and maxillary sinuses. The patients generally present with stasis and crusting of secretions in the nasal cavity. Effective treatment includes the use of systemic antibiotics and nasal irrigations using warm saline or a specially formulated nasal irrigation solution (Alkalol). Humidification of the inspired air using a bedside vaporizer is also recommended. This regimen is effective in the majority of cases.

Membrane thickening or opacification of the sinuses is frequently noted on an initial sinus roentgenogram. These findings in association

Table 14-6. *Types of Rhinologic Disease*

Diagnosis	Number	Percent
Chronic rhinitis	27	33.75
Trauma	17	21.25
Sinusitis	12	15.00
Nasal fracture	7	8.75
Epistaxis	6	7.50
Nasal polyposis	5	6.25
Septal deviation	2	2.50
Skin lesion	2	2.50
Septal perforation	2	2.50
Total	80	100.00

with purulent rhinitis suggest the presence of sinusitis. Appropriate management includes 3 weeks of a systemic antibiotic such as erythromycin or cephalexin and an initial 4-day application of a topical nasal decongestant.

A unilateral purulent rhinorrhea with or without opacified ipsilateral sinuses represents an intranasal foreign body until proven otherwise.[13,16] These foreign bodies, if clearly visualized and located anteriorly, can often be removed in the clinic after application of a topical decongestant and anesthetic such as 4% cocaine. Removal is achieved using a large Frazier suction tip or a Hartman forceps. If granulation tissue has formed around the foreign body or if it is posteriorly located, removal under general anesthesia is necessary to facilitate adequate hemostasis and safe removal with concomitant airway protection.

Nasal Trauma

Treatment for nasal trauma in this population is identical to that for the general population. The patient is evaluated initially, and if a significant external or septal deformity exists, a reduction is recommended.

Most patients do not have significant anatomic deformities that mandate operative intervention. The risk of possible complications from a general anesthetic should be weighed against any anticipated cosmetic or functional airway improvement.

The septum and columella should be carefully examined for evidence of hematoma. If a septal hematoma is discovered, it should be promptly drained and the nasal cavities packed. A broad-spectrum systemic antibiotic is routinely prescribed for 2 weeks. An external dressing should be applied to the nose to prevent probing fingers from removing the packing.

Epistaxis

Epistaxis is usually caused by crust-induced bleeding in Kisselbach's area of the anterior na-

Table 14-7. *Types of Oral Disease*

Diagnosis	Number	Percent
Ptyalism	4	25.0
Papilloma	4	25.0
Cleft palate	3	18.8
Tonsillar hypertrophy	2	12.5
Cleft lip	1	6.3
Upper respiratory infection	1	6.3
TM joint dysfunction	1	6.3
Total	16	100.2

Percentage total does not add to 100 due to rounding.

sal septum. This was true in each of the six cases treated. It is difficult to maintain an anterior nasal pack in this population; identification and cauterization of the bleeding vessel is the preferred treatment.[3,14]

Sedation followed by topical anesthesia with 4% cocaine should precede chemical cautery with silver nitrate. Absorbable dressing materials such as oxidized cellulose (Oxycel), gelfoam, or microfibrillar collagen (Avitene) can be inserted for additional hemostasis. Continuing care includes application of an emollient such as petrolatum or mineral oil to the anterior nares and the use of humidification.

Other

Bilateral nasal polyposis is often a sign of allergic rhinitis. Polyps can often be effectively treated using topical steroids such as dexamethasone or beclomethasone without the need for operative removal. Unilateral nasal polyps should be removed surgically for biopsy in order to rule out the presence of a neoplasm such as inverted papilloma.

Nasal septal deviations, particularly the S-shaped bilaterally obstructive types causing symptomatic airway obstruction, can be treated with operative intervention. Less obstructive septal deviations should be treated conservatively.

Newborn infants found to have bilateral choanal atresia require immediate airway management.[4] Infants are obligate nasal breathers, and

Table 14-8. *Types of Lower Throat Disease*

Diagnosis	Number	Percent
Dysphonia	28	45.9
Chronic laryngitis	23	37.7
Dysphagia	8	13.1
Vocal cord nodule	2	3.3
Total	61	100.0

an oral airway such as a McGovern nipple must be provided for infants with complete nasal obstruction. Unilateral choanal atresia can be managed conservatively. Bilateral atresia requires the creation of a nasal airway using the transpalatal approach. In some cases the reconstructed airway will stenose and revision will be necessary.

Oral and Pharyngeal Disease

A total of 16 patients examined at the state school ENT clinic were found to have problems associated with anatomic sites in the mouth or pharynx (Table 14-7). These included chronic drooling, the presence of benign, verrucoid squamous papillomas in one or more anatomic sites, the presence of a cleft lip and/or cleft palate, and the presence of palatine tonsillar hypertrophy.

A larger group of 61 patients presented at the same clinic with problems involving the lower pharynx or larynx (Table 14-8). More than 80% of this group were seen for problems associated with the larynx.

Oral Cavity Disease

Four patients were seen with severe drooling, manifest by soaking of clothing despite the use of absorbent bibs. Management of this problem is controversial and includes: behavioral modification, anticholinergic medications, salivary gland irradiation, and various surgical procedures including rerouting of salivary ducts, salivary gland excision, and salivary gland denervation.[18]

Behavioral modification involves reminding the patient, who often has bulbar dysfunction, to swallow frequently. This measure can be successful in highly motivated individuals with persistent family or attendants.

Anticholinergic medications do dry up salivary secretions but produce undesirable drying of the mucous membranes along with cardiovascular hyperactivity. They have also been associated with adverse personality changes.

Salivary gland irradiation, though effective, has been discontinued after the publication of studies suggesting that low-level head and neck irradiation is associated with development of thyroid neoplasia.

Of our four patients, three were treated conservatively and successfully with behavioral modification. One patient underwent bilateral total tympanic neurectomies with an excellent result over a 3-year follow-up period.

Oropharyngeal Disease

Smaller groups of older patients were seen at the state school ENT clinic with various problems including cleft palate and isolated papillomata of the oral cavity and oropharynx. Tonsillar hypertrophy was a relatively uncommon presenting problem, and no patients were seen with sleep apnea due to airway obstruction.

Patients with palatal clefts were more frequently evaluated and treated at the hospital-based ENT clinics. Each patient undergoes initial ENT and plastic surgical examinations as well as speech and language evaluations. The nasopharynx is examined either directly using a fiber-optic pharyngoscope or indirectly with a fluoroscopic radiologic evaluation. Children with mild velopharyngeal insufficiency undergo speech therapy. Those with a more severe problem are considered for construction of a pharyngeal flap to narrow the size of the nasopharyngeal inlet.

Oropharyngeal obstruction of varying degrees is common in patients with Down syndrome because maxillary hypoplasia produces a limited pharyngeal cross-sectional diameter. Space is reduced further by tonsillar and adenoid hypertrophy.

Indications for tonsillectomy with concomitant removal of adenoid tissue include significant airway obstruction with sleep apnea, oropharyngeal obstruction leading to slow or uncomfortable deglutition, or evidence of bacterial colonization of lymphoid tissue leading to recurrent pharyngitis. There is no evidence that removal of tonsils and adenoids favorably affects middle ear disease.

Laryngeal Diseases

Nearly half of the patients seen at the state residential school ENT clinic with disorders of the lower throat had dysphonic speech patterns, and their speech pathologists requested a diagnostic evaluation prior to the institution of speech therapy (Table 14-8). Patience and repeated examinations produced a complete view of the hypopharynx and larynx in the majority of patients.

Of the 61 patients seen with lower throat problems, 25 underwent a direct laryngoscopy using a fiberoptic pharyngoscope.[12] In each case the patient was kept NPO for 6 hours prior to the procedure. Cocaine 4% was used for topical anesthesia within the nasal cavity. Benzocaine spray (Cetacaine) was used for topical anesthesia of the hypopharynx and larynx.

This procedure was unusually well tolerated by the patients, and in only one of 25 cases was the procedure terminated without complete visualization of the pharynx and larynx. All patients with dysphonia were found to have chronic laryngitis or early vocal cord polyps. The procedure obviated the necessity for a laryngoscopic examination under general anesthesia.

Infants and young children with developmental disabilities may also have delayed development of portions of the respiratory tract, particularly the larynx. Laryngomalacia, the most common cause of inspiratory stridor in the infant, usually becomes symptomatic within 3 to 6 weeks after birth and ultimately resolves spontaneously by 6 to 12 months of age. Children with persistent stridor require evaluation including a complete ENT examination, a radiologic airway evaluation, and a barium swallow to check for the presence of a vascular ring. If the stridor progresses or persists longer than expected, direct examination should ultimately be carried out. Topical anesthesia and a rigid or flexible laryngoscope-tracheoscope should be used in the neonate or young infant. General anesthesia and a rigid laryngoscope and bronchoscope should be used to examine the older child.

A neonate requiring prolonged intubation for respiratory support is at risk for developing subglottic stenosis. If such a child develops frequent stridor or recurrent croup-like illnesses, he or she should undergo a radiologic examination of the airway and, if necessary, formal endoscopy.

Dysphagia

Patients referred for dysphagia underwent an initial ENT evaluation and subsequently underwent a barium swallow. All patients were found to have abnormal esophageal motility, and further endoscopic workup was not carried out.

Patients were seen by a gastroenterologist and underwent further studies including esophagoscopy-gastroscopy and direct esophageal motility studies.

REFERENCES

1. Brooks, D., Wooley, H., and Kanjilal, G.: Hearing loss and middle ear disorders in patients with Down Syndrome. J. Ment. Defic. Res., *16*:21, 1972.
2. Fairbanks, D.: Otic topical agents. Otolaryngol. Head Neck Surg., 88:327, 1980.
3. Fletcher, M., and Fisher, J.: Nasal hemorrhage. Resident Staff Physician, 5:86, 1980.
4. Hall, B.: Choanal atresia with associated multiple anomalies. J. Pediatr., 95:395, 1979.
5. Healy, G.B., and Smith, H.G.: Concepts in the management of middle ear effusions. J. Otolaryngol., 2:138, 1981.
6. Igarashi, M., Takahashi, M., and Alford, B.: Inner ear morphology in Down Syndrome. Otolaryngology, *83:* 175, 1977.
7. Kodera, K., Yamani, H., Yomada, O., and Suzuki, K.: BSR audiometry at speech frequencies. Audiology, *16:* 469, 1977.

8. Martin, R., Yonker, A., and Yarington, C.: Perichondritis of the ear. Laryngoscope, *86*:654, 1976.

9. Menyuk, P.: Effects of hearing loss on language acquisition in the babbling stage. *In* Hearing Disorders in Children. Baltimore, MD, University Park Press, 1977, p. 621.

10. Paradise, J.: Management of middle ear effusions in infants with cleft palate. Ann. Otolaryngol. (Suppl. 25), *85*:285, 1976.

11. Roche, A., Roche, P., and Lewis, A.: The cranial base in Trisomy 21. J. Ment. Defic. Res., *16*:7, 1972.

12. Sacker, M.: State of the art bronchofibroendoscopy. Am. Rev. Respir. Dis., *111*:62, 1975.

13. Smith, H.: Foreign bodies of the nose and pharynx. *In* Current Pediatric Therapy. 12th Ed. Edited by S. Gellis, and B. Kagan. Philadelphia, W.B. Saunders, 1986, pp. 103, 104.

14. Smith, H.: Epistaxis. *In* Current Pediatric Therapy. 12th Ed. Edited by S. Gellis, and B. Kagan. Philadelphia, W.B. Saunders, 1986, pp. 101–103.

15. Smith, H.G., et al.: Otologic surgery for mentally retarded and multiply handicapped patients (unpublished).

16. Stool, S., and McConnel, C.: Foreign bodies in pediatric otolaryngology: Some diagnostic and therapeutic pointers. Clin. Pediatr. (Phila.), *12*:113, 1973.

17. Strome, M.: Down Syndrome: A modern otorhinolaryngological perspective. Laryngoscope, *91*:1581, 1981.

18. Townsend, G., Morimoto, A., and Kralemann, H.: Management of sialorrhea in mentally retarded patients by trans-tympanic neurectomy. Mayo Clin. Proc., *48*:776, 1973.

15

ENDOCRINE DISORDERS

Ann Cutler, M.D. □ *Rita Benezra, M.D.* □ *Frank Crantz, M.D*

Developmental disabilities are often associated with endocrine abnormalities. This relationship can be viewed from two different perspectives: (1) some endocrinologic diseases will cause mental retardation if left untreated; and (2) recognized syndromes include both mental retardation and endocrine problems (e.g., Down syndrome). This chapter reviews the more common endocrine problems among the developmentally disabled.

ENDOCRINE CAUSES OF DEVELOPMENTAL DISABILITIES

The early diagnosis and appropriate treatment of endocrine disorders can enhance functional potency. Features such as mental retardation should not preclude treatment, but should (in instances such as Down syndrome) raise the clinician's index of suspicion for the presence of endocrine dysfunctions. Ongoing research, particularly in the areas of autoimmunity and growth disorders, may ultimately serve to prevent some of the clinical problems described below.

Congenital Hypothyroidism

Congenital hypothyroidism signifies thyroid hormone deficiency present from birth. Multiple etiologies are known, including thyroid gland dysgenesis (85 to 95% of cases),[32] metabolic blocks in hormone synthesis, hypothalamic-pituitary-thyroid axis abnormalities, endemic cretinism, transplacental transmission of antithyroid agents, and peripheral resistance to thyroid hormone. Since the institution of mass neonatal screening programs the frequency of congenital hypothyroidism has been shown to be 1 in 4,000 to 1 in 5,000.[47] This is significantly more than previously estimated, and congenital hypothyroidism is now recognized to be one of the most common treatable causes of mental retardation if treatment is instituted early. The benefits of newborn screening are underscored when it is realized that fewer than 5% of patients with congenital hypothyroidism present with the classic signs.[27]

The vast majority of infants with congenital hypothyroidism appear normal at birth. However, if untreated, by age 1 to 2 months they develop symptoms including hypothermia, poor weight gain, constipation, and prolonged jaundice. By 3 months, the classic low-pitched hoarse cry and enlarged tongue (secondary to myxedema of the larynx and tongue, respectively) begin to appear and the skin becomes coarse and dry. An umbilical hernia is common, and deep tendon reflexes show delayed relaxation. Between 3 and 6 months, physical and developmental retardation are evident. Irreversible mental retardation occurs if treatment is not begun in the early neonatal period.[32]

In 1972, Jean Dussault developed a simple radioimmunoassay that measured the L-thyroxine (T_4) concentration in the filter paper blood spot specimens obtained for phenylketonuria (PKU) screening.[47] Three years later a method to determine thyroid stimulating hormone (TSH) concentration in filter paper blood spots was developed to help confirm the diagnosis of congenital hypothyroidism in infants with low T_4. With these developments, screening of newborns was begun in North America in the mid 1970s. Most programs perform T_4 measurements initially and TSH measurements on samples with a low T_4.

Results of the outcomes of treatment of children with congenital hypothyroidism detected in the first few years of the screening program are now becoming available. The New England Congenital Hypothyroidism Collaborative (NECHC) found that Stanford Binet scores on 63 infants diagnosed in the New England Screening program and treated at 25 ± 15 days (*before* clinical manifestations) had a mean IQ of 106 ± 16.[60] The four children who were clinically hypothyroid at birth had IQs of 110, 50, 64, and 76.[60] A more recent follow-up of 112 infants from New England found a mean IQ of 104 ± 16. Inadequate treatment was the only factor found to have a significantly adverse effect on cognitive prognosis in children treated prior to clinical manifestations.[59] Therefore, frequent TSH and T_4 determination (to keep the serum T_4 in the upper half of the normal range) is advocated. Treatment should be initiated as early as possible (preferably before age 6 weeks) because treatment begun after 3 months has a much poorer intellectual outcome.[43]

Acquired Hypothyroidism

Acquired hypothyroidism is generally thought of as occurring after the second year of life. This is the most common endocrine cause of short stature. Although there may be some decrease in cognitive abilities along with growth failure, obesity, cold intolerance, lethargy, and constipation before the hypothyroidism is detected, these symptoms resolve completely with appropriate treatment.[4]

Hypoglycemia

Hypoglycemia is defined as a blood glucose concentration lower than 40 mg/100 ml. Somewhat lower levels of glucose are tolerated in normal newborns and low-birth-weight infants (glucose values less than 30 mg/100 ml and 20 mg/100 ml, respectively, are considered to be significant).[17] Symptoms of hypoglycemia are variable and nonspecific. Hypoglycemic neonates commonly present with apnea, cyanosis, tremors, or tachypnea.[50] Seizures, confusion, or lethargy (which can progress to coma or death) can occur at any age.[18] Elderly patients with

decreased cerebral perfusion may manifest stroke-like symptoms of hemiparesis and ataxia.[53]

Pathologically, severe hypoglycemia results in an irregular focal necrosis of the cerebral cortex. The subcortical gray matter (caudate nucleus and putamen) is also susceptible to adverse effects, but the white matter is generally spared.[53] The brain stem is the last area to be affected.[50] Prolonged or recurrent hypoglycemia can lead to significant neurological deficits, including mental retardation. Infants less than 6 months of age are thought to be the most susceptible to CNS damage. The degree and duration of hypoglycemia that results in permanent neurological impairment is controversial. Follow-up studies on these patients are often confused by the presence of other factors (e.g., asphyxia).[50]

There are multiple causes of hypoglycemia, and an outline of etiologies follows. Data for the outline were obtained from McMillan et al.[49] and Cornblath.[17]

Causes of Hypoglycemia

Transient; neonatal onset
  Decreased production and increased
        utilization of glucose
    Stress (asphyxia, hypothermia)
    Low birth weight
  Excess insulin production
    Infants of diabetic mother
    Erythroblastosis
Persistent hypoglycemia; neonatal/infancy
        onset
  Metabolic
    Glycogen storage disease
    Galactosemia
    Hereditary fructose intolerance
    Fructose 1,6-diphosphate deficiency
  Excess insulin production
    Beta cell hyperplasia
    Nesidioblastosis
    Islet cell adenoma
    Beckwith-Wiedemann syndrome
Hypoglycemia, childhood and adult onset
  Hormone deficiencies (the concentration in
        whole blood is approximately 15%
        less than that of plasma and serum)
    Growth hormone deficiency
    Hypopituitarism
    Adrenal disorders
      Addison's disease
      Congenital adrenal hyperplasia
  Hepatic disease
    Malnutrition
    Cirrhosis/hepatitis

Reye syndrome
Miscellaneous
  Poisons/toxins
    Alcohol
    Salicylates
    Hypoglycemic agents/factitious insulin administration
  Extrapancreatic tumors
    Fibrosarcoma
    Hepatoma
    Neuroblastoma
    Mesothelioma
    Wilms' tumor
  Malabsorption
  Idiopathic
    Ketotic hypoglycemia
    Glucagon deficiency

Treatment of hypoglycemia varies with the underlying disorder. Supplemental glucose generally relieves symptoms in patients who have not progressed to brain stem involvement. The nonspecificity of the symptoms requires that clinicians maintain a high index of suspicion in order to detect hypoglycemia before CNS damage occurs.

SYNDROMES ASSOCIATED WITH ENDOCRINE DYSFUNCTION

Certain syndromes have clinical features that can obscure the symptoms of endocrine disorders. Hence, health care professionals working with the handicapped must be particularly careful to watch for these disorders, many of which occur more frequently in the handicapped than in the general population.

Down Syndrome

Down syndrome occurs in 1 in 800 to 1 in 1,000 live births. Several endocrine disorders should be screened for in Down syndrome because they occur more often in these individuals than in the normal population.

Hypothyroidism has been reported to occur in 13 to 54% of adults with Down syndrome.[37,57,68,74] Several cases of hyperthyroidism in Down syndrome are also documented.[84] Recent studies have found thyroid dysfunction in 8 to 18% of children with Down syndrome, though the latter figure represents chemical, not clinical, abnormalities.[14,73] An increased prevalence (1 in 147 children or 28 times that of the general population) of congenital hypothyroidism in Down syndrome has also been observed.[30]

The etiology of the thyroid disease in Down syndrome is not well understood. The prevalence of positive antithyroglobulin and antimicrosomal antibodies ranges from 13 to 40%, so autoimmunity may play an etiologic role. Benda performed careful pathologic studies on the thyroid glands from 48 patients with Down syndrome and found only two that were normal. The rest were hypoplastic, showing increased colloid formation or fibrosis.[6]

Because many of the signs of hypothyroidism overlap with characteristics of Down syndrome (e.g., hypotonia, constipation, and short stature), it is important that routine periodic screening thyroid function tests be performed by physicians caring for individuals with Down syndrome and that appropriate treatment of hypo- or hyperthyroidism be instituted as indicated (see Fig. 15-1).

Diabetes mellitus is also found more frequently in persons with Down syndrome than in the general population, especially in the younger age groups.[55] The reasons for this are unknown. It is possible that abnormal autoimmune mechanisms predispose to the development of diabetes and hypothyroidism. Although the majority of people with Down syndrome have normal carbohydrate metabolism the potential for developing this disease should be kept in mind.

Almost all people with Down syndrome are of short stature. Although birth length is somewhat below the mean, the growth velocity is most significantly reduced between 6 and 24 months so that, by age 3 years, the mean length is greater than 2 standard deviations below that of controls. For this reason specific growth curves have been developed for children with Down syndrome (see Fig. 15-2). Between ages 7 and 18 years, growth velocity is similar to control children, though absolute height is reduced about 2 standard deviations from the mean.[67]

Males with Down syndrome have thus far been found to be sterile, and the testes are abnormal on histologic examination. The penis and scrotum are usually small.

Benda found hypoplasia of the ovaries in females with Down syndrome.[6] In a study using cervical smears twice a week, no evidence of ovulation was found in 30%, definite ovulation in 39%, and possible ovulation was found in the remainder. There are varying reports on the age of menarche, and amenorrhea or irregular menses are noted in many women with Down syndrome who have normal secondary sex characteristics. Late development of axillary and pubic hair has been noted by several authors.[67] There have also been reports of women with

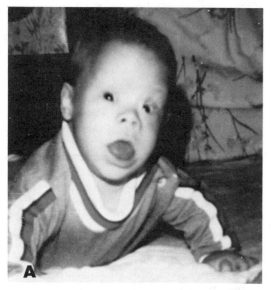

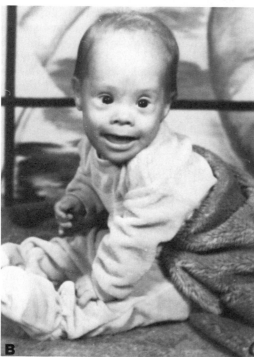

FIG. 15-1. *A.* A 10-month-old child with trisomy 21 and hypothyroidism. *B.* The same child, 1 year old, 1 month after commencement of thyroid supplementation.

Down syndrome who have conceived and given birth.

XXY Syndrome

The Klinefelter, or XXY, syndrome occurs in 1.7 per 1,000 newborn males, making this the second most common chromosomal anomaly.[11] In the adult, the syndrome is characterized by small testes, eunuchoid body proportions, tall stature, incomplete virilization, and gynecomastia. Testicular histology is abnormal, with resulting azoospermia and inadequate testosterone production. The intelligence of these males is variable but tends to be significantly lower than that of their normal siblings.[80] Behavioral difficulties are frequently encountered. The clinical features may not be obvious in prepubertal children. The diagnosis should be suspected in boys with school problems and tall stature, particularly if the testes and penis are low-average to below-average in size.[11] Early diagnosis allows age-appropriate testosterone replacement, which may inhibit gynecomastia and facilitate normal sexual maturation. Testosterone replacement is continued throughout adulthood, although lower dosages are required after puberty. The majority of these men are sterile.[86]

Overt thyroid disease is unusual in this syndrome although laboratory studies (radioactive iodine uptake and TSH response to thyrotropin releasing hormone) indicate a low thyroid reserve. Diabetes mellitus occurs 5 times more frequently among men with XXY syndrome than among the general population. The diagnosis of diabetes is usually made before the age of 50. The disease tends to be easily controlled in this population.[38] There is an increased incidence of breast carcinoma and mediastinal germ cell tumors, but these men are not considered more susceptible to testicular cancer.[81] Scoliosis may present during adolescence.[80]

The presence of XY/XXY mosaicism tempers the clinical features of Klinefelter syndrome. In these cases, testicular function is less impaired and the diagnosis is often made when the middle-aged patient presents with a complaint of decreased potency.[79]

Other variants include XXXY and XXXXY karyotypes. These men are more likely to be mentally retarded and growth deficient and to have other somatic anomalies. XXYY karyotypes have also been reported. These males have the phenotypic features of Klinefelter syndrome, and mental retardation is usually present. In addition, they are at increased risk for development of peripheral vascular disease.[35,79]

Turner Syndrome

In 1938 Henry Turner described seven girls with short stature, lack of secondary sexual characteristics, "webbing" at the neck, and cubitus valgus. Although unaware of the explanation for these findings, Turner successfully used estrogen therapy to promote sexual development.[87]

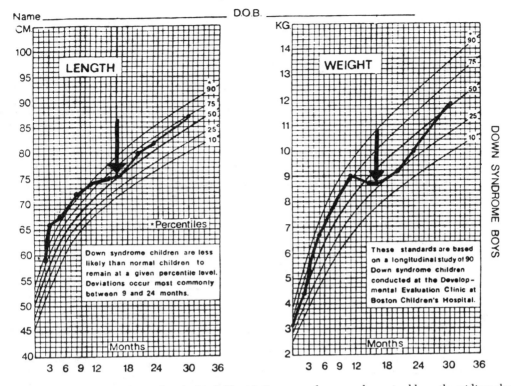

Name_____ D.O.B. _____

FIG. 15-2. Growth curve (heavy lines) of a child with Down syndrome and acquired hypothyroidism showing plateau in growth before treatment and improved growth after thyroid hormone replacement began (indicated by arrows). Percentile growth curves for boys with Down syndrome; chart developed by Cronk[19] to track growth of children with Down syndrome.

Further studies of this syndrome showed the women involved to have varying degrees of ovarian dysgenesis with elevated gonadotropin levels.[25] In 1959, Ford demonstrated the absence of an X chromosome in this syndrome.[10] Females with the Turner, or XO, syndrome are generally within the average range of intelligence; however, they have an increased frequency of perceptual organization and fine motor difficulties, either of which may present as a learning disability.[7]

The vast majority of these girls require estrogen and progesterone replacement beginning at the age of puberty to initiate and sustain sexual maturation. Though a few women with mosaicism have menstruated spontaneously and have borne children, most women who have Turner syndrome are infertile.[25] Unfortunately, estrogen replacement does not alleviate the problem of short stature. Individuals with Turner syndrome are small at birth and remain so.[62] Growth velocities are at the 10th to 25th percentiles during childhood; the average height of these girls by puberty is 4.5 standard deviations below the mean.[10] Treatment for the short stature remains controversial. Growth hormone supplements alone have not proven efficacious although there is evidence of decreased growth hormone levels in older girls (ages 9 to 20 years) with Turner syndrome.[70] Androgens cause an increase in growth velocity while being administered, but their effect on ultimate height is negligible according to some controlled studies.[71,83,88] Any hormonal treatment should be carefully monitored by an experienced endocrinologist. The risks and benefits of treatment must be discussed with the child and her parents

There is an increased incidence of inflammatory thyroid disease among women with Turner syndrome.[9] Though most reports have been of adult patients, children may also be affected.[61] Since poor growth is characteristic of this syndrome, further compromise due to hypothyroidism may be overlooked. For these reasons, routine screening of thyroid function is recommended for individuals with Turner syndrome.[9]

Poly X-Syndromes

Females with XXXX and XXXXX (penta X) karyotypes are mentally retarded and have facial features suggestive of Down syndrome (midfacial hypoplasia, epicanthal folds, upwardly slanted palperbral fissures). Minor skeletal anomalies, including radioulnar synostosis, may be present. XXXX women usually have normal stature, whereas those with the penta-X syndrome are short. Amenorrhea may or may not be present. A few women with the XXXX syndrome have been fertile.[72,80]

Noonan Syndrome

Noonan syndrome, like Turner syndrome, is characterized by short stature, webbing of the neck, and occasional renal anomalies, but the karyotype appears normal. Sporadic cases and familial modes of inheritance have both been described. Intellectual development is varied: borderline or mild retardation is common.[15] The cardiac anomalies (most frequently pulmonic stenosis) are usually right-sided (this is in contrast to the Turner syndrome, in which left-sided cardiac defects predominate). Autoimmune thyroiditis has been reported in both syndromes.[90]

Noonan syndrome has been described in both sexes, but it is more extensively documented in males. Cryptorchidism is common. Boys with Noonan syndrome exhibit variable development; puberty may be normal, delayed, or it may not occur at all without hormonal replacement. Males who do not enter puberty have primary gonadal failure with impaired spermatogenesis.[15,85,89] Females generally develop secondary sexual characeristics, although menarche may be delayed.

Congenital Rubella Syndrome

Although the frequency of congenital rubella syndrome has dramatically decreased since the licensure of live attenuated rubella vaccine in 1969, sporadic cases still occur and survivors of the last epidemic in 1964 are now adults. The classic description of the rubella syndrome by Gregg and others in the 1940s included intrauterine growth retardation, congenital heart disease, sensory impairment, and mental retardation.[45] Further studies have also documented endocrinological complications.

Diabetes mellitus occurs more frequently in persons with congenital rubella. The reported frequency varies, but it may be as high as 20% by the third decade of life.[29,51] The onset is generally in adolescence or adulthood, though young children may also be affected.[52] This population is also at increased risk of acquired thyroid dysfunction, presenting as either Hashimoto's or Grave's thyroiditis.[94] A study of 200 adolescents with rubella syndrome found 5% of the cohort to have abnormal thyroid function. Over one-fifth

of these teens had positive antithyroid antibodies.[13] The thyroid and pancreatic disease may be triggered by a virus-induced immune reaction in the target organ.[77,95]

Growth deficiency is a common manifestation of congenital rubella. The majority of infants are small for gestational age. Although the growth velocity is usually normal, the children tend to remain small. Infants infected late in gestation may show catch-up growth, whereas maternal infection in the first trimester may result in a fall-off in growth rate by age 3 years.[54] Though there have been sporadic cases of growth hormone deficiency in this syndrome this does not appear to be the usual cause of the growth failure.[66] The rubella virus has been shown to inhibit cell multiplication; this is the presumed basis of the decreased somatic growth.[58]

An individual with congenital rubella syndrome should be observed for symptoms of diabetes mellitus and routinely screened for the presence of antithyroid antibodies. If antibody titers are elevated, thyroid function tests must be obtained; these may be abnormal even in the absence of symptoms.[13] Growth hormone secretion should be evaluated in the children with low growth velocities.[66]

Prader-Willi Syndrome

The Prader-Willi syndrome (PWS) (see also Chap. 10) is characterized by severe hypotonia and failure to thrive in infancy, progressing to obesity secondary to compulsive overeating in childhood. In addition, people with this syndrome have short stature, mental retardation, small hands and feet, hypogonadism and cryptorchidism. Facial features include upslanting almond-shaped palpebral fissures, epicanthi, a narrow bitemporal diameter, and a triangular shaped upper lip The diagnosis is clinical though deletion of part of the long arm of chromosome #15 may be found in some.[34]

Hypogonadism is present in both sexes but is more frequently diagnosed in males. Males with Prader-Willi syndrome have small penises and testes as well as cryptorchidism. Females can have hypoplastic labia and/or clitoris.

Sexual maturation is abnormal and varies from precocious to delayed puberty, the latter being more common. Even when there is precocious onset of pubertal changes, complete maturation is protracted. In females, oligomenorrhea and primary and secondary amenorrhea are all frequently found. Males usually have incomplete sexual development.[12]

The question of hypothalamic-pituitary dysfunction has been raised to explain the voracious appetite, hypotonia, and abnormal sexual development. Thyroid function and thyrotropin releasing hormone (TRH) responses have been shown to be normal. Similarly, there is no evidence for any abnormality in the hypothalamic-pituitary-adrenal axis. Insulin, arginine and dopa provocative tests of growth hormone are blunted, as in simple obesity.[1] The hypothalamic-pituitary-gonadal axis has been studied extensively in people with Prader-Willi Syndrome with some variability in results. In general, however, basal levels of testosterone, estradiol, luteinizing hormone (LH) and follicle-stimulating hormone (FSH) are low.[12] There is a subnormal response of LH and FSH to luteinizing hormone releasing hormone (LH-RH), indicating pituitary or hypothalamic disease. However, clomiphene or repeated LH-RH injections result in normal LH and FSH responses, suggesting that the pituitary is normal but understimulated secondary to longstanding LH-RH deficiency. Since clomiphene restores LH and FSH responsiveness, the defect is more likely secondary to hypothalamic dysfunction rather than irreversible LH-RH deficiency.[42]

Some authors believe that a primary gonadal disorder is also present. In adult males, the testicular histology suggests primary testicular dysgenesis.[1] At this point, only one histologic study of ovarian tissue from a woman with Prader-Willi syndrome has been reported.[8] This showed small ovaries without corpus lutea or follicular development despite a history of regular menses.

No definite statements about the etiology of hypogonadism in PWS can be made at this time because there is evidence pointing to both hypothalamic and primary gonadal dysfunction.

Some individuals with Prader-Willi syndrome have diabetic manifestations, usually presenting after puberty. The reported incidence ranges from 7%[12] to 33%.[1] The diabetes is usually non-insulin-dependent and is considered to be secondary to obesity,[1] rather than an intrinsic feature of the syndrome. Reduction of caloric intake is the most effective treatment.[12]

Pseudohypoparathyroidism

Manifestations of pseudohypoparathyroidism include hypocalcemia, metastatic ossification in subcutaneous tissues, moon-shaped facies, and mental retardation. Skeletal abnormalities characterized by short stature and short, wide, and coarsely trabeculated metacarpals and metatarsals (especially 1, 4, and 5) are also typical (see Fig. 15-3). This syndrome is most commonly inherited as a sex-linked dominant trait.

These individuals have increased amounts of parathyroid hormone (PTH). Although the bone and gastrointestinal response to PTH may be normal, the renal response is quite decreased. Consequently, urinary phosphate excretion is not enhanced when PTH is administered, in

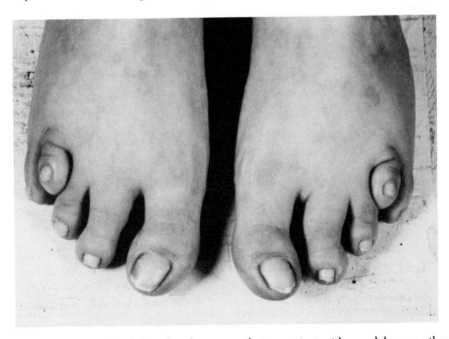

FIG. 15-3. A dramatic example of short fourth metatarsals in a patient with pseudohypoparathyroidism.

contrast to people with true hypoparathyroidism, who exhibit a supranormal response to this test. The diagnosis is made by the lack of renal response to PTH in an individual with hypocalcemia and increased circulating PTH.[44]

Treatment is aimed toward maintaining a normal serum calcium with crystalline dihydrotachysterol $(1,25 \ (OH)_2 D_3)$. If this approach is unsuccessful, then aluminum hydroxide (which decreases phosphate absorption from the gastrointestinal tract) and calcium gluconate are used.[44]

Beckwith-Wiedemann Syndrome

In 1963, Beckwith described the autopsy results of three infants with macroglossia, omphalocoele, and visceromegaly. The following year, Wiedemann described three siblings with similar findings. Subsequently, hypoglycemia has been found with an estimated frequency of 33 to 50% in these children.[76] Associated findings include facial capillary hemangiomas at birth (typically on the glabella, eyelids, and tip of the nose), hemihypertrophy, high incidence of malignancy (with and without associated hemihypertrophy), mild microcephaly, and cryptorchidism.[40]

Moderate mental retardation has been attributed to hypoglycemia. The prognosis for normal cognitive development is good in patients without hypoglycemia.[1] Islet cell hyperplasia (found at autopsy) and hyperinsulinism, along with hyperresponsiveness to glucose and glucagon, have been reported as the etiology of the hypoglycemia in some patients.[1] Because the prognosis of normal intellectual outcome is good with early treatment of hypoglycemia, the importance of early recognition is evident. Diazoxide therapy usually suppresses serum insulin levels and helps maintain euglycemia. One infant has been reported who was not adequately controlled by diazoxide until susphrine (long-acting epinephrine) was added.[76] Commonly, spontaneous regression of the hypoglycemia occurs, though it can persist throughout childhood and into adulthood.

Because these patients are macrosomic, growth hormone levels have been studied but have been found to be normal.[1] The etiology of the large stature remains unknown.

Septo-Optic Dysplasia

The term septo-optic dysplasia was coined by DeMorsier in 1956 to describe the frequent association of optic nerve hypoplasia (not necessarily associated with decreased visual acuity) and absence of the septum pellucidum.[80] A variable degree of hypopituitarism ranging from isolated growth hormone deficiency to panhypopituitarism with diabetes insipidus has been found.[82] Absence of the septum is no longer considered to be necessary for the diagnosis.[63]

The neonatal period is characterized by hypoglycemia, with or without seizures, hypotonia, and jaundice. In the untreated infant, growth failure and psychomotor retardation follow. Replacement of the hormone deficiencies improves the prognosis.

DiGeorge Syndrome

In the 1960s DiGeorge described the association of hypoparathyroidism, cellular immune deficiency, and aplasia of the thymus and parathyroid glands.[21,22] This syndrome is now recognized to have a variable spectrum of associated abnormalities including cardiovascular anomalies, hypertelorism, micrognathia, and low-set ears. The degree of thymic and parathyroid hypoplasia or malformation is variable. The majority of individuals who survive infancy are mildly to moderately retarded.

Neonatal hypocalcemia frequently occurs secondary to hypoparathyroidism. As expected, patients with severe hypocalcemia are more likely to have aplasia of the parathyroids.[16] Treatment with parathyroid hormone usually normalizes serum calcium; vitamin D and calcium supplementation may also be necessary. Although hypocalcemia can be severe during infancy, there is often remission during childhood. These remissions are thought to reflect a partial DiGeorge with hypertrophy of the small amounts of parathyroid tissue occurring over time.

Tuberous Sclerosis

Tuberous sclerosis is an autosomal dominant phakomatosis with a variable clinical spectrum including mental retardation (with tubers throughout the cortical gray matter), seizures, adenoma sebaceum, hypopigmented cutaneous macules, shagreen patches, and periungual fibromas.[56] (See also Chaps. 8 and 18.) Hamartomas have been found in the pancreas, thyroid, adrenals, and hypothalamic area. Patients with precocious puberty and adrenal hyperplasia have been described as having hypoglycemia secondary to pancreatic adenomas.[75] One case of acromegalic gigantism has been reported in an individual with tuberous sclerosis. Pathologic studies revealed an eosinophilic adenoma.[36]

A small series of institutionalized patients with tuberous sclerosis were evaluated, and three of

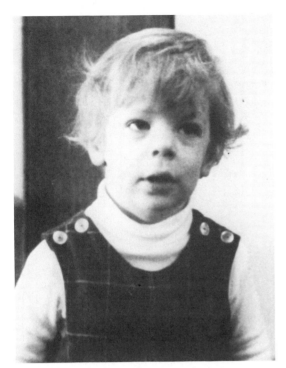

FIG. 15-4. Williams syndrome: characterized by developmental delay, supravalvular aortic stenosis, and elfin facies.

seven were found to be hypothyroid. The pituitary adrenal function was abnormal in several, and five of the seven had abnormal responses to an intravenous glucose-tolerance test.[75] These data suggest that endocrine dysfunction may be more frequent in tuberous sclerosis than previously realized.

Laurence-Moon-Bardet-Biedl Syndrome

The Laurence-Moon-Bardet-Biedl (LMBB) syndrome consists of mental retardation, pigmentary retinopathy, obesity, polydactyly, and hypogonadism.

Hypogonadism with delayed or incomplete pubertal development is attributed to a hypothalamic-pituitary disorder rather than a primary gonadal abnormality. Absent or arrested spermatogenesis has been shown on testicular biopsy. In a few patients, plasma testosterone levels are low to low-normal but increase normally in response to human chorionic gonadotropin (hCG). LH and FSH are also low to low-normal but increase significantly after LH-RH.[1] Males with LMBB syndrome have various genital abnormalities including small phallus, bifid scrotum, hypospadias, and cryptorchidism. In females, there is a range from absence of puberty to normal ovarian function and fertility.[5]

Glucose intolerance has been described but may simply be secondary to obesity. Occasional cases of diabetes insipidus, tall and short stature, and advanced and retarded bone age have been reported. Adrenal and thyroid function are usually normal.[5]

Williams Syndrome

This syndrome is characterized by features first described by Williams in 1961: mental deficiency; supravalvular aortic stenosis; and elfin facies, that is, eyebrow flare, flattened nasal bridge, anteverted nares and prominent mouth (Fig. 15-4).[92] A transient hypercalcemia may appear in the first years of life. Recent data suggest that the elevated calcium levels are secondary to an abnormal regulation of 1,25-dihydroxyvitamin D.[33] Systemic hypertension has also been reported in individuals with this syndrome. The elevated blood pressure has, in some cases, been attributed to nephrocalcinosis secondary to hypercalcemia. Peripheral vascular anomalies, such as renal artery stenosis or aortic coarctation, may also contribute to hypertension in this syndrome. Patients with Williams syndrome should have their blood pressure monitored, and it should be measured at least once in all extremities.[20]

DISORDERS OF GROWTH AND MATURATION

Disordered growth is a feature of many of the developmental disabilities. Slow growth with ultimate short stature is a general characteristic of the major chromosomal abnormalities. The tall males with XXY and XYY syndromes are notable exceptions to this rule. Isolated gene defects (e.g., osteochondrodysplasias)[46] can also inhibit somatic growth. Degenerative diseases must be ruled out when initially normal growth and development deteriorate. Children with Hurler syndrome provide a striking example of a degenerative phenomenon: their growth velocity is above average in the first years of life, with subsequent marked decline (see Fig. 15-5). In the above cases, the causes of impaired growth are attributable to the underlying genetic/metabolic problem.

Prenatal influences are a significant cause of growth disturbance. Poor maternal nutrition, smoking, infections, drugs, and placental dysfunction all play a role. The fetal alcohol syndrome is an example of teratogen that causes permanent growth and cognitive impairment (see Fig. 15-6). Infants who are small for gestational age may show catch-up growth in their first two years of life.[91] This catch-up phenomenon is more likely to occur in infants who have

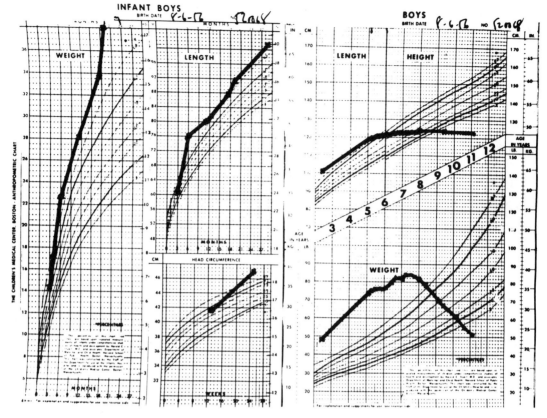

FIG. 15-5. Growth curves of a child with Hurler syndrome. Note accelerated growth in first year of life, with subsequent decline of growth in mid-childhood.

decreased weight alone than in those having general growth retardation.[48] Animal studies have suggested that intrauterine insults occurring early in pregnancy are more likely to cause permanent growth impairment than later gestational difficulties.[93] Infants who are small due to prematurity alone (appropriate for gestational age) are generally said to have a good chance of showing catch-up growth.[26] However, the catch-up may not be complete; Sherman and Miller found lower percentiles for weight, height, and head circumference in 2-year-old children who had been premature (birth weights of 1 to 1.5 kg) when they were compared with a normal population.[24,39]

Children with CNS abnormalities such as microcephaly or severe cerebral palsy may show poor growth velocities with ultimate stunting. This has been described even in the presence of adequate caloric intake. The onset of puberty is variable. For example, individuals with hydrocephalus may manifest delayed or, less frequently, precocious puberty. This has been attributed to a hypothalamic-pituitary effect, but the pathophysiology remains unknown.[28] Hypo-

thalamic dysfunction with delayed maturation is well documented in CNS anomalies such as septo-optic dyslpasia and Kallman syndrome.[32]

Malnutrition is a poignant cause of growth failure in the handicapped. Motor impairment is associated with chewing difficulties, esophageal dysmotility, and gastroesophageal reflux. Dramatic growth may follow the provision of adequate nutrition. Puberty may subsequently occur, even at mid-adult chronological ages (see Chap. 10).

Psychosocial dwarfism is an unusual cause of developmental delay and failure to thrive. These children will typically manifest bizarre behaviors such as rumination or bulimia. Marked improvement in growth and development occurs following placement in a nurturing environment.[64]

Health care professionals working with the developmentally disabled need to be familiar with patterns of growth and maturation present in syndromes encountered and investigate deviations from the expected pattern. Associated endocrine disorders or structural anomalies (e.g., cardiac malformation) must be ruled out. Drug effects should be considered. Familial patterns,

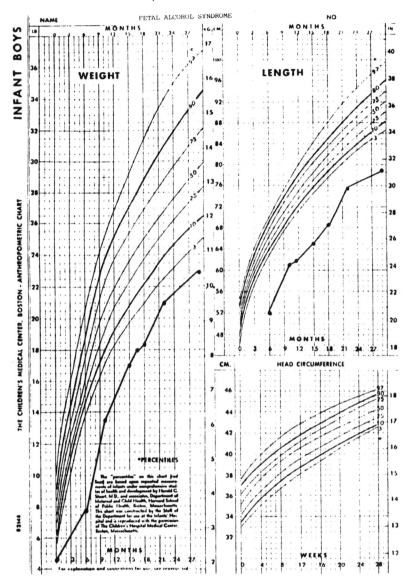

FIG. 15-6. Growth curves of a child with fetal alcohol syndrome. Note low birth weight and persistent growth impairment.

chronic illness, and malabsorption can affect the growth of any child; these factors should not be overlooked in the handicapped population. Abnormal growth and sexual development are sensitive issues for *any* individual; tact and compassion are necessary when these problems are encountered. Psychosocial supports (e.g., counseling and peer group discussion) should be offered.

MEDICATIONS AFFECTING ENDOCRINE FUNCTION AND ENDOCRINE TESTS

A number of medications that can affect endocrine function and endocrine test results are fre-

quently used when treating the manifestations of central nervous system dysfunction (see Chaps. 8 and 20). It is important that the physician caring for persons with developmental disabilities have a thorough knowledge of these effects.

Phenytoin

Phenytoin is associated with several endocrinologic effects. First, patients being treated with phenytoin typically have a 20 to 30% reduction in total serum thyroxine (T_4), but occasionally T_4 levels may be as low as 2 to 3 μg/dl. Serum free T_4 levels may fall to the same extent.[41] Thyroid status of the patient remains normal, and basal and TRH-stimulated TSH levels are in the chronic illness, and malabsorption can affect the normal range. Serum tri-iodothyronine (T_3) levels are not greatly affected by phenytoin. Phenytoin probably has multiple effects on thyroid hormone economy, including increased rate of transport of T_4 into peripheral tissues, accelerated metabolism and excretion of T_4, and some inhibition of the binding of T_4 to thyroxine-binding globulin (TBG). Typical thyroid function tests in a patient on phenytoin therapy would include low total T_4, low free T_4, normal TSH, and normal T_3 by radioimmunoassay. T_3 resin uptake (T_3RU) or equivalent test, an indirect measure of thyroxine binding proteins, may be normal or slightly increased.

Phenytoin inhibits the secretion of insulin at the level of the pancreatic beta cell and may therefore exacerbate hyperglycemia in diabetics.[65] Phenytoin has also been implicated as a cause of hirsutism, though the mechanism by which this occurs is not entirely clear. Finally, phenytoin has been noted to cause impaired bone metabolism in patients taking the medication for long periods of time.[31] The mechanism by which this occurs is still not clear. The plasma levels of 25 $(OH)D_3$ have been low, possibly the result of hepatic cell microsomal enzyme induction leading to formation of inactive vitamin D metabolites. 1,25 $(OH)_2D_3$ levels have been reported to be normal in one study. Since small doses of vitamin D by mouth appear to be protective and since there is a significant risk of developing osteomalacia among long-term phenytoin users, it is recommended that such patients receive approximately 2,000 units of vitamin D daily as a prophylactic measure.

Phenobarbital

Phenobarbital has been implicated as a cause of impaired bone metabolism in long-term users of the drug.[3] The mechanism is probably similar to that of phenytoin, and recommendations for prophylactic administration of vitamin D are the same.

Phenothiazines

Phenothiazines and related major tranquilizers routinely cause an elevation of serum prolactin levels and are a frequent cause of galactorrhea among females taking the medication.[69] Elevations of serum prolactin up to 100 ng/ml are not uncommon, and higher values may be seen. Pro-

lactin levels rapidly revert to normal within 48 to 96 hours following cessation of therapy. Values tend to be higher in women treated with phenothiazines than in men.

It is important to evaluate each phenothiazine-treated patient with galactorrhea individually. Particularly in patients with phenothiazine levels greater than 100 ng/ml and those in whom other endocrinologic dysfunction is suggested, a more thorough evaluation is warranted. In patients with minimal elevations, careful watching or a repeat prolactin level after 5 days of therapy is usually sufficient.

Long-term treatment with the phenothiazine drug, perphanazine (Trilafon) may be accompanied by an elevation of TBG. As a result, total T_4 and total T_3 may be elevated in patients treated with perphenazine. T_3 resin uptake and free thyroxine index may be low.[2] Thyroid-stimulating hormone should be normal. Since free hormone levels are normal, patients treated with perphenazine are normal, patients treated with perphenazine are euthyroid.

Several patients treated with the phenothiazine thioridazine (Mellaril) were reported to have low total T_4 levels with normal T_3 resin uptakes and normal levels of TSH. T_3 levels by radioimmunoassay are normal. The reason for the low total T_4 levels is unexplained.

Lithium Carbonate

Treatment with lithium carbonate for manic depressive or other affective disorders results in serum lithium ion levels that are able to inhibit the action of TSH on the thyroid gland and the synthesis and release of T_3 and T_4. This results in increased levels of TSH with somewhat decreased levels of T_4 and T_3.[2] Because patients are treated with lithium over a period of months, most tend to normalize on thyroid function tests. Up to 6% of patients treated with lithium carbonate will, however, develop frank hypothyroidism, which resolves when lithium is discontinued. An even larger group of patients, perhaps 15%, will have elevated TSH levels with or without thyroid enlargement. A few cases of hyperthyroidism have occurred during treatment with lithium.[69] Given this high incidence of thyroid function abnormalities, baseline T_4, T_3 resin uptake, and TSH levels should be obtained prior to beginning lithium therapy and repeat studies should be done after 6 months. If the patient develops any symptoms suggesting hypothyroidism, serum thyroid function tests should be repeated.

Methylphenidate Hydrochloride

Methylphenidate hydrochloride (Ritalin) is a stimulant that is effective in the treatment of children with hyperkinesis. A side effect of growth retardation has been reported.[78] In 1979 a Food and Drug Administration review concluded that a moderate reduction in weight and a minor decrease in linear growth occur during the first few years of treatment. Higher doses given over prolonged periods appear to have the most effect. Drug vacations (e.g., weekends, summer holiday) are recommended by some investigators to lessen the detrimental effects on growth.[23,78]

REFERENCES

1. Aarskog, D.: Dysmorphic syndromes. *In* Clinical Paediatric Endocrinology. Edited by C.G.O. Brook. Boston, Blackwell, 1981, pp. 159-190.
2. Abramowicz, M., et al.: Effect of drugs on thyroid function tests. Med. Lett. Drugs Ther., *23*:30, 1981.
3. Aurbach, G.D., Marx, S.J., and Spiegel, A.M.: Parathyroid hormone calcitonin and the calciferols. *In* Textbook of Endocrinology. Edited by R.H. Williams. Philadelphia, W.B. Saunders, 1981, p. 1003.
4. Bacon, G.E., Spencer, M.L., Hopwood, N.J., and Kelch, R.P.: Hypothyroidism. *In* A Practical Approach to Pediatric Endocrinology. Edited by G.E. Bacon, and M.L. Spencer. Chicago, Year Book Medical Publishers, 1982, pp. 139-215.
5. Bauman, M., and Hogan, G.: Laurence-Moon-Biedl syndrome. Am. J. Dis. Child., *126*:119, 1973.
6. Benda, C.E.: The Child with Mongolism. New York, Grune & Stratton, 1960.
7. Bender, B., Puck, M., Saldenblatt, J., and Robinson, A.: Cognitive development of unselected girls with complete and partial X monosomy. Pediatrics, *73*:175, 1984.
8. Bray, G.A., Dahms, W.T., Swerdloff, R.H.: The Prader-Willi syndrome: A study of 40 patients and a review of the literature. Medicine, *62*:59, 1983.
9. Bright, G.M., Blizzard, R.M., Kaiser, D.L., and Clarke, W.L.: Organ specific autoantibodies in children with common endocrine diseases. J. Pediatr., *100*:8, 1982.
10. Brook, G.C.D., Murset, G., Zachmann, M., and Prader, A.: Growth in children with 45 XO Turner's syndrome. Arch. Dis. Child., *49*:789, 1974.
11. Caldwell, P.D., and Smith, D.W.: The XXY (Klinefelter's) syndrome in childhood: Detection and treatment. J. Pediatr., *80*:250, 1972.
12. Cassidy, S.: Prader-Willi syndrome. Curr. Probl. Pediatr., *14*:3, 1984.
13. Clarke, W.L., et al.: Autoimmunity in congenital rubella syndrome. J. Pediatr., *104*:374, 1984.
14. Coleman, M., and Lentz, G.A. (Eds.): Down Syndrome: Papers and Abstracts for Professionals, *16*:1, 1983.
15. Collins, E., and Turner, G.: The Noonan syndrome: A review of the clinical and genetic features of 27 cases. J. Pediatr., *83*:941, 1973.
16. Conley, M.E., Beckwith, J.B., Mancer, J.F.K., and Tenckhoff, I.: The spectrum of the DiGeorge Syndrome. J. Pediatr., *94*:883, 1979.
17. Cornblath, M.: Hypoglycemia in infancy and childhood. Pediatr. Ann., *10*:49, 1981.
18. Cornblath, M., and Poth, M.: Hypoglycemia. *In* Clinical Pediatric and Adolescent Endocrinology. Edited by S. Kaplan. Philadelphia, W.B. Saunders, 1982, pp. 157-170.
19. Cronk, C.E.: Growth of children with Down syndrome: Birth to age three years. Pediatrics, *61*:564, 1978.
20. Daniels, S.R., Loggie, J.M.H., Schwartz, D.C., Strife, J.L., and Kaplan, S.: Systemic hypertension secondary to peripheral vascular anomalies in patients with Williams Syndrome. J. Pediatr., *106*:249, 1985.
21. DiGeorge, A.M.: New concept of cellular basis of immunity. J. Pediatr., *67*:907, 1965.
22. DiGeorge, A.M.: Congenital absence of thymus and its immunologic consequences: Concurrence with congenital hypoparathyroidism. Birth Defects, *4*:116, 1968.
23. Dulcan, M.K.: Attention deficit disorder: Evaluation and treatment. Pediatr. Ann., *14*:383, 1985.
24. Ernst, J.A., et al.: Growth outcome of the very low birthweight infant at one year. J. Am. Diet. Assoc., *82*:44, 1983.
25. Feingold, D.S., and Parris, E.E.: Disorders of sexual development. N. Engl. J. Med., *277*:387, 1967.
26. Fischer, R.: Growth patterns of low birthweight infants. Pediatr. Ann., *7*:104, 1979.
27. Fisher, D.A., et al.: Screening for congenital hypothyroidism: Results of screening one million North American infants. J. Pediatr., *94*:700, 1979.
28. Ford, F.R.: Diseases of the Nervous System. Springfield, IL, Charles C Thomas, 1973.
29. Forrest, J.M., Menser, M.A., and Burgess, J.A.: High frequency of diabetes mellitus in young adults with congenital rubella. Lancet, *ii*:332, 1971.
30. Fort, P., et al.: Abnormalities of thyroid function infants with Down syndrome. J. Pediatr., *104*:545, 1984.
31. Frame, B., and Parfitt, A.W.: Osteomalacia: Current concepts. Ann. Intern. Med., *88*:966, 1978.
32. Frasier, S.D.: Abnormalities of growth. *In* Pediatric Endocrinology. Edited by S.D. Frasier. New York, Grune & Stratton, 1980, pp. 55-118.
33. Garabedian, M., et al.: Elevated plasma 1,25-dihydroxyvitamin D concentrations in infants with hypercalcemia and an elfin facies. N. Engl. J. Med., *312*:948, 1985.
34. Goodman, R., and Gorlin, R.: The Malformed Infant and Child. New York, Oxford University Press, 1983.
35. Grumbach, M.M., and Feliz, A.C.: Disorders of sex differentiation. *In* Textbook of Endocrinology. Edited by R.H. Williams. Philadelphia, W.B. Saunders, 1981, pp. 423-506.
36. Hoffman, W., et al.: Acromegalic gigantism and tuberous sclerosis. J. Pediatr., *93*:478, 1978.
37. Hollingsworth, D.R., McKean, H.E., and Roeckel, I.: Goiter, immunological observations, and thyroid function tests in Down syndrome. Am. J. Dis. Child., *127*:524, 1974.
38. Hsueh, W.H., Hsu, T.H., and Federman, D.D.: Endocrine features of Klinefelter's syndrome. Medicine, *57*: 447, 1978.
39. Hunt, C.E., and Deddish, R.B.: Medical and neurobehavioral outcome in low birthweight infants. Birth Defects, *19*:103, 1983.
40. Ichiba, Y., and Gardner, L.: Metabolic and genetic syndrome of overgrowth. *In* Endocrine and Genetic Diseases of Childhood and Adolescence. Edited by L. Gardner. Philadelphia, W.B. Saunders, 1975, pp. 1314-1338.

41. Ingbar, S.H., and Woeber, K.A.: The thyroid gland. *In* Textbook of Endocrinology. Edited by R.H. Williams. Philadelphia, W.B. Saunders, 1981, p. 159.

42. Jeffcoate, W., Laurance, B., Edwards, C., and Besser, G.: Endocrine function in the Prader-Willi syndrome. Clin. Endocrinol., *12*:81, 1980.

43. Klein, R.: History of congenital hypothyroidism. *In* Neonatal Thyroid Screening. Edited by G. Burrow. New York, Raven Press, 1980, pp. 51-59.

44. Klein, R., and Haddow, J.: Hypoparathyroidism. *In* Endocrine and Genetic Diseases of Childhood and Adolescence. Edited by L. Gardner. Philadelphia, W.B. Saunders, 1975, pp. 415-425.

45. Krugman, S, and Katz, S.: Infectious Disease of Children. Edited by S. Krugman, and S. Katz, St. Louis, C.V. Mosby, 1981, pp. 315-331.

46. Levitsky, L.L., and Edidin, D.V.: Growth disorders in children. Compr. Ther., *6*:22, 1980.

47. Levy, H.L., and Mitchell, M.L.: The current status of newborn screening. Hosp. Pract., *17*:89, 1982.

48. Lubchenko, L.U.: The High Risk Infant. Philadelphia, W.B. Saunders, 1976.

49. McMillan, J.A., Nieburg, P.I., and Oski, F.A.: The Whole Pediatrician Catalog. Philadelphia, W.B. Saunders, 1977, pp. 98-99.

50. Menkes, J.H.: Child Neurology. 2nd Ed. Philadelphia, Lea & Febiger, 1986, pp. 458-460.

51. Menser, M.A., Dods, L., and Harley, J.D.: A twenty-five year follow-up of congenital rubella. Lancet, *2*:1347, 1967.

52. Menser, M.A., Forrest, J.M., and Bransby, R.D.: Rubella infection and diabetes mellitus. Lancet, *1*:57, 1978.

53. Meyer, J., and Meyer, J.F.: Medical Neurology. New York, Macmillan, 1975, pp. 95-101.

54. Michaels, R.H., and Kenny, F.M.: Postnatal growth retardation in congenital rubella. Pediatrics, *43*:251, 1969.

55. Milunsky, A., and Neurath, P.: Diabetes mellitus in Down syndrome. Arch. Environ. Health, *17*:372, 1968.

56. Monaghan, H., Krafchik, B., MacGregor, D., and Fitz, C.: Tuberous sclerosis complex in children. Am. J. Dis. Child., *135*:912, 1981.

57. Murdoch, J.C., et al.: Thyroid function in adults with Down syndrome. J. Clin. Endocrinol., *44*:453, 1977.

58. Naeye, R.L., and Blanc, W.: Pathogenesis of congenital rubella. J.A.M.A., *194*:1277, 1965.

59. New England Congenital Hypothyroidism Collaborative. Characteristics of infantile hypothyroidism discovered on neonatal screening. J. Pediatr., *104*:539, 1984.

60. New England Congenital Hypothyroidism Collaborative. Effects of neonatal screening for hypothyroidism: Prevention of mental retardation by treatment before clinical manifestations. Lancet, *2*:1095, 1981.

61. Pai, G.S., et al.: Thyroid abnormalities in twenty children with Turner syndrome. J. Pediatr., *91*:267, 1977.

62. Park, E., Bailey, J.D., and Cowell, C.A.: Growth and maturation of patient with Turner's syndrome. Pediatr. Res., *17*:1, 1983.

63. Patel, H., et al.: Optic nerve hypoplasia with hypopituitarism. Am. J. Dis. Child., *129*:175, 1975.

64. Patton, R.G., and Gardner, L.I.: Deprivation dwarfism: Disordered family environment as cause of so-called idiopathic hypopituitarism. *In* Endocrine and Genetic Diseases of Childhood and Adolescence. Edited by L.I. Gardner. Philadelphia, W.B. Saunders, 1975, pp. 85-98.

65. Porte, D.P., Jr., and Halter, J.B.: The endocrine pancreas and diabetes mellitus. *In* Textbook of Endocrinology. Edited by R.H. Williams. Philadelphia, W.B. Saunders, 1981, p. 765.

66. Preece, M.A., Kearney, P.J., and Marshall, W.C.: Growth hormone deficiency in congenital rubella. Lancet, *2*:842, 1977.

67. Pueschel, S.M., and Rynders, T.E.: Down syndrome. *In* Advances in Biomedicine and the Behavioral Sciences. Cambridge, MA, Ware Press, 1982, pp. 181-183.

68. Quinn, M.W.: Down syndrome and hypothyroidism. J. Med. Sci., *1*:19, 1980.

69. Rose, R.M., and Sachar, E.: Psychoendocrinology. *In* Textbook of Endocrinology. Edited by R.H. Williams. Philadelphia, W.B. Saunders, 1981, p. 666.

70. Ross, J.L., Long, L.M., Loriaux, D.L., and Cutler, G.B.: Growth hormone secretory dynamics in Turner syndrome. J. Pediatr., *106*:202, 1985.

71. Rudman, D., Goldsmith, M., Kutner, M., and Blackston, D.: Effect of growth hormone and oxandrolone singly and together on growth rate in girls with X chromosome abnormalities. J. Pediatr., *96*:132, 1980.

72. Salmon, M.A., and Lindenbaum, R.H.: Developmental defects and syndromes. England, H.M. and M. Publishers, 1978, p. 376.

73. Samuel, A.M., et al.: Thyroid function studies in young Down syndrome children. Ind. J. Med. Res., *73*:223, 1981.

74. Sare, Z., Ruvelcaba, R.H.A., and Kelley, V.C.: Prevalence of thyroid disorders in Down syndrome. Clin. Genet., *14*:154, 1978.

75. Sareen, C., et al.: Tuberous sclerosis. Am. J. Dis. Child., *123*:34, 1972.

76. Schiff, D., Colle, E., Wells, D., and Stern, L.: Metabolic aspects of the Beckwith-Wiedemann syndrome. J. Pediatr., *82*:258, 1973.

77. Schopfer, K., Matter, L., Flueder, U., and Werder, E.: Diabetes mellitus, endocrine autoantibodies and prenatal rubella infection. Lancet, *2*:159, 1982.

78. Shaywitz, S.E., and Shaywitz, B.A.: Diagnosis and management of attention deficit disorder: A pediatric perspective. Pediatr. Clin. N. Am., *31*:429, 1984.

79. Simpson, J.L.: Disorders of Sexual Differentiation. New York, Academic Press, 1976, pp. 316-321.

80. Smith, D.W.: Recognizable Patterns of Human Malformation. Philadelphia, W.B. Saunders, 1982, pp. 64-71, 466.

81. Sogge, M.R., McDonald, S.D., and Cofold, P.B.: The malignant potential of the dysgenetic germ cell in Klinefelter Syndrome. Am. J. Med., *66*:515, 1979.

82. Stelling, M.W., Goldstein, D.E., Johanson, A.J., and Blizzard, R.M.: Hypopituitarism and dysmorphology. *In* Problems in Pediatric Endocrinology. Edited by K. LaCouza, and A.W. Root. New York, Academic Press, 1979, pp. 101-112.

83. Sybert, V.P.: Adult height in Turner's syndrome with 5and without androgen therapy. J. Pediatr., *104*:365, 1984.

84. Takahashi, H., Brady, M.D., Sharma, V., and Grunt, J.A.: Hyperthyroidism in patients with Down's syndrome. Clin. Pediatr., *18*:273, 1979.

85. Theintz, G., and Savage, M.D.: Growth and pubertal development in five boys with Noonan's syndrome. Arch. Dis. Child., *57*:13, 1982.

86. Topper, E., et al.: Puberty in twenty-four patients with Klinefelter syndrome. Eur. J. Pediatr., *139*:8, 1982.

87. Turner, H.H.: A syndrome of infantilism, congenital webbed neck, and cubitus valgus. Endocrinology, *23:* 566, 1938.

88. Urban, M.D., Lee, P.A., Dorst, J.P., Plotnick, L.P., and Migeon, C.J.: Oxandrolone therapy in patients with Turner syndrome. J. Pediatr., *94:*823, 1979.

89. Van Meter, Q.L., and Lee, P.A.: Evaluation of puberty in male and female patients with Noonan syndrome. Pediatr. Res., *14:*485, 1980.

90. Vesterhaus, P., and Aarskog, D.: Noonan's syndrome and autoimmune thyroiditis. J. Pediatr., *83:*237, 1973.

91. Westwood, M., et al.: Growth and development of full-term non-asphyxiated small for gestational age newborns: Follow-up through adolescence. Pediatrics, *71:* 376, 1983.

92. Williams, J.C.P., Barratt-Boyes, B.G., and Lowe, J.B.: Supravalvular aortic stenosis. Circulation, *24:*1311, 1961.

93. Winick, M.: Malnutrition and brain development. J. Pediatr., *74:*667, 1969.

94. Ziring, P.R., and Fedun, B.A.: Thyrotoxicosis in congenital rubella. J. Pediatr., *87:*1002, 1975.

95. Ziring, P.R., et al.: Chronic lymphocytic thyroiditis: Identification of rubella virus antigen in the thyroid of a child with congenital rubella. J. Pediatr., *90:*419, 1977.

16

GYNECOLOGIC PROBLEMS

Kirtly Parker Jones, M.D. □ *Jocelyn Douglass, R.N.-C., M.S.*

In providing gynecologic care for women with severe emotional, physical, and intellectual handicaps, routine examinations and the evaluation of problems pose difficulties. Often, the history is unobtainable, the examination poorly tolerated by the patient, and the differential diagnosis confused because of the patient's many other medical problems.

This chapter elaborates on these difficulties and offers an approach to the patient and a discussion of frequently encountered gynecologic problems. The final section discusses one way to utilize personnel to provide quality routine gynecologic care in a large residential institution.

THE HISTORY AND THE
PHYSICAL EXAMINATION

The patient with developmental disabilities is not usually able to express her concerns or physical symptoms, and documentation in her record may be scanty. The menstrual history is a significant portion of the data base for gynecologic evaluation. Not having a history or having one that is inaccurate can be a potential handicap for health care providers. Those who provide daily care—parents, nurses, the supportive staff of institutions—should be strongly encouraged to keep a menstrual record of all women in the reproductive age.

Past medical history, including the etiology of the disability, is important in establishing the differential diagnosis of the gynecologic problems to be addressed. Specific physical, meta-bolic, and chromosomal disorders can predispose the patient to a range of gynecologic problems. Important in the patient's developmental record are the ages at which she developed pubic hair and began having noticeable breast tissue and her age at onset of menses. Age at menopause is also important. A history of chronic or acute weight gain or loss can also be helpful in evaluating menstrual irregularities associated with changes in body fat.

Pertinent to the patient's history are medications she may be taking. Thyroid hormone replacement and major tranquilizers are commonly prescribed; these medications may reflect an underlying endocrinopathy, and they can also cause menstrual irregularities.

The physical examination begins with an overall assessment of the patient's general health and nutrition, factors that can have profound effects on the patient's menstrual pattern. The breast examination, also part of the gynecological examination, includes palpation for masses, but it should also focus on the developmental stage of the breast and the presence or absence of galactorrhea. Both factors are important in the differential diagnosis of primary and secondary amenorrhea.

Palpation of the abdomen is usually disappointing in its yield of clinically useful information because these patients are often anxious, tense, and tend to guard. They may have spastic rectus muscles, or distended bowel from chronic constipation.

Vulvovaginal examination of these patients requires flexibility on the part of the physician and supportive staff regarding positioning of the patient. The standard lithotomy position with legs in stirrups is almost never achieved either because of the patient's anxiety or physical limitation (e.g., flexion contractures, paralysis, spasticity). The examination can be most successfully achieved with a table with a flexed or removed lower end, and two attendants supporting the patient's legs in the lithotomy position. Often the patient is examined in the Sims' position if hip flexion or abduction is inadequate for visualization with the patient on her back.

Many women with severe developmental disabilities have been in institutional care since childhood, and few have had sexual intercourse. Most have an intact hymen and a very narrow vagina. After examination of the vulva, the size of the vaginal opening, the length of the vagina, and position of the cervix can usually be estimated with the examiner's finger. A variety of specula should be available, including the standard Graves speculum, the long extra narrow Pederson speculum, and the very narrow and short (smaller than an index finger) Smith-Pederson speculum. The speculum may be placed upside down if the patient is on her back but has moved away from the end of the table, leaving no room between the patient and the table surface for the handle of the speculum.

The cervix in nulliparous women, especially those who are postmenopausal, is often very small and difficult to identify. A standard Pap smear is performed if indicated and possible. Aspiration of vaginal pool secretions may be performed when the speculum examination is not possible. Although the false-negative rate of this procedure is very high and it is not suggested as a method of routine cervical cell sampling, it may be the only possible alternative short of general anesthesia and hymenotomy.

Bimanual examination is rarely informative because the abdominal musculature is usually tense, but rectovaginal examination or just a rectal examination is usually adequate for defining masses of significant size and is well tolerated by most patients. For patients with an introitus that is not wide enough to allow a tiny speculum or finger, the rectal examination must suffice. Most such patients who require endometrial sampling for diagnosis of irregular or postmenopausal bleeding will require a hymenotomy, but routine hymenotomy for the purpose of facilitating a routine examination and Pap smear is not necessary. Although the routine Pap smear as a screening test for cervical cancer has become part of the standard of good medical care in the United States, the woman with severe developmental disabilities who has never had sexual intercourse is at extremely low risk for cervical cancer.

When the physical examination is too limited by anatomy or poor compliance to evaluate a suspected pelvic mass, pelvic ultrasonography can be helpful. The availability of this diagnostic procedure, its use in evaluating the uterus and ovaries, and the acceptability of the procedure to most patients makes this noninvasive technique quite helpful.

Occasionally there is a request for a routine gynecologic examination of a patient who has been uncooperative and probably frightened during previous attempts to perform such an examination. The decision by the administration of a given institution or the guardians of a patient who is severely retarded that good medical care includes screening tests and examinations means that occasionally a patient must be sedated. The choice of sedatives is usually made by the patient's primary physician or primary care provider who has referred her to the gynecology clinic, but the usual choice is oral chloral hydrate and diazepam. This use of mild sedation, plus a careful gentle approach to the patient and the supportive presence of caretakers whom she knows, allowed examination of all but one of the 132 patients noted in Table 16-2. This patient was a young woman with irregular bleeding for whom oral sedatives were inadequate, and with the help of paramedics and with resuscitation equipment available, the patient was sedated with intravenous diazepam. This approach is not recommended without ancillary medical facilities and respiratory support available in the immediate area.

COMMON PROBLEMS

In reviewing the experience of a gynecology consultation service at a large state residential facility, it was apparent that there were problems typical of those seen in any office practice, problems unique to the population, and problems commonly seen in a general practice but which have aspects of diagnosis or therapy that specifically apply to a woman with severe handicaps. The following section discusses some of the problems in the latter two categories. Table 16-1 shows the age distribution of 132 consecutive patients seen for gynecologic consultation. This distribution is not significantly different from that seen in the general population of women seeking gynecologic care. Table 16-2 lists the

Table 16-1. *Age Distribution of Women with Developmental Disabilities in an Institutional Setting Referred for Gynecologic Evaluation (N = 132)*

Age	Percent
Under 20	2.3
20-29	28.8
30-39	20.5
40-49	27.3
50-59	13.6
60-69	6.8
70 or older	0.8

problems for which these patients were referred. As indicated in this table, it is clear that the gynecologic problems in developmentally disabled women are quite different from those addressed by most large gynecology clinics serving the general population (e.g., requests for birth control, pelvic pain, and vaginitis).

Amenorrhea

Primary and secondary amenorrhea may be seen more frequently in the setting of an institu-

Table 16-2. *Presenting Problems in 132 Women in an Institutional Setting Requiring Referral for Gynecologic Consultation*

Problem	Percent
Excessive bleeding	20
Routine examination (previous practitioner unable to examine)	19
Suspected genital lesion	15
Dysmenorrhea and behavior disturbance with menses	11
Contraception	8
Amenorrhea	8
Abdominal or pelvic mass	7
Postmenopausal bleeding	7
Uterine enlargement	6
Amenorrhea or galactorrhea	5
Oligomenorrhea	5
Vaginal discharge	4
Stress urinary incontinence	2
Hirsutism	2
History of DES exposure	2
Rule out pregnancy	<1

tion for the emotionally or physically disabled, but the differential diagnosis and evaluation are the same anywhere. Common causes of amenorrhea in this population include central nervous system abnormality, feeding difficulties, and congenital anomalies:

1. Central nervous system lesions from birth trauma or secondary CNS lesions from hydrocephalus or meningitis can lead to primary hypothalamic amenorrhea or precocious puberty.
2. Many patients who are chronically ill or who have severe cerebral palsy, for whom adequate nutrition is a problem, may be too underweight to establish menarche or maintain regular ovulation. Several patients over 20 years old who were severely underweight because of feeding difficulties did not begin menses until feeding gastrostomies were placed and the patients attained a critical amount of body fat. (See Chap. 10.)
3. Some chromosomal anomalies, inborn errors of metabolism, and congenital syndromes are associated with gonadal dysgenesis or premature ovarian failure and subsequent failure to develop secondary sex characteristics. (See Chap. 15.)

Failure to establish menses by age 16 is an indication for a gynecologic consultation. Appropriate laboratory studies include evaluation of nutritional status, thyroid function tests, a serum prolactin test to rule out pituitary tumor, and a follicle-stimulating hormone (FSH) test. Elevated FSH would suggest ovarian failure or gonadal dysgenesis. An elevated FSH in a young amenorrheic woman is an indication for a karyotype if this has not been done as part of the patient's evaluation of her developmental disability. Young women with a Y chromosome should have their gonads surgically removed after they reach their early teens because they have a high probability of developing a gonadoblastoma in a dysgenetic testis.

Many patients hospitalized with major psychotic disturbances are taking phenothiazines or antidepressants. These medications are dopamine inhibitors. Dopamine is thought to be important in the tonic inhibition of prolactin production, and because dopamine action is inhibited by the major tranquilizers (most markedly by the phenothiazines and buterophenones), prolactin levels rise and can lead to oligomenorrhea or amenorrhea and galactorrhea in some cases. These medications are a frequent cause of amenorrhea in the patients referred for gynecologic consultation. At what point should a patient taking phenothiazines who has amenorrhea and an elevated prolactin level be evaluated for a pituitary tumor? What are the expected levels of serum prolactin that can be attributed to medication, and at what levels should a primary pituitary problem be considered? Patients with schizophrenia have baseline levels of prolactin in the normal range. Studies evaluating the effect of chlorpromazine hydrochloride have shown a dose-response curve with respect to serum prolactin with a limit to the stimulation of prolactin at a dose of 1,500 mg per day. The maximum serum prolactin measured at this dose is 150 to 200 ng/ml (normal in most laboratories is less than 20 ng/ml). Patients with pituitary adenomas definable by computerized tomography (CT) are associated with prolactin levels from 50 to 1,000 ng/ml, but most adenomas definable on CT scan are associated with prolactin levels over 200 ng/ml. Patients with amenorrhea who are taking medications known to elevate prolactin should have their prolactin measured yearly, and those with levels over 100 ng/ml should have a CT scan of the pituitary for baseline. If the baseline film is normal, and the prolactin does not continue to increase over the years, no further radiologic evaluation is probably necessary.

Irregular Bleeding

The pathophysiology of irregular bleeding among the developmentally disabled is no different from that in the general population. A stable, reasonable weight and good general health are important in maintaining regular ovulation. Sudden changes in caloric intake leading to weight gain or loss can lead to anovulation and subsequent anovulatory bleeding.

In many cases in a general gynecology practice, an endometrial biopsy performed with local anesthesia in the office is adequate to diagnose anovulatory bleeding or endometrial hyperplasia. If performed carefully, biopsy is at least 90% accurate in ruling out endometrial cancer. Our experience with women who have limited understanding has shown that these patients tolerate endometrial biopsy under paracervical block very poorly. The fact that most of these patients have a virginal entroitus limits the ability to visualize the cervix within the tolerance of the patient. Although transportation to the hospital is disruptive to the patients and their caretakers, and general anesthesia adds some risk to the chronically ill, it has been necessary to perform endometrial biopsies and dilation and curettage in a controlled hospital setting. As previously mentioned, these patients usually require a hymenotomy to allow instruments into the vagina.

Young women (under 35 years old) with irregular heavy bleeding that is presumed to be anovulatory can benefit from a trial of progestin or several months of cycle control with a combination estrogen/progestin pill as found in the oral contraceptives. Although pregnancy is a common cause of irregular uterine bleeding in the general population, it is a rare cause in this population. If there is any question about a patient's sexual experience, however, a pregnancy test should be performed.

Irregular or heavy vaginal bleeding in the older woman requires careful diagnostic evaluation. This is particularly true in the postmenopausal woman because endometrial cancer often presents in this fashion. Uterine leiomyomata or endometrial polyps can cause irregular and heavy bleeding in the premenopausal woman. The erratic ovulation of the perimenopausal woman can lead to irregular and heavy bleeding, and endometrial sampling is necessary to rule out endometrial hyperplasia or cancer.

Even normal menstrual flow can pose a serious problem of perineal hygiene for some women with severe physical handicaps. Hormonal therapy for endometrial suppression (high-dose or long-acting progestin) may be tried. Often, however, after consultation with the patient or her guardians, a hysterectomy is indicated.

Vaginal Discharge

Developmentally disabled patients referred for gynecological consultation rarely complain of vaginal discharge. The problem is usually identified by the patient's caretaker, who notes that the patient has a foul odor or has been uncomfortable and has perineal excoriations. Foreign bodies placed in the vagina or the rectum by the patient are not uncommon, and patients with these behaviors over a long period of time have had strictures and scarring in the vagina and rectum.

Vaginitis from Gardnerella vaginalis or Trichomonas vaginalis, pathogens extremely common in a general gynecology practice, is rarely seen in a population of women who are not sexually active. Moniliasis is more commonly seen. This problem is easily diagnosed with a culture or a wet mount of the discharge plus a drop of 10% potassium hydroxide. It is treated with vaginal suppositories or vulvar creams. If this is technically difficult in a patient, oral antifungal agents are successful.

Occasionally, patients have been referred for "incontinence" or "profuse watery discharge" and have had urine pooling in the vagina (rare, but found in some incontinent, immobile patients) or have gram-negative organisms in the vagina causing a profuse watery discharge (e.g., E. coli, Klebsiella, Proteus). These can be successfully treated with oral antibiotics.

Dysmenorrhea and Premenstrual Disturbances

As noted on Table 16-2, a large number of the consultations were for dysmenorrhea or behavior disturbances before or during menses. This can be very difficult to document because most of the patients are nonverbal, and the problem must be identified through observation of behavior. What are thought to be painful periods may be manifested by withdrawn behavior, rocking motions, vocalizations of a distressed nature, aggression toward caretakers, or self-abuse. Whether this behavior is caused by painful uterine contractions or whether the patient is distressed by the sight of vaginal bleeding is difficult to discern. It can be presumed that most primary dysmenorrhea occurs on the day before the onset of vaginal bleeding and the first one or two days of the period. A diagnostic and therapeutic trial of prostaglandin inhibitors (starting the day before menstruation is expected if the patient has regular, predictable menses) is often successful. There is no reason to assume that these nulligravid patients should have a lower or higher incidence of endometriosis than any group of patients of similar age and parity in a private gynecologic practice, but diagnostic laparoscopy is not recommended for any patient referred for apparent dysmenorrhea unless there are physical findings of extensive disease at the time of pelvic examination.

Premenstrual behavior disorders were the reason for consultation for some patients. Several women became extremely violent, physically abusive to the staff and to themselves. After careful documentation of this problem and its relationship to their menses, and after failed trials of prostaglandin inhibitors, cycle control with a long-acting progestin (Depo-Provera) was initiated with good results. Premenstrual tension is a controversial subject in both the medical and the lay press, and the etiology and therapy for this syndrome are unclear. Various other therapies may be available in the future.

Fertility Control

In the series of severely developmentally disabled patients in Table 16-2, only one was evaluated for the possibility of pregnancy. Women who are institutionalized for chronic care rarely engage in sexual intercourse with members of the opposite sex, although masturbation and other behaviors of a sexual nature are common. The problem of fertility control (temporary or permanent sterilization) is a complex medical and legal question. Laws differ from state to state, and sterilization is beyond the scope of this discussion. For females who are sexually active, however, sexual education programs should be provided at the appropriate level of comprehension.

The general medical guidelines that apply to the dispensing of any means of contraception also apply to these patients. Barrier methods (condoms, foam, diaphragms) are unreliable for these patients. The low-dose oral contraceptive, however, is safe for the young sexually active female and can be administered daily by her caretakers. Intrauterine devices are difficult to insert, frequently cause increased bleeding and cramping, and increase the potential for pelvic inflammation. The best contraceptive may be the most effective: a long-acting injectable progestin. This method is used around the world with good patient acceptance and excellent success. The most difficult management problem is the frequent but light irregular bleeding. This bleeding is a nuisance, but it rarely becomes a medical problem and does not usually require evaluation or treatment. Long-acting progestins are approved by the Food and Drug Administration for other indications, but they have yet to be approved for contraception. They should be considered within the framework of the needs of the patient, her caretakers, and the medical practice of the community.

ORGANIZATION OF GYNECOLOGIC SERVICES IN RESIDENTIAL FACILITIES

In the United States, there are thousands of women in large institutions for persons with mental retardation. Guidelines for routine and emergency medical care vary from one institution to another, but most chronic care facilities have protocols for yearly physical examinations that include a pelvic examination and Pap smear. The following discussion outlines the organization of an efficient and successful program for routine gynecologic care and problem referral in a residential institution.

Nurse practitioners and physician assistants provide primary health care for residents of the institution. These mid-level practitioners are encouraged to do screening pelvic examinations and Pap smears as part of the annual physical examination. The gynecologic examination includes breast examination, abdominal examination, speculum examination (including Pap smear), bimanual pelvic examination and/or bimanual rectovaginal examination. If the examination is difficult because of inadequate examination facilities or equipment, anxiety on the part of the patient, or lack of practitioner experience, we have established a peer support system called the Women's Health Care Clinic, which can provide technical assistance and equipment that facilitate complete gynecologic screening. If the examination is still unsatisfactory, or if any abnormality is identified, a referral is initiated for formal gynecologic review and consultation.

The peer support system was designed to address the following areas of concern:

Nonthreatening Surroundings. The Women's Health Care Clinic generally goes to the woman's residence or usual health care delivery site to perform the examination. The presence of familiar surroundings and familiar supportive caregivers appears to calm anxiety associated with the examination experience.

Patient Instruction. A teaching module, adaptable to varying levels of client interest and intellectual development, is used to acquaint the woman with the examination equipment, the techniques of the physical examination, and her own anatomy and physiology. Interested lay staff are encouraged to participate in this process.

Equipment Adapted to Patient Needs. An adequate variety of specula, suitable to examine comfortably the adult or aging sexually inactive woman as well as the immature young adult, has been essential to an effective evaluation.

Problem Identification and Referral. Problems identified by the Women's Care Clinic practitioners are referred to a gynecologist at a scheduled consultation clinic at the institution.

This model of gynecologic care is facilitated by the help of the direct-care staff, who assist in preparing the woman for the examination, make her feel more at ease, and often contribute valuable historical information about her that may not be available in the written record. It is important to include a menstrual calendar as part of the routine data base.

Whether in a residential institution, a nursing home, or the gynecologist's or family physician's office, the principles outlined here (proper equipment, a thoughtful and gentle manner, and the reassuring presence of families and caring people) can be helpful in providing an environment for the gynecologic examination which is the least stressful for the care providers and, above all, the patient.

BIBLIOGRAPHY

Daywood, M.Y.: Overall approach to the management of dysmenorrhea. *In* Prostaglandins and Dysmenorrhea. Edited by M.Y. Daywood. Baltimore, Williams & Wilkins, 1981.
Daywood, M.Y.: Dysmenorrhea. Clin. Obstet. Gynecol., 26:719, 1983.
Gidwani, G.P.: Vaginal bleeding in adolescents. J. Reprod. Med., 29:417, 1984.
Goldzieher, J.W., and Bengiano, G.: Long-acting injectable steroid contraceptives. *In* Advances in Fertility Research. Vol. 1. Edited by D. Mishell. New York, Raven Press, 1982, pp. 75-115.
Kaplan, S. (Ed.): Clinical Pediatric and Adolescent Gynecology. Philadelphia, W.B. Saunders, 1982.
Speroff, L., Glass, R., and Kase, N.: Clinical Gynecologic Endocrinology and Infertility. Baltimore, Williams & Wilkins, 1983.
Worley, R.T.: Dysfunctional uterine bleeding: clarifying its definition, mechanism and management. Postgrad. Med., 79:101, 1986.

17

UROLOGIC DISORDERS

Ellen Roy Elias, M.D. □ *Stuart B. Bauer, M.D.*

This chapter focuses on two main categories of genitourinary problems in children and adults with developmental disabilities. The first category includes congenital disorders, specifically anomalies of the genitourinary (GU) tract, with indices of suspicion that abnormalities are present and suggestions as to diagnosis. Also included in this section are the genitourinary problems associated with spinal cord abnormalities (myelodysplasia, sacral agenesis, and spinal dysraphisms) and suggestions for appropriate diagnosis and management.

The second category covered in this chapter includes some of the less serious but more common GU disorders seen in individuals with developmental disabilities. This section covers enuresis, incontinence, toilet training, and urinary tract infections, with suggestions for management. The chapter concludes with a brief discussion of renal failure and the issues it raises in the handicapped individual.

CONGENITAL GENITOURINARY AND RENAL ANOMALIES

It has been estimated that approximately 10% of all live-born infants in the United States have a malformation of the urinary system, although only about 1% of these malformations are significant. The embryology of the kidneys and lower urinary tract is amazingly complex. It involves three embryonic structures: the pronephros, the mesonephros, and the metanephros. The pro-

nephros and mesonephros become vestigial, but function to induce the development of the metanephros, which becomes the definitive kidney. The collecting system derives from the ureteral bud, which arises from the Wolffian duct and branches as it enters the metanephric tissue, inducing nephron formation. Description of renal embryogenesis is beyond the scope of this chapter, but an understanding of its complexity leads to an appreciation of the many ways that faulty development may occur.

Associated Anomalies

Teratogenic influences on renal development often affect other organ systems that are developing concurrently. Because of this, many nonrenal malformations are associated with renal and lower urinary tract anomalies. Some malformations may be present on a familial or hereditary basis. The nonrenal anomalies listed in Table 17-1 are commonly associated with renal or GU tract anomalies. If any of these nonrenal malformations is present, the clinician should have a high index of suspicion about the possibility of a urologic abnormality. The nonrenal anomalies associated with renal malformations can be divided into three main groups: craniofacial anomalies (head, eyes, ears, and palate), skeletal anomalies (extremities and vertebrae), and visceral anomalies (heart, liver, genitalia, reproductive tract, and gastrointestinal tract).

Craniofacial

The association between otic and renal anomalies is very well documented but poorly understood. It is clear that individuals with abnormally shaped pinnae have an increased incidence of nonspecific renal abnormalities. Abnormalities in ocular structure are also associated with renal anomalies, often within the context of a well-defined syndrome (e.g., several autosomal recessive oculorenal syndromes are well described). There are a number of syndromes with peculiar facies, unusual head shape, or palatal clefts with known associated renal anomalies. Examples include Potter syndrome, Fraser syndrome, and Meckel syndrome.

Skeletal

Vertebral anomalies are commonly associated with abnormal renal development, for example, in myelodysplasia, Goldenhar syndrome and Smith-Lemli-Opitz syndrome. One-quarter of individuals with horseshoe kidneys also have vertebral anomalies, and approximately 14% of individuals with unilateral renal agenesis have abnormalities of their vertebrae. Limb anomalies and abnormally shaped digits, particularly polydactyly or syndactyly, are seen in association with renal anomalies in a number of syndromes including Rubinstein-Taybi, Robert, and Apert syndromes.

Visceral

Embryologic development of the heart occurs at the same time as that of the kidneys. Many syndromes include both congenital heart disease and renal anomalies, e.g., Down syndrome, cardiofacial syndrome, and neurofibromatosis. The VATER syndrome (Vertebral anomalies, Anal atresia, TracheoEsophageal fistula, and Radial dysplasia) is a good example of the complexity of extrarenal involvement that may be found in association with renal anomalies. The prune-belly syndrome, a triad of inadequately formed abdominal musculature, cryptorchidism, and renal abnormalities, is another example. Certain female genital anomalies (bifid or septate vagina, didelphia, uni- or bicornuate uterus) are frequently associated with unilateral renal agenesis or upper urinary tract abnormalities. Polycystic kidney may be found in association with hepatic or pancreatic cysts. For a comprehensive reference of syndromes which contain a urologic component, see Chantler's review.[8]

Table 17-1. *Nonrenal Anomalies Associated with Urologic Defects*

Craniofacial Anomalies	
Retinal dysplasia	Abnormal pinnae
Cataracts	Middle ear anomalies
Aniridia	Cleft lip/palate
Cryptophthalmos	Macroglossia
Retinitis pigmentosa	Dysmorphic facies
Craniosynostosis	

Skeletal Anomalies	
Syndactyly	Spina bifida
Polydactyly	Sacral agenesis
Phocomelia	Vertebral anomalies
Hemihypertrophy	

Visceral Anomalies	
Congenital heart disease	Visceromegaly
Liver cysts	Single umbilical artery
Pancreatic cysts	Tracheoesophageal fistula
Imperforate anus	Hirshsprung's disease
Female reproductive tract anomalies	Absent abdominal musculature with cryptorchidism
Ambiguous genitalia	
Tuberous sclerosis	Neurofibromatosis

Chromosomal

Some syndromes of chromosomal aberrations also contain known urologic pathology. Examples include Turner syndrome (XO), which is associated with various renal anomalies in 60% of cases; Down syndrome (trisomy 21), in which 7% of individuals have cystic and other renal abnormalities; cat-eye syndrome (extra material from chromosome #22), which is associated with renal agenesis and other anomalies in 60 to 100% of individuals; and cri-du-chat syndrome (deletion of short arm of #5 chromosome), which is also associated with various anomalies. Inborn errors of metabolism, although not usually associated with anatomic abnormalities, are often associated with renal dysfunction. The renal problems associated with these disorders include renal tubular dysfunction, calculi, enlarged kidneys, and aminoaciduria.

Clinical Presentation

Renal anomalies may be suspected prenatally, in early infancy, or childhood. Evidence of urologic problems may be apparent on a prenatal sonogram, including oligohydramnios, abnormal renal, ureteral, or bladder size and shapes, and hydronephrosis. Some clues in infancy include failure to thrive, acidosis, anemia, and unexplained dehydration. Another sentinel sign during early infancy is an abdominal mass. The most common signs that should alert the clinician to the possibility of a renal or lower urinary tract anomaly in older children include persistent abdominal pain, hematuria, a urinary tract infection in a male, recurrent infections in females, persistent enuresis, and an abnormal urinary stream. Although these signs may be present, renal anomalies are often asymptomatic and may go undiagnosed for long periods of time, sometimes even into adolescence or adulthood. It is therefore important to know what other clues point to a potential anomaly.

Screening and Diagnosis

In the screening of individuals suspected of having renal or urinary tract anomalies, it is important to obtain a routine urinalysis and serum electrolytes, including urea nitrogen and creatinine. A urine culture is also indicated, because urinary tract infections are a common sign of anatomic abnormality and should be carefully documented and treated. It is also useful to measure calcium, phosphorus, and alkaline phosphatase, because hypocalcemia, hyperphosphatemia, and hyperphosphatasia are common findings in chronic renal disease. A hemoglobin and hematocrit are also helpful, because anemia often occurs in renal disease. These studies indicate the degree of functional impairment, but of course they provide no information concerning type of anomaly.

The two mainstays of screening for anatomic aberrations are ultrasonography and the renal scan. Ultrasonography is noninvasive, equipment is easily available, and it provides informa-

Table 17-2. *Recommended Studies for the Evaluation of Urologic Defects*

Urine Tests

Routine urinalysis
Urine culture
24-hour collection for creatinine clearance and protein excretion if earlier studies abnormal

Blood Tests

Serum electrolytes: sodium, potassium, bicarbonate, chloride
Blood urea nitrogen, creatinine
Calcium, phosphorus, alkaline phosphatase
Hematocrit

Anatomic Tests

Ultrasound
Renal scan
Intravenous pyelogram (in some locations more readily available than renal scan)
Roentgenogram of kidney, ureter, and bladder (KUB)
Voiding cystourethrogram (VCUG)

---

tion about size, density, and location of kidneys. It can also be used to assess the presence of ureteral dilation and bladder size and shape. Renal scanning is a radioisotope imaging technique. There are two types: the DTPA (diethylenetriamine pentacetic acid) scan, which provides information about renal function from which creatinine clearance can be calculated, and the DMSA (dimercaptosuccinic acid) scan, which, like the intravenous pyelogram (IVP), provides structural information about the kidney and gives an indication of tubular function. The advantages of a renal scan over an IVP include reduced exposure to radiation and avoidance of a potential allergic reaction to the dye. A simple radiologic procedure, the abdominal flatplate, or KUB, may be helpful in selected instances. For example, medial deviation of the splenic flexure gas pattern is a sign of an absent or malpositioned left kidney.

Table 17-2 lists the recommended laboratory and radiologic studies that aid in the diagnosis of suspected renal or urinary tract abnormalities.

Management

The medical (nonsurgical) management of renal and GU tract anomalies is very important and is directed toward maintaining optimal chemical balance and preventing infection. The definite management of most anomalies entails surgical correction. The earlier an anomaly is suspected, diagnosed, and corrected, the greater the chance of controlling infection (preserving renal function) and preventing further complications.

The common urologic problems of cryptorchidism, hernia, hydrocele, and hypospadias are described in Table 17-3 with a recommended timetable for surgical repair. Circumcision is described in Table 17-4. Table 17-5 describes the evaluation and management of obstructive uropathies.

Recent advances in perinatology and neonatology have made it possible for more newborns with multiple congenital anomalies to survive into infancy, early childhood, and even into adulthood. The goals of long-term management of individuals with urologic anomalies are to preserve renal function, to prevent infection, and to attempt to provide a socially acceptable lifestyle.

Vesicoureteral Reflux

Vesicoureteral reflux is one of the more common conditions seen in pediatric urology. It is due to an abnormally short course of the ureter through the bladder muscle, so that the valve-like mechanism of the ureterovesical junction is incompetent and urine can freely reflux from the

Table 17-3. *Urologic Problems*

Problem	Frequency and Evaluation	Complications	Management
Cryptorchidism	Full-term infant, 3% One-year-old, 0.7% Adult, 0.7% Location: Inguinal canal 60% Prescrotal 22% Intra-abdominal 8% Ectopic 10% Must differentiate between retractile testicle (can be milked into scrotum), undescended testicle, and absent testicle Confirm absent testicles with hormonal studies: Elevated LH, FSH Decreased testosterone Negative hCG stim. test	If found in association with hypospadias, 50% chance of abnormal sex chromatin Infertility in up to 70%; histologic changes develop after age 1, increase with age 35% increased risk of malignancy (incidence 2%); usually found in males 20-35 years of age Commonly associated with hernias Increased incidence of testicular torsion	Orchiopexy prior to age 1½ If hypospadias is also present, do karyotype and buccal smear Laparoscopy useful to locate abdominal testes
Hypospadias	Live male births, 0.82% Less severe forms more common Importance of family history: 12% chance of occurrence if another family member has hypospadias; 26% risk if brother or father has hypospadias Increased incidence if mother took progestational agents Increased incidence if fetus has abnormality of testosterone, chromosomal abnormalities, Beckwith-Wiedemann syndrome	Usually associated with chordee If found in association with cryptorchidism, 50% chance of abnormal sex chromatin Seen in association with Wilms' tumor, aniridia, hemihypertrophy	Correct between 9 and 18 months of age If associated with cryptorchidism, do karyotype and buccal smear If associated with aniridia and hemihypertrophy, evaluate for Wilms' tumor, continue surveillance for Wilms' tumor every 6 mos. until age 10 with renal ultrasonography
Hernia and hydrocele	Hernia 8 times more frequent in males than in females Peak incidence 0-1 year of age	Incarceration of intestines more common in younger patients. In girls, herniation of ovary or fallopian tube more common than bowel herniation	Bilateral exploration in boys to 2 years old, in girls to age 6 Small hydroceles may resolve spontaneously—wait 6 mo for repair Weigh risk of incarceration vs. risk of anesthesia in deciding appropriate time for surgical repair of hernia

bladder into the ureter during both filling and emptying of the bladder. It is commonly seen in girls with urinary tract infection. In fact, 15 to 35% of girls with infection have vesicoureteral reflux. Although urinary infection is less common in boys, vesicoureteral reflux is found up to 50% when these children are investigated because of a urinary infection.[7]

Although reflux has been seen experimentally in some animals, it should never be considered a normal phenomenon. Reflux with infection can have a devastating effect on renal function. Before the availability of diagnostic studies, reflux was the cause of chronic renal failure in one-third of the patients undergoing renal transplantation. Today, with greater emphasis placed on

Table 17-4. *Circumcision*

Incidence and Evaluation	Complications	Management
1.5 million operations per year	Frequency 1 to 35%	General anesthesia required if performed in child older than 2 weeks
Medical indications (phimosis, paraphimosis, balanitis) are rare	Bleeding	
	Separation of wound	
Ability to retract foreskin usually increases with age	Cyanosis of penis	
	Injury to glans	
Adhesions of prepuce occur in 10% of boys 6 years old, less than 1% of postpubertal males	Iatrogenic hypospadias or epispadias	
	Urethral fistula	
Children with neurogenic bladders who require intermittent catheterization: family must make private decision	Lymphedema	
	Penile loss	
	Meatal stenosis (8 to 30%)	
	Phimosis (if insufficient skin is removed)	
	Concealed penis (if too much shaft is excised)	
	Psychological trauma (if performed in older children)	

obtaining urine cultures in children with any signs of disease, urinary infection and consequently vesicoureteral reflux are being discovered sooner and the sequelae of chronic infection prevented.

Grading

It is best to grade the reflux according to its severity. An international classification has been devised recently with reflux being graded on a scale of one to five, with five being the most severe, and one the least[14] (see Fig. 17-1). Most children present with mild to moderate grades of reflux, and 80% of these children outgrow their reflux in time. Thus it is a disease that tends to get better with age, and most patients with reflux of grade three or less can be managed with long-term antibiotic therapy to prevent infection while the reflux is present. An international study is being conducted to assess the frequency of spontaneous resolution of grade-four reflux.

Pathologic Consequences

Reflux with infection can produce renal parenchymal damage. Inoculation of the kidney papillae with bacteria from the refluxed urine can result in colonization. The inflammatory response to this bacterial growth leads to pyelonephritic scarring, papillary damage, and eventual cortical loss. Therefore antibiotics should be used to prevent infection while reflux exists. Most children with reflux must remain on antibiotics for prolonged periods.

Diagnosis

The diagnosis of vesicoureteral reflux is best made with a voiding cystogram using fluoroscopic imaging and should include a voiding phase. Often reflux will not occur during filling of the bladder but massive regurgitation may be seen during voiding. Radionuclide cystography is being used with increasing frequency to screen for reflux in children with suspected infection, in siblings of children with reflux, and as follow-up for children with a past history of reflux. It is not good, however, for delineating other anatomic conditions associated with the reflux. Excretory urography (IVP) alone is not a good screening test for reflux in children with infection because 60% of children with reflux will have a normal excretory urogram but an abnormal voiding cystourethrogram (VCUG).

Management

All boys with one urinary tract infection, all girls under the age of 2, and older girls with an unusual organism, symptoms of pyelonephritis, or difficulty in clearing their first infection should undergo radiologic evaluation. Older girls with more than one infection should also undergo investigation. Once the diagnosis of grade 1, 2, or 3 reflux is established, antibiotic therapy is begun, as long as there is no evidence of upper urinary tract damage.

Table 17-5.   *Obstructive Uropathy*

Location	Presentation	Diagnosis	Treatment

Ureteropelvic junction	Prenatal: sonogram
	Newborns:
	  Abdominal mass
	  Urinary tract infection
	Older children:
	  Abdominal mass
	  Gastrointestinal symptoms
	  Urinary tract infection
	  Hematuria following mild
	    abdominal trauma
		Excretory urogram
		Renal sonogram
		Renal scan to determine renal function
			If 10% renal function is preserved, surgically correct obstruction
			Remove kidney if less than 10% of function remains

Ureterovesical junction	Urinary tract infection at any age May be found in association with distal bladder obstruction or neurogenic bladder	Renal ultrasound and/or excretory urogram	Removal of abnormal portion of urethra, reimplantation Nephroureterectomy rarely necessary

Posterior urethral valves	Prenatal: Ultrasound—see hydroureteronephrosis
	Newborns:
	  Renal failure
	  Electrolyte imbalance
	  Abnormal urinary stream
	Infants and young children:
	  Failure to thrive
	Older children:
	  Incontinence
	Any age:
	  Urinary tract infection
		Voiding cystourethrogram
		Cystoscopy
			Transurethral fulguration of valves
			Urinary diversion in small infants

Meatus	Does not usually produce obstructive uropathy Usually see irritative symptoms (frequency, dysuria, dribbling) Incidence: 10% of circumcised boys	Urinary stream: fine, forceful, directed upward	Urethral dilatation

Urine cultures are obtained every 3 months, or whenever there is a change in the child's condition suggesting a possible infection. Follow-up radionuclide studies are obtained on a yearly basis with renal ultrasonography performed periodically to assess renal growth. Indications for anti-reflux surgery include breakthrough infection while the child is on an adequate dose of antibiotics; a worsening in the degree of reflux with an anatomic abnormality at the ureterovesical junction; development or progression of renal parenchymal scarring despite absence of clinical urinary infection; poor compliance in taking antibiotics; and reflux persisting into puberty.

Surgery

Anti-reflux surgery involves removal of the affected ureter(s) from the bladder and replacement in such a way as to create a longer tunnel through the bladder wall to prevent reflux. Various operations have been devised to achieve this result. The ureter can be repositioned somewhat higher in the bladder and advanced toward the trigone, or the same ureteral hiatus can be maintained with the ureter advanced either across the trigone toward the opposite side or downward toward the bladder neck. Bilateral surgery need not be performed for unilateral disease.

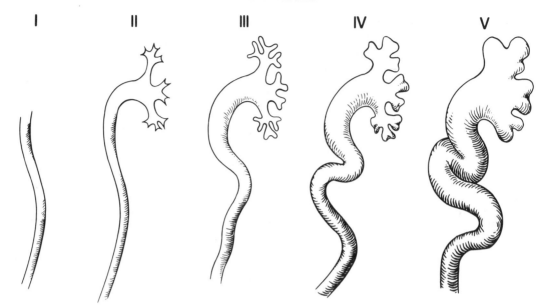

FIG. 17-1.   Grades of vesicoureteral reflux.

Postoperatively, all children are maintained on antibiotics. Assessment of the upper urinary tract is made 2 to 6 weeks following surgery, and a radionuclide cystogram is performed approximately 4 months after surgery to see if the reflux has been corrected. In general, antibiotics can be discontinued at that point if the operation has been successful. Some children do develop postoperative urinary infection (approximately 15% of girls and 1% of boys), but pyelonephritis is an extremely rare phenomenon.[23] These children are now similar to children with normal anatomy who are prone to urinary infection as a result of abnormal voiding patterns and/or inappropriate hygiene.

Myelodysplasia

It is well known that the leading cause of death in children with myelodysplasia after the first year of life is upper urinary tract damage resulting in renal insufficiency. With appropriate therapy, much of this deterioration of renal function can be prevented. This section delineates the recommended urologic management of an infant born with myelodysplasia. It concludes with a brief discussion of two related defects, sacral agenesis and spinal dysraphisms.

Management of Infants

Most infants born with myelodysplasia undergo surgical repair of the meningomyelocele sometime between 24 and 48 hours of life (see

Figs. 17-2 and 17-3). As soon as the neurosurgical condition stabilizes, it is important to assess urinary tract function. Over 95% of newborns have normal appearing and functioning kidneys. However, the higher the spinal cord lesion, the greater the incidence of upper tract abnormalities.

The initial workup includes a serum creatinine, urinalysis, urine culture, urodynamic evaluation, and renal ultrasonography (or an IVP).[19] In one study of 68 infants born with meningomyelocele, the blood urea nitrogen (BUN) was normal in all patients and had no diagnostic significance. Significant bacteriuria was common in this study (seen in 32 of 68 patients), but it was not correlated with radiologic findings. A VCUG is always done even with a normal IVP or ultrasonograph, because significant reflux may be present even with normal renal anatomy. The VCUG can probably be safely deferred until 4 to 6 weeks of age if the initial IVP or ultrasonograph is normal. In the event of a nonvisualized IVP, a renal scan is mandatory and may be preferred in the neonatal age group.

Following neurosurgical repair, trauma to the spinal cord may induce cord shock with urinary retention. This is often temporary (lasting up to 4 to 6 weeks), and the recommended treatment includes clean intermittent catheterization (CIC). Alpha-adrenergic blockers, which may be helpful in the older child, are contraindicated in the newborn period. Some authors also recommend the Crede maneuver,[19] but this is controversial

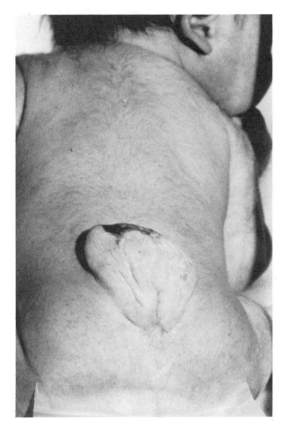

FIG. 17-2. Newborn girl with skin covering myelodysplasia defect.

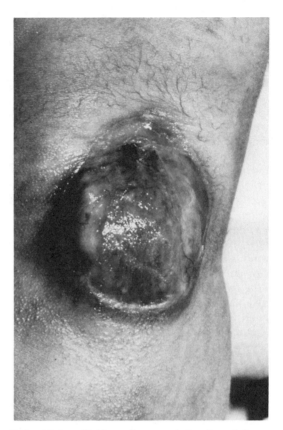

FIG. 17-3. Child in whom myelodysplasia defect is covered by thin transparent membrane.

when reflux is present because the increased abdominal pressure that results from external palpation of the bladder exacerbates the vesicoureteral reflux and causes renal damage. After 4 to 6 weeks the CIC should be stopped and the baby retested for urine residuals and reflux, because the cord shock may have resolved.

During the first 3 years of life, there are 4 main goals of management: to minimize urine residuals, to control vesicoureteral reflux, to prevent urinary tract infection, and to keep the perineal area free of rash. To minimize urine residuals, most centers use clean intermittent catheterization. This has been shown to be a safe and effective technique that can be used at any age (even in neonates) and in both sexes.[17] Although only clean technique is necessary, the success of this procedure depends on frequent and regular catheterization to empty the bladder. It is recommended that residuals be checked every 6 months. An IVP or renal ultrasonography is recommended at 6 months and at 1 year of age to monitor vesicoureteral reflux. In infants, reflux is suspected if hydronephrosis is

seen on renal ultrasonography or IVP. The most common presenting sign of reflux in the slightly older child is infection. Urine cultures are recommended every 3 months, or more often if the child develops symptoms of infection. These symptoms include nonspecific fever, vomiting, diarrhea, and failure to thrive in infants. The family should be taught the importance of good perineal hygiene. Acidification of the urine via dietary manipulation is helpful in preventing diaper rash, and tables of appropriate foods are available. Protective ointments are used on the skin, and if cloth diapers are used, they can be soaked in vinegar.

Damage to the kidneys from reflux and infection is thought to occur at a very early age. Therefore good urologic management beginning at birth is crucial to the prevention of renal parenchymal loss.

Vesicoureteral Reflux

Vesicoureteral reflux (VUR) is considered to be directly responsible for the renal parenchymal scarring that may occur in patients with myelodysplasia. Management of reflux in individuals with myelodysplasia is identical to management in individuals with reflux from other causes and has been detailed in an earlier section of this chapter. Table 17-6 shows a 60% success rate for intermittent catheterization in treating reflux in 45 children with myelodysplasia.[5] As can be seen in Figure 17-4 reflux in a patient with myelodysplasia may resolve if the bladder is emptied on a regular basis (i.e., with CIC).

When antibiotics plus CIC prove ineffective in controlling VUR and in preventing recurrent urinary tract infection, surgical intervention is necessary. Occasionally a cutaneous vesicostomy (often a temporary measure) is necessary in young babies, in whom it is impractical to perform clean intermittent catheterization on a routine basis (see Fig. 17-5). Indications for surgery in older children include recurrent infection, progression of renal scarring, persistent hydroureteronephrosis, and a documented anatomic abnormality of the ureterovesical junction.

In the 1960s and early 1970s, ileal conduit diversion was the therapy of choice for VUR. Studies have shown that many complications can result from this procedure, including recurrent pyelonephritis, nephrolithiasis, renal insufficiency, loop strictures, and stomal stenoses.[9,16,19] These complications occur in up to 80% of patients with ileal conduits. Since 1972, when Lapides introduced the concept of CIC, ileal conduits are no longer the recommended therapy for individuals with myelodysplasia. In fact, many individuals whose urinary tracts had been diverted are now being considered for undiversion procedures.

Neurogenic Bladder

The neurogenic bladder dysfunction present in children with myelodysplasia may be varied

Table 17-6. *Treatment of Myelodysplasia and Vesicoureteral Reflux with Intermittent Catheterization in 45 Patients*

Result	Number	Percent
Success (complete resolution of reflux)	27	60
Stable (persistent reflux but no urinary tract infection)	16	36
Failure (recurrent infection or pyelonephritis)	2	4

From Bauer, S.B., Colodny, A.H., and Retik, A.B.: The management of vesicoureteral reflux in children with myelodysplasia. J. Urol., *128*:102, 1982.

and complex. The abnormality may involve the nerves to the bladder, the internal and external sphincters, and the spinal cord itself above the sacral nerve roots. The two main types of problems are failure to retain urine (caused by hypertonic or uninhibited detrusor contractions, excess parasympathetic activity, or inadequate sphincter function) and excess urinary retention (caused by an adynamic detrusor and/or spastic sphincters). Many individuals have an intermediate picture and thus have mixed degrees of incontinence and retention. Most individuals do not have the ability to voluntarily control bladder or sphincter function.

Anticholinergic medications, e.g., oxybutynin hydrochloride (Ditropan) and propantheline bromide (Pro-Banthine), are helpful when there is an inability to retain urine. These medications increase the bladder capacity, and in conjunction with CIC, can be very effective in achieving continence. Children with a neurogenic bladder can do well with CIC alone as long as there is sufficient resistance in the sphincter to allow storage of urine between each bladder emptying. Sometimes alpha-sympathomimetic drugs, e.g., phenylpropanolamine (Ornade) and ephedrine, are useful in increasing resistance at the bladder neck or internal sphincter mechanism.

Incontinence

Starting at preschool age, a self-care toileting program should be introduced. Achieving bowel hygiene is the first priority. The second step is to achieve dryness. Because the neurologic abnormalities are quite variable, each child needs to be studied urodynamically and an individual program developed depending on the particular pathology present.

The majority of children use a combination of CIC and chemical agents. The technique can be mastered by 5- to 7-year-old children as long as they have free use of their hands, can maintain an appropriate position, and have mature adaptive skills. The Crede or Valsalva maneuvers may be employed alternatively if the child can empty the bladder in this manner.[2,19] When neither of these techniques is successful, surgical intervention is necessary. If there is some reactivity in the external sphincter, the bladder neck can be reconstructed to improve urethral resistance and prevent leakage of urine. If the external sphincter is completely denervated and urethral resistance is very low, an artificial urinary sphincter can be implanted to achieve continence. When detrusor function is not improved with medication, partial removal of the bladder

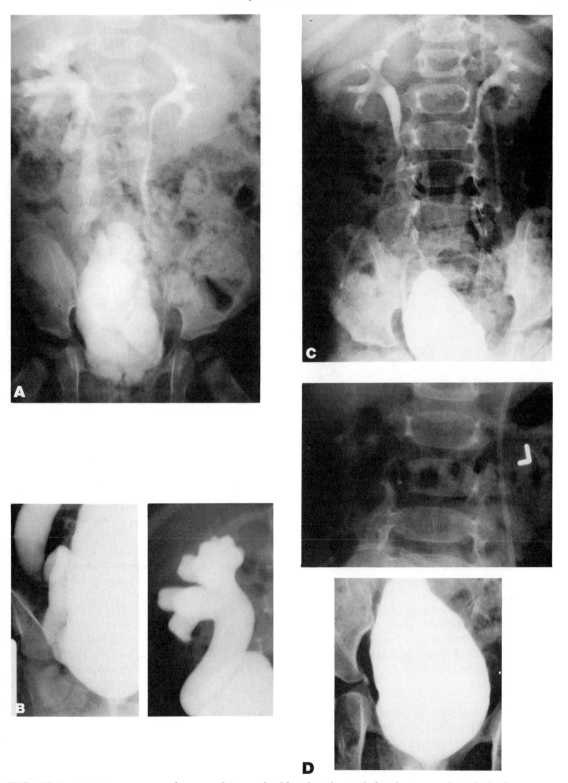

FIG. 17-4. *A.* Intravenous pyelogram of 8-month-old girl with myelodysplasia reveals right hydroureteronephrosis. *B.* Voiding cystogram demonstrates severe right reflux. *C.* and *D.* After intermittent catheterization for 3 years, IVP shows normalization of right collecting system and voiding cystourethrogram (*D*) shows resolution of reflux.

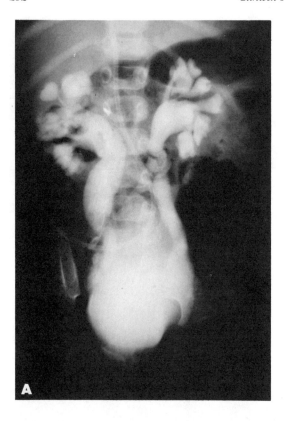 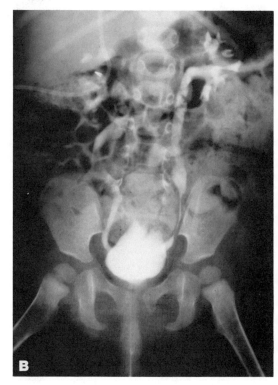

FIG. 17-5. *A.* Intravenous pyelogram (IVP) of newborn girl with myelodysplasia reveals bilateral hydro-cereteronephrosis. *B.* IVP after a vesicostomy demonstrates improved drainage of upper urinary tract.

and augmentation with a segment of bowel may be necessary. These operations are usually combined with drugs and CIC to achieve continence and complete bladder emptying. Pantyliner inserts are available for the child with constant dribbling (seen with low outlet resistance, a hypertonic detrusor muscle, or uninhibited detrusor contractions).

Urinary incontinence is the most difficult problem to manage. The goals of training are to prevent embarrassment, ensure cleanliness and freedom from odor, and to preserve renal function. The child, parents, and teachers must all cooperate for optimal success.

Sexuality

It is important to address issues of sexuality with the growing child as well as with parents, who are sure to be concerned but often will not address these issues without prompting.

Menarche often occurs at a very early age (i.e., 8 to 10 years), and fertility is possible. Girls can be assured that they can be normal sexual partners. There are some risks, however, during pregnancy. Complications include urinary tract infection, hydronephrosis, worsening urinary tract pathology, back pain, disk herniation, and even loss of neuromuscular function. The risk of recurrence (having an infant with myelodysplasia) is the same for females and males, and is 5%.[4,19] It is, therefore, recommended that women have a serum alpha-fetoprotein determination between the 16th and 19th weeks of gestation.

The issues in males are more complex.[4,19] There is a decreased fertility rate among males with myelodysplasia which may be secondary to a number of problems including the neurologic injury affecting potency and ejaculation, chronic urinary tract infections, mechanical trauma to the urethra, particularly at the point of entry of the ejaculatory ducts, and testicular hypoplasia (in conjunction with cryptorchidism). Some males can achieve erections (but sometimes not until puberty). About 30% can ejaculate, but usually ejaculation occurs in a retrograde direction into the bladder (these patients are treated with renacidin 10% solution 2 to 3 times per week). If the sperm can be recovered, the wife of an individual with meningomyelocele can be artificially inseminated. The psychological issues for boys can be most devastating, because of an altered body image and low self-esteem. It is important for the physician to be supportive during the difficult teenage years.

Sacral Agenesis

Sacral agenesis is similar to myelodysplasia in the types of urologic problems that are seen. If sacral nerves 2 through 4 (S_{2-4}) are involved, a neurogenic bladder is usually present. However, the amount of injury to the nerve roots is variable, and more subtle problems may occur.

Sacral agenesis is a rare anomaly and has a known association with maternal diabetes. It is seen in 1% of infants of insulin-dependent diabetic mothers, and the incidence increases if diabetes is present in other close family members.[3] Other anomalies are associated with sacral agenesis, including orthopedic deformities, imperforate anus, and renal ectopia or agenesis. The sacral defect is usually apparent by palpation (see Fig. 17-6), but the diagnosis is commonly missed because innervation of the lower extremities is not affected and gait is normal. Sacral agenesis is often not diagnosed until after age 3, when the child comes to medical attention because of delays in toilet training (see Fig. 17-7).

The recommended diagnostic workup for suspected sacral agenesis is as follows:

Lateral and AP spine films
IVP
VCUG
Urodynamic studies
    Cystometrogram
    Urethral pressure profile
    Electromyogram of external urethral sphinc-
       ter (striated muscle component)
Neurologic examination

In addition to roentgenograms of the spine (Fig. 17-8), a workup for associated renal anomalies, and a urodynamic assessment of bladder function, a complete neurologic examination and evaluation of gait are also important.

In a study by Bauer et al.,[6] the neurologic level had little correlation with the vertebral bony defect, particularly if the lesion was below S_2. Motor roots were affected more often than sensory afferents (75% of the patients had normal sensation). All the patients had an abnormal VCUG.

Management of the patient with sacral agenesis is similar to that for the patient with myelodysplasia. It includes CIC, artificial urinary sphincters, and pharmacologic (anticholinergic) agents.

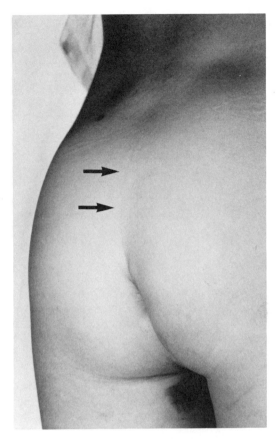

FIG. 17-6. Boy with sacral agenesis. Absence of the gluteal cleft is typical of this anomaly.

Spinal Dysraphism

Spinal dysraphism is the term applied to a group of abnormalities of the caudal spinal cord including diastematomyelia (sagittal splitting of the spinal cord from an intravertebral bony spur or fibrous band), lipoma, dermoid cyst or sinus, aberrant spinal roots, and fibrous tethering of the conus medullaris or filum terminale. These lesions are grouped together because they produce a similar urologic and neurologic picture.

The classic presentation of spinal dysraphism is the association between gait disturbance, an abnormality of the lower extremities, a skin lesion of the lumbosacral area, and urinary incontinence. The gait is usually broad-based. The patient may experience pain and/or numbness radiating down the lower extremities, particularly after awakening. Deformities of the lower extremities include high arched feet, clawing of the toes, and leg length or muscle mass discrepancy (see Fig. 17-9).

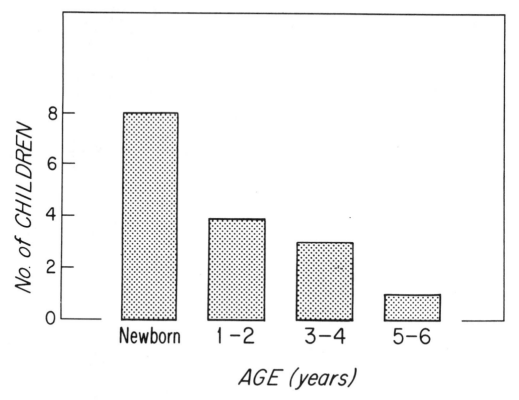

FIG. 17-7. Age at diagnosis of sacral agenesis. Most cases are discovered in newborn period but some are not diagnosed until after age 3, when they fail to become toilet-trained.

Cutaneous lesions overlying the spinal cord abnormality are seen in three-quarters of patients with spinal dysraphism, the most common lesion being hypertrichosis (hairy patch) followed by hyperpigmentation.[3,13] Lipomas (see Fig. 17-10) or skin dimples are also presenting signs.

Twenty to forty percent of children with spinal dysraphism develop neurogenic bladder dysfunction. There may also be diminished sensation in the perineal region resulting in urinary incontinence. Lower urinary tract dysfunction caused by a spinal dysraphism commonly presents with continuous dribbling during infancy, day and night incontinence in the older child, and/or urinary tract infection. The type of lesion is variable and depends on which nerve roots and/or segments of the spinal cord are involved. Therefore it is important for each child to have a complete urodynamic evaluation so that the therapeutic intervention is individualized and appropriate. Subtle signs of neurologic disease often associated with urologic problems are

Urinary and/or fecal incontinence
Urinary infection
Hyperactive reflexes/Babinski sign
High arched feet
Abnormal gait
Cutaneous lower back lesion
Fine motor incoordination
Nonfamilial left-handedness or crossed
  dominance
Learning disabilities
Sleep disorders
Abnormal head size or shape

ACQUIRED DISORDERS

Enuresis

Enuresis is defined as an episode of wetting that usually occurs during stage-4 sleep in children between 3 and 10 years of age, who have no other overt neurologic or structural urologic abnormality. Urinary incontinence, in contrast, occurs in the setting of urinary tract or neurologic pathology.

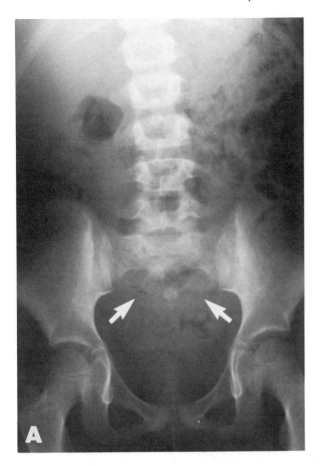
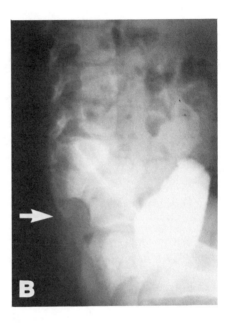

FIG. 17-8. Lateral spine film clearly demonstrates absence of sacral bones.

In order to understand abnormal patterns of voiding, it is helpful to first understand the normal development of bladder control. In infants, the bladder functions automatically. When it is filled to capacity (usually about 2 ounces), the stretch reflex activates a detrusor contraction, causing a forceful stream of urine that fully empties the bladder. An infant does not appreciate bladder fullness and can neither voluntarily stop nor start voiding. With maturation of the central nervous system (CNS), a toddler gradually becomes aware of the act of micturition and the sensation of bladder fullness. A child of 2 to 2½ also develops the ability to hold urine for brief periods of time and acquires the verbal ability to communicate the need to void. A 2-year-old still may not be able to voluntarily initiate voiding, or to void if the bladder is not full. By age 2½ to 3, a normal child has the motor skills to independently get to a lavatory and remove clothing.

By age 3, control over the levator ani and other pelvic muscles has developed, allowing the child to more successfully postpone voiding, and to limit the number of voids to 6 to 10 per 24 hours. The bladder capacity also gradually increases during this time, to at least 7 ounces. Thus, by age 2½ to 3, most children can achieve daytime (diurnal) dryness. Nocturnal dryness occurs a little later, usually by 3 to 4 years. Some time between ages 3½ and 6 the child learns to contract the diaphragm and abdominal muscles while simultaneously relaxing those of the pelvic floor, to voluntarily initiate voiding at varying degress of bladder filling. The child of 4½ also learns that he can voluntarily stop the urinary stream by contracting the levator ani muscles.

Classification and Etiology

There are several classifications of enuresis. The first distinction is between primary enuresis, when a child has never achieved bladder control, and secondary enuresis, when a child has been dry for a prolonged period of time and then resumes wetting. Another distinction refers to what time the enuresis occurs; diurnal

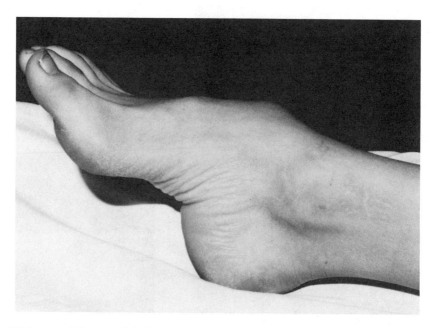

FIG. 17-9. High arched feet, a subtle but telltale sign of an occult spinal dysraphism.

uresis is bedwetting. The vast majority of enuretics (about 85%), have nocturnal, primary enuresis. Encopresis is an associated problem in about 10 to 25% of children with enuresis. The majority of enuretic children are boys (3:2 ratio).

There are many hypotheses to explain the etiology of enuresis.[18,21] Some consider that environmental factors play a major role, because there is an increased incidence of enuresis in children from broken homes and lower socioeconomic groups. There is a genetic component as well, because (1) studies of twins show an increased incidence of enuresis in monozygotic versus fraternal twins, and (2) a child has a greater likelihood of having enuresis if either one or both of his parents were also enuretic. Some investigators think that enuresis occurs as a result of a disorder of arousal in the normal sleep cycle (stage 4). Others think that psychologic factors play a major role, particularly in children with known emotional disturbances. In addition, a small number of children develop a decreased bladder capacity after eating certain foods and whose enuresis improves when these foods are withheld from the diet.

The most accepted hypothesis to explain enuresis suggests that it is caused by a delay in maturation of the central nervous system.[18,21] Evidence to support this hypothesis includes the persistence of an infantile curve on the cystometrogram (uninhibited bladder contractions or reduced functional capacity) in about half of enuretics. Other authors cite an increased incidence of delays in other developmental processes such as walking, cognitive function, and fine motor coordination. The smaller functional bladder capacity results in increased diurnal frequency and urgency commonly seen in children who have nocturnal enuresis. Finally, there is an increased incidence of minor abnormalities in the electroencephalogram of children with enuresis, thought to be another manifestation of the immaturity of the CNS.[18]

Clinical Evaluation

Evaluation of an individual with enuresis includes a history, physical examination, and several laboratory studies. The history helps to differentiate primary from secondary, and diurnal from nocturnal enuresis. In the history, it is important to elicit symptoms of possible urinary tract infection, because this is the most common organic cause of enuresis, and to check for any concurrent disorders of sleep, relationship to certain foods, or history of recent emotional stress. The family history is significant because the likelihood of enuresis increases from 15% if neither parent was enuretic to 44% if one parent was enuretic and to 77% if both parents were enuretic.[18]

The physical examination includes abdominal palpation to rule out a mass (e.g., hydronephrosis, hydroureter, large bladder), a genital examination to rule out anomalies, and a rectal examination to rule out a pelvic mass, assess rectal tone and sensation, and check for evidence of chronic constipation. A bimanual rectoabdominal examination provides an easy way to check for urine residuals. A careful neurologic examination, including examination and palpation of the lower spine, is important to rule out occult vertebral anomalies or sacral agenesis. The neurologic examination should also include assessment of perineal sensations, high arched feet, lower-extremity deep tendon reflexes, and discrepancy in muscle mass and leg length. Last, it is important to observe the urinary stream.

Laboratory Investigation

The initial laboratory examination includes a urine culture as well as urinalysis, which should include checks for blood, protein, and glucose, measurement of specific gravity (to assess renal concentrating ability), and a microscopic examination to rule out renal disease or infection.

No further workup is necessary if the physical examination is normal, residual low, the normal urinary stream and urinalysis are normal, the urine culture is negative, and particularly if the family history is positive. Further evaluation is indicated for an abnormal urinary stream, diurnal incontinence, an abnormal physical examination, urinary residual found on palpation, or a diagnosed UTI.

Organic causes of nocturnal enuresis are rare. Urinary tract lesions are found in 2 to 10% of individuals with nocturnal enuresis. Bladder outlet obstruction is also rare.[18] If a further evaluation is indicated, the workup should involve an IVP, renal and bladder ultrasonography, and a VCUG.

Management

Many remedies for enuresis have been tried, with varying rates of success. Some methods, such as psychotherapy for children with known emotional problems, and dietary therapy (eliminating food such as eggs, chocolate, or colas) are only useful in certain children. More generalized treatments include behavioral modification, medications, conditioning techniques, and urodynamic biofeedback approaches.[21]

Behavioral modification techniques include "responsibility reinforcement" (rewarding dryness with prizes or working toward a desired goal), and "bladder training" (keeping a daily log of voided volumes, forcing fluids, and gradually increasing the time interval between voidings).[21] These are the treatments of choice for enuresis,

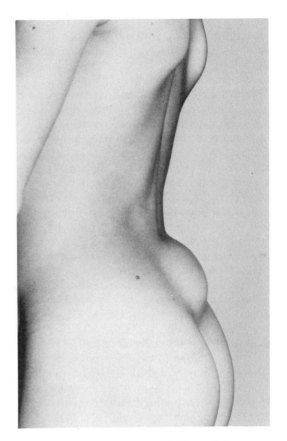

FIG. 17-10. Boy who also had small lipomeningocele in lumbosacral area, which can easily be missed unless the lower spine is inspected.

because they can be implemented by the pediatrician and are effective about 80% of the time. The relapse rate is about 20%.[18]

Drug therapy is useful in some instances. Imipramine, a tricyclic antidepressant, is the drug most commonly used. Its mechanism of action is poorly understood, although it has known anticholinergic, anti-histaminic, antiserotonin, and central nervous system effects. The dosage is 0.9 to 1.5 mg/kg/day, which usually works out to 25 mg for 5- to 8-year-olds and 50 mg for older children, given once a day.[18] There is no consensus as to the appropriate duration of therapy, but a trial of 6 to 8 weeks is usually initiated. About one-half of enuretic children are cured with imipramine, and another 10 to 20% improve. The relapse rate is very high, however: about two-thirds resume wetting once the medication is stopped.[18] There are also many known side-effects, including sleep disorders, personality changes, dry mouth, and gastrointestinal symptoms. Other tricyclic antidepressants have effects similar to imipramine and can be tried if imipramine fails. Other drugs such as oxybutynin hydrochloride (Ditropan) and flavoxate hydrochloride (Urispas), alone or in combination with imipramine, have been used with reasonable rates of success when single-drug therapy fails.[18]

"Conditioning therapy," and "nonbiofeedback biobehavioral management" are the terms used for the approach in which behavioral modification techniques are used in conjunction with an alarm system. The alarm is a sensing apparatus (or pad) that is placed either in the bed or inside the child's undershorts; it is activated by moisture voiding, to set off a bell, light, buzzer, music, or a combination of the above. Ideally the alarm awakens the child, who turns it off, finishes voiding in the bathroom, and then returns to bed. This method can be somewhat cumbersome and requires cooperation and motivation on the part of the child and his family. The average duration of treatment is long; 8 to 12 weeks as reported by some clinicians, 16 to 17 weeks by others. The cure rate is 75 to 80%, however, almost twice as good as for imipramine, and the cited relapse rate of 25 to 30% is much lower.[18]

These techniques are all based on the presumption that the person with enuresis has normal anatomy, physiology, and cognitive and motor abilities. Several techniques of behavioral management have been adapted for training the individual with cognitive limitations. Several papers by Azrin et al. (e.g., ref. 1) are good sources of behavioral management techniques in this special population.

An individual with a disability may have cognitive, neurologic, physical, or emotional limitations that preclude development of bladder control. For example, a person with mental retardation or a language disorder may not have the verbal ability to communicate his needs. He may not have the neurologic maturity to appreciate or control his body signals, or he may have actual neurologic impairment (e.g., myelodysplasia) that prevents normal bladder function. A person with cerebral palsy may not have the mobility to get to a lavatory or to remove his clothing independently. It is known that enuresis and encopresis are both common manifestations of emotional disturbance in children. Therefore, when evaluating abnormal micturition in an individual with a disability, it is important to consider not only the common causes of enuresis, but each person's particular limitations as well.

Incontinence

Individuals with physical handicaps that preclude toilet training present a special challenge. These individuals have incontinence rather than enuresis. Incontinence may be associated with obstruction (secondary to congenital urethral valves, urethral stricture, sphincter dysfunction, or prostatic enlargement), retention (secondary to neuromuscular disease such as meningomyelocele, transverse myelitis, or spinal cord trauma), or both. The incontinence may be congenital or acquired, total or partial, continuous or intermittent.

Evaluation of incontinence includes the identical history, physical examination, and laboratory studies as for enuresis but with more emphasis on details of the incontinence. Some additional modifications may also be indicated. For example, leakage of urine occurring with an anatomic anomaly of the genitalia may be ascertained using an intravenous injection of indigo carmine. The laboratory studies should include cystourethroscopy in addition to the roentgenograms recommended in the evaluation of enuresis. Sophisticated urodynamic studies are now available, including uroflowmetry (which measures urine flow rate and voided volume), cystometry, urethral pressure profilometry, and external urethral sphincter electromyography. These studies may be needed to precisely define the neuromuscular abnormality.

Achieving continence is now possible in some individuals with an organic lesion, with the advent of new urodynamic biofeedback techniques. These techniques consist of monitoring detrusor pressure or external urethral sphincter activity using a visual or auditory feedback mechanism in conjunction with behavioral modification. Biofeedback techniques were first used primarily in individuals with "non-neurogenic bladder," or bladder-sphincter dysfunction despite normal neurologic function. Biofeedback techniques have been successful in individuals with normal anatomy and physiology whose enuresis was refractory to the usual behavioral approaches and pharmacologic agents. A new hope for the future is the recent use of urodynamic biofeedback techniques in individuals with spinal cord trauma, sacral agenesis, and meningomyelocele. Some of these children have actually achieved continence despite neurologic pathology. A review of these techniques can be found in ref. 21.

Urinary Tract Infection

Urinary tract infection (UTI) is the most common urologic problem in the developmentally disabled population. One recent study has shown that residents of a state institution for the mentally retarded had a 14% incidence of UTI, which is almost three times greater than the 5% incidence cited for the general adult population.[10] There are several possible reasons why disabled individuals are prone to urinary tract infection.

A urinary tract infection is defined as bacteriuria equal to or greater than 100,000 colonies of a single organism obtained from a clean voided midstream specimen of urine. There are a number of symptoms of urinary infection, which often vary with the age of the patient. Small infants and young children may have fever, vomiting, diarrhea, and/or failure to thrive. Preschoolers often present with fever, enuresis, and abdominal pain. The triad of increased frequency, increased urgency, and dysuria is often only seen in the older child and adult who develops a UTI.

Most uncomplicated first UTI is caused by sensitive strains of E. coli, a common fecal resident that ascends into the urinary tract via the urethra. Hematogenous spread of bacteria causing a UTI is usually seen only in neonates. Other urinary tract pathogens include resistant strains of E. coli, Klebsiella, Enterococcus, Salmonella, Proteus mirabilis, Staphylococcus (especially in boys), Hemophilus influenzae, and Pseudomonas.

Associated Factors

Many factors are thought to contribute to the development of urinary tract infection. These include anatomic anomalies, abnormal voiding patterns (e.g., overt or occult neurogenic bladder dysfunction), hormonal influences (e.g., pregnancy, birth control pills), VUR, urinary obstruction, and trauma (e.g., foreign body, sexual intercourse).[11,16] The frequency of anatomic abnormalities, VUR, and neurogenic bladder dysfunction is greater in the disabled population than in the general population.[10]

Diagnosis

The most important first step in diagnosing a UTI is to suspect it. As stated earlier, the symptoms are often nonspecific, particularly in young children. They may also be insidious in the nonverbal, nonambulatory, incontinent adult, who may present with fever, anorexia, or a change in urine odor or color. The urine culture is the definitive test for diagnosing a UTI. In older patients who are able to provide a "clean catch" midstream specimen, this sample is appropriate for culture. In younger children, a suprapubic aspiration or bladder catheterization is recommended. Urine from bag collections is easily and rapidly contaminated; therefore this is not a preferred means of obtaining a urine sample. If a culture from a bag specimen is negative, however, it usually signifies the absence of infection. In older individuals who cannot provide a clean catch urine, catheterization using sterile technique is the method of choice for procuring urine for culture.

A urinalysis is important in the workup of a suspected UTI, because the presence of leukocytes, red blood cells, and bacteriuria increases one's suspicion that an infection is present. It is always important to confirm this with an appropriately collected specimen sent for culture. Several assays have been developed to detect bacteriuria and to localize the infection to the upper or lower tract. These include Uricult slides, nitrite indicator strips, antibody-coated bacteria, sedimentation rate, C-reactive protein, LDH isoenzyme, and antibodies against Tamm-Horsfall protein. The Uricult slides are particularly useful in following the child with an anatomic abnormality, because the parents can screen the urine at home with this inexpensive test, and any growth can then be sent for culture. The other tests are not all completely reliable, and some are not easily obtainable. The urine culture remains the one absolute indicator of an infection of the urinary tract.

Management

Treatment depends on the culture results and sensitivity of the infecting organism. Ampicillin, sulfisoxazole (Gantrisin), and trimethoprim-sulfamethoxasole (Bactrim) are the usual drugs of choice for the uncomplicated infection. In the case of recurrent infections, organisms resistant to ampicillin are often the pathogens. Medications such as Bactrim, nitrofurantoin, nalidixic acid, carbenicillin, and tetracyclines are used. Aminoglycosides are very effective against gram-negative organisms, but they must be used parenterally, and doses must be modified in the individual with renal insufficiency. The usual course of therapy is 7 to 10 days, although a single oral dose has been shown to be effective in some adult studies. In the disabled population, however, the incidence of anomalies and other predisposing factors is so high (45% in one recent study) that the full 10-day course is recommended.[15] A repeat urine culture after 72 hours of treatment is recommended to establish the efficacy of therapy. Follow-up cultures are also recommended; they should be obtained 3 to 4 days after completing therapy, and then periodically thereafter for 1 year.

Any neonate who develops a UTI should be treated for presumed sepsis with parenteral ampicillin and gentamycin pending culture results. Neonates with a UTI also should be investigated for a potential urinary tract anomaly. Older children and adults deserve a workup for an anomaly if one infection is seen in a male, or recurrent infection in a female.

Patients with an anatomic abnormality, VUR, neurogenic bladder, or documented multiple infections should be placed on long-term (months to years) antibacterial prophylaxis. Agents used include Bactrim, nitrofurantoin, and mandelamine (which should not be used in renal insufficiency). Urinary acidification is also helpful and can be accomplished with vitamin C and dietary modification.

There are predisposing factors to developing a UTI other than an anatomic aberration. Individuals with mental retardation and cerebral palsy seem at particular risk for acquiring a UTI. There are a number of possible explanations for this, which include: difficulty in achieving adequate perineal hygiene; chronic constipation (thought to cause a functional obstruction to urine flow as well as increasing the potential for soiling and feeding the lower urinary tract with fecal bacteria); abnormal voiding patterns; and the increased predisposition to infectious diseases inherent in a residential setting. Individuals with cerebral palsy severe enough to have developed joint contractures of the hip are at particular risk for poor perineal hygiene, chronic vaginitis, and recurrent UTI. Patients who require an indwelling catheter are at extremely high risk. Other predisposing factors include benign prostatic hypertrophy in older males and postsurgical instrumentation. Prostatitis has been shown to be a cause of recurrent infection in males. It may not respond to the customary 10-day course of antibiotics and can cause chronic seeding of the bladder with bacteria if not treated for a prolonged period (3 to 4 months) with antibiotics (Bactrim or oxytetracycline).

Antibiotics alone may not be effective in controlling infection. Other measures are also important. These include vigorous measures to control constipation, improvement of perineal hygiene, and local treatment of chronic vaginitis. Decreasing (voluntary) urinary retention by increasing voiding frequency and improving toilet practices is also an important strategy. Physical therapy is paramount in individuals with cerebral palsy, because tight hip adductors preclude good perineal hygiene.[10] Some orthopedists have even recommended surgical procedures to release contracted hips in order to improve perineal care and help prevent urinary tract infection.

Benign Prostatic Hypertrophy

Enlargement of the prostate is a common problem in men over 50 years of age. Its inception is insidious, with minimal symptoms that progress slowly until one day an individual realizes his voiding characteristics have changed. In someone with other mental and physical handicaps, this realization may not become apparent until an obvious sign occurs, such as urinary incontinence, infection, hematuria, or retention.

The initial symptoms include frequency, urgency, nocturia, hesitancy, decreasing stream size and force, straining to void, and postvoid dribbling. Other signs may include hematuria and urinary infection. Acute urinary retention is a rather late manifestation of the disease.

Benign prostatic hypertrophy (BPH) is a disease of aging males. It is rarely present in men under 50, but its prevalence increases steadily with age; by the time they are 80, most men have some signs of obstruction. A male with recent and rapidly developing symptoms (less than 6 to 9 months) raises one's suspicion of carcinoma of the prostate.

Size of prostate as noted on rectal examination is not always indicative of the degree of impediment to the flow of urine. A large intravesical portion of the gland can never be determined by palpation, and is only evident by radiography or cystoscopic visualization of the bladder and posterior urethra. Observation of voiding with measurement of the flow rate and postvoid residual urine are important adjunctive objective tests to assess the degree of obstruction. An excretory urogram or renal ultrasonogram should be obtained in every patient suspected of having BPH to assess the effect, if any, on the upper urinary tract.

Today, most operations are performed transurethrally to remove the hyperplastic elements of the gland, the open (suprapubic or retropubic) approach is reserved for men with an excessively large prostate.[22]

Renal Failure

Renal failure is the endpoint of many of the conditions mentioned earlier in this chapter, including congenital anomalies, VUR, and recurrent UTI.

Classification and Etiology

There are two categories of renal failure, acute and chronic. Acute renal failure is caused by three main types of pathology—decreased glomerular filtration (e.g., dehydration, hypotension), injury to renal parenchyma (e.g., nephrotoxic drugs, acute tubular necrosis), and obstructive uropathy (much more common in adults than in children). Depending on its etiology, acute renal failure is usually reversible, particularly in children. Chronic renal failure, in contrast, is usually progressive and leads to end-stage renal disease (ESRD). Urizar's text of pediatric nephrology presented a helpful mnemonic for remembering the causes of renal failure, VITAMIN C. The V includes vascular causes, I infections (e.g., chronic pyelonephritis), T for traumatic, A for allergic, M for metabolic, I for iatrogenic, N for neoplastic, and C for congenital etiologies.

The five most common causes of chronic renal failure (CRF) in children include glomerular disease, obstructive uropathy occurring prenatally, renal hypoplasia, hereditary nephropathies, and vascular nephropathies.[12] The prevalence of obstructive uropathies (e.g., secondary to myelodysplasia or a congenital anomaly and renal hypoplasia) is greater in individuals with a disability than in the general population; thus these conditions are likely to be a cause of renal failure in the disabled population.[19]

Clinical Features

Renal failure presents with two main features, oliguria and azotemia. Other important signs include seizures, hyperkalemia, acidosis, hypertension, hyponatremia, hyperuricemia, hypocalcemia, and altered mental status.

Some of the clinical features of renal failure deserve special mention in reference to the patient with physical or cognitive disabilities. The first of these is growth failure. Growth deficiency is thought to be secondary to deficient caloric intake, acidosis, vitamin D deficiency, and low levels of somatomedin. Children with a developmental disability often have feeding difficulties that contribute to caloric deficiency, and they may have little exposure to sunlight, which contributes to vitamin D deficiency.

Children with renal insufficiency tend to have delayed secondary sexual development. This is commonly seen in the individual with disabilities who is also malnourished. Lack of sexual development is an additional social handicap to an individual with a physical disability who already suffers from an altered body image.

One must not overlook the important area of psychosocial development. Individuals with renal failure may have problems coping with the chronic nature of their disease, the painful medical procedures, frequent hospitalizations, dietary restrictions, and dependency on dialysis. Individuals with anatomic abnormalities may find the frequent surgical and medical focus on the genital area to be upsetting and invasive. These problems may be particularly acute in the individual with cognitive limitations who cannot understand the procedures, the individual with an emotional disturbance who cannot adjust to them, and the individual with a physical handicap who may also have to cope with other surgical and medical therapies.

Management

The medical treatment of renal failure is the same for any individual regardless of the presence of a handicap. It involves correcting the chemical abnormalities, normalizing fluid status, controlling neurologic complications, and treating hypertension.

Because the disease states that cause chronic renal failure progress over time, the final outcome is end-stage renal disease. When this point is reached, conservative medical therapy alone is no longer effective. Two alternatives are then available to support life—dialysis and transplantation. There are two forms of dialysis, hemodialysis and peritoneal dialysis. Hemodialysis may be difficult to perform in small children because it requires vascular access. This can be created (surgically) via either a subcutaneous arteriovenous (A-V) fistula, a synthetic A-V graft, or an external A-V shunt. Peritoneal dialysis is another alternative that is particularly useful in small infants, because no vascular access is necessary. The major advantage of peritoneal dialysis is the potential for performing continuous ambulatory peritoneal dialysis (CAPD) through permanent peritoneal catheters. Parents and patients can be taught to perform daily CAPD at home, which saves triweekly trips to a dialysis center. Recurrent peritonitis is the major risk of indwelling peritoneal catheters.

Renal transplantation is the other alternative to dialysis. Organs are obtained either from living related donors or from cadavers. Transplantation can be performed relatively safely. It is favored over dialysis in the pediatric age group because it leads to improve somatic growth and offers a greater chance for a normal lifestyle. Transplantation is also less expensive than a chronic dialysis program. The morbidity and mortality associated with the surgical procedure and the necessity of taking immunosuppressive drugs indefinitely are its major disadvantages.

Ethical Concerns

When one is considering dialysis in a person with a severe physical or cognitive disability, there are some issues of ethical concern. Dialysis is painful and requires a considerable investment of time. The patient must either be transported to a dialysis center three times a week for hemodialysis or be in the care of trained personnel who can perform CAPD. Chronic dialysis is costly. The number of dialysis centers is limited, and they may not be geographically or physically accessible to persons with severe handicaps. Patients who elect dialysis do so after weighing the desire to prolong life with the diminished quality of life inherent in being dependent on a dialysis machine. All these factors merit consideration before the decision to dialyze can be made. The decision to withhold dialysis in severely disabled individuals is usually made by the patient when possible, and the family or caretakers who know the patient best.

The same questions arise when transplantation is considered. The individual with cognitive limitations may not be able to give informed consent or to understand the risks of surgery and long-term immunosuppression. Resources for transplantation are even more limited than those for dialysis. The waiting period for a cadaveric kidney is approximately 12 months in Boston, for example, and some individuals must wait much longer. Most medical centers will not withhold transplantation on the basis of cognitive or physical disabilities, particularly if a family member is willing to donate a kidney. It is usually the patient and family who make the ultimate decision about transplantation in an individual with severe handicaps. If neither dialysis nor transplantation is an appropriate option, early diagnosis and good medical management can ensure relatively long-term survival and a reasonable lifestyle for many individuals with renal disease.

REFERENCES

1. Azrin, N.H., Bugle, C., and O'Brien, F.: Behavioral engineering: Two apparatuses for toilet training retarded children. J. Appl. Behav. Anal., 4:249, 1971.
2. Barrett, D.M., and Furlow, W.L.: The management of severe urinary incontinence in patient with myelodysplasia by implantation of the AS 791/792 urinary sphincter device. J. Urol., 128:484, 1982.
3. Bauer, S.B.: Pediatric Neuro-Urology. In Clinical Neuro-Urology. Edited by R.J. Krane, and M.B. Siroky. Boston, Little Brown, 1979, pp. 275-293.
4. Bauer, S.B.: Genitourinary problems in adolescence. J. Reprod. Med., 29:385, 1984.
5. Bauer, S.B., Colodny, A.H., and Retik, A.B.: The management of vesicoureteral reflux in children with myelodysplasia. J. Urol., 128:102, 1982.
6. Bauer, S.B., et al.: The unstable bladder of childhood. Urol. Clin. N. Am., 7:321, 1980.
7. Belman, A.B.: The clinical significance of vesicoureteral reflux. Pediatr. Clin. N. Am., 23:707, 1976.
8. Chantler, C.: Syndromes with a renal component. In Pediatric Nephrology. Edited by M.I. Rubin, and T.M. Barratt. Baltimore, Williams & Wilkins, 1975, pp. 891-902.
9. Crooks, K.K., and Enrile, B.G.: Comparison of the ileal conduit and clean intermittent catheterization for myelomeningocele. Pediatrics, 72:203, 1983.
10. Elias, E.R., and Rubin, I.L.: Abstract: Urinary tract infections in patients with cerebral palsy. Developmental Medicine and Child Neurology, 38th Annual Meeting of the American Academy of Cerebral Palsy and Developmental Medicine, Washington, DC, October 1984.
11. Friedland, G.W.: Recurrent urinary tract infections in infants and children. Radiol. Clin. N. Am., 15:19, 1977.
12. Gauthier, B., Edelmann, C.M., Jr., and Barnett, H.L.: Nephrology and urology for the pediatrician. Boston, Little Brown, 1982.
13. Gusman, L., et al.: Evaluation and management of children with sacral agenesis. Urology, 22:506, 1983.
14. Heikel, P.E., and Parkkulainen, K.V.: Vesico-ureteric reflux in children: A classification and results of conservative treatment. Ann. Radiol., 9:37, 1966.
15. Kunin, C.M.: Duration of treatment of urinary tract infections. Am. J. Medicine, 71:849, 1981.
16. Lapides, J.: Mechanisms of urinary tract infection. Urology, 14:217, 1979.
17. Perez-Marrero, R., Dimmock, W., Churchill, B.M., and Hardy, B.E.: Clean intermittent catheterization in myelomeningocele children less than three years old. J. Urol., 128:779, 1982.
18. Perlmutter, A.D.: Enuresis. In Clinical Pediatric Urology. Vol. 1. Edited by P.P. Kelalis, L.R. King, and A.B. Belman. Philadelphia, W.B. Saunders, 1976, pp. 166-181.
19. Shurtleff, D.B.: Myelodysplasia management and treatment. In Current Problems in Pediatrics. Vol. 10. Edited by L. Gluck. Chicago, Year Book Publishers, 1980, pp. 53-64.
20. Urizar, R.E., Largent, J.A., and Gilboa, N.: Pediatric Nephrology: New Directions in Therapy. New Hyde Park, NY, Medical Examination Publishing Co., 1983.
21. Varni, J.W.: Urinary and fecal incontinence. Clinical behavioral pediatrics. An Interdisciplinary Biobehavioral Approach. Elmsford, NY, Pergamon Press, 1983, pp. 217-243.
22. Walsh, P.C.: Benign prostatic hypertrophy. In Campbell's Urology (5th Ed.). Edited by P.C. Walsh, R.F. Gittes, A.D. Perlmutter, and T.A. Stamey. Philadelphia, W.B. Saunders, 1986, pp. 1248-1267.
23. Willscher, M.K., Bauer, S.B., Zammuto, P.J., and Retik, A.B.: Renal growth and urinary infection following antireflux surgery in infants and children. J. Urol., 115:722, 1976.

BIBLIOGRAPHY

Belman, A.B.: Early surgery for hypospadias. Hosp. Pract., 19:192, 1984.

Bergsma, D., and Duckett, S.W. (Eds.): Urinary system malformations in children. Birth Defects, 13, 1977.

Bergstrom, L., Thompson, P., and Wood, R.P.: New patterns in genetic and congenital otonephropathies. Laryngoscope, 89:177, 1979.

Billie, B., Eriksson, B., and Gierup, J.: Early bladder training in patients with spina bifida. Acta Paedr. Scand., 73:60, 1984.

Campbell, M.F. (Ed.): Urology. 4th Ed. Philadelphia, W.B. Saunders, 1979.

Crocker, J.F.S., Brown, D.M., and Vernier, R.L.: Developmental defects of the kidney. A review of renal developmental and experimental studies of maldevelopment. Pediatr. Clin. N. Am., *18*:355, 1971.

Culp, O.S.: Hydronephrosis and hydroureter in infancy and childhood. J. Urol., *88*:443, 1982.

Davis, C.A., Petti, S., and Dixon, M.S.: Correlations between ancillary assays and bacteriuria in children with myelodysplasia and ileal conduit urinary diversion. J. Urol., *128*:546, 1982.

Ellenberg, M.: Urinary tract infection in diabetes: Pathogenesis and treatment. Pract. Cardiol., *8*:123, 1982.

Garibaldi, R.A., et al.: Meatal colonization and catheter-associated bacteriuria. N. Engl. J. Med., *303*:316, 1980.

Gates, G.F.: Ultrasonography of the urinary tract in children. Urol. Clin. N. Am., 7:215, 1980.

Gaum, L.D., et al.: Radiologic investigation of the urinary tract in the neonate with myelomeningocele. J. Radiol., *127*:510, 1982.

Gillenwater, J.Y., Harrison, R.B., and Kunin, C.M.: Natural history of bacteriuria in schoolgirls. N. Engl. J. Med., *301*:396, 1979.

Hallett, M., Bauer, S.B., Khoshbin, and Dyro, F.: Reflexes of the external urethral sphincter in children. Arch. Neurol., *41*:942, 1984.

Hrish, D.D., Fainstein, V., and Musher, D.M.: Do condom catheter collecting systems cause urinary tract infection? J.A.M.A., *243*:340, 1980.

James, J.A.: Embryology and structural anomalies of the urinary tract. *In* Renal Diseases in Childhood. Edited by J.A. James. St. Louis, C.V. Mosby, 1976, pp. 91-125.

Kaplan, W.E., and Firlit, C.F.: Management of reflux in the myelodysplastic child. J. Urol., *129*:1195, 1983.

Kunin, C.M., Polyak, F., and Postel, E.: Periurethral bacterial flora in women. J.A.M.A., *243*:134, 1980.

McNeal, D.M., Hawtrey, C.E., Wolraich, M.L., and Mapel, J.R.: Symptomatic neurogenic bladder in a cerebral-palsied population. Dev. Med. Child Neurol., *25*:612, 1983.

Mahoney, K., Van Wagenen, R.K., and Meyerson, L.: Toilet training of normal and retarded children. J. Appl. Behav. Anal., *4*:173, 1971.

Nicolle, L.G., Bjornson, J., Harding, G.K.M., and MacDonell, J.A.: Bacteriuria in elderly institutionalized men. N. Engl. J. Med., *309*:1420, 1983.

Platt, R.: Quantitative definition of bacteriuria. Am. J. Med., *75*:44, 1983.

Ramirez-Manguia, M., and Gordira-Paniagua, G.: Urinary tract infection associated with local predisposing factors. Bull. Med. Hospital Infante, *24*:767, 1977.

Resnick, M.I., and King, L.R.: Urinary incontinence. *In* Clinical Pediatric Urology. Vol. 1. Edited by P.P. Kelalis, L.R. King, and A.B. Belman. Philadelphia, W.B. Saunders, 1976, pp. 144-165.

Retik, A.: Urinary tract disorders in children: New approaches. Hosp. Pract., *19*:121, 1984.

Royer, P.: Embryological development of the kidney and genetic factors. *In* Pediatric Nephrology. Edited by A.J. Schaffer. Volume 11 in the series Major Problems in Clinical Pediatrics. Philadelphia, W.B. Saunders, 1974, pp. 3-8.

Schaeffer, A.S., Jones, J.M., and Dunn, J.K.: Association of in vitro Escherichia coli adherence to vaginal and buccal epithelial cells with susceptibility of women to recurrent urinary tract infections. N. Engl. J. Med., *304*:1062, 1981.

Shopfner, C.E.: Urinary tract pathology associated with constipation. Radiology, *90*:865, 1968.

Smith, J.W., et al.: Recurrent urinary tract infections in man. Ann. Intern. Med., *91*:544, 1979.

Stafford, S.J., et al.: Hydronephrosis in the asymptomatic neonate with myelodysplasia. J. Urol., *129*:340, 1983.

Stamm, W.E., et al.: Antimicrobial prophylaxis of recurrent urinary tract infections. Ann. Intern. Med., *92*:770, 1980.

Stamm, W.E., et al.: Causes of the acute urethral syndrome in women. N. Engl. J. Med., *303*:409, 1980.

Stamm, W.E., et al.: Treatment of the acute urethral syndrome. N. Engl. J. Med., *304*:956, 1981.

Warren, J.W., Muncie, H.L., Berquist, G.J., and Hoopes, J.M.: Sequelae and management of urinary infection in the patient requiring chronic catheterization. J. Urol., *125*:1, 1981.

Warren, J.W., et al.: Antibiotic irrigation and catheter-associated urinary tract infections. N. Engl. J. Med., *299*:570, 1978.

18

DERMATOLOGIC PROBLEMS

Allen I. Berliner, M.D.

Dermatologic diagnosis and treatment of developmentally disabled children and adults is often more challenging than that of other patients. The nature of the underlying neurologic disorder, the behavior of the patients, and certain environmental factors can lead to dermatoses seldom seen elsewhere. The inability of some adults to contribute historical information such as duration, symptoms, and family history can make differential diagnosis more difficult. Behavioral problems can interfere with the performance of many simple diagnostic tests, and treatment is made more complicated by the fact that most topical agents need to be applied by parents, attendants, and the nursing staff.

Despite these problems, successful skin care can be achieved if the clinician is aware of some of the more unique problems and if he is prepared to be flexible and at times even creative in treatment.

The majority of dermatologic problems seen in patients with disabilities are not rare. The prevalence of these problems has been looked at by Butterworth and Wilson, who systematically examined the entire skin of each patient at the Pennhurst State School.[7] Their findings indicate that acne, pigmented nevi, tinea, and pyoderma were the most common skin problems. In my review of patients referred to the dermatologic clinic of Wrentham State School between 1978 and 1982, acne, pigmented nevi, tinea, and seborrheic dermatitis were by far the most common diagnoses (A.I. Berliner, unpublished). Seventy percent of all the diagnoses made in both reviews could be included in the 10 most common diseases of the skin.

A discussion of dermatosis found in the developmentally disabled population is best divided into three major categories: (1) dermatoses that are diagnostic of a neurological problem, (2) dermatoses that are found more frequently among patients with neurologic diseases but are not diagnostic of the disease, and (3) dermatoses that are present because they are common in large groups of young people living together in a close environment.

DERMATOSIS DIAGNOSTIC OF NEUROLOGIC DISORDERS

There are many neurocutaneous syndromes in which the diagnosis is made from skin findings alone (see Chap. 8). Tuberous sclerosis and neurofibromatosis, the two most common examples, will be discussed in detail. This discussion will be followed by a summary of less common entities presented in table form.

Tuberous Sclerosis

Tuberous sclerosis is the epitome of a dermatosis that is diagnostic of a neurologic condition. The cutaneous manifestations can be divided into two groups—major ones, which are specific for the syndrome, and minor ones, which are commonly found but are not diagnostic. The major manifestations are

Hypopigmented macules
Adenoma sebaceum
Shagreen patches
Fibromas (periungual, oral)

The minor manifestations are

Café-au-lait spots
Skin tags, polyps

Over 50% of patients with tuberous sclerosis have hypopigmented macules, and these are the earliest manifestations, usually present at birth.[21] The lesions increase in size and number with age and persist into adult life. The classic lesion is 1 to 3 cm, dull white, does not tan, but becomes red with irritation.[23] The lesions can be found anywhere on the skin but are concentrated on the abdomen, back, and anterolateral aspects of the legs. As illustrated in Figure 18-1, most macules are oval with irregular borders, some having a classic "ash leaf" appearance. There is, however, a great variety in the potential size and shape of macules. One patient was described as having one 7-cm lesion; others had hundreds of 2- to 3-mm macules (white freckles).[27]

The hypopigmentation represents a decrease in function of the melanocytes, which are present in normal numbers (in vitiligo the melanocytes are totally absent). Examination of fair-skinned patients with a Wood's (long-wave ultraviolet) light will reveal otherwise undetectable macules by increasing their contrast with normally pigmented skin.

Tufts of white or grey hair (poliosis) occur in 18% of patients,[38] and these may be analogous to the hypopigmented macules. Because these hairs are sometimes easier than the macules to detect in very fair-skinned infants, they can be an important sign.

The most familiar of the cutaneous lesions of tuberous sclerosis is the angiofibroma, which has the misnomer "adenoma sebaceum." Histologically the lesions do not represent tumors of sebaceous glands, but hamartomas of fibrous and vascular tissue occurring in areas where many large sebaceous glands are normally found.[38] They are therefore best called angiofibromas. These red to brown, smooth nodules, illustrated in Figure 18-2, are found in 90% of patients over the age of 4 years.[38] In some cases the lesions are topped with dilated blood vessels (telangiectasias) and have a blood-red appearance.[35] They average 4 mm in diameter but can coalesce to form irregular masses. The earliest lesions start in the nasolabial folds as individual pink papules and

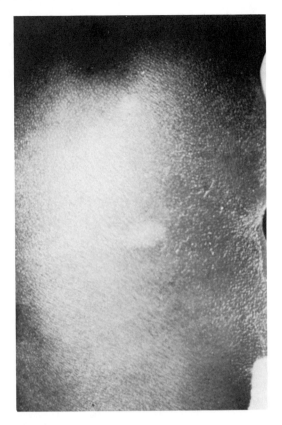

FIG. 18-1. Hypopigmented macule of tuberous sclerosis.

tend to develop symmetrically on the nose, cheeks, and chin. Eventually the temples, forehead, and eyelids can become involved.[8] The lesions rarely appear on the upper lip except immediately beneath the nose.[38]

The angiofibromas usually appear between the ages of 2 and 8,[35] but they may be present at birth and have been reported to appear as late as age 26.[38] They undergo progressive growth until adulthood, at which time they remain stable.[38]

The lesions are often confused with those of acne vulgaris, but they can be differentiated by their prepubertal appearance and the lack of pustules and comedones.[25] The differential diagnosis also includes acne rosacea, multiple trichoepitheliomata, and sebaceous hyperplasia.

Although the angiofibromas are for the most part asymptomatic, they can be of severe cosmetic concern. Dermabrasion can provide considerable improvement, but the lesions can recur.[33]

Fibrous plaques, known as shagreen patches, occur in approximately 20% of patients, usually appearing at the same time as the angiofibromas. They are flat to slightly raised plaques, flesh-

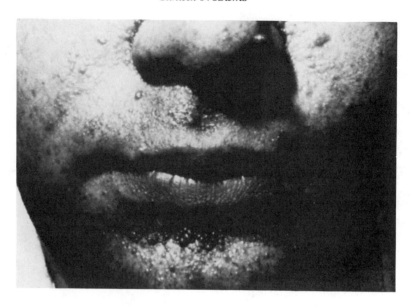

FIG. 18-2.   Adenoma sebaceum (angiofibromas of tuberous sclerosis).

colored, with a surface like pigskin or orange peel. The name derives from the appearance of untanned leather or "peau chagrine."[38] Although they are most often palm-sized and singular, they can be much smaller, and multiple lesions can occur. The lumbosacral region is the usual location. The plaques histologically represent avascular proliferations of connective tissue.[38]

Smaller fibrous plaques occur on the forehead and scalp. These are soft, pink to brown plaques that can be confused with pigmented nevi.[8]

Fibromas of the nail region occur in 17% of patients,[35] usually starting at puberty.[38] These growths are firm, red to flesh-colored nodules growing either periungually or subungually.

Fibromas of the oral region are most commonly found on the gingivae but may also be located on buccal, palatal, and tongue surfaces.[8] Their prevalence in one series was 22%.[37]

Café au lait spots occur in 9.27% of patients[8,25] and may be present at birth. These flat, tan macules are less common and fewer in number than in neurofibromatosis. They are not specific for tuberous sclerosis.

Soft, flesh-colored to tan polyps and skin tags are found in 18 to 39% of all patients.[37,38] These are clustered over the neck, shoulders, axillae, and eyelids and are most common over the age of 15.[38]

The recognition of these skin manifestations will result in prompt diagnosis of the syndrome. The two most important yet most easily overlooked signs are the earliest, the hypopigmented macules, and the most common, the angiofibromas. The former will be found if a Wood's light examination is routinely performed, and the latter will be diagnosed if one's index of suspicion is kept high. The presence of shagreen patches, fibrous plaques of the forehead, scalp, and nail, and oral fibromas help to confirm the diagnosis.

Neurofibromatosis

Neurofibromatosis, or von Recklinghausen's disease, is another neurologic disease primarily diagnosed on specific cutaneous findings.

Although the disease is thought to be inherited in an autosomal dominant fashion, 50% of cases appear to be mutations.[18] Neurologic manifestations include mental retardation (10%), seizures (10%), and tumors.[11] The degree of mental retardation, if present, while occasionally severe, is usually mild to moderate and not progressive. The retardation may appear before the skin lesions appear.[45] In addition to these problems, precocious puberty, acoustic and optic nerve tumors, bone changes, and pheochromocytomas may occur.

Two major skin findings occur, café au lait spots and cutaneous neurofibromas. The former, illustrated in Figure 18-3, are flat, light brown, oval patches of hyperpigmentation. They are usually present at birth but can take up to 1 year to appear. During the first 2 years of life the spots increase in size and number, in some cases continuing for the first decade.[42] They average 2 to 5 cm in length but can range from a few milli-

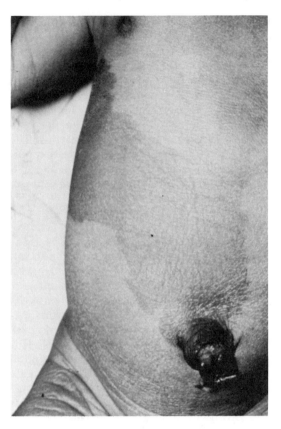

FIG. 18-3. Café au lait spot.

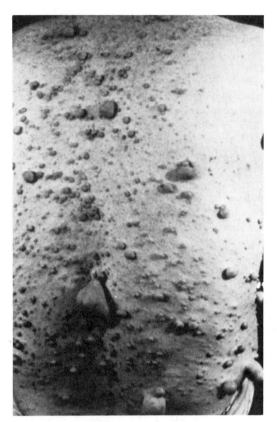

FIG. 18-4. Neurofibromas.

meters to 15 cm.[18] The café au lait spots of von Recklinghausen's disease can be found anywhere on the skin and have well-defined, smooth ("coast of California") borders. They differ from the café au lait spots in Albright's fibrous polyostotic dysplasia, which tend to follow dermatomal distributions on the neck and buttock, stop at the midline, and have irregular ("coast of Maine") borders.[13]

Ten to 20% of normal individuals have one or more café au lait spots. The larger the number and size of the spots, the more suggestive of neurofibromatosis. Ninety-five percent of patients with the syndrome have at least one spot, and 78% of them have 6 or more.[18] The presence of 6 or more spots, 1.5 cm or greater in size, is almost diagnostic.[17] Since fewer than 1% of normal children have 3 or more spots, the presence of 5 or more lesions 0.5 cm in size is significant in children 5 years old or younger.[47] Axillary freckling (i.e., multiple 1- to 4-mm café au lait spots in the axillae) is found in 20% of neurofibromatosis patients and is probably specific for the entity.[16] The lack of sun exposure in the axilla makes normal freckling unlikely. Other nondiagnostic pigmentary changes that may occur include nonaxillary freckling, hypopigmented patches, and diffuse bronze discoloration.[5]

Neurofibromas are tumors derived from Schwann cells of peripheral nerve sheaths. Solitary neurofibromas are not unusual in the normal population and are not indicative of von Recklinghausen's disease. In the latter condition, the tumors begin to appear in late childhood or early adolescence and increase in size from 1 or 2 mm to 2 or 3 cm. As shown in Figure 18-4, patients may have thousands of them.[18] They are soft, skin-colored or violaceous tumors that can appear in a variety of shapes. The lesion can be invaginated by applying finger pressure to the overlying skin. This is called a positive "button hole" sign and can be used to differentiate a neurofibroma from other tumors.

Occasionally subcutaneous tumors appear, firm nodules attached to a nerve, or, rarely, large, pendulous flabby masses in which thickened nerves can be felt. These are called plexiform neuromas and can lead to marked deformity.

The diagnosis of neurofibromatosis is usually not difficult because almost 80% of patients will

have 6 or more large café au lait spots. Of the
remaining 20%, those older than 21 will usually
have multiple cutaneous tumors and a few pigmented spots. Younger patients without tumors
and only a few spots must be diagnosed by noncu-
taneous factors such as family history, presence
of precocious puberty, radiographic evidence of
bone cysts, or cranial nerve involvement.[18]

The presence of bilateral iris Lisch nodules is
suggestive of the syndrome. Neurofibromatosis has
recently been classified into three types: neuro-
fibromatosis-1, or von Recklinghausen's neurofibromatosis; neurofibromatosis-2, or bilateral
acoustic neurofibromatosis; and neurofibromatosis-
3, all others. It may not be possible to classify some
patients without use of neuroimaging studies.[43]

Other Syndromes

Table 18-1 summarizes the features of other
cutaneous diseases that can be associated with
mental retardation and/or seizures. I have tried
to list only well-established syndromes that can
be diagnosed or strongly suspected on the basis
of skin manifestations alone. Syndromes diagnosed on developmental abnormalities with only
minor skin changes have not been included. The
degree of mental retardation present within a
syndrome may vary greatly, and in some syndromes only a small minority of patients are retarded. More detailed information about these
syndromes can be found in Dermatology in General Medicine,[22] from which parts of this table
have been adapted.

DERMATOSIS ASSOCIATED WITH BUT
NOT DIAGNOSTIC OF SYNDROMES
AND CONDITIONS

This section will discuss a loose collection of
dermatoses that are for various reasons associated with neurologic diseases. Its largest part
deals with the various nondiagnostic dermatologic
problems found in Down syndrome. Following
this, self-induced dermatosis, scabetic infection,
and an interesting dermatosis, cutis verticis gyrata,
will be discussed briefly.

Dermatoses Associated with
Down Syndrome

Patients with Down syndrome often have a
number of interesting skin changes. Most of the
skin changes are found with higher frequency
than in the general population.

Cheilitis

One of the more common skin problems found
is that of cheilitis, or inflammation of the lips.[49]

The lips are enlarged and develop vertical fissures and crusting. This condition is not present
in infancy but develops and worsens with age.
The incidence of cheilitis is higher in patients
with deeply fissured, enlarged tongues known as
"scrotal" tongue.[9] The etiology of cheilitis is unknown, but it may be caused by holding the
mouth slightly ajar to accommodate the relatively large tongue or the protruding lips. The
lips become inflamed because this position permits drooling, especially during sleep, alternating with dryness due to increased exposure to
the air during the day.

Xerosis

The skin of infants with Down syndrome is soft
and velvety, but it gradually becomes dry with
age.[49] Most adults have some manifestations of
dry skin ranging from simple, mild xerosis to the
"fish scale" appearance of ichthyosis vulgaris. Accompanying these changes may be hyperkeratosis, or thickening of the palms and soles. This
latter observation is important because it often
must be differentiated from the hyperkeratotic
form of tinea pedis.

As is often the case with very dry skin, patients
with Down syndrome tend to develop eczematous eruptions. One of the most common types is
lichen simplex chronicus, a condition involving
well-defined plaques of thickened, red, scaling
skin showing accentuation of the normal skin
markings. This dermatitis is usually found on the
upper arms, anterior thighs, ankles, wrists, back
of the neck, and knuckles.[30]

Eczema

In nummular eczema, round, dry, scaling or
vesicular, crusted patches occur. The condition
occurs frequently in patients with xerosis. This
eruption appears to favor the extremities, especially the dorsa of the hands and feet.

Atopic eczema; i.e., eczematous skin changes
associated with a personal or family history of
hayfever or asthma, is thought by some observers to be found more frequently in persons with
Down syndrome than in the general population.[12]

Vascular Instability

The vascular instability of the skin is hall-
marked by acrocyanosis, a bluish discoloration of
the extremities found in up to 90% of patients.[49]
In addition, cutis marmorata, a transient, reticu-
lated, blue mottling of the extremities has been
noted in 8.4% of patients.[12]

Table 18-1. *Cutaneous Manifestations of Miscellaneous Developmental Disorders*

Name	Intelligence	Seizures	Hereditary	Skin Manifestations	Associated Features
Sturge-Weber syndrome	Normal or decreased	Yes	Not familial	Unilateral angioma (port wine stain) in area of ophthalmic division of fifth cranial nerve	Ipsilateral glaucoma
Ataxia telangiectasia	Decreased	No	Autosomal recessive	Telangiectasia of conjuctivae, ears, neck, face, extremities. Sclerodermatous skin, café au lait and hypopigmented spots, eczema, gray hair	Immune defects, cerebellar atoxic choreoathetosis
Incontinentia pigmentosa	Normal or decreased	Yes	X-linked dominant	Vesicles at birth to 2 weeks, replaced by verrucous plaques, then replaced by whorls of hyperpigmentation; alopecia, nail abnormalities	Teeth and eye defects
Anhidrotic ectodermal dysplasia	Decreased	No	X-linked recessive	Skin dry, shiny, absence of eccrine sweat glands, alopecia	Teeth absent, eye abnormalities
Hidrotic ectodermal dysplasia	Normal or decreased	Yes	Autosomal dominant	Normal eccrine sweating, hyperkeratosis of palms and soles, alopecia, dystrophic nails	Neural deafness
Epithelial nevus syndrome	Decreased	Yes	?	Multiple linear, warty verrucous plaques	Skeletal abnormalities
Rothmund-Thompson syndrome	Decreased	No	Autosomal recessive	Atrophy and telangiectasia (poikiloderma), photosensitivity, pigmentary change, nail defects, cutaneous tumors	Cataracts, macrodontia, adontia, skeletal abnormalities, hypogonadism, immune defects
Menke's syndrome (kinky hair)	Decreased	No	X-linked recessive	Sparse kinky hair	Growth retardation, copper malabsorption
Lesch-Nyan syndrome	Decreased	No	X-linked recessive	Self mutilation	Increased uric acid, cerebral palsy, choreoathetosis
Xerodermic idiocy of DeSanctis and Cacchione	Decreased	No	Autosomal recessive	Xeroderma pigmentosum, freckled, telangiectasia, atrophy, multiple actinic keratoses, basal cell CA, squamous cell CA, melanoma	Ocular abnormalities, retarded growth and sexual development, defective repair of ultraviolet light damaged DNA
Phenylketonuria	Decreased	Yes	Autosomal recessive	Fair skin, eczema, photosensitivity, inability to tan well, acrocyanosis, sclerodermatous skin	Blue eyes, blond hair
Hartnup syndrome	Decreased	No	Autosomal recessive	"Pellagra like" dermatitis in sun exposed areas	Cerebral ataxia
Sjogren-Larsson syndrome	Decreased	Yes	Autosomal recessive	Lamellar ichthyosis (thick, large scales over most of body)	Spastic paralysis, retinitis pigmentosa
Conradis syndrome	Decreased	No	Autosomal recessive	Scaling of skin in whorled pattern eventually leaving atrophic lesions	Skeletal abnormalities, cataracts

Table 18-1. *Continued.*

Name	Intelligence	Seizures	Hereditary	Skin Manifestations	Associated Features
Rud syndrome	Decreased	Decreased	Autosomal recessive	Lamellar ichthyosis	Dwarfism, hypogonadism
Netherton syndrome	Decreased	No	Autosomal recessive	Eczema, ichthyosiform dermatitis, bamboo like hair shaft defect (trichorrhexis invaginata)	
Argenosuccinic-aciduria	Decreased	Yes	Autosomal recessive	Brittle, friable hair with nodules on hair shaft (trichorrhexis nodosa) or beaded hair (monolethrix)	
Leopard (Moynahan) syndrome	Decreased	No	Possibly autosomal recessive	Multiple hyperpigmented macules (lentigines)	EKG abnormalities ocular hypertelorism, pulmonic stenosis abnormal genitalia, deafness, retardation of growth

Seborrheic Dermatitis

Seborrheic dermatitis occurs more frequently in the presence of a variety of neurologic diseases, e.g., epilepsy, Parkinson's disease, stroke,[4] and Down syndrome.[3] It can also occur with phenothiazine treatment.[6] This red-yellow eruption with fine dry to thick yellow scale involves the scalp, retroauricular skin, auditory meatus, eyebrows, cheeks, nasolabial folds, eyelids, and presternal skin.

Follicular Eruptions

Approximately 50% of male patients between 20 and 40 years of age have an erythematous, papular follicular eruption of the presternal and interscapular skin.[20] This may represent a follicular variety of seborrheic dermatitis, but it may be an independent dermatosis because many patients have normal scalps. It should not be confused with acne vulgaris.

Alopecia Areata

Alopecia areata (Figure 18-5) has been found in up to 8.9% of patients with Down syndrome as compared to less than 1% of the general population.[12] This form of hair loss occurs in round, well-circumscribed patients without evidence of erythema, scaling, or scarring. "Exclamation point" hairs are often found at the periphery of the patch and are a diagnostic feature. These are short hairs that are thinner at the scalp surface than they are distally. The scalp is usually involved, but occasional hair loss can be found in other areas such as the beard, eyelashes, or eyebrows. The hair may regrow spontaneously, the alopecia may remain for many years, or, rarely, progress to total loss of scalp hair (alopecia totalis) or all body hair (alopecia universalis). Although some evidence suggests an autoimmune mechanism, the etiology of alopecia areata is unknown.

Syringoma

Syringomas, benign tumors derived from eccrine sweat glands, are extremely common, although they are often overlooked. These have been found in 13 to 26% of males and 26 to 58% of females with Down syndrome.[10,12] These growths are first noted at puberty and most frequently involve the eyelids and periorbital areas. The individual growths are 0.5 to 3.0 mm, skin-colored to yellowish brown, slightly elevated papules. If the clinical picture is not clear, a small cutaneous biopsy will reveal a diagnostic histopathology.

Elastosis Perforans Serpiginosa

Elastosis perforans serpiginosa, which is a relatively rare disorder in the general population, appears to be associated with Down syndrome.[41] The lesions consist of small, hyperkeratotic papules often arranged in serpiginous lines, in circles, or in arcs as seen in Figure 18-6. While in the classic disease the papules involve a single anatomic site, most often the nape of the neck or the upper arms, a more generalized variety has been described in Down syndrome.[41] The dermatosis is chronic but usually involutes spontaneously, leaving atrophic scars. Skin biopsy is diagnostic, revealing an abnormal dermal elastic tissue being extruded through the epidermis.

Skin Care in Down Syndrome

The cheilitis and xerosis in these patients can often be controlled with proper skin care. Petroleum jelly should be applied to the lips daily, especially before bedtime. If the cheilitis is symptomatic, 1% hydrocortisone ointment can be used to control inflammation.

Emollient creams must be applied daily to the entire skin surface, preferably after bathing. Soaps should be cream-based and used in minimal amounts. In areas of the country with cold, dry winters, an attempt should be made to humidify the air of the living quarters. The ideal frequency of bathing is variable, some patients doing best with bathing limited to one to two times a week and others with daily baths followed by an emollient cream.

If eczematous changes occur they are usually relatively refractory to treatment, but topical corticosteroid therapy is sometimes successful.

Seborrheic dermatitis of the scalp is best treated with regular shampooing with preparations containing zinc, seleneum, or tar. Refractory cases can be treated with corticosteroid lotions after shampooing. If the facial or presternal skin is involved, 1% hydrocortisone cream can be helpful. The papular, follicular eruption of the chest and back does not appear to be responsive to topical steroids.

Alopecia areata is best not treated because the hair can regrow spontaneously. Topical or intralesionally injected corticosteroids can sometimes induce hair growth. Systemic steroid therapy can result in hair regrowth but should be avoided because large doses are required and relapse often occurs while the patient is still on treatment.

There are no simple, effective treatments for either syringomas or elastosis perforans serpiginosa.

Self-Induced Dermatosis

Skin changes produced by either direct or indirect actions of the individual are common in people with behavioral or emotional disturbances. In institutionalized patients, direct observation of the causative behavior makes such a diagnosis simple. In other cases one's index of suspicion should be raised by such clues as the presence of bizarre arrangements of linear excoriations, ulcers, and scars with geometric shapes

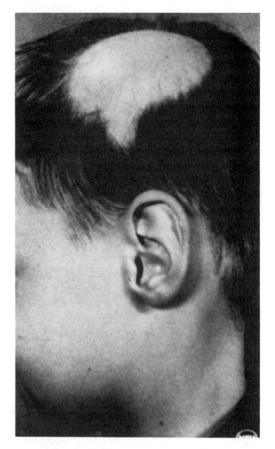

FIG. 18-5. Alopecia areata.

and sharply defined margins. These are often unilateral and involve large amounts of destruction in localized areas.[24]

Biting of the nails, lips, and skin are frequent behavioral problems. The forearms, hands, and fingers are the most common skin areas attacked. The skin, repeatedly traumatized in this way, can thicken, dry, darken, and occasionally develop increased hair growth.[6]

Some patients are subject to trichotillomania. Hair loss most often involves the scalp and occasionally the eyebrows and eyelashes. Plucking or twirling is usually responsible, although repeated rubbing can also result in hair loss. Ill-defined patches of hair loss occur, often triangular in shape. The diagnosis is suggested by the presence of short regrowing hairs, too short for the patient to grasp. If in doubt, scalp biopsy can confirm the diagnosis.[36]

Other dermatosis-inducing behavior patterns include hand clenching, leading to swollen and purpuric fingers; finger sucking, causing red, macerated, hemorrhagic, and possibly hypertro-

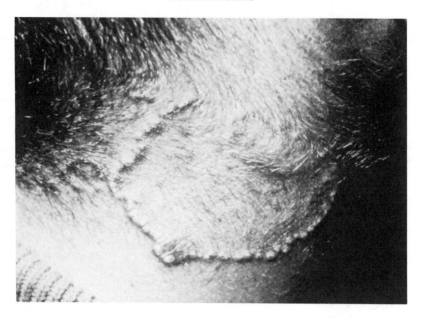

FIG. 18-6. Elastosis perforans serpiginosa.

phied digits; and prolonged sitting postures, resulting in calloused, thickened plaques on the lateral aspects of the ankles and feet.[6]

Dermatologic treatments of these dermatoses are usually of no avail unless the behavior can also be modified (see Chap. 20). Applications of gel cast bandages protecting the abused skin and shaving off the scalp in trichotillomania can occasionally divert the patient's attention from these areas, but this is most often temporary.

Scabies

Scabies is a common cutaneous infection with a mite, Sarcoptes scabieis var. hominis. The typical case is marked by intense itching, often worse at night, and a rash involving the fingers, web spaces, wrists, elbows, axillary folds, nipples, buttocks, knees, and occasionally the feet. It spares the face except in young infants. A linear burrow is the primary lesion, but the eruption consists mostly of papules, pustules, and eczematous patches. It is not more common among the mentally retarded, but once introduced into an institution, this very contagious disease can become widespread.

Norwegian scabies is a rare variant of scabies found only in certain susceptible hosts including patients with Down syndrome. It has also been reported in trisomy E syndrome, diabetes (especially with neuropathy), leprosy, and immunosuppression.[26] The eruption is hyperkeratotic and involves predominately the palms, soles, face, scalp, nails, elbows, and knees. Pruritus is not always present,[19] but this may be hard to judge objectively in patients with either severe mental retardation or neuropathy. Whereas scabetic patients are usually infected with only several mites, Norwegian scabies is distinguished by the presence of thousands of mites.[20] The lack of pruritus, often leading to a delayed diagnosis, and the large number of organisms make Norwegian scabetics a potential source for widespread epidemics. Because the causative mite is the same, healthy individuals exposed to the patient will develop classic scabies.

Treatment of both types of scabies is with 1% lindane (Kwell) lotion or cream applied to all skin except scalp and face and left on for 8 to 24 hours. Norwegian scabies requires scalp and face treatment as well as repeat applications. Infants and pregnant women should be treated with either crotamiton (Eurax) cream or 5 to 10% sulfur in petrolatum. It is wise to treat close contacts prophylactically and to wash underwear, night clothes, sheets, towels, etc. at the time of treatment. It is not necessary to attempt to further disinfect the environment.

Cutis Verticis Gyrata

Cutis verticis gyrata (CVG) is a disorder of the skin, classically the scalp, characterized by a furrowing and convoluted folding. This gives the area a brain-like or cerebriform appearance. The folds are permanent and cannot be flattened with traction on the skin.[44] It can be localized or involve the entire scalp.

The disorder may be primary and idiopathic or secondary to a large number of dermatologic and medical conditions. These can include acromegaly, pachydermoperiostosis, myxedema, tuberous sclerosis, large intradermal nevi, and others.[39]

The incidence of CVG in institutionalized handicapped men has been estimated at 0.21 to 1%.[39] One-quarter of the cases of primary generalized CVG occur in patients with mental deficiency and epilepsy.[1] The remaining cases are associated with combinations of schizophrenia, cerebral palsy, cranial abnormalities, and cataracts. It is rare in the general population.[39]

DERMATOSIS OF YOUNG INSTITUTIONALIZED PEOPLE

This section will discuss dermatosis found in any group of young people living together in a close environment. Because medical personnel in this population encounter these dermatologic problems far more than any other, diagnosis and treatment are discussed in detail.

Acne Vulgaris

Acne was the most common skin problem found by Butterworth at Pennhurst State School[7] and is the most common problem at the dermatology clinic at Wrentham State School. The majority of patients with acne are between 15 and 20 years of age, but the disease can be seen at birth and can smoulder on into the seventh decade.

Diagnosis

Because the disease is so familiar, its diagnosis is, for the most part, not difficult. The face and trunk are involved with a polymorphous eruption consisting of both inflammatory and noninflammatory lesions on a background of oily skin. The latter lesions are comedones, either raised papules with a central dark plug, i.e., open comedones or blackheads, or light-colored, small papules without visible plugs, i.e., closed comedones or whiteheads. The inflammatory lesions consist of papules, pustules, and deep subcutaneous, red, tender masses called acne cysts.

Pathophysiology

Treatment of acne is easier if one has some understanding of its pathogenesis. The exact etiology is unknown, but the pathology involves the sebaceous follicles. These follicles are present in highest numbers on the face but are also found on the back and chest. They are very wide, have very small, rather insignificant vellus hairs within them, and are connected to large sebaceous glands. Sebum, keratinous material, and a normal flora consisting of propionibacterium acnes and pityrosporum yeasts[28] fill the follicular canal.

In patients with acne, the wall of the sebaceous follicle keratinizes abnormally. It produces a dense, coherent horny material that seems to clog the normal passage of material within the canal. The follicle now dilates with the buildup of the material, producing what is seen clinically as a closed comedo or whitehead. If the most distal part of the follicle dilates, an open comedo forms. The material in the distal part of the open comedo will darken, hence the name blackhead. Ruptures can occur in the wall of closed comedones, enabling the follicular contents to escape. This material is extremely irritating to surrounding skin, and an inflammatory response will occur. The inflammation is seen clinically as an acne papule, pustule, or cyst, depending on the degree and depth of the reaction. The higher the bacterial content of the follicle, the greater the inflammation that can occur. The amount of sebum produced by the sebaceous gland and excreted into the follicle to fuel this bacterial reaction is controlled hormonally; androgenetic stimulation is predominant. Thus hormonal stimulation, sebaceous gland activity, bacterial content of the follicular canal, and the keratinizing activity of the sebaceous follicular wall are all interrelated in the pathophysiology of acne vulgaris.

Environmental Influences

Dirt and bacteria on the surface of the skin have no influence on the underlying sebaceous follicles. Washing more frequently or with special soaps will do nothing other than temporarily dry the surface of the skin. Certain oils and chemicals that are found in moisturizers, makeups, etc. can flare acne in some patients; therefore only products labeled "noncomedogenic" should be used in acne patients. There is no good scientific evidence that changes in the diet can influence acne, but frequent anecdotal reports from patients suggest that diet should be given individual consideration. The hormonal influences on the sebaceous gland can be noted clinically with the frequent premenstrual flare of acne and with the improvement or flare that can occur with pregnancy or with oral contraceptives. Factors like emotional stress, lack of sleep, and fatigue may flare acne through hormonal activity, but this link is uncertain. In addition to oral contraceptives, other medications can influence acne. The two most common ones in our patient population are diphenylhydantoin (Dilantin)[28] and lithium carbonate,[34] both of which can induce or flare acne. It appears that many other anticonvulsant medications can have adverse effects. Isonicotinic Acid has been reported to cause acne.[15] Iodides, bromides, and corticosteroids can induce acne-like eruptions.

Treatment

Most patients can get significant improvement with therapy. It must be understood that after treatment has begun, it may take 3 to 8 weeks to see clearing and that after this has been achieved, some sort of maintenance program must be continued.

The common acne treatments can be divided into three major categories. These are (1) benzoyl peroxide, topical preparations that reduce follicular bacterial content and dissolve comedones; (2) retinoic acid, a topical preparation that reverses abnormal follicle wall keratinization; and (3) topical or systemic antibiotics, which reduce follicular bacterial concentrations.

In most patients, acne can be controlled with combinations of these three types of medications. The first step in deciding on a treatment is to decide if the acne is noninflammatory (comedonal) or inflammatory (papules, pustules, cysts). Purely comedonal acne responds best to topical retinoic acid (Retin-A). This agent can be very irritating and must be applied carefully in low concentration. The 0.01% gel or the 0.05% cream can be used initially by applying it sparingly to all involved skin every other night for 1 to 2 weeks, and if no irritation develops, every night. No improvement may be seen for 4 to 12 weeks, and a small number of patients will exhibit an initial, temporary flare of inflammatory lesions.

Mildly inflammatory acne can be treated with topical benzoyl peroxide gel 5% or 10%, applied to all the involved skin nightly. Benzoyl peroxide may cause an irritant reaction in some patients, and, less often, an allergic contact dermatitis. If the inflammatory component responds but the comedones remain after 4 to 6 weeks, topical retinoic acid can be added, one product being applied in the morning and the other in the evening. Irritation of the skin is the limiting factor in this combination treatment.

Topical antibiotic therapy is used if patients with inflammatory acne do not respond to or cannot tolerate benzoyl peroxide. Antibiotics can be used in combination with retinoic acid or benzoyl peroxide. As with all topical agents, antibiotics should not be applied solely to acne lesions but must be applied to all acne-prone skin in an attempt to suppress the development of new inflammatory lesions. Clindamycin (Cleocin-T), erythromycin (Staticin, A.T.S., Eryderm), tetracycline (Topicycline), and meclocycline (Meclan) are the currently available topical antibiotics. Scattered case reports of diarrhea and pseudomembranous colitis have been reported with topical Cleocin; therefore patients, attendants, and the nursing staff need to be made aware of this remote, potential complication.[34] Meclan cream, a topical antibiotic in a nonalcohol cream vehicle, can be used more easily in patients with very dry skin.

Systemic antibiotics should be used if topical therapy fails. They can be used while benzoyl peroxide and/or retinoic acid are applied topically. Tetracycline should be used initially at a dosage of 500 mg bid. If there is a decrease in the number of new inflammatory lesions after 1 month, the dosage can be reduced by 250 mg each 2 to 4 weeks. This reduction should be continued to find the lowest daily dosage needed to suppress inflammatory lesions. Many patients who need only 250 mg to 500 mg a day can be switched to a topical antibiotic for maintenance treatment. Patients who do not respond to 4 to 6 weeks of tetracycline therapy should be switched to erythromycin 500 mg bid, and if that fails after 4 to 6 weeks, minocycline 50 mg bid.

Patients who fail to respond to the above regimen will need dermatologic referral for either more intensive antibiotic therapy, hormonal therapy, or 13-cis retinoic acid (Accutane) therapy.

Warts

Warts are common cutaneous infections with human papova virus. These benign tumors are very common in the general population but several studies indicate that their prevalence may be up to 2.5 times greater in institutionalized groups.[32] If individual warts are followed untreated, two-thirds will resolve spontaneously in 2 years. Susceptible patients, however, will continue to develop new warts, so that only approximately one-half of untreated patients with warts will be totally free of warts in 2 years.[32]

If treatment is attempted, the modality chosen will depend on the morphology and location of the wart. Common warts are usually found on the hands, fingers, arms, and legs. These are best treated with liquid nitrogen cryosurgery, or, if that fails, electrodesiccation after lidocaine (Xylocaine) anesthesia. The pain associated with these procedures can make them impractical with many young or disabled patients, so alternative, painless approaches must be taken. A preparation containing salicylic and lactic acids in flexible collodion (Duofilm) has been helpful. This should be applied to the wart after the area has been soaked in hot water for 5 to 15 minutes. The wart is then covered with adhesive tape, which should be left in place for 24 hours. The treatment should be repeated daily.

If this method fails, cantharidin should be used. This chemical, derived from the blister beetle, is available in flexible collodion (Cantherone) and should be applied over the wart. After drying, the wart should be covered with a waterproof tape such as Blenderm for 24 hours. A blister should form within 1 to 3 days, and further treatment should be withheld until the blister heals. One potential complication of this therapy is the formation of "doughnut" warts, or rings of warts that form at the edge of the healing blister.

Common warts on the fingers can at times respond dramatically to the simple procedure of applying waterproof adhesive tape. The tape should cover the wart completely, making a relatively airtight seal, and should be left on for 2 weeks. If this is unsuccessful, the wart can be covered with either trichloracetic acid or Duofilm and the tape reapplied.

Flat warts are small brown to flesh-colored, flat-topped papules commonly seen on the face or dorsa of the hands. The fact that they tend to occur in large numbers makes the use of traditional wart treatments impractical. The use of peeling agents can cause resolution of these lesions: retinoic acid cream 0.05% should be applied once or twice a day in an attempt to get the skin red and somewhat dry. This treatment should be continued for 2 to 6 weeks, and if the warts have not shown any sign of resolution, salicylic acid in propylene glycol (Keralyt gel) can be used in a similar fashion.

Plantar warts, the hyperkeratotic, often painful lesions studded with black dots found on the plantar surfaces of the feet, are the most difficult of all warts to treat. The best, least painful approach is the daily application of Duofilm or 40% salicylic acid plasters. This should be done on a daily basis after the foot is soaked in hot water for 15 minutes. Adhesive tape is applied after the acid, and this is left on for 24 to 48 hours. When the tape is removed, the foot is again soaked in hot water and the soft white keratin that forms over the wart is gently debrided with a pumice stone. If the patient is cooperative, every 2 weeks the hyperkeratotic material over the wart should be totally removed by a physician using a sterile scalpel.

Molluscum contagiosum is marked by dome-shaped, smooth papules with umbilicated centers that are caused by a pox virus. They are etiologically unrelated to warts, but they are similar in that they are self-limiting and contagious. Molluscum lesions will respond to much less vigorous therapy, usually resolving with Duofilm applied daily until mild erythema or crusting appears.

Tinea Infection

Fungal infections were found to be the third most common dermatosis in both the Pennhurst State School study[7] and at the Wrentham State School dermatology clinic (A.I. Berliner, unpublished). The types of infections varied greatly, however. At Pennhurst, tinea versicolor represented greater than 50% of the total number of fungal cases and tinea pedis caused 22%. At Wrentham, tinea pedis and tinea infections of the nails, onychomycosis, were the most common infections seen, causing 73% of the cases; tinea versicolor caused 7.5%. Tinea capitis was an epidemiologic problem at Pennhurst in 1938, but not one case was diagnosed at Wrentham skin clinic between 1978 and 1982.

The clinical type of fungal infection depends on the species of dermatophyte and the degree of the patient's cell-mediated immunity. Three clinical varieties of tinea pedis exist. The least common is the vesicular type, presenting as tense vesicles with erythema and scaling on the instep and sole. The most common form in all population groups is the interdigital form, usually involving the third and fourth but occasionally all of the webspaces. These areas can simply exhibit scaling, but maceration, exudation, and erythema will appear if secondary bacterial infections occur. The form of tinea pedis most problematic at Wrentham State is the chronic or "moccasin pattern" form. This form presents as chronic hyperkeratosis and scaling of the soles with minimal erythema. Often one palm is involved in a similar pattern. It is rare to have palmar involvement without any evidence of sole involvement or to have all four extremities involved. This type of tinea pedis is most likely to be accompanied by the thickened, crumbly, discolored nails of onychomycosis. At times patients, especially those with Down syndrome who have hyperkeratosis plantaris, a genetically determined thickening of the soles, will be misdiagnosed as having tinea pedis. Individuals with chronic tinea pedis have an impaired degree of cell-mediated immunity,[29] require systemic rather than topical therapy, and are subject to frequent reinfection.

Tinea cruris can be found as an isolated condition or associated with chronic tinea pedis. The red to brown, annular, scaling patches involve the inguinal fold and upper inner thighs. As in tinea corporis ("ringworm"), the outer border of the patch can be more "active," with elevation, erythema, and scaling.

Monilia is also a common pathogen in this area but differs from tinea in its tendency to involve the scrotum or labia and the presence of red, raw patches with white exudate and peripheral satellite pustules.

Tinea versicolor infection appears as brown, red, or white scaling patches, most often on the trunk, neck, and upper arms.

Diagnosis of all fungal infections should be confirmed with a positive potassium hydroxide smear or culture before instituting therapy. Treatment of most cases of tinea pedis, cruris, and corporis consists of the twice a day application of an antifungal cream or lotion with tolnaftate, haloprogin, clotrimazole or miconazole nitrate. This should be continued for 2 weeks after all clinical signs of infection are gone. If monilia is suspected, tolnaftate should not be used. Chronic tinea pedis and onychomycosis require systemic therapy with griseofulvin. Nail infections respond poorly, but fingernail treatment can usually be accomplished with microsized griseofulvin 500 mg bid for 4 to 6 months or until the nail grows out normally. Toenails respond so poorly, require 12 to 18 months of systemic therapy when they do respond, and relapse so often that oral treatment should not be attempted except under very special circumstances. White blood count and liver function need to be monitored with the use of oral antifungal drugs.

Tinea versicolor therapy is somewhat different because of the large area involved. Although all of the previously mentioned topical agents can eradicate tinea versicolor, its widespread nature makes their use expensive. Systemic griseofulvin is not effective. Fortunately its causative agent, the hyphal form of the normally occurring Pityrosporum yeast, can be suppressed with a variety of detergents and keratolytic agents. Sodium hyposulfate 25% solution (Tinver) twice a day for 1 to 2 weeks or selenium sulfide 2.5% applied and left on 2 to 3 hours for 2 or 3 nights are simple and relatively successful treatments. Therapy should involve all the involved skin, not just the visible macules. The first sign of successful treatment is the absence of scaling, because the discoloration, especially the hypopigmentation, can take months to fade and its presence is not necessarily an indication of residual active disease.

Drug Reactions

Patient populations with neurologic, emotional, or behavioral problems are often exposed to multiple drugs (see Chaps. 8, 20, and 26). These medications can have adverse cutaneous reactions that vary from self-limiting cosmetic problems to life-threatening dermatosis.

The diagnosis of such a reaction is a clinical one, based on a high index of suspicion for drugs that cause rashes and a knowledge of the morphology of those rashes. Once a drug rash has been diagnosed, identification of the offending drug may be difficult in patients on multiple medications. Since most drug reactions, with a few exceptions, tend to occur within the first week of exposure, the most recently added drug should be suspected first. The next fact to consider is the frequency with which certain drugs have caused reactions in the past. For example, antibiotics probably cause cutaneous reactions more than any type of drug, whereas digoxin rarely causes such reactions. The frequency at which various drugs cause cutaneous reactions can be found in the review by Arndt and Jick.[2] This article may be helpful in dealing with rashes in the multiply medicated patient.

Although drugs can cause any type of eruption, some forms are more common. A brief description of these common patterns is given in Table 18-2.

Some medications are used so commonly in this population that it is important to discuss them in more detail. The remainder of the section will discuss the types of reaction seen with these frequently administered medications.

Phenothiazines

These drugs are not associated with a high rate of cutaneous reaction. Arndt and Jick found that chlorpromazine caused no reactions when given to 622 patients.[2] Nevertheless, phenothiazines can cause urticaria, fixed drug eruption, morbilliform eruptions, erythema multiforme, vasculitis, exfoliative dermatitis, lichenoid eruptions, a lupus erythematosus–like eruption, and photoeruptions. Phenothiazines can also cause contact dermatitis in medical personnel administering them.

The photosensitivity is of two types. A severe sunburn-like eruption can occur after sun exposure. This is a phototoxic eruption resulting from a direct action of ultraviolet light on the drug in the skin. It does not directly involve the immune system. The type of ultraviolet light involved is the long-wave type, or UVA (320 to 400 nm).

Because most sunscreens contain PABA or its esters, which produce little if any blocking action of this wavelength, they are useless to prevent this adverse effect. A non-PABA sunscreen giving some UVA protection, or, better yet, physical protection (long sleeves and a hat) may protect some patients.

The second type of light-associated reaction is a slate gray hyperpigmentation seen in exposed areas following the ingestion of large amounts of chlorpromazine over a prolonged period of time. This pigmentation appears to be a result of deposition of complexes of melanin and chlorpromazine in the skin. Autopsy studies have found similar pigmentation in many internal organs, perhaps deposited there by macrophages removing the cutaneous complexes.[31] Because it is unclear which wavelength of light is responsible for catalyzing this complex formation, strict physical protection from light is prudent in patients taking large dosages.

Benzodiazepines

Benzodiazepines do not tend to cause severe cutaneous reactions, but they can cause rashes. Arndt and Jick found that chlordiazepoxide caused 4.2 reactions per 1,000 recipients and diazepam, 3.8 reactions.[2] The most distinct type of eruption appears to be a chlordiazepoxide lichenoid eruption. Photosensitivity to this drug can also occur.

Amitriptyline

This tricyclic antidepressant is not a very common cause of rashes, reacting in none of 290 patients in the study by Arndt and Jick.[2] However it has been reported to cause hives, including angioedematous swelling of face and tongue, and a photosensitivity (Merck, Sharpe and Dohme: Elavil package insert).

Lithium

The most characteristic cutaneous problem with lithium is instigation or exacerbation of acne vulgaris[48] and folliculitis. These flares of acne can be severe. In addition psoriasis can be significantly worsened with the administration of the drug. I have seen one patient with a widespread, purpuric eruption associated with leukocytosis and adenopathy that was thought to be lithium-induced (A.I. Berliner, unpublished).

Barbiturates

Barbiturates are fairly common inducers of rash and can produce a wide spectrum of cutaneous changes. They produced a reaction rate of 4.7 per 1,000 patients, but their common use makes the absolute number of reactions quite high. Barbitu-

Table 18-2. *Common Forms of Drug Rash*

Urticaria	"Hives," well defined, red, edematous wheals that usually itch. Individual lesions rarely persist for more than 24 hr
Morbilliform eruption	"Measles-like," symmetrical, red-pink maculopapular rash becoming confluent in areas—very common
Photo eruption	"Sun reaction," red, edematous to blistering areas starting in sun-exposed areas but occasionally spreading beyond
Vasculitis	"Palpable purpura," classically a papule that does not blanch or lose its color with pressure, often accompanied by red macules, papules, and wheals and can show hemorrhagic blisters
Erythema multiforme	"Target lesions," eruptions starting on extremities and spreading centrally. Classically the "bull's eye" lesion on the palms and soles, although many other patterns can be present. Mucous membrane involvement occurs (when severe, termed Stevens-Johnson syndrome)
Erythema nodosum	Red, warm, subcutaneous nodules, usually on anterior aspects of lower legs. Become purple-brown as they resolve
Fixed drug eruption	Round or oval, red, occasionally vesicular patches that recur in the same location with rechallenge of the drug; when they resolve they leave a long-standing hyperpigmentation
Eczematous eruption	"Eczema-like," red, scaling to vesicular patches, many round in shape
Lichenoid eruption	"Lichen planus like," multiple red to violaceous, flat-topped papules
Exfoliative dermatitis	Generalized erythema and scaling involving most of skin surface. Patient may have chills and fever

rates were the fifth most common drug given to the inpatients surveyed by Arndt and Jick.[2]

The drugs can cause urticaria, morbilliform eruptions, exfoliative dermatitis, fixed drug eruptions, and erythema multiforme, including Stevens-Johnson syndrome. A stomatitis can occur without cutaneous involvement.[46]

Phenytoin

Although the reaction rate of diphenylhydantoin (Dilantin) is relatively low, 1.1 per 1,000 patients,[2] this drug can cause a number of extremely severe reactions. A morbilliform rash is the most common type of benign reaction, others including exacerbation of acne vulgaris and hypertrichosis. Severe exfoliative dermatitis, vasculitis, or Stevens-Johnson syndrome can be life-threatening and require hospitalization.

One extremely severe reaction to phenytoin is toxic epidermal necrolysis. This eruption presents with painful red skin that forms blisters that erode, leaving large sheets of denuded skin. These patients begin to resemble burn patients and are often best cared for in burn units. Systemic steroids have been used with mixed results.

The pseudolymphoma syndrome caused by phenytoin consists of a generalized red macular or papular pruritic rash, lymphadenopathy, hepatosplenomegaly, fever, arthralgias, abnormal liver function, and eosinophilia. The histology of the lymph nodes can be benign or suggestive of lymphoma. The disease is most often self-limiting once the drug has been stopped, but a rare patient may develop malignant lymphoma.[14]

REFERENCES

1. Adams, R.D.: Neurocutaneous diseases. In Dermatology in General Medicine. Edited by T. Fitzpatrick et al. New York, McGraw-Hill, 1979, p. 1231.
2. Arndt, K.A., and Jick, H.: Rates of cutaneous reaction to drugs. J.A.M.A., 235:918, 1976.
3. Brant, P.W., and McCallum, D.I.: Cutaneous aspects of Mongolism: A clinical study. Br. J. Dermatol., 93(suppl.): 11, 1975.
4. Brauner, G.J.: Seborrheic dermatitis. In Dermatology in General Medicine. Edited by T. Fitzpatrick et al. New York, McGraw-Hill, 1979, p. 804.
5. Butterworth, T.: Neurocutaneous syndrome—von Recklinghausen's disease. In Clinical Genodermatology. Edited by T. Butterworth. Baltimore, Williams & Wilkins, 1962, pp. 101-105.
6. Butterworth, T.: Dermatologic disorders in institutionalized mental defectives. Birth Defects, 7:178, 1971.
7. Butterworth, T., and Wilson, McC.: Incidence of diseases of the skin in feebleminded persons. Arch. Dermatol. Syph., 38:203, 1938.
8. Butterworth, T., and Wilson, McC.: Dermatological aspects of tuberous sclerosis. Arch. Dermatol. Syph., 43:1, 1941.
9. Butterworth, T., et al.: Cheilitis of Mongolism. J. Invest. Dermatol., 35:347, 1960.
10. Butterworth, T., et al.: Syringoma and Mongolism. Arch. Dermatol., 90:483, 1964.
11. Callen, J.P.: The skin, the eye and systemic disease. Cutis, 24:501, 1979.
12. Carter, D.M., and Jegasothy, B.U.: Alopecia areata and Down syndrome. Arch. Dermatol., 112:1397, 1976.
13. Carter, D.M., and O'Keefe, E.J.: Hereditary cutaneous disorders. In Dermatology. Edited by S.L. Moschella et al. Philadelphia, W.B. Saunders, 1975, p. 1022.

14. Charlesworth, E.W.: Phenytoin induced pseudolymphoma. Arch. Dermatol., 113:477, 1977.
15. Cohen, L.K. et al.: Isoniazide induced acne and pellagra. Arch. Dermatol., 109:377, 1974.
16. Crowe, F.W.: Axillary freckling as a diagnostic aid in neurofibromatosis. Ann. Intern. Med., 61:1142, 1964.
17. Crowe, F.W., and Schull, W.J.: Diagnostic importance of cafe au lait spots in neurofibromatosis. Arch. Intern. Med., 91:758, 1953.
18. Crowe, F.W., Schull, W.J., and Neel, J.V.: Clinical Pathological and Genetic Study of Multiple Neurofibromatosis. Springfield, IL, Thomas, 1956.
19. Derbes, V.J.: Arthropod bites and stings. In Dermatology in General Medicine. Edited by T. Fitzpatrick et al. New York, McGraw-Hill, 1979, p. 1660.
20. Finn, O.A., et al.: A singular dermatosis of Mongols. Arch. Dermatol., 114:1493, 1978.
21. Fitzpatrick, T., et al.: White leaf-shaped macules. Arch. Dermatol., 98:1, 1968.
22. Fitzpatrick, T., et al. (Eds.): Dermatology in General Medicine. New York, McGraw-Hill, 1979.
23. Gold, A.P., and Freeman, J.M.: Depigmented nevi: The earliest sign of tuberous sclerosis. Pediatrics, 35: 1003, 1965.
24. Griesemer, R.D., and Nadelson, T.: Emotional aspects of cutaneous disease. In Dermatology in General Medicine. Edited by T. Fitzpatrick et al. New York, McGraw-Hill, 1979, p. 1355.
25. Halprin, K.M.: The "acne" of tuberous sclerosis. J.A.M.A., 199:152, 1967.
26. Hubler, W.R., and Clabaush, W.: Epidemic Norwegian scabies. Arch. Dermatol., 112:179, 1976.
27. Hurwitz, S., and Braverman, I.M.: White spots in tuberous sclerosis. J. Pediatr., 77:587, 1970.
28. Jenkins, R.B., and Ratner, A.C.: Diphenylhydantoin and acne. N. Engl. J. Med., 287:148, 1972.
29. Jones, H.E., et al.: Acquired immunity of dermatophytes. Arch. Dermatol., 109:840, 1974.
30. Kersting, D.W., and Rapaport, I.F.: A clinicopathologic study of the skin in mongolism. Arch. Dermatol., 77: 319, 1958.
31. Lever, W., and Shaumberg-Lever, G.: Histopathology of the Skin. Philadelphia, J.B. Lippincott, 1983, p. 261.
32. Massing, A., and Epstein, W.: Natural history of warts. Arch. Dermatol., 87:74, 1963.
33. Menon, P.A.: Dermabrasion for the management of angiofibromas in tuberous sclerosis. J. Dermatol. Surg. Oncol., 8:984, 1982.
34. Milestone, E.B., et al.: Pseudomembranous colitis after topical application of clindamycin. Arch. Dermatol., 117:154, 1981.
35. Monaghan, H.P., et al.: Tuberous sclerosis complex in children. Am. J. Dis. Child., 135:912, 1981.
36. Muller, S.A., and Winkelmann, R.R.: Trichotillomania. Arch. Dermatol., 105:535, 1972.
37. Nevin, N.C., and Pierce, W.G.: Diagnostic and genetical aspects of tuberous sclerosis. J. Med. Genet., 5:273, 1968.
38. Nickel, W.R., and Reed, W.B.: Tuberous sclerosis. Arch. Dermatol., 85:209, 1962.
39. Orkin, M., et al.: Cerebriform intradermal nevi, a cause of cutis verticis gyrata. Arch. Dermatol., 110:575, 1984.
40. Plewig, G., and Liggman, A.M.: Acne. Berlin, Springer-Verlag, 1975, p. 38.
41. Rasmussen, J.E.: Disseminated elastosis perforans serpingosa in four Mongoloids. Br. J. Dermatol., 86:2, 1972.

42. Riccardi, V.M.: von Recklinghausen neurofibromatosis. N. Engl. J. Med., *305:*1617, 1981.
43. Riccardi, V.: Neurofibromatosis. Arch. Dermatol., *123:* 882, 1987.
44. Robinson, J.: Cutis verticis gyrata. *In* Clinical Dermatology. Vol. 1. Edited by J.D. Demis et al. Hagerstown, MD, Harper & Row, 1987, p. 3.
45. Rosman, N.P., and Pearle, J.: The brain in neurofibromatosis. Brain, *90:*829, 1967.

46. Sneddon, I.B., and Leishman, A.W.D.: Severe and fatal phenobarbital eruptions. Br. Med. J., *1:*1276, 1952.
47. Whitehouse, D.: Diagnostic value of the cafe au lait spot in children. Arch. Dis. Child., *41:*316, 1966.
48. Yoder, F.: Acne, form eruption due to lithium carbonate. Arch. Dermatol., *109:*377, 1974.
49. Zeligman, I., and Scalia, S.: Dermatologic manifestations of Mongolism. Arch. Dermatol. Syphilol., *69:*342, 1954.

19

DENTAL MANAGEMENT

Joel Pearlman, D.M.D.

In the past, many thought that dental disease was an inevitable problem for the handicapped. And, historically, dental treatment has been called one of the greatest unmet health needs of the developmentally disabled.[8,33] The correlation is an important concept to understand, but only from a historical perspective.

The old notions are being supplanted by recognition of the fact that although many developmentally disabled individuals have suffered from dental disease and its resultant discomfort, disfigurement, dysfunction, and social and psychological isolation, much of their suffering was needless. The developmentally disabled deserve and can have good oral health. It is unnecessary and unfortunate for things to be otherwise; it is only a compounding of their problems. Dental disease is preventable and therefore avoidable, rather than inevitable.[12,18,23,25,36,41]

Any current philosophy of dental care adopts the belief that the handicapped have the right to good oral health, and that they deserve the same kind of treatment we expect for ourselves. Such assumptions are indisputable. The cornerstone supporting this right is a commitment to a program of prevention: a program that combines early intervention when possible, consistent effective daily oral hygiene, and thorough, comprehensive professional care.[33]

NATURE OF DENTAL PROBLEMS

Congenital Anomalies

Most disturbances of growth and development have a genetic basis and are sometimes traceable to a specific prenatal problem in embryogenesis; these include cleft lip, cleft palate, median rhomboid glossitis, bifid tongue, amelogenesis, and dentinogenesis imperfecta. Such conditions may appear at birth or sometime after and can be transitional or permanent. Abnormal oral conditions may also be caused by environmental teratogens.

In conditions like amelogenesis and dentinogenesis imperfecta, teeth have defective structures and are therefore more prone to decay. Congenital rubella can have directly associated dental morphologic abnormalities such as defective enamel and fused teeth.[26] Cleft lip and palate can be accompanied by an increased frequency of congenitally missing teeth, supernumerary teeth, and teeth that are fused, malformed, or malposed. Dental texts cover in detail the characteristics of medical problems and syndromes that can have dental implications.[4,5,17,18,24] These conditions, however, are more of an exception than a rule.

Oral Lesions

Oral lesions are primarily due to reactions of the oral tissues. They are a response to a developmental event with either a traumatic, irritational, or pathologic component and generally do not have a hereditary basis.[42] Such lesions include moniliasis, white sponge nevus, primary herpetic gingivostomatitis, hemangiomas, and papillomas.[5]

These abnormalities occur in handicapped and nonhandicapped individuals with equal frequency. Only a few handicapping conditions have directly associated dental problems. At an early stage, most individuals are dentally comparable. With age, a number of factors related to different disabilities make prevention more difficult.[3]

Dental Problems Associated with Common Disorders

Dental disease for the most part falls into two general categories, caries and periodontal disease. Both are chronic conditions that can involve acute episodes and can afflict individuals over their entire lifespan. When dealing in generalities, however, it is important to keep in mind that each person is an individual, and therefore unique, and that actual dental findings vary from person to person.

Down Syndrome

Experience has shown the dental profile of an individual with Down syndrome would take the following form: A low caries index or incidence of decay, a predisposition for periodontal disease with early onset and greater severity, malocclusion with delayed eruption of the primary and permanent dentition, spacing or diastemas between teeth, and malformed or congenitally missing permanent teeth.[11,13]

The tongue of many individuals with Down syndrome assumes a forward position caused by underdevelopment of the maxilla and chronic mouthbreathing often secondary to persistent rhinitis. The result is a pseudomacroglossia.[35]

The lower incidence of decay can be attributed to the spacing between teeth, the excessive wear of occlusal surfaces, and the increased buffering capacity of saliva.

Periodontal disease tends to have an earlier onset in most handicapped and retarded persons than in the nonhandicapped population. In persons with Down syndrome, it is caused in part by the physical characteristics of the syndrome and in part by a decreased immunologic response, whereas in most other handicapped persons the main contributing factor is poor oral hygiene.

Several factors predispose a person with Down syndrome to develop early periodontitis: (1) Poor occlusal relationships place inordinate stress on the developing periodontium. (2) High labial frenum attachments lead to mucogingival defects, resulting in early detachment of the gingiva from the mandibular incisors. (3) The anterior position of the tongue, as mentioned, creates abnormal forces on the teeth. For the above reasons, treatment considerations should include frenectomy and interceptive orthodontics when possible.[35]

Cerebral Palsy

Individuals with cerebral palsy encounter a higher incidence of dental problems than their normal counterparts. Enamel hypoplasia in primary teeth, higher rates of decay, gingivitis, malocclusion, bruxism, and temporomandibular joint (TMJ) dysfunction are some common findings.

The hypoplastic enamel corresponds to the dentochronology or time of insult in odontogenesis. Individuals with both athetoid and spastic cerebral palsy tend to brux and abrade their teeth,[30,31] and the result is a decreased vertical dimension or overclosure of the bite, which can ultimately contribute to a TMJ problem.

ASSOCIATED COMPLICATING FACTORS

The individual with developmental disabilities is at higher risk to develop dental problems for a variety of factors and reasons.

Feeding Difficulty and Diet

The abnormal function of the tongue, lips, and cheek and the abnormal patterns of swallowing adversely affect mastication and deglutition. These problems lead to diet selections that are soft, easy to eat, and rich in carbohydrates, with resulting overretention of food debris in the oral cavity. Retention of food debris, combined with the individual's general coordination problems, makes oral hygiene a difficult task. As might be expected, caries and periodontal disease are more prevalent and more severe. Trouble swallowing can also mean difficulty drinking, which leads to a decreased fluid intake, less cleansing and rinsing action of liquids, and less than optimal intake of fluorides if the water is fluoridated.

This is the type of interplay of variables many handicapped children experience and which increases the likelihood of dental disease.

Meal Patterns

As infants, children with metabolic disorders may use a bottle longer before developing regular meal patterns. They are at greater risk of developing "nursing bottle syndrome" if allowed to fall asleep with a bottle of juice or formula. When not nursing, they must have carbohydrate-rich diets at frequent intervals. It is well known that the consistency and texture of foods and the frequency of intake can affect decay rates.[6] This has the same risk as snacking: exposing the teeth to more and more acid attacks.

Diet imbalances and inadequate nutritional intake can also contribute to the development of periodontal disease or a decreased resistance to it, and even a diminished response to its treatment.

For all individuals with developmental disabilities, early intervention is necessary, with specific preventive treatment plans including fluoride supplements, affirmative dental health dietary practices, and effective plaque control.[38] In conjunction with these home measures, clinical preventive procedures such as oral prophylaxis, topical fluoride treatments, and pit and fissure sealants should be used to maintain good oral health.[36]

Motivators and Rewards

Handicapped children may be indulged by parents and other adults who give them candy and sweets. Sometimes this is done intentionally in conjunction with behavior modification through rewards; at other times it is just too much babying. Alternatives to these rewards should be encouraged that are less harmful to oral health. Anyone aware of the regular use of sweets as rewards should insist on breaking this habit.

Medications

Hidden Sugars

The sugar contained in syrup-based medications can promote decay, especially if medications are taken often or for a long period of time. Two commonly prescribed anticonvulsants, phenytoin (Dilantin) and valproic acid (Depakene) in liquid form, contain 1 g and 3 g of sucrose per tsp, respectively. Two commonly prescribed agents, chloral hydrate and hydroxyzine hydrochloride (Atarax), contain 3.5 g, and 5.9 g of sucrose per tsp, respectively.

Phenytoin

Drug therapies or prescribed medications taken on a regular basis increase the risk for dental problems. The most obvious association is that between phenytoin therapy and gingival hyperplasia.

Gingival hyperplasia is the overgrowth of the tissue surrounding the teeth seen in individuals with seizure disorders treated with phenytoin therapy. With effective oral hygiene, the thickened fibrotic tissues can remain pink and firm, thus avoiding the secondary inflammation and hyperemic condition that can grossly exaggerate this condition.[4,22]

Advanced gingival hyperplasia in the severely retarded, however, presents an especially difficult treatment and management problem. The grossly enlarged gingiva can obscure the clinical crowns, causing teeth to drift and rotate. When surgical treatment cannot be followed by controlled oral hygiene and other anticonvulsant therapies cannot be substituted for phenytoin, then the generally accepted treatment modalities do not apply.[35] If surgery is undertaken, excessive bleeding, difficulty in tissue-contouring, difficulty with periodontal pack placement and retention, and postoperative tooth mobility and sensitivity are all complications that can be anticipated.

Other Common Medications

Antianxiety medications (Valium, Tranxene, Xanax) and the common preparations for coughs and colds (Dimetapp, Robitussin, Actifed, and Triaminic) can cause motor restlessness and irritability. This can adversely affect behavior and interfere with the delivery of dental care. Barbiturates can cause dizziness, drowsiness, and lethargy. The neuroleptics and antidepressants both have been known to result in orthostatic hypotension. Constipation, the chronic side effect of all these medications, cannot be overlooked as contributing to irritability and motor restlessness as well.

Saliva Flow

Xerostomia (reduced saliva flow) induced by drugs can make teeth more vulnerable to decay. Anticholinergics reduce secretions, and widely used antidepressants such as amitriptyline (Elavil), imipramine (Tofranil), and trazodone (Desyrel) have this as a major side effect. The neuroleptic medications including the phenothiazines (e.g., Thorazine, Mellaril, Stelazine, and Trilafon) all may cause xerostomia.

Saliva also acts as a lubricating medium, and in the edentulous geriatric or chronically ill debilitated patient, a dry mouth increases the potential for trauma. Wearing dentures can be difficult and uncomfortable for a person with a dry mouth, and the oral mucosa may exhibit a lowered resistance to irritation.

Physical Limitations

Individuals with a convulsive disorder are more prone to trauma during a seizure, and often anterior teeth are fractured, avulsed, or devitalized as a result. The same is true of people with cerebral palsy, muscular dystrophy, and of other persons with physical handicaps and impaired motor function. These physical limitations can also mean a higher risk of developing dental disease because of the person's inability to care for his own oral hygiene needs.[31]

Impaired muscle function can also result in poor oral hygiene. If the physical handicap prevents adequate performance of daily care, even with adaptive aids, the handicapped individual becomes totally or partially dependent on caregivers. This dependency can also add to the risk of dental disease if care is erratic and irregular. The longer the plaque is in contact with the teeth and gums, the greater the risk of dental disease. Toothbrushing and other proven oral hygiene techniques should be totally familiar to the parent, surrogate, or institutional staff in order to provide the necessary care. Whenever it is possible, independent activity is preferable. Handicapped individuals should be encouraged to clean their own teeth, and their effectiveness should be assessed. Goals that are practical and realistic can be set to develop self-care skills.

If the individual is hindered by the mental or physical limitations of his handicap, then his oral health maintenance plan should always strive for maximum effectiveness in any combination of self-care and direct care.

Oral Problems and Habits

A number of commonly encountered oral habits can be frustrating to caregivers. Individually or in combination, they can make it difficult to achieve and maintain good dental hygiene.

The spastic, clonic jaw movements of the individual with cerebral palsy can result in biting on the toothbrush or gagging as a result of it. Tight perioral musculature can almost certainly frustrate anyone unaware of techniques for retracting the lips. Some disabled individuals are hypersensitive about having their mouths and lips touched and become resistive when any attempt is made to do so. The chronic irritation of the mouth breather and tongue thruster are two additional problems that can result in less than optimal oral hygiene.

Social and Economic Factors

The arrangement of a family's priorities may also be a risk factor for the developmentally disabled individual. Parental indifference and stress on general health needs without regard for dental health are often encountered.[3,37] If home preventive measures and routine dental care are not high priorities, then acute problems may be the first and only initiating cause for seeking dental treatment.

It is unfortunate, but appearance alone can lead to a certain degree of social ostracism and arouse stereotypical attitudes. Both are barriers to dental care and result in poor dental health.[3]

A number of treatment barriers make it difficult for the developmentally disabled to attain good dental health. These limit both access to care and the type and frequency of care received. They include the following: the limited number of dentists willing to accept developmentally disabled patients,[28] either because of insufficient training in behavior management techniques or because these patients' maladaptive behavior can disrupt routine office procedure; negative stereotypical attitudes; lack of appropriate transportation to dental offices; and physical accessibility limitations and architectural barriers of the offices themselves. Add to these barriers the socioeconomic impediments and financial disincentives of the publicly financed health system and one can begin to understand the substantial vulnerability of this population as a whole.[8]

Because of their disabilities, many developmentally disabled individuals are not gainfully employed. As young and older adults, these people have the least amount of expendable funds and often require some of the most expensive care. Unable to pay for needed care, they must rely on Medicaid. Low fees, limited benefits, and slow administrative procedures create inherent barriers to care.[39] These limit the value of dental care provided and even limit the number of participating providers, thus restricting the individual's choice for care.[29]

A MODEL FOR PROVISION OF DENTAL SERVICES

The experiences of a university-affiliated dental service program for handicapped people can serve as a model for service provision. These facilities represent a statewide network of dental programs funded on a contractual basis through an agreement with the Massachusetts Department of Public Health. As a dental care program for the developmentally disabled, it offers and provides comprehensive clinical care in all specialty areas and in preventive education. It is equally accessible to developmentally disabled patients in institutions and in the community. An ADA-accredited program, it operates much like a large multispecialty group practice. The program is characterized by the advanced level of training of its providers, qualified personnel, adequate staff, state-of-the-art equipment, and supplies and clinical facilities that are adapted to meet special needs (architecturally barrier free).[25]

Population Served and Treatment Modes

Statewide, the population served numbers over 7,000 persons with developmental disabilities, who either live in institutions or in community residences, supervised apartments, halfway houses, group homes, with parents or relatives, under foster care, or in surrogate relationships.

Practice Management

Over the past 10 years a wealth of pragmatic experience has accumulated. Certain routine activities are mentioned because, collectively, they constitute good practice management when treating the developmentally disabled in a dental treatment facility.

All relevant nondental considerations (e.g., medical, pharmacologic, behavioral, and physical) should be integrated when planning treatment.[24] Review of the problem-oriented record and consultation with other treatment planners should be commonplace.

Record Keeping

The sequence of treatment and its documentation follow a prescribed format.[25] Starting with the medical history review and including the results of a complete head and neck examination and radiographs whenever possible, a treatment plan is developed. Reports of consultations and regular treatment provided are sequentially recorded in abbreviated fashion on a record-of-treatment sheet and in considerably more detail as a continuing-progress note. Signed and dated, the progress note serves to identify behavioral responses, including the reaction to premedication, treatment provided, prevention measures needed or provided, and recommendations for future visits. A separate medication log identifies the premedication ordered, dosage and form given, the patient's response to it, and recommendations for successive visits. Review of the medication log helps the prescribing dentist decide whether to increase, decrease, modify, or discontinue premedications.

Precaution stickers placed on the record covers alert providers to drug allergies, idiosyncracies, and special care considerations.

Scheduling

Patients' complex health needs, their care programs, and their involvement in school, sheltered workshop activities, and real jobs all require scheduling consideration. An attempt is made to coordinate services in the most sensitive and least disruptive manner. Those holding jobs may be the last hired and first fired, so scheduling becomes a delicate compromise.

Frequent recall is an important adjunct to the prevention program. The optimal interval is that which a dentist or hygienist considers to be the most likely to be successful for any individual's oral health maintenance program.

Standard of Care

Because the staffing patterns of the clinic are similar to that of a large multispecialty group practice, and because of the advanced level of training of the providers and the educational nature of this accredited program, constant peer review tends to take place. To supplement this internal review process, the quality of care is periodically reviewed by an external review committee of unbiased dental service providers. The quality and quantity of services provided, appropriateness of treatment plans, and accuracy of records are assessed.[43] In addition to current competence in cardiopulmonary resuscitation (annual recertification), continuing education is encouraged, required, and supported. All of the above seem to establish or ensure a certain standard of care.

At the community level, the quality and nature of dental care is not checked. There is no regular system or format. Usually, the only control is the conscience of the provider. This lack of review represents a potential weakness in the process of normalization and mainstreaming. A review mechanism should exist to protect individuals unable to make competent decisions concerning their own health needs.

Changing Dental Needs

In the institutional setting, with a stable patient population and a program providing comprehensive dental care, the demand for services has changed over time. Initially, when the dental program began, the institutionalized population was not unlike new community patients; both had a backlog of unmet oral health needs. As their basic needs were addressed, there were fewer restorations and extractions necessary and a greater emphasis on prevention and increased frequency of maintenance therapies. After the institutionalized population was put on a maintenance schedule, the demand for prosthetic services increased.

Because of the institutions' adopted policy of no new admissions and the state's policy of deinstitutionalization, the institutionalized population is aging, and the disabilities are apparently concentrating at the profound and severe end of the continuum. Outpatients tend to be higher functioning and younger and represent about one-quarter of total patients served. To provide comprehensive dental care, a variety of settings and modes of treatment are used. If adequate treatment cannot be provided in the dental clinic on an outpatient basis either with or without premedication, relative analgesia, or intravenous sedation, elective dental procedures under general anesthesia must be considered. Therefore, affiliation with a hospital with a well-equipped operating room is a necessary part of the delivery of care.

Complementing the clinical component is a dental health education program designed to be responsive to and responsible for the preventive care of the developmentally disabled. This is accomplished through in-service training programs for patients, parents, and other caregivers.[32] Through ongoing instruction, supervision, motivation, and follow-up, coordinated with periodic clinical assessments, an accountable preventive program is leading to improved oral health.

The types and number of providers in an active dental hygiene program can continually be expanded. This starts with a core of primary providers, which includes dental health educators, dentists, and hygienists. Dental assistants and dental students can augment this core of primary providers. A network of generic care providers can ensure the delivery of effective dental care.[41] This involves the use of allied health care professionals, e.g., nurse practitioners, registered nurses, direct care staff, and program coordinators. Annual reviews of individual treatment plans can establish realistic goals and objectives.

Dental students and student hygienists can be especially helpful. They usually exhibit a high degree of enthusiasm and eagerness to improve the patient's level of oral hygiene. They also tend to have a certain naiveté that offsets the biases many practitioners have. A student's presence means an ongoing explanation and justification for methods and materials. It also broadens the base of familiarity with the disabled, thus breaking down treatment barriers.

Treatment Goals

In many cases the treatment and management of the developmentally disabled clients and their responses are not unlike that of their normal peers. This is especially true for the mildly retarded, but some profoundly retarded individuals also respond well in a dental treatment situation.

Treatment planning is designed basically to respond immediately to the elimination of pain, followed by restoration and maintenance of existing dentition, achieving an acceptable level of oral hygiene, and restoration and maintenance of function and esthetics. This, combined with frequent recall, staff inservice training, and dental health education, constitutes total patient care.[12,32]

Treatment Approaches and Rationale

Initially, all treatment is attempted on an outpatient basis. Various management adjuncts such as behavior modification, nitrous oxide, premedication, protective restraints (e.g., pediwrap, papoose board), and mild physical restraint are commonplace. Mouth props and headrests are used routinely to maximize access.

In a clinical situation the presence of direct care staff who accompany and often know a patient, extra dental assistants, and other dental personnel can offer a staff-to-patient ratio that generally does not exist in private practice. In addition, the lack of time constraints and costs to the patient are positive factors that help to establish a successful treatment program for the handicapped.

Treatment that places inordinate demands on the time and patience of the operator is likely to be excluded from the generic formula of community practice.

Another important consideration in treating the special needs patient, is weighing the risks, benefits, and costs of mild physical and chemical restraints versus general anesthesia. The ability to provide routine prophylaxis on an outpatient basis is important if it can prolong the intervals between reliance on general anesthesia. Frequent recalls, even for this group, may, over time, reduce resistance and lead to gradual acceptance or tolerance. In any event, frequent visits (2- or 3-month intervals) can ensure that acute or potentially acute problems are carefully monitored and kept to a minimum.

Some patients, particularly the more profoundly and severely handicapped, require general anesthesia and hospital admission for any definitive treatment. Also included in this group are the physically hyperactive patients, whose impulsive behavior can be harmful to self and others, and the resistive patients, who clench their jaws, purse their lips, or otherwise aggressively avoid treatment. Patients with concomitant behavioral problems can present real problems in dental management.[9]

In private practice, excessive noise can be very disruptive and any unusual degree of physical restraint is disconcerting; two additional reasons why the standard practice mode of treatment is not always possible.

PRACTICAL ASPECTS OF SERVICE

Familiarization/Conditioning

Without fee and time constraints, the long-term goals of patient compliance and tolerance can be attained through the technique of familiarization, a form of behavior modification, positive reinforcement, and operant conditioning; over time, the handicapped individual can learn to accept the dental setting and dental treatment. Serious consideration should be given to this method of gaining patient cooperation when evaluating other options such as premedication and intravenous sedation.[34] Enlisting the cooperation of parents or staff to participate in practice sessions between visits with patients deemed capable of learning simple tasks may make the use of other behavior modifiers unnecessary.

Doctor-patient rapport is not always easily established. A safe, nonthreatening examination can be conducted while one brushes the patient's teeth. The toothbrush is a familiar object, and its introduction is not likely to cause apprehension when used, resulting in more compliant behavior. It can provide a baseline response and can even be used in conjunction with other instruments to maintain the level of familiarity. Swabbing with gauze impregnated with fluoridated mouthrinse serves the same purpose.

The success of a visit often depends on criteria that have been predetermined. If a patient's limited attention span precludes extensive treatment, the treatments can be broken down into units. The cleaning of one quadrant and rescheduling the client for additional treatment may be a more "successful" approach than attempting to clean all four quadrants during the same visit.

Management

Some individuals will accept conventional treatment in an unconventional manner. They may be totally cooperative if allowed to stand up, or sit on the floor or on a chair other than the dental chair. Patients with idiosyncratic behaviors should be identified; it is useful to know that a specific patient can be pacified by merely holding a doll, toy, or other familiar object, or by being accompanied by a specific individual. Although the delivery of clinical care may be easiest for the dentist and assistant in a conventional sit-down, four-handed approach, the client's comfort should come first. It is often necessary to treat patients on stretchers and in wheelchairs.

Individuals with gastrostomies and those with kyphosis, scoliosis, osteoporosis, quadriplegia, or joint contractures all require special consideration when positioning. Many patients, including those who are blind,[27] are easily startled and are especially aware of postural changes, so even seating and positioning the patient in the dental chair require care and understanding.

Idealism must be balanced with reality, and the ability to improvise is essential to successfully treat patients who are not always totally cooperative. Flexibility, perseverence, patience, humor, and dedication, combined with a practical yet casual informality that mixes care and concern with a modicum of firmness, usually constitutes "management."

In most forms of treatment, management is the variable and the dental procedure the constant. Treatment plans may have to be altered according to the physical and mental aspects of the condition, but the principles of good dental care do not.

A thorough individual assessment, based on the medical, physical, emotional, and social history, helps shape the management aspects of the treatment plan. What may be more helpful in the long run is documentation of patient tolerances: responses, both positive and negative, to sounds, instruments, and touching; to premedication dosages and combinations; and time tolerances for treatment. One should approach the patient with an open mind, always willing to review patient needs and treatment options.

Treatment Modifications

Modifications in the delivery of treatment usually must be made due to client difficulties regarding mobility, stability, communication, and medical problems (see Table 19-1).

Most disabilities have no direct dental manifestations and therefore treatment is usual and customary. However, modifications in treatment must be made in the following clinical situations: congenital or hereditary disabilities that have dental manifestations, disabilities that limit jaw mobility, psychomotor imbalances with predisposition for facial trauma, conditions that cause attrition and abrasion of the dentition, congenital or acquired physical disabilities limiting maintenance of oral hygiene, and congenital or acquired mental disabilities that render individuals dependent.[15]

Table 19-1. *Modifications in Dental Treatment*

Disabilities with No Direct Dental Manifestations

Hemiplegia	Blindness	Deafness
Poliomyelitis	Autism	Juvenile diabetes
Klinefelter syndrome	Mild muscular dystrophy	Congenital heart disease
Turner syndrome		Cystic fibrosis
Hemophilia		

Hereditary or Congenital Disabilities with Dental Manifestations

Amelogenesis imperfecta	Dentinogenesis imperfecta
Dentinal dysplasia	Severe enamel hypoplasia

Disabilities Limiting Oral Opening

Juvenile rheumatoid arthritis	TMJ ankylosis
Facial burn contractures	Discoid lupus erythematosis
Scleroderma	Trismus
Myositis ossificans	Cicatricial trismus

Conditions that Render Persons Trauma-Prone

Epilepsy	Cerebral palsy
Chronic vertigo	Lesch Nyhan syndrome

Disabilities Accompanied by Abrasion

Cerebral palsy	Epilepsy
Psychogenic disturbances	Chorea

Congenital or Acquired Physical Disabilities Limiting Maintenance of Oral Hygiene

Cerebral vascular accident	Amputation
Paralysis	Cerebral palsy
Muscular dystrophy	Parkinson's disease
Multiple sclerosis	Rheumatoid arthritis

Congenital or Acquired Mental Disabilities Limiting Maintenance of Oral Hygiene

Congenital	Acquired
Severe mental retardation	Meningitis
Hydrocephaly	Cranial trauma
Down syndrome	Anoxia
	Encephalitis
	Brain tumor
	Senility
	Alzheimer's disease
	Cerebral vascular accident

Compiled from information in Ettinger, R.L., and Pinkham, J.R.: Modification in restorative dentistry for the handicapped patient. *In* Dentistry for the Handicapped Patient. Edited by A.J. Nowak. St. Louis, C.V. Mosby, 1976.

Treatment Limitations

Treatment plans generally reflect current modalities. Treatment limitations relate directly to the patients' ability to cooperate, with or without special delivery modifications. Lack of cooperation can mean a paucity of intraoral radiographs and impede other diagnostic procedures as well as necessitating restraint. When it is necessary to control body movements, the use of physical restraints should be explained so that their purpose is not misinterpreted as punishment or undue force. When one uses chemical restraint in the form of premedication, one must be aware of possible drug interactions because many developmentally disabled patients are on daily medications. Phenothiazines and their derivatives can potentiate sedatives and narcotic analgesics. Antidepressants can enhance the effects of barbiturates and other central nervous system depressants. Anesthetics containing epinephrine should be avoided or used cautiously because tricyclic antidepressants can potentiate the effect of catecholamines.[35]

In cases in which lack of cooperation ultimately leads to performing elective dental procedures under general anesthesia, the preoperative workup and hospital admission may be the first comprehensive medical evaluation a patient has ever received. Often, previously unknown medical problems are revealed. When possible, day surgery is preferable as the least disruptive procedure for patients who react adversely to unfamiliar settings and situations. In addition, it represents an attempt at cost containment and reduces the demands on hospital staff, who are less familiar with handling behavioral problems.

Uncommunicative patients lack the ability to reliably express symptoms and thus place a greater responsibility on the dentist and hygienist to accurately diagnose dental problems. One should communicate with patients according to their mental and neurologic level rather than chronological age, but it is equally important to avoid infantilizing speech.[14] Those groups especially susceptible are the high-functioning retarded, individuals with cerebral palsy, and handicapped geriatric patients.

Replacing Missing Teeth

Usually the lack of cooperation and limited patient comprehension, understanding, and desire are the determining factors for the replacement of missing teeth. Other considerations are the existing esthetics of lack thereof, the patient's ability to function as is, and his potential ability to adapt to a prosthesis. It is most difficult to predict long-term client response to either fixed or removable prostheses.

If a patient indicates a definite desire to have missing teeth replaced, this is a fairly good indication that the prosthesis will be worn. Many times, however, the request for tooth replacement is generated by parents or other caregivers. In any event, the dentist must ultimately decide whether to undertake the steps involved in fabrication of a removable prosthesis. If serious doubts surround a particular case, starting it may clear up the uncertainty. Usually at least one appointment is necessary before the expenditure of a laboratory fee. These visits enable the dentist to become more familiar with the patient, and vice-versa. The dentist is then in a better position to assess patient tolerances, gag reflex control with and without premedication, and to predict whether the patient will tolerate a prosthetic device.

The clinical procedures can be accomplished one way or another. But when the denture is made and delivered, or when the etched-metal-resin retained bridge is inserted, or when the temporary crowns or bridges are cemented, or when the ceramic bridge is cemented, then the real challenge begins. One-to-one coverage for the first 24 to 48 hours has worked with some success. Phased-in delivery of prostheses, when possible, has also made transition and adjustment easier. There are still many cases, however, of complete dentures and partial dentures that are not worn. Partial dentures are probably the most complicated prosthesis for the developmentally disabled to adjust to.

Bent or broken clasps and frameworks are not uncommon, and represent forced or incorrect insertion or removal, or damage from dropping. High-impact or impact-resistant acrylics reduce breakage, and should be part of a lab prescription. In addition, the patient's name should be placed in each removable prosthesis by the lab before final insertion.

When prostheses are worn regularly, sudden behavior changes often result in removable prostheses being thrown, discarded, or flushed, and so-called "fixed" prostheses actually being removed.

Prosthetic replacement of missing teeth can be the most rewarding dental service for the developmentally disabled. And it can be the most frustrating for both doctor and patient. Some patients inadvertently lose their dentures after many weeks or months of successful wear and care. This is particularly common in an institutional setting. It is possible to have a duplicate denture or jump case made by the dental laboratory at the time of remaking the denture. This can reduce the number of appointments needed in the future if a remake again becomes necessary. Considerable care must be taken by the dentist and laboratory in the fabrication of a removable dental prosthesis for a developmentally disabled person. The chances of success are enhanced if the device initially fits properly with minimal adjustment and is esthetically pleasing. Both are motivating factors that encourage wear.

For the questionable full-denture candidate, the dentist may elect to fabricate only the upper denture, and if this is successful, then make a lower one at a later time. The upper denture generally tends to be more easily retained and more stable, and, as a result, easier to adjust to.

Frequent recall is in order for the edentulous and partially edentulous handicapped person with prosthetic tooth replacement. Many patients are unaware of trauma caused by their dentures, and they are not usually conscious of inflammation and edema of the mucosa. The motivational responses and postinsertion tolerances of the developmentally disabled to dental prostheses are probably similar to their tolerance for similar devices such as eyeglasses and hearing aids.

The questions of appropriateness of treatment, what constitutes over-treatment, and when is a case considered successful, all span a large gray area.

The recent development of the etched-metal-resin retained bridge is of considerable importance to the developmentally disabled. In some cases it can be an alternative to either a removable partial denture or a fixed bridge. It is essentially a reversible procedure when compared with a conventional bridge. The remaining teeth are not significantly altered and need no further treatment if the bonded bridge cannot be tolerated. Fabrication of a resin-bonded bridge requires less appointment time, can be done on minimally cooperative patients, and does not require the administration of local anesthetics.

For the client requiring extensive maxillofacial reconstruction or orthognathic surgery, a team workup representing various disciplines is indicated. Again, the results can be profound and dramatic, but serious questions must be asked, answered, and reviewed before treatment is attempted.

Clinical Examples

Consider the following examples: (1) A psychotic, autistic, mentally retarded young woman with periodontosis presented for dental care. After treatment under general anesthesia, an immediate denture was fabricated and significant behavioral changes were achieved, attributable to improved appearance and comfort. (2) A moderately retarded institutionalized middle-aged woman with gross disfigurement from a protrusive and flared maxilla was initially resistive. After treatment in the operating room involving an osteotomy and the eventual fabrication of a prosthesis, she responded to her improved appearance and now willingly accepts outpatient treatment. (3) The denture case that took 17 visits to complete. (4) The apprehensive, over-anxious moderately retarded man whose extensive dental needs were treated under general anesthesia, with minimal time away from work. He remains gainfully employed and has been successfully maintained postoperatively through a preventive program subscribed to by his employer. He is followed up by frequent outpatient recall visits. (5) An institutionalized patient keeps clinic visits only when the dentist promises to take him out for lunch after the visit. This patient is now on regular recall after completing moderate restorative procedures. (6) A community patient who was referred by her dentist for endodontic therapy and crown and bridge, while the dentist remained the primary provider of regular dental care. (7) A cerebral palsy patient whose missing anterior maxillary teeth were replaced with an etched-metal-resin retained bridge, thus contributing to the psychologic welfare of patient and family alike.

In each case, an assessment of the patient's needs and limitations was made (see Fig. 19-1). Judgment, perseverance, and a continuum of treatment options, without time or financial constraints, enabled the treatment to be carried out.

EMERGING PATTERNS AND ISSUES

Over the past decade, a pattern has emerged in issues associated with the developmentally disabled population. Some issues are due, in part, to an increased awareness, sensitivity, and responsiveness to the needs and rights of the disabled. Other issues result directly from the policy of deinstitutionalization.

Individuals who previously depended on institutional services are being encouraged to seek care in the community in which they live. Those who previously would have sought admission to institutions are also part of the same system. They require supervision and cannot monitor their own health needs with total independence. Over a short period of time a significant number of community placements have reduced the institutional population. The community resources may not necessarily be in place to handle this population's special needs.[16]

Access to Care

From the standpoint of dental services, access to care in the community has not yet been evaluated. Those providers most qualified to treat the handicapped, (pedodontists and general practitioners who have completed internships emphasizing special patient care) are not necessarily the ones who treat this group. They may not be providers for Medicaid, on which the majority of special needs individuals depend. In addition, although it has been demonstrated that the deinstitutionalized and developmentally disabled population can be treated successfully by private practitioners,[23] for various reasons previously discussed, many elect not to participate. Therefore, the treatment pool is reduced, and access to treatment is diminished at a time when increased access is needed. From a dental viewpoint, a major concern is whether the deinstitu-

Tufts Dental Facility For The Handicapped At Wrentham

Oral Hygiene Clinical Evaluation

Client's Name:_____

Date: _____   Time of Appt.: _____

Building:_____

Cooperation Factor: Poor   Fair   Good

Premed: Yes   No

Oral Hygiene Condition: Poor   Fair   Good   Excellent

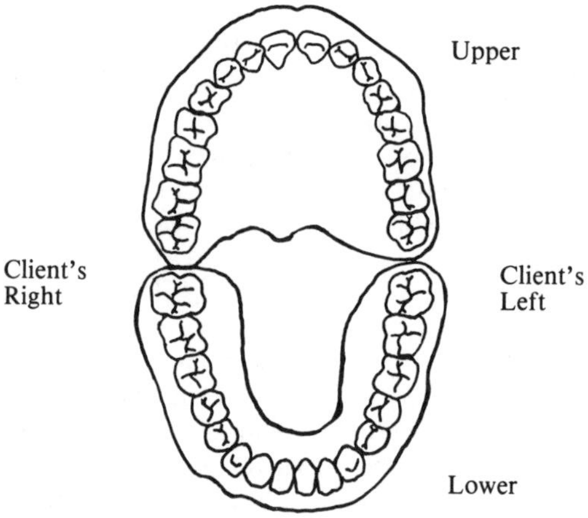

Upper

Client's Right   Client's Left

Lower

Area(s) Needing Improvement:

1. Upper Right   4. Lower Right
2. Upper Left   5. Lower Left
3. Upper Anteriors   6. Lower Anteriors

7. All Areas

Additional Comments:

_____

_____

_____

FIG. 19-1.   Oral hygiene clinical evaluation form, used to communicate relevant oral hygiene information at Tufts Dental Facility for the Handicapped at Wrentham State Hospital.

tionalized individual can find appropriate and adequate dental care in the community.

Many states do not have differential Medicaid rates that recognize the added demands of providing care for a population that is difficult to manage. Furthermore, Medicaid is the primary source of coverage of the deinstitutionalized. This results in financial disincentives that limit provider participation and thus restrict choice and access.[16] The scope of services covered by insurance is not sufficient for the needs of the handicapped population. A high percentage of this group requires recall scalings and prophylaxis at intervals of 1, 2, 3, or 4 months rather than the standard 6.

Given the financial disincentives, the lack of special competencies of the private practitioner, the inherent difficulties of managing this population, and the impossibility of monitoring the quality of services, the potential for supervised neglect becomes a real concern.

Mutual Access

By maintaining an open-door policy for the deinstitutionalized client, and by eliminating fee and predetermination barriers, the university-affiliated dental facilities for the handicapped represent an important program for this special patient group. The system can provide the necessary continuity of care that the deinstitutionalized client needs. The clinic can also serve as a referral center that the private practitioner can use to supplement community care, and thus avoid the pitfall of supervised neglect. A patient can be referred for a specific procedure that the practitioner is not comfortable performing, or for multiple scalings, which Medicaid does not cover. A treatment fund has been established to bridge the gap and cover a wider range of services, but there is still a substantial difference from usual and customary fees.

Dental Health as a Priority

In an institutional setting, in-service training and dental health education have, over the last several years, obviously raised the level of dental awareness or "dental IQ" of all caregivers. This advocacy action has made dental health a higher priority in daily care.

Similarly, the response is the same when a prevention program is offered to community-based programs. At the family level, studies have shown that if dental health is important to parents and their normal children, then dependent children are treated with equal concern. Therefore, counseling parents and other caregivers is an important process. It is basic to stress good home care, a proper dietary regime, and early intervention as the initial processes in prevention. In any event, a realistic and practical approach is usually what most caregivers are interested in; e.g., positioning, finger rests, and mouth propping.[1,23]

Continuity of Care

Assuming that the institutionalized patient is scheduled for as many visits as necessary for treatment and optimal recall, the question must be asked whether private practitioners are willing to do the same. Thus the issue of continuity of care once an individual seeks care in the community remains in question.

Type of Care

Another issue, related to the type and frequency of care received, is whether the dental services delivered meet the requirements of the developmentally disabled as a group, and whether the individual can obtain quality dental care.[19] In the past, dental care for this population has often been crisis-oriented. It would be to their detriment if periodic preventive therapies were limited or curtailed.

Levels of Need

Obviously, just as there are different degrees of disability, there are different levels of need.[40] Some developmentally disabled individuals are comparable with their peers in the general population. This group should have the least amount of difficulty finding appropriate care. The next group (e.g., persons with Down syndrome) require more frequent care, sometimes of greater intensity, to maintain an acceptable level of oral health.[20] Increased needs and demands for treatment put this group at greater risk because of their limitations of independence. Such a risk undermines the appropriateness of their community placement.

A third group, the multiply handicapped, requires a delicacy of management skill in the coordination of services. For this group, and for those with concomitant communication, behavior, and social problems, a team approach is necessary to compensate for their inability to communicate subjective sensations and make decisions regarding self-preservation. For this group the strain of finding appropriate care is greatest.

Dental Health Education

The implementation and continuity of preventive programming rest almost exclusively on a group of relatively new dental health personnel—dental health educators. Although the overall objective is to improve the oral hygiene of the patient, the dental health educator (DHE) carries out a number of related responsibilities and activities.

The DHE's role in the overall provision of care for the developmentally disabled cannot be classified as totally one-dimensional. Because teaching is the primary responsibility of an educator, that person must develop multifaceted approaches when dealing with direct care staff and/or professionals who have a direct or indirect role in providing treatment for the developmentally disabled individual. The DHE selects, designs, and presents materials and audiovisual aids in conveying the message of proper oral physiotherapy. In addition, the DHE must (1) be an efficient administrator to oversee any structured oral hygiene program and provide detailed, concise, and appropriate records to measure the progress of that program; (2) implement constructive programs that may benefit individual clients or groups of clients; (3) become sensitive and open-minded in the area of public relations as it applies to participation in the administration of the institution and/or the individual residences in the community setting; and (4) become totally familiar with all departments in the institution and work closely with them to expedite complete care, to correct perceived program deficiencies, and to collaborate on policy making. In short, the DHE must be able to do a little of everything, mainly concentrating on his or her expertise, but proficient in all aspects of care provision to the developmentally disabled.

Consent

Authorization for treatment is another issue one encounters. Normally, in a private practice, the very presence of a patient in the dental office or chair implies consent[37]; treatment is generally performed at the patient's request or according to a treatment plan that the dentist judges to be in the best interest of the patient. When given by a minor or individuals considered mentally incompetent, however, the authorization for treatment is not considered legally acceptable.

Uncertainties exist concerning the forms of consent appropriate for mentally handicapped and retarded individuals. Often the issue is a legal one concerning who can represent the client (e.g., parent, guardian, superintendent, medical director). In such cases a court must appoint a legal guardian. Consent plays an important role and is necessary to protect all parties concerned. Consent forms should be in order to avoid legal action. To expedite matters, a standard consent and procedure should be developed and adhered to. Delay of treatment, even in emergency cases, is not unusual. At present, discrepancies and uncertainties over consent may well be an additional treatment barrier the developmentally disabled individual must overcome, especially in community settings.

Risk of Infection

Dental personnel who deal with the institutionalized (and possibly noninstitutionalized) handicapped may be at greater risk for exposure to hepatitis B, intestinal parasites, and tuberculosis and other respiratory ailments. Total sterilization and disinfection of instruments and work areas, combined with the use of disposable needles, masks, and gloves, helps protect patients and staff alike from infection and other contaminants.[2,25] The recent availability of a hepatitis vaccine and immunization program should eventually prove to significantly reduce the risk of hepatitis among dental health workers.

As part of routine dental care, practitioners treating patients with disabilities should be familiar with a number of commonly encountered problems. Specifically, the higher frequency of patients with valvular heart disease, congenital heart disease, mitral valve prolapse, idiopathic hypertrophic subaortic stenosis, and prosthetic heart valves requires subacute bacterial endocarditis prophylaxis regimen. For patients with scoliosis, impaired respiratory function due to postural limitations or depressed function secondary to premedication deserves attention. The chronic nature of periodontal disease means that it cannot be overlooked in any differential diagnosis of head and neck problems.[7,20,21]

The author wishes to acknowledge the following people for their help and suggestions: Mr. Robert Hammond, R.D.H., B.S., Mr. Andrew Marcoux, R.Ph., Richard G. Miller, D.M.D., and Joseph P. O'Donnell, D.M.D., M.S. Special thanks are extended to Ms. Brenda Markel for typing this manuscript.

REFERENCES

1. Albertson, D.: Prevention and the handicapped child. Dent. Clin. N. Am., 18:595, 1974.
2. American Dental Association: Accepted Dental Therapeutics. 38th Ed. Chicago, 1979, pp. 5-22.
3. American Dental Association: Caring for the Disabled Child's Dental Health. Chicago, 1982.
4. Baer, P.N., and Benjamin, S.D.: Periodontal Disease in Children and Adolescents. J.B. Lippincott, 1974, pp. 255-264.
5. Bhaskar, S.N.: Synopsis of Oral Pathology. 4th Ed. St. Louis, C.V. Mosby, 1973.
6. Bibby, B.G.: Cariogenicity of snack foods and confections. J. Am. Dent. Assoc., 90:121, 1975.
7. Butts, J.E.: Dental status of mentally retarded children. J. Public Health Dent., 27(4):195, 1967.
8. Campaign of Concern. National Foundation of Dentistry for the Handicapped, Denver, CO, 1976.
9. Capute, A.J.: Developmental disabilities. Dent. Clin. N. Am., 18:557, 1974.
10. Cohen, M.M., Sr.: Stomatologic alterations in childhood. J. Dent. Child., 44:396, 1977.

11. Cohen, M.M., Sr., and Winer, R.A.: Dental and facial characteristics in Down's Syndrome. J. Dent. Res., *44*:197, 1965.

12. Center for Development and Learning Disorders: Dental Care for the Mentally Retarded: A Handbook for Ward Personnel. Birmingham, University of Alabama in Birmingham, 1967.

13. Dicks, J.L.: Dental Implications of Down's Syndrome. Atlanta, Georgia Retarded Center, 1978.

14. Dolinsky, E.H., and Dolinsky, H.B.: Infantilization of elderly patients by health care providers. Spec. Care Dentist, *4*:150, 1984.

15. Ettinger, R.L., and Pinkham, J.R.: Modifications in restorative dentistry for the handicapped patient. *In* Dentistry for the Handicapped Patient. Edited by A.J. Novak. St. Louis, C.V. Mosby, 1976.

16. Garrard, S.D.: Health services for mentally retarded people in community residences: Problems and questions. Am. J. Public Health, *72*:1226, 1982.

17. Gellis, S.S., and Feingold, M.: Atlas of Mental Retardation Syndromes. Washington, DC, HEW, 1968.

18. Gorlin, R.J., and Pindborg, J.J.: Syndromes of the Head and Neck. New York, McGraw Hill, 1964.

19. Gotowka, T.D., Johnson, E.S., and Gotowka, C.J.: Costs of providing dental services to adult mentally retarded: A preliminary report. Am. J. Public Health, *72*:1246, 1982.

20. Goyings, E.D., and Riekse, D.M.: Periodontal condition of institutionalized children: Improvement through oral hygiene. J. Public Health Dent., *28*:5, 1968.

21. Gullikson, J.S.: Oral findings of mentally retarded children. J. Dent. Child., *36*:59, 1959.

22. Jenson, L.G.: Clinical management of the epileptic dental patient. *In* Phenytoin Induced Teratology and Gingival Pathology. Edited by T.M. Hassell et al. New York, Raven Press, 1980, pp. 129-132.

23. Johnson, R., and Albertson, D.: Plaque control for handicapped children. J. Am. Dent. Assoc., *84*:824, 1972.

24. Kamen, S.: Mental retardation. *In* Dentistry for the Handicapped Patient. Edited by A.J. Novak. St. Louis, C.V. Mosby, 1976, pp. 39-53.

25. Kay, L., et al.: Guidelines for Dental Programs in Institutions for Developmentally Disabled Persons. Denver, National Foundation for Dentistry for the Handicapped, 1982.

26. Kraus, B.S., Clark, G.S., and Oka, S.W.: Mental retardation and abnormalities of dentitions. Am. J. Ment. Defic., *72*:905, 1968.

27. Lebowitz, E.J.: An introduction to dentistry for the blind. Dent. Clin. N. Am., *18*:3, 1974.

28. Leviton, F.J.: The willingness of dentists to treat handicapped patients: A summary of eleven surveys. J. Dent. Handicapped, *5*(1):13, 1980.

29. Lindemann, R.A., and Henson, J.L.: Acceptance of dental prophylaxis by the institutionalized patient. Spec. Care Dent., *4*:77, 1984.

30. Massler, M.: Review of problems in dealing with the handicapped. J. Dent. Educ., *21*:62, 1957.

31. Miller, J.B., and Taylor, P.P.: A survey of the oral health of a group of orthopedically handicapped children. J. Dent. Child., *37*:31, 1970.

32. Nicolaci, A.B., and Tesini, D.A.: Improvement in the oral hygiene of institutionalized mentally retarded individuals through training of direct care staff: A longitudinal study. Spec. Care Dent., *2*(5):217, 1982.

33. Nowak, A.J.: Dental disease in handicapped persons. Spec. Care Dent., *4*:66, 1984.

34. O'Donnell, J.P.: Dental familiarization for the handicapped. J. Dent. Handicap., *1*:1, 1975.

35. O'Donnell, J.P., and Cohen, M.M., Sr.: Dental care for the institutionalized retarded individual. J. Pediatr., *9*:3, 1984.

36. Plotnick, S.: A survey of preventive dental programs for the handicapped child. NY J. Dent., *45*(5):160, 1975.

37. Posnick, W.R., and Posnick, I.H.: Dental care in private practice. *In* Dentistry for the Handicapped Patient. Edited by A.J. Nowak. St. Louis, C.V. Mosby, 1976, pp. 193-208.

38. Ripa, L.: A Guide to the Use of Fluoride for the Prevention of Dental Caries, with Alternative Recommendations for Patients with Handicaps. Denver, National Foundation for Dentistry for the Handicapped, 1981.

39. Stotsky, B.A., et al.: Medicare: A disaster for the aged psychiatric patient. J. Psychol., *67*:341, 1967.

40. Tesini, D.A.: Age, degree of mental retardation, institutionalization and socioeconomic status as determinants in the oral hygiene status of mentally retarded individuals. Community Dent. Oral Epidemiol., *8*:355, 1980.

41. Tesini, D.A.: Developing Dental Health Education Programs for the Handicapped: A Training Manual and Reference Text. Springfield, MA, Area Health Education Center of Pioneer Valley, 1982.

42. Wei, S.H.Y. (Ed.): Pediatric Dental Care: An Update for the Dentist and for the Pediatrician. New York, Medcom, 1978, pp. 6-12.

43. Weintraub, J.A.: Utilization review and quality assessment of Tufts Dental Facilities for the Handicapped. Boston, Massachusetts Department of Public Health, 1983.

20

BEHAVIORAL AND PSYCHIATRIC DISORDERS

MILDLY AND MODERATELY RETARDED PERSONS

Ludwik S. Szymanski, M.D.
Mairin B. Doherty, M.D.

The field of mental retardation was neglected by psychiatry for many years,[3] but recently there has been a resurgence of interest in children who are both retarded and emotionally disturbed. To a large extent this has been due to the pioneering work of workers such as Potter, Tarjan, Chess, and Menolascino. However, there has been much less interest in adults who are mentally retarded and mentally ill. If Potter[21] could call mental retardation the Cinderella of Psychiatry, one could consider a mentally disturbed and mentally retarded adult as a Cinderella among the Cinderellas. This lack of interest might be due to a lack of training for psychiatrists in mental retardation, or to preoccupation with early stimulation of young children, perhaps with an underlying hope for "cure," whereas an adult is seen as permanently deficient and may arouse guilt for not effecting a "cure."

Another reason for the poor availability of psychiatric services for retarded persons is the resistance of some caregivers to mental health professionals. The politicization of the field of mental retardation should be mentioned as well. Psychiatry has been singled by some as responsible for the "tragic interlude"[7] in the first half of this century, when many retarded persons were warehoused in large institutions frequently directed by psychiatrists. Also, as a part of medicine, psychiatry has been opposed by those hostile to the "medical model" of the care of retarded persons. The role of psychiatry in the care of retarded persons is often still misunderstood, and, not infrequently, in some places psychiatrists are told that they should limit themselves to signing prescriptions. Fortunately, it is now generally acknowledged that the complexities of problems presented by most retarded persons require input by an interdisciplinary team. Psychiatrists, by virtue of training in both biologic and psychological aspects of medicine, are important members of such teams, especially as synthesizers of the information on these two aspects of human behavior.

MENTAL ILLNESS AND MENTAL RETARDATION

Mental health professionals traditionally relied on verbal communications by patients in order to diagnose mental disorders; such disorders would often be explained in terms of a disturbance in the thought processes. As an extension of such a view, possession of adequate intelligence was considered a prerequisite for vulnerability to mental disorders. In fact, the current psychiatric diagnostic system still relies to a considerable extent on verbalizations as a basis for diagnosis. Thus some psychiatrists would doubt that retarded persons could develop a mental disorder. Their disturbed behaviours would be seen as an inevitable part of the retardation, caused by "organicity."[20] On the other hand, others would see all disturbed behaviors of retarded persons as learned attention-getting, devices, to be remedied only by behavior modification. Both these views in fact deny that retarded persons experience emotions (and that they are human).

The importance of the recognition, treatment, and prevention of mental disorders in this population has become more apparent in the recent years. Mental disorders have been recognized as a leading factor in the failure of integration into the community after deinstitutionalization.[19]

Profound changes have taken place in the care of retarded persons in institutions. In the wake of court decisions in such cases as Youngberg[36] and Rogers,[24] standards for the use of psychotropic medications have been established. In particular, it has been recognized that they should be employed to treat mental disorders rather than nonspecific behaviors objectionable to the caregivers. As a result, the need has been recognized for an accurate diagnosis established by qualified professionals.

In the community, universal acceptance of the principles of P.L. 94-142 (Education for All Handicapped Children Act) has meant that a child's disturbed behavior is seen as requiring appropriate services, rather than as a reason for exclusion from school. Proper diagnosis of the child's mental disorder is the first step to these services. Also, a "new" group of retarded persons has emerged. These are retarded adults who always lived with their families. As they grow older, they often exhibit symptoms such as withdrawal, aggression, and rebelliousness. At the same time their parents become aged and unable to manage the "child," who might be of middle age, and they often turn for help to mental health agencies. Not infrequently these individuals are found to suffer from a mental disorder, particularly treatable depression.

Although some mental health professionals in the field of retardation dismiss formal psychiatric diagnosis as a meaningless label, an accurate diagnosis may be critical in resolving caregivers' doubts, confusion, and anxiety about an individual's disturbed behavior. It may also be prerequisite to providing appropriate treatment and avoiding improper management. For instance, the disorganized behavior of a retarded and psychotic individual might be considered by an angry and frustrated caregiver as an attention-getting behavior to be treated only with behavior modification, even an aversive one, and an aggressive individual reacting to a depriving institutional environment might be seen as "crazy" and unnecessarily treated with large doses of neuroleptics.

EPIDEMIOLOGY OF MENTAL ILLNESS IN RETARDED PERSONS

Existing diagnostic epidemiologic studies (reviewed by Webster[35] and Szymanski[30]) have focused mainly on retarded children and adolescents. They suffer as a rule from methodological faults such as biased study populations (for instance, describing preselected patient populations in institutions or special clinics), inconsistent use of diagnostic criteria for retardation and mental disorder, and lack of control groups. There appears, however, to be a general agreement among the various studies that the prevalence of mental disorders in retarded persons is several times higher than in nonretarded populations, mostly in the 30% to 60% range. Currently it appears that the prevalence among institutionalized retarded persons is on the increase because those who are functioning better (and are less disturbed) are apt to be placed in the community, leaving the more disturbed ones in the institution. Our own data on mildly and moderately retarded patients seen in a developmental disabilities clinic (in a nonpsychiatric setting but with an integral psychiatric service) indicate that 73% of children and 75% of adults manifested symptoms severe enough to establish a formal psychiatric diagnosis (Axis I in DSM III R).

This high vulnerability of retarded persons to emotional disturbance may be reasonably expected. They are subjected to increased environmental stresses and expectations, particularly if "mainstreamed" in the community, where human exceptionality is less tolerated. They may be rejected by their families and in addition may experience inner stresses such as unsatisfied sexual drives, repeated experiences of failure, wishes to be like a "normal" person, and awareness of their own limitations. Institutionalized persons frequently have little stimulation and live in environments where passivity and deindividualization are implicitly encouraged and aggressive behavior may be the means of attracting staff attention. Last but not least, the neurologic dysfunction that leads to retardation may also contribute to the genesis of mental disorders.

PSYCHIATRIC DIAGNOSTIC ASSESSMENT OF RETARDED PERSONS

The psychiatric diagnostic process and techniques as applied to retarded persons, especially the mildly and moderately retarded, were extensively described by Menolascino and Bernstein,[17] Szymanski,[29,30] and Szymanski and Crocker.[32] They are basically a modification of standard psychiatric diagnostic approaches. These have to be adapted to special life circumstances and developmental skills, especially abilities to communicate. The context and the scope of the assessment should be comprehensive. Past test results (both medical and psychological) should be critically reviewed and repeated if necessary, considering new developments (e.g., chromosomal testing for fragile-X syndrome). It is important to understand the caretakers' expectations of the evaluation, not only those they express but their "hidden" agenda as well. Behavioral observations and interviewing techniques (both verbal and nonverbal) are used as appropriate to the patient's developmental level and language skills. Generally, concrete and directive approaches are necessary, combined with liberal support and empathy with the patient. The interview with the family, other caregivers, and service providers is a most important part of the evaluation process: as a source of information that the patient may be unable to provide, as a way of understanding the emotional climate in which the patient lives, and as a means of establishing rapport with those responsible for implementing the recommendations.

The assessment of the diagnostic data and the diagnostic formulation should be made in the context of the patient's specific developmental levels in various areas, not merely within the framework of an intelligence quotient. Realities of the patient's life should be considered, especially the training received and individual life experiences.

Diagnosis of mental disorders in retarded individuals has been seriously hampered by the lack of an appropriate diagnostic classification system. The previously used Diagnostic and Statistical Manual of Mental Disorders (DSM II)[4] often relied on presumed etiology in its definition of various disorders. Many clinicians were hesitant to diagnose a "neurotic" disorder in retarded individuals, presuming that at least average intelligence was necessary in order to develop a conflict that would be at the root of such a disorder. On the other hand, diagnosis of chronic organic brain disorder was frequently used, on the presumption that the retardation was an evidence of "organicity."

The DSM III[5] is more helpful in the diagnosis of mental illness in retarded persons, because it relies on specific criteria descriptive of clinical presentation rather than presumptive etiology. The multi-axial system permits recording of multiple diagnoses in parallel with that of mental retardation. For example, Axis III permits the recording of coexisting relevant physical disorders such as Down syndrome and seizure disorder without the need to imply that they have a causal relationship with the primary psychiatric diagnosis.

The DSM III has its drawbacks, however. It is not easily adaptable to varying developmental levels. Its criteria often rely on the patient's verbalized productions, and if the patient is nonverbal, at best one may make a diagnosis of an "atypical" disorder. It has been pointed out that the diagnosis of mental retardation should not be made on Axis I and that a separate axis should be used to describe the level of cognitive functioning[27] or a cognitive profile.[30] These problems have been partly rectified in the Revised Version of the Diagnostic and Statistical Manual (DSM III R), which was published in the spring of 1987.[6] It creates the category of developmental disorders, coded on Axis II, which groups together mental retardation, pervasive developmental disorders, and specific developmental disorders.

INDIVIDUALIZED APPROACH TO PSYCHIATRIC DIAGNOSIS

Mentally retarded persons are not a homogeneous group merely by virtue of carrying the diagnosis of retardation. In fact, the spectrum of individual differences in discrete developmental levels, cognitive skills, and personality traits is much broader than in the nonretarded population. At one end of the spectrum there are profoundly retarded persons, nonverbal, requiring close to total care, virtually all with gross signs of neurologic disorder and often with associated physical handicaps. At the other end are mildly retarded individuals who, with appropriate education, can become self-supporting and mainstreamed in the community, where they may acquire, through adaptive behavior, a "cloak of competence"[9] to the point that the diagnosis of mental retardation may be no longer appropriate. Potter[21] has pointed out that mildly retarded persons may be more similar to the nonretarded than to those with severe and profound retardation. The symptoms and signs of a mental disorder in mildly retarded persons may be the same as in the nonretarded, and the usual diagnostic and interviewing techniques can be used, with minor adaptations to the patient's level of communication.[29,30] In contrast, in persons with severe and profound retardation, the emotional disorder may manifest itself primarily through changes in bodily functions and behavioral disorganizations (as occurs with young children). Individuals with moderate retardation may fall in between, primarily depending on the level of communicative skills. The environment where the person grew up can also modify the clinical presentation. Large institutions may encourage bizarre behaviors (such as self-stimulatory behaviors) that may substitute for the deprivation and help in obtaining staff attention.

In the following section the diagnostic process is reviewed as it applies to several representative and most important psychiatric diagnostic categories.

Psychotic Disorders

The literature on psychotic disorders in retarded individuals, although still modest, is considerably more comprehensive than the literature on other mental disorders in this population. Many mental health professionals still tend to diagnose psychosis in retarded individuals on the basis of behaviors such as self-stimulation, talking to self, or aggressive outbursts, which appear strange to them in comparison with the behavior of a nonretarded person. Reid[22] has reviewed the literature on this subject. He points out the early controversy among psychiatrists, whether schizophrenia and retardation in an individual were two separate illnesses and whether the former could cause the latter. Some had even believed that manneristic movements of retarded patients were diagnostic of catatonia.[8,14,15] In a recent study on this topic Russell and Tanguay[26] have shown that psychotic process in children might reduce their performance on intelligence testing. Their findings may be relevant to the not infrequent cases of institutionalized adults whose early records show that they were admitted because of presentation consistent with schizophrenia in the presence of normal intelligence, but who currently function at a retarded level. Of course, one also has to consider the effects of an educationally and socially depriving institutional environment.

The diagnosis of schizophrenia in retarded persons is not easy if one adheres to the recognized diagnostic criteria. Reid[22] described 12 schizophrenic-retarded patients, and Heaton-Ward[12] reported on 42 such patients referred for psychiatric evaluation from an institutionalized population of 1,251. These authors concluded that schizophrenia in retarded patients could be diagnosed on the basis of usually accepted criteria, and that one can distinguish hebephrenic, paranoid, and catatonic subtypes. They also considered that such diagnosis would be impossible in patients unable to communicate sufficiently verbally, but they did not discuss the question whether these disorders might have, in these patients, a different clinical presentation. Heaton-Ward[12] pointed out the inadequacy of the diagnostic criteria for psychosis accepted at that time, which required, among others, absence of insight. The DSM III diagnostic system did not do much to alleviate these difficulties. The DSM III criteria require, among others, evidence for the presence of delusions, hallucinations, or a thought disorder. These may be difficult to document unless the patient has sufficient verbal language. For many retarded patients who are nonverbal, considering symptoms such as gross disorganization of behavior and behavioral episodes suggesting hallucinations, one has to utilize the residual category of "atypical psychosis" (in DSM III R: psychotic disorders not otherwise specified). In these cases the history provided by caregivers and documented in clinical records is of particular importance. The history may show whether there has been a deterioration in the patient's clinical presentation and functioning. Positive family history may also help in establishing the diagnosis. The diagnosis may be particularly difficult if the recent symptoms are superimposed on a preexisting developmental disorder (besides the retardation), as exemplified by the following case.

CASE 1

A 19-year-old moderately retarded woman was referred because of management difficulties of half a year duration, mainly aggressive behavior and a poor attention span. In the last two years she developed a variety of other behaviors. These included inducing others to say something negative to her, to which she would then react with aggression or self-abuse. She engaged in intermittent motor mannerisms with a driven, anxious quality. She related poorly. Her speech was pressured, staccato, and robot-like. She frequently interrupted her activity and appeared for several minutes preoccupied with internal stimuli, possibly hallucinating, and out of reach. Her previous treatment had been based on behavior modification techniques aimed at reducing behaviors objectionable to the caregivers, which resulted in a transient, minor improvement. Review of the past history disclosed that in her childhood infantile autism had been diagnosed. Behaviors such as self-stimulation, stereotypies, and poor relatedness had been long-standing and were consistent with the diagnosis of autism. The more recent symptoms, such as increased behavioral disorganization, high levels of anxiety, bizarre preoccupations, and possibly hallucinations, were thought to represent a separate psychotic disorder. The diagnosis of "atypical psychosis" was made both because of clinical presentation and inability to document the presence of a thought disorder with any certainty because of the patient's language limitations. Thioridazine,

300 mg/day, resulted in marked decrease of agitation, explosive speech, and aggression. However, she remained manipulative, disruptive, and manneristic.

Pervasive Developmental Disorders

The category of pervasive developmental disorder (PDD) is a relatively new category, established by the DSM III, which includes infantile autism, pervasive developmental disorder of childhood onset, and a residual "atypical" category. It is mentioned here because the majority of persons with this diagnosis are also mentally retarded.[33]

PDD has come under considerable criticism as a separate category on the grounds that it does not reflect clinical realities. Age of onset before 30 months is used as an important criterion distinguishing autism from the other two categories, but clinicians are well aware that in many children with classical autism the symptoms are first noticed after that age.

In the DSM III R, the differentiation between infantile autism and pervasive developmental disorder, childhood onset has been eliminated. These two have been combined under the category of autistic disorder, which, together with pervasive developmental disorders NOS (not otherwise specified), forms the category of pervasive developmental disorders, which is now coded on Axis II.

Of the disorders included in the PDD category, clinicians are most familiar with infantile autism. It was first formally described by Kanner in 1943.[13] In the following decades considerable literature was devoted to it, primarily psychoanalytical, which today is mainly of historical significance. According to it autism was seen as a specific disorder related to early disturbances of the mother-child relationship. Autistic children were viewed as potentially intelligent, due to "islands of intelligence" demonstrated by some of them; many studies of autism excluded subjects who were retarded.

At present we see autism as a behavioral syndrome that probably includes a number of different subsets, possibly with different etiologies and pathogeneses. It is known to be associated with some disorders such as congenital rubella, inborn errors of metabolism, tuberous sclerosis, and possibly the fragile-X syndrome. In subsets of children with autism, abnormalities in the neurotransmitter systems (such as hyperserotonemia) and neurophysiologic abnormalities (delayed auditory brain stem transmission) have been demonstrated, but their role in the pathogenesis of autism is unclear. The importance of genetic factors is suggested by a 50-fold increased prevalence of autism in siblings of autistic persons.

About three-quarters of autistic persons are functioning in the retarded range, although some show higher functioning in areas such as recall of trivial, unrelated bits of information. The most prominent and pathognomonic clinical feature is severe disturbance in interpersonal relatedness. These infants lack social smile, anticipatory posture when picked up, attachment to caregivers, stranger anxiety, and response to being comforted. What some clinicians do not realize is that when autistic children become older, they may relate more, although not necessarily more normally. They may interact more, respond to commands, give affection on request, and eye contact may be more frequent but still fleeting and empty. Language may be absent, or, if present, it lacks interpersonal communicative intent and is characterized by abnormalities such as echolalia, perseverations, and reversal of personal pronouns. Nonverbal language such as gestures are also deficient. Characteristic perceptual inconsistencies include over- and under-reactivity to sensory stimuli and preference for proximal stimuli (e.g., preference for smell and touch). Ritualistic behaviors, intolerance of change, and efforts to maintain sameness were described in the original article by Kanner.[13] Motor abnormalities such as self-stimulation, self-abuse, and mannerisms (often described incorrectly as "autistic tendencies") are frequent, and their presence usually leads to suspicion of autism, although they are not the cardinal feature.

Mental retardation professionals are typically concerned about differentiating autism from mental retardation, psychosis, and major language disorder. Strictly speaking, mental retardation is not a true differential diagnosis, because these two conditions coexist so frequently. Mildly and moderately retarded nonautistic persons typically can relate well interpersonally, appropriate to their developmental level, as can persons with aphasia. By definition, the diagnosis of psychosis (except "atypical") requires presence of thought disorder, delusions, and hallucinations. Typically there is a history of premorbid normal development, as opposed to the case in most, if not all, autistic children. However, a psychotic illness may later be superimposed on infantile autism, as demonstrated by case 1. The problems involved in the diagnosis of autism are illustrated in the following case.

CASE 2

Seven-year-old John was referred because of overactivity, self-stimulatory behavior, and poor language development. His early motor development was normal, but at $3\frac{1}{2}$ years he had only some jargon words. As an infant he was "distant" and did not reach to his mother. More recently he started to relate better to his parents, although he still ignored other children. He had no sense of danger and would run out of the house into the street. He had some language, which he used to communicate his needs. He had a trial of methylphenidate, on which he became more disturbed and enuretic. On psychological testing he scored in the mildly retarded range. He attended a school for language-disordered children. His teachers believed that his behavior problems were related to his mother's emotional difficulties and recommended residential placement. During the interview he was mildly to moderately overactive and tested limits, but he responded to structure and firm limits. He could relate and establish eye contact, but in an immature fashion. He engaged in various motor stereotypies. He liked to feel textures of objects and to self-stimulate with a stick, which he would wave or use to hit his hands. His parents were devoted to him, overprotective and inconsistent. They felt that the school had not given them any guidance on how to manage John's behavior. Recommendation was made for placement in a more structured school for autistic children.

Affective Disorders

Szymanski and Biederman[31] have pointed out two obstacles to professionals' ability to recognize depression in retarded persons. The first obstacle is the misconception that depression (as an illness) does not occur in this population. Although most clinicians will recognize that a patient looks sad, this would be frequently interpreted as a transient reaction to an environmental event. Only recently has there been gradual recognition that retarded persons are "able" to suffer from affective disorders just as nonretarded ones (reviews by Sovner and Hurley[28] and Szymanski and Biederman[31]). The earlier literature on this subject has been reviewed by Gardner,[10] who noticed lack of definite data in published studies, as well as theoretical predictions of high vulnerability of retarded individuals to depression, due to their experience of rejection, failure, and inconsistent mothering. On the other hand, some authors cited by Gardner posited that retarded persons would not be able to develop depression, because their low intelligence precluded development of an understanding that their functioning was below the normally expected level. Reid,[22] Heaton-Ward,[12] and Rivinus and Harmatz[23] reported on series of retarded patients with diagnosis of manic-depressive illness. Heaton-Ward[12] observed occurrence of paranoid features with delusions of bodily malfunction in the depressive phase. Some of his patients had ideas of guilt and unworthiness and made suicidal threats.

The second obstacle to the correct diagnosis is lack of recognition that the clinical presentation might be somewhat different from one encountered in nonretarded persons. Of interest is that already in 1919 Gordon observed that depression in psychotic retarded patients was not as profound as in nonretarded ones, but was characterized by more indifference and apathy.[11] In our experience, a patient's level of communicative skills, particularly verbal-conceptual, will affect the clinical presentation of depression. Higher functioning, more verbal patients have a clinical presentation of depression similar to the presentation seen in nonretarded persons. However, even they may complain more of feeling "sick" than of depressed mood. Increase in dependency, apathy, lack of motivation, withdrawal, and various somatic symptoms including sleeping and eating disorders, are also manifested. In more retarded and less verbal individuals, behavior and somatic presentations dominate the clinical picture. Additionally, self-stimulatory, self-abusive, and aggressive behaviors may appear, or increase, if pre-existing. This topic is discussed in detail in the section on self-injurious behavior later in this chapter.

Some of the problems involved in diagnosing depression in retarded persons are illustrated by the following case.

CASE 3

Claire, a young woman in her twenties, with Down syndrome, was referred because of depression. She had been cheerful, friendly, and outgoing until about a year prior to referral, at which time she started to regress. This coincided with her alcoholic father being told by the mother to leave the house. She refused to walk and preferred instead to sit on the floor, talked progressively less and in a whisper, ate poorly and lost about 20 pounds, refused to leave her home, became stubborn and uncooperative, slept poorly, complained of headaches, cried, and was preoccupied with the fear that her mother would leave her.

During the first interview Claire cried and whined continuously. She exhibited a variety of motor mannerisms. There was no evidence of psychotic thought disorder, disorientation, or loss of memory. Medical assessment was noncontributory. Differential diagnosis of presenile dementia was not supported because of intact memory, lack of definite neurological signs, and lack of evidence of loss of skills. Claire was treated with doxepin and supportive psychotherapy, individually and jointly with her mother. She improved gradually. Her mood changed and became more appropriate and cheerful. She became more active, attended social activities in her community, and later a sheltered workshop program.

DIFFERENTIAL DIAGNOSIS

In retarded persons several conditions have to be kept in mind while considering a diagnosis of an affective disorder.

Physical Illness

Disturbed behavior may be a form of communicating pain and other discomfort and distress by a person not able to communicate verbally. This is particularly frequent in severely and profoundly retarded persons and is discussed in detail in the next section of this chapter. In some subgroups, specific disorders, such as hypothyroidism in persons with Down syndrome, may present with symptoms of depression.

Dementia

If depression is expressed mainly through changes in behavior and adaptation, the differential diagnosis of a dementia should be considered. This is particularly relevant to adults with Down syndrome, in whom Alzheimer's disease has been described as occurring more frequently than in the general population.[18] (See also Chap. 8.) Neuropathologic changes consistent with Alzheimer's disease have been found in up to 100% of adults over 40 years of age who had Down syndrome,[16] but they are not necessarily accompanied by a clinically significant dementia. For instance, Ropper and Williams[25] found neocortical plaques and neurofibrillary tangles in all of 20 patients over 30 with Down syndrome whom they studied, but they reported clinical dementia in only 3.

Precipitous diagnosis of dementia in these patients should be avoided, because it might convey to the staff an attitude of therapeutic nihilism and lead to abandoning the patient, which would be particularly tragic if the patient suffers from a treatable depression. Careful history and observation of the patient, sometimes over a period of time, should document loss of memory and of ability to perform a particular task, characteristic of dementia, versus loss of motivation of a depressed patient. Neurologic examination, including computerized tomography and perhaps a positron emission tomography (PET) scan will be important.

Reaction to Major Environmental Stress

In geriatric patients relocated within or outside institutions as well as in retarded persons in similar situations, symptoms related to precipitous changes in daily routine and environment, such as weight loss, withdrawal, confusion, and disorientation, have been described.[1,2] These are usually related to the precipitousness of the change and might be avoided by careful and gradual preparation of the patient, although some of these patients might also be genuinely depressed. Related to this may be similar symptoms that appear in retarded persons in whom major bodily changes occur rapidly and lead to loss of a particular function (such as loss of vision).

REFERENCES

1. Carsrud, A.L., et al.: Effects of social and environmental change on institutionalized mentally retarded persons: The relocation syndrome reconsidered. Am. J. Ment. Defic., 84:266, 1979.
2. Cochran, W.E., Sran, P.K., and Varano, G.A.: The relocation syndrome in mentally retarded individuals. Ment. Retard., 15(2):10, 1977.
3. Cushna, B., Szymanski, L.S., and Tanguay, P.E.: Professional roles and unmet manpower needs. In Emotional Disorders of Mentally Retarded Persons. Edited by L.S. Szymanski and P.E. Tanguay. Baltimore, University Park Press, 1980.
4. DSM II: Diagnostic and Statistical Manual of Mental Disorders. Washington, DC, American Psychiatric Association, 1968.
5. DSM III: Diagnostic and Statistical Manual of Mental Disorders. Washington, DC, American Psychiatric Association, 1980.
6. DSM III R: Diagnostic and Statistical Manual of Mental Disorders. Revised version. Washington, DC, American Psychiatric Association, 1987.
7. Donaldson, J.Y., and Menolascino, F.J.: Past, current and future roles of child psychiatry in mental retardation. J. Am. Acad. Child Psychiatry, 3:352, 1977.
8. Earl, C.J.: The primitive catatonic psychosis of idiocy. Brit. J. Med. Psychol., 14:231, 1934.
9. Edgerton, R.B.: The Cloak of Competence. Berkeley, University of California Press, 1967.
10. Gardner, W.I.: Occurrence of severe depressive reactions in the mentally retarded. Am. J. Psychiatry, 124:386, 1967.
11. Gordon, A.: Psychoses in mental defect. Am. J. Insanity, 75:489, 1919.
12. Heaton-Ward, A.: Psychosis in mental handicap. Br. J. Psychiatry, 130:525, 1977.
13. Kanner, L.: Autistic disturbances of affective contact. New Child, 2:217, 1943.
14. Kraepelin, E.: Psychiatrie. Leipzig, 1896.
15. Kraepelin, E.: Clinical Psychiatry. Transl. by A.R. Diefendorf. New York, Macmillan, 1902.
16. Malamud, N.: Neuropathology of organic brain syndromes associated with aging. In Aging and the Brain. Edited by C.M. Gaitz. New York, Plenum Press, 1972.
17. Menolascino, F.J., and Bernstein, N.R.: Psychiatric assessment of the mentally retarded child. In Diminished People. Edited by N.R. Bernstein. Boston, Little, Brown, 1970.
18. Miniszek, N.A.: Development of Alzheimer disease in Down syndrome individuals. Am. J. Ment. Defic., 87:377, 1983.
19. Pagel, S.E., and Whitling, C.A.: Readmission to a state hospital for mentally retarded persons: Reasons for community placement failure. Ment. Retard., 16:164, 1978.
20. Philips, I.: Children, mental retardation and emotional disorder. In Prevention and Treatment of Mental Retardation. Edited by I. Philips. New York, Basic Books, 1966.
21. Potter, H.W.: Mental retardation, the Cinderella of psychiatry. Psychiatr. Q., 39:537, 1965.

22. Reid, A.H.: Psychosis in adult mental defectives. Br. J. Psychiatry, *120:*205, 1972.
23. Rivinus, T.M., and Harmatz, J.S.: Diagnosis and lithium treatment of affective disorder in the retarded: Five case studies. Am. J. Psychiatry, *136:*551, 1979.
24. Rogers versus Okin: 738 F.2d 1387 (10th Cir. 1984), 9 MPDLR 528.
25. Ropper, A.H., and Williams, R.S.: Relationship between plaques, tangles, and dementia in Down's syndrome. Neurology, *30:*639, 1980.
26. Russell, A.T., and Tanguay, P.E.: Mental illness and mental retardation: Cause or coincidence? Am. J. Ment. Defic., *85:*570, 1981.
27. Rutter, M., and Shaffer, D.: DSM-III a step forward or back in terms of the classification of child psychiatric disorders? J. Am. Acad. Child Psychiatry, *19:*371, 1980.
28. Sovner, R., and Hurley, A.: Do the mentally retarded suffer from affective illness? Arch. Gen. Psychiatry, *40:*61, 1983.
29. Szymanski, L.S.: Psychiatric diagnostic evaluation of mentally retarded individuals. J. Am. Acad. Child Psychiatry, *16:*67, 1977.
30. Szymanski, L.S.: Psychiatric diagnosis of mentally retarded persons. *In* Emotional Disorders of Mentally Retarded Persons. Edited by L.S. Szymanski and P.E. Tanguay. Baltimore, University Park Press, 1980.
31. Szymanski, L.S., and Biederman, J.: Depression and anorexia nervosa of persons with Down syndrome. Am. J. Ment. Defic., *89:*246, 1984.
32. Szymanski, L.S., and Crocker, A.C.: Mental retardation. *In* Comprehensive Textbook of Psychiatry. Edited by H. Kaplan and B.J. Sadock. Baltimore, Williams & Wilkins, 1985.
33. Tanguay, P.E.: Early infantile autism and mental retardation: Differential diagnosis. *In* Emotional Disorders of Mentally Retarded Persons. Edited by L.S. Szymanski and P.E. Tanguay. Baltimore, University Park Press, 1980.
34. Tanguay, P.E.: Toward a new classification of serious psychopathology in children. J. Am. Acad. Child Psychiatry, *23:*373, 1984.
35. Webster, T.G.: Unique aspects of emotional development in mentally retarded children. *In* Psychiatric Approaches to Mental Retardation. Edited by F.J. Menolascino. New York, Basic Books, 1970.
36. Youngberg versus Romeo: 457 U.S. 307 (1982), 6 MDLR 223.

SEVERELY AND PROFOUNDLY RETARDED PERSONS: A CONCEPTUAL FRAMEWORK FOR ASSESSMENT AND TREATMENT

Mairin B. Doherty, M.D.
Ludwik S. Szymanski, M.D.

When Grunewald described severely and profoundly retarded persons as the "lost generation" of the retarded,[9] he was referring to the failure to provide this population with much of anything from a psychological and habilitative point of view, creating for them an existence that tragically reflects the results of lifesaving without developmental activation. It remains to be clarified to what degree the emotional and behavioral presentations commonly identified in severely and profoundly retarded persons can be ameliorated by vigorous implementation of early intervention programs, but support for social, emotional, and cognitive development must occur in harmony with a health care plan that recognizes the magnitude of the treatment requirements of a population that has a psychiatric morbidity of 50% compared to 7% in the nonretarded population.[20] Rutter and his associates, in their classic epidemiologic study of the nonselected population of the Isle of Wight, identified a strong and clinically important association between mental retardation and psychiatric disturbance and showed that the prevalence of such disturbance increases with the degree of retardation.[20] In the severely and profoundly retarded, the mechanism for the association between their intellectual handicap and the psychiatric disturbance relates to many factors that compromise their adaptive capacities including organic brain dysfunction and deviant temperamental attributes,[18] language failure, and the frequent association with other handicapping conditions such as seizure disorder, blindness, deafness, cerebral palsy, and neuromuscular disturbances. Virtually all persons with an IQ below 50 have demonstrable brain disease,[3] and Eisenberg[5] draws attention to the complexity of the psychophysiologic relationships in brain damage, where interference with functional areas of the brain can lead to disinhibition and failure of higher integrating mechanisms. Therefore, the contribution of organic brain damage to the clinical presentations of the retarded person is more on the order of a propensity for emotional or behavioral disturbance rather than a direct one-to-one relationship with a specific psychiatric disorder.

The prevalence of psychiatric disturbance is higher in institutional settings. Before attributing the high prevalence of emotional and behavioral disturbance to the poor quality of institutional care, however, it is important to review the reasons for admission of retarded persons to residential treatment and the institutional policy with regard to discharge planning and return to community care. It is recognized that preexisting psychiatric and behavioral problems are potent reasons for institutionalization.[14] However, adverse psychiatric disturbance can jeopardize the retarded person's ability to achieve or maintain a community placement even where deinstitutionalization is being vigorously pursued.

In the course of providing psychiatric consultation to an institutionalized population of severely and profoundly retarded adults and their interdisciplinary caregivers, one quickly appreciates the magnitude of the challenge to psychiatry to develop conceptual models for the assessment and treatment of these patients. Although the patients are obviously psychologically distressed and impaired in their interpersonal functioning, their clinical presentations rarely resemble commonplace psychiatric syndromes, and each patient encounter challenges the relevance of standard clinical theory and practice. However, as one becomes more familiar with the patient population, one increasingly recognizes that their psychopathology needs to be primarily assessed in the context of their developmental level and that the traditional conceptual framework used for adult patients requires adaptation to incorporate the principles of psychiatric assessment of nonretarded persons at similar social, emotional, and cognitive levels, e.g., those of infants and toddlers. In this section we will elaborate on some of these conceptual adaptations as they relate to biopsychosocial assessment, mental status evaluation, categorical diagnosis, and treatment approaches.

BIOPSYCHOSOCIAL ASSESSMENT

The experienced clinician approaches psychiatric assessment with a repertoire of skills that involve observation, elucidation, and decision-making along a number of different lines including assessment of developmental level, review of psychosocial stressors in the environment, exploration of psychodynamic themes, and identification of categorical or syndromal diagnoses. The difficulty and complexity of this process increases with the degree of the patient's retardation. In the severely and profoundly retarded patient, multiple levels of normal, delayed, and deviant development can coexist, and the clinician must depend on nonverbal clues and nonspecific behavioral symptoms to gain access to the etiology of the patient's distress. An approach to assessment that draws on a biopsychosocial data base[6] increases the probability of achieving diagnostic accuracy. Costello[2] has emphasized that good psychiatric assessment usually requires a pooling of several different sources and types of information. The importance of this approach will be highlighted in the following case example.

Psychiatric consultation was requested for a young man whose oppositional, disruptive, and at times assaultive behavior was jeopardizing his continuation in a prevocational workshop program. Although the young man's chronological age was 28 years, his mental age was estimated to be at the level of 18 months, and he was nonverbal except for occasional unintelligible sounds and some limited gestures. His social and emotional development was not only delayed but deviant, with evidence of apathy and social withdrawal, and he walked with a shuffling, constricted gait, rarely lifting his gaze from the ground. Although he was physically mature, his physiologic functions of eating, sleeping, and eliminating were poorly regulated and his sexual drives, although age-appropriate, were uninhibited and socially unacceptable. Cognitively, he was assessed to have an aptitude for sensory motor activity, and this was the reason he was referred for prevocational training. His problematic behaviors occurred shortly after his workshop placement.

A baseline review of this patient's strengths, weaknesses, delays, and deviance along various lines of human growth and development (e.g., chronological, biological, social, emotional, and intellectual) is critical to the formulation of a diagnostic understanding of his presentation. The initial information presented on referral suggested that his oppositional, disruptive, and assaultive behavior reflected a nonspecific stress response to placement in a group setting that challenged his most seriously delayed or impaired areas of functioning, i.e., social and emotional maturity. However, closer inquiry into the context of his problematic behaviors revealed that they occurred when workshop personnel intervened to interrupt his masturbation, which had increased at the time of his new assignment. This new information did not negate the previous diagnostic speculation but expanded the clinicians' understanding to include contextual or environmental factors that contributed to the behavior. It might be speculated that this increase in masturbation served as a self-soothing mechanism to allay distressful feelings, but the nature of the distress needed further clarification. Direct clinical observation revealed that the young man's mental status presentation was remarkable for its sadness, apathy, withdrawal, and psychomotor retardation and its resemblance to a depressive presentation. Subsequent review of historical data from the patient's primary caregivers highlighted the fact that few people were knowledgeable about his past history because of a recent change in caretaking personnel. Perusal of the patient's record supplied critical information that indicated that this was not the patient's usual presentation but that his mental state and functioning had deteriorated when he lost a caretaker who had been a source of affection, stimulation, and advocacy for him in a long-term relationship. This person had initiated a referral for workshop training prior to leaving employment with the institution. Before the placement was implemented, however, the change in the patient's presentation had already occurred, with apathy, withdrawal, and emergence of vegetative symptoms such as sleep disturbance and weight loss. This historical information highlighted the temporal association between a significant loss for the patient and the onset of depressive symptoms. Because of the patient's early developmental level and the onset of profound depressive symptomatology following a disruption in primary attachment, the clinical presentation had many of the features of an anaclitic (i.e., "dependent") depression described by Spitz.[22] However, the clinical presentation also met many of the diagnostic criteria for major depressive disorder.

A treatment plan in this case might involve any or all of the following interventions: staff training on the significance and management of increased masturbation, review of patient's developmental readiness for group placement and modification of his educational goals until emotional issues could be addressed, reinstitution of a primary caretaking model, arrangement for visits by his previous caretaker, monitoring of changes in, or persistence of, affective symptoms following these psychosocial interventions, and, ultimately, consideration of antidepressant medications if the depressive presentation persisted.

Thus it can be seen that a biopsychosocial and developmental approach to assessment involves a continuing process of evaluation along many parameters. An organized approach works from the specific difficulties identified in the referring complaint to pursue lines of inquiry that include past history, changes in presentation over time, recent psychosocial stressors in the environment, review of patient's adaptive coping efforts and defenses against psychological distress, formal mental status assessment, generation of hypotheses about etiologic factors, and treatment approaches that test these hypotheses. It will be appreciated that implementation of such an approach in the assessment of severely and profoundly retarded persons requires considerable clinical skill in order to accurately formulate a diagnostic impression and select a treatment approach.

MENTAL STATUS ASSESSMENT

A confounding factor in the mental status assessment of severely and profoundly retarded persons is the nonspecificity of the behavioral symptoms by which they communicate their distress. Affective states of anxiety, depression, and psychosis will be conceptualized, experienced, and symptomatically expressed in accordance with the retarded person's developmental level, which in the case of the severely and profoundly retarded is usually at or below the sensory-motor stage, with a very limited repertoire of higher-level functions including speech and language.

Piaget[13] has described how affect during the sensory-motor stage of development is predominantly linked to motoric expression and that pathological affective states therefore tend to be linked to presentations of apathy or motor discharge. Heaton-Ward[10] commented how the majority of profoundly retarded persons, and some severely retarded individuals, could be considered psychotic if one made the diagnosis of psychosis on the basis of emotional lability, noisy outbursts, and continuous or periodic disorganized purposeless activity, including aggression, destructiveness, and self-mutilation. This description does highlight the linking of affective states to motoric expression, which is commonplace in this population, although not all such symptoms indicate a psychotic state. Looking at symptom formation at the earlier developmental level before ambulation, Anna Freud[7] noted how frequently one encounters psychophysiologic presentations in very young children, who have few pathways other than the somatic for expressing symptoms of distress. Thus, it will be appreciated that symptoms of emotional distress in severely, profoundly retarded persons of necessity present with affecto-motor or somatic disturbances.

In reviewing current clinical practice in the assessment of the retarded person, it is noteworthy how frequently an exclusive focus on behavioral assessment eclipses the critical link between behavioral presentations and underlying affects or emotions. Similarly, somatic presentations are frequently ascribed to the vicissitudes of ill health or organic conditions associated with the patient's retardation. In both of these situations, the patient's clinical presentation is frequently inadequately or imprecisely diagnosed unless the underlying affective disturbance leading to the behavioral or somatic presentation is correctly identified.

The following case vignettes highlight the nonspecificity of many somatic or behavioral symptoms in this population and the necessity for clinicians to review such symptoms within the context of a comprehensive mental status assessment in order to diagnose the appropriate clinical syndrome. This approach underscores the fact that significant psychiatric disturbance is manifested by a constellation of symptoms related to the patient's affective state, behavioral presentations, and somatic disturbances, which coexist as concomitant aspects of the same diagnosis. However, it is commonplace for the presenting complaint to highlight a major disturbance in one area which in turn overshadows less prominent but no less important disturbances in other systems. Thus, in important aspects, a comprehensive mental status assessment in the severely and profoundly retarded will be similar to that used in the assessment of infants and toddlers, i.e., identification of disturbed affective/emotional states, observation of deviant behavioral/interactional patterns, and recognition of psychophysiologic/somatic presentations.[17]

CASE VIGNETTE WITH A PROMINENT
BEHAVIORAL PRESENTATION

A 20-year-old man with Down syndrome had created a large wound in his mandibular region by persistently picking the area with his forefinger. At the time of psychiatric consultation, he had been hospitalized and placed in partial arm restraints to allow his face to heal. His face presented a cavernous wound from this self-injurious behavior, but the key to his categorical diagnosis lay not in this behavior, but in his affective state. He was noted to have little capacity for interpersonal relatedness, was unresponsive to environmental manipulation, and appeared to be preoccupied and distressed by an internal source of anxiety and disorganization. His agitation was extreme, and his picking behavior was only one of many recurring movements in a body that seemed to be in constant motion. A review of somatic disturbances in this man revealed a profound weight loss; he was indeed emaciated, with a history of chronic chest infections which at times were life-threatening. A diagnosis of atypical psychosis was made on the basis of a comprehensive mental status assessment and the patient's affective presentation of pervasive disorganizing anxiety. Treatment with thioridazine was begun, and over a 2-week period divided doses of 75 mg daily brought about a dramatic change in his psychotic state. The young man became alert, purposeful, and interactive with his environment. With this change in his mental state and the calming of his agitation, his self-injurious behavior ceased and the wound healed. In addition, he began to gain weight and eventually over a period of months achieved his ideal body weight. He returned to full participation in the educational and rehabilitative aspects of his program.

Self-injurious behavior is a symptom with important developmental, organic, and psychiatric aspects. Self-biting and scratching are commonplace in early infancy, and the severely and profoundly retarded populations are at risk for remnants of this behavior, or regression to this behavior, at times of stress because of their immature development level. Over a 3-year period, Schroeder et al.[21] found a consistent prevalence of self-injurious behavior in 10% of the population of a state facility for the retarded and found that the patients with these behaviors had

more seizure disorder, severe language handicap, visual impairment, and more severe or profound retardation than the rest of the patient population. When the behavior is viewed in the context of a comprehensive mental status assessment, however, it is frequently apparent that behaviors such as head-banging, face-slapping, skin-picking, hair-pulling, self-biting, and excessive painful masturbation serve as potent modes of communicating distress. The nature and intensity of that distress may be the most important clinical factor in choosing the treatment intervention most likely to lead to a successful outcome. Therefore, self-injurious behavior can be viewed as a nonspecific indicator of such diverse diagnostic entities as habit, self-stimulation, situational anxiety, psychotic anxiety, or affective disturbance. A behavior modification approach produces impressive results in terms of treating the specific symptom,[21] but a treatment approach that defines the psychiatric diagnosis in addition to a behavioral diagnosis has the potential to identify a treatable disorder and can therefore lead to improvement not only in the symptomatic behavior but also in the patient's affective state and somatic/physical health. Reports of successful treatment attributed to psychoactive medication[21] are difficult to evaluate when only a behavioral diagnosis or monosymptomatic target symptom is identified and more comprehensive mental status information is lacking.

CASE VIGNETTE WITH PROMINENT
AFFECTIVE PRESENTATION

An 18-year-old girl was referred for psychiatric consultation because of management problems related to her restlessness, excitement, and tireless energy. Staff reported that she was active to the point of exhaustion, slept little, and was eating nonfood substances, in particular cigarette ends. The patient was noted to have increased sexual drive that led her to masturbate indiscriminately on both people and objects. Staff found her to be mischievous and elusive, but she quickly became irritable and aggressive when thwarted and frequently hit out at caretakers and other patients. This presentation of excitement and drive was initially attributed to a nicotine effect from cigarette ingestion and a treatment approach of greater supervision and containment was implemented. However, one month later a second psychiatric consultation was requested because of recurrence of symptoms, and the interim history was reviewed. It emerged that the patient had entered a phase of inactivity, withdrawal, and disinterest during that time, with a noticeably depressed mood and periods of tearfulness. This fluctuation in mood raised the possibility that the patient suffered from a manic-depressive psychosis, and this diagnosis was confirmed over time. Careful charting of the patient's behaviors, affect, sleep pattern, and appetite documented a cyclical disturbance in which the patient showed periodic changes in activity level, mood, and vegetative symptoms. It was possible to modulate the mood swings by occasional use of thioridazine, and this in turn modified the behavioral disruptions. Lithium was also considered in the management of this patient, but its use was not necessary, and the more problematic side effects and monitoring were avoided.

Reid and Naybr[15] reported in precise clinical detail the cyclical patterns of change in mentally retarded patients with short-cycle manic-depressive psychosis. They postulated that manic-depressive psychosis can occur and be diagnosed in mentally retarded persons of all degrees of retardation including the most severe, but contended that the conceptual model of schizophrenic and paranoid psychosis has little significance below an IQ of 45 because of the retarded person's inability to verbalize hallucinatory or delusional states. They made the diagnosis of manic-depressive psychosis in profoundly retarded individuals on the basis of a prolonged study of behavior and physiologic functions backed up by knowledge of the family history. In their patients periods of overactivity tended to correlate with a reduction in the number of hours spent asleep, tachycardia, and rise in temperature. Short-cycle manic-depressive psychosis was identified in 4% of the profoundly retarded population of their hospital, and they speculated that brain damage might act as a precipitating or releasing factor for manic-depressive psychosis in individuals with appropriate genetic loading, giving this relatively high frequency. Treatment approaches included antipsychotic medications and lithium.

CASE VIGNETTE WITH A PROMINENT SOMATIC DISTURBANCE

A profoundly retarded 24-year-old man was referred for psychiatric consultation because of life-threatening deterioration in his physical state, which included profound weight loss, emaciation, rumination, and copious regurgitation of food. This deterioration was accompanied by emotional withdrawal and deterioration in his mental status, with signs of anxiety and agitation. In reviewing the history, it was noted that the patient had developed rumination and regurgitation as early as 3 months of age, and prior to his institutionalization at 3 years had many hospitalizations for vomiting, dehydration, and hypochromic anemia secondary to esophagitis. This clinical picture reoccurred periodically after institutionalization, and intercurrent chest infections frequently placed him on the critically ill list. He had been hospitalized in critical condition at the time that psychiatric consultation was requested. On mental status assessment, he was noted to be pale, marasmic, overanxious, and vigilant, scanning his environment with the wide-eyed appearance described by Richmond, Eddy, and Green[16] as a "radar-like gaze." He demonstrated a low-intensity agitation with occasional stereotypical flicking of his fingers and could be seen to be actively ruminating by maneuvering his jaw to facilitate the reentry of food into his mouth. The biomedical model of intervention had tended to attribute his clinical presentation to organic factors related to his retardation and focused on physical investigation of his gastrointestinal tract, with nutritional supplementation as a treatment approach when findings were negative. Following psychiatric consultation, however, the diagnostic understanding of the patient's condition was expanded to that of nonorganic failure to thrive, and treatment interventions were sought primarily to remediate social and emotional factors in his environment. A psychodynamically oriented treatment plan sought to eliminate multiple unfamiliar caregivers, reinforce a primary caretaking system, and reorganize his feeding schedule to allow for a relaxed and unhurried approach to both the meal and postprandial time. The importance of empathy and synchronicity in the dyadic relationship between the feeding caretaker and the patient was emphasized. A centrally acting antiemetic medication, prochlorperazine, was administered rectally to stabilize the patient's vomiting and then discontinued as the caretaking relationship became more effective in stabilizing the patient's affective and nutritional status. On this regime the patient gained 16 pounds in 2 months, and his mental status changed from an overanxious constricted presentation to that of a more relaxed, sociable young man who showed affective reciprocity in his relationship with his caregivers. Diagnosis in this case was rumination disorder, a condition frequently encountered at early stages of human development.

Rumination and failure to thrive are psychophysiological disorders most frequently ascribed to deprivation syndromes in infancy and childhood which in turn can lead to failure of physical growth, retardation of social and emotional development, malnutrition, and even death.[8,11,12] These clinical presentations pose a difficult diagnostic problem requiring differentiation between subtle organic disease in the patient and complex social and emotional factors in the patient's environment. Seasoned clinicians acknowledge how frequently the diagnosis can go unrecognized while sophisticated diagnostic interventions are pursued in search of more esoteric diseases. However, emotional and environmental disturbances so frequently lie at the root of growth failure that Bewick[1] suggests physicians consider these nonorganic etiologies in parallel with and often before the search for occult organic disease. Our experience suggests that poorly differentiated distress states in severely and profoundly retarded persons are frequently manifested by disturbance in gastrointestinal functions, with presentations of mouthing, rumination, and regurgitation serving to discharge organismic tension and self-soothe.

One of the most important criteria in establishing a diagnosis of nonorganic failure to thrive has been the achievement of significant weight gain when the child is hospitalized. However, it is recognized that clinical improvement can only be maintained if the interpersonal aspects of feeding are addressed within the primary caretaking relationship. Interpersonal qualities that accommodate to the patient's individual style

Table 20-1. *DSM III Axis I Psychiatric Diagnoses*

Psychiatric Diagnoses	Retardation Level: Severe/Profound (N = 92)	
	N	%
Psychotic disorders	28	30
Pervasive developmental disorders	18	20
(i) Autism	7	8
(ii) Autism with psychosis	3	3
(iii) Childhood-onset PDD	5	5
(iv) Childhood-onset PDD with psychosis	3	3
Affective disorders	12	13
(i) Depressive disorder	9	9
(ii) Bipolar, manic, cyclothymic	3	3
Anxiety disorders	9	9
(i) Overanxious	6	6
(ii) Phobic	2	2
(iii) Obsessive-compulsive	1	1
Adjustment disorders	12	13
Movement disorders (stereotypies)	15	16
Psychological factors affecting physical condition	7	7
(i) Eating disorders	4	4
(ii) Failure to thrive	3	3
Conduct disorder	7	7
No Axis I diagnosis	9	9

Table 20-2. *DSM III Axis III Physical Diagnoses*

Diagnosis	Retardation Level: Severe/Profound (N = 92)
Seizure disorder	23
Blindness	16
Impaired vision	7
Cerebral palsy	15
Down syndrome	15
Hearing impaired	9
Emaciation	6
No Axis III diagnosis	24 = 26%

Other diagnoses: Phenylketonuria, tuberous sclerosis, neurofibromatosis, systemic lupus erythematosus, myeloma, CNS malformation, CNS trauma, post-meningitis, hypothyroidism, hypertension.

DSM III[4] with its multi-axial approach to evaluation was used in 92 severely and profoundly retarded adult patients ranging in age from 16 to 65 years who were referred for psychiatric consultation. DSM III, Axis I describes the clinical psychiatric syndromes, and conditions not attributable to a mental disorder, that were the foci of attention and treatment (see Table 20-1). Axis III describes coexisting physical disorders and conditions in the patients (see Table 20-2). Axis II diagnoses, e.g., personality and specific developmental disorders, were considered to be virtually impossible to assess in this population.

It can be seen that psychotic disorders accounted for 30% of the diagnoses. The patients were nonverbal and could not demonstrate the necessary hallucinations or delusions of a formal thought disorder; therefore they did not meet the criteria for schizophrenia, and the diagnosis was usually an atypical psychosis. Psychosis usually presented with such features as perplexity, egocentricity, profound withdrawal, flat, unpredictable, or incongruous affect, behavioral disorganization and agitation, and grimacing or unusual mannerisms.

Pervasive developmental disorders (PDD) accounted for 20% of the diagnoses with 10 autistic patients (3 with intercurrent psychosis, including 1 with bipolar disorder) and 8 with childhood onset pervasive developmental disorder (3 with intercurrent psychosis). Age of onset differed between these two groups, autism presenting before 30 months of age and childhood-onset PDD after 30 months of age, information that could be gleaned from the records. Degree of impairment in social relationships also differed, autistic patients showing pervasive lack of social responsiveness

and preference are critical in establishing the emotional harmony necessary for synchronous exchanges in the feeding situation. Scheduling of assisted feeding, which is often required for the severely or profoundly retarded person, should allow for a relaxed, unhurried approach to meals that does not overtax the patient's ability to integrate the feeding experience into a satisfying physical and interpersonal exchange. It should also be recognized that multiple unfamiliar caretakers present problems in mutual adaptation and increase the risk of failure to thrive in developmentally immature patients who are irregular and dysrhythmic in their physiologic functions.

SPECTRUM OF CATEGORICAL DIAGNOSES

A categorical approach to diagnosis does not state all that could, and should, be said about a patient, but it does provide a data base for comparison of characteristics within patient groups. The objective descriptive diagnostic criteria of and childhood onset PDD patients showing inappropriate responsivity, which might include clinging, asociality, or lack of empathy. These patients also differed in their responses to aspects of the environment, the autistic patients showing bizarre responses to the environment or peculiar interest in animate or inanimate objects, and patients with childhood-onset PDD showing unusually strong anxiety responses and sensitivity to sensory stimuli. Both groups showed resistance to change in routine, and self-mutilation.

Thirteen percent of patients had an affective disorder, including 9% with depressive disorder, 1 with bipolar, 1 with manic, and 1 with cyclothymic disorder. The depressed patients were for the most part sad, apathetic, and joyless, with psychomotor agitation or retardation and vegetative symptoms of appetite and sleep disturbance. Anxiety disorders were present in 9% of patients, who were notable for their vigilance, hyperattentiveness, motor tension, and autonomic hyperactivity. Adjustment disorder or situational disturbance accounted for 13% of cases, and 16% showed movement disorders, including motor tics and stereotypies, which often included self-injurious behavior. Seven percent had psychophysiological disorders, including 4 with eating disorders and 3 with failure to thrive. Another 7% had conduct disorders, usually with aggressive behavior, with or without social attachment to their peer group. Only 9% of this population had no psychiatric diagnosis in addition to their retardation, and this probably reflected their preselection for psychiatric services. The 92 patients were part of a potential referral pool of approximately 300 patients (the numbers fluctuated over the 2-year period of the study as deinstitutionalization was being vigorously implemented).

The distribution of diagnostic categories suggests that this population has a notably high prevalence of pervasive developmental disorder, psychotic disturbance, and movement disorder in addition to other psychiatric diagnoses.

DSM III, Axis III diagnoses of physical disorders and conditions are noted in Table 20-2 and highlight the high incidence of seizure disorder, cerebral palsy, blindness, and Down syndrome in this population, with an interesting 26% of patients showing no specific physical diagnosis but having at least hypothesized CNS dysfunction because of their level of retardation.

OBSERVATIONS

A broad spectrum of acute, recurrent, and chronic psychiatric conditions can be identified in severely and profoundly retarded persons. When these conditions are recognized and treated, the patients' physical health, adaptive capacities, and ability to participate in educational and rehabilitative programs can be improved. Health care professionals need to be aware of the limited but nevertheless significant repertoire of affective, behavioral, and somatic symptoms by which this nonverbal population communicates emotional distress so that critical presentations can be referred for psychiatric assessment. When these presentations are unrecognized and untreated, psychiatric disturbance in the severely and profoundly retarded may fall prey to either therapeutic nihilism or overly conscientious pursuit of inappropriate interventions. Psychiatry in turn needs to become more cognizant of the special problems that complicate the mental status assessment and bio-psycho-social evaluation of this population so that opportunities for therapeutic intervention are not missed. Experiences reported in this study suggest that close involvement by psychiatry can help to clarify the developmental and psychopathological mechanisms that underly clinical manifestations of distress in the severely and profoundly retarded and that treatment approaches evolving from these perspectives have important benefits for this patient population.

REFERENCES

1. Bewick, D.M.: Non-organic failure to thrive. *In* Pediatrics in Review. Vol. 1. Edited by R.J. Haggerty. Elk Grove Village, IL, American Academy of Pediatrics, 1980, pp. 265-270.
2. Costello, A.: Assessment and diagnosis of psychopathology. *In* Psychopathology in the Mentally Retarded. Edited by J.L. Matson and R.P. Barrett. Orlando, FL, Grune & Stratton, 1982.
3. Crome, L.: The brain and mental retardation. Brit. Med. J., *1*:897, 1960.
4. DSM III: Diagnostic and Statistical Manual of Mental Disorders. 3rd Ed. Washington, DC, American Psychiatric Association, 1980.
5. Eisenberg, L.: Psychiatric implication of brain damage in children. Psychiatr. Q., *31*:72, 1957.
6. Engel, G.L.: The need for a new medical model: A challenge for biomedicine. Science, *196*:129, 1977.
7. Freud, A.: Normality and Pathology in Childhood. New York, Hallmark Press, 1965, pp. 150-153.
8. Glaser, H.H., Hegarty, M.C., Bullard, D.M., Jr., and Pivchik, E.C.: Physical and psychological development of children with early failure to thrive. J. Pediatr., *73*:690, 1968.
9. Grunewald, K.: International trends in the care of the severely profoundly retarded and multiple handicapped. *In* Beyond the Limits: Innovations in Services for the Severely and Profoundly Retarded. Edited by F.J. Menolascino and P.H. Pearson. Seattle, Bernie Straub, 1974.

10. Heaton-Ward, A.: Psychosis in mental handicap. Br. J. Psychiatry, 130:525, 1977.
11. Menking, M., et al.: Rumination, a near fatal psychiatric disease of infancy. N. Engl. J. Med., 280:802, 1969.
12. Newberger, C.M., Newberger, E.H., and Harper, G.P.: The social ecology of malnutrition in childhood. In Malnutrition and Intellectual Development. Edited by J.D. Lloyd-Still. Littleton, MA, Publishing Sciences Group, 1976.
13. Piaget, J.: Play, Dreams and Imitation in Childhood. New York, W.W. Norton, 1962.
14. Lakin, K.C., et al.: New admissions and readmissions to a national sample of public residential facilities. Am. J. Ment. Defic., 88:13, 1983.
15. Reid, A.H., and Naylor, G.J.: Short-cycle manic depressive psychosis in mental defectives: A clinical & physiological study. J. Ment. Defic., 20:67, 1976.
16. Richmond, J.B., Eddy, E., and Green, M.: Rumination: A psychosomatic syndrome of infancy. Pediatrics, 22:49, 1958.
17. Rosenthal, P.A., and Doherty, M.B.: Pre-school Depression Scale. Paper presented at annual meeting of American Academy of Child Psychiatry, San Francisco, October 1983.
18. Rutter, M.: Psychiatry. In Mental Retardation. Vol. 3. Edited by J. Wortis. New York, Grune & Stratton, 1971.
19. Rutter, M.: Maternal Deprivation Re-assessed. Harmondsworth, Penguin, 1972.
20. Rutter, M., Graham, P., and Yule, W.: A neuropsychiatric study in childhood. Clin. Dev. Med., 35/36 London SIMP/Heinemann, 1970.
21. Schroeder, R.S., Schroeder, C.S., Smith, B., and Dalldorf, J.: Prevalence of self-injurious behavior in a large facility for the retarded: A three-year follow-up study. Journ. Autism Child. Schizophrenia, 8(3):269, 1978.
22. Spitz, R.A.: Anaclitic depression. An enquiry to the genesis of psychiatric conditions in early childhood. Psychoanal. Study Child, 2:313, 1946.

PSYCHOTROPIC MEDICATION
Mai-Lan Rogoff, M.D.

Mental retardation does not confer immunity to psychiatric disorders, and the problems suffered by the mentally retarded range from minor adjustment reactions to schizophrenia. When diagnosable psychiatric disorders are present, mentally retarded patients respond to appropriate medications in much the same way as do patients in the general population. The major obstacle to optimal use of psychotropic medications with mentally retarded patients lies in the difficulty of making accurate diagnoses. Mentally retarded individuals often have communication difficulties, associated central nervous system abnormalities, and maladaptive coping behaviors. These all contribute both to the problem of making diagnoses and to that of evaluating side effects of medications. In addition, mentally retarded patients may respond to unusually low doses or require unusually high ones, as in many conditions involving central nervous system dysfunction.

The physician prescribing psychotropic medications for mentally retarded patients must weigh more than the usual risks and benefits. The risk of further compromising cognitive ability or ability to respond to behavioral programming through the use of tranquilizers is an often cited caveat. Conversely, the benefit of being able to remain in the community rather than being reinstitutionalized or being "demoted" to a more supervised living situation is not trivial. There may also be consequences to having the neighbors call the police yet another time to a community residence. Families, guardians, judges, other professionals on the team, and the patient himself often have strong feelings regarding the use of psychotropic medications. Capabilities beyond the actual effects of the drugs, both beneficial and negative, are often attributed to them.

The courts have also entered the arena of prescription of psychotropic medications, providing both needed protection against abuse to some mentally retarded clients and constraints on the prescribing physician that may not serve others. Wyatt versus Stickney[77,78] established minimal and reasonable guidelines against indiscriminate use of psychotropic medication. Many other cases have followed this approach. Other decisions, such as Welsch versus Likens[74,75] or Doe versus Hudspeth,[17] take upon the legal system prerogatives usually assumed by the physician, such as mandating yearly drug-free periods or prohibiting the giving of neuroleptics in divided doses. Constraints may also be imposed on the prescribing physician by other agencies, such as the prohibition of prn schedules, further complicating the picture. The physician can easily be caught between the Scylla of attempting to respond to all behavioral ills with psychotropic medications and the Charybdis of therapeutic nihilism.

It is important to keep in mind that drug intervention is only one component of an integrated treatment plan in which environmental support and behavioral/psychodynamic therapies play a prominent role. Psychotropic medications are not a substitute for adequate staff, consistent and supportive environment or consideration of intrapsychic factors, but they are very helpful in conjunction with all these factors. When appropriately used, they can help mentally handicapped people to function as effectively as possible in the community and to feel accepted as useful members of society.

This section of the chapter will examine evidence for effectiveness of psychotropic medications in the treatment of common behavioral syndromes in mentally retarded patients, current prescribing practices, and the question of the effect of psychotropic medications on learning.

EFFICACY OF PSYCHOTROPIC MEDICATION IN MENTALLY RETARDED PATIENTS

Psychotropic medications are widely used with mentally retarded patients. Among institutionalized retarded people, 40 to 50% have been shown to be receiving neuroleptics.[16,39,50,62,67,71] Thioridazine, chlorpromazine, and haloperidol account for most of this drug use. The prevalence of use of other classes of psychotropics in institutions is less than 10%.[11,39,40,67] Fewer studies of drug use in noninstitutionalized mentally retarded people have been done. Davis, Cullari, and Breuning[14] found that almost 60% of mentally retarded people in supervised community residences were taking neuroleptics, less than 10% were taking anxiolytics or stimulants, and very few were given antidepressants or lithium.

Despite the widespread use of psychotropic medications by retarded individuals, controversy regarding the effectiveness of these drugs continues to exist. Studies attempting to measure the effectiveness of medications in this population are hampered by several factors. Evaluation of drug effects has to take into consideration the level of retardation, past and present experience of institutional living, and indications for which the medication was originally prescribed. Many of the early studies did not use placebo controls, random assignment of patients, or blind raters. In addition, most studies of the effectiveness of psychotropic medications have been done in institutions, despite the fact that most retarded people do not live in this setting.

Several comprehensive reviews of the literature regarding use of psychotropic medications with mentally retarded individuals have suggested that no medication improves the level of intellectual functioning but that, for well-selected individuals, psychotropic medications are helpful in improving feelings of well-being and in decreasing some maladaptive behaviors.[20,40,58,69] Although medications are most effective when prescribed on the basis of psychiatric diagnosis, consultation requests are generally made on the basis of symptoms. Some of these symptoms, such as aggression, can be quite compelling, leading to an almost inevitable temptation to try to control target symptoms without adequate regard for diagnosis. The nonspecific nature of the effect of psychotropics on agitation, shifting criteria for psychiatric diagnoses, and overlap of symptoms in some of the psychiatric syndromes compounds the problem. When used to treat specific psychiatric syndromes, medications are quite effective: they maintain their effectiveness over time and prevent recurrence of symptoms, which often follow discontinuation of the drug.[81]

Once a diagnosis has been made and the appropriate medication selected, the easiest way to assess the usefulness of medications is by following target symptoms. It may be useful to think of the clinical trial of medication in an individual as a study of the usefulness of that particular medication in a population with an "n" of one. Although placebo controls and a double-blind design are difficult to achieve in the clinical setting, a standardized way of evaluating outcome and the use of several observers are helpful. Target behaviors should be well enough defined that they can be reliably reported by different observers, they should be valid symptoms of the syndrome for which the drug is being prescribed, and should be capable of being changed by the drug. The length of time required for drug washout should also be kept in mind: from about 24 hours for stimulants to 4 to 6 weeks for neuroleptics. Some standardized scales, such as the Brief psychiatric rating scale, the Hamilton scale for depression, or the Connors scale for hyperactivity, are readily available. These are often useful, but items on these scales may not be applicable to some mentally retarded people, especially those who are nonverbal. In this case, modifications of the scales or even simple lists of target behaviors can be used.

SYNDROMES

Behavioral syndromes can be divided into those that are mainly client-reported (e.g., depression, anxiety) and those that tend to be observer-reported (e.g., aggression, agitation, impulsivity). At different levels of mental retardation, the same syndrome may present with different symptoms. With more severely impaired, nonverbal individuals, thought processes and feelings may need to be inferred from behaviors such as hypervigilance, mood lability, or new inappropriate responses. Vegetative signs such as sleep disturbance or change in appetite may become the major evidence of psychiatric disturbance. The problems of adequate diagnosis are amply discussed in the previous section in this chapter by Doherty and Szymanski.

Psychosis

The syndromes causing psychotic symptoms of loss of contact with reality and accompanying agitation or confusion are the major affective disorders (manic illness, psychotic depression), schizophrenia, atypical psychosis, and the organic psychoses. The possibility of psychotic symptoms on the basis of dementia is of particular concern in individuals with Down syndrome.[10,52]

Neuroleptics have been shown to have nonspecific effects on such symptoms as hyperactivity, aggression, appetite, and sleep disturbances,[40] and some patients improve when neuroleptics are discontinued.[42,47] Of the three most commonly used neuroleptics, thioridazine, chlorpromazine, and haloperidol, none has been shown to be more effective than another in treating psychotic symptoms. Choice of medication thus depends more on history of previous response to a drug and to desirable or unwanted side effects such as sedation. The more sedating neuroleptics (e.g., thioridazine and chlorpromazine) have a higher incidence of anticholinergic side effects such as dry mouth, urinary retention and constipation, and postural hypotension than the high-potency neuroleptics such as haloperidol. These have a higher incidence of central nervous system side effects such as akathisia. It has not been demonstrated that any one group has a lower incidence of tardive dyskinesia.

Movement disorders, both iatrogenic and pre-existing, are a major concern in the mentally retarded population. There have been some suggestions that the brain damage often associated with mental retardation may predispose to tardive dyskinesia.[2,29] Tardive dyskinesia has also been described in mentally retarded children taking long-term neuroleptics.[24,26] The more-sedating aliphatic and piperidine phenothiazines may have less tendency to exacerbate preexisting movement disorders[58] and should probably be used in these conditions.

Other side effects may present in novel ways. The discomfort of akathisia may manifest as aggression[33] or as agitation and mood lability. Corneal and lenticular opacities[25] may present as self-injurious behavior or agitation if they proceed to the stage in which vision becomes disturbed. Side effects are of particular concern when they are persistent, as in tardive dyskinesia, and in the rare but potentially fatal case of neuroleptic malignant syndrome. Vigilance on the part of the physician is necessary in monitoring for side effects in mentally retarded individuals who may not be able to describe them accurately.

Psychotic symptoms may also be a part of the manic phase of bipolar illness, which has been well described in mentally retarded individuals.[27,51,59] Manic hyperactivity and irritability are more likely to be the presenting symptoms than are flight of ideas or grandiosity. Although the nonspecific effects of the neuroleptics may be used in the acute treatment of manic excitement, lithium remains the more definitive treatment and prophylaxis against future episodes.[46,59] Again, caution must be exercised in monitoring for side effects of lithium. Gastrointestinal discomfort, for example, may present as irritability and aggression rather than as loss of appetite.

Institutionalized patients may have trouble maintaining fluid and electrolyte balance if they do not have free access to water or if drinking water is involved in control issues with staff. The problem of reversible encephalopathy despite a lithium blood level in the therapeutic range may be more common in patients already suffering from cerebral dysfunction.[57] When lithium is used with appropriate caution, however, it is an extremely useful adjunct to other forms of treatment and environmental management.

Antidepressants have been shown to be useful in treatment of depression in mentally retarded patients.[20,40,69] Considering the frequency of this illness in retarded and nonretarded populations,[51,66] the low reported use of antidepressants with mentally retarded individuals is surprising. It may be that depression is not being diagnosed as often as it occurs. Unlike the neuroleptics and possibly lithium, tricyclics have not been shown to have nonspecific effects. Newer uses for antidepressants such as attention-deficit disorder[38] and panic disorder[63,64] have yet to be investigated with the mentally retarded population.

Anxiety Disorders

Anxiety and its more severe cousin agitation are two of the most common behavioral problems in mentally retarded people. The benzodiazepines and related compounds have been the traditional drugs of choice for the syndrome of simple anxiety, whereas the neuroleptics are generally used in the management of agitation. Benzodiazepines may produce paradoxical effects of rage instead of calm. This effect may be more common in patients such as those with mental retardation, who often have central nervous system compromise.[72]

Use of benzodiazepines for management of anxiety in the nonretarded population is generally done on a prn schedule to minimize the amount of drug used and to decrease the probability of physical dependence. Mentally retarded patients, however, may have defects in judgment and are often prevented from regulating their own medication schedules. On the other hand, allowing the staff to choose when to administer medication raises the fear of chemical restraint. The unfortunate consequence is that prn schedules are often prohibited in this population, making management of anxiety with benzodiazepines more difficult. Low-dose neuroleptics are often substituted. These may be effective, but they expose the patient to an increased risk of side effects, including tardive dyskinesia.

Data on frequency of physical dependence on benzodiazepines are conflictual.[23,76] These drugs remain optimal for short-term management of anxiety. Longer-term use of benzodiazepines, especially on a regular schedule, requires frequent medication review with attention to the possibility of development of tolerance and dependence.

The other major group of medications used in anxiety management are the beta blockers such as propranolol. In small doses (10 mg qid) these agents are thought to reduce anxiety by blocking the peripheral manifestations.[12] Part of the mechanism of anxiety reduction may be the reduction of anticipatory anxiety, raising questions about the efficacy of beta blockers with mentally retarded people.

Aggressive Behavior

Aggressive behavior in mentally retarded patients tends to represent difficulty with impulse control rather than premeditated violence. Aggressive and assaultive behavior is a frequent reason for psychiatric consultation and makes community placement difficult. Aggressive mentally retarded individuals may have impulse-control disorders on the basis of frontal or temporal lobe dysfunction and often have past or present environmental stresses or aggressive role models. The DSM III lists at least 20 syndromes in which aggressive behavior may be one of the symptoms. These include manic excitement, adjustment disorders, attention-deficit disorder with hyperactivity, conduct disorder, organic personality syndromes, and the psychotic disorders. In addition, aggressive behavior in severely retarded individuals may represent a developmental phase which would be normal in a 2-year-old, for example, but which becomes more threatening in a 250-lb man.

Unfortunately, no medication has nonspecific, reliable antiaggressive effects. Early drugs used included the barbiturates, which may themselves produce a behavioral syndrome including irritability, mood lability, and assaultiveness.[31,55] Similar problems attend the use of benzodiazepines for rapid control of agitation and aggression,[22] although benzodiazepines are useful in some cases.[28] Neuroleptics have been shown to be effective in many cases of impulsive, assaultive behavior.[19–21,30,34–37,70] Their major drawbacks are the risk of serious side effects, possibility of decreased learning, and amount of sedation required to produce behavioral control. Nevertheless, the neuroleptics remain useful first-line drugs.

Lithium has been used successfully in the treatment of aggressive states.[13] Because aggression may be part of a manic presentation, it is unclear whether this effect of lithium represents a nonspecific effect on irritability and aggression or whether the subjects who respond to lithium have an atypical presentation of a bipolar illness. DeLong[15] has reported successful use of lithium in treatment of aggression in children with organic encephalopathy and without evident manic symptoms other than aggression, suggesting that there may be at least some nonspecific effect. Use of lithium in the absence of manic symptoms, however, remains experimental.

Propranolol has been described as useful in treatment of explosive rage and aggression in patients with acute and chronic brain syndromes.[18,61,65,79,80] The mechanism is unclear, although Yudofsky has speculated that there may be some central disinhibition of the rage response or that the peripheral actions of the beta blockers may act to diminish the intensity of the stress response. Rage then decreases as a secondary response to perceived stress. Propranolol is contraindicated in patients with bronchial spasm and various cardiac conditions. Toxic psychosis has also been reported in patients taking even low doses of propranolol,[54] and use of propranolol in combination with a neuroleptic has been reported to lead to toxic effects.[43]

Other medications have been tried in the management of rageful, impulsive behavior. Stimulants have been reported to be successful in patients with attention-deficit disorder with hyperactivity and aggression as part of their syndrome.[56] DeLong[15] notes that children who respond to stimulants with reduction of aggressive behavior do not respond to lithium, and vice versa. Anticonvulsants have been used in treatment of epileptiform episodic dyscontrol syndrome,[41,44] although this syndrome appears to be rare, at best, in mentally retarded patients. An interictal syndrome of intense affects and responses has been described in temporal lobe epilepsy, which is not uncommonly seen in retarded patients.[73] Management of this syndrome is complex because it appears even in the face of adequate control of seizures.

Recently, the anticonvulsant carbamezine has come under investigation for its behavioral effects, mainly as an anti-manic agent[6,45] and in excited schizophrenia.[32] It also has been described as effective in reducing lifelong symptoms of hyperactivity and irritability in a group of severely retarded adults.[53] Because of the possible interrelationships of aggression and temporal lobe dysfunction,[5,48,49,60] carbamezine may represent another medication to use in certain cases of aggression.

EFFECT OF PSYCHOTROPIC MEDICATIONS ON LEARNING

There has been much interest in the question of whether psychotropic medications impair or aid learning when used with mentally retarded patients. This group is already at a cognitive disadvantage, and quieting behavior would not be an adequate trade for decreased learning. In addition, there is concern that neuroleptics may decrease response to behavioral programming. Behavioral methods have been shown in numerous studies to be helpful in decreasing maladaptive behaviors in retarded individuals. If, on the other hand, medications increase concentration, either directly or by decreasing interfering thoughts and feelings, this effect would be very helpful.

Methylphenidate has been found to increase alertness, attention, and concentration in mentally retarded patients.[7,8] Similar improvements have been described with amphetamines.[1,4]

Methylphenidate is usually prescribed for attention-deficit disorder, many of the symptoms of which are found in patients with mental retardation even without attention-deficit disorder. This is especially true of associated features such as stubbornness, negativism, low frustration tolerance, temper outbursts, and low self-esteem, but it is also true of the primary symptoms of poor concentration and high distractibility. Caution therefore needs to be exercised in making this diagnosis in the presence of mental retardation. The DSM III suggests that it not be made in the presence of severe or profound retardation. Because of the possibility of decreased rather than increased learning and because of

other side effects of methylphenidate such as precipitation of organic psychosis or manic attacks, use of stimulants should be restricted to instances in which there is an attention and concentration deficit beyond the normal range for that level of retardation. Stimulants have been described as less effective for the associated symptoms of attention-deficit disorder and are not indicated when symptoms such as stubbornness and negativism are the primary concern.[68]

The major class of psychotropics suspected of causing impaired learning is the class most frequently prescribed: the neuroleptics. Several studies have suggested that neuroleptics may decrease both learning and response to behavioral programming.[20,40,58,69] Discontinuation of neuroleptics will at times result in an improvement in learning behavior performance,[42] particularly if they have been inappropriately prescribed. A similar situation has been reported for diazepam.[3]

The absolute effect of neuroleptics on learning and speed of information processing is unclear. Chlorpromazine has been shown to aid certain types of information processing in normal subjects, and Braff and Saccuzzo[9] demonstrated similar effects in schizophrenic subjects. Agitation, depression, and psychotic loss of concentration also impair learning; presumably when psychotropic medications improve these underlying conditions they leave the patient more available for learning. Nevertheless it appears that attention has to be paid to a possible decrease in capacity for learning and response to behavioral programming when psychotropics are prescribed.

REFERENCES

1. Alexandris, A., and Lundell, F.: Effect of thioridazine, amphetamine, and placebo on hyperkinetic syndrome and cognitive area in mentally deficient children. Can. Med. Assoc. J., 98:92, 1968.
2. Ananth, J.: Drug induced dyskinesia: A critical review. Int. Pharmacopsychiatry, 14:21, 1980.
3. Angus, W.R., and Romney, D.M.: The effect of diazepam on patients' memory. J. Clin. Psychopharmacol., 4:203, 1984.
4. Anton, A.H., and Greer, M.: Dextroamphetamine, catecholamines, and behavior: The effect of dextroamphetamine in retarded children. Arch. Neurol., 21:248, 1969.
5. Ashford, J.W., Schulz, C., and Walsh, G.O.: Violent automatism in a partial complex seizure: Report of a case. Arch. Neurol., 37(2):120, 1980.
6. Ballenger, J.C., and Post, R.M.: Carbamezine (Tegretol) in manic-depressive illness: A new treatment. Am. J. Psychiatry, 1137:782, 1980.
7. Blackridge, V.Y., and Ekblad, R.L.: The effectiveness of methylphenidate hydrochloride (Ritalin) on learning

and behaviour in public school educable mentally retarded children. Pediatrics, *47*:923, 1971

8. Blue, A.W., Lytton, G.J., and Miller, O.W.: The effect of methylphenidate on intellectually handicapped children. Am. Psychologist, *15*:393, 1960.

9. Braff, D.L., and Saccuzzo, D.P.: Effect of antipsychotic medication on speed of information processing in schizophrenic patients. Am. J. Psychiatry, *139*(9):1127, 1982.

10. Burger, P.C., and Vogel, F.S.: The development of the pathologic changes of Alzheimer's disease and senile dementia in patients with Down's Syndrome. Am. J. Pathol., *73*:457, 1973.

11. Cohen, M.N., and Sprague, R.L.: Survey of drug use in two midwestern institutions for the retarded. Paper presented at the Gatlinburg Conference on Mental Retardation, Gatlinburg, TN, March 1977 as cited in Matson, J.L., and Barrett, R.P.: Psychopathology in the Mentally Retarded. New York, Grune & Stratton, 1982, p. 209.

12. Cole, J.O., Altesman, R.I., and Weingarten, C.H.: Beta blocking drugs in psychiatry. McLean Hosp. J., *4*:40, 1979.

13. Dale, P.G.: Lithium therapy in aggressive mentally subnormal patients. Br. J. Psychiatry, *137*:469, 1980.

14. Davis, V.J., Cullari, S., and Breuning, S.E.: Drug use in community group foster homes. *In* Drugs and Mental Retardation. Edited by S.E. Breuning and A.D. Poling. Springfield, IL, Charles C Thomas, 1982.

15. DeLong, R.: Use of lithium in impulsive disorders in children. Paper presented at Psychiatry Grand Rounds, University of Massachusetts Medical Center, Worcester, MA, 1984.

16. DiMascio, A.: An examination of actual medication usage in retardation institutions. Paper presented at the American Association on Mental Deficiency Conference, Portland, OR, May 1975.

17. Doe v. Hudspeth. Civil No. J75-36 (S.D.Miss., filed Feb. 17, 1977).

18. Elliott, F.A.: Propranolol for the control of belligerent behavior following acute brain damage. Ann. Neurol., *1*:489, 1977.

19. Ferguson, D.G., and Breuning, S.E.: Antipsychotic and antianxiety drugs. *In* Drugs and Mental Retardation. Edited by S.E. Breuning and A.D. Poling. Springfield, IL, Charles C Thomas, 1982.

20. Freeman, R.D.: Psychopharmacology and the retarded child. *In* Psychiatric Approaches to Mental Retardation. Edited by J. Menolascino. New York, Basic Books, 1970, pp. 294-368.

21. Grabowski, S.W.: Safety and effectiveness of haloperidol for mentally retarded behaviorally disordered and hyperkinetic patients. Curr. Ther. Res., *15*:856, 1973.

22. Greenblatt, D.J., and Shader, R.I.: Psychotropic drugs in the general hospital. *In* Manual of Psychiatric Therapeutics. Edited by R.I. Shader. Boston, Little Brown, 1975, pp. 1-26.

23. Greenblatt, D.J., and Shader, R.I.: Dependence, tolerance and addiction to benzodiazepines. Drug Metab. Rev., *8*:13, 1978.

24. Gualtieri, C.T., Barnhill, J., McGinsey, J., and Schell, D.: Tardive dyskinesia and other movement disorders in children treated with psychotropic drugs. J. Am. Acad. Child Psychiatry, *19*(3):491, 1980.

25. Gualtieri, C.T., Lefler, W.H., Guimond, M., and Staye, J.I.: Corneal and lenticular opacities in mentally retarded young adults treated with thioridazine and chlorpromazine. Am. J. Psychiatry, *139*:1178, 1982.

26. Gualtieri, C.T., Quade, D., Hicks, R.E., Mayo, J.P., and Schroeder, S.R.: Tardive dyskinesia and other clinical consequences of neuroleptic treatment in children and adolescents. Am. J. Psychiatry, *141*:20, 1984.

27. Hasan, M., and Mooney, R.P. Three cases of manic-depressive illness in mentally retarded adults. Am. J. Psychiatry, *136*:1069, 1979.

28. Itil, T.M., and Wadud, A.: Human aggression with major tranquilizers, antidepressants and newer psychotropic drugs. J. Nerv. Ment. Dis., *160*:83, 1975.

29. Jeste, D.P., and Wyatt, R.J.: Tardive dyskinesia: The syndrome. Psychiatr. Ann., *10*:6, 1980.

30. Kaplan, S.: Double blind study at state institution using thiorizadine in program simulating out-patient clinic practice. Penn. Psychiatry Q., *9*:24, 1969.

31. Kirman, B.: Drug therapy in the mentally handicapped. Br. J. Psychiatry, *127*:545, 1975.

32. Klein, E., Bental, E., Lerer, B., and Belmaker, R.H.: Carbamezine and haloperidol versus placebo and haloperidol in excited psychoses. Arch. Gen. Psychiatry, *41*:165, 1984.

33. Kumar, B.B.: An unusual case of akasthisia. Am. J. Psychiatry, *136*(8):1088, 1979.

34. Lacny, J.: Mesoridazine in the care of disturbed mentally retarded patients. Can. Psychiatry Assoc. J., *18*:389, 1973.

35. LeVann, L.J.: Haloperidol in the treatment of behavioral disorders in children and adolescents. Can. Psychiatry Assoc. J., *14*:217, 1969.

36. LeVann, L.J.: Clinical experience with Tarasan and thioridazine in mentally retarded children. Appl. Ther., *12*:30, 1970.

37. LeVann, L.J.: Clinical comparison of haloperidol with chlorpromazine in mentally retarded children. Am. J. Ment. Defic., *75*:719, 1971.

38. Linnoila, M., Gualtieri, C.T., Jobson, K., and Staye, J.: Characteristics of the therapeutic response to imipramine in hyperactive children. Am. J. Psychiatry, *136*(9):1201, 1979.

39. Lipman, R.S.: The use of pharmacological agents in residential facilities for the retarded. *In* Psychiatric Approaches to Mental Retardation. Edited by F. Menolascino, New York, Basic Books, 1970.

40. Lipman, R.S., DiMascio, A., Reatig, N., and Kirson, T.: Psychotropic drugs and mentally retarded children. *In* Psychopharmacology, a Generation of Progress. Edited by R.S. Lipman, A. DiMascio, and K.F. Killam. New York, Raven Press, 1978, pp. 1437-1449.

41. Maletsky, B.M., and Klotter, J.: Episodic control: A controlled replication. Dis. Nerv. System, *35*:175, 1974.

42. Marholin, D., Touchette, P.E., and Stewart, R.M.: Withdrawal of chronic chlorpromazine medication: An experimental analysis. J. Appl. Behav. Anal., *12*(2):159, 1979.

43. Miller, F.A., and Rampling, D.: Adverse effects of combined propranolol and chlorpromazine therapy. Am. J. Psychiatry, *139*(9):1198, 1982.

44. Monroe, R.: Anticonvulsants in the treatment of aggression. J. Nerv. Dis., *160*:119, 1975.

45. Moss, G.R., and James, C.R.: Carbamezine and lithium carbonate synergism in mania. Arch. Gen. Psychiatry, *40*:588, 1983.

46. Naylor, G.J., Donald, J.M., and LePoidevin, D.: A double-blind trial of lithium therapy in mental defectives. Br. J. Psychiatry, *124*:52, 1974.

47. Paul, G.L., Tobias, L.I., and Holly, B.L.: Maintenance sychotropic drugs in the presence of active treatment programs: "Triple blind" withdrawal study with long term mental patients. Arch. Gen. Psychiatry, *27*:106, 1972.

48. Pinel, J.P., Treit, D., and Rovner, L.I.: Temporal lobe aggression in rats. Science, *197*(4308):1088, 1977.

49. Post, R.M., Uhde, T.W., Ballenger, J.C., and Bunney, W.E., Jr.: Carbamezine, temporal lobe epilepsy, and manic-depressive illness. *In* Advances in Biological Psychiatry. Vol. 8. Temporal Lobe Epilepsy, Mania and Schizophrenia and the Limbic System. Edited by W.P. Koella and M.R. Trimble. Basel, Switzerland, S. Karger, pp. 117-156.

50. Pullman, R.M., Pook, R.B., and Singh, N.: Prevalence of drug therapy for institutionalized mentally retarded children. Austr. J. Ment. Retard., *5*:212, 1979.

51. Reid, A.H.: Psychosis in adult mental defectives: I. Manic-depressive psychosis. Br. J. Psychiatry, *120*:205, 1972.

52. Reid, A.H., and Aungle, P.G.: Dementia in aging mental defectives: A clinical psychiatric study. J. Ment. Defic. Res., *18*:15, 1974.

53. Reid, A.H., Naylor, G.J., and Kay, D.S.G.: A double-blind, placebo controlled, crossover trial of carbamezine in overactive, severely mentally handicapped patients. Psychol. Med., *11*:109, 1981.

54. Remick, R.A., O'Kane, J., and Sparling, T.G.: A case report of toxic psychosis with low-dose propranolol therapy. Am. J. Psychiatry, *138*:297, 1981.

55. Reynolds, E.: Antiepileptic toxicity: A review. Epilepsia, *16*:319, 1975.

56. Richmond, J.S., Young, J.R., and Groves, J.E.: Violent dyscontrol responsive to d-amphetamine. Am. J. Psychiatry, *135*:365, 1978.

57. Rifkin, A., Quitkin, F., and Klein, D.F.: Organic brain syndrome during lithium carbonate treatment. Comp. Psychiatry, *14*:251, 1973.

58. Rivinus, T.M.: Psychopharmacology and the mentally retarded patient. *In* Emotional Disorders of Mentally Retarded Persons. Edited by L.S. Szymanski, and P. Tanguay. Baltimore, University Park Press, 1980, pp. 195-221.

59. Rivinus, T.M., and Harmatz, J.S.: Diagnosis and lithium treatment of affective disorder in the retarded: Five case studies. Am. J. Psychiatry, *136*:551, 1979.

60. Rodin, E.A.: Psychomotor epilepsy and aggressive behavior. Arch. Gen. Psychiatry, *28*(2):210, 1973.

61. Schreier, H.A.: Use of propranolol in the treatment of postencephalitic psychosis. Am. J. Psychiatry, *136*:840, 1979.

62. Sewell, J., and Werry, J.S.: Some studies in an institution for the mentally retarded. N.Z. Med. J., *84*:317, 1976.

63. Sheehan, D.V.: Current concepts in psychiatry: Panic attacks and phobias. N. Engl. J. Med., *307*(3):156, 1982.

64. Sheehan, D.V., Claycomb, J.B., and Kouretas, N.: Monoamine oxidase inhibitors: Prescription and patient management. Int. J. Psychiatry Med., *10*(2):99, 1980-81.

65. Sheppard, G.P.: High dose propranolol in schizophrenia. Br. J. Psychiatry, *134*:470, 1979.

66. Sovner, R., and Hurley, A.D.: Do the mentally retarded suffer from affective illness? Arch. Gen. Psychiatry, *40*(1):61, 1983.

67. Sprague, R.L.: Overview of psychopharmacology for the retarded in the United States. *In* Research to Practice in Mental Retardation—Biomedical Aspects. Vol. 3. Edited by P. Mittler. Baltimore, University Park Press, 1977.

68. Sprague, R.L., and Sleator, E.K.: Methylphenidate in hyperkinetic syndrome: Differences in dose effects on learning and social behavior. Science, *198*:1274, 1977.

69. Sprague, R.L., and Werry, J.S.: Methodology of psychopharmacological studies with the retarded. *In* International Review of Research in Mental Retardation. Vol. 5. Edited by N.R. Ellis. New York, Academic Press, 1971, pp. 147-219.

70. Tischler, B., Patriasz, K., Beresford, J., and Bunting, R.: Experience with pericyazine in profoundly and severely retarded children. Can. Med. Assoc. J., *106*:136, 1972.

71. Tu, J., and Smith, J.T.: Factors associated with psychotropic medication in mental retardation facilities. Compr. Psychiatry, *20*:289, 1979.

72. Walters, A., Singh, N., and Beale, I.L.: Effects of lorazepam on hyperactivity in retarded children. N.Z. Med. J., *86*:473, 1977.

73. Waxman, S.G., and Geschwind, N.: The interictal behavior syndrome of temporal lobe epilepsy. Arch. Gen. Psychiatry, *32*:1580, 1975.

74. Welsch v. Likens. 373 F. Supp. 487 (1974).

75. Welsch v. Likens. 550 F. 2d 1122 (1977).

76. Winokur, A., and Rickels, K.: Withdrawal from long-term, low-dosage administration of diazepam. Arch. Gen. Psychiatry, *37*:101, 1980.

77. Wyatt v. Stickney. 344 F. Supp. 373 (1972) (a).

78. Wyatt v. Stickney. 344 F. Supp. 387 (1972) (b).

79. Yorkstone, N.J., Zaki, S.A., and Pitcher, D.R.: Propranolol as an adjunct to the treatment of schizophrenia. Lancet, *2*:575, 1977.

80. Yudofsky, S., Williams, D., and Gorman, J.: Propranolol in the treatment of rage and violent behavior in patients with chronic brain syndromes. Am. J. Psychiatry, *138*:218, 1981.

81. Zimmerman, R.L., and Heistad, G.T.: Studies of the long term efficacy of antipsychotic drugs in controlling the behavior of institutionalized retardates. J. Am. Acad. Child Psychiatry, *21*(2):136, 1982.

SELF-INJURIOUS BEHAVIOR

Stephen B. Sulkes, M.D.

Philip W. Davidson, Ph.D.

Self-injurious behavior (SIB) is one of the most pervasive and difficult to manage of the behavior problems prevalent among developmentally disabled individuals. In addition to being socially disagreeable and leading to increased isolation from typical persons, SIB by its very nature results in tissue damage and, in extreme cases, additional disability and even death.

DEFINITION

Self-injurious behavior is defined as "repetitive self-inflicted action by an individual, encompassing a number of behaviors and resulting in physical harm and tissue damage."[5] This obviously broad definition reflects the breadth of clinical manifestations that can be shown by SIB as well as the uncertainty among researchers concerning underlying etiologies.

Self-injurious behavior in developmentally disabled persons is apparently different from that seen in psychiatrically impaired individuals with normal intelligence.[41] Unlike the suicidal person who may make repeated attempts to hurt himself, the developmentally disabled patient with SIB abuses himself at a high frequency, from once or twice daily to rates reaching hundreds of times per hour. Moreover, the latter patient usually engages in a particular type of SIB in a highly repetitive and sometimes predictable manner.

PREVALENCE

Variability in definition has resulted in variation in institutional prevalence figures for SIB. In studies from the 1970s,[22,34,38] prevalence rates in the neighborhood of 10 to 15% of clients in long-term residential facilities were common. At present, however, this figure may be an underestimate, because many higher functioning clients have been moved into community settings, leaving as institutional residents persons with behavior problems such as SIB as their major barrier to community living. Moreover, persons with lower cognitive function constitute another group less likely to move out of institutions, and this group is also the one most susceptible to SIB. It is suggested that the fraction of institutional populations with SIB will therefore approach 40% within this decade.

Prevalence data collected in institutional populations consistently show that SIB is more common with increasing cognitive impairment. In various studies,[22,34] it has been found that about 95% of persons with severe SIB function in the severe or profound range of mental retardation. Although several studies have shown a slight female:male predominance,[22] this finding is not supported by other prevalence studies.[34,38] Maisto et al.[22] have reported associations between particular types of SIB and gender (self-biting in females, head-banging in males), but there is much crossover.

THEORIES OF CAUSATION

There is dispute among researchers as to whether the similarity between SIB and stereotypic behavior reflects an organic or behavioral etiologic link between these phenomena.[5] One view is that SIB is an extension of less-injurious stereotypy, with both related to attempts to maintain homeostasis or to reduce stress. In this view, the same underlying forces lead to the aberrant behavior, with the SIB developing as habituation develops to the "less potent" self-stimulus.[5]

Behavioral Precipitants

Behaviorists note a variety of apparent precipitants for SIB. One, as mentioned above, is the "escape from stress" response, in which the patient uses SIB as a diversion from a noxious or stressful situation. This diversion may be external, as in the case of the student who engages in SIB whenever the teacher makes demands, thus "redirecting" the attention of the caretaker from the lesson to protecting the student from harm. Alternatively, the self-injurious individual may be responding to internal cues, engaging in the painful behavior in order to reduce stress caused by other uncomfortable feelings.

Traditionally, SIB has been reported in higher prevalence in long-term residential care facilities than in community settings. One conclusion drawn from this is that SIB is an extreme form of self-stimulation in the less-stimulating environment of the residential facility. Similarly, the view of residential living as being stressful in other ways and leading to SIB for the reason described above also stems from this observation. No data exist, however, to describe the prevalence and severity of this problem in community settings. Moreover, the presence of SIB as a chronic problem may be a precipitant to institutionalization or a barrier to deinstitutionalization, thus reinforcing the perception that this is an institutional problem. Further epidemiologic research is needed to clarify this issue.

When one considers the potency of personal attention as a behavioral reinforcer, it is easy to see that SIB could develop as an attention-getting behavior. Naturally and appropriately, caretaking staff intervene to abort the behavior as quickly as possible. Unfortunately, this well-intentioned reaction may, in the long run, reinforce the undesirable behavior and ultimately make it more difficult to treat.

It has been repeatedly noted that SIB can be seen transiently in developmentally normal infants in the form of head banging or head hitting. In many cases this is associated with the presence of otitis media, but sometimes it is associated with teething. The severely or profoundly retarded individual may still be functioning on the level of such an immature child, and thus SIB could be viewed as an immature coping mechanism. In this model, SIB is seen as an aberrant developmental response.

Normal adults also show occasional self-injurious behaviors in times of stress. An example is the culturally based response of striking a hard object such as a table or wall with the fist when angry or frightened. Whether such a cultural basis is related to SIB in the developmentally disabled population is unclear.

Freudian theory suggests that SIB represents re-creation of an old trauma as a mediator in times of stress. The lack of apparent cognitive abilities to support such a model in the severely or profoundly retarded individual and the lack of communication abilities to analyze such behavior make this theory difficult to substantiate.

It is well recognized that mentally retarded persons with associated sensory handicaps show a higher prevalence of SIB. Of interest is that the SIB in such cases is commonly directed at the organ system that is impaired (e.g., eye-gouging in visually impaired patients, ear-boxing in hearing-impaired clients). That this reflects an attempt to elicit the equivalent of a form of sensory input is a theory that is attractive but difficult to prove. Nevertheless, eye-poking, a relatively uncommon form of SIB in general (0.9% of all SIB in one study), increases 10 times in frequency in visually impaired individuals.[41]

Organic Precipitants

Several identifiable medical conditions have been associated with SIB. The most well known is Lesch-Nyhan syndrome,[7–9,19,26] an X-linked disorder of purine metabolism (deficiency of hypoxanthine-guanine phosphoribosyl transferase). Serum uric acid levels are elevated, and uric acid crystals are excreted in the urine. Patients with this disorder commonly have severe SIB with self-biting as a predominant feature. Such persons chew their lips, tongue, and fingers despite attempts to regulate uric acid excretion, necessitating dental extraction in some cases for protection.[9] In the absence of uric acid as the offending metabolite, abnormalities in two groups of neurotransmitters, serotoninergic and dopaminergic, have been sought, with promising preliminary results both in terms of pathologic correlation[28] and treatment.[20] Although behavioral management is the mainstay of SIB treatment in most cases, it has met with variable success at best in Lesch-Nyhan syndrome.

Another well-described syndrome with SIB as an associated finding is Cornelia De Lange syndrome. This syndrome, without clear underlying etiology, has a number of specific physical features including brachycephaly, hypertrophy of brows and lashes with synophrys (eyebrows meeting over the nasal bridge), small hands and feet (micromelia), and syndactyly. In addition, many persons with this syndrome engage in high rates of SIB. Any of the usual varieties of SIB are

seen here, including self-biting, self-hitting, and head-banging.[25,35]

Another disorder associated with SIB is the Riley-Day syndrome (familial dysautonomia), an autosomal recessive disorder found in descendants of Ashkenazi Jews and occurring at a rate of about 1:10,000 in American Jews. Among the abnormalities found in this syndrome is congenital insensitivity to pain. As in Lesch-Nyhan syndrome, abnormalities in dopaminergic systems have been implicated in several of the findings of Riley-Day syndrome, including SIB.[9,42]

Dopaminergic abnormalities have also been reported in an individual with XXXXY syndrome who engaged in SIB (head-hitting).[18] Whether this is a specific association with this syndrome and whether this patient's dopaminergic abnormalities were endogenous or related to antipsychotic drug (haloperidol, mepazine) treatment require further investigation.

In seeking common organic causes for SIB, several researchers have sought abnormalities in neurotransmitter systems that may be medically treatable. Primrose[30] has suggested abnormalities in neurologic pathways involving gamma-amino-butyric acid (GABA), a neurotransmitter involved largely with inhibitory neuroregulation.

Another neurotransmitter system being investigated vis-à-vis SIB is the endogenous opiate system.[4,10,31,32] Starting from the supposition that persons engaging in SIB on a highly repetitive basis might perceive painful stimuli less markedly than unaffected individuals, the question was raised whether this neurotransmitter/neuroendocrine system involving endogenously produced substances (endorphins) functioning like morphine and other opiate drugs might play a role in the development or maintenance of SIB. A second theory suggests that an associated euphoric effect of these endogenous opiates might act as a positive reinforcement, making the painful self-injury "worthwhile" as a means of stimulating endorphin production. The studies performed to date have used opiate antagonists to block the effects of any endogenous opiates being produced, and have met with success, varying from quantitative decreases in SIB frequency[32] to qualitative decreases in intensity of self-striking.[10] Auto-stimulation of endogenous opiate secretion has been suggested in other settings such as in long-distance runners, who experience a "runner's high," describe feelings of dysphoria when not able to run, and have had elevated serum beta-endorphin levels measured following races.[3] It has been suggested recently that SIB can be reduced by engaging the self-injurious patient in a program of regular exercises, including running, presumably fulfilling the patient's endogenous opiate needs through less destructive means.

CONSEQUENCES OF SELF-INJURIOUS BEHAVIOR

The physical consequences of SIB are seldom insignificant. They may range from relatively mild contusions and callus development to increased disability and even death.

As described above, individuals with Lesch-Nyhan syndrome commonly experience marked damage to the lips and fingers due to self-biting. Bite injuries are commonly associated with infection, which compounds the tissue damage and inhibits healing. Direct treatment can include protection of body parts at risk (e.g., using protective mittens, covering the teeth with mouthguards, or dental extraction).[9] Biting injuries can also be found in other SIB-associated disorders. In Riley-Day syndrome, chewing of fingers, tongue, and cheeks has been described. Other types of gingival and dental injuries have been associated with oral digging[29] and with bruxism and recurrent seizure activity,[13,44] and these should be considered whenever oral lesions are recurrent in the developmentally disabled patient.

Eye injuries are a second area of pervasive problems. The individual who is already visually and cognitively impaired (e.g., in congenital rubella syndrome) and who eye-gouges is at high risk of further loss of vision. "Keratoconjunctivitis artefacta," a term that also includes voluntary self-mutilation, has been used to describe conjunctivitis secondary to recurrent trauma caused by eye-rubbing.[16] Self-enucleation has occurred, as well as uni- or bilateral papilledema due to meningitis of the optic nerve.[23] Other types of eye damage include vitreous hemorrhage, retinal detachment, glaucoma, and corneal laceration.[27]

Injuries to the head are the most common (18.6% of all SIB in one institutional study)[24] and potentially the most damaging effects of SIB. Head-banging on hard surfaces and head-slapping or hitting can occur, with development of skull defects.[40] Thickening of the calvaria can occur due to repeated subperiosteal hemorrhage and separation of cranial sutures, soft-tissue reactions such as skin thickening can take place, and cartilagenous hypertrophy as in cauliflower ear deformity can also occur.[45] Breakdown of the skin can occur, with development of cellulitis or with additional bony trauma, and osteomyelitis can be a complication. With high-intensity SIB to the head, intracranial injury can occur, with attendant increase in neurologic impairment, although this fortunately is an uncommon complication.

Injury directed against other body parts, particularly the extremities, has a prevalence similar to that of head-related injuries.[24] Self-biting, especially common in Lesch-Nyhan syndrome, also occurs in other settings, along with scratching, rubbing, or pinching. Such injuries may involve active hitting of one body part with another, or banging against some inanimate object with an extremity or even the whole torso. Damage to tendon, bone, skin, and soft tissue can occur, as well as damage to internal organs. In such cases the differential diagnosis between patient-abuse and self-injury must be considered.

Yet another cause of chronic injury is digging at orifices and body cavities such as rectum, vagina, or urethra.[24,43] Although these types of SIB may begin as efforts at masturbation (which may also be a concomitant of other SIB types), they may result in blood loss, disordered elimination, decreased hygiene, and loss of support-structural integrity leading to organ prolapse. Again, molestation (by both staff and peers) must be considered in the differential diagnosis for this type of SIB. Naturally, such external abuse may coexist with self-induced trauma, confounding efforts at diagnosis. It should be remembered that persons engaging in SIB generally maintain typical patterns over long periods of time, so the observer should be specially alerted to new or atypical types of trauma.

Some researchers include rumination of regurgitated gastric contents as an additional form of SIB. Although fitting most of the criteria as to high frequency and potential for tissue damage, rumination does not appear to be an inherently painful behavior. Nevertheless, it may have a similar behavioral basis in stereotypy or self-stimulation, and efforts at finding acceptable and safe treatment regimens have been similarly unrewarding.

TREATMENT APPROACHES

Because of the predominantly low cognitive levels of most persons with SIB, most approaches involving volitional teaching, counseling, or psychodynamic methods are impractical or impossible. Moreover, with tissue damage occurring and increasing disability at stake, quick and (one hopes) effective managements must be utilized. Therefore, treatment approaches to management of SIB take two forms: the pharmacologic approaches, which presume that SIB has an organic (presumably neurophysiologic) etiology, and the behavioral techniques, which work on the assumption that SIB, like any behavior, can be modified.

Pharmacologic Approaches

As mentioned above, some forms of SIB have clearly defined etiologies. In Lesch-Nyhan syndrome, for example, attempts to lower uric acid levels in blood and tissues have met with poor results. Theories regarding abnormalities in serotoninergic neurologic pathways have led to the use of 5-hydroxytryptophan, a serotonin precursor, in combination with carbidopa and imipramine to enhance CNS uptake.[20,28] This approach has met with short-lived but promising effects on self-biting in patients with Lesch-Nyhan syndrome.

Increased levels of serotonin have been found in some autistic patients by Geller et al.[15] In preliminary data, interfering behaviors (including SIB) and cognitive function have improved in autistic patients with higher baseline levels of cognitive function with the use of fenfluramine, a sympathomimetic drug used as an appetite suppressant and having the effect of decreasing serum serotonin levels.

Dopaminergic neurons have also been implicated as possible mediators of SIB, particularly on the basis of pathologic findings in Lesch-Nyhan syndrome. Of interest, several of the major phenothiazines (e.g., chlorpromazine) and butyrophenones (e.g., haloperidol) have the effect of blocking dopaminergic receptors. Nevertheless, these are the drugs most commonly used to control SIB in clinical settings.

Work with the gamma-aminobutyric acid (GABA) neurotransmitter system has shown initial promise. Primrose has reported striking improvements in selected patients with SIB with the use of baclofen, a GABA-mimetic agent. Unfortunately, these results have not been replicated to date. Similarly, benzodiazepines, which potentiate the effects of GABA, can sometimes be useful in management of SIB.[14]

It should be recognized that in sufficient doses to result in sedation, any of the above psychoactive drugs will be effective in reducing SIB. In emergency situations when severe damage to life or increased disability is imminent, they should be made available. When used in such doses, they should be considered as short-term management at best, and they should be handled as any other form of pharmacologic restraint in terms of close monitoring and clear, informed consent from responsible advocates.

Other drugs that have been tried in the management of SIB include reserpine,[1] methylphenidate,[2] lithium,[39] mesoridazine,[46] and droperidol.[6] In each case, replication data are needed in order to validate the reported findings.

As mentioned above, another promising area for pharmacologic intervention involves the endogenous opiate system. Although studies to date are preliminary, the possibility of using opiate antagonists to block the effects of endorphins and thus allow the self-induced pain to be perceived may result in marked decreases in injury. Utilizing such blockers as adjuncts to behavioral programs, the euphoric effects may be lessened, allowing for extinction of the undesirable behavior and differential reinforcement of other, more appropriate behaviors. Similarly, using other noninjurious activities such as exercise to stimulate production of endogenous opiates will allow the individual with SIB to continue to self-stimulate, albeit with less injurious and more socially acceptable behaviors.[10,31,32]

Methodological problems are common in drug studies in this population.[36] Variabilities in identification of etiology and target behavior, standardization of observations, and consistency of data collection can make such trials difficult to evaluate. Few studies are placebo-controlled or include crossover designs. Often it is impossible to establish conditions in which those administering drugs or collecting data are blind to treatment regimens. Usually, behavior programs already in place continue during drug treatment, making it difficult to establish which intervention is having an effect. Sample sizes are often small, and controls and minimization of confounding variables are difficult to establish. SIB can vary greatly in frequency and severity over time, and the short-term view may be inadequate while the longer study may suffer from confounding circumstances such as changes in habilitative program or living situation, which are known to precipitate increases in SIB in susceptible individuals. Finally, since most studies are taking place in residential institutions, administrative barriers (often appropriate) erected for client protection may further obstruct "neat" experimental design. All of these factors combine to make it difficult to evaluate the efficacy of drug studies to date. However, research must continue in a well-organized way if conclusive pharmacologic managements for SIB are to be found.

Behavioral Approaches

Behavioral approaches to treatment of SIB fall into four categories: direct suppression and reduction techniques, substitution of competing behaviors, noncontingent techniques, and combinations. Implementation of all of these procedures is quite technical. Also, they will almost always require a setting for administration that permits substantial control over the patient's environment and a high degree of consistency. Each technique is based upon the assumption that the SIB was initially a learned response, or at least that its maintenance depends on the existence of some reward system. In other words, SIB is a response that leads to some reward, from an internal or environmental source, or a combination of the two. As long as the reward is available, the SIB will continue. Each technique is designed to alter the learned bond between occurrence of the SIB and delivery of the reward.

Direct Suppression and Reduction Techniques

Punishment

These techniques involve attempts to reduce the value of emitting SIB responses by arranging negative consequences on each emission. One method of direct suppression of ongoing behavior is punishment. This involves the application of a stimulus perceived by the client as noxious immediately following the occurrence of the undesirable response. Various punishment techniques have been reported in the SIB treatment literature. Physically harmless electric shock, delivered either directly by a hand-held prod or wand or remotely by means of radio-controlled signals to surface electrodes, has been used extensively in a number of treatment programs.[34] Other punishing consequences that have been reported include slapping and verbal reprimands. Punishment procedures, especially those perceived by the client as very noxious, often produce immediate and impressive suppression, but such procedures generally do not lead to permanent suppression of SIB. Only electrical stimulation has been reported to have any durable suppressive effect, usually lasting several months. However, soon after the threat of punishment is removed, the SIB returns.

Extinction

A second, widely used suppression technique is extinction, defined as the removal of positive consequences following emission of the undesirable response. The use of extinction presumes that there is a known or at least suspected reinforcing event maintaining the SIB response. For instance, if the SIB is thought to be instrumental in gaining attention for the patient, extinction would consist of ignoring the patient each time SIB occurs. Extinction as an isolated treatment requires consistent application over many weeks or months, often at a risk of injury to the patient. When used in combination with other techniques, however, its effects can be accelerated.

Time Out from Positive Reinforcement

Suppression can be achieved through time out from positive reinforcement. Time out involves the removal of reward opportunities contingent upon SIB. It differs from extinction in that it is not specific to the stimuli maintaining the SIB. This procedure has been reported as more effective than extinction, but it is logistically difficult to implement because of interference with other habilitative program activities. Also, the isolation situation may actually be rewarding to some patients, making the procedure counterproductive.

Physical Restraint

Physical restraint also suppresses SIB.[37] Different levels of restraint are in wide use, including articles of clothing that constrain movement and protective helmets and gloves. All methods of restraint may reduce or eliminate SIB by removing the opportunity or means for it to occur; almost always, however, removal of the restraints results in eventual return of the undesirable behavior. It also poses dangers to the patient's physical well-being and developmental progress and should be avoided when possible.

In general, suppression techniques teach the patient only that SIB leads to negative consequences. They teach nothing about alternative ways to be rewarded. Removal of the threat of the negative consequence always results in an increased frequency of SIB.

Substitution of Competing Responses

These techniques involve the assumption that SIB is instrumental in obtaining reward. If the same quality and quantity of reward were to follow a response other than the SIB, the positive response would replace the SIB. Some substitution techniques, such as differential reinforcement of other behavior, involve reinforcement only of behaviors that are incompatible with SIB. Substitution procedures yield promising results, so long as the SIB is not so intense and frequent as to preclude any intervention other than suppression. They require at least as much consistency as suppression techniques, but they must also be modified as the patient makes progress, thus demanding frequent review.

Noncontingent Techniques

These strategies are based on the premise that the stimuli that select and maintain SIB are too complex and diffuse to be identified. Therefore, treatment does not focus on altering the reward for a specific response, but rather on a modification of the patient's total ecology. Examples of such approaches include placement of the patient in a 24-hour controlled environment that consistently reinforces appropriate behaviors,[17] providing sensory or motor stimulation in a noncontingent manner,[12] placement of the patient in a noncontingent time-out,[21] and involving patients in physically exerting activities such as jogging. These approaches have been attempted only on a limited basis, so their value is not yet certain. They seem promising, however.

Combinations

The best results in treatment of SIB involve combinations of several behavioral approaches, or of behavioral approaches with pharmacologic interventions. Frequently, a suppressive technique is combined with substitution techniques. This approach is best suited to patients whose SIB is so frequent and intense that little or no opportunity exists to reinforce appropriate behavior. The suppressive technique is used to create the opportunity to reinforce behavior other than SIB. Drug therapy may be employed to accomplish the same goal as suppressive techniques in some cases where the latter procedures are dangerous to implement.

At the present time, combinations of pharmacologic and behavioral therapies in a setting allowing for close, consistent monitoring and data collection appear to offer the best hope for reduction of SIB.[11] Clearly, current resources for such treatment are predominantly limited to facilities with high staff-patient ratios in residential settings. It is hoped, however, that ongoing research and critical evaluation of therapeutic results will lead to more effective treatment or prevention techniques.

REFERENCES

1. Adamson, W., et al.: Use of tranquilizers for mentally deficient patients. J. Dis. Child, 96:159, 1958.
2. Aman, M., and Singhy, N.: Methylphenidate in severely retarded residents and the clinical significance of stereotypic behaviors. Appl. Res. Ment. Retard., 3:345, 1982.
3. Appenzeller, D.: What makes us run? N. Engl. J. Med., 305:578, 1981.
4. Barron, J., and Sandman, C.: Relationship of sedative-hypnotic response to self-injurious behavior and stereotypy by mentally retarded clients. Am. J. Ment. Defic., 88:177, 1983.
5. Barron, J., and Sandman, K.C.: Self-injurious behavior and stereotypy in an institutionalized mentally retarded population. Appl. Res. Ment. Retard., 5:499, 1984.
6. Burns, M.: Droperidol in the management of hyperactivity, self-mutilation, and aggression in mentally handicapped patients. J. Int. Med. Res., 8:31, 1980.
7. Cataldo, M., and Harris, J.: The biological basis for self-injury in the mentally retarded. Anal. Intervent. Dev. Disabilities, 2:21, 1982.
8. Christie, R., et al.: Lesch-Nyhan disease: Clinical experience with nineteen patients. Dev. Med. Child. Neurol., 24:293, 1982.
9. Cudzinowski, L., and Perreault, J.: The Lesch-Nyhan syndrome: Report of a case. J. Dentistry Child., 46:143, 1979.
10. Davidson, P., et al.: Effects of naloxone on self-injurious behavior: A case study. Appl. Res. Ment. Retard., 4:1, 1983.
11. Durand, V.: A behavioral/pharmacological intervention for the treatment of severe self-injurious behavior. J. Autism Dev. Disorders, 12:243, 1982.
12. Favell, J., McGimsey, J., and Schell, R.: Treatment of self-injury by providing alternative sensory activities. Anal. Intervent. Dev. Disabilities, 2:83, 1982.
13. Fenton, S.: Management of oral self-mutilation in neurologically impaired children. Spec. Care Dentistry, 2:70, 1982.
14. Galambos, M.: Long-term clinical trial with diazepam on adult mentally retarded persons. Dis. Nerv. Syst., 26:305, 1965.
15. Geller, E., Ritvo, E., and Freeman, B.: Preliminary observations on the effect of fenfluramine on blood serotonin and symptoms in three autistic boys. N. Engl. J. Med., 307:165, 1982.
16. Jay, J., and Grant, S.: Keratoconjunctivitis artefacta. Br. J. Ophthalmol., 66:781, 1982.
17. Jones, F., Simmons, J., and Frankel, F.: An extinction procedure for eliminating self-destructive behavior in a 9-year-old autistic girl. J. Autism Child. Schizophrenia, 4(3):241, 1974.
18. Korten, J., et al.: Self-mutilation in a case of 49, XXXXY chromosomal constitution. J. Ment. Defic. Res., 19:63, 1975.
19. Lesch, M., and Nyhan, W.: A familial disorder of uric acid metabolism and central nervous system function. Am. J. Med., 36:561, 1964.
20. Lloyd, K., et al.: Biochemical evidence of dysfunction of brain neurotransmitters in the Lesch-Nyhan syndrome. N. Engl. J. Med., 305:1106, 1981.
21. Lovaas, I., and Simmons, J.: Manipulation of self-destruction in three retarded children. J. Appl. Behav. Anal., 2(3):143, 1969.
22. Maisto, C., et al.: Analysis of variables related to SIB among institutionalized retarded persons. J. Ment. Defic. Res., 22:27, 1978.
23. Margo, C., and Adams, R.: Bilateral papilledema and self-mutilation. Arch. Neurol., 39:604, 1982.
24. Maurice, P., and Trudel, G.: Self-injurious behavior prevalence and relationships to environmental events.

In Life Threatening Behavior Analysis and Intervention. Edited by John J. Hollis and C. Edward Meyers. Washington, DC, American Association on Mental Deficiency, 1982.

25. Menolascino, F., et al.: Behavioural dimensions of the De Lange syndrome. J. Ment. Defic. Res., 26:259, 1982.
26. Mizuno, T., and Yugari, Y.: Letter: Self-mutilation in Lesch-Nyhan syndrome. Lancet, 1(860):761, 1974.
27. Noel, L., and Clarke, W.: Self-inflicted ocular injuries in children. Am. J. Ophthalmol., 94:630, 1982.
28. Nyhan, W., et al.: Serotoninergic approaches to the modification of behavior in the Lesch-Nyhan syndrome. Appl. Res. Ment. Retard., 1:25, 1980.
29. Pattison, G.: Self-inflicted gingival injuries. J. Periodontol., 54:299, 1983.
30. Primrose, D.: Treatment of self-injurious behavior with a GABA analogue. J. Ment. Defic. Res., 23:163, 1979.
31. Richardson, J., and Zaleski, W.: Naloxone and self-mutilation. Biol. Psychiatry, 16:99, 1983.
32. Sandman, C., et al.: Naloxone attenuates self-abusive behavior in developmentally disabled clients. Appl. Res. Ment. Retard., 4:5, 1983.
33. Schroeder, S., Rojahn, J., and Mulick, J.: Ecological organization of developmental day care for the chronically self-injurious. J. Pediatr. Psychol., 3:81, 1978.
34. Schroeder, S., et al.: Prevalence of self-injurious behaviors in a large state facility for the retarded: A three-year follow-up study. J. Autism Child. Schizophrenia, 8:268, 1978.
35. Singh, N.: Behavioural dimensions of the De Lange syndrome: Attribution of mystique and a question of cause and effect. J. Ment. Defic. Res., 27:237, 1983.
36. Singh, N., and Millichamp, C.: Effects of medication on the self-injurious behavior of mentally retarded persons. Psychiatr. Aspects Ment. Retard. Rev., 3:13, 1984.
37. Singh, N., et al.: The effects of physical restraint on self-injurious behaviour. J. Ment. Defic. Res., 25:207, 1981.
38. Sinon, N.: Prevalence of mental retardation in institutionalized retarded children. N.Z. Med. J., 36:325, 1977.
39. Sovner, R., and Hurley, A.: The management of chronic behavior disorders in mentally retarded adults with lithium carbonate. J. Nerv. Ment. Dis., 169:191, 1981.
40. Stuck, K., and Hernandez, R.: Large skull defect in a headbanger. Pediatr. Radiol., 8:257, 1979.
41. Sweeny, S., and Zamecnik, K.: Predictors of self-mutilation in patients with schizophrenia. Am. J. Psychiatry, 138:1086, 1981.
42. Thompson, C., and Park, R.: Oral manifestations of the congenital insensitivity to pain syndrome. Oral Surg., 50:220, 1980.
43. Thomson, H., and Hill, D.: Solitary rectal ulcer: Always a self-induced condition? Br. J. Surg., 67:784, 1980.
44. Turley, P., and Henson, J.: Self-injurious lip-biting: Etiology and management. J. Pedod., 1:209, 1983.
45. Williams, J., et al.: Roentgenographic changes in headbangers. Acta Radiol. [Diagn.] (Stockh.), 13:37, 1972.
46. Zaleski, W.: A clinical evaluation of mesoridizine in mentally retarded patients. Can. Psychiatr. Assoc. J., 154:319, 1970.

PICA

Aruna Sachdev, M.D.
Catherine McNiff, R.N.

The word pica is derived from the Latin word for magpie, a bird known for gathering a variety of objects to satiate its hunger or curiosity. In humans the term is usually used to describe the habitual eating of nonfood items, though some authors have included the ingestion of food items when food is picked off the floor or eaten in excess.[2,7,13] It is an eating disorder that occurs throughout the world in adults and in children. Pica may be nonspecific, when a person will eat different nonfood items indiscriminately, or it may be specific for a certain item, as in geophagia (clay and dirt ingestion), amylophagia (laundry starch ingestion), pagophagia (ice ingestion), trichophagia (hair ingestion) and coprophagia (feces ingestion).

CULTURAL AND HISTORICAL PERSPECTIVES

In the United States, pica occurs among people from various backgrounds.[25] Its occurrence in a community or ethnic group has been attributed to cultural and socioeconomic reasons. In a study done in rural Mississippi,[25] geophagia was found among children of both sexes from 1 year of age through 4. Between 4 years and adolescence it did not occur. It was then seen to reemerge in pubertal females and during pregnancy, and continue through adulthood. It was not seen in adult males. The authors reported that the women in the household played a primary role in the continuation of this cultural tradition. They were unable to correlate the geophagia to nutritional needs or to find any deleterious effect on the health of the people who practiced it. A report from Australia noted that pica had become a conspicuous behavior among aboriginal women past childbearing age. This was seen as a regressive phenomenon and attributed to a change in the social structure that caused these women to lose their importance in the community.[9]

POSSIBLE PATHOGENETIC ASSOCIATIONS

Mouthing of objects by an infant is a part of normal development, and this mode of exploration continues into the second year of life, when a toddler will suck on or bite objects. A thumb or pacifier may be used for comfort and security,

Table 20-3. *Distribution of Pica by Level of Retardation*

Retardation Level	Total Population (%)	Patients with Pica (%)
Profound	405 (43.8)	45 (66.1)
Severe	276 (29.9)	20 (29.4)
Moderate	135 (14.6)	1 (1.5)
Mild	46 (5.0)	1 (1.5)
Borderline	18 (1.9)	1 (1.5)
Untestable	44 (4.8)	0 (0)
All	924 (100.0)	68 (100.0)

particularly in times of stress. After the second year of life, however, persistence of this habit may be considered deviant behavior.[3]

General Population

Several factors have been implicated in the pathogenesis of pica in infants and children. Children who have pica have been found to come from unstable homes where there was an inappropriate mother-child relationship, inadequate childcare, paternal deprivation, parental separation, and child abuse.[21,24] Also, children who had problems during weaning, or whose mothers had pica, were more likely to have pica.[21] Pica has been associated with psychosis, and as many as 65% of psychotic children in one study had pica.[20] Other authors have also reported pica in association with psychosis, though this has usually not been found to be suicidal in intent.[18]

Iron deficiency has been implicated as a cause of pica, and the pica in these cases has resolved with oral administration of therapeutic doses of iron.[14]

Mental Retardation

Children with mental retardation, who have extensive histories of finger feeding, are more likely to have pica than those who have been able to use utensils early in their development.[1] It has been hypothesized that these children are unable to progress beyond this developmental stage and hence the habit persists.

In state institutions, severely and profoundly retarded individuals demonstrate a much higher prevalence of nonfood pica than those who are mildly or moderately retarded.[8] In a survey by Sachdev and McNiff, 96% of the patients with pica were profoundly or severely retarded as compared to 74% in the total population at the state school (Table 20-3).

There is probably a multifactorial etiology for this relationship. One hypothesis is that the cognitive development of these individuals has possibly not progressed much beyond the oral stage, and they find in pica a means of readily accessible self-gratification. Other contributing factors could be a lack of environmental stimulation, frustration, and hunger, particularly in the early stages of their development. As a behavior that often attracts the attention of caregivers it may create secondary gains and thus become self-perpetuating. In the case of the ingestion of cigarettes or cigarette stubs, there may be physiologic gratification as well, and individuals addicted to cigarettes are often very aggressive in their pursuit of this item.

CLINICAL PROBLEMS ASSOCIATED WITH PICA

Individuals with pica have been reported to ingest a variety of nonfood objects including thread, string, rags, stones, dirt, clay, leaves, twigs, cigarettes, buttons, insects, and paint chips.

Plumbism

In children, the ingestion of lead-containing substances is a significant problem, and has been widely studied because of the serious consequences. It is found to occur most commonly in poor neighborhoods with substandard housing, where lead-containing paint is peeling and crumbling, making it readily available to young children with pica.[21] Other sources of lead are pencils coated with lead paint, printed material with an increased amount of lead, and toys with lead-containing paint.[21] The most serious consequence of lead ingestion is encephalopathy, but it also causes anorexia, hyperirritability, microcytic hypochromic anemia, and nephropathy.[6] In children with chronically increased lead absorption, an increased frequency of behavioral and cognitive defects has been noted, affecting their classroom performance.[6]

Parasitic Infection

Parasitic infections are another problem associated with pica. Visceral larva migrans, caused by the ingestion of soil contaminated with infective dog roundworm (Toxocara canis) and cat roundworm (T. cati), and ascariasis have been reported in children who eat dirt.[22] In children with pica, several cases of concurrent visceral larva migrans and lead poisoning have been reported.[16]

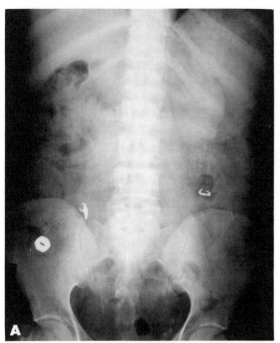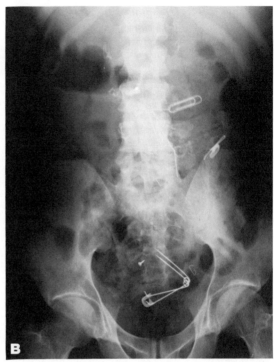

FIG. 20-1. Radiographs following episodes of pica behavior. These two radiographs illustrate the clinical phenomenology of pica. The individual in Fig. 20-1B has a long history of pica, with a predilection for safety pins. Some of the safety pins have been passed, but he has required three surgical procedures, two to remove safety pins and one to remove a rubber glove, which caused obstruction. His episodes of pica have decreased since a formal program was established.

Metabolic and Nutritional Disorders

A syndrome characterized by geophagia, iron deficiency anemia, growth retardation, hypogonadism, and zinc deficiency has been observed in both sexes in Turkey.[5] It is thought to be due to malabsorption of zinc and iron, caused by the ingestion of Turkish clay. Treatment with zinc corrected growth retardation and delayed puberty. It is also thought that the nutrient intake of vitamins C and D and phosphorous and iron may be decreased in persons with pica. Hence, patients with a history of pica should be screened for these dietary factors.[13] Persons who chronically consume nicotine can develop toxic organic brain syndrome, and severe states of nicotine poisoning can lead to myocardial infarction.[18]

Mechanical and Local Factors

Trichobezoars,[14] mechanical obstruction and perforation of the intestine,[8,9] gastrointestinal hemorrhage, aspiration, and dental erosions have been reported to occur in association with pica.[18] Ingested foreign bodies usually pass through the intestinal tract without symptoms, and less than 1% lead to perforation.[23] Long-term ingestion of foreign materials may, however, lead to chronic ileitis, in which the histopathologic picture mimics Crohn's disease in some respects.[23]

In a survey of residents at a state school, we found that 41% of the 68 who were identified as exhibiting pica behavior were hospitalized for problems occurring as a result of pica behavior (Table 20-4). Thirteen percent had to undergo surgery to alleviate problems caused by the ingestion of nonfood items (Table 20-5), and 17% underwent invasive procedures for diagnosis and/or treatment following a pica episode (Table 20-5). More than half (51.5%) of these individuals (Table 20-6) had to have radiographs (see Fig. 20-1) following episodes of pica or suspected pica.

Table 20-4. *Hospitalization Following Pica Episodes*

Number of patients hospitalized	28 (41.2%)
Total number of hospital admissions	71
Number of patients hospitalized for pica on 5 or more occasions	5

Table 20-6. *Radiographs Following Episodes of Pica or Suspected Pica*

Number of patients	35 (51.5%)
Number of patients with more than 5 radiographs	20
Number of patients with more than 10 radiographs	10

MANAGEMENT

General Population

Treatment of pica in young children requires a multifactorial approach. It is important that parents be made aware of the dangers of pica and the need for prevention. Counseling around issues of child development, nutrition, and adequate supervision of children is essential.[21] Marital issues, where they exist, may need to be resolved, and appropriate housing provided when families are living in poorly maintained houses with lead-containing paint. In cases in which a pet may be the source of Toxocara infection, parents need to be made aware of this.[19] Children are not usually brought to physicians with a history of pica, and it is important that this issue be explored in cases suggestive of problems associated with pica.

Behavior modification techniques and environmental enrichment have been used to reduce pica in children. In young children, interaction with the environment is essential for normal development and learning, and it is important to use the least restrictive treatment approach. In a study done by Madden, Russo, and Cataldo[15]

Table 20-5. *Surgery and Other Invasive Procedures Following Episodes of Pica*

Surgery for pica	
Number of patients who underwent surgery	9 (13%)
Total number of operations	12
Invasive procedures following episodes of pica	
Number of patients	12 (17%)
Procedures	
Bronchoscopy	7
Endoscopy	4
Gastroscopy	2
Laryngoscopy	2
Colonoscopy	1
Total number of procedures	16

the mouthing behavior of children was found to be higher in environments where a minimum of stimulation was available, whereas in an environment enriched with toys and adult contact, or even one of these, little or no mouthing was observed. Hence it seems possible that environmental manipulation could help to reduce pica.

In a study by Finney, Russo, and Cataldo,[10] children with high lead levels received a sequential training program of discrimination, differential reinforcement for behavior other than pica, and overcorrection. This program was effective in reducing each child's pica behavior in the hospital. In some cases, when parents followed through at home after appropriate instruction, the effect continued after discharge. Although these techniques are extremely time-consuming and require that the parents continue to enforce them after the therapist's initial intervention, they could be an effective means of treatment with enough support for the family.

Mental Retardation

Management of pica in mentally retarded individuals has been focused primarily in two areas—behavioral programs and environmental control.

Behavioral Programs

Several techniques have been used to eliminate or reduce the frequency of pica in mentally retarded individuals. These include (1) time out and reinforcement of nonpica behavior,[2] (2) overcorrection,[11] and (3) brief physical restraint to control the pica behavior.[4]

All these methods produced a reduction in frequency of pica and in some cases totally eliminated the behavior. They are time-consuming, however, and need intensive work over long periods of time. In all these cases, once the patient was returned to his usual environment, it was necessary to continue enforcing the above methods in order to maintain the improvement achieved during the intensive phase of the program, otherwise regression could occur. Programs requiring physical restraint depend on the availability of staff and compliance of patients and may not be feasible in all situations.

Environmental Control

In group residences and in large institutions, an important factor in decreasing the frequency of pica is environmental control. This involves education of the staff in order to ensure that cigarette ends and other potentially harmful materials are not left lying around in areas accessible to the residents.

Structured Activities

In a survey of individuals with pica in a large institution, 45% of the group exhibited pica only when not occupied with any interesting activity. Involvement in programmed activities reduced the frequency of pica in several cases. Well organized programs also provide these individuals with the attention from their caregivers that they need. This eliminates the necessity for drawing the attention of direct-care staff by less desirous habits, such as pica, which can be potentially dangerous.

The cost of care for individuals with pica is considerable, both in terms of staff time and the medical intervention often required after pica episodes. Besides the high staff-to-patient ratio required in programs aimed at decreasing pica behavior, a ratio of one-to-one may be necessary either when the pica is so severe as to be life-threatening or when a patient becomes self-abusive or aggressive towards others. When frequent physician involvement is necessary to monitor and manage potentially harmful pica episodes, the total cost can be considerable. Hence there is a definite need for programs aimed at eliminating or decreasing this behavior.

Long-Term Follow-up

Individuals with pica need to be monitored closely for problems that may arise in the future. It has been shown that children with a history of chronic lead ingestion may have poor classroom performance even though they were asymptomatic in the preschool years.[17] An awareness of this relationship is essential in order that the problem be identified early and appropriate measures taken to assist the child. In children with Toxocariasis the ocular manifestations may not appear for many years, and they need to be followed closely for them.[12] The long-term ingestion of foreign bodies itself can be detrimental, and patients should be monitored for signs of malabsorption, mineral and vitamin deficiency, and constipation. Patients who ingest large items, especially metal and plastic objects, are at much greater risk for intestinal obstruction and perforation and need to be monitored so that timely intervention can be made. Close monitoring is helpful in reducing morbidity due to pica, but probably cannot eliminate it altogether.

REFERENCES

1. Albin, J.B.: The treatment of pica (scavenging) behavior in the retarded: A critical analysis and implications for research. Ment. Retard., *15*:14, 1977.
2. Ausman, J., Ball, T.S., and Alexander, D.: Behavior therapy of pica with a profoundly retarded adolescent. Ment. Retard., *12*(6):16, 1974.
3. Bicknell, J.D.: Pica, a Childhood Symptom. London, Butterworth, 1975, p. 4.
4. Bucher, B., Reykdahl, B., and Albin, J.B.: Brief physical restraint to control pica in retarded children. J. Behav. Ther. Exp. Psychiatry, *2*:137, 1976.
5. Cavdar, A.O., et al.: Geophagia in Turkey: Iron and zinc deficiency, iron and zinc absorption studies and response to treatment with zinc in geophagia cases. Prog. Clin. Biol. Res., *123*:71, 1983.
6. Chisolm, J.J., Jr.: Increased lead absorption and lead poisoning. *In* Nelson Textbook of Pediatrics. Edited by R.E. Behrman and V.C. Vaughan III. 12th Ed. Philadelphia, W.B. Saunders, 1983, pp. 1800-1803.
7. Crosby, W.H.: Food pica and iron deficiency. Arch. Int. Med., *127*:960, 1971.
8. Danford, D.E., and Huber, A.M.: Pica among mentally retarded adults. Am. J. Ment. Defic., *87*(2):141, 1982.
9. Eastwell, H.D.: A pica epidemic: A price for sedentarism among Australian exhunter-gatherers. Psychiatry, *42*(3):264, 1979.
10. Finney, J.W., Russo, D.C., and Cataldo, M.F.: Reduction of pica in young children with lead poisoning. J. Pediatr. Psychol., *7*(2):197, 1982.
11. Foxx, R.M., and Martin, E.D.: Treatment of scavenging behavior (coprophagy and pica) by overcorrection. Behav. Res. Ther., *13*:153, 1975.
12. Glickman, L.T., Chaudhry, I.U., and Constantino, J.: Pica patterns, toxocariasis and elevated blood lead in children. Am. J. Trop. Med. Hyg., *30*(1):77, 1981.
13. Kalisz, K., Ekvall, S., and Palmer, S.: Pica and lead intoxication. *In* Pediatric Nutrition in Developmental Disorders. Edited by S. Palmer and S. Ekvall. Springfield, IL, Charles C Thomas, 1978, pp. 150-155.
14. McGehee, F.T., and Buchanan, G.R.: Trichophagia and trichobezoar: Etiologic role of iron deficiency. J. Pediatr., *97*(6):946, 1980.
15. Madden, N.A., Russo, D.C., and Cataldo, M.F.: Environmental influences on mouthing in children with lead intoxication. J. Pediatr. Psychol., *5*(2):207, 1980.
16. Moore, M.T.: Human Toxocara canis encephalitis with lead encephalopathy. J. Neuropathol. Exp. Neurol., *21*:201, 1962.
17. Needleman, H.L., et al.: Deficits in psychologic and classroom performance of children with elevated dentine lead levels. N. Engl. J. Med., *300*:689, 1979.

18. Neil, J.F., Horn, T.L., and Himmelhoch, J.M.: Psychotic pica, nicotinism and complicated myocardial infarction. Dis. Nerv. Sys., *38*(9):724, 1977.

19. Newton, R.W., et al.: Pets, pica, pathogens and preschool children. J. R. Coll. Gen. Pract., *31*(233):740, 1981.

20. Oliver, B.E., and O'Gorman, G.: Pica and blood lead in psychotic children. Develop. Med. Child Neurol., *8*: 704, 1966.

21. Pueschel, S.M., et al.: Pathogenetic considerations of pica in lead poisoning. Int. J. Psychiatry Med., *8*(1):13, 1977-78.

22. Schantz, P.M., and Glickman, L.T.: Toxocaral visceral larva migrans. N. Engl. J. Med., *298*:436, 1978.

23. Segal, I., Nouri, M.A., and Hamilton, D.G.: Foreign body ileitis: A case report. S. Afr. Med. J., *58*(10):421, 1980.

24. Singhi, S., Singhi, P., and Adwani, G.B.: Role of psychosocial stress in the cause of pica. Clin. Pediatr., *20*(12):783, 1981.

25. Vermeer, D.E., and Frate, D.A.: Geophagia in rural Mississippi: Environmental and cultural contexts and nutritional implications. Am. J. Clin. Nutr., *32*(10): 2129, 1979.

21

RECONSTRUCTIVE SURGERY FOR MULTIPLE CONGENITAL CRANIAL, FACIAL, AND HAND ANOMALIES

Joseph E. Murray, M.D.

The birth of a child with visible anatomic deformity is a shock to parents and family, and their initial responses vary. Some reject the child either totally or partially; others deny the existence of the defect and consider the child special or cute. Most parents learn to cope and accept the situation, with varying degrees of understanding and rationalization.

During this initial response period, professional opinions and gratuitous advice from well-meaning friends and relatives may confuse the picture. The first physician advisors are usually obstetricians or pediatricians. The questions posed are: How serious is this? Can it be repaired? How many operations will be required? What is the optimal time for surgical correction? How good will the result be? Will the condition be passed on to others in this or future generations?

Wrong advice can cause catastrophic consequences and may lead to underestimation of normally intelligent children. Children who look funny are often treated as such. Abnormal-looking children only slightly below normal in intelligence may be denied full access to educational opportunities. It is critical that these complex problems be properly evaluated at the earliest possible time.

THE SURGICAL TEAM

Because of the complexity of these situations, no one physician can master all the potential ramifications of the problem. An integrated team of physicians, nurses, social workers, and other clinical specialists is required to provide full diagnosis and treatment. These deformities must be evaluated in three anatomic dimensions, i.e., length, width, and depth. A fourth dimension, time, is needed to anticipate the changes resulting from growth. The psychosocial development of the patient can be considered a fifth dimension. The whole picture must be integrated in the mind of the team leader and then articulated with sensitivity, confidence, and compassion to the parents and family.

A fully organized craniofacial team includes a plastic and maxillofacial surgeon, neurosurgeon, ophthalmologist, otolaryngologist, anesthesiologist, psychiatrist and psychologist, speech and hearing personnel, dental professionals including orthodontists and prosthodontists, nurses, social workers, and an administrative coordinator. Considering the rare nature of some of these defects, their complexity (they may involve the cranium, brain, orbits, nose, mouth, ears, palate, lips, and the extremities) and the number and variety of the personnel required, it is no wonder that parents may have difficulty comprehending the future possibilities for their child's growth and development. Not all the participating disciplines are required for each patient, but the expertise of all should be available when needed.

TREATMENT GOALS

The goal of treatment is to give the patient the best chance to lead as normal a life as possible. The team leader must know what can be repaired; the limitations, optimum time, and sequence for the surgical operations; and the likelihood of complications. In addition, he must strive to determine the degree of understanding and the reality of the expectations of the patient and/or parents.

When planning treatment, patient safety is the primary consideration. Correction should be performed as early as possible in order to minimize secondary growth defects and to maximize normal sensory and motor input during the child's development and psychosocial growth.

Body image is a result of a person's inherent cognitive ability, the quality of his sensory and motor input, his comparison of self with others, and his reaction to the responses of others. Consider the normal child greeted and fondled with unadulterated joy and love by parents, able to suck and swallow, hear and see without distortion, and explore the outside world with intact tongue and hand. Then contrast this child, at any age, with one born as the center of emotional stress of parents, with defective sensory input from eyes, tongue, hands, ears, or nasal airway. Regardless of innate cognitive ability, his development is bound to be conditioned by his impaired sensory and motor input and by comparison of his body with those of others who are normal. In addition, he is affected either consciously or subconsciously by reactions from the outside world—his parents, siblings, playmates, teachers, and strangers.

The decision to try to correct a deformity involves a great deal more than planning a surgical exercise, such as suturing together two parts of a cleft lip, separating webbed fingers, or moving one orbit closer to the other. The decision to operate disturbs the inner fabric of the individual's self. It may unbalance a delicately adjusted defense mechanism. Nevertheless this worrisome surgical responsibility cannot be put aside because the benefits of successful, well-planned surgical correction can literally release a new individual into the main pathways of life.

To summarize, the specific goals of treatment are to restore function and improve appearance, maximize growth potential, improve self-image, and achieve optimal psychosocial adjustment. Early repair consistent with safety is practically always preferable in order to optimize vision, hearing, speech development, mastication, breathing, and nutrition.

Improved appearance has a major bearing on gains in self-image, which has received considerable study in the Craniofacial Program at the Children's Hospital.[1,9] It has been found that the change in body image following operation demonstrates its adaptability, and that change occurs in four phases. First, there is a complex decision to undergo surgery. The timing of this decision is based on social awareness, self-recognition, parental and peer pressure, emotional state, and the surgeon's assessment. The second phase, the operative experience, provides concrete evidence that a change in physical appearance has taken place. The reality of intervention is now acknowledged. Prior to intervention there is always the opportunity to indulge in fantasies. The third phase, the immediate postoperative period, involves physical pain, increased rather than decreased distortion of physical appearance, and reexamination of the decision and expectations. This postoperative phase is a psychological crisis with an opportunity to lay better groundwork for subsequent integration. Disruption of the previous psychological defense often leads to introspection, with acknowledgment of the previously existing deformity. During the fourth or reintegration phase, the psychological defenses reorganize, with increased intellectual freedom, a changing of social priorities, and increased interpersonal relationships. Change in body image does not necessarily correlate with the degree of anatomic improvement. In addition, intellectual function is often improved despite the absence of any organic change. Consequently children perform better at home, and in school some children can be transferred from specialized programs to regular classroom.

DECISIONS ABOUT SURGICAL INTERVENTION

Currently the improvements in hospital skills and surgical techniques allow a corrective approach to almost every facial deformity. Although only a few can be totally corrected, most can be improved to such a degree that patient and family satisfaction is high. Even the most severe deformity can be improved to some degree. The major problem is decision-making.

Can the person be helped enough to justify the risk, discomfort, and disturbance of psyche that any operation entails? These questions can be answered only on an individual basis after all areas of expertise have been consulted and evaluated. Final decisions are always with the patient and family, but firm guidance and recommendations must be given by the craniofacial team leader. This leader, who is in contact with the family, does not have to be the operating surgeon. Often it is the psychiatrist, orthodontist, or nurse. The main responsibility of the chief of the craniofacial team is to assure that every available hospital talent has considered the patient, that sufficient time has been allowed for planning, and that communication with family and patient has been thorough and sensitive.

PROBLEMS SEEN AT CHILDREN'S HOSPITAL

The variety of clinical problems being seen by the craniofacial group at the Children's Hospital continues to increase. The largest number of young people are the cleft lip and palate population; these all require operation at an early age, and some need secondary procedures during growth or as adults. The craniofacial deformities seen may be grouped into two major categories, congenital and acquired. Approximately 80% of the patients at the craniofacial clinic present with congenital malformations of the following major types: (1) craniosynostosis (including Crouzon and Apert syndromes), (2) orbital hypertelorism, (3) mandibulofacial dysostosis (Treacher Collins syndrome), and (4) hemifacial microsomia (1st and 2nd branchial arch deficiency). Twenty percent of the patients present with acquired deformities, consisting of defects secondary to tumors (15%) and trauma (5%).[7] In addition, all types of facial deformities are evaluated and treated. These deformities include neurofibromatosis (von Recklinghausen syndrome), vascular and lymphatic malformations, fibrous dysplasias, unilateral facial hypertrophy, Romberg lipodystrophy, and myriad isolated nonclassifiable facial clefts and fusions.

Treatment of three specific deformities—cleft lip and palate, Crouzon and Apert syndromes, and hemifacial microsomia—will be discussed in this chapter.

CLEFT LIP AND CLEFT PALATE

The most common congenital deformity is cleft lip and palate, occurring about 1 in 800 live births for whites. The deformity is less frequent in blacks and more frequent in Asians. Although cleft lip and palate are usually isolated (90%), they are sometimes associated with lip pits and with hemifacial microsomia. The condition varies from a minimal, almost invisible, clefting of one side of the lip to a bilateral failure of fusion of both sides of the upper lip and palate.

Repair of the minimal incomplete cleft lip is practically always done for cosmetic reasons, although subsequent distortion of the nose can occur, leading to asymmetry of the alae nasi and septum and impairment of breathing. Surgical realignment of the oral musculature can minimize subsequent dento-alveolar defects that can contribute to impaired chewing and speaking.

A complete cleft lip, unilateral or bilateral, always causes dento-alveolar distortion and nasal asymmetry. Technical improvements in surgical repair have now reached the point where some of the most severe defects of the lips are nearly undetectable after repair; nevertheless, complete correction of the nasal defect with the short columnella and flaring wide nostrils is almost impossible to obtain (Fig. 21-1).

In addition to the improvement in appearance, correction of these complete clefts of the lip and palate allows for optimal speech development, produces better function of the eustachian tubes draining the middle ears, and, with proper dental guidance, facilitates eruption of teeth. Separation of the nasal cavities from the mouth improves breathing, chewing, and oral and nasal hygiene.

Ideally, one operation should suffice for lip repair at about 6 to 12 weeks of age and another for palate repair at 9 to 14 months. In actuality, repair of a wide cleft lip usually requires a preliminary lip-adhesion operation within the first few weeks of life in order to allow the lip musculature to act on the separated palatal segments to bring them into better alignment.[5] This not only allows a more precise anatomical closure of the lip, it also gives better subsequent dental alignment.

The closure of the palate is also a one-stage procedure under ideal circumstances. The purpose is to produce a functioning, mobile palate capable of contributing to a nasopharyngeal sphincter mechanism that can prevent the escape of expired air during sibilant speech production. As in cleft lip repair, a second or even third operation may be required to achieve the best possible palatal function. Often the repaired palate may require lengthening attachment of its free margin to the posterior pharyngeal wall, termed a pharyngeal flap. Varieties of palatal operations have been described; regardless of the techniques used, the purpose is to achieve optimal speaking, dental, and auditory functions.

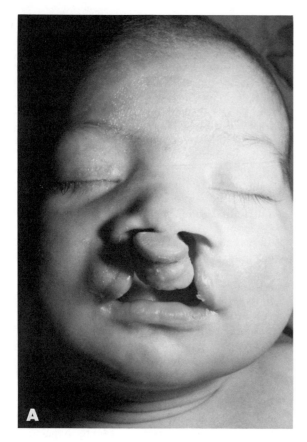
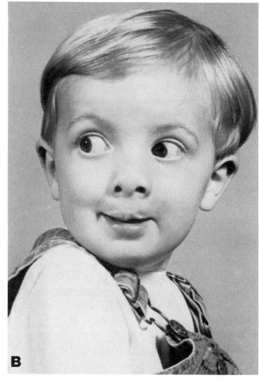

FIG. 21-1. Bilateral complete cleft lip. *A.* Preoperative view, in early infancy. *B.* The child at $3\frac{1}{2}$ years of age, following a two-stage lip and nasal correction. (From Mulliken, J.B.: Principles and techniques of bilateral complete cleft lip repair. Plast. Reconstr. Surg., 75:477, 1985.)

The stages in dental development play a vital role in planning for treatment of the patient with cleft lip and palate. During the deciduous period (from birth to 6 years), dental hygiene must be maintained in order to gain maximum stimulus for alveolar growth. During mixed dentition (6 to 12 years), midface growth is accelerated and permanent teeth are starting to erupt. Surgical intervention during this time can impair skeletal growth. Therefore indications for surgery during this stage are to aid normal growth potential, but with the awareness that harm can result from ill-conceived surgical intervention. In the adult, deformity is stable or fixed. At this time operative correction can be performed with precision, with the knowledge that the surgical result will not be changed by subsequent growth.

Most persons with cleft lip and palate have midfacial underdevelopment. Often other family members without clefts show flattened cheeks, retruded upper lips, or a class III dental occlusion with the upper incisor teeth being posterior to the lower ones. There seems to be an inherent growth deficiency of the maxillary bones as well as the clefting, which is failure of fusion of the maxillae and pre-maxilla. Surgical correction of the lip and palate, no matter how skillfully and delicately done, always has a potential of injury to subsequent growth. The part that surgical correction plays in the final adult deformity can never be determined in the individual patient. Most patients who receive good, consistent care end up with normal appearance, normal function, and normal psychosocial development. Nevertheless, many who have a severe deformity are damaged further by the surgical trauma. Studies from developing countries, where large numbers of untreated clefted patients can be evaluated, reveal clearly that persons with cleft palates who are not treated practically always end up with the maxillae in normal anterior and lateral positions in relation to the mandible.

CRANIOSYNOSTOSIS WITH ASSOCIATED FACIAL SKELETAL DEFORMITY

The estimated incidence of craniosynostosis is 1 per 1,000 live births; the facial skeleton is affected in only 9 to 10% of cases.[10] The configuration of the skull deformity in the craniosynostoses depends on the suture or sutures involved. Thus, premature synostosis of the sagittal suture prevents lateral expansion of the calvarium (perpendicular to the fused suture) but permits expansion anteriorly at the coronal suture and posteriorly at the lambdoidal suture. The result is a long, narrow skull (scaphocephaly). Oxycephaly, turricephaly, or acrocephaly, all indicating a tall or "tower" skull, would therefore result from premature fusion of the coronal sutures. Other common skull deformities in craniofacial dysostosis include trigonocephaly (metopic synostosis) and plagiocephaly (unilateral coronal synostosis).

Crouzon, in 1912, first described a group of patients with craniosynostosis and severe midface hypoplasia. A variety of skull types may be seen in Crouzon syndrome; depending on the cranial suture involved, however, oxycephaly and brachycephaly are the most often observed. The shallow bony orbits produce the characteristic exorbitism and divergent strabismus. The diminished orbital volume is the result of the anterior position of the greater wing of the sphenoid bone, the ballooning of the ethmoid sinuses, and the foreshortening of the floor (maxillary hypoplasia) and roof (recession of the frontal bone) of the orbit. During the first 3 years of life, progressive visual loss may occur in patients with Crouzon syndrome secondary to constriction of the osseous optic canals.[13] This phenomenon is rare later in childhood, although the possibility of corneal damage from exposure keratitis always is a threat. Prolapse of the frontal sinus, an inferior position of the cribriform plates, and widening of the ethmoid sinuses can produce orbital hypertelorism. Another significant physical finding is the relatively low position of the lateral palpebral ligaments (secondary to hypoplasia of the zygomatic bones), giving a slant to the eyelids with the lateral canthus depressed.

The maxilla is deficient in three dimensions, producing relative prognathism (the mandible is normal) and the characteristic drooping lower lip. The nose has a typical "parrot's beak" deformity. The narrow, inverted V-shaped maxillary dental arch results in bilateral crossbite. The palate usually has an extremely high vault, but there is a low incidence of bony palatal clefts.[12]

In 1906, Apert described a group of patients with craniosynostosis, midface hypoplasia, and peculiar extremity deformities, a syndrome known today by the eponym or as acrocephalosyndactyly. The facial deformities of Apert syndrome are in many ways similar to those of Crouzon syndrome. However, there are significant differences between the two groups.[11] Patients with Apert syndrome more commonly have (1) isolated involvement of the coronal suture, producing oxycephaly (turricephaly, acrocephaly) and a transverse forehead skin furrow; (2) asymmetric exorbitism; (3) more severe lateral canthal dystopia; (4) a significant incidence of clefts of the secondary palate (30% of patients); and (5) anterior open bite. The major distinguishing characteristic of Apert syndrome is the complex syndactyly of the hands and/or feet, with interphalangeal synostosis, symphalangism, and other anomalies producing a "mitten" deformity.[3]

The genetic aspects of the two syndromes are similar. Crouzon syndrome is inherited as an autosomal dominant condition, occurring in a frequency of 1 in 10,000 live births; however, 25% of these patients are fresh mutations. Apert syndrome is less common than Crouzon syndrome, with an estimated frequency of 1 in 160,000 live births. Apert syndrome appears to have an autosomal dominant inheritance with low penetrance, and the spontaneous mutation rate is higher than in Crouzon syndrome.

Treatment of the posteriorly positioned midface consists of detaching a monoblock of the orbits, maxilla, and nose from the skull and repositioning this bony unit to an anterior site. The forehead may be included in this osseous unit if necessary. Thus, in one maneuver, the bony orbits are enlarged, correcting the exorbitism, opening the nasal passages, improving breathing and eustachian tube function, and placing the upper jaw and teeth in a more normal relation with the mandible. The oral cavity is also made more spacious; this accommodates the tongue and reduces drooling. Accompanying all these functional changes is a striking change in appearance (Fig. 21-2). Patients and families may require up to two years to adjust to the "new" person. During this period unexpected behavior patterns may develop. For example, one previously well-behaved teenage male with Crouzon syndrome became rebellious and moved out of his parents' home after successful surgical repair. The clinic's psychiatric consultant explained that he had been denied the usual chances to express himself during adolescence and was now enjoying the new-found freedom

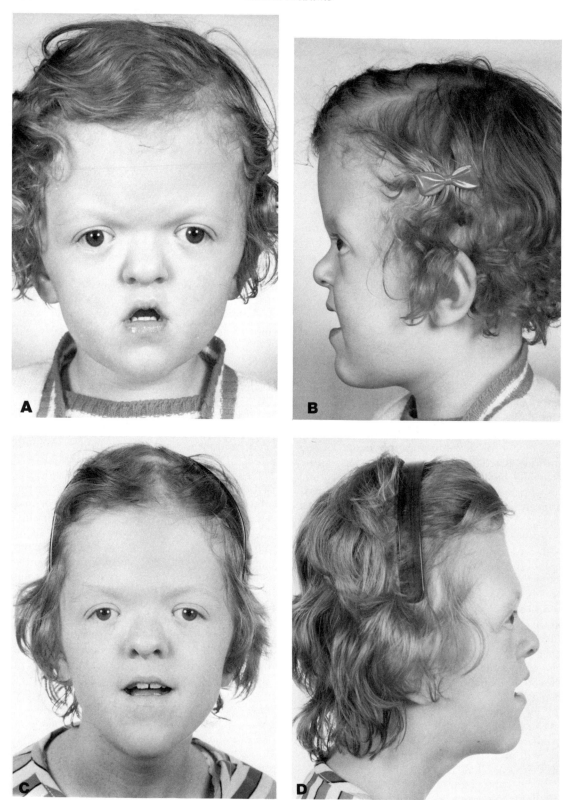

FIG. 21-2. Child with Apert syndrome. *A* and *B*. Appearance at $2\frac{1}{2}$ years of age. *C* and *D*. Child at 10 years of age, 4 years following mid-face advancement operation.

that accompanied his more normal facial appearance. Within nine months he rejoined his family and pursued college studies.

The physical features of a person with Apert syndrome are more distorted than in Crouzon syndrome. The nose is more bulbous, the alar bones more sunken, the palatal arch higher, and, most significantly, the hands are fused and malaligned. The functional deficits from the hands deprive the young person of full sensory and motor feedback even after the most successful surgical repair. The usual defects include side-to-side fusion of the distal phalanges (acrosynostosis), symphalangism, delta phalanx of the thumb, and synostosis between the fourth and fifth metacarpals. Repair of the hands in persons with Apert syndrome should start as early as possible. The border digits, i.e., the thumb and fifth finger, must be freed from the fused mass, the distorted phalanges and joints realigned, and motion restored as well as possible. Usually a three-digit hand gives the best function. Joints are fused surgically in positions of function, and individual metacarpals and/or phalanges may be lengthened or realigned. The appearance of these hands is never normal after repair, but most hands can be made useful for ordinary tasks (Fig. 21-3). The cognitive ability of patients with Apert syndrome is usually found to be less than that of those with Crouzon syndrome. Some of the difference, however, may be due to the worse facial appearance, poorer sensory input, and decreased expectations on the part of family and teachers, leading to self-fulfilling prophesies of poorer performance.

HEMIFACIAL MICROSOMIA

Hemifacial microsomia is the term commonly used to describe a spectrum of anomalies involving structures derived from the first and second branchial arches.[2] It is the second most common facial birth defect after cleft lip and palate. Other designations include otomandibular dysostosis, first and second branchial arch syndrome, and lateral facial dysplasia. The Goldenhar syndrome (oculoauriculovertebral dysplasia) is usually considered a variant of hemifacial microsomia. Historically, treatment has been directed toward the jaw or ear, the choice depending on the patient, family concern, and the surgeon's interest and experience.[6] Because of the complex interrelationships between the affected structures and fragmentation of medical care, a systematic and unified therapeutic plan for hemifacial microsomia has developed slowly.[8]

Classification of the deformities is arbitrary and utilitarian. At birth, the defect often appears mild; with growth, asymmetry becomes more marked because of progressive development of the normal side. Only after full growth of the patient is the end-stage deformity evident.

Two major anatomic components exist: the skeleton and the soft tissues. Three types of skeletal deformity can be distinguished: type I has a normally shaped miniature mandible and glenoid fossa. Type II has a functioning temporomandibular joint, usually displaced anteriorly and medially; the contour of the joint cavity is never normal, and the ramus is short and abnormally shaped. Type III has complete absence of the ramus and glenoid fossa; there is no temporomandibular joint. In all three types the adjacent facial skeleton is distorted. The temporal bone and glenoid fossa are usually displaced medially and anteriorly, the zygomatic arch may be small or absent, and the orbit may be underdeveloped and inferiorly displaced. The maxilla can be hypoplastic with an oblique occlusal plane and piriform opening reflecting the decreased distance between the infraorbital rim and the maxillary occlusal plane.[4]

Facial soft tissues on the affected side vary from normal to severely deficient. For descriptive purposes, patients with minimal deformity, without auricular or cranial nerve involvement, are termed mild, those with major soft-tissue deficiency associated with ear distortion, seventh nerve deficits, and clefts of the face or lips are classified as severe, and those between are called moderate. There is a wide spectrum of external ear anomalies, varying from a normal ear to total absence. The severity of the ear deformity does not parallel that of the mandibular defect. All muscles of mastication are underdeveloped or absent, especially in the patient with type III deformity.

All of the affected facial structures in patients with hemifacial microsomia have diminished growth potential. Because the inborn morphogenetic error cannot be treated, the best one can do is to create an environment that potentiates normal facial growth and minimizes secondary distortion. Regardless of the patient's skeletal type, the first priority is correction of the mandibular deformity. The fundamental technical principle is to rotate the mandible into a normal position in three planes: frontal, lateral, and horizontal. The final operative plan is based on the type of deformity, the person's age, and analyses of photographs, radiographs, and dental models (Fig. 21-4).

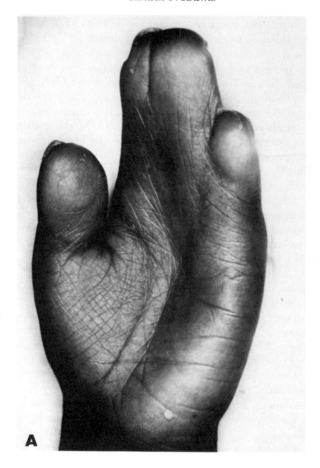

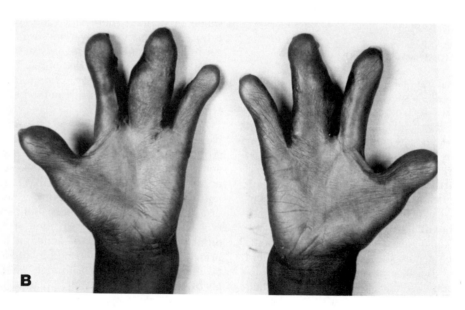

FIG. 21-3. Hand anomalies in a child with Apert syndrome. *A.* Preoperative, 4 years of age. *B.* At 5 years, following release of syndactyly. (Courtesy of Dr. Joseph Upton.)

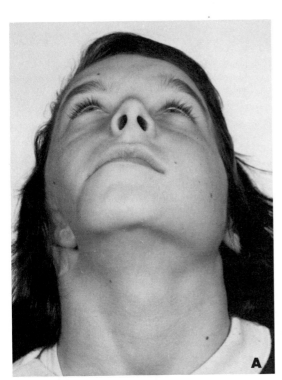
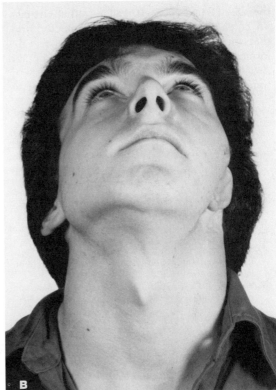

FIG. 21-4. Young man with left hemifacial microsomia. *A.* Submental view at 12 years of age. *B.* Same view at age 16 years, 4 years after surgical correction that included construction of the left zygomatic arch, glenoid fossa, and ramus of the mandible, and 2 years after skin and muscle grafting to the left postauricular area and revision of the helix of the external ear.

Patients with type I deformity may require one or two ramus-lengthening procedures at intervals of several years. If proper orthodontic appliances are used sequentially, and if adequate lengthening occurs, no further surgical treatment is necessary. With unimpeded downward growth, the maxilla will maintain a normal horizontal occlusal plane. If the patient is first seen as an adult, mandibular elongation, rotation, and advancement may be sufficient. In patients with type II deformity the time for surgical correction is determined by the occurrence of secondary deformities and is usually during mixed dentition age. A major decision involves the site selection for the future temporomandibular joint. A type III skeletal deformity, if untreated, results in a displaced, flattened, distorted maxilla, mandible, and zygoma, often with a concavity of the midface on the affected side. For children with type III deformity, construction of a glenoid fossa, ramus, temporomandibular joint, zygomatic arch, and body of the mandible is performed at ages 2 to 4 years, or whenever there is a full complement of deciduous teeth.

Construction of the external ear is deferred, whenever possible, until the mandibular and zygomatic osseous framework has been established. The earliest age for repair of isolated microtia has been 6 to 8 years. Marked deficiencies of subcutaneous fat and facial musculature are corrected by placement of an omental free flap in specially designed subcutaneous pockets. In patients with mild deficiencies, onlay bone grafts to the mandible and/or zygoma or subcutaneous dermal fat grafts can be used effectively. Although many patients present with seventh nerve paresis or palsy, especially the frontalis and mandibular branches, neuromuscular transfers or nerve grafts have not yet been used.

Formerly at the Boston Children's Hospital the operations for hemifacial microsomia dealt only with the external ear anomaly. Surgery on the facial skeleton was avoided in these children for fear of disturbing "growth centers." In following these children, it was noted that the skeletal deformities increased, probably as a result of growth of the normal side. Therefore we now operate on the mandible as early as possible after the age of 2 to 4 years. It is of note that virtually no "catch up" growth occurs on the affected side, that these patients always become more deformed with age if there is not intervention, and that the psychologic problems increase with time and progression of the facial deformity.

REFERENCES

1. Belfer, M.L., and Lukens, P.F.: Body image: Impacts and distortions. In Developmental-Behavioral Pediatrics. Edited by M.D. Levine, W.B. Carey, A.C. Crocker, and R.T. Gross. Philadelphia, W.B. Saunders, 1983, pp. 623-632.
2. Gorlin, R.J., Pindborg, J.J., and Cohen, M.M.: Syndromes of the Head and Neck. New York, McGraw-Hill, 1976, pp. 546-552.
3. Hoover, H.G., Flatt, A.E., and Weiss, M.W.: The hand and Apert's syndrome. J. Bone Joint Surg., 52A:878, 1970.
4. Kaban, L.B., Mulliken, J.B., and Murray, J.E.: Three dimensional approach to analysis and treatment of hemifacial microsomia. Cleft Palate J., 18:90, 1981.
5. Mulliken, J.B.: Principles and techniques of bilateral complete cleft lip repair. Plast. Reconstr. Surg., 75:477, 1985.
6. Munro, I.R.: One-stage reconstruction of the temporomandibular joint in hemifacial microsomia. Plast. Reconstr. Surg., 66:699, 1980.
7. Murray, J.E., Kaban, L.B., and Mulliken, J.B.: Craniofacial abnormalities. In Pediatric Surgery. Edited by M.M. Ravitch et al. Chicago, Year Book Medical Publishers, 1979, pp. 233-248.
8. Murray, J.E., Kaban, L.B., and Mulliken, J.B.: Analysis and treatment of hemifacial microsomia. Plast. Reconstr. Surg., 74:186, 1984.
9. Murray, J.E., Mulliken, J.B., Kaban, L.B., and Belfer, M.: Twenty year experience in maxillocraniofacial surgery. Ann. Surg., 190:320, 1979.
10. Shillito, J., and Matson, D.D.: Craniosynostosis: A review of 519 surgical patients. Pediatrics, 41:829, 1968.
11. Tessier, P.: The definitive plastic surgical treatment of the severe facial deformities of craniofacial dysostosis. Plast. Reconstr. Surg., 48:419, 1971.
12. Tessier, P.: Orbital hypertelorism. I. Successive surgical attempts, materials and methods, causes and mechanisms. Scandinav. J. Plast. Reconstr. Surg., 6:135, 1972.
13. Wood-Smith, D., Epstein, F., and Morello, D.: Transcranial decompression of the optic nerve in the osseous canal in Crouzon's disease. Clin. Plast. Surg., 3:621, 1976.

22

ANESTHESIA

Kristen L. Johnson, M.D.

There are two major challenges to the anesthesiologist in dealing with children and adults with developmental disabilities. First, the patient may not respond to the stress of a visit to the operating room in a manner predicted by his age and may require special considerations to maximize cooperation and minimize psychologic trauma. Second, the patient may have associated disease states that necessitate the most sophisticated pharmacologic, physiologic, and technologic practices.

The anesthesiologist must be well informed about a patient prior to choosing and then administering an anesthetic. Because some of these complex patients have rare disorders, choice of anesthetic can be difficult. The patient's physicians and nurses, knowledgeable of the anesthesiologist's concerns, are in a unique position to communicate this important information.

PREOPERATIVE PREPARATION

Approach to the Patient

In order to plan an approach that will permit emotional comfort and cooperation, the anesthesiologist must first assess the patient's level of mental functioning. Vissintainer and Wolfer[64] have categorized the major threats and fears of the hospitalized child as (1) fear of separation, (2) fear of physical harm or bodily injury, (3) fear of the strange and unknown, (4) uncertainty about limits and expected acceptable behavior, and (5) fear of loss of control, autonomy, and competence. The patient's emotional response to these fears is influenced by mental age, previous hospital experience, cultural and family background, and personality. The anesthesiologist experienced in caring for children is accustomed to adopting different approaches based on the age of the patient. When the mental age differs from the chronologic age, or when physical disabilities obscure a brief assessment of mental ability, the intuition of the anesthesiologist is best supplemented by information from the patient's caretakers regarding anticipated responses to the stress of a visit to the operating room.

All patients benefit from the time taken to develop rapport. A patient is likely to respond to a gentle tone of voice and a reassuring touch on remeeting in the operating room. Fear of separation is best dealt with by making provisions for predictability. For the less mentally sophisticated patient, this may involve having a parent, a favorite nurse or physician, or a case worker accompany him to the operating room suite. Security objects from home such as a toy, blanket, or stuffed animal may help create some sense of the familiar. For the older or more sophisticated patient, predictability is also provided by information. Informing the patient honestly about what to expect in the operating room (e.g., seeing doctors and nurses in OR scrubs with hats and masks, the application of monitoring devices, an intravenous line if necessary, breathing air from the space mask) will help make it familiar and predictable. This information can be supplemented by the patient's primary caretakers, but only after consulting with the anesthesiologist regarding the specifics of care for that particular patient. For example, although it is fairly routine to induce anesthesia in children by the inhalation of anesthetic gases delivered by a mask prior to starting an intravenous (IV) line, there are many situations in which this is potentially hazardous and an IV line must be started with the patient awake. If the primary physician relies on experience with the routine and tells the patient that no IV line will be started, the patient will be upset when the security of his knowledge is lost, and it may be difficult to regain his trust.

For the child, fear of physical harm is most frequently the fear of "needles" and "shots." For this reason, many pediatric anesthesiologists avoid premedication. This approach requires the exercise of patience and interpersonal skills that can tax the efficiency orientation of any operating room, but it is worth the effort. There are patients, however, who require premedication, as for example the very anxious patient or the mentally disabled patient who cannot understand or cooperate and who is at risk of harming himself (or others) when brought into a frightening and strange environment. These patients can receive oral or rectal premedication on the ward, or intramuscular (IM) injections if necessary. Supplementation to their sedation may be required on arrival in the OR suite. Sometimes it is best to premedicate a patient with the anesthesiologist's observation. Rectal methohexitol, IM ketamine, or a barbiturate or narcotic infused through a small intravenous catheter can be given in the operating room area prior to separating the patient from caretakers. The patient brought to an operating room feels physically vulnerable. Allowing patients to wear their own underwear or pajamas and respecting their modesty is a simple but often overlooked technique in dealing with these fears.

Patients' fear of the strange and unknown and their uncertainty concerning acceptable behavior is best handled by providing appropriate information.

The fear of loss of control and autonomy also requires sensitivity. Allowing the patient to experience a feeling of mastery by clearly defining a "job" for him in the OR and positively rewarding him for a job well done permits him to retain a sense of control. When appropriate, allowing the patient to participate in decision-making is helpful. This may be, for example, asking him to choose a flavor of "air"—cherry, chocolate, watermelon, etc. The flavor of choice can then be applied to the anesthesia mask, with a compliment on the patient's good taste, and this can be used as a takeoff for a story during the induction of anesthesia.

These approaches to the patient require the anesthesiologist to assess the mental and emotional level of functioning of the patient, which is best done in consultation with the primary caretakers who best know the patient.

Medical History

Having assessed the mental age of the patient and designed a plan of approach based on this age and related factors, the anesthesiologist is then interested in a medical history. The anesthesiologist needs to know the current complaint, the planned surgical procedure, and all of the patient's diagnoses, because all have anesthetic implications. The history of previous surgical and anesthetic procedures and the family history of responses to anesthesia are both obtained, to screen for pharmacogenetic disorders such as malignant hyperthermia, atypical plasma cholinesterases, or acute intermittent porphyria. The patient with a family history of malignant hyperthermia deserves very special attention because this disorder, if not anticipated and not aggressively managed, has a 70% mortality. These patients can receive a relatively safe anesthetic if known triggering agents are avoided and if dantrolene is available for prophylaxis or treatment. Patients with atypical cholinesterases may have prolonged apnea after the administration of succinylcholine, and it should be avoided. Barbiturates can exacerbate acute intermittent porphyria and should be avoided. Finally, the patient's allergies and current medications are noted.

Almost all drugs should be continued through the time of surgery with the exceptions of anticoagulants if surgical hemostasis is needed and routine insulin in diabetics. The decision to administer or to withhold a drug preoperatively should be made by the anesthesiologist, who will then be responsible for the anesthetic implications of the decision. Of special concern are anticonvulsants, antihypertensives, mood-altering drugs, sympathomimetics, anticoagulants, chemotherapeutic agents, antiarrhythmic drugs, endocrinologic preparations, antibiotics, digitalis, and organophosphates. Withholding anticonvulsants for prolonged periods is potentially hazardous. Phenobarbitol and phenytoin (Dilantin) are hepatic enzyme inducers and alter the metabolism of some drugs and potentially increase the dose requirement of Thiopental sodium (Pentothal). The thiazide diuretics are associated with hypochloremic alkalosis, hypokalemia, hyperglycemia, and hypercalcemia. Beta-adrenergic receptor blockers (e.g., Inderal) block in a dose-related fashion the effects of norepinephrine and epinephrine in increasing the heart rate and the force of the heart's contractions, and withdrawal can be accompanied by a hyper-beta-adrenergic condition. Reserpine and guanethidine deplete brain stem and peripheral storage granules of norepinephrine, epinephrine, and dopamine. Alpha-methyldopa (Aldomet) produces false neurotransmitters and decreases anesthetic requirements 20 to 40%. Prazosin (Minipress) is an alpha-1-adrenergic receptor blocker that causes both venodilation and arteriodilation, dizziness, weakness, and anticholinergic effects. Clonidine (Catapres), an alpha-adrenergic stimulant that lowers blood pressure through central brain stem stimulation, can result in a hypertensive crisis if withdrawn suddenly. Monoamine oxidase inhibitors, used to treat depression, are potentially problematic. They irreversibly bind to monoamine oxidase and thereby increase intraneuronal levels of amine neurotransmitters.

Despite a recent report of uneventful anesthetics in patients on chronic monoamine oxidase inhibitors,[16] caution is indicated in administering anesthesia. There are case reports of severe hypertension, hypotension, convulsions, hyperpyrexia, and coma in patients on these drugs who receive general anesthesia. The tricyclic antidepressants block adrenergic reuptake and decrease noradrenergic catecholamine stores. They have atropine-like effects and can cause electrocardiographic abnormalities—including arrhythmias—and have been associated with fatal arrhythmias in the presence of the anesthetic drugs halothane and pancuronium. The phenothiazines and butyrophenones have dopamine receptor blocking action in addition to varying degrees of alpha-adrenergic blocking action and parasympathetic stimulation. They produce sedation, depression, antihistaminic, antiemetic, and hypothermic responses and are associated with cholestatic jaundice, dystonic reactions, photosensitivity, orthostatic hypotension, and electrocardiographic abnormalities.

The CNS depressant action of barbiturates and narcotics is enhanced by phenothiazines, and the seizure threshold is lowered by these drugs. Lithium prolongs neuromuscular blockade and may decrease anesthetic requirements. The sympathomimetics (e.g., aminophylline) used to treat asthma can interact with the volatile anesthetics to cause arrhythmias. Halothane, for example, sensitizes the myocardium to exogenous catecholamines, and these xanthines act by the production of beta-adrenergic stimulation. (Experimentally, aminophylline decreases the threshold of ventricular fibrillation: 75% of dogs anesthetized with a routine concentration of halothane (1%) developed ventricular arrhythmias after receiving aminophylline boluses.)[62]

Anticoagulants need to be reversed in the face of the need for surgical hemostasis. Antiarrhythmic drugs should be continued perioperatively, and their indications and pharmacology are well appreciated by the anesthesiologist. Patients receiving chemotherapy should have current hematologic, hepatic, and renal studies. Patients who have had bleomycin therapy require evaluation of their pulmonary status and careful monitoring of their intraoperative oxygen requirement (with transcutaneous oxygen monitoring, pulse oximetry, or arterial blood gases) to minimize the potential exacerbation of lung pathology with oxygen therapy. Patients who have received doxorubicin (Adriamycin) (especially over 450 mg/m^2) should have an echocardiogram to evaluate ventricular function. They may require invasive intraoperative cardiac monitoring. Patients on corticosteroids with suppression of their adrenal axis require supplemental perioperative steroid coverage. Antibiotics (with the exception of penicillin G and the cephalosporins) prolong neuromuscular blockade. Digitalis can be continued perioperatively, and should be when used to treat supraventricular arrhythmias, but toxicity in the form of diverse arrhythmias can occur. And, the organophosphates (echothiophate and isofluophate), used to treat glaucoma, inhibit serum cholinesterase, which is responsible for the inactivation of succinylcholine and the ester local anesthetics. These anesthetic drugs should be avoided in patients so treated.[20,21,50]

Review of Systems

The anesthesiologist must thoroughly review the patient's respiratory, cardiac, hepatic, hematologic, gastrointestinal, and neurologic systems (Table 22-1). A problem with any of these warrants a thorough investigation because there are definite anesthetic implications. The patient with a developmental disability may have had a complicated neonatal course. Ventilatory support in the neonatal period suggests the possibility of chronic lung disease (bronchopulmonary dysplasia) and an increase in airway resistance, a decrease in pulmonary compliance, ventilation/perfusion (V/Q) mismatching, a decrease in arterial oxygenation, tachypnea, and an increase in oxygen consumption.[7,35] A history of an intra-

Table 22-1. *Review of Systems*

System	Item
Respiratory	Exercise tolerance
	Asthma
	Pneumonia
	Croup
	Cough
	Recent upper respiratory infection
Cardiac	History of murmur, arrhythmias, hypertension
	Chest pain
	Palpitations
	Exercise tolerance
Hepatic	Jaundice
	Hepatitis
	Drug, alcohol use
Hematologic	Bruisability
	Bleeding tendency
	Transfusion history
	Anemia
Gastrointestinal	Regurgitation
	Vomiting
Neurologic	Seizures
	Motor or sensory abnormality
	Behavioral problems
	Stroke, hemorrhage

ventricular hemorrhage raises the question of hydrocephalus and an increase in intracranial pressure. Preterm infants who are less than 46 weeks of conceptual age are at risk for postoperative apnea, and their anesthesia and surgery should be delayed if possible. If surgery is urgent, they should have 18 hours of postanesthetic apnea monitoring.[38] Problems with restrictive or obstructive pulmonary disease of other etiologies, recurrent infections, congenital heart disease (surgical correction does not render the heart normal for the anesthesiologist's purposes), hepatic microsomal enzyme induction, gastroesophageal reflux, and seizures might also be anticipated in the patient with a developmental disability.

Physical Examination

The anesthesiologist's physical examination includes vital signs (weight, pulse, blood pressure, respiratory rate, and temperature). Any abnormality requires further investigation prior to administration of anesthesia. The head and neck examination focuses on head size, patency of the nares, mandibular size and mobility, tongue size, swallowing and gag reflexes, dentition, and neck length and mobility. The primary concern here is to assess the ability to ventilate with a mask and to visualize the vocal cords for endotracheal intubation. Evaluating the patient for thoracic musculoskeletal abnormalities, respiratory effort, and breath sounds screens for potential respiratory complications and may suggest the need for further evaluation with a chest radiograph, arterial blood gases, or pulmonary function testing. An abnormal cardiac examination must be determined to be unchanged from previous examinations, and the anesthesiologist will want to know the diagnosis made by a cardiologist and will want a current electrocardiogram (EKG) and a chest radiograph. The abdominal exam screens for organomegaly or masses, and the neurologic examination is typically abbreviated to observation. Finally, the patient is examined for sites for venous and arterial access.

Laboratory Evaluation

The absolute minimum preoperative laboratory information needed is hemoglobin concentration and hematocrit (Hb/Hct). For some patients this is adequate after a thorough history and physical exam. Many patients, however, will require more. The patient with pulmonary disease may require a CXR, blood gases, and pulmonary function tests. The patient with cardiac disease needs at minimum an EKG and a chest radiograph. An echocardiogram or even cardiac catheterization may be necessary. Patients with significant cardiac disease are best handled by consultation between the anesthesiologist and the cardiologist. Although supportive data diagnosing gastroesophageal reflux is important, the history is adequate to direct the anesthetic. Preoperative laboratory confirmation of hepatic or renal dysfunction will guide the usage of drugs relying on either organ for metabolism. The patient with hepatic dysfunction or with a history suggestive of a coagulation defect should have a prothrombin time/partial thromboplastin time (PT/PTT) and a platelet count. If the patient has been receiving aspirin, a bleeding time test will diagnose a possible secondary platelet dysfunction. The patient with a history of vomiting or diarrhea, diuretic use, or fluid and electrolyte abnormalities needs preoperative normalization of electrolytes (with documentation). The diabetic patient needs a fasting A.M. glucose test, and an intravenous infusion of 5% dextrose in water should be started before administration of one-half of the usual insulin dose on the morning of surgery. The asthmatic on aminophylline may require confirmation of a blood level, especially if there is clinical evidence of toxic or subtherapeutic effects. The patient with a history or physical examination suggestive of cervical spine abnormalities or airway abnormalities might require radiographs of the cervical spine or neck.

Risk Assessment

The anesthesiologist correlates the history, physical findings, and laboratory results to make an assessment of physical status. This physical status is an assessment of anesthetic risk in the presence of a skilled anesthesiologist and surgeon, optimal nursing and allied personnel, and appropriate equipment. The American Society of Anesthesiologists' classification system is useful in assessing patients.

ASA Class I: No organic, physiologic, biochemical, or psychiatric disturbance
ASA Class II: Mild to moderate disturbances which may or may not be related to the reasons for surgery
ASA Class III: Severe systemic abnormality from any cause
ASA Class IV: Systemic disturbance which is life-threatening with or without surgery
ASA Class V: Moribund patient submitted to surgery in a resuscitative effort
Emergency Class (E): Any patient in the above classes scheduled for emergency surgery

SPECIFIC DISEASES

The following discussion of the anesthetic implications of various disease entities suggests some of the concerns of the anesthesiologist.

Hereditary

Inborn Errors of Metabolism

MUCOPOLYSACCHARIDOSES

The mucopolysaccharidoses (see Chap. 2) are a heterogeneous group of progressive inherited disorders in which enzymatic defects result in accumulation of mucopolysaccharide in various tissues. The clinical features of the eight types depend on the exact enzyme deficiency. For purposes of brevity, the anesthetic implications of type I, Hurler syndrome, will be discussed and the others mentioned only if the clinical variation has anesthetic consequences. Patients with Hurler syndrome have a large head, and tonsils and adenoids are large. These patients are mouth-breathers, because the nose is often blocked by secretions. The hepatosplenomegaly, restricted chest movement secondary to skeletal abnormalities, and abnormal laryngeal and tracheobronchial cartilages predispose them to frequent chest infections. Skeletal abnormalities and thickened soft tissue may limit mouth opening.

In types IV (Morquio) and V (Maroteaux-Lamy), the atlantoaxial joint can be unstable due to hypoplasia of the odontoid process. The patients are therefore vulnerable to acute spinal cord compression, and indeed this has occurred under general anesthesia, causing permanent spastic quadriplegia.

The thickened skin and stiff joints can make venous access difficult. Cardiac involvement is usual, with thickened valve leaflets leading to incompetent or stenotic lesions. Coronary artery deposits can cause significant narrowing and ischemic heart disease at a relatively young age. Systemic and pulmonary hypertension are not unusual.

Other clinical features of the mucopolysaccharidoses include corneal clouding, progressive deafness, abnormal dentition, and varying degrees of mental retardation. These patients present the anesthesiologist with significant problems. Indeed, two recent articles reviewing the anesthetic histories of these patients in two institutions reveal that an uncomplicated anesthetic is rare. The problems encountered were primarily related to difficulties with the airway.[28,29] One of these reports estimated perioperative and postoperative mortality at 20%.[29]

An anesthesiologist should be consulted early for a patient with one of the mucopolysaccharidoses. A thorough workup (including pulmonary and cardiac) is essential, and the risks of an anesthetic must be evaluated and discussed with the patient's family and physicians. Premedication should include an antisialogogue in view of the copious upper airway secretions—and this would best be glycopyrrolate to avoid the tachycardia of atropine (and subsequent increase in myocardial oxygen consumption and decrease in diastolic filling time). A preoperative sedative can result in upper airway obstruction and as a rule should be avoided. In selected patients a light premedication with oral diazepam may be indicated. Valvular cardiac lesions suggest the need for routine antibiotic prophylaxis. Anticipated problems maintaining an airway dictate that an intravenous line be established prior to the induction of anesthesia. For the same reason, muscle paralysis is contraindicated until the airway is secured.

Anesthesia should be induced with the spontaneous ventilation of nitrous oxide, oxygen, and increasing concentrations of halothane. Difficulties in maintaining an airway with a mask may not be alleviated with an oral airway, and a nasopharyngeal airway may be helpful. It has been documented that some of these patients experience tracheal collapse when the neck is flexed, and a roll under the shoulders may provide the extension necessary for tracheal patency. Laryngoscopy is typically difficult in these patients. The anesthesiologist should be prepared with an assortment of different shapes and sizes of laryngoscope blades, a fiberoptic laryngoscope, and, as always, the capability of performing an emergency tracheotomy. If visualization of the vocal cords is not possible, an attempt at blind oral or blind nasal intubation can be made. Fiberoptic laryngoscopy by experienced hands may be the best option to intubate the trachea. If all else fails, a catheter passed via a needle through the cricothyroid membrane and advanced retrograde into the mouth can serve as a guide for insertion of the endotracheal tube.

Once the patient is intubated, ventilation should be assisted. Muscle relaxation can now be performed, preferably with metocurine iodide (Metubine Iodide), atracurium, or vecuronium bromide because of their relative cardiovascular stability. The patient with a hypoplastic odontoid process should have some type of external fixation prior to manipulation of the neck.

Maintenance of anesthesia in these patients focuses on cardiovascular stability. There is no "right" way to do this—the anesthesiologist is just ever mindful of the cardiovascular lesions of the patient and the cardiovascular effects of the drugs chosen, closely monitors the interaction, and titrates accordingly.

Recovery from anesthesia may be slow. The patient should not be extubated until airway reflexes are intact. Postoperative airway obstruction is a definite concern, and these patients require close observation. Pain medication should be given very cautiously, and, again, only with close observation. Aggressive chest physiotherapy postoperatively (and preoperatively) is indicated, considering the risk of pulmonary infection.[26,28,29,58]

LIPIDOSES

The lipidoses are progressive disorders characterized by various enzymatic defects resulting in lysosomal accumulation of sphingosine-containing lipids; they are not often seen in the operating room.

Patients with gangliosidoses (types 1, 2, and 3), with their progressive CNS deterioration, present problems with seizures and history or risk of respiratory complications. They are probably at risk for aspiration with induction of anesthesia and should receive no preoperative sedation. They should have their airway protected during anesthesia with endotracheal intu-

bation, and this should be done by an awake intubation or by the rapid-sequence technique with cricoid pressure.

Patients with Niemann-Pick disease have sphingomyelin and cholesterol accumulation in many organs. Accumulation in the marrow, liver, and spleen can lead to anemia and thrombocytopenia, and these should be corrected. Infiltration of the lungs can lead to pulmonary insufficiency and pneumonia, and a test of pulmonary function and an EKG should be obtained prior to operation. Dysfunction would dictate more aggressive intraoperative monitoring.[27,48,66]

PHENYLKETONURIA

Patients who are on a PKU (phenylketonuria) diet should have their blood phenylalanine levels measured before operation. Excessive levels might predispose them to seizures, and low levels might lead to hypoglycemia; either can result in abnormal neurologic and/or psychologic behavior. These patients should not have an excessive preoperative fasting period because care must be taken to avoid a catabolic state and consequent increases in blood phenylalanine. An intravenous infusion of glucose should be started in the operating room before or after the induction of anesthesia and should be continued until the patient can resume oral feedings. Patients who have developed CNS sequelae of phenylketonuria will have varying degrees of mental retardation, and the patient's inability to cooperate may be a challenge.

Patients with seizure disorders should continue to receive perioperative anticonvulsant medication, and the anesthesiologist will avoid, if possible, epileptogenic anesthetics such as ketamine or enflurane. Phenobarbital and phenytoin are hepatic-enzyme-inducing agents, and their effect on the metabolism of anesthetic drugs must be kept in mind. Finally, some of these patients have very sensitive skin, and the anesthesiologist should be cautious in application of tape and use of a face mask.[25]

Other Genetic Disorders

THE MUSCULAR DYSTROPHIES

The muscular dystrophies are characterized by painless degeneration and atrophy of skeletal muscle. There is progressive muscle weakness, but no evidence of muscle denervation. Duchenne's muscular dystrophy is the most common and the most severe. These patients present between 2 and 6 years of age with weakness of the pelvic girdle, followed rapidly by atrophy of other proximal muscles. Creatinine phospho-kinase levels are elevated, reflecting muscle necrosis and an increased permeability of the muscle membrane. Cardiac abnormalities are common, degeneration of cardiac muscle resulting in a decrease in myocardial contractility and mitral regurgitation from papillary muscle dysfunction. EKG changes are present in most patients, presumably reflecting progressive myocardial necrosis. Pulmonary function testing reveals a restrictive pattern, implicating intercostal involvement.

Preparation of a patient with Duchenne's muscular dystrophy for a general anesthetic must take into consideration the psychological impact of the diagnosis (and its associated perioperative morbidity and mortality) on the patient and the family, and the physiologic implications of an increased skeletal muscle membrane permeability and decreased cardiac and pulmonary reserves. There is also an increased risk of malignant hyperthermia under general anesthesia.

Families of patients with Duchenne's muscular dystrophy typically ask for a more factual explanation of the perioperative anesthetic experience than most, and their questions and concerns should be answered with a straightforward and sensitive honesty. The anesthetic risks and the plans to minimize them should be addressed with the family. The patients will have varying levels of understanding depending in part on their age, or, more accurately, the duration of disease in themselves or other family members, and the anesthetic should be discussed with them accordingly. These patients require preoperative pulmonary function testing, a chest radiograph, an EKG, and, possibly, an echocardiogram. A preoperative introduction to chest physiotherapy may not only improve the preoperative pulmonary status of the patient, but may also facilitate its early postoperative introduction. In view of their decreased respiratory reserve, these patients should receive minimal or no premedication. Ideally, an intravenous line should be started prior to the induction of anesthesia.

Use of the potent inhalational agents (halothane, enflurane, isoflurane) is controversial. These drugs are contraindicated in patients susceptible to malignant hyperthermia, and there seems to be an increased risk of malignant hyperthermia in patients with muscular dystrophy. Succinylcholine, a quick-acting depolarizing muscle relaxant, is associated with an exaggerated potassium release leading to cardiac arrhythmias or cardiac arrest, and rhabdomyolysis

with the potential for myoglobinuria and renal failure. It is wisely avoided in these patients. The nondepolarizing muscle relaxants can result in prolonged responses, necessitating cautious titration of these drugs and, potentially, postoperative mechanical ventilation. Marginal pulmonary reserve dictates an anticipation of significant postoperative dysfunction, a conservative and monitored approach to pain relief, and aggressive pulmonary therapy.

Myocardial involvement is problematic in patients with Duchenne's muscular dystrophy, and the contractility-depressant effects of some anesthetic agents (the potent inhalational agents) may not be tolerated; the anesthesiologist must cautiously titrate the various agents. Many of these patients come to the operating room for major surgery (e.g., scoliosis repair) with large fluid shifts, and if they have myocardial dysfunction, they may require a pulmonary artery catheter in addition to a central venous catheter and the routine arterial catheter for continuous blood-pressure monitoring. The decision to use a pulmonary artery catheter will be based on the clinical history, the EKG, the cardiac ECHO, and the proposed surgical procedure.

The other muscular dystrophies (Becker's, limb-girdle, and facioscapulohumeral) carry the same implications though cardiac involvement is less often a concern.[6,12,19,20,22,23,39–41,47,52,53]

NEUROFIBROMATOSIS

Neurofibromatosis, with an incidence of 1 in 3,000 live births and with a progressive pattern of growth of neurofibromas of peripheral, cranial, or autonomic nerves, not infrequently brings patients to the operating room and to an anesthesiologist. Although histologically benign, the neurofibromas can be functionally compromising and cosmetically disfiguring. The anesthesiologist is concerned that the pharynx, larynx, and the peritracheal area are free of involvement. If they are not, the anatomy needs definition by radiographic studies and direct visualization before the patient is anesthetized. Patients with airway involvement should never be paralyzed prior to securing an airway and demonstrating that controlled ventilation is possible; some of these patients may require a tracheostomy. Pulmonary parenchymal involvement with a fibrosing alveolitis is a possibility, resulting in ventilation-perfusion mismatching, a decrease in pulmonary compliance, and pulmonary hypertension, and these patients require preoperative pulmonary function testing, an EKG, and intraoperative blood gas analysis to guide ventilatory assistance. Patients with scoliosis should also have this testing.

An increase in intracranial pressure secondary to an intracranial tumor must be considered, and patients with this must receive an anesthetic technique that will not further increase intracranial pressure. Patients on seizure medications should continue on them in the perioperative period.

A finding of hypertension necessitates a preoperative workup for a pheochromocytoma (1% of patients with neurofibromatosis) and renal artery stenosis (from perivascular neurofibromas). The patient who is diagnosed with a pheochromocytoma must be treated with an alpha-blocking agent (e.g., phenoxybenzamine), and in the presence of persistent tachycardia and/or cardiac dysrrhythmias *after* alpha blockade, a beta blocker. Surgical excision of the pheochromocytoma should then follow. (The complex anesthetic management of these patients is discussed in the anesthesia textbooks.) A pheochromocytoma with its characteristic episodic hypertension may in fact be suspected for the first time under anesthesia, when the patient has continual blood pressure monitoring for the first time. The patient with renal artery stenosis and hypertension requires preoperative medical control of the hypertension, and this should be continued through the time of surgery. Renal function should be evaluated so that the anesthesiologist can use the appropriate precautions with drugs that are excreted by the kidneys.

There are reports of an increased sensitivity to muscle relaxants in patients with neurofibromatosis, and they should be used with careful monitoring. Regional anesthesia in these patients may be difficult because of the presence of neurofibromas, and one must recognize the potential for the future development of spinal cord involvement and the confusion that may result with presentation of symptoms referable to the spine.[4,9,17,33,36,63,70]

TUBEROUS SCLEROSIS

Patients with tuberous sclerosis present with a classic triad of mental retardation, epilepsy, and fibroangiomas. Lesions are most commonly seen on the skin, but they may also occur in the heart, lung, or kidneys. The anesthesiologist is concerned with maintenance of anticonvulsant therapy, and the presence of lesions in the heart (potential for arrhythmias), lung (potential for rupture of lung cysts), and the kidneys (potential for impaired function).[25]

Early Alterations of Embryonic Development

Chromosomal

TRISOMY 21

Down syndrome, or trisomy 21, is a relatively common disorder, occurring in 1 in 1,000 live births. Patients with Down syndrome frequently present for surgical procedures requiring general anesthesia, and some of the anomalies associated with this syndrome are of great significance to the anesthesiologist.

The frequency of cardiac malformations is up to 40%; the most common are endocardial cushion defects (36%) and ventral septal defects (33%) (see Chaps. 2 and 12). Atrial septal defects, tetrology of Fallot, and patent ductus arteriosus are found in less than 10% of patients. Thirty percent of patients with Down syndrome with cardiac disease have multiple cardiac defects. Without surgical correction morbidity and mortality are high. Congestive heart failure, pulmonary hypertension, and pulmonary vascular obstructive disease are complicating factors.

Early surgical correction is now the treatment of choice, but for complete arterio-venous canal, mortality remains high and residual cardiovascular dysfunction in the form of mitral insufficiency, left-to-right shunting, pulmonary artery hypertension, conduction abnormalities, and ventricular dysfunction are potential problems. An early transatrial correction of a VSD, on the other hand, typically results in excellent postoperative hemodynamics.

Pulmonary artery hypertension is reported to occur more frequently in patients with Down syndrome, both with and without cardiac malformations. The reason for this, in patients without cardiac malformations, is unknown but current hypotheses implicate chronic upper airway obstruction secondary to tonsilar and adenoidal hypertrophy, laryngomalacia, obstructive sleep apnea, enlarged tongue, and midfacial hypoplasia. These can all result in alveolar hypoventilation, hypoxemia, and hypercapnia and can chronically or acutely result in an elevation of pulmonary artery pressures. In addition, patients with Down syndrome may have a diminished number of alveoli with a loss of capillary surface area, and this can result in development of pulmonary artery hypertension.

Clearly, all patients with Down syndrome should have an EKG, an echocardiogram, and a chest radiograph before operation to screen for cardiac disease. Patients with cardiac disease should be evaluated by a cardiologist. The interest here is to know the functioning physiology for the particular patient. A simple "ok for surgery" is not very useful information; specifics of ventricular function, shunt fractions, pulmonary and systemic pressures, and conduction abnormalities, on the other hand, will guide the choice of anesthetic drugs and monitoring.

The pediatrician can facilitate the care of the patient with cardiac disease by appreciating that the specifics of a cardiology evaluation are required (for example, a history of a repaired VSD is inadequate in itself; it is important to know when it was repaired, whether there was congestive heart failure, and whether there was any evidence of pulmonary hypertension or residual hypertension). The anesthesiologist will want to see a current EKG, chest radiograph, and possibly an echocardiogram (depending on the cardiac lesion). The anesthetic care of the patient with uncorrected or residual cardiac disease may be prolonged and invasive, even for simple surgical procedures.

Patients with Down syndrome have airways that may be problematic for the anesthesiologist. They typically have a narrow nasopharynx and relatively large tonsils, adenoids, and tongue that can make ventilation with an anesthetic mask difficult and may necessitate the avoidance of preoperative sedation and necessitate close postoperative observation. Patients with Down syndrome have an increased frequency of subglottic stenosis, and they may require a smaller endotracheal tube than anticipated—actual size is dictated by the quantification of a leak around the tube with positive-pressure ventilation.

Children with Down syndrome are prone to respiratory infections, possibly because of B and T lymphocyte abnormalities and/or repeated exposure to infectious agents in an institutional setting. It may be difficult to find a time when they are not symptomatic with a rhinorrhea, and the guidelines of timing for anesthesia and surgery should possibly be modified to proceeding if the patient is at baseline. An antisialogogue before operation may facilitate airway management.

Ten percent of patients with Down syndrome have atlantoaxial joint instability (see Chap. 8), and they are at risk of spinal cord injury with laryngoscopy or positioning for surgery. Patients with gait disturbances, abnormalities of neck motion, or excessive laxity of more readily examined joints should have neck radiographs preoperatively to diagnose the need for neck stabilization. Exaggerated neck motion is probably best avoided in any of these patients.

Persistent primary congenital hypothyroidism occurs 28 times more frequently in infants with Down syndrome than in the general population, and this diagnosis, as well as hypothyroidism of later onset, should be kept in mind (see Chap. 15). If the patient is so affected, elective surgery should be postponed until the patient is euthyroid. If surgery cannot be delayed, the anesthesiologist must anticipate an increased sensitivity to depressant drugs, a hypodynamic cardiovascular system, slowed drug biotranformation, unresponsive baroreceptor reflexes, a decreased intravascular volume, impaired ventilatory responses, delayed gastric emptying, hyponatremia, hypothermia, anemia, and hypoglycemia.

Historically, it has been held that patients with Down syndrome have an increased sensitivity to the cardioacceleratory effects of atropine. Several studies have now demonstrated that this is not the case and that atropine can safely be used.[65]

With all of these potential problems, one might expect a significant frequency of complications with anesthesia in patients with Down syndrome. Fortunately, this does not seem to be the case. Kobel, Creighton, and Steward[31] reported in 1982 on 100 consecutive operations (including cardiac) involving anesthesia in patients with Down syndrome, and found a low incidence of complications—14 patients, to be exact, with postintubation croup, requirement for airway support, or postoperative respiratory depression. These patients in fact seem to do rather well with general anesthesia.[1-3,5,10,11,13,18,31, 37,51,53,55,59-61,65,67,68]

TRISOMY 13

In the context of micrognathia with or without cleft lip or palate, patients with trisomy 13 can be difficult to intubate, and they may require an awake intubation to insure airway control. Associated cardiac disease in 80% of patients necessitates a complete preoperative cardiac workup to decide on appropriate anesthetic technique.[8,57]

TRISOMY 18

Again, micrognathia (80%) may make intubation difficult and may dictate an awake intubation. Congenital cardiac disease (95%) must be diagnosed and defined. Renal function should be assessed to guide in choice of drugs.[8,56]

PRADER-WILLI SYNDROME

Prader-Willi syndrome (see also Chap. 10), with neonatal hypotonia, mental retardation, genital hypoplasia, and later hyperphagia and obesity, presents several anesthetic problems.

Neonatal hypotonia carries a risk of aspiration, and care should be exercised in preventing this by either performing an awake intubation or a rapid-sequence induction of anesthesia with cricoid pressure. No abnormal responses to muscle relaxants have been reported, but certainly cautious titration of these drugs with monitoring is indicated.

Some patients with Prader-Willi syndrome exhibit disturbances in thermoregulation, and the anesthesiologist must be prepared to provide external sources of heating and cooling. Hyperthermia under general anesthesia always raises the question of a malignant hyperthermia reaction, and this must be evaluated aggressively if hyperthermia occurs.

Obesity, from any cause, carries a significant increase in perioperative morbidity. These patients have an increase in O_2 consumption and CO_2 production, a decrease in chest wall compliance and functional residual capacity, and ventilation/perfusion mismatching. Cardiac output and blood volume are increased, resulting in progressive cardiac hypertrophy. Some of these patients suffer from obesity hypoventilation syndrome (pickwickian syndrome) with cardiac enlargement, polycythemia, hypoxemia, and hypercapnia. There is a linear increase in intraabdominal pressure with increasing weight, and these patients are at risk of aspiration. In fact, most obese patients have a gastric pH below 2.5 and a gastric volume greater than 25 ml at the time of anesthesia induction, increasing the morbidity of an aspiration if it occurs. An obese person should not be premedicated with drugs that depress ventilation—oral diazepam is a good alternative. A preoperative EKG, CXR, and arterial blood gas are indicated. The risk of aspiration suggests the advantage of preoperative treatment with cimetidine, and the patient should be intubated awake after topical anesthesia or with a rapid-sequence induction with cricoid pressure.

The morbidly obese patient requires controlled ventilation intraoperatively, and analysis of the efficacy of that ventilation should be confirmed with blood gas analysis. Morbidly obese patients are at postoperative risk of hypoxemia and atelectasis, and care should be taken to assure that oxygen is administered by nasal prongs or a mask and that these patients receive aggressive chest physiotherapy. Venous thrombosis occurs with twice the frequency in obese patients, and prevention with early ambulation is indicated. Postoperative analgesia should be administered with caution because it can precipitate respiratory depression.

Hyperphagia in itself can be a problem. Patients coming to the operating room must not have anything by mouth 6 to 8 hours prior to surgery (4 hours in infancy). The patient with Prader-Willi syndrome might not appreciate the import of the food restriction, and the nursing staff will have to watch closely that nothing is taken orally.[42,45,69,71]

Prenatal Influence Syndromes

Potential anesthetic problems in patients disabled because of prenatal TORCH infections or maternal drug or alcohol use relate to the particular manifestations of pathology in a given patient. The anesthesiologist is concerned with the presence of hydrocephalus (is it effectively treated with a shunt?), microcephaly (probable decrease in anesthetic dose requirements), seizure disorders (maintenance of adequate anticonvulsant levels and possibility of microsomal enzyme induction), level of mental functioning (how best to maximize patient cooperation and minimize psychologic trauma), visual impairment (need for verbal and tactile communication and/or arrangements for eyeglasses to accompany patient to operating room), hearing impairment (need for visual and tactile communication and arrangements for hearing aides to accompany patient), congenital heart disease (requirement for preoperative definition of functional status, antibiotic prophylaxis, appropriate anesthetic agents, and monitoring), airway reflexes (adequate to prevent aspiration?), and midface and mandibular anatomy (potential problems with intubation or anesthesia mask ventilation with loss of consciousness). The presence of these or other manifestations should be communicated, personally or by record, to the anesthesiologist.

Structural Defects

CRANIOSYNOSTOSIS

Premature closure of cranial sutures should be diagnosed and treated before a patient develops intracranial pathology. The possibility of increased intracranial pressure should be considered, however, in any patient with craniosynostosis. If it is present, the anesthesiologist will want to use a technique that minimizes an increase in intracranial pressure: a Pentothal induction, muscle relaxation, lidocaine anesthesia for the endotracheal intubation (to prevent tachycardia and hypertension and a subsequent increase in intracranial pressure), appropriate doses of narcotics for analgesia, low doses, if any, of inhalation agents, and hyperventilation. The major intraoperative complication of this surgical procedure is hemorrhage. Blood should be immediately available for transfusion. An arterial catheter is indicated for continuous blood pressure monitoring and blood sampling. Depending on the degree of head tilt and the area of surgery, intraoperative air embolization is a possibility and the anesthesiologist, after discussion with the surgeon of these factors, may want to monitor for this with a precordial doppler, continuous end tidal CO_2 monitoring, and prepare for treatment by aspiration from a central venous catheter.[34]

KLIPPEL-FEIL SYNDROME

Patients with Klippel-Feil syndrome, whose cervical vertebrae are congenitally fused, are very difficult to intubate. Spontaneous ventilation must be maintained during the intubation, either with the patient awake or breathing inhalation agents. Direct visualization of the vocal cords is unlikely—a blind or fiberoptic technique is usually required.

HYDROCEPHALUS

Placement, revision, or removal of ventricular shunts for hydrocephalus are common operative procedures in a pediatric anesthesia practice. Some of these children will have an increase in intracranial pressure and will require the techniques mentioned above. These children, symptomatic with headache and vomiting, are at risk of aspiration, and anesthesia should be induced by the intravenous rapid-sequence technique with cricoid pressure. Some patients present in the operating room as true emergencies with apnea and bradycardia necessitating aggressive intervention; thiopental sodium and hyperventilation are effective in quickly decreasing intracranial pressure. Potential intraoperative problems include cardiovascular instability with decompression of the ventricles. After operation these patients should be maintained in a slight head-up position to facilitate free drainage of cerebrospinal fluid.[44]

MYELODYSPLASIA

The infant with dysraphism of the spine (myelodysplasia) or of the head (encephalocele) can be difficult to position for induction of anesthesia and for endotracheal intubation. In some cases, it is possible to position the defect in a soft doughnut-shaped support, allowing the ideal supine position for these procedures. When this is not possible because of the size or position of the defect, intubation with the patient in a left lateral position is indicated. The anesthetic technique must take into consideration the possibility that the neurosurgeon may want to directly stimulate neural tissue. If this is the case, neuromuscular blocking agents should be avoided. These patients commonly have an associated hydrocephalus and Arnold-Chiari malformation (a downward displacement of brain stem structures into a deformity of the upper cervical spine). An increase in intracranial pressure necessitates techniques to lower the pressure, and the signs of brain stem compression (swallowing difficulty, stridor secondary to vocal cord paralysis, and apnea) must be closely observed, especially with positioning of the head in flexion.

Neurologic deficits frequently bring these children to the operating room for orthopedic, urologic, and ventricular shunt procedures. The psychological impact of repeated surgical procedures is considerable, and these children and young adults are often fearful and require special consideration.[30,34,43,46,49]

Cerebral Palsy

The primary caretakers of a patient with cerebral palsy can do a great deal for their patient by explicitly informing the anesthesiologist if mental retardation is present (or absent). An erroneous assumption of mental retardation can easily lead to an inappropriate approach to the patient with cerebral palsy.

The nonprogressive abnormalities of motor function and posture or the aberrant movement disorders that characterize cerebral palsy can present problems of positioning for surgery. These patients should be intubated for surgery because of their propensity for gastroesophageal reflux and poorly functioning laryngeal and pharyngeal reflexes. Temperature monitoring and means of heating are especially important because these patients are particularly susceptible to intraoperative hypothermia.

Patients with an associated seizure disorder may be on drugs that stimulate hepatic microsomal enzyme activity, and the response to anesthetic drugs that are biotransformed in the liver may be altered. The concern for a hyperkalemic response to succinylcholine has been recently addressed in a study which reported that succinylcholine did not cause hyperkalemia in patients with cerebral palsy. These patients are at increased risk of pulmonary complications after operation, and aggressive attempts at prevention are indicated.[15]

GUIDELINES FOR THE PRIMARY CARE PHYSICIAN

The primary physician's guidelines in preparing any patient for anesthesia, but especially these more complicated patients, are (1) consult with the anesthesiologist early—careful planning is the best way to avoid problems, (2) communicate knowledge of the patient's mental and emotional status to the anesthesiologist—this is sometimes difficult in brief encounters, and progress notes are typically not very helpful for this, (3) know that the anesthesiologist's dictum is to have the patient in the best medical condition possible prior to an anesthetic, and (4) remember that there is no such thing as "a little anesthesia"—all anesthetics, even those for minor surgery or diagnostic tests, are "major" and require the same degree of preparation.

REFERENCES

1. Aggarwal, K.C., et al.: Cor pulmonale due to laryngomalacia in Down syndrome. Indian Pediatr., *18*:914, 1981.
2. Barroeta, O., et al.: Defective monocyte chemotaxis in children with Down syndrome. Pediatr. Res., *17*:292, 1983.
3. Baxter, R.G., et al.: Down syndrome and thyroid function in adults. Lancet, *2*:794, 1975.
4. Berryhill, R.E.: Skin and bone disorders. In Anesthesia and Uncommon Diseases. Edited by J. Katz, J. Benumof, and L. Kadis. Philadelphia, W.B. Saunders, 1981, p. 571.
5. Bird, T.M., and Strunin, L.: Anaesthesia for a patient with Down's syndrome and Eisenmenger's complex. Anaesthesia, *39*:48, 1984.
6. Brownell, A.K., et al.: Malignant hyperthermia in Duchenne muscular dystrophy. Anesthesiology, *58*:180, 1983.
7. Bryan, M.H., et al.: Pulmonary function studies during the first year of life in infants recovering from the respiratory distress syndrome. Pediatrics, *52*:169, 1973.
8. Carey, J.C.: Chromosomal disorders. In Pediatrics. Edited by A.M. Rudolph. East Norwalk, CT, Appleton Century Crofts, 1982, p. 245.
9. Chang-lo, M.: Laryngeal involvement in von Recklinghausen's disease. Laryngoscope, *87*:435, 1977.
10. Chi, T., and Krovetz, L.J.: The pulmonary vascular bed in children with Down syndrome. J. Pediatr., *86*:533, 1975.
11. Clark, R.W., et al.: Sleep induced ventilatory dysfunction in Down's syndrome. Arch. Intern. Med., *140*:45, 1980.
12. Cobham, J.E., and Davis, H.S.: Anesthesia for muscular dystrophy patients. Anesth. Analg., *43*:22, 1964.
13. Conney, T.P., and Thurlbeck, W.M.: Pulmonary hypoplasia in Down's syndrome. N. Engl. J. Med., *307*:1170, 1982.
14. Cottrell, J.E., and Turndorf, H.: Anesthesia and Neurosurgery. St. Louis, C.V. Mosby, 1979.
15. Dierdorf, S.F., and McNiece, W.L.: Effect of succinylcholine on plasma potassium in children with cerebral palsy. Anesthesiology, *61*:A432, 1984.
16. El-Ganzouri, A.R.: Monoamine oxidase inhibitors: Should they be discontinued preoperatively. Anesth. Analg., *64*:592, 1985.
17. Fisher, M.M.: Anaesthetic difficulties in neurofibromatosis. Anaesthesia, *30*:648, 1975.
18. Fort, P., et al.: Abnormalities of thyroid function in infants with Down syndrome. J. Pediatr., *104*:545, 1984.
19. Genever, E.E.: Suxamethonium induced cardiac arrest in unsuspected pseudohypertrophic muscular dystrophy. Br. J. Anaesth., *43*:984, 1971.
20. Gibbs, P.S., and Kim, K.C.: Skin and musculoskeletal diseases. In Anesthesia and Co-Existing Disease. Edited by R.K. Stoelting and S.F. Dierdorf. New York, Churchill Livingstone, 1983, p. 583.
21. Gilman, A.G., et al.: The Pharmacological Basis of Therapeutics. New York, Macmillan, 1980.
22. Henderson, W.A.: Succinylcholine induced cardiac arrest in unsuspected Duchenne muscular dystrophy. Can. Anaesth. Soc. J., *31*:444, 1984.
23. Heymsfield, S.B., et al.: Sequence of cardiac changes in Duchenne's muscular dystrophy. Am. Heart J., *95*:283, 1978.
24. Jackson, S.H.: Genetic and metabolic disease. In Anesthesia and Uncommon Diseases. Edited by J. Katz, J. Benumof, and L. Kadis. Philadelphia, W.B. Saunders, 1981, p. 35.
25. Kadis, L.: Neurologic disorders. In Anesthesia and Uncommon Diseases. Edited by J. Katz, J. Benumof, and L. Kadis. Philadelphia, W.B. Saunders, 1981, p. 504.
26. Kadis, L.B.: Neurologic disorders. In Anesthesia and Uncommon Diseases. Edited by J. Katz, J. Benumof, and L. Kadis. Philadelphia, W.B. Saunders, 1981, p. 496.
27. Kadis, L.B.: Neurologic disorders. In Anesthesia and Uncommon Diseases. Edited by J. Katz, J. Benumof, and L. Kadis. Philadelphia, W.B. Saunders, 1981, p. 499.
28. Kempthorne, P.M., and Brown, T.C.: Anaesthesia and the mucopolysaccharidoses: A survey of techniques and problems. Anaesth. Intensive Care, *11*:203, 1983.
29. King, D.H., Jones, R.M., and Barnett, M.B.: Anaesthetic considerations in the mucopolysaccharidoses. Anaesthesia, *39*:126, 1984.
30. Kirsch, W.M., et al.: Laryngeal palsy in association with myelomeningocele, hydrocephalus, and the Arnold-Chiari malformation. J. Neurosurg., *28*:207, 1968.
31. Kobel, M., Creighton, R.E., and Steward, D.J.: Anaesthetic considerations in Down's syndrome: Experience with 100 patients and a review of the literature. Can. Anaesth. Soc. J., *29*:593, 1982.
32. Krane, E.J., and Rockoff, M.A.: Pediatric neuroanesthesia. Semin. Anesth., *3*:117, 1984.
33. Krishna, G.: Neurofibromatosis, renal hypertension, and cardiac dysrhythmias. Anesth. Analg., *54*:542, 1975.
34. Krishna, G., et al.: The pediatric patient. In Anesthesia and Co-existing Disease. Edited by R.K. Stoelting and S.F. Dierdorf. New York, Churchill Livingstone, 1983, p. 766.
35. Krishna, G., et al.: The pediatric patient. In Anesthesia and Co-existing Disease. Edited by R.K. Stoelting and S.F. Dierdorf. New York, Churchill Livingstone, 1983, p. 753.
36. Krishna, G., et al.: The pediatric patient. In Anesthesia and Co-existing Disease. Edited by R.K. Stoelting and S.F. Dierdorf. New York, Churchill Livingstone, 1983, p. 771.
37. Levine, O.R., and Simpser, M.: Alveolar hypoventilation and cor pulmonale associated with chronic airway obstruction in infants with Down syndrome. Clin. Pediatr., *21*:25, 1982.

38. Liu, L.M.P., et al.: Life threatening apnea in infants recovering from anesthesia. Anesthesiology, *59*:505, 1983.

39. McKishnie, T.D., and Girvan, D.P.: Anesthesia induced rhabdomyolysis. Can. Anaesth. Soc. J., *30*:295, 1983.

40. Miller, E.D., et al.: Anesthesia induced rhabdomyolysis in a patient with Duchenne's muscular dystrophy. Anesthesiology, *48*:146, 1978.

41. Miller, J., and Lee, C.: Muscle diseases. *In* Anesthesia and Uncommon Diseases. Edited by J. Katz, J. Benumof, and L. Kadis. Philadelphia, W.B. Saunders, 1981, p. 530.

42. Moorthy, S.S.: Metabolism and nutrition. *In* Anesthesia and Co-existing Disease. Edited by R.K. Stoelting and S.F. Dierdorf. New York, Churchill Livingstone, 1983, p. 507.

43. Myers, G.J.: Myelomeningocele: The medical aspects. Pediatr. Clin. N. Am., *31*(1):165, 1984.

44. Newfield, P., and Cottrell, J.E. (eds.): Handbook of Neuroanesthesia: Clinical and Physiologic Essentials. Boston, Little Brown, 1983.

45. Palmer, S.K., and Atlee, J.L. III: Anesthetic management of the Prader-Willi syndrome. Anesthesiology, *44*:161, 1976.

46. Park, T.S., et al.: Experience with surgical decompression of the Arnold-Chiari malformation in young infants with myelomeningocele. Neurosurgery, *13*:147, 1983.

47. Perloff, J.K., et al.: The cardiomyopathy of progressive muscular dystrophy. Circulation, *3*:625, 1966.

48. Robinson, A., Goodman, S.I., and O'Brien, D.: Genetic and chromosomal disorders, including inborn errors of metabolism. *In* Current Pediatric Diagnosis and Treatment. Edited by C.H. Kempe, et al. Los Altos, CA, Lange Medical, 1984, p. 1021.

49. Rockoff, M.A.: Pediatric neurosurgery. *In* Handbook of Neuroanesthesia: Clinical and Physiologic Essentials. Edited by P. Newfield and J.E. Cottrell. Boston, Little Brown, 1983, p. 368.

50. Roizen, M.F.: Preoperative evaluation of patients with diseases that require special preoperative evaluation and intraoperative management. *In* Anesthesia. Edited by R.D. Miller. New York, Churchill Livingstone, 1981, p. 29.

51. Rowland, T.W., et al.: Chronic upper airway obstruction and pulmonary hypertension in Down syndrome. Am. J. Dis. Child., *135*:1050, 1981.

52. Sanyal, S.K., et al.: Dystrophic degeneration of papillary muscle and ventricular myocardium. Circulation, *62*:430, 1980.

53. Scott, J.G., and Allan, D.: Anaesthesia for density in children: A review of 101 surgical procedures. Can. Anaesth. Soc. J., *17*:391, 1970.

54. Seay, A.R., et al.: Cardiac arrest during induction of anesthesia in Duchenne muscular dystrophy. J. Pediatr., *93*:88, 1978.

55. Semine, A.A., et al.: Cervical spine instability in children with Down's syndrome. J. Bone Joint Surg., *60*:649, 1978.

56. Smith, D.W.: Recognizable Patterns of Human Malformation. Philadelphia, W.B. Saunders, 1982, p. 14.

57. Smith, D.W.: Recognizable Patterns of Human Malformation. Philadelphia, W.B. Saunders, 1982, p. 18.

58. Smith, D.W.: Recognizable Patterns of Human Malformation. Philadelphia, W.B. Saunders, 1982, pp. 334-349.

59. Spicer, R.L.: Cardiovascular disease in Down syndrome. Pediatr. Clin. N. Am., *31*(6):1331, 1984.

60. Spina, C.A., et al.: Altered cellular immune functions in patients with Down syndrome. Am. J. Dis. Child., *135*:251, 1981.

61. Strome, M.: Down syndrome: A modern otorhinolaryngological perspective. Laryngoscope, *91*:1581, 1981.

62. Takaori, M., and Loehning, R.W.: Ventricular arrhythmias induced by aminophylline during halothane anaesthesia in dogs. Can. Anaesth. Soc. J., *14*:79, 1967.

63. Triplett, W.W.: Case report: Anesthetic considerations in von Recklinghausen's disease. Anesth. Prog., *27*:63, 1980.

64. Vissintainer, M.A., and Wolfer, J.A.: Psychological preparation for surgical patients. Pediatrics, *56*:187, 1975.

65. Ward, H.J., et al.: The safety of atropine premedication in children with Down's syndrome. Anaesthesia, *38*: 871, 1983.

66. Wenger, D.A.: Defects in metabolism of lipids. *In* Textbook of Pediatrics. Edited by R.E. Behrman, V.C. Vaughan, and W.E. Nelson. Philadelphia, W.B. Saunders, 1983, p. 476.

67. Whaley, W.J., and Gray, W.D.: Atlantoaxial dislocation and Down's syndrome. Can. Med. Assoc. J., *123*:35, 1980.

68. Wilson, S.K., et al.: Hypertensive pulmonary vascular disease in Down syndrome. J. Pediatr., *95*:722, 1979.

69. Yamaguchi, M., et al.: Anesthetic experience of Prader-Willi syndrome. J. Clin. Anesth., *5*:411, 1981.

70. Yamashita, M., et al.: Anaesthetic considerations on von Recklinghausen's disease. Anaesthesia, *26*:117, 1977.

71. Yamashita, M., et al.: Anaesthetic considerations in the Prader-Willi syndrome. Can. Anaesth. Soc. J., *30*:1791, 1983.

23

MANAGEMENT OF CHILDREN AND ADULTS WITH SEVERE AND PROFOUND CENTRAL NERVOUS SYSTEM DYSFUNCTION

I. Leslie Rubin, M.D.

The term mental retardation and its descriptions of degree—severe or profound—are not only inappropriate in this context in that they do not fully qualify what they set out to do, but they also deny the realities of what they set out to define. By using the terms in describing a group of individuals by tested IQ, one ignores the etiology, nature, and implications of the underlying pathology. This may well be part of the reason that the medical (including psychiatric) services to this population have lagged behind the other services. Nowhere is this more striking than in that group of children and adults who have severe and profound degrees of involvement.

As shown in Chapter 5, mental retardation is but one manifestation of central nervous system dysfunction—whatever the etiology. The important consideration when addressing the issue of medical care is the reflection on the direct, indirect, and interrelated implications and effects of the central nervous system dysfunction. The greater the degree of (CNS) dysfunction, the more dramatic will be its manifestations and the greater will be the complexity (Table 23-1).

Although the population under discussion represents a relatively small number of individuals, they present with a challenging and compelling set of personal, social, and medical needs.[11,15]

CHARACTERISTICS

Crocker and Nelson[6] have eloquently teased out the features that characterize this group of people:

Limited Self-Care and Survival Skills

This group of people needs constant supervision, with attention to such basic needs as bathing, dressing, feeding, and toileting. Their dependency on caretakers will extend beyond childhood and indeed for the rest of their lives because their potential for development or learning is severely compromised.

Limited Educational Potential

Given the severity of their disability along with the right of all children to public education, it becomes a challenge to parents, caretakers, teachers, vocational and rehabilitation counselors, and all professionals involved in the care of this population to determine what services and programs are appropriate. Providing intervention for this population requires extraordinary sensitivity and creativity and demands great expenditures of time and energy.

Impaired Abilities to Communicate

It is implicit in the designation that verbal and nonverbal language will be minimal. This major handicap in socialization requires caretakers who are sensitive to minor nuances in behavior that can be interpreted as signals of need or distress.[5] The inability to communicate becomes particularly significant when changes in mood or behavior occur that might represent clinical disorders.

Disorders of Socialization and Behavior

Along with the limited ability in communication there often exist disorders of behavior (see Chap. 20, section by Doherty and Szymanski). These behaviors may represent attempts to react to or interact with the environment or people but will manifest in universal, nonspecific ways. They may also be nondirected, repetitive, and self stimulatory (e.g., rocking, twirling), or even self-injurious (e.g., head-banging) and medically relevant behaviors such as rumination and aerophagia.[1]

Serious Organic Handicaps

When presented with the serious organic handicaps that can affect this population, the physician must adapt and exercise knowledge and clinical acumen in order to provide ongoing health care as well as to provide information and insight to parents, caretakers, therapists, teachers, and advocates. In order to begin to understand the complexity of clinical challenges it is useful to consider that the medical problems fall into three major categories:

1. conditions directly attributable to severe central nervous system dysfunction, e.g., seizures, disorders of motor function, and sensory impairment
2. conditions indirectly attributable to CNS dysfunction, e.g., orthopedic handicaps, feeding problems, and disorders of gastrointestinal motility
3. conditions relating to the underlying etiology of the CNS dysfunction, be it progressive, e.g., mucopolysaccharidosis, or nonprogressive, e.g., chromosomal anomalies or congenital infections

AGE AT PRESENTATION

Although it is difficult to predict the developmental future for infants and young children

Table 23-1. *Rates of Associated Handicaps in Swedish School Age Children with Mental Retardation*

Handicap	Percent Handicapped, by IQ Level	
	Under 50	50 to 70
Cerebral palsy	21	9
Epilepsy	37	12
Hydrocephalus	5	2
Severe impairment of hearing	8	7
Severe impairment of vision	15	1
One or more associated neurologic handicap	40	24

Adapted from Hagberg, B., and Kyllerman, M.: Epidemiology of mental retardation—a Swedish survey. Brain & Development, 5:441, 1983.

(even for neonates with low Apgar scores) it is useful to consider that the underlying pathophysiologic process is that of severe CNS dysfunction. With this in mind it is helpful to begin to anticipate the clinical problems that can be encountered. Only with a firm and concise clinical diagnosis and the passage of time will the evolution of the clinical picture with its attendant prognostic implications become evident.

It is useful at this point to consider the age at which various clinical syndromes present.

Neonatal Period

In the neonatal period there are three groups of infants who present with particular challenges: (1) infants with multiple congenital anomalies, particularly those involving cerebral dysgenesis, be they sporadic or due to chromosomal aberrations or intrauterine insults (Chap. 6); (2) infants with severe birth asphyxia, particularly if the symptoms of CNS involvement persist beyond the first week of life (first section of Chap. 5); and (3) infants of very low birth weight, particularly if they have large interventricular hemorrhages (first section of Chap. 5).

Infancy and Childhood

In this age group there are two major etiological considerations: (1) infants and children with genetically determined conditions that may only become clinically evident later, e.g., inborn errors of metabolism (Chap. 2); (2) those with acquired conditions (Table 23-2). These conditions include CNS infections, CNS tumors and accidental events which can occur at any age.

Table 23-2. *Postnatal Causes of Profound CNS Dysfunction in a Group of Children from a Pediatric Nursing Center*

Cause	Number
CNS infection	7
Asphyxial accident	4
Cardiac arrest	4
Drowning	3
Motor vehicle accident	2
Trauma X	2
Reye syndrome	1
All causes	23

Adolescence

The conditions that occur during adolescence relate mainly to trauma, particularly from motor vehicle accidents, but can also result from other acquired diseases or hereditary progressive neurologic diseases such as the muscular dystrophies.

CLINICAL PROBLEMS

There have been a number of surveys of associated medical problems that can be found in populations with mental retardation,[17,20] cerebral palsy,[16] and other conditions (Chap. 2). These surveys usually specify the orthopedic handicap, seizure disorders, sensory handicaps (hearing and vision), and nutritional issues. For the population with profound disability, however, the disorders are compounded because of the severity of CNS involvement. Also, it may be easy enough to examine one aspect of the individual's array of medical problems, but it becomes more difficult when one has to appreciate that, more often than not, any one individual will have at least three or more complex medical problems (see Hagberg and Kyllerman[11] and Chap. 2). Table 23-3 lists the medical problems and procedures encountered in a group of pediatric patients from a pediatric nursing home[10] (see section by Staub in Chap. 4). There are many children, however, cared for at home by their parents or in specialized foster homes. For the parents (biological, foster, or adoptive), keeping up with the medical needs of their children is a particularly challenging task. It is therefore important to bear this in mind and facilitate the situation by scheduling as many appointments as possible at one time to avoid repeated trips to the same place. Also, it is important to remember that parents can become depleted, and that encouragement and emotional support

Table 23-3. *Survey of Medical Problems of 75 Children in a Pediatric Nursing Center*

Total number surveyed	75
Number of surgical procedures performed in 3-yr period	43
Orthopedic	24
Myringotomies	6
Gastrostomies	6
Fundal plications	4
Dental	3
Tonsillectomy and adenoidectomy	2
Laparotomies	2
Cystotomy	1
Nephrectomy	1
Chronic medical problems	
Number of children with orthotic devices	64
Hand splints	35
Body jackets	31
Leg casts	59
Arm and shoulder splints	5
Milwaukee brace	3
Neurological disorders	
Seizures	62
On 1 anticonvulsant only	19
On 2 anticonvulsants	33
On 3 anticonvulsants	10
Shunted hydrocephalus	11
Urinary tract infections	15
Gastrostomies	44
Fundal plications	19
Recurrent medical problems: number of episodes over 17-month period	
Pneumonia (in 21 patients)	34
Upper gastrointestinal bleeds	8
Hypothermia	8
Fractures (over 3 yr for 9 patients)	12
Clinic visits (over 5 mo)	
Orthopedic	85
Neurology/neurosurgical	13
Dental	17
Other	21
Admissions to tertiary hospitals over 5 mo	13
Total number of radiographs over 5 mo	50

Data prepared by M. Maki and N. Nichols at Children's Extended Care Center, Groton, MA, presented at 1984 annual meeting of the American Association of Mental Deficiency by I.L. Rubin.

should be given at each visit. In some situations, parents may benefit from the support services of parents' groups, or from individual counseling with social workers or therapists. In addition, respite care may be necessary to help families regain strength and composure and just get away for a while.

Although Table 23-3 represents the problems of one group of children, it can serve as a model not only for children at home or in other settings but for adults as well. Chapters 26, 27, and 28 deal with adults in an institutional setting, and

Table 26-7 ("infirmary" group) presents the clinical problems of a population comparable to those children presented in Table 23-3. What can be seen is that many conditions are common to both age groups, e.g., seizure disorders, orthopedic problems, feeding and nutrition problems, respiratory problems, urinary tract infections, skin problems, ear disease, dental care, hypothermia, and dehydration.

Seizure Disorders

Seizure disorders represent a common neurologic disorder in the general population. When relating the prevalence of epilepsy in relation to mental retardation, Alvarez (Chap. 8) makes the distinction of degree of mental retardation. In this population the prevalence of seizure disorders is extremely high. Approximately 80% of this group have seizure disorders, 70% of whom are on more than one anticonvulsant to control the seizures.

Orthopedic Problems

When a CNS disorder translates into disorders of movement and posture the term used is cerebral palsy. This condition manifests, and is identified clinically, in orthopedic problems. As Menkveld (Chap. 9) points out, all joints can be affected, and the management of these problems is one of maintaining optimal function.[18]

Although cerebral palsy and orthopedic problems are not diagnosed per se in Table 23-3, the frequency of orthopedic problems in this population can be appreciated when one considers that 85% of these children require orthotic devices, with an average of 2 devices per child (see Drennan and Gage[8] for information on orthotics). The number of orthopedic clinic visits and number of orthopedic surgical procedures also attests to the magnitude of this problem. The dilemmas involved in making decisions about surgery are discussed by Menkveld (Chap. 9) and Staub (Chap. 4).

It should be noted that the maintenance of function as a philosophical guideline in this population relates mainly to seating rather than ambulation. Although independent bipedal ambulation is by definition not an issue for this population, walkers and motorized wheelchairs should be thoughtfully considered.[2,19] Such devices increase the opportunity for exploration, enhance the developmental potential for children, and help provide an opportunity for socialization for both children and adults.

Feeding and Nutrition

Maintaining an adequate nutritional status for this population can be difficult. Linear growth is frequently impaired, and attempts to maintain appropriate body weight for length or height can be difficult because there are no good standards for this population. Staub uses height age, weight age, and triceps skin fold as his yardsticks (R.U. Staub, personal communication, 1983). Walsh and Feigelman (Chap. 10) present a strong case for biochemical and endocrinologic parameters to assess adequacy of nutrition in adults. Nonetheless, even when these goals are sought and attained, some patients remain underweight by any standards. Some of the explanation for low weight may reside in the low muscle bulk and the tendency to osteoporosis, but undernutrition is a real consideration. Many factors are involved, including feeding difficulties, rumination and gastroesophageal reflux, and chronic constipation.

Feeding difficulties, discussed by Shishmanian and Tomlinson (Chap. 10), include difficulties with sucking, chewing and coordination of swallowing, and nasopharyngeal aspiration.

The problem of rumination and gastroesophageal reflux has been increasingly appreciated by gastroenterologists, but the explanation for the high prevalence of gastroesophageal reflux in this population remains elusive (see sections in Chap. 10 by Roberts and by Walsh and Feigelman). In this survey (Table 23-2), almost 60% had gastrostomy feeding tubes, and almost half had fundal plications as well. In the adult population (see Table 26-7), 22% had rumination and aerophagia and 51% had documented reflux.

It should be noted that because of the commonly associated problem of gastroesophageal reflux in this population it is advisable to perform a fundal plication when gastrostomy feeding is considered.[13,14] As Feigelman and Walsh (Chap. 10) point out, there may be no reasonable alternative method of maintaining adequate nutrition and preventing complications. Upper gastrointestinal bleeds are frequent, recurrent problems, and in almost all cases bleeding is caused by reflux esophagitis. When bleeding occurs at a subclinical level, iron-deficiency anemia will result; therefore, if an unexplained anemia is detected, reflux esophagitis should be considered as a possible cause.[3]

Chronic and serious degrees of constipation are a major problem in this population (see section by Roberts in Chap. 10). Antanitis (Chap. 27) asserts that constipation can present clini-

Table 23-4. *Causes of Death by Level of Retardation for Ages 1 to 24 Years*

	Level of Retardation		
Cause of Death	**Mild and Moderate**	**Severe**	**Profound**
	Mortality rate		
Respiratory infections (e.g., pneumonia)	18	58	71
Accidents (e.g., choking, fire, drowning)	29	22	7
Congenital anomalies (e.g., hydrocephalus, heart defects)	18	4	6
Central nervous system diseases (e.g., epilepsy, meningitis)	3	0	4
Other (e.g., other infections, other organ systems)	32	16	12
	Mortality rate compared to general population		
All causes	2×	7×	31×

Adapted from Herbst, D.S., and Baird, P.A.: Survival rates and causes of death among persons with non-specific mental retardation. *In* Perspectives and Progress in Mental Retardation. Vol. 2, Biomedical Aspects. Edited by J.M. Berg and J.M. DeJong. Baltimore, University Park, 1984.

cally in many ways. As the admissions to hospital for this population show, impaction and volvulus can have serious implications (Chap. 28). Indeed, constipation may contribute to failure to thrive by resulting in vomiting or by some other unspecified mechanism. For all these reasons it should be aggressively prevented and managed.

Respiratory Problems

Pneumonia is the single most significant cause of mortality[4,12] (Table 23-4) and a substantial cause of morbidity in this population (see section by Gavriely in Chap. 11, and Chap. 28). Although intercurrent infections may take their toll in the very young infant and in the geriatric patient, chronic aspiration syndrome is by far the most significant factor in this population. Recurrent pneumonias were recorded on 34 occasions in 21 patients over 17 months in this pediatric population. The source of aspiration may be from swallowing incoordination or, more commonly, from chronic gastroesophageal reflux. Gastroesophageal reflux therefore becomes implicated again as a significant problem that requires thoughtful medical and/or surgical management.

Urinary Tract Infections

Urinary tract infections are being identified as a significant recurrent clinical problem.[9] As Elias and Bauer (Chap. 17) point out, the factors involved relate to bladder dysfunction (most commonly neurogenic bladder), to severity of orthopedic handicap (as a manifestation of the severity of the CNS involvement), to constipation, and to poor perineal hygiene, particularly in females. As can be seen from Table 23-3, one patient required nephrectomy for chronic pyelonephritis and cystostomy for obstructive uropathy, both presumably from a neurogenic bladder. None of the patients in this group had myelodysplasia or any other identifiable spinal cord lesion. It should be appreciated, therefore, that urinary tract infection needs to be actively considered and aggressively managed.

Skin Problems, Ear Disease, and Dental Care

Decubitus skin lesions are a common problem in the patient who is unable to change position. Fortunately the care has improved, and no lesions were documented. Other common problems relate to bruising through trauma and cellulitis, particularly in the older age group (Chap. 28).

Ear disease is a problem in the pediatric age group, as can be seen by the number of myringotomies performed (Table 23-3; see also Chap. 14). Recurrent middle ear infections are a common problem and may have a pathogenetic basis in disordered anatomy and physiology, particularly with nasopharyngeal aspiration.

Dental care is an issue of general health care; tooth brushing must be performed by a caretaker. Aspects of feeding and oral hygiene can be a problem, and Dilantin can cause gum hypertrophy; therefore periodontal disease is a major problem. Regular dental visits are encouraged (Chap. 19).

Hypothermia

Hypothermia is documented as a common recurrent clinical problem (also see Chap. 28). Although CNS regulation of temperature may be implicated, the problem may be more complex. The poor subcutaneous tissue, limited ability to shiver, and dependence on caretakers to pay attention to warmth are all factors. Hypothermia is particularly prevalent in the winter months for obvious reasons, but it can occur during the warmer months and may be the only manifestation of an infection.

Dehydration

Although dehydration is not listed in Table 23-3, it is a significant problem, particularly in hot summer months when fluid requirements are higher (Chap. 28). The reasons are simple. The individuals cannot request fluids and may also have difficulty drinking. Inability to take in adequate fluid may be a consideration for a gastrostomy feeding tube as a supplement. Dehydration can also be a factor in constipation.

Other Clinical Considerations

For a number of reasons, laboratory and radiologic investigations may be more frequent in this population. First, nonspecific manifestation of intercurrent illnesses may require elucidation with the help of hematologic, biochemical, or radiologic studies (see also section by Antanitus in Chap. 27). Second, there are complex underlying clinical problems, e.g., orthopedic problems that need radiologic monitoring and recurrent pneumonias necessitating radiographs (50 radiographs in 5 months!) (Table 23-3). Third, multiple medications are necessary, e.g., anticonvulsants, which may have hematologic, biochemical, or enzymatic effects that require monitoring.

In addition, frequent hospitalizations are necessary (see Chap. 28) for surgery or for intercurrent illnesses, e.g., pneumonias and dehydration. In this survey there were 13 hospital admissions over a 5-month period!

As can be seen from Tables 23-3 and 27-7, other clinical problems occur that may relate to the underlying pathology. For example, fractures can result from osteoporosis, which may be a result of immobility, from inadequate exposure to sunlight, and, theoretically, from anticonvulsants. Fractures can occur with vigorous manipulation or even with sudden spontaneous movement, such as a seizure.

What emerges from the understanding of the multiple and complex problems that can and do occur in this population is that there must be a conceptualization of the underlying pathophysiologic processes and an attempt to anticipate adequately the health care needs (Fig. 23-1). A number of points should be stressed.

First, although the data presented represent surveys of institutionalized children and adolescents, problems can just as likely be encountered in the community, while living at home, and in specialized foster care situations.

Second, given the complexity of the problems, it is implicit that a number of specialty medical services will be involved, e.g., orthopedics, neurology, neurosurgery, and gastroenterology, and that coordination of these services with communication between involved physicians is vital to optimal management.

Finally, the approach to optimal management should be seen in the context of the patient's other needs, be they therapeutic (e.g., physical therapy), educational, or social, because it is only with this philosophy that care can be provided in such a way as to ensure maintenance of functional well-being.

CONSIDERATIONS REGARDING MORTALITY

In the general population, mortality rate and causes of death are intimately linked with quality of health care. This linkage is relevant to industrialized societies with improvement in knowledge and technology particularly over the last 50 years. Improvements in health care have resulted in a decline in infant mortality and an unprecedented life expectancy. In populations where there is not enough food and the quality of health care is inadequate, as in developing countries, mortality rates remain high for all ages.[7]

For the population with severe and profound mental retardation and the complex set of associated medical problems, including congenital anomalies (Chaps. 2 and 6) and inborn errors of metabolism (Chap. 2), mortality is influenced by the nature and extent of the underlying pathology as well as by the availability of optimal health care.

In their review of mortality in British Columbia, Herbst and Baird[12] report that the average death rate for those between the ages of 1 and 19 with nonspecific mental retardation was 11 times higher than the general mortality rate for the same age group. When they examined the mortality rate by level of retardation, they found that for those with mild and moderate retardation it

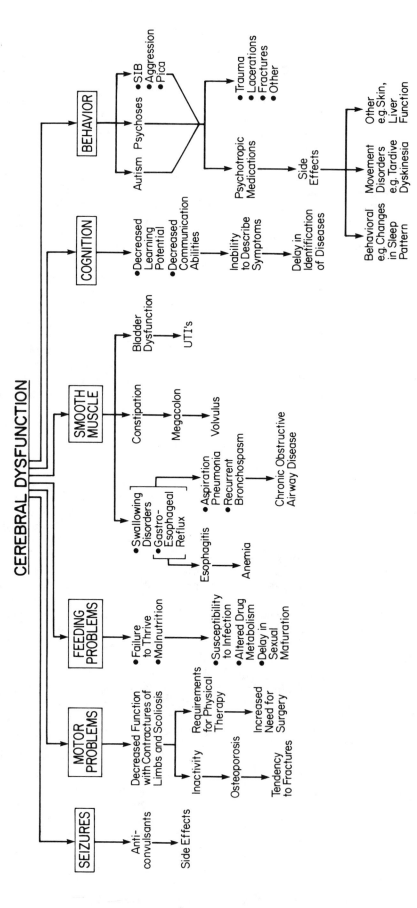

FIG. 23-1. Underlying pathophysiologic processes of cerebral dysfunction. UTI = urinary tract infection. SIB = self-injurious behavior.

was only twice as high, whereas for severe retardation it was increased 7-fold and for profound retardation it was increased 31-fold (Table 23-3).

Herbst and Baird translated their data into the probability for survival to age 20 years for those who had at least reached age 1 year. This was 97.7% for the mild to moderate group (compared to 98.8% for the general population), 91.8% for the severely retarded group, and 67.9% for the profoundly retarded group. There is no question, therefore, that mortality risks are significantly higher for this population.

When the causes of death were analyzed (Table 23-3), there were also significant differences for the degree of retardation, the most striking finding being in the respiratory causes, which increased with severity of retardation at all ages from 1 to 19 years. Respiratory infections were the cause of death for at least half of all cases.

These facts illustrate the enormity of the challenges in this population, in which the clinical entities can be seen across a spectrum of severity. Through the understanding and appreciation of these factors, the health care needs of this group of children and adults can be better served.

REFERENCES

1. Berkson, G., et al.: The relationship between age and stereotyped behaviors. Ment. Retard., 23:31, 1985.
2. Butler, C.: Effects of powered mobility on self-initiative behavior of very young locomotor-disabled children. Presented at the American Academy of Cerebral Palsy and Developmental Medicine in Washington, DC, October 1984.
3. Byrne, W.J., et al.: A diagnostic approach to vomiting in severely retarded patients. Am. J. Dis. Child., 137:259, 1983.
4. Carter, G., and Jancar, J.: Mortality in the mentally handicapped: A 50 year survey at the Stoke Park Group of Hospitals (1930–1980). J. Ment. Defic. Res., 27:143, 1983.
5. Cirrin, F.M., and Rowland, C.M.: Communicative assessment of non-verbal youths with severe/profound mental retardation. Ment. Retard., 23:52, 1985.
6. Crocker, A.C., and Nelson, R.P.: Mental retardation. In Developmental-Behavioral Pediatrics. Edited by M.D.

Levine, W.B. Carey, A.C. Crocker, and R.T. Gross. Philadelphia, W.B. Saunders, 1983.
7. Dogramaci, I.: Parameters of child health. S. Afr. Med. J., 60:49, 1981.
8. Drennan, J.C., and Gage, J.R.: Orthotics. In Comprehensive Management of Cerebral Palsy. Edited by G.H. Thompson, I.L. Rubin, and R.M. Bilenker. New York, Grune & Stratton, 1983.
9. Elias, E.R., and Rubin, I.L.: Urinary tract infections in patients with cerebral palsy. Presented at the American Academy of Cerebral Palsy and Developmental Medicine in Washington, DC, October 1984.
10. Glick, P.S., Guyer, B., Burr, R., and Gorbach, I.E.: Pediatric nursing homes. N. Engl. J. Med., 309:640, 1983.
11. Hagberg, B., and Kyllerman, M.: Epidemiology of mental retardation—A Swedish survey. Brain Dev., 5:441, 1983.
12. Herbst, D.S., and Baird, P.A.: Survival rates and causes of death among persons with non-specific mental retardation. In Perspectives and Progress in Mental Retardation. Vol. 2—Biomedical Aspects. Edited by J.M. Berg and J.M. DeJong. Baltimore, University Park Press, 1984.
13. Mollitt, D.L., Golladay, S., and Seibert, J.J.: Symptomatic gastroesophageal reflux following gastrostomy in neurologically impaired patients. Pediatrics, 75:1124, 1985.
14. Raventos, J.M., Kralemann, H., and Gray, D.B.: Mortality risks of mentally retarded and mentally ill patients after a feeding gastrostomy. Am. J. Ment. Defic., 86:439, 1982.
15. Richardson, S.A., Koller, H., Katz, M., and McLaren, J.: Patterns of disability in a mentally retarded population between ages 6 and 22 years. In Perspectives and Progress in Mental Retardation. Vol. 2—Biomedical Aspects. Edited by J.M. Berg and J.M. DeJong. Baltimore, University Park Press, 1984.
16. Shapiro, B.K., Palmer, F.B., Wachtel, R.C., and Capute, A.J.: Associated dysfunctions. In Comprehensive Management of Cerebral Palsy. Edited by G.H. Thompson, I.L. Rubin, and R.M. Bilenker. New York, Grune & Stratton, 1983.
17. Smith, D.C., Decker, H.A., Herberg, E.N., and Rupkel, K.: Medical needs of children in institutions for the mentally retarded. Am. J. Public Health, 8:1376, 1969.
18. Thompson, G.H., Rubin, I.L., and Bilenker, R.M.: Comprehensive management of cerebral palsy. New York, Grune & Stratton, 1983.
19. Verburg, G., et al.: Providing powered mobility to two to five year olds: The effects on child and family. Presented at the American Academy of Cerebral Palsy and Developmental Medicine in Washington, DC, October 1984.
20. Wright, S.W., Valente, M., and Tarjan, G.: Medical problems on a ward of a hospital for the mentally retarded. Am. J. Dis. Child., 104:142, 1962.

24

MANAGEMENT OF THE GERIATRIC POPULATION

I. Leslie Rubin, M.D. □ *Frances Medaglia Dwyer, R.N.*

The improvement of health care and "quality of life" in the U.S. has increased life expectancy and resulted in the fact that more than 10% of the population is over 65. The proportion is expected to rise to 20% by the year 2020.[2] This change has resulted in an appreciation of the physiology of aging,[2] the neurology of aging,[7] and the pathology of aging.[9]

This improvement in health care has been translated into improved life expectancy for individuals with developmental disabilities. Over the last 50 years, longevity has increased by 40 years for people with Down syndrome and by 30 years for persons with other developmental disorders (Table 24-1).[1] Carter and Jancar note that their findings have "important implications for the planning of future services for the ageing mentally handicapped population, in hospital and in the community alike, with associated geriatric ailments, and pre-senile and senile dementias."[1] Another striking finding in the same study is that deaths due to carcinoma, myocardial infarction, and cerebrovascular accident are increasing, bringing the health care issues of this population in line with what is expected for the general population (Table 24-2). In addition the data were collected from the whole of the country and not specifically from institutions. The improvement in health care in institutions and in the community (particularly for children) has seen an increase in life expectancy for all individuals with mental retardation, regardless of etiology.[5] The mortality for those with severe and profound retardation, however, is higher (Chap. 23).

To some extent the social and biomedical factors that pertain to individuals with developmental disabilities and those who do not have developmental disabilities but are at the extreme end of the age spectrum are similar: both groups are likely to be dependent on others for some basic needs, and both groups are likely to have a coexisting set of significant disabilities. Rowe[10] states that elderly persons living in the community have 3.5 important disabilities per person and that the hospitalized elderly have 6 disabilities per person. The coexistence of multiple medical problems in children and adults with developmental disabilities is well documented.[4] (See also Chaps. 2, 23, and 26.) For an excellent review of the social and biomedical aspects of aging in persons with developmental disabilities the reader is referred to the book by Janicki and Wisniewski.[6]

The health care needs of the developmentally disabled aging population have similarities and differences when compared with the health care needs of the nondevelopmentally disabled aging population. In this population the underlying etiologies of disabilities are different, and there are allied medical and psychosocial factors that must be considered. The underlying etiology of the disability confers on the clinical picture considerations that may not be necessary under other circumstances. The example of the population with Down syndrome illustrates this point.

Table 24-1.   *Distribution of Ages at Death, 1930–1980*

Period	Sex	Age Range (Years)									Total Patients
		0–10	11–20	21–30	31–40	41–50	51–60	61–70	71–80	80+	
1931-35	M	18	32	18	4	0	0	0	0	0	72
	F	5	26	14	6	1	0	0	0	0	52
1936-40	M	33	42	15	10	0	0	0	0	0	100
	F	17	33	17	15	5	1	0	0	0	88
1941-45	M	8	28	12	9	0	0	0	0	0	57
	F	5	20	16	13	7	2	0	1	0	64
1946-50	M	10	20	27	6	3	0	0	0	0	66
	F	12	16	22	11	13	6	0	2	0	82
1951-55	M	21	15	12	8	9	2	1	0	0	68
	F	12	11	19	13	7	12	1	1	0	76
1956-60	M	3	10	8	8	9	12	0	0	0	50
	F	4	4	5	4	6	11	11	4	0	49
1961-65	M	3	6	8	10	12	8	9	1	0	57
	F	7	4	4	10	4	10	8	1	0	48
1966-70	M	6	4	6	7	18	13	12	1	0	67
	F	4	6	7	7	11	19	23	6	0	83
1971-75	M	3	6	7	9	10	9	30	7	0	81
	F	2	1	2	5	10	11	19	20	2	72
1976-80	M	3	3	6	6	7	18	9	8	0	60
	F	1	2	4	6	10	13	21	22	12	91
Total	M	108	166	119	77	68	62	61	17	0	678
	F	69	123	110	90	74	85	84	56	14	705
		177	289	229	167	142	147	145	73	14	1383

From Carter, G., and Jancar, J.: Mortality in the mentally handicapped: A 50 year survey at the Stoke Park Group of Hospitals (1930–1980). J. Ment. Defic. Res., 27:143, 1983. With permission of Blackwell Scientific Publications Limited.

There are frequently multiple underlying chronic medical problems that affect both diagnostic and therapeutic considerations. And there are additional psychosocial factors, which should influence the decision-making process but should in no way compromise provision of health care.

PHYSIOLOGICAL PHENOMENA OF AGING

Data have accumulated on the effects of aging on various physiologic processes. These data have provided an understanding of what constitutes normal aging and what symptoms would suggest underlying pathologic processes.[2,7,10] Rowe[10] stresses this distinction by stating that "anemia of old age" and loss of intellectual skills are not inevitable. If present, these conditions are likely to have a pathologic etiology and clinical investigation is therefore mandatory. A sound basis of knowledge in the physiology of aging as well as in the common clinical conditions that affect this age group will help to make these important distinctions and result in an appropriate course of management.

In Table 24-3, three groups were selected to illustrate the following: (1) Certain clinical conditions increase with age irrespective of the etiologic diagnosis of the developmental disabilities (e.g., hearing loss, cataracts, arthritis, constipation, hemorrhoids, urinary tract infection and varicose veins) although some conditions such as hearing loss and cataracts occur a little more commonly in the Down syndrome group. (2) Some conditions are specific to or occur more commonly in persons with Down syndrome (e.g., Alzheimer's disease, hypothyroidism, neutropenia, mitral valve prolapse, and aortic regurgitation). In this particular group none of the patients with Down syndrome had hypertension or generalized connective tissue disorders.

Central Nervous System

Contrary to many views of the effects of aging on the central nervous system, longitudinal studies have demonstrated a remarkable integrity in the intellectual ability of older individuals, particularly comprehension, vocabulary, processing of

Table 24-2. Causes of Death, 1931–1980

Cause of Death	1931-35	1936-40	1941-45	1946-50	1951-55	1956-60	1961-65	1966-70	1971-75	1976-80	Total Deaths
Respiratory tract infections	53	72	53	62	66	55	53	67	78	76	635
Tuberculosis	41	70	38	46	27	9	4	2	0	0	237
Sudden deaths	8	11	12	18	21	14	22	31	31	36	204
Carcinomas	1	3	3	4	6	10	11	23	20	22	103
Cardiac failure	12	16	7	6	12	6	4	12	8	7	90
Gastrointestinal causes	1	8	2	7	5	2	5	6	6	3	45
Metabolic causes	3	3	4	1	4	2	4	5	5	3	34
Other causes	5	5	2	4	3	1	2	4	5	4	35
Total	124	188	121	148	144	99	105	150	153	151	1383

From Carter, G., and Jancar, J.: Mortality in the mentally handicapped: A 50 year survey at the Stoke Park Group of Hospitals (1930–1980). J. Ment. Defic. Res., 27:143, 1983. With permission of Blackwell Scientific Publications Limited.

information, and manipulation of digits.[7] Any loss of intellectual skills, therefore, should be viewed as pathological, and an etiology should be sought with a view to possible remediation.

Roughly 15% of patients with losses of mental skills have treatable medical causes, e.g., metabolic disturbances, 15 to 25% have cerebrovascular disease, and 70% have Alzheimer's disease.[10] These data are particularly important for adults with developmental disabilities because of their limited ability to communicate. In this group, many clinical conditions frequently present with a loss of function with very little explanation. Whereas a cause would likely be sought in a younger individual, such conditions in the older individual may erroneously be attributed to aging. Indeed, because nutritional disorders are more likely to be a problem in the geriatric population, and because their immunity and physiologic resilience to infection are likely to be reduced, these problems commonly arise and may present insidiously. The symptoms and signs are frequently nonspecific, and loss of appetite may aggravate the situation. It is therefore crucial that any geriatric patient with developmental disabilities who presents with a sudden or gradual loss in skills should have a complete and comprehensive clinical workup.

The increased prevalence of Alzheimer's disease among persons with Down syndrome makes it an important clinical entity among the older population with developmental disabilities (see Chap. 8). Although statistics vary, it appears that (1) neuropathologic findings consistent with Alzheimer's disease are universally present in individuals with Down syndrome after the third decade of life; (2) the clinical syndrome usually does not present until after the fourth and fifth decades of life and is by no means universal, affecting only 10 to 20% of those with Down syndrome; and (3) the presenting features are those of a change in personality with depressive elements and withdrawal as well as the classical features of memory loss and confusion.

If an individual with Down syndrome who is 50 years or older presents with a personality change, it is clear from consideration (2) above that the change is not necessarily Alzheimer's disease and that a thorough clinical evaluation is essential.

If there is intellectual or functional deterioration in an older individual with or without Down syndrome and no obvious pathophysiologic process can be identified, emotional and psychiatric disturbances should also be considered. As with the general population, depression is the most likely diagnosis, and response to antidepressants would be confirmatory.

Although the foregoing discussion assumes that there is no "natural" deterioration in central nervous system function, this is not totally true. There is a decline in functions that involve a complex system of sensory input, with reactions and activities relating to fine motor and gross motor coordination and muscle strength. These, however, relate more to disturbances in peripheral nerve conduction and a reduction in muscle mass than to a central problem.

Hearing

Progressive hearing impairment does occur with increasing age and in most cases is secon-

Table 24-3. *Percentage of Patients with Selected Medical Conditions in Three Patient Groups*

	Group		
	Patients with Down Syndrome		Geriatric Patients (Ages 60–79, Average 66)
Condition	Ages 24–48 (Average 36)	Ages 50–71 (Average 56)	
Alzheimer's disease	0	19	0
Hearing loss	38	42	35
Cataract	45	65	42
Arthritis	3	13	15
Constipation	16	29	26
Hemorrhoids	7	13	12
Urinary tract infections	10	29	22
Prostatism	0	6	20
Hypothyroidism	19	19	5
Diabetes	1	3	11
Benign neutropenia	6	13	0
Generalized connective tissue disorders	0	0	6
Mitral valve prolapse	12	16	0
Aortic regurgitation	4	10	0
Hypertension	0	0	12
Varicose veins	4	6	16

Data compiled from computerized information on patient population at Wrentham State School, Wrentham, MA (see Chap. 26). Clinical entities were selected as representing conditions that increase in likelihood with age.

dary to receptor organ change.[11] It should be noted, however, that a variety of treatable disorders of hearing (e.g., cerumen impaction) should be sought clinically when a patient presents with hearing loss. Hearing loss is important at any age, but it is particularly important at an older age because it affects social communication and interaction and can lead to disorientation and confusion. Although audiologic evaluations are performed on a routine basis in some settings (see Chap. 27), this is by no means a universal practice. Whereas individuals with intellectual and communication skills will readily identify hearing loss, those with developmental disabilities and intellectual impairment might not be able to identify even severe hearing loss. Hearing loss in such persons may result in social withdrawal, depression, and even anger or aggression. It is therefore important not only to examine the ears but also to obtain an audiologic evaluation. In older individuals, audiologic evaluations should be done routinely at the annual physical checkup, along with all the other tests. Hearing impairment occurs with increased frequency in association with certain conditions, e.g., Down syndrome and congenital rubella.

Vision

The most common manifestations of aging that significantly impair vision are cataracts, glaucoma, and macular degeneration.[15] These conditions can compromise function and hence independence, so attention to visual acuity is most important.

Visual impairment is a frequent concomitant of many syndromes associated with developmental disabilities, the most notable of which are congenital rubella, retrolental fibroplasia associated with prematurity, and Down syndrome. Of these three the individuals with congenital rubella are currently in their early 20s, and those with retrolental fibroplasia are also in their 20s. This leaves the group who have Down syndrome as the major clinical older group with a higher than average frequency of ocular problems and visual impairment. The spectrum of conditions is broad—refractory errors, strabismus, keratoconus, and cataracts. For those who have had cataracts removed, complications include glaucoma, fibrosis, and even retinal detachment with eventual phthisi bulbi (Chap. 13).

Cataracts are a particular problem with aging and occur more commonly in individuals who have Down syndrome. In addition, those who are on phenothiazines have an increased likelihood of developing cataracts.

It is therefore important that visual function be assessed annually, preferably by an ophthalmologist. For individuals who have visual impairment, referral to a low-vision clinic may be helpful.

Skeletal System

There are two major manifestations of aging on the skeletal system, osteopenia and aging arthropathy.[12]

Osteopenia

Osteopenia, or osteoporosis, represents a loss of bone density and consequently bone strength. For individuals with developmental disabilities who are ambulatory, this condition mainly affects postmenopausal women, with the frequent clinical complication of hip fracture. The other manifestation of this disorder is in vertebral compression, which may result in kyphosis and bone pain or nerve root compression and nerve pain. Both these conditions set up a vicious cycle of inactivity, with further loss of strength and function, or dependence on analgesics with their consequent complications.

For individuals with cerebral palsy or myelodysplasia, the picture is different. These patients already have osteoporosis, and many have contractures and scoliosis as well. In addition, there is frequently a history of orthopedic surgery or of fractures. In this situation, attention to diet, exposure to sunlight, and appropriate physical therapy or activities are vital to maintain function and prevent complications.

Aging Arthropathy

Aging arthropathy can result in progressive motor disabilities. The common conditions are osteoarthritis, periarticular rheumatism, and chondrocalcinosis. Aging arthropathy is more of a problem in three groups: (1) those with cerebral palsy, particularly of the choreoathetoid type (see Chap. 8); (2) those with stereotypic behavior disorders in which the stereotypy involves a spe-

cific activity, e.g., hand wringing; and (3) those who have seizure disorders of the akinetic type, who may fall frequently, e.g., onto their knees. Not included in this group but of particular importance is the condition of atlantoaxial subluxation associated with Down syndrome (see Chap. 8).

Gastrointestinal System

Decrease in taste, dental problems, and difficulty in ability to chew can all affect eating behavior. Disorders of digestion, with decreased gastric acid production and absorption, can affect nutritional status. Chronic disorders of the large bowel include constipation, diverticulosis, and hemorrhoids.[3]

Many of these disorders may have been present for many years in individuals with developmental disabilities, even from childhood. Attention to dental hygiene, diet, nutritional status, and bowel function are important at all ages. What is relevant here is that a change in any of the above factors can occur at any time. Therefore, attention to details should be constant.

Urogenital and Other Systems

Urinary incontinence is a prevalent and particularly distressing symptom in the elderly. In approximately 50% of cases, this is an urge incontinence in which the individual is unable to control the bladder contraction. This condition can sometimes be controlled, e.g., by smooth muscle relaxants but there are problems with side effects of the drugs. Other types of incontinence may be reversible, e.g., overflow incontinence due to urinary retention as a result of constipation. These conditions may have existed for many years. In the population with musculoskeletal complications of severe cerebral palsy, problems relating to chronic urinary tract infections are important considerations.[10] In males, of course, there is the problem of prostatic enlargement and consequent urinary retention.

Decrease in pulmonary, cardiac, and renal function occur and are variable. A decrease in immune response also occurs, leading to susceptibility to infections, autoimmune phenomena, and neoplasia.[2,9]

CUMULATIVE EFFECT OF ORGAN SYSTEM INVOLVEMENT

Promotion of health during infancy, childhood, adolescence, and adulthood encourages health in old age and is in part responsible for increased longevity. Disease processes that affect any organ system, e.g., respiratory, cardiac, or gastrointestinal tract, adversely affect health in old age and decrease longevity. Pervasive disease processes that can affect many or all organ systems, such as diabetes, are more obviously pernicious. Medical or surgical intervention can also add to the cumulative effects of organ system involvement.

It therefore becomes a major task, when evaluating an elderly patient, to review an often extensive history to determine how clinical events in the past are related to present symptoms.

THERAPEUTIC INTERVENTIONS

Before contemplating any medical or surgical treatment, much thought must be given to the underlying disability, the past history, the relative physiologic and pathologic aspects of aging, and the benefits of the intervention. This is particularly the case in determining drug dosage, because the patient's weight might suggest a lower dose as well as the consideration that absorption may be erratic. Metabolic rate may be reduced, thus affecting the pharmacokinetics of the drug being considered, particularly the half-life and the adverse effects.[9,14] In this population special consideration should also be given to drug interaction, because many individuals are on two or more medications.

PSYCHOSOCIAL CONSIDERATIONS

Two main factors must be considered in accounting for the presence of a large number of older persons with developmental disabilities in institutions. One factor is the reason for admission to the institution. For this age group it is likely that admission to the institution took place more than 50 years ago. At that time reasons for admission to state schools reflected social policy as well as cognitive or physical problems (see Chap. 25).

The second factor is the reason for remaining in the institution despite the societal pressure for deinstitutionalization. The reasons for remaining in institutions may be related to geographic and political factors or to health status and behaviors profiles that would make living in the community difficult.[8]

Most individuals with developmental disabilities now live in the community and outside institutions, and it appears that many older individuals with developmental disabilities within the community enjoy social and recreational activities within foster family situations.[13]

Not only is it necessary to pay attention to health related issues as they arise, but in the broader context of the WHO definition of health, i.e., "physical, emotional, and social well-being," it is necessary to help ensure a full and meaningful life. The factors included here involve the considerations of companionship, of meaningful social and recreational activities, of vocational pursuits where appropriate, and, most important of all, a respect for the individual and his independence. These factors, along with the monitoring of chronic health-related problems, ensuring of optimal function, and prompt and thoughtful responses to acute medical problems, will add not only to increased longevity but to greater enjoyment of life as well.

REFERENCES

1. Carter, G., and Jancar, J.: Mortality in the mentally handicapped: A 50 year survey at the Stoke Park Group of Hospitals (1930-1980). J. Ment. Defic. Res., 27:143, 1983.
2. Gambert, S.R.: A clinical guide to the physiology of aging. Sci. Med., 82:13, 1983.
3. Huber, A.M.: Nutrition, aging and developmental disabilities. *In* Aging and Developmental Disabilities. Edited by M.P. Janicki and H.M. Wisniewski. Baltimore, Brookes Publishing, 1985.
4. Jacobson, J.W., and Janicki, M.P.: Observed prevalence of multiple developmental disabilities. Ment. Retard., *21*:87, 1983.
5. Jacobson, J.W., Sutton, M.S., and Janicki, M.P.: Demography and characteristics of aging and aged mentally retarded persons. *In* Aging and Developmental Disabilities. Edited by M.P. Janicki and H.M. Wisniewski. Baltimore, Brookes Publishing, 1985.
6. Janicki, M.P., and Wisniewski, H.M.: Aging and Developmental Disabilities. Baltimore, Brookes Publishing, 1985.
7. Katzman, R., and Terry, R.D.: The Neurology of Aging. Philadelphia, F.A. Davis, 1983.
8. Lakin, K.C., Hill, B.K., Hamber, F.A., and Bruininks, R.H.: New admissions and readmissions to a national sample of public residential facilities. Am. J. Ment. Defic., 88:13, 1983.
9. Rowe, J.W.: Physiological changes of aging and their clinical impact. Psychosomatics, 25:6, 1984.
10. Rowe, J.W.: Health care of the elderly. New Engl. J. Med., *312*:827, 1985.
11. Ruben, R.J., and Kruger, B.: Hearing loss in the elderly. *In* The Neurology of Aging. Edited by R. Katzman and R.D. Terry. Philadelphia, F.A. Davis, 1983.
12. Rudelli, R.D.: The syndrome of musculoskeletal aging. *In* Aging and Developmental Disabilities. Edited by M.P. Janicki and H.M. Wisniewski. Baltimore, Brookes Publishing, 1985.
13. Sherman, S.R., Frenkel, E.R., and Newman, E.S.: Foster family care for older persons who are mentally retarded. Ment. Retard., 22:302, 1984.
14. Thompson, T.L., Moran, M.G., and Nies, A.S.: Psychotropic drug use in the elderly. New Engl. J. Med., *308*:134, 1983.
15. Wright, B.E., and Henkind, P.: Aging changes and the eye. *In* The Neurology of Aging. Edited by R. Katzman and R.D. Terry. Philadelphia, F.A. Davis, 1983.

Part III

HEALTH SERVICES IN STATE
RESIDENTIAL FACILITIES

25

CHANGING CONDITIONS AND THE PROVISION OF CARE

Harold L. May, M.D.

EARLY INSTITUTIONS

Many state residential facilities for individuals with developmental disabilities opened in the late 1800s and early 1900s, a time when society knew that something must be done but had limited understanding of appropriate solutions. Some persons were admitted to institutions because families could not handle the demands of care at home or because of problems at school. Some were confined on the advice of physicians who sought to maintain normal life in the home by separating out a family member who might be a disrupting influence. Many persons were institutionalized inappropriately; the label "mental retardation" was sufficient.

The chief executive officer of the institution was usually a physician. All persons admitted to the facility were considered patients, but medical attention was concentrated on those who were sick. The focal point for medical treatment was a hospital on the grounds that was staffed by nurses. Because many of those who were admitted were children, most facilities were called state schools. Unfortunately, massive overcrowding and understaffing limited the effective teaching in these "schools." For persons who were not acutely ill, the goal was to provide food, clothing, shelter, and whatever basic protection could be offered. Many members of these pitifully small staffs were dedicated, sometimes to a heroic degree.

The design of most institutional buildings reflected a lack of understanding of the services that should be provided in facilities for such large populations of individuals, many of whom had serious disabilities. Not surprisingly, residential structures were patterned after the open ward, the design for most hospital-based medical care at that time. Though these facilities were society's well-intentioned response to the needs of developmentally disabled individuals, they compounded the problems presented by the disabilities themselves. The allocation of materials and human resources was painfully insufficient. As though by design, institutions became eddies off the mainstream. Like their charges, they were underdeveloped, and in many ways disabled. Over time, buildings gradually fell into disrepair. More important, the condition of many residents deteriorated as well. Care was provided for acute medical problems, but many chronic disabilities progressed unnoticed; deaths occurred that could have been avoided, and complications developed that could have been prevented.

NEW FACILITIES

After the election of John F. Kennedy in 1960, there was an awareness that more should be done for mentally retarded persons. In 1963 a panel of distinguished scientists, educators, and laymen, appointed by the president, completed a national plan, and in March of 1974 the federal regulations for Intermediate Care Facilities for Mentally Retarded (ICF-MR) were adopted. These called for an interdisciplinary team which would conduct periodic assessments of residents, at least annually, so that realistic goals might be set and appropriate programs implemented for each individual. State residential facilities had to meet standards for certification as intermediate care facilities in order to be eligible for federal reimbursement for services. The resulting infusion of funds made it possible to improve staffing levels, renovate buildings, and improve the quality of the care that was provided. The formerly unfortunate group of "patients," now called residents and clients, were the subject of class action suits that sought to correct conditions that had violated their civil rights. Many who had been inappropriately institutionalized were discharged into the community.

Most state residential facilities are now working hard to rectify the past deficiencies that are the legacy of society's benign neglect for many decades. While the strong wave of deinstitutionalization has been gathering force, an equally powerful and seemingly opposite movement is underway to transform some state residential facilities into developmental centers. It is ironic that many residents are being discharged into the community at a time when developmental centers finally can meet their institutional goals for enhancing the quality of life and for providing health services, habilitative programs, and residential services that will enable residents to function as independently as possible. Class action litigations, in addition to assuring appropriate community placement for residents, have also made it possible to renovate institutional buildings and to attract and hold necessary staff. The achievement of institutional goals is limited by the constraints of each individual's disabilities and also by the human and environmental resources that society provides for care. The future points neither to the community nor to the developmental center as a final answer. It points instead to a system of care that includes both and that builds on the availability of potential resources wherever they are.

INSTITUTIONAL STAFF

Wherever a mentally retarded individual receives care, whether in the community or in a developmental center, those who provide care, generally as a team, must know and understand the person holistically. Identifying strengths and potential gains as well as areas of disability and

vulnerability, the care team must develop individual service plans that are appropriate, realistic, and achievable. Responsibility for developing and implementing plans must be assigned to staff members who have appropriate credentials, training, and experience, including those who provide direct care. The staff also works closely with guardians or responsible family members whenever possible. To maximize its chance of success, the plan must be monitored carefully. Effective, ongoing, and periodic assessments should determine whether its objectives are being met, and appropriate changes should be made when necessary.

It is universally understood that the health and medical status of residents represents only a portion of the spectrum of needs that must be addressed. Residents may also require habilitative services and attention to difficult behavior problems in order to enable them to function at an optimal level in spite of impairments that limit them. Developing and implementing plans effectively requires a staff of professionals who are qualified in their disciplines and committed to working as members of interdisciplinary teams.

A total service system in health care responds to the needs of all the individuals served. Environmental elements, residential and program staffs, special services, and consultation, transportation, and referral services should be organized so that the system of care will be as effective as possible, both in achieving the goals set for each individual and also in cost effectiveness.

Physicians

Some physicians who staffed state residential facilities in the past were extraordinarily dedicated and competent while others, unfortunately, were not professionally qualified. This situation has changed in recent years as links have been established with medical centers and as the quality of care in state residential facilities has improved.

In improving health services the first priority has clearly been to attract and retain highly qualified and dedicated physicians. Although the first responsibility of primary care physicians is to supervise and provide care, their experience, energy, and thoughtful attention can also be channeled into the broad-based movement to improve care for all developmentally disabled individuals. This can enhance a physician's professional and personal satisfaction and growth.

No developmental center is free of problems or devoid of challenges. One responsibility of the director of medical services is to work with physicians in an attempt to match their professional experience, personal interests, and aspirations with an appropriate area in developing solutions to the problems of developmentally disabled individuals. Staff physicians should be given the opportunity to work individually or with others to improve or develop projects and programs, for example, in infection control, coordination of specialty services, medical education, or clinical research.

Mid-Level Practitioners

Mid-level practitioners are the backbone of medical services in many centers. During the past decade, the importance of these workers has been clearly demonstrated, not only in developmental centers, but also in many other fields of medical practice. As discussed in the section of Chap. 27 by Browne and Walsh, whether they are nurse practitioners or physician assistants, they perform many of the functions that in the past were performed only by physicians.

Nurses

Health care in residential facilities has always depended on the 24-hour availability of nursing care for residents who have serious medical needs. Skilled nursing continues to be a vital ingredient. In centers where mid-level nurse practitioners and physician assistants have joined the medical team, nursing roles have been complemented and the care of the residents has been reinforced. (Nursing roles are discussed in Chap. 27 by Curtis et al.)

TYPES OF CARE

Primary Care

The first responsibility of the staff of a developmental center is to preserve the life of its residents. This requires that the care team identify the health needs of each resident and plan and implement an appropriate therapeutic response. Although most decisions are medical, many cannot or should not be made without close consultation with other members of the interdisciplinary team and with responsible members of the family or guardians. In normal medical practice, the physician recommends a particular form of therapy, but can carry it out only if the patient gives informed consent. In developmental centers, the residents are often unable to give such informed consent because of mental retardation. Where necessary, a guardian should be appointed to make informed medical decisions on behalf of the resident. In some jurisdictions, such a guardian *must* be appointed. Such consent is especially important in the care of residents whose psychiatric problems require the use of psychotropic medication.

Consultation Services

Dermatologic disorders, cardiac disease, respiratory, orthopedic, and other such disorders are common in developmentally disabled individuals. If the quality of care is to be maintained at the highest level, consultations must be timely and must be provided directly at the facility whenever possible. Consultants must be well qualified specialists. Neurologic and psychiatric consultations are of particular importance because of the high prevalence of related problems in mentally retarded individuals. One of the most effective ways to obtain good reciprocal benefits from the consultation process is to establish links between developmental centers and medical centers. Such ties are so advantageous that distances of 40 or 50 miles between institutions should not ordinarily be considered an impediment. Cooperating institutions can benefit, learning from each other while teaching each other. Piece by piece, they can dismantle the walls of separation that previous generations have mistakenly built.

Emergency Care

Seizures, choking injuries that are self-induced or caused by other mechanisms, and other emergencies must be anticipated in developmental centers. All staff members should be able to perform choke-saving maneuvers and cardiopulmonary resuscitation, to monitor and provide supportive care during seizures, and to provide initial control of external bleeding. An emergency medical and nursing response team must be available on a 24-hour basis. In many developmental centers emergency medical technicians are an important part of the emergency response team. Protocols of action must be developed in order to assure as smooth and coordinated a response as possible. In addition to an appropriate staff that responds in a timely fashion, emergency equipment must also be available at the scene when needed.

Care for Acute Medical Problems

Medical Unit

Pneumonia, hematemesis associated with low-grade gastrointestinal bleeding, status epilepticus, infections, and many other acute medical problems that frequently occur in developmental centers can be cared for safely and effectively in an acute-care medical unit on the grounds (Chap. 28). This is by far the most cost-effective method that does not require the facilities of a hospital intensive-care unit. Such care does, however, require a team that includes a qualified physician, preferably an internist, a mid-level practitioner, and nurses, all of whom are experienced in providing acute care. Laboratory and radiologic services must also be available. The organization of acute on-grounds medical care is discussed in Chap. 28.

Referral

The level of care should always be appropriate to the need. If the patient can be cared for effectively in the institution's medical unit, that is where the care should be given. When it is clear that the need clearly exceeds the capabilities of the on-grounds unit, the patient must be transferred to a referral center. Within the limits of good judgment, the process of correcting acute dehydration and hypotension should be initiated prior to transfer. When necessary, appropriate intravenous therapy should be started, decompressing tubes should be inserted, and appropriate oxygen therapy should be initiated in order to improve the condition of the patient and increase the safety of the transfer without delaying it unduly. In addition to meeting the needs of the patient, such preparation contributes to the development of a sense of respect between the staffs of the developmental center and the referral center. This, in turn, contributes to the well-being of the resident and to the efficiency of the health care system. The resident is in the appropriate place at all times, whether it be the residential unit, the institution's acute-care unit, or the referral center. Mutual respect between staff members at various levels prevents delay in moving from one level of the system to another. Such respect is not bestowed automatically; it must be earned.

Convalescent Care

Many complications of developmental disabilities can be reduced, though few can be cured. They progress inexorably unless their course is interrupted, which is usually by a surgical procedure such as fundoplication to correct gastroesophageal reflux or the Girdlestone procedure to assure a comfortable sitting position. After such procedures, patients can be returned from referral hospitals expeditiously because of the monitoring of hospital bed utilization, now current practice nationwide. Transfer should be made to the acute-care unit in the developmental center as soon as the condition of the patient indicates that the move can be safe and relatively comfortable. The resident should be attended in that unit until it is safe for transferral to the living unit.

Preventive Care

At the opposite end of the spectrum, preventive care must be a high priority for individuals whose defense mechanisms are underdeveloped and whose reserves for the function of various physiologic systems are impaired. Any precautions observed regarding the elderly must also be observed in debilitated mentally retarded persons, regardless of age. Immunizations are guided by recommendations of the Public Health Service Advisory Committee on Immunization Practices and the Committee on the Control of Infectious Diseases of the American Academy of Pediatrics; tuberculosis control should conform to the recommendations of the American College of Chest Physicians; and communicable diseases and infections should be reported in accordance with applicable laws of the state in which the facility is located.

Disaster Planning

Unfortunately, disasters can and sometimes do occur in any area where large numbers of people are concentrated, especially if some of them are not ambulatory or are incapable of practicing self-preservation. Planning imposes the responsibility of preparedness. Although an effective response depends primarily on the alert exercise of good judgment by those on the scene, it also requires the organization and coordination of a large group of people who do not ordinarily work together. They must understand the fundamentals of setting up a command post and organizing a response. Normal fire drills are required at frequent intervals by regulation. An extension of this is the disaster drill, which needs to be held periodically to make sure that the disaster plan is kept up to date and that the staff is familiar with it.

26

DEMOGRAPHICS AND HEALTH CARE

I. Leslie Rubin, M.D.

Examining the health care needs of individuals who remain in large institutions is an aid, first of all, in planning for optimal care. Second, it helps identify specific clinical entities that might otherwise have escaped notice. In addition, it benefits the greater community of similar individuals outside of institutions by bringing to light clinically relevant patterns of health-related problems.[9]

The history of medical services within large state residential facilities for individuals with mental retardation reveals that provision of health care cannot be seen in isolation.[7] (See also Chap. 25.) Because complex major handicapping conditions affect all aspects of an individual's daily life, physicians must be aware of how health affects function.

With declining populations in large institutions (Fig. 26-1) and the transference into the community of the most competent individuals, those who remain can be divided into four groups: people with severe and profound physical and/or cognitive limitations; people with severe behavior problems; older people; and people who are being prepared for community placement. The demographics of the population at the Wrentham State School in Wrentham, Massachusetts indicate an older and more severely impaired population. (Tables 26-1 and 26-2). In addition, because of improvements in health care, these people are living longer; hence, the clinical challenges that have to be faced become more complex as the physiologic process of aging becomes superimposed on the existing set of disabilities (Chap. 24).

Crocker (Chap. 2) points out that the diagnosis of mental retardation carries with it a set of additional clinical problems in at least two-thirds of the individuals; and half of these will have two or more added problems. Furthermore, the more severe the level of retardation, the more the likelihood of additional multiple problems (see Chap. 23). Indeed, there have been a number of surveys on the medical needs of institutionalized populations, and all report very similar findings (Table 26-3).[7,12,13] The findings are similar not only for chronic health problems but for acute problems as well.

MORTALITY, LONGEVITY, AND CAUSES OF DEATH

Because of improvements in the provision of health care through advances in clinical practice and access to services, a significant change has occurred in the overall health status of individuals residing in institutions.[14] This is reflected in statistics on mortality rates, longevity, and causes of death.

Carter and Jancar[2] surveyed the causes of death and ages of death in a group of institutions in England over a 50-year period from 1930 to 1980. At the beginning of the period, tuberculosis was the second most common cause of death after respiratory infections. Between 1936 and 1940 the rates were almost equal (about 40%). At that time almost half the deaths occurred during

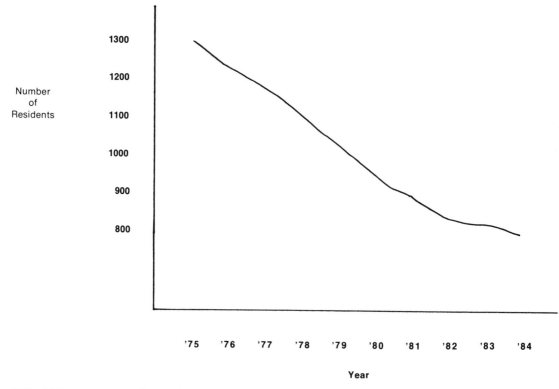

Number
of
Residents

1300
1200
1100
1000
900
800

'75 '76 '77 '78 '79 '80 '81 '82 '83 '84

Year

FIG. 26-1. Patient population of Wrentham State School, Wrentham, Massachusetts, between 1975 and 1984.

the second decade of life. While this survey reflected the medical problems of the times, the living conditions probably played no small role. In contrast, the statistics from the period between 1976 and 1980 show that although respiratory tract infections accounted for almost half of all deaths, the other half were almost all sudden deaths (presumably mostly cardiac) or a result of malignancies. During this period 60% of deaths occurred in individuals over 50 years of age, and almost half in people over 60—a 40-year increase in longevity for people with Down syn-

drome and a 30-year increase for others. In their explanation for this improvement, Carter and Jancar included improved diet, overall care, environment, and improved drug therapy.

RECORD KEEPING AND DOCUMENTATION

At a very basic level, collection of pertinent data is crucial to the function of any system, particularly such a complex one as health care. As an example, the data recorded by a pharmacy can be extremely helpful not only in providing information on what medications are currently being used, but also in monitoring use of medications in a system of quality control (see Chap. 29). Table 26-4 is a very simple one and records the number of individuals in the institution, the number receiving medications, and specifically the medications that reflect seizure disorders and psychiatric disorders. One can see at a glance what the statistics are for any given population for any disorder where the treatment requires medication. This requires good documentation and a good system of data collection, retrieval, and analysis.

The recording of specialty clinic visits, shown in Table 26-5, is a useful indicator of chronic

Table 26-1. *Age of Individuals at Wrentham State School (October 1984)*

Age	Male	Female	Total	Percent of Total
21 and under	14	12	26	3
22–29	91	63	154	19
30–39	140	96	236	29
40–49	124	68	192	24
50–59	60	50	110	14
60–69	30	38	68	8
70 and over	10	11	21	3
Total	469	338	807	100

Table 26-2. *Level of Retardation at Wrentham State School (July 1985)*

Level of Retardation	Number	Percentage
Mild	55	7
Moderate	86	11
Severe	281	37
Profound	326	45
Total	749	100

Table 26-4. *Medications for Wrentham State School (July 1985) (Total Population 736)*

Patients on Medications	Number	Percent
All medications	599	81
Psychoactive medications	178	24
Anticonvulsants	250	34

Average number of medications per person per day = 2.7.
Statistics supplied by Pharmacy Department (see Chap. 29).

medical problems; it provides another example of the complexity and multiplicity of chronic and acute medical problems for the institutional population. Reasons for hospitalizations at tertiary care facilities (see Table 28-1) also illustrate this complexity.

Information about health-related problems is vital in making accurate clinical diagnoses. The general population may be able to rely on their faculties of memory recall and speech; but for individuals with limited cognitive and communicative ability, documentation is of the utmost importance. Additional reasons for careful documentation are the multiplicity of disabilities and chronic and acute medical problems in this population, the possible variety of health-care providers over time, and movement of individuals from one facility to another or from institutional care into the community.

A continual review and updating of health-related information is generally accomplished by an annual physical examination and, as mandated by Title XIX, an interdisciplinary review process.

COLLECTION AND ANALYSIS OF DATA

The process of data collection should be simple, the data should be readily retrievable, and should provide information on the total institutional population, on selected groups of individuals within the institution, and on selected clinical entities. A system that would meet these standards was set up at the Wrentham State School. The process included the following:—

1. Documentation of all relevant clinical information, historical and current
2. Coding of clinical information, using the World Health Organization's International Classification of Diseases, 9th Revision (ICD 9)
3. Setting out of information in specific areas for systematic practical application:
   Level of retardation
   Etiology
   Psychiatric diagnosis
   Chronic medical problems
   Routine health issues

Table 26-3. *Representative Medical Problems in Institutionalized Mentally Retarded Persons*

Chronic Problems	Percent with Problem
Behavior problems	56
Seizures	34
Physical handicaps	33
Hearing loss	24
Obesity	19
Respiratory disease	13
Eye problems	13
Dental problems	11
Visual deficit	10

Adapted from Nelson, R.P., and Crocker, A.C.: The medical care of mentally retarded persons in public residential facilities. Reprinted by permission of The New England Journal of Medicine, *299*:1039, 1978.

Table 26-5. *Wrentham State School On-Campus Outpatient Clinics, 1980*

Clinic	No. of Visits in 1 Year
Ophthalmology	396
Orthopedic	312
Podiatry	297
Surgical	289
Otolaryngology	272
Urology	107
Cardiology	93
Neurology	72
Gastroenterology	69
Gynecology	52
Dermatology	46
Hematology	27

Total patient population = 999.

Wrentham State School Medical Survey

- - - - - - - - - - - - - - - - - - - -

NAME: BIRTH DATE: 6/10/35   SEX: Female
CERIS #:   ANNUAL REVIEW: BLDS:
                               DATE ABSTRACTED: UNIT:

- - - - - - - - - - - - - - - - - - - -

LEVEL OF MENTAL RETARDATION:
312   Moderate (36-51)

ETIOLOGICAL DIAGNOSIS:
758.0   Down Syndrome—Trisomy 21.

PSYCHIATRIC DIAGNOSIS:
296.3   Depression

CHRONIC MEDICAL PROBLEMS:
331.0   Rule out Alzheimer's Disease
244.9   Hypothyroidism—1980
839.01   At Risk for Atlantoaxial Subluxation
366.0   Aphakic
424.0   Mitral Valve Prolapse
627.9   Post Menopausal Bleeding

ROUTINE HEALTH PROBLEMS:
389   Hearing Loss (Moderate)
704.01   Alopecia Areata
523   Periodontal Disease
278.0   Obesity
288.0   Neutropenia

EPISODIC MEDICAL PROBLEMS:
486.0   Pneumonitis RUL—1978
041.9   Shigellosis 1979
818.0   Fracture Right Wrist 1981
599.0   Urinary Tract Infections 1976, 1985

DIAGNOSTIC OR SURGICAL PROCEDURES:
29.99   Tonsils and Adenoids Removed 1947
17.99   Cataracts Removed 1984

IMMUNE STATUS:
V02.6   Hepatitis B carrier—HBsAg positive—1985.
         Mantoux negative—1982
         Allergy—No known allergies.

Comments:

FIG. 26-2. Wrentham State School medical survey form.

Episodic medical problems
Diagnostic and surgical procedures
Immune status
4. Entering information into word processor or computer
5. Annual updating of clinical information

In the Wrentham system, relevant clinical data for each individual are available on 1 or 2 printed pages (see Fig. 26-2). This concise data summary is invaluable in transmitting clinical information to health care providers, e.g., specialty clinic or emergency room personnel.

Table 26-6. *Chronic Medical Problems of the Resident Population at Wrentham State School, by Group (1983)*
All numbers represent percentages of the relevant group

Demographics	Group			
	Down Syndrome	**Geriatric**	**Infirmary**	**Social Adjustment**
Total surveyed	125	65	81	79
Average age (yr)	40	66	43	39
Age range (yr)	21–69	60–79	27–75	20–63
Male:female	81:44	28:37	40:41	70:9
	Percent of residents with problem			
Level of retardation				
Borderline/mild	1	18	0	1
Moderate	12	11	0	3
Severe	48	34	22	41
Profound	38	37	78	54
Etiology				
Unknown	0	60	30	52
Known syndrome	0	6	11	6
Down syndrome	100	8	7	13
Perinatal	0	11	36	19
Postnatal	0	15	15	8
Psychiatric/behavioral				
Autism	0	0	0	19
Schizophrenia	0	6	4	1
Self-injurious behavior	2	8	11	52
Pica	2	5	12	22
Aggression	0	0	0	16
Side effects from medications	0	0	0	20
Other	7	2	0	0
Cardiorespiratory				
Total	45	49	17	23
Minor cardiac (ECG changes)	*	31	11	23
Major cardiac (e.g., valvular disease, myocardial ischemia)	*	18	6	0
Hypertension	0	12	1	3
Varicose veins	5	15	0	5
Chronic pulmonary	15	20	33	4
Central nervous system				
Seizures	14	23	62	46
Cerebral palsy	5	28	85	15
Alzheimer's disease	4	2	4	0
Orthopedic				
Scoliosis	10	42	77	11
Arthritis	5	15	6	5
Fractures	21	29	17	25
Atlanto-axial subluxation	10	0	0	0
Eye				
Cataract	42	42	15	27
Other, minor (e.g., strabismus)	43	34	15	30
Other, major (e.g., keratoconus)	22	17	26	11
Ear				
Hearing loss	36	35	37	18
Middle ear pathology	25	0	0	4
Dental				
Periodontal	32	25	70	46
Edentulous	31	38	5	13
Caries	2	0	0	4

* Data not separated out from the total.

Table 26-6. *Continued.*

	Group			
Demographics	Down Syndrome	Geriatric	Infirmary	Social Adjustment
Gastrointestinal				
Aerophagia/rumination	3	5	22	6
Gastroesophageal reflux	6	18	51	6
Peptic ulcer	0	0	0	3
Upper GI bleeding	0	8	21	1
Gallbladder	2	9	2	0
Constipation	19	26	65	6
Hemorrhoids	8	12	4	6
Hernia	9	12	4	5
Other	0	8	0	0
Nutritional/metabolic				
Underweight	8	11	31	22
Overweight	29	29	14	15
Thyroid disorders	16	5	2	1
Diabetes	2	11	2	0
Other	5	11	2	1
Hematologic				
Anemia	6	21	12	14
Neutropenia	8	0	4	3
Other	4	0	2	0
Connective tissue	0	6	5	0
Neoplasia	0	9	0	0
Genitourinary tract				
Infections	11	22	37	4
Prostate and other	2	20	4	8
Skin				
Dry skin	22	0	0	20
Seborrheic dermatitis	26	14	30	11
Fungal problems	34	15	1	13
Acne	4	0	2	5
Cellulitis	5	12	2	6
Alopecia	6	0	0	0
Decubitus ulcers (by history)	0	11	23	0
Immune status				
Hepatitis B Ag	44	6	12	23
Hepatitis B Ab	22	28	4	33
Chronic hepatitis	9	2	2	4
PPD-positive	16	71	33	32
History of tuberculosis	2	9	4	9

* Data not separated out from the total.

Once data on the whole institutional population are collected in a readily retrievable manner, it is possible to examine statistically any medical problem or group of problems. At Wrentham hitherto unreported or poorly reported clinical associations were investigated and analyzed, for example, mitral and aortic valve lesions in Down syndrome[4] and urinary tract infections in cerebral palsy (see Chap. 17).

Because general surveys of institutional populations had already been reported, it was decided to compare the medical problems in four groups of individuals: those with Down syndrome, the geriatric group, infirmary residents (a severely multiply handicapped population), and those with severe behavior problems. Table 26-6 shows the results of this exercise. The reader is referred to chapters in this book that discuss in detail the specific medical problems and their significance within each group. What remains for the reader to appreciate is that all too often statistics are generated for large populations of individuals all grouped together under a nonspecific label such as mental retardation or developmental disabilities. An examination of subgroups within such populations is necessary to determine the prevalence of specific diseases and the best approach to the overall provision of health care for selected populations.

PROJECTIONS OF INSTITUTIONAL AND COMMUNITY NEEDS

There is a flux of individuals in and out of institutions despite the goal of total deinstitutionalization.[8] The most common reasons for admission or readmission are (1) to obtain the best specialized program or the most appropriate one; (2) an insufficient or deteriorating capability to care for the individual (includes abuse and neglect); (3) unmanageable and/or intolerable behavior, psychosis, or dementia; (4) family factors; (5) severe and/or complex physiologic impairment that requires specialized care (e.g., blindness); (6) geographical and other such factors.[1,6]

These reasons indicate that there is currently a continuing need for institutions with special skills in serving this population and that the medical and other services in such institutions may be of significantly better quality than those available in the home, in community facilities, or other public residential facilities. What is needed is the creativity and energy to utilize the services, skills, and knowledge accumulated in large public residential facilities and to transfer them to the community. This can be done while continuing to strive toward improvement in quality of care. Cohen[3] describes how improvements have already evolved; and Schor, Smalky, and Neff[10] describe how medical services are being provided for children who had previously been institutionalized. Evidence shows that community placement can have a beneficial effect on adaptive behavior[5] and that older individuals enjoy foster home placements.[11]

As far as medical issues are concerned, it is through the appreciation of the complex problems identified among larger groups of individuals in institutions (Table 26-7) that services can be designed and implemented in the community. The significant clinical problems that have been identified and managed can be shared with physicians and health care providers in the community, thereby ensuring optimal health care for people discharged from institutions. This will help create a situation whereby individuals with more complex problems who remain in institutions will have services available in the community. It will also limit to some extent the number of admissions and readmissions to institutions.[1,6]

REFERENCES

1. Carter, G.: Why are the mentally handicapped admitted to hospital? A ten year survey. Brit. J. Psychiatry, *145*:283, 1984.
2. Carter, G., and Jancar, J.: Mortality in the mentally handicapped: A 50 year survey at the Stoke Park group of hospitals (1930-1980). J. Ment. Defic. Res., *27*:143, 1983.
3. Cohen, H.: Trends in service delivery and treatment of the mentally retarded. Pediatr. Ann., *11*:458, 1982.
4. Goldhaber, S.T., et al.: Valvular heart disease (aortic regurgitation and mitral valve prolapse) among institutionalized adults with Down's syndrome. Am. J. Cardiol., *57*:278, 1986.
5. Kleinberg, J., and Galligan, B.: Effects of deinstitutionalization on adaptive behavior of mentally retarded adults. Am. J. Ment. Defic., *88*:21, 1983.
6. Lakin, K.C., Hill, B.K., Hauber, F.A., and Bruininks, R.H.: New admissions and readmissions to a national sample of public residential facilities. Am. J. Ment. Defic., *88*:13, 1983.
7. Nelson, R.P., and Crocker, A.C.: The medical care of mentally retarded persons in public residential facilities. N. Engl. J. Med., *299*:1039, 1978.
8. Rotegard, L.L., Bruininks, R.H., and Krantz, G.C.: State operated residential facilities for people with mental retardation. Ment. Retard., *22*:69, 1984.
9. Rubin, I.L.: Health care needs of adults with mental retardation. Ment. Retard., *25*:201, 1987.
10. Schor, E.L., Smalky, K.A., and Neff, J.M.: Primary care of previously institutionalized retarded children. Pediatrics, *67*:536, 1981.
11. Sherman, S.R., Frenkel, E.R., and Newman, E.S.: Foster family care for older persons who are mentally retarded. Ment. Retard., *22*:302, 1984.
12. Smith, D.C., Decker, H.A., Herberg, E.N., and Rupke, L.K.: Medical needs of children in institutions for the mentally retarded. Am. J. Public Health, *59*:1376, 1969.
13. Wright, S.W., Valente, M., and Tarjan, G.: Medical problems on a ward of a hospital for the mentally retarded. Am. J. Dis. Child., *104*:142, 1962.
14. Ziring, P.: Health planning for handicapped persons in residential settings. *In* Planning for Services to Handicapped Persons: Community, Education, Health. Edited by P. MaGrab, and J. Elder. Baltimore, Paul H. Brookes, 1979.

27

PROFESSIONAL ROLES IN THE HEALTH CARE DELIVERY SYSTEM

DELIVERY OF NURSING SERVICES IN AN INTERMEDIATE CARE FACILITY FOR THE MENTALLY RETARDED

Sandra J. Curtis, R.N.
Barbara A. Begin, R.N.
Paula L. Blinkhorn, R.N.

Nurses have traditionally been the largest single group of professionals employed in institutions for individuals with mental retardation. Their broad basic educational preparation provided them with the flexibility needed to assume a variety of roles and functions within the facility.

In the traditional medical model, the roles of both physicians and nurses were clearly defined. Physicians prescribed medications, treatments, laboratory tests, and activities for patients. Nurses noted, transcribed, and implemented these orders. Through the vehicle of the physician's order sheets, physicians shaped and directed nursing practice. Because of the severe staffing shortages among physicians and nurses, this practice was, by necessity, geared to the treatment of patients with acute medical problems and behavioral crises.

In order to ensure that services could be delivered, nurses functioned as building managers, physicians' aides, and direct-care supervisors. They also generated the voluminous amount of paperwork that was seen as essential in the daily operation of the institution. These activities became functional barriers that prohibited nurses from exploring new roles or using their unique competencies and skills to the maximum benefit of each patient. There was little time for nurses to provide direct service to clients, and many traditional nursing activities were role-released to direct-care staff. Because of nursing and direct-care staffing constraints, the training, clinical support, and supervision needed by direct-care staff to assume these responsibilities effectively could not be provided.

CHANGES IN FEDERAL POLICY

In the 1960s, heightened public interest in mental retardation promoted investigation of the services provided in large state institutions. When the physical, psychological, and social deprivation existing in institutions was publicized by the media, there was a public outcry for reform. Landmark legal decisions followed, and these decisions established the legal rights of the retarded to habilitation.

The 1970s heralded dramatic and innovative changes in the delivery of services to mentally retarded people in institutions. The passage of the Intermediate Care Facility Amendment of the Social Security Act in 1974 provided this population the opportunity to participate in the Medicaid Program. The intent of Congress in developing this program was to "ensure that individuals are receiving more than custodial care, to improve institutional care and services to clients with mental retardation and to provide adequate safeguards for federal funds expended."[5]

FEDERAL POLICY AND THE STATE OF MASSACHUSETTS

In 1975 a series of class-action suits were filed against the Governor of Massachusetts on behalf of individuals living in state schools. The intent of these suits was to establish the rights of such individuals to constitutionally acceptable care and treatment.[4] The lawsuits resulted in consent decrees between the plaintiffs and the state and provided major entitlements for active treatment. The consent decrees mandated close monitoring by the U.S. District Court for the next decade to ensure consistent progress in implementation of all requirements of the decree. Through federal legislation and the consent decree, large sums of money were made available to the facilities. These monies were earmarked for the hire of additional staff, capital improvement projects, expanded professional services, and development of community programs. In order to meet the requirement for comprehensive health and habilitative services, the state schools signed contracts with major teaching hospitals. These contracts provided the facilities with the broad array of highly qualified professional staff needed to meet their mandates for change.

FEDERAL POLICY AND WRENTHAM STATE SCHOOL

The changes at the federal and state levels signaled the demise of the medical model and the beginning of a developmental approach to service delivery at Wrentham State School. The mandated changes affected every aspect of the organizational structure. The impact on the Nursing Department was profound; nurses struggled to meet the mandated changes while still maintaining stability through the delivery of traditional nursing services to patients. The abrupt transition from medical to developmental model was traumatic for many nurses who encountered difficulties in accepting the philosophic and organizational change and in defining a nursing role to fit professionally into the new organizational structure. Some of the initial difficulty in adjusting to the changing scope of practice related to the roles in which nurses had been cast prior to this time.

As facility reorganization proceeded, new decentralized management systems were implemented. The new systems relieved nurses of all responsibilities for building management and supervision of direct-care personnel. For the first time in their long history of providing service in institutions, nurses were free to design and develop a comprehensive system for the delivery of nursing services.

REORGANIZATION OF THE NURSING DEPARTMENT

In designing a system to meet the health care needs of patients, nursing administrators were guided by several basic prerequisites. First, the design would need to support the unitization model adopted by the facility. The institution was divided into multiple units and managerial authority was decentralized and delegated to unit directors. Professional departments were retained, however, and department directors were held responsible for professional role development and practice. The scope of responsibility and how this would be translated into actual nursing practice within the facility would need to be clearly defined and articulated by nursing administrators and supported by facility executives.

The second factor to be considered was the need to identify the external forces that would affect nursing roles and functions. Title XIX standards, consent decree requirements, and regulations promulgated by the Massachusetts Department of Mental Health and the Massachusetts Board of Registration in Nursing would need to be reviewed and interpreted in the light of nursing practice.

The third and most important factor to consider was the assessed health care needs of individuals residing within the facility. The role of the nurse would need to be interpreted and focused on each individual's health care needs, and nurses would need to acquire skill in interdisciplinary collaboration and planning if these needs were to be met.

The final factor to be considered in planning was the need for additional nursing staff if the transition from custodial care to active treatment in nursing was to be achieved. The new system would place increased demands on nurses in their performance and documentation of nursing practice activities. Establishment of standards for nursing practice was both professionally and fiscally imperative to the future viability of the nursing department because Title XIX funds were tied to the facility's compliance with federal requirements, and the loss of funds due to nursing's organizational inability to comply would be catastrophic. High standards of practice were also essential in overcoming the low status associated with long-term care and play a major factor in the recruitment and retention of professional nursing staff. Without sufficient resources to accomplish the task, nurses would feel defeated, powerless, and ineffectual.

PRESENT ORGANIZATION OF THE NURSING DEPARTMENT

The Nursing Department is organized to ensure that adequate numbers of administrative and direct-service nursing personnel are available to deliver nursing services three shifts per day, seven days per week. The structure of the department is a modified decentralized design that complements the dual departmental/unit system that is in use in the facility.

Head nurses and licensed practical nurses constitute 80% of the total nursing staff, and all of these positions are assigned to residential units. A nursing supervisor is assigned to each unit to organize nursing services within the unit on a 24-hour-per-day basis. Nursing staffing requirements have been set for each unit on all shifts, and these staffing patterns are met on a consistent basis.

In addition to the nursing supervisor, who assumes clinical control and decision-making responsibility for the delivery of nursing services on a unit level, a clinical nursing instructor is also assigned to each unit. The nursing instructor plays a major role in increasing the competencies and skills of direct-care personnel and nursing staff through training during orientation and throughout their employment. Administrative leadership is provided by the director of nursing and three assistant directors assigned to the core Nursing Department. As the Nursing Department changed from a highly centralized operation to a unit-management system, authority and accountability for clinical decision-making were decentralized to unit-assigned nursing staff. Nurses became members of the unit's interdisciplinary team and focused on planning services for a small group of clients.

The core Nursing Department was organized to ensure that all nurses functioning in a nursing capacity, regardless of assignment, are accountable to the director of nursing or her designee for nursing practice. The Nursing Department retains responsibility for the hiring, assigning, orienting, and training of new staff. Staff promotions, transfers, and performance appraisals are initiated by the Nursing Department with input from the unit director in the decision-making process. The Nursing Department is responsible for formulating policy that defines the role and guides the practice of unit-assigned nursing staff. Through this organizational structure, unit-assigned nurses have developed a strong sense of professional identity with both the Nursing Department and the unit interdisciplinary team.

This organizational structure requires close and frequent collaboration between nursing administrators and unit directors. It also requires the unrelenting commitment of both parties to the missions and goals of the facility. Changes in the role or functions of a nurse will have a direct impact on the delivery of services within the residential unit. For this reason, neither nursing administrators nor unit directors can make decisions in isolation.

To be effective, the Nursing Department must be fully integrated into the organizational structure of the institution. Collaborative practice requires sensitivity, flexibility, strong professional and managerial identity, and a mastery of the fine art of negotiating.

The service delivery system that has evolved within the facility is a dynamic and challenging model that requires the participation of clinicians and managers at every level.

SPECIALTY SERVICES IN THE CORE NURSING DEPARTMENT

The reorganization of the Nursing Department required the development or expansion of specialty practice areas that would be organized and managed by nurses. These areas include recruitment, community hospital liaison, supervision of employee health services, coordination of supplies and staff, coordination of emergency transport, medical unit supervision, infection control, and liaison with Developmental Services.

Recruitment and Retention

Historically, the difficulties in recruiting nursing staff to intermediate care facilities parallel the problems seen in nursing homes and other long-term-care facilities.[1] The reasons for these problems have been documented in nursing literature. The first reason relates to the unrealistic staffing patterns established within the facilities.[6] All too often, staffing was based on availability of staff at a given time rather than on staffing ratios based on the identified needs of patients. Nurses skilled in need identification and assessment became frustrated in a practice area that could not provide adequate staff to support professional nursing practice.

The second reason for the shortage of nurses had to do with the low level of professional status accorded to nurses who work in long-term care.[6] Nurses working in technologically complex acute care areas achieve the highest level of status among their peers. Technological complexity is not a characteristic of long-term care, and nurses practicing in this field are sometimes perceived as less competent than their peers in acute care.

A third reason for the nursing shortage is the lack of understanding of the roles and functions of nurses in long-term care.[6] The curriculum in schools and colleges of nursing is almost totally devoid of meaningful content related to the health care needs of adults with mental retardation. A search of the literature reveals a paucity of textbook references or nursing journal articles dealing with the provision of nursing services to this population. For this reason, many nurses seek employment because of geographic convenience rather than from motivation based on knowledge of the field.

The Nursing Department developed the position of nurse recruitment and retention specialist in 1982. In order to provide support to new staff, this nurse also functions as an ombudsman for staff during their initial 4 months of employment. Although the ombudsman function was initially designed for newly hired personnel, it has become a service that all nursing staff feel free to use and has proven to be an effective tool in the retention of nursing personnel. Within 12 months, the nursing vacancy rate was reduced to 3%. An additional 14 positions were allocated to the Nursing Department by facility administration, and all positions were filled within 3 months.

Liaison with Community Hospitals

The nurse liaison position was developed to provide linkage between the unit interdisciplinary team in the facility and the acute care providers in community general hospitals. The nurse liaison coordinates the transfer of information between facilities and arranges special services required by residents of the facility when they require hospitalization. Through frequent visits to the hospitalized patients, this nurse assists the hospital staff in identifying, understanding, and meeting the specialized needs of these patients.

The nurse liaison submits daily written reports on hospitalized patients' current status to the directors of medicine and nursing. These reports are reviewed and forwarded to the unit-

assigned nursing supervisor, who shares this information with the unit team. The provision of factual, current data on the patient's status allows the team to engage in planning prior to the patient's return. If new procedures are to be used in the care of the patient when he returns to the facility, the nurse liaison arranges for inservice training for unit nursing staff at the community general hospital.

Supervision of Employee Health Services

The nursing supervisor assigned to the employee health services program works with a physician to plan and deliver health care services to employees. These services include pre-employment screening, first-aid to ill and injured employees, referral of staff to outside agencies as needed, and evaluation of employee health status prior to return to duty. The nurse assigned to employee health services also coordinates screening programs for tuberculosis and hypertension and provides counseling and support to staff with health problems. The physician and nurse assigned to this service also plan and coordinate all screening and immunization programs.

Coordination of Supplies and Clinic Staff

The coordinator of central supply and ambulatory care clinics is responsible for ensuring that supplies and equipment used in the care of patients are safe, effective, and representative of products currently in use in the health care market place. This nurse works closely with the business manager in the procurement, storage, distribution, processing, and evaluation of supplies and equipment. Her responsibilities also include adapting equipment to meet the special needs of the developmentally disabled. She is a resource to facility staff, and her knowledge of equipment has been invaluable in selecting products designed to meet needs of specific patients. This nurse also coordinates the daily operation and staffing of the ambulatory care clinics.

Coordination of Emergency Medical Transport Service

The emergency medical transport service is responsible for emergent and nonemergent transport of patients by ambulance, for implementing systems of response to medical emergencies, and for maintenance and operation of vehicles in compliance with standards set by the State Office of Emergency Medical Services. The service is directed by the facility's medical director and is coordinated by an assistant director of nursing. At present, 12 certified emergency medical technicians are assigned to this service to provide 24-hour coverage to all residents of the facility.

Supervision of Medical Unit Nursing Services

The facility's medical unit is a 29-bed hospital designed to provide inpatient treatment to facility residents with serious acute medical and psychiatric illness (see Chap. 28). Nurses assigned to this center function in a primary-care role, and registered nurse coverage is provided on all shifts. Nursing services within this unit are coordinated by a nursing supervisor, who ensures that standards of practice specific to an acute-care setting are maintained.

Infection Control

The nurse assigned to infection-control services works with a physician in the design, implementation, and monitoring of an infection-control program (see Chap. 30). Policies and procedures have been revised to incorporate the Centers for Disease Control standards. The responsibilities of the infection-control nurse include development of audit tools to measure the facility's compliance with standards, training of facility personnel, and consultation services to unit staff whenever a communicable disease is diagnosed.

The infection-control nurse also acts as a resource to community-based staff and provides them with training in a variety of infection-control topics and procedures.

Liaison with Developmental Services Department

A nursing supervisor was assigned to the Developmental Services Department in 1983 to facilitate entry of nurses as providers of role-appropriate services to residents in the day-activity program. The Developmental Services Department is interdisciplinary in structure and function and is responsible for overseeing the development of program services for all residents in the facility.

The nurse assigned to this department has been instrumental in assisting unit-based nurses to develop systems for delivering services to patients in this setting. All nurses in the facility are oriented to the day-activity programs. They receive training in program prototypes, and they are provided with a clinical practicum in a unit program. The Developmental Services Department nurse also works closely with the infection-control nurse in implementing an infection-control surveillance program that has standards and procedures specifically designed for program sites.

DELIVERY OF NURSING SERVICES

The chronic health needs of residents in this facility are complex, and when they are not met they constitute the largest single barrier to attainment of full and satisfying lives.

Health Care Needs

Approximately 49% of the residents have mobility problems that require staff support and assistance. Staff assistance in personal hygiene is required by 66% of the residents if basic hygiene needs are to be met. Approximately 61% have serious limitations in ability to express basic needs, and 47% have episodes of unstable behavior at least once each month. These episodes have the potential for risk to the patient or others and require program support. Eighty-one percent function in the severely or profoundly retarded range (see Chap. 26).

Statistics from 1984 about disease chronicity and severity indicate that 36% of the patients had chronic health problems that required monitoring and continuing intervention on a daily basis and that 81% of the patients were scheduled to receive medication or treatments several times each day (see Chap. 29).

Medication administration studies were conducted by the Nursing Department in 1982 and 1985 to determine the intensity of medication use within the facility and the number of patient-nurse encounters this would generate. These studies revealed the statistics shown in Table 27-1. This study showed that in spite of an 11% decrease in client population, the number of doses of medication administered increased by 16%. The 20% increase in the number of patient-nurse encounters required to administer medications is of special significance because this figure reflects an increase in the amount of direct nursing time required.

Identification of the chronic health care needs of the patients helped to shape the role of the nurse, because these needs dictate the need for primary care nursing assignments.

Federal Requirements

The nursing services mandated by the Title XIX regulations[7] have played a major part in shaping the role and defining the functions of nursing personnel. These regulations mandate the following activities to nursing personnel:

Participation in the preadmission and admission study and plan

Ongoing evaluation of the type, extent, and quality of service and programs

Involvement in the discharge plan including referral to appropriate community resources

Training in habits of personal hygiene, human sexuality, and family planning

Control of communicable disease and infection through surveillance, early identification of infection-control hazards, and implementation of protective and preventive measures

Development of a written nursing service plan for each patient as part of the total habilitation program

Participation in the training of personnel in the basic skills needed to meet the health needs of patients, respond appropriately to accidents and injuries, and detect signs of illness and dysfunction

The Title XIX regulations require extensive documentation by nurses on a monthly and quarterly basis. The responsibility for assessing each patient's response to his current drug regimen is done quarterly and is shared by registered nurses and pharmacists.

Licensed practical nurses and registered nurses assess each patient's response to nursing interventions on a monthly basis, and these findings are documented in the monthly nursing review. A quarterly nursing review is done by registered nurses to interpret and summarize these findings.

Primary Care Nursing Model

In order to meet the primary health care needs of developmentally disabled adults, emphasis must be placed on long-range planning for the promotion and maintenance of health. The primary care model in use in general hospitals has the longitudinal focus on health management that is essential in meeting the needs of patients with a multiplicity of chronic health problems.[2] The model requires modification, however, if it is to fit into the organizational structure of the unit. Primary care in this facility is the result of a collaborative planning process that relies heavily on the contributions of all members of the interdisciplinary team. An annual review is conducted for each client on a yearly basis, and the individual service plan generated provides the framework for all services planned for the client in the coming year. Prior to the review, assessments are done by representatives of each discipline, and these assessments are shared with other numbers of the team at the annual review.

Table 27-1. *Medication Administration Data for 1982 and 1985*

	Year	
	1982	1985
Patients receiving daily medication		
Number	680	676
Percent of total population	79	89
Number of doses administered per week	22,330	25,809
Number of nurse-patient encounters per week required for administration of medications	12,180	14,672
Mean number of doses per patient per week	33	38

Measurable objectives are established for each need, objective managers are selected, and the interdisciplinary plan is formulated.

Responsibilities of the Primary Care Nurse

Each patient is assigned a primary nurse. It is the responsibility of the primary nurse to generate the assessment prior to the review and to attend the review as the client's nursing representative on the interdisciplinary team. The primary nurse develops the nursing care plan following the annual review, and, in this plan, defines all nursing interventions to be used in meeting the client's health care objectives. Participation in clinical and program meetings scheduled for the client during the next year is also part of the primary nurse's responsibilities. The primary nurse works closely with nurses on other shifts to maintain awareness of any changes in the patient's health status. Nursing care required by the patient because of episodic illness or injury is planned or reviewed by the primary nurse and documented in the progress notes. Significant changes in the patient's health status caused by major illness or surgery require revision of the nursing care plan and interdisciplinary team input.

The primary nurse administers medication, performs treatments, and makes referrals to the nurse practitioner, physician, or physician assistant whenever medical problems are identified. The federal requirements for documentation are consistently met by the primary nurse on a monthly and quarterly basis.

The primary nurse cannot implement the nursing care plan in isolation, however, because many of the interventions planned are implemented by direct-care staff. Indeed, the responsibility for implementation of the individual service plan rests heavily with direct care staff. Mental retardation assistants and technicians have contact with clients 24 hours per day, 7 days per week. They are directly assigned to clients and interact with them more than any other group in the facility. If nurses are to successfully plan and manage major segments of the health care plan, they must develop collaborative work relationships with the providers of care—the direct-care staff. This can be done when the application of nursing process is organized to include the contributions of direct care staff. The mental retardation assistant is frequently the initial identifier of a health-related problem, and the observations made are referred to nurses for interpretation. These referrals provide nurses an optimal opportunity for teaching direct care staff, and learning is the most meaningful when it is done in the clinical context.

Task Delegation

In implementing the primary care model, it was necessary for nurses to formally role-release specific tasks to direct-care staff. Through the delegation of tasks, nurses gained the additional time required to plan and manage care and established joint accountability with direct-care staff in the provision of care. This placed major responsibility on nurses for "properly and adequately teaching, directing and supervising the delegates and the outcomes of the delegation."[3] To meet this responsibility, extensive training programs were conducted for all direct-care staff. A system for documenting health-maintenance tasks performed by direct-care staff was developed, and documentation and task performance are supervised by nursing personnel. This training has been incorporated into the basic orientation program for newly hired staff to ensure competency in task performance.

Evolution of the Nursing Model

The design of the nursing-practice model is continually evolving in response to change within the facility. Through this model, we have achieved significant improvements in the quality of client care and in the utilization of nursing staff in a professional role. The Nursing Department achieved full compliance with federal standards on the most recent survey, and this accomplish-

ment must be attributed to the efforts of all staff who worked to create and support change.

FUTURE NEEDS

The shift in focus from institutionally based services for the developmentally disabled to community-based services has major implications for all health care providers. The role of institutions as providers of service is being restructured, and nurses must play a proactive role in shaping future service delivery systems. Institutional and community-based services are not mutually exclusive entities, and both systems will need to evolve and change in order to develop a comprehensive network of services for people who are developmentally disabled.

In the past decade, the role and responsibilities of nurses practicing in intermediate care facilities have been more clearly defined and structured. What has evolved from this process is a variety of roles to address the great diversity of needs within this population. Although each individual shares the common characteristic of a developmental disability, this is not a homogenous population. On a daily basis, nurses within the facility interact with adolescents, adults, and the elderly. They provide services to persons who are capable of assuming greater autonomy over their own health care as well as to those who are totally dependent on staff for even the most basic needs. They provide care to patients with life-threatening medical problems as well as patients with disabling psychiatric illness.

The future role of the nurse in this setting requires creative contemplation as well as planning. The nurse will play a large role not only for those who remain in the institution, but also for those who achieve community placement. Community programs will need the services and experience of nurses who have practiced in the institution. The institution will seek input from those who have developed systems in the community that allow the developmentally disabled to make the transition from the institution and live in the community. Both will need to teach one another and plan together to achieve successful results. Nurses will make significant contributions to this process.

Ideally, the institution will become a learning center where both facility staff and community-based staff can apply their knowledge and skills to benefit the developmentally disabled and to learn from each other. Nurses will follow patients into the community and practice with them to acquire the knowledge required in this setting. The evolution of the relationship between institutional and community services is anticipated by nursing, and we are preparing to meet this challenge.

In planning for the future, it will be essential to incorporate health assessment skills into the basic preparation of nurses working with a developmentally disabled population. Assessment is the first phase of nursing process and is the basis of nursing diagnosis and all subsequent health care planning done for and with clients. Because assessment relies heavily on the patient's ability to verbally relate health care information, the nurse is especially challenged in assessing the needs of the severely and profoundly retarded, nonverbal, physically handicapped client. Nurses rely heavily on direct-care staff as collectors and providers of factual data. Thus, nurses must be trained to obtain and utilize the knowledge and observations of other service providers through interviewing techniques. As nurses increase their skills in these areas, there will be less inappropriate utilization of physicians and mid-level practitioners in the evaluation of minor health care problems that are responsive to management by nurses. As nurses expand their skills in collecting and interpreting data and formulating nursing diagnosis, they will be more effective in planning holistic care within the interdisciplinary framework.

REFERENCES

1. Aiken, L.H.: Nursing priorities for the 1980's. Hospitals and Nursing Homes. Am. J. Nursing, *81*:324, 1981.
2. Fagin, C.M.: Nature and scope of nursing practice and meeting primary health care needs. *In* Primary Care by Nurses: Sphere of Responsibility and Accountability. American Nurses Association, Publication Code G127-7M, 1977, pp. 35-48.
3. Massachusetts Board of Registration in Nursing: Regulation 244 CMR, 3:02. Responsibilities and Functions—Registered Nurse and 3:02 Responsibilities and Functions—Licensed Practical Nurse. Boston, 1982.
4. Massachusetts Department of Attorney General: Massachusetts Association for Retarded Citizens, Inc. et al. v. Michael Dukakis, et al. Civil Action nos. 75-52.1 OT (Dever) and 75-5023, Wrentham, MA, December 18, 1978.
5. Massachusetts Department of Mental Health, Division of Mental Retardation: Massachusetts Department of Mental Health Fact Sheets—State Schools. Boston, 1982.
6. Shields, E., and Kirk, E.: Nursing care in nursing homes. *In* Nursing in the 1980's. Edited by L. Aiken. Philadelphia, J.B. Lippincott, 1982, p. 199.
7. United States Department of Health, Education and Welfare. Federal Regulations for Intensive Care Facilities for Mentally Retarded Persons. Washington, DC, U.S. Government Printing Office, 1974.

MID-LEVEL PRACTITIONERS: EXPANDED ROLES

Christina M. Browne,
R.N.-C., B.S.N., M.S., M.M.H.S.
Carol A. Walsh, R.N.-C., B.S.N., M.P.H.

In the United States in the 1980s, nurse practitioners (NPs) and physician assistants (PAs) are practicing in ever-increasing numbers and in a wide variety of settings. They can be referred to collectively as mid-level practitioners (MLPs). For the past 10 years, MLPs have formed the foundation of health care in Massachusetts state mental health and retardation facilities. Their role has evolved to emphasize continuous access to the client, accountability for health care, and availability to family and staff. Today, there are over 80 MLPs serving 4,500 clients in these facilities. A model MLP program at Wrentham State School, a large residential facility, is described here, along with a discussion of the present and future roles of mid-level practitioners in similar institutions.

THE MID-LEVEL PRACTITIONER PROGRAM

A staff of 20 NPs and PAs is headed by a nurse practitioner who is the program director. The presence of a program director ensures the autonomy of the MLP staff and identifies it as being distinct from the physician and nursing staff. The director can provide assistance to the medical director in the development of health care services, work collaboratively with the director of nurses, and provide a link with MLPs at other state facilities.

ROLE AND RESPONSIBILITIES OF MID-LEVEL PRACTITIONERS

The MLPs are assigned to teams in residential units comprised of about 100 residents. Because the MLP staff has been one of the most stable professional groups within the institution, with an average length of tenure of 5 years, MLPs have assumed major decision-making roles in the interdisciplinary team. In many situations the MLP is called on to provide expertise in areas far outside of the traditional medical realm.

In most situations the MLP assumes almost total responsibility for the provision of primary care and utilizes the physician preceptor in a collaborative model. General responsibilities include:

Well Care. Completion of the annual physical exam, ordering and review of screening labo-

Table 27-2. *MLP Time Study Data Review*

	Percent of Total Time						
	By Year			By Patient Group*			
Work Category	1982	1983	1984	Medically Involved	Behavioral Ambulatory	Adult Ambulatory	Infirmary
Direct care	11	19	12	13	11	13	9
Indirect care	30	22	38	40	35	45	43
Documentation	32	22	20	·23	25	18	7
Institutional work	6	12	15	12	11	8	11
In-service training	0	2	2	1	2	0	13

* Data for 1985.

ratory studies, chart review, and development of plan of care.

Screening and Triage. Evaluation of episodic illness, trauma, behavior changes, and initiation of workup or treatment regimen.

Management and Monitoring of Chronic Disease. Follow-up of long-term illnesses such as hypertension, pulmonary and bowel problems, and seizure disorders. Evaluation or initiation of laboratory investigation and specialty consultations.

Collaboration. Collaboration with nursing and other professionals to assist in development of plans of care.

Communication. Communication with the family, nursing, and other team members regarding health issues and interpretation of their impact on daily activities.

Documentation. Documentation, on a regular basis, of health issues, and periodic review of the plan of care. Preparation of admission summaries to acute care facilities and discharge summaries to the community. Review and updating of monthly medical orders in collaboration with the nursing staff and assigned physician.

Participation. Participation in case conferences, such as psychiatric meetings.

Advocacy. Advocacy for health care needs.

Teaching. Teaching sessions, both formal and informal, with direct-care staff regarding health care issues.

Committee Membership. The MLP's involvement in institution-wide committees is encouraged. MLPs are members of human rights, pharmacy and therapeutics, ethics, quality assurance, medical records, emergency disaster, and other committees. Through participation in such committees quality-of-life issues can be addressed. The MLPs are thus able to influence institutional policy regarding health care issues.

Preceptorship of NP Students. Functioning as preceptors for NP students from affiliated graduate programs in an effort to broaden the exposure of other professionals to this population.

Annual time-motion studies document shifts in allocation of time and practice functions and provide the program director with data regarding staff assignments. It has been found that direct-care activities take up approximately 12% of the MLPs' time, while indirect care such as meetings, documentation, and committee work consume about 75% (Table 27-2). The high percentage of time spent on indirect care activities can be attributed to efficient management of chronic medical problems, introduction of preventive health care measures, and routine institutional demands. Statistical analysis of activities allows identification of subtle shifts in practice (Fig. 27-1).

CASELOAD MANAGEMENT

The MLPs depend on the nursing and direct-care staff for problem identification and for feedback regarding treatment regimens (see section in this chapter by Curtis et al.). Due to programming schedules, clients are not always accessible at morning rounds; therefore, necessary exams, etc., are usually scheduled during periods that do not conflict with program activities.

Morning activities also include laboratory and consultation review, writing of orders, and meetings. Providing health care in an interdisciplinary setting results in mandatory attendance at many meetings to assure that other professionals and direct-care staff are informed of health care issues. The MLP generally arranges set times during the day with the physician for client evaluation and case review. The day's events are often unpredictable, and times set aside for scheduled activities may be filled with acute

STATISTICS WORKSHEET NP/PA Name Week	Title XIX Exams	Title XIX Meetings	Family Contact	MEDICAL SUMMARIES		PATIENT CONFERENCES		IN-SERVICE ACTIVITIES		COMMUNITY-RELATED ACTIVITIES						
				Quarterly/Semiannual	Other	Psych Review	Other	Attended	Presented	Placement Summary	Referral/Placement Mtg.	Group Home Visit	Visit to Off-Grounds Clinic, etc.	Community-Based In-service Activities	Family Visit	Other Activities (Specify)

FIG. 27-1. Statistics worksheet.

medical and behavioral problems. All MLPs and physicians are accessible by page so that they can discuss cases by phone. Phone consultation is often necessary because physicians practice with more than one MLP and assume caseloads of 150 to 200 clients (see section in this chapter by Antanitus).

Each MLP must develop a system for monitoring care and assuring follow-up of laboratory data, procedures, and specialty consultations.

STAFF DEVELOPMENT

Continuing-education opportunities exist for refinement of skills through discussion of un-

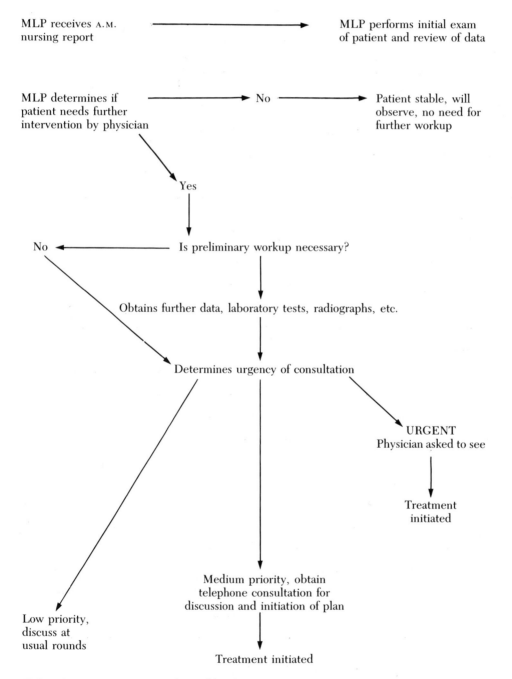

FIG. 27-2. Decision matrix for mid-level practitioners.

usual clinical presentations as well as exposure to current practice methods in the nonretarded population. Such exposure is necessary because of the isolation that institutional practice can foster. The responsibility for health care regimens assumed by the MLP necessitates maintenance of up-to-date knowledge and practice skills.

Formal teaching sessions are given by members of the medical and consultation staff on such topics as radiographic interpretation, evaluation of neurologic problems, and evaluation and treatment of seizure disorders. MLP staff are also encouraged to attend seminars, conferences, and professional association activities.

Sharing ideas on clinical practice are an ongoing part of the program and add to its vitality. Each NP and PA is encouraged to develop an area of interest such as gynecology, dermatology, or genetics and to join physicians on special projects.

ROLE EXPECTATIONS, ACCOUNTABILITY, AND DECISION-MAKING

Role expectations fall into three overlapping categories: the MLP's personal expectations, the expectations of other professionals and the administration, and the expectations of the physician preceptor.

MLPs view their role as providers of primary and preventive health care and as client advocates. The assumption of such a role allows the physician to concentrate on medically more complex and sicker patients, and on duties that must, by regulation and degree of sophistication, be performed by the physician.

Other professionals view the MLP as the medical representative to the interdisciplinary team as well as a decision-maker in health care issues. The expectations of administration have varied depending on perceived needs.

Physician expectations also vary depending on the length of time the physician has worked in the institution or with MLPs and the physician's own style of practice. For some physicians this means that the MLP has primary and ongoing responsibility for the case load while the physician acts as consultant. For others, the expectation is for a joint-practice model in which responsibility and work are shared equally.

The level of independent decision-making varies with each MLP and with experience, knowledge, and the length of time the MLP has practiced in the institution gaining familiarity with the patient population. It can also vary with the presenting complaint—for example, an MLP may feel more comfortable working with a gynecologic problem than a problem of anemia or weight loss. Most teams have a mutual understanding of the level of independent decision-making that is acceptable. A typical format for decisions regarding care issues is displayed in the decision matrix shown in Fig. 27-2.

The most productive teams are those in which professional expectations, accountability, and decision-making are mutually shared. The model is collaborative, rules are well-delineated yet fluid, and professional growth is dynamic. There is efficient use of each professional's time according to individual strengths and expertise.

INTERFACE WITH OTHER PROFESSIONALS

Nursing

Health care in the institution is provided through the collaboration among physicians, MLPs, and the nursing staff. MLP practice provides the team with a model different from the traditional medical or nursing approach. Both the NP and PA are viewed as autonomous, responsible decision-makers. They collaborate with nurses in creative ways to provide quality care. Their close proximity to the patient and to the nursing staff makes health care delivery easier. The MLPs encourage the nursing staff to explore and redefine their practice, responsibility, and the context in which health care decisions are made. NPs are especially able to anticipate the concerns and issues of providing nursing care to this population. Because NP practice falls within both medical and nursing realms, however, team members must avoid ambiguity of overlapping of roles.

The Interdisciplinary Team

The team process, vastly different from the traditional medical model, poses a unique set of challenges. The size and structure of the team can be cumbersome, but generally the more people involved in decision-making, the more creative the solution may be. Struggles within the team, however, are faced daily. The MLP must often maintain a delicate balance between the roles of client advocate and medical representative. Teams may want to assume all health care decision-making, or, when solutions are not readily available, delegate sole responsibility for solutions to the medical members of the team.

The primary responsibility of the MLPs to the team is interpretation of health care problems and explanation of their impact on daily activities. Working within the team takes time and energy and requires creative interpersonal and problem-solving skills, and, sometimes, patience and self-control.

COMMUNICATION WITH CLIENTS' FAMILIES

A result of a stable health care staff has been the ability to develop relationships with families. The MLP informs family members of changes in health status, explains and answers questions about needed procedures, and, often for the first time, provides an understanding of the ramifications of a chronic or acute illness. Such an educational role allays family members' anxieties and often assists them to accept the patient's disability. The MLP works closely with the social worker in the ongoing communication with family members, although there are times when conflicts arise over who should assume responsibility for ongoing communication regarding medical concerns.

A UNIQUE POPULATION

The definition of health for this population differs from that for the general population. Traditional definitions of health include "the absence of disease" and subjective perceptions of harmony between the psyche and the soma. In the institutionalized mentally retarded population health is broadly interpreted; for example, the profoundly retarded, totally dependent patient whose recurrent pneumonia has been eliminated by the placement of a feeding gastrostomy tube can be viewed as having attained his optimal state of health.

Developmentally disabled individuals respond unpredictably to illness and to treatment. A patient may present with fever when constipated or become hyperactive when sedated for dental care. Clinical issues are rarely straightforward, and their presentations may not be typical. Long-term familiarity with a client may be the only way to recognize individual responses to illness or pain. Indeed, the evaluation of patients with sensory and/or severe mental deficits necessitates learning new and creative diagnostic skills. Problem-solving takes perseverance as well as ingenuity.

The MLP must often seek unlikely resources for aids in diagnosis, using a pediatrician for some problems, an internist for others. Most patients present with both pediatric and adult problems, even though most are over the age of 20.

Problem identification and discrimination between cause and effect of illness can be extremely difficult. Many patients suffer from severe sensory impairment and are unable to communicate verbally. The presentation of a potentially life-threatening problem may be only a staff member's observation that the individual is "not himself." Sequelae of chronic disease may make determination of the etiology of acute illness unclear. Injuries may be caused by acute illness, neurologic impairment, behavior problems, or the risks entailed in life in the institutional setting.

Addressing health care issues can involve negotiation with direct-care staff whose concept of health may be naive, or it may mean convincing the administration to change procedures, such as the handling of soiled linens.

INSTITUTIONAL PRIMARY CARE

If the definition of health has its unique interpretation within an institutional setting, so does the definition of primary care. As defined by Stoeckle, primary care is coordinated, comprehensive, and personal care available on both a first encounter and a continuous basis. It incorporates several tasks—medical diagnosis and treatment, psychological assessment and management, personal support, communication of information about illness, prevention, and health maintenance.[2] Mundinger points out that primary care has three essential elements: (1) recognition of all socioeconomic, cultural, and environmental aspects of the individual, family, or community; (2) patient access to the system; and (3) provision of personnel who offer continuous coordination and management of basic health care.[1]

Primary care takes time and attention to detail. It takes familiarity with the individual and the milieu. To ensure that primary care is carried out effectively, case loads are kept at a manageable level—about 50 clients per MLP. Because the MLP is based in the residential unit, access and accountability are continuous. Long-term stability of staff helps provide continuity of care.

COORDINATION OF CARE

In the institutional setting there are multiple determinants of the need for hands-on care. These include federally mandated annual physical examinations and problem updates, management of acute health care problems, followup of episodic illnesses, and routine checks to determine if a plan of care is therapeutically sound.

Optimally, patient evaluation should be away from the living area. The examination room should have running water, an appropriate examination table (with stirrups), adequate lighting, and necessary equipment. Obtaining such facilities often requires reeducating administrators in the importance of adequate examination areas for the delivery of quality care and patient privacy.

Examination of the patient presents its own set of problems. If the patient is difficult to examine, the MLP relies on the direct-care or nursing staff members whom the patient best knows and trusts. These individuals are usually most able to allay anxiety and elicit cooperation. For a crucial examination, it may be beneficial to wait until a familiar staff person is available.

Despite the best staff efforts, there may be times during which minimal patient cooperation can be elicited. If the procedure to be performed is of short duration, physical restraint may be appropriate. In other situations, sedation may be necessary. In these instances every attempt should be made to coordinate its use with multiple purposes. For example, obtaining of laboratory work and a visit to a specialty clinic can be scheduled in the same morning. Some procedures, such as dental work or evaluation and testing at an outside facility, may mandate sedation. Referral facilities usually have had minimal exposure to this population, and it is unfair to expect them to deal with an individual who refuses to even enter the X-ray suite. Sedation should always be used with discretion, however, and the risk of parodoxical reactions must be recognized. Medications found to be successful are listed in the monthly order sheets.

SPECIALTY CONSULTATION

Consultation services are available at regularly scheduled clinics at the institution and occasionally at outside facilities. There are a number of benefits in having specialty consultants available to the primary care staff:

1. availability of clinical expertise in the diagnosis and management of often complex medical and surgical problems
2. opportunities for formal and informal education and the ability to bring a more academic analysis to medical problems
3. collaboration with primary care staff in the investigation of medical problems unique to this population

To assist the consultant in patient evaluation and record review, a physician or MLP is assigned as a liaison to each specialty clinic. The liaison reviews and prioritizes consultations and communicates recommendations to the primary care providers. The liaison also provides insights into institutional constraints, which may have significant impact in the carrying out of a recommended treatment plan. These insights help the consultant to put the clinical assessment and management into perspective.

The addition of psychiatric consultation services has been invaluable in diagnostic evaluation and the use of psychotherapeutic agents. Each psychiatrist has a designated patient case load. In some instances, the same psychiatrist has been able to provide care to a defined population for long periods of time, which further ensures appropriate diagnosis and treatment. Regular psychiatric case conferences are held with both direct-care and professional staff in attendance. The interdisciplinary team input provides a clearer understanding of the patient's behavior and response to medication.

USE OF ACUTE CARE FACILITIES

Individuals with severe impairment may be admitted to tertiary facilities for surgical or medical procedures. The nursing and medical care staff of these facilities are usually unfamiliar with this population. They may be uncomfortable in providing care, or even hostile regarding the utilization of services for individuals with mental retardation.

Communication concerning a patient's problems and needs should not be exclusively transmitted via written materials because these are often lost or not read. Verbal communication with the admitting resident and receiving nursing staff can facilitate patient evaluation and care. Responsibility for transfer referrals is assumed by the medical care provider most familiar with the patient and his presenting problem. For the patient with severe psychiatric disturbance, utilization of the admitting facility's psychiatric nurse can be extremely valuable. In our institution, a member of the nursing staff has been assigned liaison duties to tertiary care facilities. Important information can thus be channeled between the institution and the outside facility. Such a communication network has enhanced the quality of patient care and informally expanded the education of other professionals.

DOCUMENTATION—THE INTERDISCIPLINARY RECORD

As the expectations of quality care in large state facilities increase, so do those related to documentation. Indeed, documentation is one of the most time-consuming activities of most professionals in institutions. In conformity with our interdisciplinary process, the record is integrated. Such integration provides the opportunity to gain vital information from other perspectives, although it must be admitted that following a medical problem through the records can be tedious. A problem-oriented system is also maintained. Medical entries are made in SOAP format, and acute and long-term care problems, once identified, are entered onto a master list.

Both state and federal regulations dictate stringent documentation procedures. These apply to all patients, regardless of the severity of their medical problems. Episodic illnesses and their resolutions must be documented. Annual, semi-annual, or quarterly reviews of the plan of care must be entered as well as acknowledgments of laboratory reports and consultations.

One issue with which the MLP staff struggles constantly is qualitative versus quantitative documentation. Excessive documentation often results in records of inferior quality. In an effort to make medical entries more appropriate, individual patients are reviewed in accordance with their medical needs, and documentation is more individually determined.

Health care documentation must conform to the traditional medical model, yet be intelligible to other team members. In addition, data concerning the unique responses of the individual to illness, pain, and therapeutic measures must be entered to ensure that such valuable information will not be lost to future care providers. The availability of a word processor system allows for computerization of important patient information (see Chap. 26).

Federal Title XIX requirements specify that each patient have an annual review of the medical plan of care. Patient evaluation, record review, and the written summaries can take 1 to 4 hours. To save time, a checklist is available for documentation of routine health care (Fig. 27-3). A separate page is used to summarize patient status (Fig. 27-4). The development and availability of up-to-date and accurate medical histories are major accomplishments of the program.

INSTITUTIONAL BARRIERS TO CARE

As has been mentioned, delivery of primary care in a large institutional setting can present unique challenges. Regulations and rules abound. Such regulations are created for the general institutional population and may have little relevance to the care of an individual. Challenging of regulations may mean negotiations between the administrators and state and federal agencies.

VALUE OF A MID-LEVEL PRACTITIONER PROGRAM

In the 10 years since the introduction of the MLP program and its growth from a 2-member staff to one of 20, the quality of institutional care has been greatly improved. The benefits derived from MLP intervention include:

1. Improved access to health care. The assignment of manageable case loads and the close proximity of the MLP to the patient population has resulted in early detection and improved management of health care problems.
2. Introduction of the concepts of health promotion and disease prevention.
3. Early resolution of health problems, which has led to a general decrease in complications. Chronic disease is managed more consistently, thereby reducing the use of the infirmary and tertiary care facilities.
4. Continuity of care through the stability of the MLP staff.
5. Expertise in providing primary care to mentally retarded adults. Such expertise deserves special emphasis because there are currently no training programs that prepare NPs or PAs for this specialty practice.
6. Development of several specialty services as a direct result of NP/PA advocacy (e.g., gynecologic and podiatric services provided within the institution).

IMPLICATIONS FOR THE FUTURE

It is likely that nurse practitioners and physician assistants will continue to be important providers of health care in institutions. There is now a significant number of professionals with 5 to 10 years' experience in providing primary care to the mentally retarded adult population. A unique body of knowledge has evolved from this experience.

As the populations of institutions decrease, the needs of the remaining residents will also change. MLPs will be providing health care to patients who will be older, and whose conditions will be more medically complex. For these patients, transition to the community will not be an option because of their severe medical or behavioral problems. The challenge will be to maintain the quality of services and avoid the isolation and stagnation that institutional practice can foster, and to continue to provide advocacy for the developmentally disabled.

Changing federal and state regulations and standards may mean an expansion of tasks and functions. In Massachusetts, a prescription-writ-

ROUTINE HEALTH CARE CHECK LIST

Client's Name: _____

Subjective: _____

Unit: _____

Evaluator's Name: _____

Objective: _____

Menstrual History _____

Physical Findings (See physical exam for details) _____

Title: _____

Discipline:
MEDICINE _____

Labs:	Date:	Results:
Chemistries:		
CBC:		
Urinalysis:		
HBsAg:		
Anti-HBs:		
HBeAg:		
Anti-HBe:		
HAV:		
Pap:		
CXR:		
EKG:		
EEG:		
PPD:		
Immunizations:		

Need Area Title:
Routine Health Care _____

Need # or Letter _____

Chronic Stable Problems: _____

Date of Evaluation: _____

	Date:	Results:
Dental:		
Audiology:		
Ophthalmology:		
Allergies & Sensitivities:		
Weight:	IBW:	
Diet:		
Diet Supplements:		
Risk Factors:		

FIG. 27-3. Checklist for documentation of routine health care.

STATUS ASSESSMENT SHEET

Assessment

_____

_____

_____

_____

_____

_____

Annual Objective(s): (Statement of objectives should include actions to be performed, condition, and criteria)   Priority #

_____   _____

_____   _____

_____   _____

_____   _____

_____   _____

Recommended Plan/Intervention: (Specific manner by which each objective will be attained, e.g., approach, methodology, level of assistance, mode of data collection, in-service training, and special materials)

_____

_____

_____

_____

_____

_____

_____

_____

_____

_____

Recommended frequency of review of medical care plan:

(   ) Quarterly   (   ) Semiannual

FIG. 27-4. Status assessment sheet.

ing bill has been enacted; it gives nurse practitioners and physician assistants in long-term-care facilities the authority to write prescriptions and medical orders.

In addition, as some individuals leave institutions and move to community-based facilities and residences, the mid-level practitioner's future role can be envisioned as a consultant to care providers not familiar with the unique problems and needs of this population. Where health care services are particularly difficult to obtain, the MLP may develop a community-based model of practice.

Mid-level practitioners are in a position to continue to broaden and expand the education of nurse practitioner and physician assistant students through preceptorship and teaching affiliations with universities. They are able to prepare others to enter this challenging and unique area of service, whether in the institution or in the community.

REFERENCES

1. Mundinger, M.: Automomy in Nursing. Germantown, Maryland, Aspen Systems, 1980, p. 110.
2. Stoeckle, J.D.: Tasks of primary care. *In* Primary Care Medicine. Edited by A.H. Goroll, L.A. May, and A.G. Mulley. Philadelphia, J.B. Lippincott, 1981, p. 1.

PRIMARY CARE PHYSICIAN
Dale Antanitus, M.D.

As the process of deinstitutionalization continues, conditions in some institutions have improved dramatically. Complex medical demands are now met with increasingly effective answers by a growing number of experienced physicians. Some institutions are developing into centers that can offer their experience and expertise to professionals working with this population outside the institution. Under the current conditions there is still a large population of individuals whose medical needs are currently best met within the institution. Primary care physicians may indeed ensure that retarded citizens receive optimum care both within and outside of the institution. Ideally, as the institutions become a community resource instead of an embarrassment, physicians should care for patients both within the institution and in the community.

Direct medical care for individuals living in institutions can be divided into four categories: preventive care, acute care, chronic care, and miscellaneous care. In providing such care, primary care physicians work with mid-level practitioners, institutional psychiatrists, and consultants.

The experience summarized here applies only to severely and profoundly retarded individuals, most of whom have multiple physical disabilities.

PREVENTIVE CARE

Screening

An important aspect of preventive medical care is the judicious use of screening laboratory tests for early detection of disease. Each individual has at the minimum a yearly complete blood count, full blood chemistry profile (SMAC-25), thyroid function tests (especially important in trisomy 21), and a urine analysis with culture. (The urine is requested only if a clean catch can be obtained.) Catheterization for yearly urinalysis is done only if the patient has a history of recurrent urinary tract infection.

In addition, each patient over the age of 50 or with a history of cardiac disease has an annual cardiogram and chest radiogram. Those who have had a previous diagnosis of successfully treated tuberculosis or skin test (PPD) conversion have a chest radiogram only if symptoms suggest the reactivation of disease.

Though none of the above-mentioned tests is mandatory, baseline data and documentation of long-term trends can become valuable in the acute situation. Many patients with chronic diseases such as epilepsy have routine blood work done as often as every 3 months (see Chap. 8).

Routine immunization is also an important aspect of preventive care. Tetanus toxoid is given routinely every 10 years. Pneumococcal vaccine (Pneumovax) and yearly influenza vaccine are given to those with a history of pulmonary problems. Hepatitis B vaccine has also been administered to those identified as being antibody-negative (the great majority were found to be antibody-positive) (see Chap. 30).

Early Identification of Problems

The detection and reporting of initial signs and symptoms is vital. This important first step in health care is the responsibility of the direct-care staff, who, through their daily efforts of bathing, feeding, and providing activities and companionship to the patients, develop a keen awareness of even subtle changes in their health. Their concerns and observations are then reported to the nursing staff, who in turn perform nursing assessments and report significant findings to the physician and/or the mid-level practitioner (nurse practitioner or physician assistant).

This reporting system is optimized by ensuring open lines of communication among *all* the members of the health care team and by a program of basic medical education for the direct-care staff.

Interdisciplinary Conferences and Medical Meetings

General topics such as symptoms of urinary tract infections or common skin problems can be covered by the nursing staff. Conferences on individual patients and their specific clinical problems are provided by the physician or the mid-level practitioner. In addition, weekly medical meetings are held at which medical topics of current interest are presented by visiting lecturers, clinical pathologic conferences are discussed, and management of particularly difficult patients is reviewed.

Annual Interdisciplinary Review

Once a year, under the mandate of federal law (Title XIX), a conference is held on each patient, during which all aspects of care are reviewed by the entire interdisciplinary team. This meeting serves as a forum in which the accomplishments and problems of the previous year are reviewed in detail and goals are set for the coming year. Though many of the issues discussed in this meeting do not necessarily involve medical problems (e.g., school programs, family involvement, recreational programs), participation of physicians in this long-range planning venture is important.

Specialty Clinics

Several periodic examinations by medical specialists are also an important aspect of preventive care. An ophthalmologic examination is done every 1 to 3 years, as is an audiologic evaluation. A pelvic examination with Papanicolaou smear is done every 3 to 5 years. The regular services of a podiatrist have also been invaluable because very few primary care physicians have experience in podiatry. Many patients use this service on a regular basis (Table 26-5).

ACUTE CARE

Presentation

The making of a rapid and accurate diagnosis of acute illness can be a challenging task for the following reasons:

(1) The presenting symptoms are vague and not usually identified by the person affected but instead by a care provider. Most often these initial symptoms are the presence of fever, change in behavior (disruptive, aggressive, self-abusive, or quiet and disinterested), not eating, vomiting, change in bowel or bladder habits, or the perception that the person "just doesn't look right."

(2) Many of the individuals needing diagnosis and treatment cannot communicate and therefore cannot give a history or description of their condition. Dealing with this aspect of initial assessment may be decidedly easier for those with pediatric training, who are comfortable evaluating nonverbal patients.

(3) The chronology of events that leads to the presentation to the physician is often detailed by different observers for every 8-hour period prior to the presentation. Variability in observers can be great.

(4) Major disease entities may present as trivial complaints; conversely, exhaustive workups for apparently ominous signs and symptoms may be negative with later spontaneous improvement. Adults, because of their size, strength, and previous unpleasant medical experiences, must be approached calmly, gently, and reassuringly. They may be not only frightened and uncooperative, but also agitated and aggressive and therefore difficult to examine. If not contraindicated, the administration of an anxiolytic or short-acting sedative may facilitate a more complete examination in selected cases.

Examination

Physical examinations do not always have to be completed during the initial assessment of the patient. Apart from life-threatening emergencies, physical examinations can take as long as necessary and can sometimes last longer than a day. Besides the traditional observation, auscultation, palpation, and percussion, the physical examination should also include careful observation of daily routines. Most importantly these include careful observations of sleep patterns, eating behavior and appetite, variations from usual physical activity, willingness to engage in pleasurable activities, and general demeanor over a prolonged period.

Diagnostic Challenge

In the absence of a traditional history and with a limited physical examination, laboratory data can play a major role in diagnosis. When considering numerous diagnostic possibilities it is often necessary to order a battery of laboratory tests or radiograms as a major aid in the differential process. However, as the amount of laboratory data increases, so does the likelihood that some of the data may confound rather than aid in making a diagnosis.

The following maxims may help in arriving at a working diagnosis in acute disease:

If the Clinical Picture Is Not Clear at First, Wait a While.   Many quite diverse disease entities share the same initial presenting signs. Diagnosis at the very outset of a disease can be difficult in any patient population; when patients can be seen in an institution on a daily basis, however, the evolution of a disease process can be monitored very closely.

A Historical Record Is Always Available, Both in the Form of the Medical Record and the Experience of Senior Direct-Care Staff.   Many conditions tend to be recurrent, and diagnostic puzzles may have been solved in the past. The only warning here is that the physician must be prepared to use the information, because solutions to past puzzles are not always easy to accept (e.g., fever of 102° F with marked diaphoresis caused by constipation and completely alleviated by a soapsuds enema). Previous physical examinations are also available in the historical record. These can be valuable in differentiating between the onset of new signs and physical findings and those that have been present before.

Rare Diseases Occur Frequently in This Population, and Problems That Seem to Defy Diagnosis Occur at Least Monthly.   This phenomenon has two major ramifications: all possibilities must be considered in differential diagnosis, and it becomes evident that one must approach the diagnostic process itself from a physiologic perspective, often arriving at a diagnosis of a disease process rather than the name of known disease.

Management (or Treatment) Plan

It is almost always more advantageous, though not always possible, to begin treatment somewhat later in the course of a disease, when a diagnosis has been established, than to blindly administer treatment without a working diagnosis. Most disease presentations fall across a broad spectrum of presenting features depending on the place in time during which medical care is sought. In the institutionalized population, however, it is very common for illness to present at both ends of the spectrum: very early in the course of the disease (the first refused meal and one episode of vomiting that precedes the picture of volvulus 24 hours later) or so late in the course of the disease process that a classical clinical picture is present even without a detailed prior history. Patience, when coupled with the knowledge that the individuals involved will always be closely monitored, will inevitably result in an effective treatment plan.

Even when all the above factors are considered, accurate diagnosis of acute disease is difficult. The initiation of treatment, however, may of necessity precede diagnosis. In some instances patients fully recover spontaneously.

CHRONIC CARE

Individuals with severe and profound retardation within the institution have a high incidence of a broad spectrum of serious chronic disease entities (see also Chap. 23 and Tables 26-3 and 26-6). The complexity of these conditions prompts the physician to utilize the expertise of available specialty consultants. Some of the more commonly encountered chronic problems are constipation, musculoskeletal conditions, skin care, ceruminosis, and weight control.

Constipation

Constipation (see section in Chapter 10 by Roberts) is a common and often neglected problem in this population. The magnitude of this problem is attested to by the realization that 40% of the Wrentham State School population is considered to have constipation and that 76% of these people are effectively controlled only by the use of two or more cathartics combined with diet modification and enemas (Table 27-3). The

Table 27-3.   *Wrentham State School Survey of Cathartic Medications in Combination with Diet (1981)*

Treatment	Number of Patients	Percent of Total
Total in survey	934	97
Total on cathartics and diet modification	385	40
High-fiber diet	19	5
Prune juice	185	48
Bran	78	20
Docusate sodium preparations	250	65
Cascara	91	24
Enemas	233	61
Suppositories	15	4
Psyllium preparations	15	4
Senna preparations	15	4
Milk of magnesia	118	31
Mineral oil	37	10
Only one of the above	94	24
2 or 3 combinations of above	165	43
4 or more combinations of above	129	33

Prepared by E. Cavallari (see Chap. 29).

reasons usually given for the high prevalence of constipation in this population are immobilization, diet, and poor fluid intake. In addition it seems likely that the severe neuromuscular involvement also involves the integrity of abdominal musculature and has an untoward effect on effective elimination.

The effects of chronic constipation are significant. Constipation can directly or indirectly result in the following: vomiting, anorexia, episodic fever (to 103), ileus, volvulus, marked respiratory compromise, singultation (hiccups), congestive heart failure, self-abusive behavior, and aspiration pneumonia. Though constipation rarely leads to complications such as these in the general population, the physician working in an institution quickly becomes aware of these potential secondary effects. It must, therefore, be a consideration in most differential diagnoses and can be a contributing factor in many clinical presentations.

Effective control of constipation can be remarkably challenging and frustrating. Care falls into two categories, prevention and treatment. Administration of treatment also falls into two categories, oral and rectal. At times the same regimen is used for both treatment and prevention and administered both rectally and orally. The best example of this is the inexpensive, safe, effective, and quite traditional concoction of milk and dark molasses (4 oz:4 oz). A daily morning dose of this elixir can be titrated to the point of ensuring elimination daily or every other day. It can also be used in enema form to relieve even some of the most stubborn impactions. All other available treatments also work some of the time, either alone or in combination with one or two other of the treatments (e.g., 4 oz citrate of magnesia po qd, 200 mg Colace po qd, and soapsuds enema every 3 days). This kind of polypharmacy approach coupled with regular enemas is a continuing source of academic annoyance to most gastroenterologists encountering this patient population for the first time. Abuse of purgatives and enemas in the general population is known to lead to dependence. This may indeed be the legacy that remains in the institution, but attempts at remedying this dependence by tapering or withholding treatments has in most cases ended in failure. There appears to be more than a simple dependence on these treatment regimens in this population. Aggressive prevention and treatment of constipation, though decidedly unglamorous, is an important aspect of chronic care in this group of individuals.

Musculoskeletal Problems

Allied health professionals play a significant habilitative role in chronic care. (See Chapter 9.) The primary care for the complex and ubiquitous musculoskeletal problems that plague this population is provided by the physical therapists, occupational therapists, and the innovative experts who design adaptive equipment.

Skin Care

Skin care is often required on a daily basis. (See Chapter 18.) Cerebral injury can affect the circulatory stability and dermal integrity of the lower extremities, especially in individuals with paraplegia or quadriplegia, and the skin is often thin, fragile, and easily injured. Emollients (Eucerin, Vaseline) applied daily after showering offer an effective method of maintaining the integrity of the skin and preventing decubiti and cellulitis.

Ceruminosis

In an individual whose hearing is already compromised, ceruminosis can contribute to additional hearing impairment. (See Chapter 14.) Emulsification of ear wax may be necessary on a recurrent basis. Use of the over-the-counter preparation Debrox is usually successful in alleviating this problem. Instilling 3 or 4 drops in each ear nightly for 5 consecutive days each month is just as effective as daily use in over 90% of patients.

Weight Control

Weight control is also important in this population; many patients' capacity for physical exercise is severely compromised. The physician, in conjunction with a dietician, monitors weight and caloric intake on a monthly basis. In many individuals, especially those with multiple contractures, determination of ideal body weight is difficult and often cannot be based on height. Though a universally accepted method of determining ideal weight for this population has yet to be developed, percentage of body fat as indicated by skinfold thickness appears to be a useful indicator.

MISCELLANEOUS CARE

Often the physician may be in the position of making day-to-day decisions that seem to bear little relationship to the practice of traditional medicine. Such decisions may include assuring warm clothing in winter (scarves and mittens) to prevent hypothermia, encouraging extra fluids and providing protection from the sun in summer (sunscreen, wide-brimmed hats, and umbrellas) to prevent sunburn and dehydration, plus an almost endless list of other mundane problems (should a bed be by a window, is it too hot to go to school, should an individual with quadriplegia wear tennis shoes or leather shoes?).

As trivial as such questions may seem, either making decisions or not making them can have considerable impact. The direct-care staff are usually well-intentioned, dedicated, and nurturing. Although they are rather unsophisticated in medical matters, they are very conscientious about making the correct decisions affecting the health of the individuals under their care. Often, however, there are opposing opinions. It must also be realized that many routine tasks require specific orders by a physician. Therefore, to assure the comfort and well-being of the patients and to ensure harmonious relationships between the members of the direct-care staff, the physician must convert into medical orders all those things his parents or grandparents used to tell him to be careful to do. It is also important to make these decisions with diplomacy, without ever giving the impression of siding with one contingent of direct-care staff against another opposing contingent. (In the question of footwear for the patient with quadriplegia, one group favored tennis shoes and another, leather shoes; the decision for footwear was bedroom slippers, which seemed to satisfy everyone.)

CONSULTANTS

As can be appreciated from the lists of chronic medical problems in Tables 26-3 and 26-6, the expertise of specialty consultants has been significant in the improved medical care in institutions (see Table 26-5 for specialty clinics). Physicians rely heavily on their advice and experience, each patient seeing between two and eight consultants from different specialties each year.

For the general health of each patient, however, the final responsibility for making all medical decisions must rest with the primary care physician. Assurance that this principle is not compromised is found in the system used for writing medical orders. Consultants, by mutual agreement with the primary care physician, do not order medication, perform investigative procedures, or order laboratory testing without discussion. This system resolves the sometimes conflicting opinions of different consultants, assures that recommendations made on specific

medical issues are consonant with the overall health of the patient, and acts as an educational vehicle between consultant and primary care physician. When as many as eight different consultations are involved in one patient, the role of the primary care physician in coordinating the eventual treatment plan is evident.

PSYCHIATRY SERVICES

Psychiatrists working in the institution share the responsibilities of the psychiatric care of patients with the primary care physician. This partnership is becoming a legal as well as professional relationship as the increasing judiciary mandates concerning the use of psychotropic medications have demanded specific accountability for their administration. Though few primary care physicians have formal psychiatric training, their familiarity with the symptomatic

Table 27-4. *Psychotropic Medication Usage March 1983*

Type of Therapy	No. of Patients
Single drug therapy	
Antipsychotic	
Thioridazine (Mellaril)	96
Haloperidol (Haldol)	33
Chlorpromazine (Thorazine)	22
Thiothixene (Navane)	7
Fluphenazine (Prolixin)	1
Trifluoperazine (Stelazine)	1
Piperacetazine (Quide)	1
Total	161
Antidepressant	
Amitriptyline (Elavil)	9
Imipramine (Tofranil)	3
Doxepin (Sinequan)	1
Total	13
Antimanic	
Lithium	4
Anxiolytics	
Diazepam (Valium)	11
Oxazepam (Serax)	2
Total	13
Combination therapy	
Antipsychotic and antidepressant	13
Antipsychotic and antiparkinson	19
Antipsychotic and lithium	6
Antipsychotic and anxiolytic	2
Lithium and anxiolytic	1
Anxiolytic and antidepressant	1
Antipsychotic, antiparkinson, and lithium	2
Total	44

Total number of clients on psychotropic medications was 235 (29%). Total client population was 803. Data supplied by E. Cavallari (see Chap. 29).

behavioral manifestations of mental retardation are important in formulating psychiatric diagnoses. Likewise, few psychiatrists have extensive experience with mental retardation, but their knowledge of traditional psychiatry is essential for both the establishment of a final diagnosis and the development of a treatment plan. Because approximately 35% of the residents of the institution carry major psychiatric diagnoses and because most of these patients are on psychiatric medications (see Table 27-4), frequent (weekly) psychiatric review meetings are held in which the primary care physician actively participates. Through this close association between primary care physician and psychiatrist, careful monitoring of all the parameters involved in caring for mentally retarded persons with major psychiatric problems is effectively accomplished.

MID-LEVEL PRACTITIONERS

Though not found in the medical care delivery systems of all institutions, nurse practitioners (NPs) and physician assistants (PAs) can play a valuable role in both chronic and acute care (see previous section in this chapter). The relationship between mid-level practitioners and the physician can be effectively developed to enhance care while making optimum use of the limited available health care resources by sharing responsibilities. Through a collaborative relationship, both NP/PAs and physicians share the satisfactions of successful treatment and accumulate the experience necessary for improving health care practice.

SUGGESTED READINGS

Nelson, R.P., and Crocker, A.C.: The medical care of mentally retarded persons in public residential facilities. N. Engl. J. Med., 299:1039, 1978.

Scheiner, A., and Abroms, I.: The Practical Management of the Developmentally Disabled. St. Louis, C.V. Mosby, 1980.

Schor, E.L., Smalky, B.S., and Neff, J.M.: Primary care of previously institutionalized retarded children. Pediatrics, 67:536, 1981.

Smith, D.C., Decker, H.A., Herberg, E.N., and Rupke, L.K.: Medical needs of children in institutions for the mentally retarded. Am. J. Public Health, 59:1376, 1969.

Thompson, G.H., Rubin, I.L., and Bilenker, R.M.: Comprehensive Management of Cerebral Palsy. New York, Grune & Stratton, 1983.

Wright, S.W., Valente, M., and Tarjan, G.: Medical problems on a ward of a hospital for the mentally retarded. Am. J. Dis. Child., 104:142, 1962.

28

INFIRMARY UNIT

Theodor Feigelman, M.D. □ *I. Leslie Rubin, M.D.*

Individuals with developmental disabilities who remain in large residential facilities tend to have more complex problems and correspondingly more complex medical needs. Their requirement for consistent, high-quality medical care continues, and increases with advancing age.[4]

The first part of this chapter outlines the framework for an acute care medical delivery system for institutionalized individuals with physical and mental handicaps. The second section describes the spectrum of acute illness routinely found in an institutional setting. Previous reports have described health care systems and the nature of diseases seen at some institutions.[6,8] This chapter describes the situation in which outpatient and inpatient medical care, usually provided in a community hospital, is delivered on the grounds of a large institution.

MEDICAL CENTER BLUEPRINT

In this chapter the area that houses the acute inpatient unit and related medical services is termed the medical center. The level of care in the medical center depends on the population of the institution (Chap. 26) and the level of medical services available. The components necessary for optimal delivery of medical services include an acute care unit (ACU) for fragile and acutely ill patients who require the most skilled nursing and physician attendance, an inpatient division for patient monitoring and observation, and an ambulatory services area for routine outpatient primary care and consultant clinics. An inpatient service is available in the ACU and inpatient division to admit sick patients, correct their medical conditions, and return them to the care of their residential team in the shortest possible time.

A complete medical center also contains an emergency room, and support services such as pharmacy, laboratory, radiology, respiratory therapy, physical therapy, and central supply.

Emergency Room

The emergency room is an area with resuscitation equipment and facilities for the management of severe medical problems such as shock from cardiovascular collapse, traumatic bleeding, or gastrointestinal bleeding. Acute surgical problems are stabilized here prior to admission to the ACU or transfer to a higher-level care facility. This room is most commonly used for repairing lacerations. During times of nonacute use, this room can be used for diagnostic procedures such as endoscopy, bronchoscopy, sigmoidoscopy, or various fluid-removal procedures such as thoracentesis, paracentesis, and arthrocentesis.

Acute Care Unit

The acute care unit is equivalent to a medical/surgical inpatient hospital service. The level of care varies according to need and the experience and training of the medical team. The ACU is staffed 24 hours per day with a nurse-to-patient ratio of no less than 1 to 5. Attending physician coverage is available at all times. Procedures usually reserved for an acute hospital setting are routine, such as intravenous fluid administration, nasogastric suctioning, cardiac monitoring, and isolation. Blood transfusion and assisted ventilation may not be available because too much ancillary expertise may be required.

The ACU is ideally located near the emergency room to facilitate emergency transport. This location also allows for the shared use of equipment such as emergency carts and monitors as well as supplies.

Inpatient Division

The inpatient division is used for recuperation from acute medical or surgical illness and can also accommodate patients with chronic care needs, such as patients with tracheostomies and feeding tubes. Daily medical rounds are conducted, with attending physician, physician assistant or nurse practitioner, and staff nurse.

Patients requiring postoperative orthopedic surgical care can be maintained in traction and receive acute rehabilitation in this setting. Specialized feeding practices can be established here (see section on alternative feeding methods in Chap. 10).

Behavioral Unit

The behavioral unit, separate from the medical areas, provides acute and respite care for management of psychiatric disturbances. Patients needing intensive evaluation and/or medication adjustment are admitted here for varying lengths of time.

Pharmacy

A pharmacy is present within the Medical Center. Pharmacists frequently participate in rounds in the ACU and inpatient division, and they are available for consultation (Chap. 29).

Laboratory Services

A basic medical laboratory is available during the day for blood drawing and the performance of urinalyses, complete blood counts, electrolyte determinations, and electrocardiograms. Additional studies are available by contractual arrangement with a private laboratory. After-hours blood specimens are analyzed at local community hospitals, which have 24-hour services.

Radiology

A radiology suite provides routine services during weekdays. If radiographs are required after hours, the patient is transported to a local hospital. Radiographic facilities include a "fast" (high voltage) static X-ray machine with a rapid-process printer/developer. High voltage reduces exposure time and decreases motion artifact, an important consideration in dealing with patients who are unable to remain still. A consulting radiologist visits regularly to interpret the radiographs.

More sophisticated radiographic techniques such as fluoroscopy and contrast studies are usually performed at the secondary care hospital. Mobile fluoroscopy, ultrasonography, and computed tomography are considered in selected situations.

Respiratory Therapy

The high frequency of pulmonary disorders and the increasing need for tracheostomies requires the presence of a respiratory therapy staff. Services routinely provided are: chest percussion, postural drainage, inhalation therapy, and tracheostomy care. Blood-gas monitoring is available.

Physical Therapy

Physical therapy is available to patients in the ACU and inpatient division. Therapists usually provide postoperative orthopedic rehabilitation and chest physical therapy.

Electroencephalography/Telemetry Unit

Seizure disorders are very common in this population. Facilities for the performance of electroencephalography with telemetry are employed to diagnose or study difficult seizure disorders in a controlled setting (Chap. 8).

Outpatient Clinic

The outpatient clinic area is staffed by a nurse, has a record-keeping system, and is used by consulting specialists. These consultation services are provided by contractual arrangement. The clinic is especially important considering the frequency of outpatient consultative visits (Table 26-5).[5]

Central Supply and Receiving Unit

A central supply and receiving unit is required for the storage and distribution of medical supplies such as feeding tubes, syringes, and intravenous equipment. Proximity to patient care areas facilitates efficient care.

Medical Records

Access to historical records and a full, comprehensive system of record-keeping are vital. Medical diagnoses are clearly outlined on a continuously updated problem list. A complete typewritten summary regarding each diagnosis is revised on an annual basis and is available at the time of an acute medical evaluation. The legal competence of the patient and the contact names of relatives and guardians are readily available in the record.

Offices, Conference Rooms, Reference Library

There are individual and shared offices for reading and writing reports. Conference rooms are available for interdisciplinary case discussions and case or topic presentations. A modest reference library is present near the ACU, with access to larger library facilities elsewhere on the grounds of the institution. Secretarial services, telephones, and desktop computers are integral parts of support services.

MEDICAL CENTER STAFF

Physicians

The role of the ACU physician is primarily in acute patient care. Patients are screened on referral, and those who are admitted to the medical center receive a full medical evaluation, including history, physical examination, and appropriate laboratory and radiologic studies. If more extensive management is needed, patients are stabilized and then transferred to tertiary care facilities.

In the event of consultation or transfer, the physician acts as liaison with the outside hospital. When patients from the institution require outside hospitalization, the physician maintains contact with colleagues and consultants to monitor progress. Visits to the referral hospitals and attendance on rounds can assist in providing optimal management.

The physician experienced in the medical care of individuals with developmental disabilities also has an educational responsibility to physicians-in-training. Didactic sessions, bedside rounds, case studies, pathophysiologic discussions, and clinicopathologic conferences are held with medical students, house officers, fellows, and other health professionals to share experiences and knowledge of medical problems in this specialized population.[2]

The ACU physician works with a nurse practitioner or physician assistant, sharing patient care in the medical center. He is also responsible for scheduling and coordination of the on-duty physicians who attend during nights and on weekends.

Mid-level Practitioners

The mid-level practitioner (nurse practitioner or physician assistant) provides medical care for the recovering and chronically ill patients (see section on mid-level practitioners in Chap. 27). Management of acute medical problems is handled by the mid-level practitioner in collaboration with the physician. Mid-level practitioners with superior clinical skills are chosen, because this level of involvement requires a sophisticated knowledge of complex medical problems and technical procedures.

Nurses

Because of their experience with developmentally disabled individuals, the nurses of the medical center can often provide better care than that offered in secondary and tertiary care facilities. Their observational skills are relied on for valuable information necessary for elusive diagnoses (see section on nursing services in Chap. 27).

Attendants

Mental retardation attendants (MRAs) who work in the medical center need specialized orientation and training. They should, for instance, have a basic knowledge of medical equipment to help identify problems. Besides being responsible for providing basic needs, their companionship and understanding can help calm the anxious hospitalized patient. MRAs provide a unique and critical service by accompanying and remaining with patients who are transferred to outside hospitals.

PATTERNS OF PATIENT REFERRAL

Referrals to the medical center are made when there is need for more intensive medical care than can be provided within the residences. Contact with the physician in the medical center is initiated either by the mid-level practitioner or by the primary care physician. This may require only a consultation for recommendations or may result in admission to the ACU or inpatient medical service. If, after evaluation, the patient's medical condition is found to be unstable or specialty services are required, then telephone consultation is obtained with relevant staff members at the tertiary hospital. On the basis of this consultation, management may continue at the medical center or the patient may be transferred out for further care (Table 28-1).

Residents may return from outside hospitals for postoperative management, which the medi-

Table 28-1. *Wrentham State School: Off-Campus Hospitalizations for 1983 (845 residents)*

Reasons for Hospitalization	Number of Admissions
Elective surgery	53
Evaluative studies	15
Gastrointestinal	15
Trauma	14
Pulmonary	11
Carcinoma	6
Cardiac	6
Genitourinary	5
Medical	4
Psychiatry	2
All	131

Table does not include dental evaluations or nonelective surgical procedures.

cal center can provide at substantially less expense and with greater convenience. Hospitalization is often less frightening in the medical center than in an outside hospital. A more comfortable environment can be provided in the medical center on "home turf," where familiar staff know the individual resident and his or her unique pattern of communication.

CLINICAL PROFILE

Admissions to the inpatient service cover a wide variety of clinical problems. Admissions to the medical center at Wrentham State School over a 1-year period were reviewed and analyzed. There were 496 separate admissions from

Table 28-2. *Acute Medical Center Admissions for a 12-Month Period (July 1981—June 1982)*

Reason for Admission	No. of Admissions	Total Hospital Days	Average Stay (Days)
Pulmonary	102	1352	13
Gastrointestinal	75	949	13
Surgical	59	1939	33
Trauma and accidents	54	1064	20
Metabolic	42	770	18
Neurologic	33	912	28
Elective workup	27	52	2
Skin infections	19	193	10
Psychiatric	15	467	31
Genitourinary	11	109	10
Cardiac	10	84	8
Miscellaneous	49	249	5
TOTAL	496	8140	16

Table 28-3. *Pulmonary Disorders*

Category	Number of Admissions	Total Hospital Days	Average Length Stay (Days)
Pneumonia	27	502	19
Respiratory distress	23	292	13
Asthma	20	189	9
Bronchitis	13	221	17
Aspiration	9	27	3
Other	7	109	16
Diagnostic procedures	3	12	4
All	102	1352	13

a residential population of 845, representing 8,140 patient-days (Table 28-2). The most common clinical presentations requiring admission were pulmonary (21%), followed by gastrointestinal (15%), surgical (12%), traumatic (11%), metabolic (9%), and neurologic (7%).

Pulmonary Disorders

Pneumonia, respiratory distress, asthma, bronchitis, and aspiration accounted for the majority of pulmonary problems, and required over 1,300 hospital days (Table 28-3). Most cases were an exacerbation of chronic pulmonary disease, reflecting some of the clinical problems present in persons with severe physical disabilities (Chap. 23).

Many of these admissions were related to pulmonary aspiration of oral contents due to dysphagia, or gastroesophageal reflux with aspiration (see section in Chap. 10 on GI problems and section in Chap. 11 on recurrent aspiration syndrome).

Gastrointestinal Disorders

Constipation was the most frequent (52%) of the gastrointestinal causes for admission (Table 28-4). In this population, serious complications can arise from this "simple" clinical entity, which may present as fever, dehydration, pneumonia, atelectasis, or even respiratory arrest. Volvulus has been found to be a particularly serious complication in older patients who have been living in institutions for a long time. Years of neglected bowel habits may contribute to a state of relative megacolon, with dilated and thinned bowel wall, resulting in a high prevalence of volvulus and intestinal obstruction (H.L. May, 1986, personal communication).

Hematemesis, the next most common gastrointestinal presentation (17%), is often a result of

Table 28-4. *Gastrointestinal Disorders*

Category	No. of Admissions	Total Hospital Days	Average Stay (Days)
Constipation, abdominal distension, fecal impaction, obstruction	22	109	5
Hematemesis	17	184	11
Gastroenteritis	13	65	5
Vomiting	7	23	3
Endoscopy	6	7	1
Liver and gallbladder	4	321	80
Other	6	240	40
All	75	949	13

Table 28-5. *Surgical*

Category	Number of Admissions	Total Hospital Days	Average Stay (Days)
Orthopedic	14	647	46
Eye	12	576	48
Genitourinary	10	62	6
Gastrointestinal	8	148	18
Ear, nose, and throat	6	72	12
Neurosurgical	2	30	15
Other	7	404	58
All	59	1939	33

long-standing gastroesophageal reflux (see section in Chap. 10 on GI problems). The availability of nasogastric suction and intravenous fluid administration in the inpatient unit frequently prevents transfers to outside hospitals. Anti-reflux surgical procedures are often indicated. Initiation of permanent ostomy-tube feedings is done in the inpatient division, with eventual transfer to the residences, which may require specialized nursing and team services (see section in Chap. 10 on alternative feeding methods).

A high prevalence of carriers of hepatitis B exists in the institutionalized population, and routine precautions are taken when handling blood or other body fluids.[1] (See section in Chap. 10 on GI problems and Chap. 30.)

Surgical

The most frequent postoperative care admissions (Table 28-5) were for orthopedic surgery (24% of surgical admissions, 33% of total postsurgical inpatient days), eye surgery (20% and 30%), and genitourinary surgery (17% and 3%). Admissions after endoscopy and other minor procedures are usually brief.

When immediate postoperative stabilization is achieved at the outside hospital, the patient is returned to the inpatient division for the remainder of postoperative care.

Support by familiar nurses and attendants in an unpressured atmosphere with appropriate physical therapy is ideal for recuperating patients, who often require lengthy postoperative management.

Trauma

Trauma (Table 28-6) was the fourth most frequent cause for admission to the Medical Center (11% of all admissions). Injuries from known causes have been most frequently related to "peer altercations," followed by falls, restraint-related injury, foreign-body ingestion, and trauma during seizures. Injury of unknown cause is frequent, and has been reported to be the most common category of accident reports.[7] The type and severity of injuries vary with patient characteristics; therefore patterns of injury differ from one institution to another. For example, at Wrentham State School, trauma most often resulted from seizures and accidents due to motor coordination difficulties.

Fractures (33% of trauma admissions) necessitated lengthy inpatient division stays, particularly when complicated or of the lower extremities. Head injuries represented 26% of admissions, but usually required only brief admissions for observation (3% of total hospital inpatient days due to trauma). Foreign-body ingestion and human bites did occur (11 and 9% of admissions, respectively), but rarely required extended stays.

Metabolic

Primary dehydration was the most common (43%) of the metabolic causes for admission (Table 28-7). It represents a frequent clinical entity

Table 28-6. *Trauma and Accidents*

Category	Number of Admissions	Total Hospital Days	Average Stay (Days)
Fractures	18	804	45
Head injury	14	37	3
Lacerations	9	82	9
Pica	6	81	14
Human bite	5	51	10
Other	2	9	5
All	54	1064	20

Table 28-7. *Metabolic*

Category	Number of Admissions	Total Hospital Days	Average Stay (Days)
Dehydration	18	155	9
Hypothermia	8	128	16
Hormonal	4	169	42
Immune/allergy	4	85	21
Toxicity	4	9	2
Hypoglycemia	3	41	14
Other	1	183	183
All	42	770	18

in populations of handicapped and nonverbal individuals who are unable to request fluids. This is more a problem in the summer months. Hypothermia (representing 19% of admissions for metabolic causes) is a problem of individuals with severe central nervous system dysfunction and is more prevalent in the cold months. Both are potentially preventable with awareness and preventive measures.

Neurologic

Most neurologic admissions (Table 28-2) were for the monitoring, management, and control of complex and incapacitating seizures that were not controllable on an ambulatory basis (see section on epilepsy in Chap. 8).

Other Medical Conditions

Among the other reasons for admission (Table 28-2), cellulitis, most often of the lower extremities, was frequent due to the need for intravenous antibiotics. Infections of other areas, especially the hands and face, were associated with self-injurious behavior.

Admissions were required for diagnostic evaluation of clinical problems such as syncope and acute onset of atypical behaviors, but frequently they did not reveal identifiable cause. Many of these patients were followed closely after discharge, continuing the search for cause.

Psychiatric

Psychiatric and behavioral admissions were uncommon (Table 28-2), but they represented a sizeable portion of total hospital patient days. Psychiatric management takes place in an inpatient area apart from the medical areas and has psychiatric supervision along with psychological and multidisciplinary management.[3]

When behaviors become too difficult to manage in the residential units, an inpatient stay with well-planned interdisciplinary monitoring and behavior management is necessary. For patients with difficult behaviors, a constant attendant (MRA) is required; two attendants are occasionally necessary for one patient. Monitoring of efficacy of psychotropic medications and behavior-shaping programs are conducted by trained staff.

When patients with behavior problems and limited understanding of medical procedures are admitted to the medical center with a physical illness, an attendant may also be necessary on a one-to-one basis. This is particularly important in situations in which intravenous lines or nasogastric tubes must be preserved. If mechanical restraint is indicated, it must be used at the discretion of the physician, with due attention to established protocols and regulations.

ADVANTAGES OF THE MEDICAL CENTER

Staff familiarity with the population, with individual patients, and experience with the presentation of illness in a developmentally disabled population improve medical care. The patients are familiar with their surroundings, and those who receive visits from their peers can more easily do so on the grounds of the institution than if alone in a referral hospital. The costs of providing these services in this setting are less than in ordinary hospital settings.

REFERENCES

1. Centers for Disease Control: Inactivated hepatitis B virus vaccine: Recommendation of the immunization practices advisory committee. Ann. Intern. Med., 97: 379, 1982.
2. Cohen, H.J., and Diamond, D.L.: Training and preparing physicians to care for mentally retarded and handicapped children. Appl. Res. Ment. Retard., 5:279, 1984.
3. Gudeman, J.E., and Shore, M.F.: Beyond deinstitutionalization: A new class of facilities for the mentally ill. N. Engl. J. Med., 311:832, 1984.
4. Nelson, R.P., and Crocker, A.C.: The medical care of mentally retarded persons in public residential facilities. N. Engl. J. Med., 299:1039, 1978.
5. Schor, E.L., Smalky, K.A., and Neff, J.M.: Primary care of previously institutionalized retarded children. Pediatrics, 67:536, 1981.
6. Smith, D.C., Decker, H.A., Herberg, E.N., and Rupke, L.K.: Medical needs of children in institutions for the mentally retarded. Am. J. Public Health, 59:1376, 1969.
7. Spreat, S., and Baker-Potts, J.C.: Patterns of injury in institutionalized mentally retarded residents. Ment. Retard., 21:23, 1983.
8. Wright, S.W., Valente, M., and Tarjan, G.: Medical problems on a ward of a hospital for the mentally retarded. Am. J. Dis. Child., 104:142, 1962.

29

PHARMACY SERVICES

Edward A. Cavallari, M.S., R.Ph.

This chapter describes the evolution of comprehensive pharmacy services at Wrentham State School, Wrentham, MA. Pharmacy services progressed beyond the traditional dispensing model after the facility contracted with a teaching hospital in 1976 to upgrade pharmacy services[8] (see Chaps. 25 and 27). Implementation of a unit-dose dispensing system provided the pharmacists with the necessary client medication information from which clinical services could evolve.

Developments made possible by these changes have brought the facility's pharmacy services into compliance with the regulations of the Medical Assistance Program under Title XIX of the Social Security Act, specifically its standards for intermediate care facilities for the mentally retarded. Pharmacy services are now a relevant component of the overall health care delivery system in the facility.

TRADITIONAL DISPENSING MODEL

Until 1976 the pharmacy service used the traditional ward stock system for procurement, storage, and dispensing of medications and other non-drug items such as sterile gauze, elastic bandages, adhesive tape, and other supplies that would have been more appropriately handled by a central supply system. The pharmacy was located on the ground floor of the hospital building and consisted of an office adjacent to a dispensing area and two storage rooms elsewhere on the same floor. Pharmacy hours were 8:00 A.M. to 4:00 P.M. Monday through Friday. It was staffed by two pharmacists and a part-time technician. The pharmacists remained in the pharmacy most of the time, and rarely visited a medication area or interacted with other professional staff.

Nurses ordered supplies on specified mornings by dropping off empty medication containers with a requisition sheet for replacement stock and returned in the afternoon to pick up the requested items. They would have to leave the client care areas to go to the pharmacy for all their medication needs.

This dispensing system provided little opportunity for useful data collection. Requisitions for tablets and capsules consisted of refilling empty containers. Because medications were not counted but simply poured from large stock containers to refill empty ward stock containers, the numbers recorded were only estimates. More important, the pharmacists had no means of knowing for whom the medication was prescribed because they did not receive copies of the physicians' orders. Consequently, maintenance of medication profiles was impossible.

EVOLUTION OF SERVICES

Improvement and expansion of pharmacy services began in 1976, when the facility contracted with a teaching hospital to upgrade health and habilitative programs.[8,10] The contract provided one full-time pharmacist and one full-time pharmacy technician. The contract staff worked with the facility's pharmacy personnel to upgrade pharmacy services to comply with the rules and regulations of the Department of Health, Education, and Welfare's Medical Assistance Program under Title XIX of the Social Security Act.[6] The contract pharmacist reported to the director of pharmacy at the teaching hospital. At the end of the first contract year, accomplishments included establishment of routine medication area inspections by a pharmacist, transfer of non-drug items to central stores inventory, completion of a unit-dose pilot study, and implementation of a formulary system.

The initial formulary listed drugs approved for use within the facility by the Pharmacy and Therapeutics Committee. Implementation of the formulary system helped to control irrational use of medication. By eliminating unnecessary duplication and outmoded drugs, the pharmacy was able to order more efficiently and to use its storage space more effectively. The Pharmacy and Therapeutics Committee established an active review process so that drugs available to the physicians would represent those considered to be the most efficacious and rational, and reflecting current therapeutic practice.[2,3]

In the second year, the contract for pharmacy services added a director of pharmacy position. The director was responsible for the planning, development, and implementation of pharmacy services at the facility as well as the management of department personnel. He reported administratively to the on-site project manager and medical director and professionally to the director of pharmacy at the teaching hospital. Because of this administrative addition to the pharmacy, along with the support provided for program development, pharmacy services progressed rapidly.

Over the course of 5 years, the physical size of the department expanded with the scope of services. The pharmacy remained on the ground floor of the hospital building, but the amount of occupied space increased from 700 to 1,500 square feet. An increase in personnel was necessary as services were developed. Comprehensive pharmacy services are now provided by a staff consisting of a director, 1 supervisor, 4 staff pharmacists, 5 pharmacy technicians, a courier, and a secretary. The hours of operation are 8:00 A.M. to 4:30 P.M. Monday through Friday and 8:00 A.M. to 4:00 P.M. Saturday and holidays.

Approximately 30 medication areas, located in several buildings, serve the needs of over 800 patients. This situation presented a problem because timely processing of physician's orders by the pharmacy is essential for an effective drug distribution system. To alleviate this problem, the pharmacy initiated a courier service to systematically obtain and process medication orders and deliver medications. A driver and a vehicle were assigned from the motor pool to the pharmacy department on a full-time basis. The courier visits each medication area of the facility twice a day, once in the morning and again in the afternoon. All medications are delivered by courier except STAT orders, which nurses can obtain at the pharmacy.

UNIT-DOSE SYSTEM

A unit-dose system of drug distribution was initiated in early 1977 with a 2-month pilot program in 2 medication areas. Approximately 1 year later, the system was implemented for all clients at the facility.

The unit-dose drug distribution system provides many advantages over the traditional ward stock system.[1] Now the pharmacist receives and reviews a direct copy of the physician's order. Pharmacy technicians perform dispensing tasks that do not require the knowledge of a pharmacist.[9]

The specified quantity of each medication is dispensed to the medication area for each patient in a drawer labeled with the patient's name. Each dose is individually labeled so that it is identifiable by a nurse up to the time of administration. These precautions combine to improve accountability and reduce the possibility of errors in administration of medications.

Medication drawers are transported between the pharmacy and medication areas in locked containers called cassettes, each containing 12 drawers (Fig. 29-1). Cassettes are placed in medication carts in the medication areas. Because medications are dispensed for a chronic care population, the system provides a 7-day supply of medication in each patient drawer. The drawers are subdivided into 7 sections, each labeled with a day of the week, into which unit doses of medication are placed. Each medication area is assigned a specific weekday for cassette exchange. If there is an order change between delivery days, a new drawer reflecting the change is prepared with medications for the remainder of the week. It is delivered to the medication area and replaces the prior drawer.

MEDICATION PROFILE

The medications for a client and the number of doses dispensed are recorded on a medication profile, which is maintained in the pharmacy. The profile records the unit-dose dispensing in-

FIG. 29-1. Medication cassette. A patient name tag is affixed to each drawer. The cassette locks and can be transported by the handle on top.

formation in addition to other pharmaceutical orders (e.g., topical preparations). A system was developed to permit the recording of medications for a 6-month period on a single profile card. After 6 months, the profile is placed into a client medication history file. A new profile for the next 6-month period is then prepared by a pharmacy technician, checked by a pharmacist, and placed in the dispensing Kardex. This system provides a readily retrievable pharmacy-based medication history for each patient in the facility. The medication profiles are continually reviewed by the pharmacists for potential adverse reactions and drug interactions. Questions or potential problems regarding prescribing or administration of medications can be brought to the attention of the physician or nurse. The profiles are also useful as dispensing records, and they are important for the tabulation of statistics on medication usage.

COMPUTERIZATION OF PHYSICIAN'S ORDERS

To facilitate the monthly review and renewal of physician's orders, a word processor system was implemented in all units except the 30-bed

acute care unit in May 1980. The decision to exclude the acute care unit from the system was made because it has many admissions, discharges, and medication order changes. Planning and implementation of the system was a collaborative effort between the Departments of Medicine, Nursing, Data Coordination, and Pharmacy. The system was initially implemented in the pharmacy. Once it was totally operational, however, it was transferred to the Data Coordination Department.

Physician's orders are printed by name of client for each building on an established 28-day schedule (Fig. 29-2). Each order sheet is printed on no-carbon-required (NCR) paper to produce a duplicate that is forwarded to the pharmacy after the nurse practitioner or physician assistant and physician have reviewed and signed the form. If the physician wishes to change an order, this can be done by writing the change below the signature and then signing again after the change.

Order changes within the following month are written on another standard NCR physician's order sheet that permits up to three sets of orders to be written per sheet. Copies of these orders

```
Page 1


                    Physician's Orders
                    ---------------------

Name:  Client                    HBsAg:              Pos, Anti-HBs: Neg
DOB:   -/--/--                   Last TD:
ID:    DMH/Ceris: 0000/0000      SBE Prophylaxis:  No
Bldg:  Cottage                   Ideal Weight:     140 lbs.
Ward:                            Actual Weight:    138 lbs.

Allerg.&Sens.:    NKA

EFF. ORDER DATE:


                       CERTIFICATION

    1.   This Client's plan of care continues to be appropriate.

    2.   Continued ICF/MR Services are necessary for this client
         who requires 24 hours habilitative residential environment.

                    D/C PREVIOUS ORDERS
         ------------------------------------------

Diet:              House/seconds/4/10-31-

Sz Meds:           No
Psy Meds:          Thorazine 50mg p.o. q.d. @ h.s.
                   Cogentin 2mg p.o. daily @ 8am.
Other Meds:        Colace 100mg p.o. @ 8pm. Give c 4-6oz water.

Med Trmts:         Tinactin Powder to feet q.d. p bath or shower.
                   Sebulex shampoo 2x/wk.
Treatments:        No

Lab:               No

P.T.:              No

O.T.:              No

Special Inst.:     May self-treat c supervision.

Activity:          Ambulatory.


ALL ABOVE ORDERS X 31 DAYS UNLESS OTHERWISE NOTED.

PHYSICIAN'S SIGNATURE_____MD_____NP/PA
```

FIG. 29-2.   Physician's orders produced by word processor, printed monthly for each patient. Original stays in patient's record; copy is forwarded to pharmacy.

are also forwarded to the pharmacy. A pharmacy technician sorts out the orders, filing them with the appropriate patient profile card after pertinent information is transcribed. If necessary, a new medication drawer is prepared for delivery.

Two or three days before the next scheduled effective order date, the pharmacy sends the medication profile Kardex, containing all order changes for the month, to the word processor operator, who then edits the data files and prints new current orders. The orders are picked up by the courier and delivered to the appropriate medication areas.

In addition to monthly physician's orders, the system can print lists of any of the category headings on the order sheet. For example, lists of diet, physical therapy, and occupational ther-

apy orders can be printed for the respective department. Patients receiving a specific medication, combination of medications, or a particular classification of medication, e.g., psychotropic medications, can be readily identified (Fig. 29-3). The system eliminates manual searching through medication profiles or patients' records.

Although the word processor does not have the data processing capability of a computer, it has been an extremely useful source of information for drug utilization reports (see Tables 27-3 and 27-4).

INTRAVENOUS ADMIXTURE SERVICE

An intravenous admixture service was implemented in May 1981. Pharmacy personnel trained in aseptic technique compound large-volume

```
NAME                    PSYCHOTROPIC MEDICATIONS               PAGE 1


Building/Ward:

   Charles              Elavil 75mg p.o. q pm.
                        Thorazine 300mg p.o. q pm.
   David                Elavil 75mg p.o. q pm.
                        Cogentin 1mg p.o. q pm.
   Robert               Haldol 15mg p.o. @ 4pm and 25mg p.o. @ h.s.
                        Cogentin 1mg p.o. b.i.d. @ 8am/h.s.

Building/Ward:

   Celia                Mellaril 100mg p.o. q.d. @ h.s.

Building/Ward:

   Mary                 Navane 7mg p.o., q pm.
                        Serax 10mg p.o., q.d. @ 4pm.

Building/Ward:

   Alan                 Mellaril 300mg p.o. @ 8am and 250mg p.o. @ 8pm.
   Raymond              Valium 5mg p.o. b.i.d.
   Robert               Mellaril 250mg p.o. @ 8pm.
                        Lithium 300mg p.o. @ 8am and 600mg p.o. @ 1pm
                        and 300mg p.o. @ 8pm.
   Joel                 Mellaril 75mg p.o. @ 8pm.
                        Elavil 75mg p.o. @ 8am/8pm.
   Walter               Haldol 1mg p.o. @ 8pm.
   William              Haldol 25mg p.o. @ h.s.
   George               Mellaril 150mg p.o. @ 8pm.

Building/Ward:

   John                 Mellaril 50mg p.o., @ 6am and 100mg p.o. @ 8pm.
   James                Thorazine 250mg p.o. @ 8am and 450mg p.o.
                        @ 8pm.
   Roland               Haldol 4mg p.o. @ h.s.
   John                 Mellaril 150mg p.o., q.d.
   Edwin                Lithium 600mg p.o. @ 8am/1pm and 900mg p.o., @ 8pm.
                        Mellaril 200mg p.o., t.i.d. @ 8am/1pm/8pm.
   Peter                Mellaril 300mg p.o., b.i.d. @ 8am/6pm.
   William              Elavil 100mg p.o., @ 8am and 75mg p.o. @ 8pm.
                        Thorazine 25mg p.o. @ 8am and 50mg p.o. @ 8pm.
   Paul                 Mellaril 100mg p.o., @ 8am and 150mg p.o., @ 8pm.
```

FIG. 29-3.   List produced by word processor showing patients receiving psychotropic medications. Such lists are useful for review of drug use.

and small-volume admixtures for six beds in the acute care unit using a vertical laminar flow hood. Also, syringes of immunization vaccines are prepared in the hood and dispensed to nurses for administration to patients throughout the facility.

The pharmacy does not provide 24-hour services. Therefore, nurses prepare initial intravenous admixtures ordered for patients admitted to the acute care unit after pharmacy hours. A pharmacy technician visits the nursing areas at 8:00 A.M. each day and picks up orders initiated the previous night. The pharmacy prepares all subsequent intravenous admixtures required for the patient.

A pharmacy intravenous admixture service provides several safeguards for patients receiving parenteral therapy.[5] The service provides a system for screening physical-chemical incom-

patibilities and for dispensing of stable preparations. It provides an aseptic environment for the preparation of admixtures, minimizes pharmaceutical calculation errors, provides standardization of labels, and provides for the preparation of solutions that are not commercially available.

EXPANDED ROLE OF PHARMACIST

Over the past decade, much attention has been focused on the use of medications, particularly psychoactive medications for the developmentally disabled. As a result of litigation and federal regulations, activities such as the performance of drug regimen reviews have been mandated.[4,6] Responsibility for monitoring the use of medication has been directed to the pharmacist.

To fulfill this expanded role, a pharmacy service model was developed that incorporates innovative dispensing systems with direct participation of the pharmacist in the interdisciplinary team at a clinical level.

The pharmacy department adopted the philosophy that first priority is given to maintaining a drug-dispensing system that ensures that patients receive their medications as prescribed in a timely and safe manner.

Clinical pharmacy services evolved out of the unit-dose dispensing system, which gave the pharmacists access to physician's orders and established channels for dialog with the medical and nursing staffs. To be effective, the pharmacy had to establish a close working relationship with the Departments of Medicine and Nursing. When developing changes in the drug distribution system, involvement and support from the Department of Nursing was necessary for successful implementation because any changes had a direct impact on this group.

As supportive personnel have assumed many dispensing tasks, the pharmacists now review physician's orders and medication profiles, perform drug regimen reviews, and consult with other professional staff regarding drug information.

Once the unit-dose system was implemented, pharmacists began spending more time in the patient-care areas conducting medication area inspections, providing drug information on request, and presenting in-service sessions on various topics to other professional staff.

The population of the institution is divided among eight administratively autonomous units, each having its own medical, nursing, human services, and support staff. The pharmacists have specific unit assignments, an arrangement that improves communication between the pharmacy and the unit staff. This relationship allows unit personnel to associate pharmacy services with specific individuals and give them ready access to drug information. Clinical services were introduced gradually as these relationships grew and matured over time.

Psychiatric Case Reviews

The psychiatric case review is an interdisciplinary team meeting conducted to review the current clinical, psychological, and environmental status of the patient with the consulting psychiatrist for the purpose of developing a treatment plan and assessing drug therapy. The team consists of a physician, mid-level practitioner, nurse, pharmacist, psychologist, social worker, teacher, and direct-care staff. On average, the review teams of each unit meet weekly for 2 hours and review 6 clients (see Chap. 27).

The pharmacist's role at the psychiatric case review is to provide drug information, monitor therapy, and make recommendations. He needs to be familiar with the patient's current medications and to review the record for pertinent drug-related information. The pharmacist is provided time prior to the meeting to conduct this record review and prepare a presentation.

The pharmacist can be helpful in distinguishing drug-related movement disorders caused by psychotropic medications from certain types of behaviors. Because many patients have medical problems requiring multi-drug therapies, the pharmacist is a resource in evaluating the combined effects of the medications. The interdisciplinary team enables the pharmacist to make clinical contributions and participate in the decision-making process.

Drug Regimen Reviews

A drug regimen review, as required by federal regulations, must be performed by either a pharmacist or a registered nurse and is documented each month by a written progress note.[7] Because there are approximately 800 clients in the facility, registered nurses perform most of the reviews. Each pharmacist has a caseload of approximately 20 patients from his assigned units which he reviews monthly. The caseload is comprised of highest-need patients—those who receive psychoactive medications or who have complex medical problems that require multiple-medication treatment regimens. Patients are added to or dropped from a pharmacist's caseload as their needs change. The review's purpose is to identify any potential problems with the patient's drug therapy and to determine whether the drug therapy is effective in achieving the physician's objectives. The patient's record is examined for past clinical history, drug administration records, progress notes, physicians' orders, laboratory reports, and medical consultations. Information from this inspection is then analyzed, and any potential drug therapy problems are cited and communicated to the responsible medical staff. If no problems are identified, this is stated in the written note.

In the process of monitoring drug therapy, the pharmacist interviews nursing and direct-care staff, observes the patient, and checks the record for effectiveness and rationale of drug therapy, adverse reactions, drug interactions, laboratory values, and documentation of use. Knowledge of the client's clinical status enables the pharmacist to make positive clinical contributions. The pharmacist discusses any recommendations that are made to correct potential drug therapy problems with the physicians.

Staff Development

Pharmacists provide in-service training on a variety of drug-related topics to many groups within the facility. This service provides multiple disciplines with a better understanding of medications and identifies the pharmacist as a resource person and educator.

Subscriptions to several pharmacy journals, purchase of current clinical reference books, and a drug information file maintained by a pharmacist comprise the department's drug information library. This library provides the resources that support the staff-development component of pharmacy services. Pharmacists use these resources when preparing in-service training presentations and when researching drug-related questions. Availability of these resources enables the pharmacists to expand their clinical knowledge and establish credibility with the medical and nursing staffs.

REFERENCES

1. American Society of Hospital Pharmacists: ASHP statement on unit dose drug distribution. Am. J. Hosp. Pharm., *38*:1214, 1981.
2. American Society of Hospital Pharmacists: ASHP statement on the formulary system. Am. J. Hosp. Pharm., *40*:1384, 1983.
3. Bell, J.E., Evans, P.J., and Standish, R.C.: Mission, role, and function of the P&T committee. Hosp. Formulary, *18*(6):639, 1983.
4. Breuning, S., and Poling, A.: Pharmacotherapy with the mentally retarded. *In* Psychopathology in the Mentally Retarded. Edited by J. Matson and R. Barrett. New York, Grune & Stratton, 1982, pp. 239-243.
5. Burke, W.A.: Justifying an I.V. additive program. Drug Intell. Clin. Pharm., *6*:111, 1972.
6. Department of Health, Education, and Welfare, Social and Rehabilitation Service: Medical Assistance Program, Intermediate Care Facility Services. Federal Register. Washington, DC, National Archives and Records Administration, January 17, 1974.
7. Health Care Financing Administration: State Operations Manual, Transmittal No. 149, Provider Certification. January 1982.
8. Nelson, R., and Crocker, A.: The medical care of mentally retarded persons in public residential facilities. N. Engl. J. Med., *299*:1039, 1978.
9. Stolar, M.H.: National survey of hospital pharmacy technician use. Am. J. Hosp. Pharm., *38*:1133, 1981.
10. Ulrey, G., and Schnell, R.: A program for developing professional services at a residential institution. Ment. Retard., *19*(4):163, 1981.

30

EPIDEMIOLOGY OF INFECTIOUS DISEASES

Marc Manigat, M.D., M.P.H.

Hepatitis is an ancient disease. Reports of infectious icterus were noted in Hippocrates' writings. Epidemic jaundice became a clinical entity as early as the eighth century, when war and scourge swept through Europe. In modern times, several epidemics called infectious hepatitis have occurred. With the increased use of inoculation during this era, however, what was considered infectious hepatitis could have been serum hepatitis. Data obtained in 1960 from the studies of the hepatitis epidemic at Willowbrook State School helped substantiate the definitive evidence of two hepatitis viruses—hepatitis A and hepatitis B.[18]

Progress has been constant and rapid since 1960. In 1970, David Dane first visualized the hepatitis B virus; approximately 3 years later, Feinstone also visualized the hepatitis A virus. The last ten years have seen numerous scientific developments in the study of viral hepatitis, from sensitive and specific radioimmunoassays to the manufacturing of hepatitis B vaccine.

Viral hepatitis, both endemic and sporadic, has long occurred in closed institutions, particularly those for the mentally retarded. Today, these schools are no longer considered as closed environments in the strict sense, because residents move freely between state schools and programs within the community. The processes of deinstitutionalization and community participation carry with them the risk of spread of any communicable disease. To minimize this ever present danger, infection-control committees were established in most institutions for the mentally

retarded. With the availability of specific radio-immunoassays and the advent of hepatitis B vaccine, prevention and control of viral hepatitis, particularly viral hepatitis B, have become more feasible.

A basic knowledge of the natural history, epidemiology, and immunology of these two types of viral hepatitis remains a prerequisite for formulating any institutional control measures. The distinct epidemiologic, clinical, and immunologic features of hepatitis A and hepatitis B warrant separate discussion.

VIRAL HEPATITIS TYPE A

Viral hepatitis, type A, formerly known as infectious hepatitis, is an acute, benign, and self-limited disease when compared with Hepatitis B. Eighty to 90% of infected individuals recover with no serious sequelae.

For many years, hepatitis A was considered endemic in closed institutions for the mentally retarded, but public health practices in institutions have changed the pattern of hepatitis A from endemic to one of periodic introduction of the hepatitis A virus (HAV) after prolonged intervals.

Hepatitis A virus (HAV) is the official name of this 27-nm RNA particle, which in many aspects resembles an enterovirus subgroup of picornaviruses. Hepatitis A virus has a worldwide distribution, with its highest prevalence in institutions and communities with substandard sanitation and overcrowding. During the past 10 years, reports of outbreaks of hepatitis A in day-care centers have been increasing.[12]

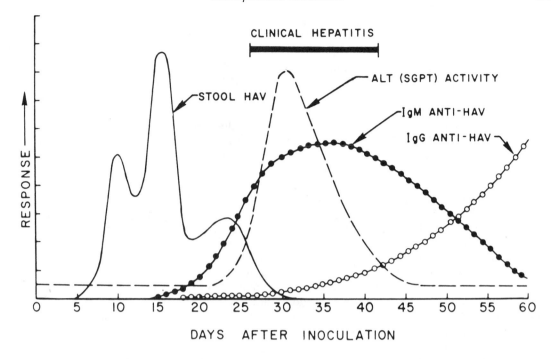

FIG. 30-1. Typical response to infection by hepatitis A virus, by number of days after inoculation.

Wrentham State School experienced its last major outbreak of hepatitis A at the end of 1980. This outbreak provided an opportunity to uncover factors facilitating the spread of hepatitis A and establish appropriate control measures in present institutional settings. During the period between December 1980 and April 1981, 42 cases of viral hepatitis type A were diagnosed at the school. Thirty-five of the 42 were residents, and the remaining 7 were members of the staff. The attack rate was 38 per 1,000 among residents and 2.6 per 1,000 among staff members. Although the average age of Wrentham State School residents was estimated to be between 40 and 49 years, the average age of resident cases was 24.5 years. About 73.5% of the residents who contracted the disease were profoundly retarded and poorly toilet-trained. Some of these residents attended training and educational programs scattered throughout eastern Massachusetts. Overall, 11 residential buildings with a total of 529 residents were affected by this outbreak when successful control measures, including immune globulin (IG) administration, were implemented.[13] The source of infection of the index case was not known.

In general, the incubation period of viral hepatitis type A ranges from 20 to 50 days, with an average of 28 days. The virus can be detected in the liver, blood, bile, and stools of infected individuals. The length of infectivity is not clear. There is agreement, however, that the period of infectivity of a patient coincides with maximal viral concentration and fecal shedding,[26] that is, 3 weeks before biochemical evidence of hepatitis A and 7 to 10 days after illness begins (Fig. 30-1).

Transmission

The mechanism of virus transmission consists in the transfer of the virus shed from the feces of an infected person to the mouth of another person. Certain behaviors observed in institutions, such as rectal digging, fecal smearing, pica, and close-contact interaction in day activity facilitate oral transfer of fecal contaminants. Parenteral transmission of hepatitis A virus is being documented more and more in hospital intensive-care nurseries,[28] but this cannot be viewed as a serious concern in institutions. The role of direct-care staff in the transmission of HAV to residents is unclear.

Diagnosis

Clinical presentation of viral hepatitis type A ranges from benign and asymptomatic to acute fulminant disease. Dark urine and jaundice are the most frequent signs noted by staff. Anorexia and lassitude in a hyperactive resident are other indexes of suspicion. The icteric/nonicteric ratio is 1:3. Hepatic transaminases raise to levels of about 4,000 international units (IU) in jaundiced patients.

Diagnosis of acute viral hepatitis type A is made by demonstrating a specific antibody response. During acute illness, anti-HAV is predominantly of the IgM immunoglobulin class; gradually it is replaced by antibody of the IgG class; it usually peaks within 1 to 3 months after illness begins. Anti-HAV IgG is associated with recovery and acquisition of immunity and can be detected many years after acute infection.

Immunologic survey of 209 residents using anti-HAV solid-phase radioimmunoassay revealed that 107 (51.2%) had anti-HAV IgG; 48.8% tested anti-HAV negative. The latter group consisted mostly of residents who had been admitted to the institution for less than 12 years. It was also observed that chronic carriership of hepatitis B virus (HBV) influences the morbidity of viral hepatitis type A. IgM anti-HAV seems to persist longer than 6 months in carriers of hepatitis B virus who have Down syndrome.

Prevention

The presence of a substantial number of susceptible residents in institutions and the growing participation of these residents in community training and recreational programs make any case of viral hepatitis, particularly Type A, a major infection-control concern. Besides the general hepatitis precautions, environmental surveillance helps maintain high sanitary standards in both residential and program areas. Handwashing before meals and after toileting is incorporated into residents' training in activities of daily living skills. Data from immunologic survey are cross-referenced with day-training programs so contacts can be readily identified. Institutional hepatitis guidelines adapted from those published by Favero et al.[10] are incorporated into the content of the hepatitis course for direct-care staff.

Prophylaxis

Until a hepatitis A vaccine is available, immunoglobulin (IG) is indicated for hepatitis A prophylaxis either before or after exposure. The recommended dose of 0.02 ml per kg of body weight is 91% effective in preventing this disease[22] provided it is given within 2 weeks of known exposure. Postexposure prophylaxis is indicated for close personal contacts and institutional contacts. In a continuous-contact setting such as in closed institutions, immunoglobulin for postexposure prophylaxis is given soon after diagnosis to direct-care staff and susceptible residents as soon as a case of hepatitis A is confirmed.

VIRAL HEPATITIS TYPE B

Hepatitis B, formerly known as serum hepatitis, is caused by a virus called hepatitis B virus (HBV), which has a worldwide distribution. Human infection with hepatitis B virus can result in significant mortality and morbidity. In the United States, where the prevalence of hepatitis B is low (0.1 to 0.5%), about 300,000 young adults are infected each year. Between 6% and 10% become chronic carriers.[5]

Hepatitis B virus is a 42-nm double-strand DNA virus consisting of a central core containing the hepatitis B core antigen and a surrounding envelope that represents the hepatitis B surface antigen.[14] The hepatitis B surface antigen (HBsAg) is antigenically distinct from the hepatitis core antigen (HBcAg), which elicits its own antibody, anti-HBc. Hepatitis B surface antigen as a marker for the virus is detected in certain body fluids (pleural, ascitic fluids), secretions (saliva, serum, vaginal secretions), and excretions (bile, urine). Except for the liver, blood has the highest concentration of hepatitis B virus, which circulates either as a complete virus or as spheres and tubules.

Transmission

Hepatitis B virus can be transmitted to a susceptible person parenterally, by percutaneous inoculation with or without a needle, nonparenterally, or by mucosal transfer via saliva or sexual contact. The prevalent condition in institutions favors the nonparenteral mode of transmission. Certain aberrant behaviors and work practices such as sharing of toys, toileting articles, kissing, and biting facilitate transfer of HBV. The virus can survive at least 7 days on inanimate objects.[2] Today, because sexual relationships are acceptable among residents in institutions, transmission via the venereal route is enhanced. The mechanism of transmission of HBV virus in direct-care staff is unclear in most cases, but human bites appear to be a significant risk factor.[3]

Serologic Markers

Compared with hepatitis A virus, which possesses only one serologic marker, anti-HAV, hepatitis B virus has 5 serologic markers, which have characteristic association with time of exposure and degree of infectivity and immunity. The general pattern is that HBsAg appears 4 weeks or more after exposure to hepatitis B virus (Fig. 30-2). HBeAg appears any time thereafter,

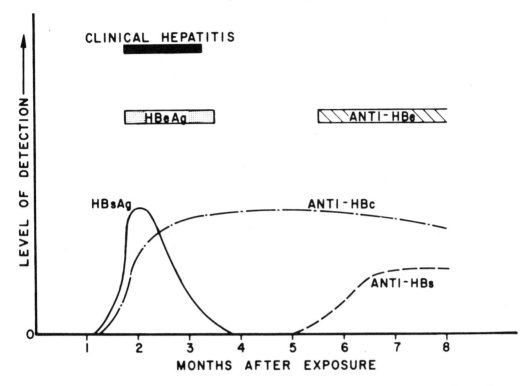

FIG. 30-2. The serologic responses of an individual with a transient HBsAG response and typical acute HB after exposure to HBsAg-positive serum (chronic carrier serum).

whereas anti-HBe is detectable only after the disappearance of HBeAg. Blood, serum, and secretions of HBeAg-positive individuals are considered highly infectious for intimate contacts and for those exposed parenterally.[25] Anti-HBc peaks during the interval between the decline of HBsAg and the rise of anti-HBs titers. Anti-HBc is considered to be a more reliable index of potential infectivity from hepatitis B virus than HBsAg.[19] Anti-HBc IgM appears also to be a specific marker of recent or ongoing hepatitis B infection. It may become a useful laboratory test in the differential diagnosis between acute hepatitis B and non A, non B hepatitis.

The period in which HBsAg and anti-HBs are both negative is called the window phase. It may last up to 3 or 4 months. Patients in window phase are usually considered infected.[15] A group from Cleveland Clinic Foundation has demonstrated the coexistence of hepatitis B surface antigen and anti-HBs in 13 patients on hemodialysis, which represents a different sequence of events. Their explanation is these patients appear to be chronic carriers who were exposed to a second HBV subtype to which they were able to mount a monotype antibody response.[11]

In general, immunity to hepatitis B infection implies negativity to all HBV markers except anti-HBs.

Diagnosis

The period of infectivity varies widely among patients with hepatitis B. Hepatitis B infection has an incubation period ranging from 40 to 180 days. The infection usually follows two clinical courses. One is a self-limited course with clinically inapparent illness. The other is characterized by acute icteric hepatitis that resolves

Table 30-1. *Hepatitis B Serologic Survey at Wrentham State School March 1983*

Status	Number	Percent
HBsAg positive (carrier)	120	15.0
HBsAg negative, anti-HBs positive (immune)	599	74.9
Anti-HBc, anti-HBs negative (at risk)	81	10.1
	800	100

Table 30-2. *Quick Interpretation of Hepatitis Serology*

	Marker						
	IgM/ Anti-HAV	HBsAg	Anti-HBc	HBeAg	Anti-HBe	Anti-HBs	Status
1)	+	−	−	−	−	−	Acute hepatitis A, patient probably infectious
2)	−	+	+	−	−	−	Acute hepatitis B
3)	−	−	+	−	−	−	Recent HBV infection, window phase, moderately infectious
4)	−	+	+	+	+	−	Acute HBV infection or carrier state, very infectious
5)	−	+	+	−	+	−	Recent HBV infection or chronic carrier state, less infectious
6)	−	−	+	−	−	+	Past infection, possibly infectious
7)	−	−	−	−	−	+	Remote infection; immune
8)	−	−	−	−	−	−	Possibility of non A/non B hepatitis

without residual damage. Ten percent of the icteric patients develop a prolonged hepatitis B infection with possibility of serious sequelae such as chronic active hepatitis, cirrhosis, and primary hepatocellular carcinoma. Most of the cases of hepatitis B seen in institutions are subclinical or chronic; therefore the diagnosis lies in appropriate laboratory testing.

Prevention

Hepatitis B virus poses a certain risk for both the direct-care staff and susceptible residents in institutions for the mentally retarded. The risk seems to increase with duration of institutionalization or employment.[8] In Massachusetts, there are about 4,867 residents in community programs whose hepatitis B status is unknown. In the past, serologic surveys were not considered necessary; now they prove to be useful in determining prevalence of serologic markers in certain groups. This information has been the cornerstone of the hepatitis B surveillance program at Wrentham State School. Hepatitis B screening was performed on 800 residents (100%) in March 1983 (Table 30-1). Tests were performed by the Bioran Laboratory under state contract. One hundred and twenty patients representing 15% of the resident population were chronic carriers.

Among the chronic carriers, 18 were positive to HBeAg. Sixteen of these 18 patients had Down syndrome. Antisocial and bizarre behaviors were also observed in some residents in this group.

The 81 susceptible residents, representing 10.1% of the school population, received a serial of three injections of hepatitis B vaccine (Heptavax B). The remaining 599 residents (74.9% of the population) were positive to antibody to the hepatitis B surface antigen.

Because of the peculiar characteristics of institutional environments, additional control measures were recommended. The immunologic survey is kept up to date by annual testing of the carriers and those who failed to respond to the hepatitis B vaccine. A standardized protocol for screening and management of susceptible persons exposed to HBV has been established. Residents slated for community placement are retested prior to their discharge if indicated, and information on their HBV status is passed on to their health care providers (see Table 30-2 for interpretation of hepatitis serology). Emphasis is also placed on staff training and education, along with effort in improving residents' activities of daily living skills.

Prophylaxis

Before 1982, the main approach to prophylaxis against hepatitis B infection was passive immunization, which depended on immune globulin (IG) and hepatitis B immune globulin (HBIG).[17]

Table 30-3. *Who's at Risk?*

Hepatitis A	Hepatitis B
High Risk	
Household contacts of infected patients	Immigrants and refugees from areas where HBV is prevalent
Sexual contacts of infected patients	Residents of institutions for the developmentally disabled
	Users of illicit parenteral drugs
	Homosexually active males
	Household contacts of carriers
	Sexual contacts of carriers
	Patients in hemodialysis units
Intermediate Risk	
Staff and children of daycare centers that have children in diapers	Male prisoners
Residents and staff in custodial care facilities (e.g., prisons and institutions for the developmentally disabled)	Staff of institutions for the developmentally disabled
Contacts of infected food handlers	Health care employees who have frequent contact with blood including: emergency department, intensive care unit, operating room, and dialysis unit nursing staff
	Nurse anesthetists
	Laboratory staff
	Pathology staff
	Surgeons
	Physicians in dialysis units
	Transplant staff
	Dentists and dental hygienists
Low Risk	
School contacts	Health care workers who have no or infrequent contact with blood
Hospital contacts	Casual social, office, or school contacts
Work contacts	
Social contacts	

Source: Immune globulins for protection against viral hepatitis. MMWR, *30*:423, 1981.

Hepatitis B immune globulin is recommended for postexposure prophylaxis of persons exposed to hepatitis B virus either via parenteral or nonparenteral route, whereas immune globulin is reserved for preexposure prophylaxis against hepatitis B in endemic settings such as institutions for the mentally retarded or hemodialysis units (see Table 30-3 for relative risk levels of various groups). The disadvantage of passive immunization with these agents is that protection against HBV infection is not complete or permanent.

With the availability of the hepatitis B vaccine, active immunity can be induced after 3 intramuscular injections. Hepatitis B vaccine derives from pooled plasma of chronic carriers of hepatitis B surface antigen and is manufactured in the United States by Merck, Sharpe and Dohme Laboratories. Field trials thus far have demonstrated that the efficacy of 3 doses of vaccine approaches 96%.[30] After the initial survey at the school, 59 of the 81 patients at risk for HBV infection were given hepatitis B vaccine (Table 30-4).

Although the hepatitis B vaccine has been proved to be safe and effective, acceptance of the vaccine among health care personnel has been very low, probably because of its exorbitant price ($100 per 3-ml vial) and the lingering although unjustified concern about vaccine safety,

Table 30-4. *Acceptance of Hepatitis B Vaccine Among Patients at Risk*

	Number	Percent
Number of vaccinees	59	72.9
Patients still at risk of HBV	22	27.1
	81	100

Table 30-5. *Guidelines for Prophylaxis Against Hepatitis in Intermediate Care Facilities for the Mentally Retarded*

Type of Prophylaxis	Hepatitis A		Hepatitis B	
	Preexposure	Postexposure	Preexposure	Postexposure
Immune globulin (IG)	0.02 ml/kg, IM, for travelers to high-risk areas; provides protection for 2 to 3 months 0.06 ml/kg every 4 to 6 months for prolonged travel	0.02 ml/kg, IM, for household and sexual contacts, staff of day-care centers, and residents and staff of custodial institutions	0.05 to 0.07 ml/kg, IM, for staff and patients of hemodialysis units and of custodial institutions for the developmentally disabled if other infection control measures fail to interrupt transmission	0.06 ml/kg, IM, or no prophylaxis, for those exposed to blood that is unlikely to be HBsAg-positive or when the source is unknown 0.06 ml/kg, IM, immediately if exposed to blood that is likely to be HBsAg-positive (HBIG is recommended once the blood is proved HBsAg-positive)
Hepatitis B immune globulin (HBIG)	Not indicated	Not indicated	Not indicated	0.06 ml/kg, IM, within 24 hr and repeat in 1 month for those exposed to HBsAg-positive blood
Hepatitis B vaccine	Not indicated	Not indicated	1.0 ml, IM, for adults; 0.5 ml, IM, for children under 10; 2.0 ml, IM, for immunosuppressed patients Repeat 1 and 6 months after first dose	

particularly in regard to the acquired immune deficiency syndrome (AIDS). New approaches bypassing the need for human blood, such as gene-splicing and cloning, have been successfully used in the production of new vaccines. Some of these vaccines, such as the recombinant DNA hepatitis vaccine, are now undergoing field trials.

Hepatitis B vaccine is recommended to high-risk groups including susceptible clients and staff of institutions for the mentally retarded, homosexual males, users of illicit parenteral drugs, household contacts and sexual partners of ABV carriers, and infants born of mothers who are HBsAg-positive (see Table 30-5 for guidelines for prophylaxis against hepatitis in intermediate care facilities for the mentally retarded).

Twelve hundred doses of hepatitis B vaccine were administered at Wrentham State School between December 1983 and June 1984. The frequency of side effects reported was only 8%. In 2 double-blind controlled trials among almost 2,500 persons, the overall rates of adverse reactions reported by vaccine recipients were 24.1% and 21.5%, which did not differ significantly from those of placebo recipients (21.4% and 18.7%). Arm soreness was the most common side effect. Other reported reactions included low-grade fever, myalgia, and arthralgia. Occasionally fever exceeded 100.2° Fahrenheit. Frequency of complications will be known with more experience with the hepatitis B vaccine. Since 1982 it is estimated that 1,400,000 persons have completed the 3-dose series (Merck, Sharp & Dohme).

Because of the high prevalence of serologic markers of hepatitis B in institutions for the mentally retarded, screening before vaccination is cost-effective; it may not, however, be cost-effective to screen health care professionals in these institutions prior to vaccination for hepatitis B. The decision whether to screen health workers before vaccination depends on the prevalence of HBV and cost-benefit factors in a given institution.

SHIGELLOSIS

Shigellosis has been a serious health problem for day-care centers and institutions, particularly institutions for the mentally retarded. Several outbreaks of shigellosis in these facilities have been reported.[8] In 1978, Wrentham State School experienced an outbreak of shigellosis involving both residents and direct-care staff. This outbreak affected 155 residents housed in old and overcrowded buildings with substandard toilet facilities. No sex predominance was noted. The majority of the cases comprised residents with poor personal hygiene and aberrant or pica behavior. Shigella flexneri accounted for 80% of the shigella serotypes. Shigella flexneri was also cultured from environmental cultures taken from the bases of toilet fixtures in some of the buildings.

Epidemiology

Organisms of genus Shigella are short, non-motile, nonencapsulated gram-negative rods. The shigellas are categorized in Groups A, B, C, and D according to their specific somatic antigen. Group A is represented by Shigella dysenteriae, Group B by Shigella flexneri, Group C by Shigella boydii, and Group D by Shigella sonnei.[16] The latter is the most common serotype encountered. Out of 14,089 shigella serotypes reported in 1983 by the Centers for Disease Control, Shigella sonnei comprised 65%.[6]

There is no intermediate host in the cycles of transmission of shigellosis. Humans are the main reservoir. The fecal-oral route is the most predominant mechanism of transmission. Person-to-person spread occurs when organisms on hands (under fingernails) or items contaminated with fecal materials (e.g., water, milk) are ingested. Because Shigella can survive in the environment for days and weeks, contaminated surfaces constitute a mechanical vehicle in the transmission of the infection, particularly in populations prone to fecal soiling. Once Shigella is ingested, it invades the colonic submucosa, where it multiplies. There, Shigella produces a toxin that interferes with protein synthesis, thus resulting in cell death. This is evidenced clinically by colitis with discharge of blood and mucus containing numerous bacteria. The period of communicability is generally 4 weeks.

Diagnosis

Shigellosis is a self-limited disease with a mortality rate less than 1% in the United States. An acute attack of shigellosis usually lasts no more than 7 days. The clinical spectrum of Shigella infection ranges from asymptomatic illness characterized by 2 or 3 loose stools to severe dysentery with high fever, chills, abdominal cramps, and watery stools with or without blood and mucus. Most patients with shigellosis observed during the outbreak at Wrentham State School had a mild illness consisting of low-grade fever and low-volume diarrheal stools. Eight residents with protracted diarrhea and severe fluid losses were admitted for intravenous hydration.

Although fever and diarrhea with mucus and blood arouse the clinical suspicion of shigellosis, definitive diagnosis is established only when Shigella organisms are isolated from stool cultures. To achieve high yields of Shigella on stool culture during the Wrentham episode, rectal swabs were taken from blood-tinged flecks of mucus on 3 alternate days. Specimens were sent to the bacteriology department within 1 hour.

Prevention and Control

Outbreaks of shigellosis can be difficult to control in an institutional environment. Control efforts in general are to maintain a clean and sanitary environment, to identify and isolate cases and carriers, and instruct staff in basic principles of personal hygiene and enteric precautions. The decision to restrict training and day programs, which foster close contacts and cross-infection, depends on failure of preliminary control measures and the occurrence of secondary cases. When patients demonstrate intermittent shedding of Shigella, a single oral dose of tetracycline is given.[20,21] This is followed by repeated stool cultures until seven consecutive negative results are obtained. At Wrentham State School, the treatment with a single dose of tetracycline has been effective in ending the carrier state. (The choice of antimicrobial agent depends on the isolated strain.) Convalescent carriers with stool cultures that are intermittently positive for Shigella need to be followed. To ensure eradication of the organism, stool cultures are done twice a week until seven consecutive negative test results are obtained. Contrary to a report by Dupont,[9] which stated that infected children shed organisms intermittently more than a year, follow-up stool cultures in 8 carriers were consistently negative after 7 months.

Shigellosis as cause of diarrheal illness in institutions is less frequently seen. An overzealous bowel regime for treatment of constipation and viral gastroenteritis seems to be the most common cause of diarrhea at Wrentham State School.

Until a Shigella vaccine offering protection against all serotypes becomes available,[20] preventive measures, including maintenance of a sanitary environment, remain the most important means of controlling infection.

ENTEROBIASIS

Parasitic infections among institutionalized individuals have received broad attention during the past decades.[27] Rational drug therapy and environmental improvement and building renovation at some of the facilities for the mentally retarded have contributed to the decrease in prevalence of parasitic infections in these settings.

Analysis of stool reports for ova and parasites at Wrentham State School in 1983 revealed a significant decrease in the frequency of intestinal parasitosis such as Trichuris trichiura, Ascaris, and Hymenolepis nana, but infection with Enterobius vermicularis appeared to be on the increase among the profoundly and severely retarded. The prevalence of pinworm in this subgroup, representing 81% of the resident population of 800, was 12.4%.

Epidemiology

Enterobius vermicularis is an intestinal nematode that is found in almost all climates. The adult male measures 3 mm, and females 10 mm. They both inhabit the large intestine, where they attach themselves to the colonic mucosa. When the female worm becomes fully gravid she migrates down the length of the intestine and passes out the anus margin, where she liberates her burden of 10 to 11,000 eggs. The eggs, which are embryonated, become infective larvae after 4 to 7 hours. It is reported that pinworm eggs can survive for days or weeks in dry dust.[22] Under ideal environmental conditions, pinworm eggs can remain viable for 1 to 2 months. Pinworm eggs are not killed by chlorination of water in swimming or wading pools. In the United States an estimated 42 million cases of pinworm are reported each year.

The principal mode of transmission of Enterobius vermicularis is the transfer of infective eggs from the anus to the mouth by means of contaminated fingers or fingernails. Nail biting and scratching of the anal area facilitate autoinfection. Sleeping accommodations in open wards and shaking of the linen, which are current practices in institutions, facilitate close contact and airborne transmission. Also, individuals become reinfected by retrograde migration of the larvae from the anus to the bowel. This form of autoinfection was described by Schüffner and Swellengrebel in 1943,[29] but it has not been demonstrated.[1]

Diagnosis

A pinworm infection is usually inapparent, but heavy infestation can cause anal itching at night, hyperirritability, loss of appetite, insomnia, and outbursts of self-abusive behavior. Diagnosis of pinworm is usually done by direct observation of the egg on a cellophane tape swab or visualization of the adult worm in the perineal area. Eggs in feces are seen in only 5% of infected individuals. Best results are obtained when a pinworm tape swab is done early in the morning or in the evening before a bath. Three consecutive pinworm paddlings have a 90% diagnostic yield.[1]

Prevention

The results of treatment and control measures preventing the spread of pinworm infection in institutions are frustrating. Cram[4] confirms the observations of others that "it is an extremely difficult matter to prevent the spread of oxyuriasis." Mebendazole (Vermox),[24] an alternative drug to pyrantel pamoate (Antiminth), is widely used in institutions, probably because it is dispensable in chewable tablets, has less hepatic toxicity, and kills worms in all stages of development. In some cases treatment with mebendazole should be repeated in 2 weeks.

Several approaches have been tried in an attempt to eradicate pinworm in institutions. The policy of mass treatment of infective wards resulted only in reduction of the infective cases but not in total eradication.[31] One of the control measures that so far has proved successful at Wrentham State School is to coordinate drug treatment with environmental sanitation and supervised personal hygiene, with major emphasis placed on clipping of fingernails and handwashing before meals and after toileting. Linen and personal clothing should be washed in hot water in order to destroy the eggs and prevent further contamination of the environment. In addition, staff have been instructed in how to recognize adult pinworms and in the perianal swab technique. Patients with pinworm reinfestation should have perianal swabs every 2 weeks. Periodic retreatment may result in eradication of the parasite.

REFERENCES

1. Beaver, P.C., and Jung, C.J.: Clinical Parasitology. 9th Ed. Philadelphia, Lea & Febiger, 1984, p. 304.
2. Bond, W.W., et al.: Survival of hepatitis B virus after drying and storage for one week. Lancet, 1:550, 1981.

3. Cancio-Bello, T.P., et al.: An institutional outbreak of hepatitis B related to a human biting carrier. J. Infect. Dis., *146*(5):652, 1982.
4. Cram, E.B.: Studies on oxyuriasis XXVIII. Summaries and conclusions. J. Dis. Child., *65*:46, 1943.
5. Center for Disease Control: Recommendation of Immunization Practices Advisory Committee: Inactivated Hepatitis B Virus Vaccine. MMWR, *31*:317, 1982.
6. Centers for Disease Control: Shigellosis United States, 1983. JAMA, *252*(20):2811, 1984.
7. Craig, C.F., and Faust, E.C.: Clinical Parasitology. 8th Ed. Philadelphia, Lea & Febiger, 1984, p. 302-306.
8. Dienstag, J.L., and Ryan, D.: Occupational exposure to hepatitis B virus in hospital personnel: Infection on immunization. Am. J. Epidemiol., *115*(1):26, 1982.
9. DuPont, H.L., et al.: Shigellosis in custodial institutions. Am. J. Epidemiol., *92*:172, 1970.
10. Favero, M.S., et al.: Guidelines for the care of patients hospitalized with viral hepatitis. Ann. Intern. Med., *91*:872, 1979.
11. Footch, G.P., et al.: Concomitant hepatitis B surface antigen and antibody in 13 patients. Ann. Intern. Med., *99*:460, 1983.
12. Hadler, S.C., et al.: Hepatitis A in day-care centers: A community-wide assessment. New Engl. J. Med., *302*:1222, 1980.
13. Hadler, S.C., et al.: Effect of immunoglobulin on hepatitis A in day-care centers. JAMA, *249*(1):48, 1983.
14. The hepatitis knowledge base. Ann. Intern. Med., *93*(1)Part 2:194, 1980.
15. Hoofnagle, J.H., et al.: Type B hepatitis after transfusion with blood containing antibody to hepatitis B core antigen. N. Engl. J. Med., *298*:1379, 1978.
16. Hornsick, R.: Shigellosis. *In* Infectious Diseases. 2nd Ed. Edited by Paul D. Hoeprich. Philadelphia, Harper & Row, 1977, pp. 549-554.
17. King, J.W.: A clinical approach to hepatitis B.. Arch. Intern. Med., *142*:925, 1982.
18. Krugman, S., Giles, J.P., and Hammond, J.: Infectious hepatitis—evidence for two distinctive clinical epidemiological and immunological types of infection. JAMA, *252*(3):393, 1984.
19. Leezy, C.M.: Hepatitis Disease Symposium: Introduction. Postgrad. Med., *68*(3):115, 1980.
20. Levine, M.M., et al.: Shigellosis in custodial institutions. II. Clinical immunologic and bacteriology response of institutionalized children to oral attenuated Shigella vaccines. Am. J. Epidemiol., *96*:40, 1972.
21. Lionel, N.D.W., and Goonewardena, C.V.: A comparison of a single dose and a five-day course of tetracycline therapy in bacillary dysentery. J. Trop. Med. Hyg., *72*:170, 1969.
22. Markell, E.K., and Voge, M.: Medical parasitology. Philadelphia, W.B. Saunders, Philadelphia, 1965, pp. 124-127.
23. Maynard, J.E.: Passive and active immunization in the control of viral hepatitis. *In* Viral Hepatitis: 1981 International Symposium. Edited by W. Szmuness, H.J. Alter, and J. Maynard. Philadelphia, Franklin Institute Press, 1982, pp. 379-384.
24. Miller, M.J., et al.: Mebendazole—an effective antihelmintic for trichuriasis and enterobiasis. JAMA, *230*:1412, 1974.
25. Miyakawa, Y., and Mayumi, M.: HBe-anti-HBe system in hepatitis B virus infection. *In* Viral Hepatitis: 1981 International Symposium. Edited by W. Szmuness, H.J. Alter, and J. Maynard. Philadelphia, The Franklin Institute Press, 1982, pp. 183-194.
26. Rakola, J., and Mosley, J.W.: Fecal excretion of hepatitis A virus in humans. J. Infect. Dis., *135*(6):933, 1977.
27. Sargent, R.G.: Parasitic infection among residents of an institution for mentally retarded persons. Am. J. Ment. Defic., *87*(5):566, 1983.
28. Sceberg, S., et al.: Hospital outbreak of hepatitis A secondary to blood exchange in a baby. Lancet, *1*:1155, 1981.
29. Schüffner, W., and Swellengrebel, N.H.: Retrofection in oxyuriasis: A newly discovered mode of infection with Enterobius vermicularis. J. Parasitol., *35*:138, 1943.
30. Szmuness, W., et al.: Hepatitis B vaccine: Demonstration of efficacy in a controlled clinic trial in a high risk population in the United States. N. Engl. J. Med., *303*:833, 1980.
31. Yoelli, M., Most, H., Hammond, J., and Scheinesson, G.P.: Parasitic infection in a closed community. Trans. R. Soc. Trop. Med. Hyg., *66*(5):746, 1972.

Part IV

POLICY AND PLANNING

31

SERIOUS VIRAL INFECTION*

Frederick B. Palmer, M.D. □ *Philip R. Ziring, M.D.* □ *Bruce K. Shapiro, M.D.*

Infection in the infant and child with developmental disabilities has become an extremely controversial topic as the prevalence of private and mandated public developmental programs has increased in the last 10 years. Concern about contagion in community developmental centers has led to an avalanche of publicity, waves of anxiety, and a variety of legal challenges. The excitement is heightened by the media attention paid to certain infections in the nondisabled population such as genital herpes, hepatitis, and acquired immune deficiency syndrome (AIDS). This chapter is intended to review briefly the current knowledge of certain infections as it relates to persons with developmental disabilities. Emphasis is placed on risk of transmission and infection control. It is hoped that this information will provide those caring for such persons with an improved understanding of contagion and contribute to effective and dispassionate efforts of infection control.

CYTOMEGALOVIRUS INFECTIONS

Cytomegalovirus (CMV) is the most common agent known to be responsible for congenital in-

fection. It is a DNA virus like the herpes viruses. Growth of CMV in human fibroplasts results in a characteristic cytopathic effect of cell enlargement and intranuclear inclusions. These inclusion cells are often visible in the urinary sediment of infected individuals and provide a simple (but only partially sensitive) method for clinical diagnosis. Until the virus had been grown in tissue culture in the 1950s, CMV infection was rarely diagnosed. With the widespread use of these techniques and serologic methods, CMV infection is now commonly and readily diagnosed and the virus is recognized as ubiquitous in the community.[10]

Clinical Syndrome

CMV infection occurs in up to 2.3% of live births. Ninety-five percent of congenitally infected infants are asymptomatic and have no sequelae. Those with symptoms experience a wide range of problems including neonatal hepatitis, purpura, and microcephaly. The most common clinical feature is intrauterine growth retardation including microcephaly. Other findings include intracranial calcifications, deafness, chorioretinitis, and various congenital anomalies. The central nervous system damage and resultant developmental disability are of greatest concern. Neurologic sequelae range from profound mental retardation, cerebral palsy and seizures, to communication disorder, hyperactivity, learning disability, and sensorineural hearing loss.[5] Infants with congenital CMV infection

* Adapted from Palmer, F.B., Ziring, P., and Shapiro, B.K.: Serious viral infection in developmentally disabled persons: Threat to normalization? *In* Developmental Handicaps: Prevention and Treatment III. Edited by E.M. Eklund. Silver Spring, MD, American Association of University Affiliated Programs for Persons with Developmental Disabilities, 1985, pp. 1-22.

may continue to excrete the virus in urine and body secretions such as saliva for a prolonged period of time (months to years). It is now apparent that symptomatic intrauterine CMV infection occurs most frequently with primary maternal infection and not as a result of secondary infection (reexposure or reactivation).[28]

There is a vast range of clinical presentation of postnatal CMV infection, from the asymptomatic to severe disseminated manifestations. Postnatal primary infections in otherwise healthy infants, children, and adults are most often innocuous and are commonly subclinical. Mild respiratory symptoms, possibly with a rash, are not uncommon. More severe infections include hepatitis and an infectious mononucleosis-like picture with fever, rash, and polyarthritis. The severe forms of infection are more likely in the debilitated or immunocompromised individual and may be acquired through blood transfusion or organ transplant. CMV often persists in the body and is excreted in the urine and other fluids years after the mildest postnatal infection. A secondary or recurrent CMV infection can result from reexposure to an antigenically different strain or from reactivation of latent virus at a time of physiologic stress such as surgery, pregnancy, illness, or the use of immunosuppressive drugs.

Transmission

Considerable concern has been expressed by parents, teachers, physicians, and public health officials about the risk to pregnant or potentially pregnant women exposed to CMV. The focus of this concern is usually the presence of a known virus excretor in a day-care or developmental center. In order to understand the issues that determine risk and to develop recommendations to control risk, it is helpful to briefly review the epidemiology of CMV infection.

CMV is ubiquitous in the community. It is not highly contagious and requires intimate or close interpersonal contact with virus excretors to be transmitted. Thirty-five to 90% of females of childbearing age are seropositive for CMV, that is, they have evidence of previous primary infection. At present, seropositivity is much more common in low socioeconomic classes, in blacks, and in situations of overcrowding, which increase the likelihood of transmission.[7, 10]

The increasing use of child day-care and developmental centers appears to be altering the epidemiology, probably by providing frequent opportunity for close, intimate contact between infants, many of whom are virus excretors. In such settings, transmission through urine and saliva is probably of greatest importance. An evaluation in a day-care center in Alabama composed primarily of white middle-income families showed that 57% of enrolled children aged birth to 5 years were excreting CMV in their urine or saliva. Further, in the 12- to 24-month age group, almost 80% were excretors. This contrasts with a comparison group of preschool-age children not attending a day-care center in whom the virus excretion prevalence was only 8%.[24] Although absolute prevalence of excretion varies from center to center and class to class, it is apparent that the increasing use of out-of-home care for normal and handicapped children increases the risk of infection in pregnant women by increasing the number of infants and preschoolers who are excreting the virus. This increased risk appears to be independent of socioeconomic class or race.

The degree of risk this exposure presents to the pregnant caretaker is unclear. Correlations have been demonstrated between CMV infections in infants and children and subsequent seroconversion of mothers and other adults in the household. However, the magnitude of increased risk for CMV infection in a parent or day-care worker, or, more important, the increased risk for intrauterine infection, is uncertain.

These uncertainties have a bearing on policy regarding day-care or developmental-center attendance of normal or handicapped infants known to be excreting CMV. Since CMV is ubiquitous in day-care centers, almost any center is likely to have children enrolled who are excretors. It is illogical to exclude known excretors when there may be many other unknown excretors in the same center. Since the prevalence of CMV excretion in developmental centers is likely to be no higher than that in day-care centers for normal children,[8] the same argument should apply to the exclusion of infants with known congenital infection. This is especially important because exclusion could deprive a child of needed developmental programming. The unavoidable risk of repeated exposure to children in the general population who are unrecognized virus excretors probably far outweighs the risk from a child with known congenital CMV.[7]

It remains likely that the most effective method of reducing the risk of transmission of CMV is careful handwashing after contact with all infants, especially contact with saliva, urine, or other bodily secretions.[7, 25] The importance of such simple sanitation measures needs to be emphasized to all child care workers and center administrators. Currently, routine serologic screening of child care workers for CMV seronegativity (and thus risk for primary infection) cannot be advocated because of the limited knowledge about actual risk and the tremendous expense that would be involved. Whether transfer of the worker to another setting would significantly influence risk is not known.[7,25]

Policy Considerations

The increased use of day care and developmental centers may be altering the epidemiology of CMV infection in young children and may result in increased opportunity for exposure to women of childbearing age. Simple infection control measures are felt to be the best method for prevention of transmission.

Accurate data quantitating risk to mothers and child care workers is necessary. With such information, rational policy to reduce transmission can be developed. Current information indicates that it is illogical to exclude infants from day care or developmental centers on the basis of CMV excretion.[7,8,25]

HERPES SIMPLEX VIRUS INFECTION

Surveying the media reveals the strong emotional feelings associated with herpes simplex virus (HSV) infection. Headlines such as "Herpes Epidemic Rages," "Mother's Kiss Causes Infant's Handicap," and "Parents Vow Boycott if Herpes Child Attends Class" indicate the fear, concerns, and misinformation of the general population. This section reviews existing data about HSV to provide information for those who are likely to deal with children who have been handicapped as a result of HSV infection.

The Virus

HSV is a large, complex virus that is related to cytomegalovirus and varicella zoster virus. All members of this class have double-stranded DNA in their core and consequently have the potential for being incorporated into cellular DNA. In addition to causing cell death by overwhelming biosynthesis of infection progeny, the HSV genome can be totally or partially incorporated into cellular DNA, with continuing cell survival. This latent (nonproductive) infection can be reactivated by a variety of stimuli such as fever, sunshine, trauma, menses, or psychic stress. Reactivation manifested by local vesicular eruptions, e.g., the common cold sore, is usually not associated with constitutional symptoms. The mechanisms of reactivation are unknown. It

is also not known whether the virus is ever cleared from the host organism.

HSV is divided into two subtypes on the basis of epidemiology and biologic effects.[22] Primary HSV1 infection occurs in young children. Ninety to 95% of HSV1 infections are not associated with clinical disease. Symptomatic HSV1 may present with lesions of mucous membranes (lips, oropharynx, eye, genitals), lesions related to direct inoculation (whitlow), or meningoencephalitis.

HSV2 is found primarily in adolescents, young adults, and neonates. It too is commonly associated with subclinical disease. HSV2 causes genital infections, but nongenital infection can be seen. Neonatal meningoencephalitis is primarily caused by HSV2 and has been associated with maternal infection. Approximately 1% of pregnant women have cytologically detectable primary or recurrent herpetic genital lesions.

Transmission

The usual route of transmission is via direct, intimate contact. HSV1 is transmitted in an unknown fashion, although respiratory spread is postulated. HSV2 is acquired through venereal contact. HSV1 is found in approximately 10% of genital infections, however, and HSV2 has been found in the pharynx. Genital herpes in a prepubertal child should raise concern of sexual abuse.

Although most persons infected with HSV do not experience clinical symptoms, those with deficient immunologic defenses, such as immunosuppressed patients or neonates, represent special risks. The degree of risk is unknown, and this uncertainty is reflected in the American Academy of Pediatrics (AAP) recommendations. For those with cold sores, not kissing newborn infants or infants with eczema is advised. The decision to relieve a person with a cold sore from direct patient care because of potential risk of infection must be balanced against the risks of compromising care by excluding personnel who are essential for operation of the unit. Further, there is a 9.6% rate of recovery of HSV from saliva samples of *asymptomatic* personnel. Persons with herpetic whitlow (HSV infection of the finger) should not work in direct patient-care activities. Personnel with genital HSV infection require no special procedures.[1]

To date the AAP has no official policy regarding techniques for dealing with recurrent HSV infection in a congenitally infected child. Intermittent shedding of virus may occur years after infection. The degree of infectivity of patients with recurrent lesions is unknown. Whether additional isolation is needed for nonhospitalized children will require better understanding of methods of transmission. The likelihood of *significant* disease resulting from healthy children (or caretakers) being together in a classroom with a child who suffered neonatal infection is remote. At present it seems prudent to cover active skin lesions with a sterile dressing to limit lesion-to-skin contact and to decrease the likelihood of bacterial superinfection.

Symptomatic HSV infections are estimated to occur in 1 birth in 7,500. This incidence figure is subject to question, but it is clear that the fetus' unique relationship with the mother and its immature immunologic system permit other modes of HSV transmission to occur. Maternal viremia may allow virus to pass through the placenta to the fetus, although transplacental infection is uncommon. Intrapartum acquisition is thought to be the major route of transmission of neonatal HSV infection. It can occur during passage through an infected birth canal or via ascending infection through ruptured amniotic membranes. Approximately one-half of children born to women with genital herpes at or near term develop an infection, and approximately half of these have severe or fatal diseases.[9]

Clinical Syndromes

Several preliminary reports have suggested that antenatal HSV infection is associated with increased rates of abortion, preterm birth, and congenital malformations. Mothers who contracted HSV prior to 20 weeks gestation had a threefold increase in spontaneous abortion.[23] Preterm birth approximated 50% in infants of mothers who evidenced HSV infection during pregnancy.[31] Several reports of microcephaly and microphthalmia associated with transplacental infection have been described.[6]

Neonatal HSV disease is primarily the result of HSV2 infection. Most of the mothers are asymptomatic and without obvious signs of HSV at the time of delivery.[31] Although primary HSV in the mother is postulated to be more likely associated with neonatal disease,[9] serologic studies have shown that prior maternal HSV exposure is common in cases of neonatal infection.[32] Therefore, neonates may be infected as a result of either primary or reactivated maternal infection.

Intrapartum acquisition is usually insidious, not becoming evident until 6 to 12 days, or as late as 1 month. Neonatal HSV can assume three forms—localized to eyes, skin, or mucosa; localized to central nervous system (CNS); or disseminated visceral disease affecting lung, liver, or other organs (including CNS). Maternal anti-

body status does not predict which form of HSV disease develops, nor does it influence long-term survival or morbidity of the infected infant.[32]

Eighty percent of babies with HSV disease present with vesicular eruptions. The appearance of vesicles is ominous because most infants progress to disseminated or CNS disease. Diagnosis may be delayed in infants who are at home and in whom the significance of the vesicles is not apparent. The appearance of vesicles may initially escape detection in hospitalized, ill premature infants. Infected infants who do not present with vesicles constitute a major diagnostic challenge.

Details of other HSV infections are outlined elsewhere.[10]

Treatment

Mortality rates in neonatal HSV infections range from 30% for localized CNS disease to 80% in disseminated forms. Profound CNS handicaps—microcephaly, seizures, quadriparesis, profound cognitive deficits, and postinflammatory eye diseases—are the rule; only 10 to 15% of neonates survive without residue. Localized disease carries a better prognosis for life but is still associated with a rate of handicap of approximately 15%.

Adenine arabinoside has become the treatment of choice for neonatal HSV infection and has decreased the mortality from 74% to 34%. The most dramatic effects have been noted in disseminated and localized CNS forms of the disease, in which mortality has decreased from 85% to 57% and from 50% to 10%, respectively. The difference in morbidity is less impressive for disseminated disease (14% versus 8%) but more encouraging for localized CNS disease (50% versus 17%).[32]

Adenine arabinoside is a purine analogue, and, although it does not show substantial long-term neurologic toxicity in adults, its effects on the developing central nervous system must be viewed with caution. It is possible that the "cure" may result in neurologic dysfunction. The number of children treated is small, however, and length of follow-up has been too short to resolve this issue. Given the extreme mortality and morbidity and the lack of a proven alternative (trials are under way to determine the efficacy of acyclovir, another nucleotide analogue), there is little choice at the current time.

The treatment of localized eye infection is urgent and requires the supervision of an ophthalmologist. Meningoencephalitis in patients outside the neonatal period is beyond the scope of this review. The remaining clinical syndromes are usually managed supportively.[10]

Policy Considerations

People who deal with handicapped children develop a biased view of HSV. Instead of seeing a disease that is usually mild or asymptomatic, they see the results of intrapartum acquisition of HSV. The profound sequelae associated with this form of HSV infection tend to overshadow the broader picture and lead to unfounded associations and emotional postures.

The most effective way to deal with handicap resulting from HSV infection is to prevent its occurrence. The method of transmission of genital HSV to the immunologically immature neonate is well established. Expectant mothers with a history of HSV infection should be examined clinically and cytologically on a regular basis to determine if lesions are present. If lesions present near term or if genital HSV lesions are noted in a woman whose amniotic membranes have been ruptured less than 4 to 6 hours, cesarean section should be considered.

Although adenine arabinoside has decreased the mortality of neonatal HSV infection, mortality is still unacceptably high in some groups and morbidity remains substantial.

The likelihood of significant disease resulting from children (or caretakers) being together in a classroom with a child who suffered neonatal infection is remote if the children (or caretaker) are immunologically competent and lesion-to-skin contact is avoided.

HEPATITIS

Hepatitis is a viral illness affecting the liver. It is prevalent throughout the world and has been responsible for serious morbidity among all age groups and socioeconomic strata.[10] It is a disease which has had a very special significance for persons with mental retardation in the United States during the past 50 years, first as an endemic illness in public residential facilities throughout the country, and more recently as a public health issue regarding the rights of mentally retarded carriers of hepatitis B surface antigen to live in the community. It will remain a problem until there is far better education of the public and mental retardation professionals regarding the natural history and means of prevention of this disease. No easy solutions for this problem are in sight, and it is a major responsibility of professional staff from all disciplines to be fully informed about the nature of this disorder, its management, and means of prevention.

Hepatitis A and Hepatitis B

Two distinct forms of viral hepatitis were not recognized until the World War II era, when infectious hepatitis (now referred to as hepatitis A) was distinguished from serum hepatitis (now referred to as hepatitis B) by some of its clinical features, such as its shorter incubation period and mode of spread. It was not until the last 20 years that the quickening pace of scientific investigation led to a number of major breakthroughs in our understanding of other important features of these diseases, their long-term consequences, and to the development of effective means of prevention.

Hepatitis A, caused by an RNA virus, is now known to be an acute illness of widespread distribution throughout the country, especially prevalent in children as an inapparent or subclinical infection, and readily spread to susceptible individuals through the fecal-oral route. It is generally *not* spread by contaminated blood or needles, is not characterized by a carrier state, and is usually a self-limited illness followed by complete recovery. Prophylaxis of exposed persons with ordinary pooled gamma globulin is often helpful in preventing serious clinical illness. Preexposure prophylaxis is also recommended under circumstances of travel to areas of the world where hepatitis A is endemic.[13] A vaccine for prevention of hepatitis A is currently under development, but it is not yet available for general use.

Hepatitis B, caused by a more complex DNA virus (HBV), is of more limited prevalence in the United States, where it is of special concern for certain high-risk groups such as intravenous drug abusers, male homosexuals, and persons in the health professions. The disease is generally spread by contact with blood contaminated by HBV. HBV can also be transmitted by mucosal contact with other infective body secretions such as saliva or semen. The disease is not spread by exposure to the stool of a carrier (unless the stool is contaminated by blood). Ordinary immune globulin is of limited efficacy as a prophylactic agent. Ninety percent of individuals contracting the disease recover fully and become immune to the disease by developing antibody to hepatitis B surface antigen. Six to 10% of individuals acquiring hepatitis B do not develop antibody but remain chronic carriers of HBV and have the capacity, under circumstances of very intimate exposure, to transmit the disease to susceptible individuals. A small minority of such carriers are more highly contagious than the remainder, and are identified by demonstrating e-antigen in their blood. These long-term carriers have significant subsequent morbidity: more than 25% develop chronic active hepatitis, and some develop cirrhosis. Furthermore, there is an association between the HBV carrier state and the occurrence of primary liver cancer later in life.[13]

Susceptible persons who have lived in public residential facilities for individuals with mental retardation and who may be intimately and repeatedly exposed to infected persons are commonly infected by HBV because of the limited hygienic practices in such settings. For example, while the prevalence of HBV carriage in the general community is approximately 3 per 1,000, in public residential facilities for persons with mental retardation it is often as high as 30%, many of these individuals also being positive for e-antigen.

The increasing trend toward normalization in the United States has seen more mentally retarded persons continuing to live in the community. They are joined in community residences, workshops, and schools by persons who have been deinstitutionalized from residential centers and who may be HBV carriers. The result often has been great anxiety on the part of parents of retarded persons that their children would become infected with hepatitis B by these carriers. Similarly, staff in special education programs, workshops, and group homes may be fearful of contracting hepatitis through their occupational exposures. Furthermore, the public at large is concerned about the possibility of the spread of hepatitis throughout the community by persons with mental retardation who are also carriers of hepatitis B surface antigen.

Available data, from public schools in which children with mental retardation who are carriers of HBV are integrated with other children susceptible to hepatitis, are contradictory.[3,33] However, where adequate hygienic practices are carried out (proper disposal of materials contaminated by body fluid, adequate handwashing), there has been little documentation of spread of hepatitis B, even under the more intimate conditions of group home living.

Prevention

The recent widespread availability of two safe and effective hepatitis B vaccines should lead to considerable reduction in the risk to susceptible clients and staff posed by their exposure to persons who are chronic carriers of HBV. A full series of three inoculations of these vaccines has been demonstrated to induce immunity in 95% of individuals. Side effects have consisted primarily of local, transient soreness at the injection site and occasional low-grade fever. One vaccine is prepared from plasma of individuals who have had hepatitis B and became carriers of the antigen, but the procedures used in preparation of the vaccine are believed to destroy all known infectious agents, including the virus believed to be responsible for causing AIDS. A new genetically engineered recombinant vaccine has recently been introduced and appears to be of similar safety and efficacy.[21]

The Immunization Practices Advisory Committee of the Centers for Disease Control of the Public Health Service recommends that persons who may be intimately exposed to carriers of hepatitis B (especially carriers demonstrated to be e-antigen positive) be given one of these hepatitis B vaccines.[13] Those individuals currently deemed to be at higher risk than the general population would include hepatitis B susceptible individuals being newly admitted to residential facilities for mentally retarded persons, health workers who have frequent contact with blood or serum-contaminated materials from carriers, and direct-care and therapy staff who have close and direct contact with carriers whose behavior makes transmission possible. This includes community group home residents and staff as well as those from larger residential facilities. Persons with Down syndrome, although no more likely to contract hepatitis B infection, are more likely to become chronic carriers. They are especially appropriate candidates for immunization.[29] In view of the present high cost of the required three doses of vaccine, persons who are candidates for the vaccine may choose to be screened serologically for evidence of existing immunity to hepatitis B, although only approximately 5% of individuals in the general population have such evidence of prior infection. Immunization of susceptible individuals as currently recommended should effectively eliminate the already low risk of exposure to persons with mental retardation who are carriers and allow for their full integration into community-based programs without fear of infection with hepatitis B virus.

ACQUIRED IMMUNODEFICIENCY SYNDROME

Acquired immunodeficiency syndrome (AIDS) has become a familiar term to most adults as a result of its continually increasing incidence, high prevalence in homosexual persons, and sensational media coverage. A pediatric form is well recognized,[26] raising issues of transmission to others similar to those raised by CMV, HBV, and HSV.

AIDS, as recognized in adults, is a syndrome of severe, generalized immunologic dysfunction. Patients are incapable of mounting effective immune responses to foreign antigens and yet have inappropriate formation of auto-antibodies and immune complexes, and therefore show autoimmune disease. The deficient immune responses result in severe, recurrent, and opportunistic infection. Although the natural history of AIDS is incompletely understood, it appears to be irreversible with a uniformly poor prognosis. Seventy-nine percent of those diagnosed before January 1985 had died by December 1986.[18]

Those at particularly high risk for AIDS include male homosexuals, drug addicts, heterosexual prostitutes, patients with hemophilia, persons receiving blood or blood-product transfusions, and certain young children.[27] The etiologic agent appears to be human T-cell lymphotropic virus (HTLV-III). HTLV-III has been isolated from blood, semen, and saliva of infected individuals. Information suggests that transmission occurs through intimate contact or contaminated blood or blood products. Routine contact such as casual kissing, hugging, or other social contact has not been shown to result in virus spread. The experience with AIDS in children has shown that transplacental infection also occurs.

As of December 1986, 394 cases of AIDS in children under age 13 had been reported.[18] Seventy-nine percent were children with parents who either had AIDS or were at increased risk for AIDS. Nineteen percent apparently contracted AIDS through blood or blood-product transfusion. Incomplete information is available regarding risk factors for the parents of the remaining infected children. Infants with apparently transplacentally acquired AIDS usually present with interstitial pneumonitis, hepatosplenomegaly, developmental delay, and failure to thrive, many before 3 months of age. They soon develop severe infections. As in adults, the prognosis is poor. Of the reported pediatric cases, 61% had died as of December 1986.[18] An AIDS prodrome occurs and is characterized by the immunologic and clinical features but without recognized opportunistic infection. This prodrome, AIDS-related complex (ARC), will probably be recognized with increasing frequency as physicians' familiarity with the AIDS spectrum grows. Whether all with ARC go on to develop full-blown AIDS with its bleak prognosis is unknown. A separate classification for HIV infection in children has been derived[19] and does not use the ARC designation. Better knowledge of the natural history of AIDS and ARC in children should emerge in the next few years.

Infants and children with AIDS have been shown to have a wide variety of neurologic and developmental abnormalities.[2,30] These abnormalities may be due to many factors including recurrent infection, nutritional compromise, prolonged hospitalization, and deprivation as well as direct involvement of the CNS. Such neurologic and developmental abnormalities will result in recommendation for placement in various developmental programs. Furthermore, the disordered social and family circumstances of many AIDS infants will require a wide range of public services such as foster care, social and protective services, and health department involvement. Each of these needs increases contact with adults and heightens anxiety about transmission of AIDS.

There are well-established guidelines for the care of hospitalized patients with AIDS and for precautions to be taken by patients with AIDS.[4,14,16,20,21] These guidelines are designed to eliminate the transmission of virus by contact with contaminated needles, blood products, or bodily secretions. When these guidelines are followed, transmission of AIDS to hospital workers caring for AIDS patients has not been a problem.[16] Because casual contact is not thought to lead to transmission of AIDS, it is reasonable to conclude that routine contact in a developmental center or foster placement also should not be a problem. In addition to careful attention to handwashing, precautions to avoid blood contact should be taken. After accidents with bleeding, surfaces contaminated with blood should be cleaned with a 1:10 solution of bleach in water. Toothbrushes, which can become contaminated with blood, should not be shared.[12] Dentists, dental hygienists, and others involved in dental care must take particular precautions because of their close exposure to saliva and blood.[15]

Neurologically impaired infants and children with AIDS who cannot control saliva and other bodily secretions pose a theoretical risk for transmission.[17] Decisions regarding their management should be made after discussion with the child's physician, parents or guardian, and school personnel.

The Centers for Disease Control have circulated recommendations for management of infants and children with AIDS in foster care and educational settings.[11] Persons caring for such children should review these and any future recommendations carefully.

As with other infections already discussed, denial of services to the child and family afflicted with AIDS seems an unnecessary additional burden to bear. Calm attention to accepted practices of infection control and an avoidance of sensationalism will result in safe delivery of necessary services to the child and family with AIDS.

REFERENCES

1. American Academy of Pediatrics Committee on Infectious Disease: Report on Infectious Disease. Evanston, IL, American Academy of Pediatrics, 1982.
2. Belman, A.L., et al.: Neurologic complications in children with acquired immune deficiency syndrome (abstract). Ann. Neurol., *16:*414, 1984.
3. Breuer, B., et al.: Transmission of hepatitis B virus to classroom contacts of mentally retarded carriers. JAMA, *254:*3190, 1985.
4. Conte, J.E., Hadley, W.K., and Sane, M.: Infection-control guidelines for patients with acquired immunodeficiency syndrome (AIDS). N. Engl. J. Med., *309:* 740, 1983.
5. Hanshaw, J.: Developmental abnormalities associated with congenital cytomegalovirus infection. Adv. Teratology, *4:*64, 1970.
6. Hanshaw, J.B., and Dudgeon, J.A.: Viral Disease of the Fetus and Newborn. Philadelphia, W.B. Saunders, 1978.
7. Hutto, C., Ricks, R., and Pass, R.: Prevalence of cytomegalovirus excretion from children in five day-care centers, in Leads from MMWR. JAMA, *253:*1236, 1985.
8. Jones, L., Duke-Duncan, P., and Yeager, S.: Cytomegalovirus infections in infant-toddler centers: Centers for the developmentally disabled versus regular day care. J. Infect. Dis., *151:*953, 1985.
9. Kilbrick, S.: Herpes simplex infection at term. What to do with mother, newborn and nursery personnel. JAMA, *243:*157, 1980.
10. Krugman, S., and Katz, S.: Infectious Diseases in Children. 7th Ed. St. Louis, C.V. Mosby, 1981.
11. Morbidity and Mortality Weekly Report: Education and foster care of children infected with human T-lymphotropic virus type III/lymphadenopathy-associated virus. *34:*313, 1985.
12. Morbidity and Mortality Weekly Report: Provisional public health service inter-agency recommendations for screening donated blood and plasma for antibody to the virus causing acquired immunodeficiency syndrome. *34:*5, 1985.
13. Morbidity and Mortality Weekly Report: Recommendations for protection against viral hepatitis. *34:*313, 1985.
14. Morbidity and Mortality Weekly Report: Recommendations for preventing transmission of infection with human T-lymphotropic virus type III/lymphadenopathy-associated virus in the workplace. *34:*682, 1985.
15. Morbidity and Mortality Weekly Report: Recommended infection-control practices for dentistry. *35:*237, 1985.
16. Morbidity and Mortality Weekly Report: Additional recommendations to reduce sexual and drug abuse-related transmission of human t-lymphotropic virus type III/lymphadenopathy-associated virus. *35:*152, 1986.
17. Morbidity and Mortality Weekly Report: Apparent transmission of human T-lymphadenopathy-associated virus from a child to a mother providing health care. *35:*76, 1986.
18. Morbidity and Mortality Weekly Report: Update: Acquired immunodeficiency syndrome—United States. *35:*757, 1986.
19. Morbidity and Mortality Weekly Report: Classification system for human immunodeficiency virus (HIV) infection in children under 13 years of age. *36:*225, 1987.
20. Morbidity and Mortality Weekly Report: Update: Human immunodeficiency virus infections in health-care workers exposed to blood of infected patients. *36:*285, 1987.
21. Morbidity and Mortality Weekly Report: ACIP. Update on hepatitis B prevention. *36:*353, 1987.
22. Nahmias, A.J., and Roizman, B.: Infection with herpes-simplex viruses 1 and 2I. N. Engl. J. Med., *289*(13):667, 1973.
23. Nahmias, A.J., et al.: Perinatal risk associated with maternal genital herpes simplex infection. Am. J. Obstet. Gynecol., *110:*825, 1971.
24. Pass, R., Hutto, C., Reynolds, D., and Polhill, R.: Increased frequency of cytomegalovirus infection in children in group day care. Pediatrics, *74:*121, 1984.
25. Pass, R., and Kinney, J.: Child care workers and children with congenital cytomegalovirus infection. Pediatrics, *75:*971, 1985.
26. Rubenstein, A., et al.: Acquired immunodeficiency with reversed T4/T8 ratios in infants borne to promiscuous and drug-addicted mothers. JAMA, *249:*2350, 1983.
27. Shannon, K.M., and Ammann, A.J.: Acquired immune deficiency syndrome in childhood. J. Pediatr., *106:*332, 1985.
28. Stagno, S., et al.: Congenital cytomegalovirus infection: The relative importance of primary recurrent-maternal infection. N. Engl. J. Med., *306:*945, 1982.
29. Troisi, C.L., Heiberg, D.A., and Hollinger, F.B.: Normal immune response to hepatitis B vaccine in patients with Down syndrome: A basis for immunization guidelines. JAMA, *254:*3196, 1985.
30. Ultmann, M.H., et al.: Developmental abnormalities in infants and children with acquired immune deficiency syndrome (AIDS) and AIDS-related complex. Dev. Med. Child. Neurol., *27:*563, 1985.
31. Whitley, R.J., et al.: The natural history of herpes simplex virus infections of mother and newborn. Pediatrics, *66:*489, 1980.
32. Whitley, R.J., et al.: Vidabrine therapy of neonatal herpes simplex infection. Pediatrics, *66:*495, 1980.
33. William, C., Weber, F.T., Cullen, J., and Kane, M.: Hepatitis B transmission in school contacts of retarded HBsAg carrier students. J. Pediatr., *103:*192, 1983.

32

PREVENTION

Allen C. Crocker, M.D.

Over the past 10 to 15 years a substantial force has gathered, dedicated to rendering more systematic the formerly scattered efforts toward prevention of mental retardation and other developmental disabilities. This qualitative change can be documented by the enhanced activity of prevention committees in local and national organizations, the proliferation of public education materials in the area of prevention, the convening of collaboratively sponsored conferences on prevention, and the generation of state plans for prevention of mental retardation and developmental disabilities. All of this activity has the characteristics of a "movement," judging from the breadth of participation and the vigor of resolve.[1] These activities have captured the special excitement of prevention, with its aspiration for improvement in the human condition and enhancement of the outlook for human achievement. The prevention movement does not detract from the need or reality of services for persons already involved with disability, and it is not really competitive in the area of resource allocation.

INTERESTED GROUPS

Much of the energy for the promotion of prevention has come from consumer groups whose members cannot directly benefit (being already involved), but who extend their hopes to "our children's children," to "tomorrow's children," or to "the right to be born well." It is not difficult to develop impressive cost-benefit tables for the

results from immunization, newborn screening, prenatal diagnosis, or intensive care of prematurely born infants—but it is abundantly apparent that economic issues are only a part of the point.[4]

The responsibility within public agencies for carrying out activities for the prevention of developmental disabilities spreads across all of the human service areas, generally at the state level. In biomedical matters the leadership currently rests with the state departments of health, particularly the "Title V" components (maternal and child health, and Services for Children with Special Health Care Needs). Departments of mental health, mental health/mental retardation, or mental retardation/developmental disabilities are typically charged with developmental screening, early intervention, and anticipatory services. Some responsibility may also rest with the departments of education, which are also involved with identification of children with sensory handicaps, design of relevant curricula, family life education, and perhaps education of the public. Social service and welfare agencies must be concerned with child abuse, deprivation, and family planning. It follows that if coordination, accountability, and sustained relations with planning groups are to be maintained, a high degree of interagency collaboration must occur. To this end a prevention task force or commission is required, not attached to any single agency, and preferably with ultimate responsibility to the governor's office (or to a developmental disabilities planning council). At present time 15 to 20 states have a discrete prevention plan; a handful of these are systematically subjected to regular analysis of effects.

The most important watchdogs of progress in prevention are the private consumer groups and the joint private-state conferences on the subject. Although much federal support can be identified in various prevention activities, there is not really an expression of a national prevention policy.[3] Federal investment is fragmented, without interagency accountability. A new coalition has been formed by the Association for Retarded Citizens/U.S. (ARC), the American Association on Mental Retardation (AAMR), the American Academy of Pediatrics (AAP), the American Association of University Affiliated Programs for Persons with Developmental Disabilities (AAUAP), and the President's Committee on Mental Retardation (PCMR), which may have the capability of achieving national commitments that match the earnest hopes of citizens and professionals.

PROGRAMS DIRECTED AT BIOMEDICAL CAUSES OF DEVELOPMENTAL DISABILITY

Primary Prevention

Primary prevention activities are designed to eliminate the occurrence of the condition which causes the disability.

Rubella Immunization

Immunization against rubella, to prevent the possibility of rubella during pregnancy with congenital infection of the fetus, is one of the most successful efforts in primary prevention. Reported instances of rubella in Massachusetts occurred at about 3,000 per year prior to vaccine licensure in 1968 (with 37,000 cases in the epidemic year of 1964), and now are down to about a dozen per year. Congenital rubella, often with severe sensorineural deafness, other central nervous system effects, and heart disease, was formerly at a level of 50 or so per year (750 deaf children alone in 1963-64); no congenital rubella has been identified in the state for several years.

Measles Immunization

Immunization against measles during childhood has also been very successful, although still just short of the elimination of measles as an endemic infection (originally targeted for 1982). Measles is no longer a major cause of encephalitis in children.

Education on Alcohol Effects

Public education about the pernicious effects of alcohol consumption on the unborn child has been useful, but fetal alcohol syndrome is still thought to occur in about 1 of every 700 births. Currently one sees it most commonly in circumstances of parental decompensation, and further prevention will depend on linkage to general social support and early education. It is important to realize that control of fetal alcohol effects requires limitation of drinking prior to the onset of pregnancy, not simply after the time when pregnancy is usually diagnosed.

Surveillance for Maternal Rh Antibodies

Surveillance for potential maternal Rh-antibody development, appropriate management, and the use of immunoglobulin have almost eradicated affirmed central nervous system pathology from "kernicterus," although some questions remain about the toxic effects of milder bilirubin levels in very small babies.

Cranial Trauma in Children

Programs to reduce head injury from accidents to small children who are passengers in motor vehicles have been vigorous, such as the American Academy of Pediatrics' "First Ride/ Safe Ride" program and the seat restraints for children pressed by law in many states. It must be noted, however, that children also suffer disabling cranial trauma as pedestrians, as bicycleriders, and in numerous types of household accidents.

Lead Poisoning

Absorption of toxic amounts of lead from contaminated dirt, dust, and paint chips (and from air, water, and food) continues to be a source of potential functional handicap for preschool children in many environments (3.9% of U.S. children from 6 months to 5 years of age had blood lead levels over 30 mcg/dl in the NHANES II 1976–1980 survey.[7] Efforts for prevention of lead poisoning currently depend on (1) studies of blood FEP or lead levels in child populations at risk, with individual intervention where appropriate, and (2) continuing attention to reduction of environmental contact with lead. Most experts feel that blood assays should be carried out on all children at ages 1 and 2 years, and beyond this in special circumstances. At the moment only about 500,000 children are tested in the U.S. each year, or about 3% of those under 6 years.

Support for Mothers with PKU

A new prevention assignment has developed, largely on the basis of previous successful management of children with PKU. Detection of PKU in newborn babies and early dietary guidance of these youngsters has established a cohort of girls now entering the child-bearing years whose fetuses are eligible for the toxic effects of their mothers' elevated blood phenylalanine levels ("maternal PKU"). Vigorous efforts are under way to locate and advise these young women so that they can approach pregnancy with appropriate supports. It is not yet certain that assurance can be given about fetal safety from low-phenylalanine diets started by their mothers prior to conception, but results to date are encouraging in this regard. A large coordinated national study has been begun (sponsored by the National Institute of Child Health and Human Development) that will explore this prospect systematically. No liability is apparent regarding the outcome of children whose fathers have PKU.

Genetic Counseling

Genetic counseling can offer significant guidance to potential parents, but there is disagreement about the breadth of applicability. The suggestion that all young couples be counseled is unrealistic in relation to the availability of appropriate professionals and the limitation of useful interpretations. Counseling is highly valuable in pedigrees with affirmed problems, such as known inborn errors of metabolism, other single-gene disorders (as in the phakomatoses), and hereditary chromosomal aberrations (fragile-X syndrome, translocations). Counseling is also useful in circumstances of multifactorial anomalies (as in neural tube defects, facial clefts, etc.), and for parents with fertility problems, fetal loss, or obscure congenital anomalies. One hopes that the ability to provide cogent counsel can gradually be extended to many further situations.

Advances in Neonatology

It is in the setting of care for the prematurely born infant that some of the most striking preventive activities have occurred. The contributions of neonatologists working in newborn intensive care nurseries have in the past 20 years set the scene for an enormously improved mortality rate for low- and very-low-birthweight infants. Regionalized newborn intensive care, physician education, and a move to maternal transport before delivery for the pregnancy at risk have greatly improved the prospects for these vulnerable infants. Beyond this, however, the percentage of survivors with developmental handicap has not increased, as had been feared.

Secondary Prevention

Secondary prevention activities are those in which there is an early identification of a relevant condition, and then intervention to avert an outcome with developmental disability.

PKU Screening

Newborn screening for treatable inborn errors of metabolism began in 1962-63 as the Guthrie filter-paper blood spot technique made mass testing feasible. Eventually all states engaged in the assay for PKU (occurrence about 1:12,000 births), and many have gone on to test for galactosemia as well (roughly 1:50,000 births). These analyses are particularly effective when carried out in regional projects in which large volumes of specimens are handled. Management of affected children by special diets serves well to prevent mental retardation, although other challenges accompany these programs.

Thyroid Screening

In the past decade screening of newborn infants for the presence of congenital hypothyroidism has followed on the PKU experience, with notable success. An unexpectedly high incidence of this abnormality has been demonstrated (1 in 4,500 births). By 1981 all 50 states had begun testing programs. Eminently successful results are occurring from the commencement of replacement therapy shortly after the newborn screen shows thyroid deficiency, and the former experience of discovering irreversible retardation in the early years of life from partial congenital hypothyroidism has now been eliminated.

Screening for High Maternal Alpha-Fetoprotein Levels

Substantial experience has been gained during the past decade with the use of elevations in maternal serum alpha-fetoprotein (MSAFP) measurement as a screen for the presence of neural tube defects in the fetus (spina bifida, myelomeningocele, anencephaly). This complex system requires a guiding program that provides carefully standardized laboratory analysis, skilled use of ultrasonographic examination, selective amniocentesis, and informed counseling of the parents. Up to 90% of babies with myelodysplasia can be thus detected, with information also obtained on other altered fetal conditions (abdominal wall defects, multiple pregnancy, etc.). In states where public education and obstetrical sharing have progressed (e.g., Maine), screening levels above 50% are now taking place. In the United Kingdom, where occurrence figures are higher than in the U.S. (here about 1:750 births), use of the assay is even more extensive. With the new interest in low MSAFP levels as an indicator of risk for a fetus with Down syndrome (see below), this double study will stimulate yet further screening effort.

Screening for Low Maternal Alpha-Fetoprotein Levels

Prenatal diagnosis of Down syndrome has traditionally been based on elective provision of amniocentesis with chromosomal study of fetal cells for women known to be at substantially increased risk (age 35 years and above). Because of changes in the numbers of older women having babies (reduction from 11% of total births to 4% from 1960 to 1980), about 80% of mothers of infants with Down syndrome are now below 35 years of age. Hence, although in many sections of the country close to 50% of older women are undergoing amniocentesis, this can be expected to produce only about a 10% reduction in births of infants with trisomy 21.

A new element in this equation has emerged with the finding that pregnancies for infants with Down syndrome may be accompanied by a lower-than-average level of alpha-fetoprotein in the maternal serum, as tested at 16 to 18 weeks of gestation.[5,8] It appears that risk tables constructed on both maternal age and serum alpha-fetoprotein level will allow a much more effective utilization of amniocentesis. On this basis a considerable further lowering of the birth incidence for Down syndrome can be anticipated.

Testing for Tay-Sachs Carrier State

It has proven workable to carry out testing for the carrier state (heterozygosity) in Tay-Sachs disease by automated measurement of the serum hexosaminidase A level, and thus identify couples at risk for having involved pregnancies. In the past 15 years almost 500,000 such tests have been accomplished[6] among persons in the group with the highest gene frequency (Ashkenazi Jews). This testing was originally carried out in publicly conducted screening sessions, but now it is more commonly included in individual prenatal care. The incidence of births of infants with Tay-Sachs disease is now said to be reduced by 85%, in part because of this vigorous effort. Outreach is currently being extended to certain non-Jewish French-Canadian populations, in which there is also an increased occurrence of the altered gene.

GENERAL PROGRAMS

Prevention activities regarding discrete biomedical causes of developmental disabilities have high individual value, but even in the aggregate they cannot be expected to produce a major decrease in overall incidence. It is clear that to achieve our ultimate goals we must depend as well on improved supports to pregnant women, protection and nurturance of the vulnerable small child, and enhancement of family life and parenthood. These more general commitments are obviously linked to societal values, and to some extent to economic stability. The medical care team has an opportunity to promote and reinforce many components of these endeavors.

Prenatal Care

Improved prenatal care is central to the production of good babies. Our understanding is incomplete of the actual supports required by the fetus for optimal outcome, but it is known that thoughtful utilization of the best current level of prenatal guidance is associated with decreases in prematurity, obstetric complications, and infant mortality. Educational materials for childbearing couples, distributed by voluntary organizations and state agencies, encourage active involvement in concern for the mother's and baby's health (Figs. 32-1 to 32-3). Good nutrition, avoidance of noxious influences (alcohol, smoking, drugs, teratogens), attention to infection, and surveillance for diabetes and toxemia are of known importance. Planning in the Title V programs of state departments of health is assisting in developing better access to prenatal care, including removal of financial barriers.

Family Life Education

Family life education is designed to alert young people to the upcoming opportunities and responsibilities of parenthood. Linked in the public mind to sex education, it has fared poorly in conservative school districts. Conclusions vary on whether early public school coursework can reduce teenage pregnancy, but the effort seems essential in the face of appalling general statistics. A joint commitment on the part of parents, schools, churches, private groups, and perhaps medical practitioners would be appropriate, but involves complex forces. Instillation of information in an atmosphere of respect for the needs of children yet to be born is the major goal.

FIG. 32-1. Educational pamphlets from associations for retarded citizens of Alabama, Indiana, Illinois, and Virginia informing pregnant women about best care for their babies. From Crocker, A.C.: Prevention of mental retardation. Ann. N.Y. Acad. Sci., 477:329, 1986. Reprinted with permission.

Family Planning Services

Making family planning services available is another component in the effort to assure that children will be born when wanted. Information about contraception of all forms, together with provision of direct assistance in contraceptive use, can be part of the investment of schools. School-based health clinics where contraceptives are available have had favorable experiences. More common are the family planning clinics run by city or state health departments in the community, and those sponsored by private organizations.

Identification of Children at Risk

Early identification and intervention for children at risk are critical in enhancing the progress of the vulnerable child and preventing complications in those with disorders. These processes include infant follow-up programs for graduates

of newborn intensive care units (see Chap. 5), maintenance of a network of early-intervention programs, home-visiting by community nursing services, and outreach by health departments and school districts to families who have concern about the developmental progress of their young children. There is much current effort to examine the different levels of effectiveness of various models of early stimulation and training programs, but their general utility in gains for children and parents is unquestioned.

Child-Abuse Surveillance

Education and surveillance regarding child abuse represents a somewhat desperate effort to assure children a life without trauma or neglect. Particularly compelling is the transgenerational disturbance of family life that characterizes some wounded or limited parents. Both the normal and the disabled child deserve a family environment which encourages self-belief. Psychosocial

FIG. 32-2. Pamphlets emphasizing effect of mother's activities on outcome of pregnancy. From Crocker, A.C.: Prevention of mental retardation. Ann. N.Y. Acad. Sci., 477:329, 1986. Reprinted with permission.

deprivation remains a significant cause of mental retardation. Regrettably, our public child-welfare organizations are nearly overwhelmed by process issues and have insufficient energy to cover some of the penetrating background components. In current times family integrity is sorely tested.

Child-Health Programs

Enhanced child-health measures are pertinent to prevention of developmental disabilities in many ways. Positive growth and development of children depend on an atmosphere of good health. Examples of deterrents include exposure to lead, undernutrition, repeated infection, and the drain of chronic illness. It is of interest that the state of Tennessee recently broadened their plan for prevention of mental retardation to a full "Healthy Child Initiative," acknowledging that he majority of pro-child supports they were sponsoring dealt jointly with good development and good health.

Alleviation of Effects of Social Disadvantage

Assistance regarding the effects of poverty and social disadvantage must be approached in thoughtfully conceived programs if the full legacy for a good childhood (with optimal personal progress) is to be secured. The suppressive effects of limited social and economic circumstances are pervasive. At present our early-intervention programs have only partial capacity to receive infants who are "environmentally at risk." The work of Head Start is a valuable addition in the preschool years.

Research

Research on causation of developmental disabilities must proceed if prevention programs are to become more encompassing. Every child-study unit is obliged to admit that a significant portion of the disabled children whom they evaluate have arrived at their altered state by

FIG. 32-3. Conference proceedings from California and New York that project the hopeful atmosphere of prevention activities. From Crocker, A.C.: Prevention of mental retardation. Ann. N.Y. Acad. Sci., 477:329, 1986. Reprinted with permission.

unknown causes (see Chap. 2). This includes the vast majority of those with congenital anomaly syndromes, the chromosomal aberrations, and autism, as well as a large number who have less-specified pictures. It is possible that environmental teratogens or intrauterine infections play a larger role than we presently appreciate. More information is also needed on the dynamics of injury in intraventricular hemorrhage of premature infants, and on the effects of divergent lifestyles and nurturance systems on growing children.

THE ROLE OF MEDICAL TEAMS IN PREVENTION ACTIVITIES

The extensive contact of physicians, nurses, and clinic staffs with disabled persons and their families allows medical teams to form special perceptions about the mechanisms and complications of developmental disorder. This situation increases the possibilities for prevention, for avoid-

ing trouble in these patients, and for enhancing general progress in the field in a number of areas:

Support to programs (and public education) regarding immunization, fetal alcohol syndrome, newborn screening, head injury, etc.

Energetic pursuit of etiologic and epidemiologic studies, with the hope of improving knowledge about causation

Encouragement of genetic counseling for couples with children who have congenital anomalies or possible genetic syndromes

Encouragement of good prenatal care, maternal transport when appropriate, use of regional newborn intensive care programs, and infant follow-up

Referral of infants at risk to early intervention programs

Strong emphasis on health maintenance and habilitative therapy of disabled children and adults, in the "tertiary prevention" mode

Diligence in detection of lead intoxication, child abuse, and inadequate nutrition

Family planning assistance (and family life education) for young persons, including those with developmental disabilities

Aid to families in finding the community-based services that will help in procuring the best progress for their family member

Participation in state agency or private group planning for prevention activities

With techniques presently available, it is possible to effect an important reduction in the incidence of developmental disabilities. Future considerations seem even more encouraging.[2] The alliance of consumer, professional, and governmental forces in this effort has been gratifying.

REFERENCES

1. Crocker, A.C.: Current strategies in prevention of mental retardation. Pediatr. Ann., *11*:450, 1982.
2. Crocker, A.C.: The thoughtful thirteen. *In* Assessment of the National Effort to Combat Mental Retardation from Biomedical Causes: Conference Proceedings. Washington, DC, Department of Health and Human Services, 1983, pp. 14-20.
3. Crocker, A.C.: Prevention of developmental disabilities: Fundamental considerations for public policy. *In* Action for Prevention: 1983 Virginia Mental Retardation/Developmental Disabilities Prevention Conference, Williamsburg, VA, 1984, pp. 52-63.
4. Crocker, A.C.: Societal commitment to prevention of developmental disabilities. *In* Advances in Prevention of Developmental Disabilities. Edited by S.M. Pueschel and J.A. Mulick. Cambridge, MA, Academic Guild Publishers, in press.
5. Cuckle, H.S., Wald, N.J., and Lindenbaum, R.H.: Maternal serum alpha-fetoprotein measurement: A screening test for Down syndrome. Lancet, *1*:926, 1984.
6. Kaback, M.M.: Annual Update of TSD Carrier Detection and Prenatal Diagnosis Experience. Report to the National Tay-Sachs and Allied Diseases Association, 1985.
7. Mahaffey, K.R., Annest, J.L., Roberts, J., and Murphy, R.S.: National estimates of blood lead levels: United States, 1976-1980. N. Engl. J. Med., *307*:573, 1982.
8. Merkatz, I.R., Nitowsky, H.M., Macri, J.N., and Johnson, W.E.: An association between low maternal serum alpha-fetoprotein and fetal chromosomal abnormalities. Am. J. Obstet. Gynecol., *148*:886, 1984.

33

PLANNING FOR MEDICAL CARE

Allen C. Crocker, M.D.

This book has discussed the wide range of medical care needs of children and adults with developmental disabilities, along with many of the settings and systems in which attention can be given to health-related factors. These include private medical practices, hospitals, schools, residences, nursing homes, state residential facilities, community nursing practices, and Services for Children with Special Health Care Needs. Funds for care come from private insurance, Title XIX (Medicaid, welfare), Title XVI (Supplemental Security Income/Disabled Children's Programs), Title V (health departments), Medicare, community and state education budgets, state departments of mental health/mental retardation, employers, and individuals. This diversity serves the involved population fairly well, but coordination, improvement, and growth are appropriate.

GAPS, BARRIERS, AND GOALS

In 1984 and 1985, a group of over 900 Massachusetts parents of children with developmental disabilities or chronic illness were surveyed as part of Project SERVE[5] and were asked whether various important special services were available to them. Their replies provide an impression of the needs and frustrations experienced in these households for the supportive elements (which complete the medical and educational programming) required for optimal personal progress. The services that they ranked as *least available* for them (in order) were:

Support groups for brothers and sisters
Help in making physical changes in the house
After-school care
Legal services
Financial help
Day care
Transportation to medical services
Information on community resources
Social and recreational opportunities

They ranked eight other components as *somewhat available*, but these clearly represented incomplete accessibility. This list included:

Parent education on rights and entitlements
Home health/nursing care
Respite care
Counseling for other family members
Counseling for child
Parent training in child's health needs
Summer camp
Parent support groups

Many medically related services were listed as *generally available*, but it is of interest that certain families had not had this desired assistance: genetic counseling (25% said "not available"), adaptive equipment (20%), early intervention (17%), occupational therapy (14%), physical therapy (12%), and speech therapy (12%). These various gaps obviously represent an ultimate systems failure, in many instances with complex explanations. It is not possible to provide a listing of deficits in the general care programs for adults with developmental disabilities, but it is reasonable to assume that some supportive features are commonly lacking.

When one considers the direct elements of planning for best medical care in this field, it must be acknowledged that a barrier exists by virtue of incomplete knowledge of all factors involved in specialized health maintenance. As discussed in Chap. 1 and in the section on private practice in Chap. 4, there is a broad unfamiliarity with the biomedical features for many of the low-incidence conditions within the developmental disabilities. This blockade occurs in physicians' offices, hospital emergency rooms, departments of health, and medical departments of insurance companies. Medical training programs have characteristically given little attention to the discerning care of persons with Down syndrome, spastic diplegia, or Hurler syndrome. It is only in current times that the natural history of optimal courses for these types of disorders is being charted. Primary care is being adequately dispensed; sustained specialty medical care is more problematic.

The families of those involved with serious functional difficulties in the developmental area, and the individuals themselves, are presently subjected to a troubling fragmentation of services. In this situation portions of "service coordination" are provided by educational or vocational services, by mental health/mental retardation services, by social services or welfare agencies, by public health agencies, by special commissions and projects, and by voluntary agencies. This phenomenon produces the potential for "five social workers or none," depending on the vagaries of the family's interactions. Medical services can become confounded in this disjointed situation.

A series of national conferences took place in 1982 and 1983, beginning with the Surgeon General's Workshop on Children with Handicaps and Their Families, which looked to the establishment of more coordinated programs for developmentally disabled children who had significant medical problems. From these evolved a consensus regarding the features that should characterize modern designs for care. Two statements of these guiding elements by important spokespersons appear in current publications; they reflect many of the features included in the American Academy of Pediatrics' Project BRIDGE code reported in Chap. 1. MacQueen[4] recommends standards that assure that

Care must be family based
Care must be personalized
Each child must have an individual plan of care
Coordinated interprofessional team care must be available because most handicapped children have more than one problem
One person will be responsible for assisting the family to carry out the program
The cost of the program must not destroy the family's finances

McPherson[3] has similar convictions, and states that to be effective in both care and cost the services must be

Family- and child-centered in approach
Developmental in focus
Interdisciplinary in scope
Individualized, active, and ongoing in nature
Least restrictive in environment
Comprehensive, continuous, and coordinated in execution

All of this implies that for the child (or adult) with multiple disabilities there must be a single "individual service plan," determined by true interagency collaboration and secured by continuing monitoring from a single responsible service coordinator. For children the major challenge is simultaneous engagement of the medical and educational components; partial acknowledgment of the health-related issues in the educational plan is not sufficient. It is not clear how this can be achieved in present times. Many workers feel that the Title V agency (health department) should take the lead, but some conceptual changes must occur before that can happen. When such a revised service plan model is established, the involved "special services" mentioned in the first part of this section can also be arranged.

The issue of payment for medical services must be considered. This is a difficult area to summarize because of the many idiosyncratic practices concerning coverage in different localities, facilities, and companies. The four major supporting systems with which individual families deal are the Blue plans (Blue Cross and Blue Shield), prepayment (HMO) plans, Medicaid, and Services for Children with Special Health Care Needs. All are similar in their opening statements regarding general coverage of physician fees, home nursing care, physical therapy, occupational therapy, speech therapy, and adaptive equipment, but obviously there are contingencies (see next page). Services for Children with Special Health Care Needs and Medicaid are more likely to support nonambulance transportation, respite care, and adaptive changes in the home. Coverage for counseling, mental health services, support groups, and parent training are irregular in all, but best with Services for Children with Special Health Care Needs. None covers special day care, after-school care, creative art therapies, or social or recreational services.

The coverage with the most hope and the most uncertainty is Medicaid. This huge but oddly restricted system is funded jointly by state and federal sources, and eligibility is determined by widely varying state regulations. For persons with developmental disabilities there is a strong bias toward payments for services based in large public facilities. The so-called institutional caseload includes nursing homes, chronic disease hospitals, and state residential facilities for persons with mental retardation. This selection can be overcome by pursuit of a special state waiver, and may be modified by legislation now being sought (the various "Community and Family Living Amendment" bills). Many families are confused about their eligibility for coverage; there are many "near poor" or "medically indigent" families who are at the borderline between private-insurance coverage and Medicaid eligibility. These persons need financial counseling. As an example of the variation in the provision of "optional" Medicaid benefits, a survey in 1981 revealed that 23 states did not cover speech and hearing services and that 12 states offered no physical therapy.

Costs for ambulatory care are unevenly covered by private insurance policies. Even with employer-sponsored group plans there may be exclusions or restrictions for "preexisting conditions," or waiting periods. It is often unclear how to regard a complication of a constitutional syndrome in terms of eligibility for coverage. Particularly discouraging is the general reluctance to provide meaningful continuing support for medical and nursing care in the home, which often represents a vastly more economical and desirable mode for dealing with the needs of a child with complex illness.

Family and individual enrollment in HMOs is growing enormously (membership now 26 million) and is expected to continue to do so. Adequate general coverage can be assumed, irrespective of diagnosis, when there has been enrollment as part of an employer's group, but definitions of essential services are locally determined. HMO trials in relatively high-demand "senior plans" have provided useful experience regarding service to special populations. Some HMOs have entered negotiations with state agencies for coverage of deinstitutionalized persons in community group homes, and this is a promising concept.

Most parents with third-party coverage who responded to the Project SERVE questionnaire[5] indicated substantial out-of-pocket costs for care of their children. These included travel expenses, medications, bills after insurance payments, lost wages due to hospitalization or medical visits, special equipment, babysitters for other children, diet food cost, and special clothing.

NEW DESIGNS

The present political climate has favored consideration of new planning for provision of medical care for persons with developmental disabilities and chronic illness. Important national leadership has come from Richmond, Koop, Hutchins, Hobbs, MacQueen, and others, encouraging fresh attention to coordinated care for children and adults. Supporting this thrust are the human rights movement, better knowledge about long-term disorders, new achievements in promoting the survival of persons with previously compromising medical conditions, professional concerns about quality assurance, and informed consumer activism. Unquestionably the accomplishments of the Education for All Handicapped Children Act (P.L. 94-142) have stirred the hopes of health care planners that the medical needs of those with disabilities might also be viewed for universal assistance. The "EHA Amendments of 1986" (P.L. 99-457) go further to extend the concept of entitlement to medical assessment and special services for children in the birth to 5-year age levels.

Areas for particular concern in this thrust for planning include (1) improved understanding of developmental disabilities by providers of medical care, (2) interagency collaboration in formation and implementation of comprehensive individual service plans for involved persons, (3) assistance to families and individuals in meeting the costs of related medical care, and (4) better education of families and the public regarding health care needs. Supplementary to these is also continuing research on causation, natural history, and therapeutic intervention, plus activities in prevention. Medical planners are also concerned with enhancement of complementary services in the educational, vocational, recreational, and other personal development fields that contribute to individual fulfillment.

One of the most ambitious and imaginative projects, which has looked at the continuing medical care needs of a relevant population with disabilities, is the "Vanderbilt Study" from the Vanderbilt Institute for Public Policy Studies in Nashville. This group, with assistance from professionals in many sections of the country, has reviewed the circumstances of children with chronic illness.[2] Their findings carry extensive analogies to the predicament of children with developmental disabilities (and, in fact, there is some joint involvement). The Vanderbilt researchers have now made available their recommendations for possible policy choices in meeting the special needs of chronically ill children, and it is appropriate to consider them for our population:

1. The greatest-good option. This option suggests devoting available resources to improving the care of all children, and in the process those with long-term health problems would benefit.
2. The research-only option. Here all new dollars would be invested in scientific study, acknowledging that the need for new knowledge is great regarding diseases, child and family development, and effective services.
3. National health care. Such a plan could be for national health insurance or a nationalization of health services, which would include universal eligibility and incentives for cost-effectiveness.
4. Add funds to the present system. This would give further support for Services for Children with Special Health Care Needs, Medicaid, school health, comprehensive specialty centers, University Affiliated Facilities, etc.
5. Reform the present system of care. A plan for incremental reform would include improved mechanisms for early identification, educational programs, teamwork and case management, related service in schools, improved insurance arrangements, and regional data systems.
6. A national community-based program for chronically ill children and their families. This approach envisages a network of community programs, federally mandated and state-based, which would define program standards, assure access, involve area-wide coordinating groups (with lead from Services for Children with Special Health Care Needs), and encourage availability of increased federal, state, and insurance funds.

There is a special courage to these Vanderbilt options, especially numbers 5 and 6 (even they agree that national health insurance is not currently politically opportune). With a slight change in the terminology of the eligible clientele, many of the same speculations could be considered for children with developmental disabilities.

When one looks progressively at human services in this country, it is apparent that we are both assisted and hindered by the categorical territorialism of our federal, state, and city agencies. If it were possible, for example, to consider for planning purposes the overall needs of "children" or "persons," without regard to special agency mandates, one could develop prescriptions for blended services which would not require such pressing negotiations. It is conceivable that the commingled funds of the departments of health, welfare, education (special services), mental health/mental retardation, and private insurance could cover the costs of an improved system of delivery of medical care and related services (free of some of the present duplication). MacQueen[4] has suggested a model whereby individual service plans for children are created in "community child councils" involving the participation of all relevant agencies. Comparable groups could plan for the provision of supports to adults with disabilities.

A review has recently been published[1] that analyzes the requirements and future directions for the health care of adults with serious mental retardation who are living in the community. It is thought that the generic medical care system can adequately provide primary care if it is given training, the support of an information network and data system, and improved financial planning. Specialty medical care is appropriately offered at "resource centers," based especially at tertiary hospitals and experienced state residential facilities. An investment is needed on the part of mental retardation departments in state government to assist in coordination and formation of standards of care. A dilemma exists at present in that nearly the entire population of adults with serious mental retardation is eligible for Medicaid but for few other third-party payment methods, and traditional Medicaid programs in the community have not been adequate for reimbursement of full or normalized services. It is clear that some degree of subsidization is necessary from the mental retardation departments, perhaps in the form of purchase of prepayment coverage for HMOs. Reforms are also being discussed regarding the capacity of Medicaid to develop particular coverage for certain "high-consuming" special populations.

It is my hope that primary care for children and adults with developmental disabilities can continue in a lively and informed fashion (private physicians and community clinics), with good information available about skilled health maintenance, and a concern for wellness. Tertiary centers should offer a devoted allegiance to these providers for specialty care and should pursue studies on improved technology. Coordination of the diverse components involved in an individual service plan is appropriately managed in the setting of true interagency collaboration; support and counseling for the family should also be accessible through such teamwork. Clarification must be achieved regarding the real obligations of public and private insurance provisions, to cover cost. And the whole system should be founded on a base of continuing planning and review among families (and individuals), clinical service providers, researchers, coordinators, payors, and other agency personnel.

REFERENCES

1. Crocker, A.C., and Yankauer, A. (eds.): Sterling D. Garrard Memorial Symposium: Community health care services for adults with mental retardation. Ment. Retard., 25:189, 1987.
2. Hobbs, N., Perrin, J.M., and Ireys, H.T.: Chronically Ill Children and Their Families. San Francisco, Jossey-Bass, 1985.
3. McPherson, M.G.: Community based services for disabled/chronically ill children and their families. In Developmental Handicaps: Prevention and Treatment III. Edited by E.M. Eklund. Silver Spring, MD, American Association of University Affiliated Programs for Persons with Developmental Disabilities, 1985, pp. 43-62.
4. MacQueen, J.C.: The integration of public services for handicapped children: Myth or reality. In Developmental Handicaps: Prevention and Treatment II. Edited by E.M. Eklund. Silver Spring, MD, American Association of University Affiliated Programs for Persons with Developmental Disabilities, 1984, pp. 116-129.
5. Project SERVE: New Directions: Serving Children with Special Health Care Needs in Massachusetts. Boston, Health Research Institute, 1985.

INDEX

Numerals in *italics* indicate a figure; "t" following a page number indicates tabular material.